DATE			

DERIVATIVES RISK AND RESPONSIBILITY

The Complete Guide to Effective Derivatives Management and Decision Making

To Loring Woodman

*Pioneer of permanently affordable
housing for Jackson Hole*

DERIVATIVES RISK AND RESPONSIBILITY

The Complete Guide to Effective Derivatives Management and Decision Making

Robert A. Klein

Jess Lederman
Editors

IRWIN
Professional Publishing

Chicago • Bogotá • Boston • Buenos Aires • Caracas
London • Madrid • Mexico City • Sydney • Toronto

This publication is designed to provide accurate and authoritative information in regard to the subject matter covered. It is sold with the understanding that neither the author or the publisher is engaged in rendering legal, accounting, or other professional service. If legal advice or other expert assistance is required, the services of a competent professional person should be sought.

From a Declaration of Principles jointly adopted by a Committee of the American Bar Association an a Committee of Publishers.

Irwin Professional Book Team

Publisher: *Wayne McGuirt*
Associate publisher: *Michael E. Desposito*
Executive editor: *Kevin Commins*
Managing editor: *Kevin Thornton*
Marketing manager: *Kelly Sheridan*
Project editor: *Rebecca Dodson*
Production supervisor: *Lara Feinberg/Carol Klein*
Assistant manager, desktop services: *Jon Christopher*
Compositor: *Weimer Graphics, Inc.*
Typeface: *11/13 Times Roman*
Printer: *Quebecor/Book Press, Inc.*

Times Mirror
Higher Education Group

Library of Congress Cataloging-in-Publication Data

Risk derivatives and responsibilities / edited by Robert A. Klein,
  Jess Lederman.
    p. cm.
  Includes bibliographical references and index.
  ISBN 1-55738-903-9
  1. Derivative securities.   I. Klein, Robert A. (Robert Arnold),
  1953–   . II. Lederman, Jess.
  HG6024.A3R57   1966
  332.6—dc20   95-38517

Printed in the United States of America
1 2 3 4 5 6 7 8 9 0   QBP   2 1 0 9 8 7 6 5

Preface

Over the last few years, we have had the privilege of working with some of the most talented practitioners and academics in the world to produce two books that have become indispensable for participants in the derivatives market: *The Handbook of Derivatives and Synthetics* (Probus Publishing, 1994) and *Financial Engineering with Derivatives* (Irwin Professional Publishing, 1995). *Derivatives Risk and Responsibility*, our third book on the derivatives market, is in some ways our most ambitious, and perhaps most important effort to date.

The critically important role that derivatives play in both profit maximization and risk reduction has recently been overshadowed by numerous well-publicized financial disasters. *Derivatives Risk and Responsibility* is intended both for the senior manager or board member who is unfamiliar with derivatives and for the seasoned professionals who, more than ever, must assure themselves that they have all the tools and knowledge necessary to avoid the mistakes that others have made. *Part One* features seven chapters that are intended for officers with oversight responsibility, but who may not necessarily have technical knowledge of the derivatives markets. *Part Two* consists of seven chapters that discuss the state of the art in derivatives risk management. The five chapters of *Part Three* cover critical accounting, tax, systems, and control issues, while the five chapters of *Part Four* deal with a wide and comprehensive range of legal and regulatory matters. The *Appendices* provide a checklist on the relative roles of the board and senior management as well as a wealth of information on derivatives software products.

Many thanks are owed to the 37 authors, who took valuable time from their hectic schedules to make this important book possible. We are also grateful to the superb staff at Irwin Professional Publishing.

Jess Lederman
Robert A. Klein

Contributing Authors

Sheila C. Bair is commissioner of the Commodity Futures Trading Commission. She has served as chairman of the CFTC's Financial Products Advisory Committee since December 1991. Previously, she was legislative counsel to the New York Stock Exchange (NYSE), and acted as legal advisor to Senator Robert Dole in a number of capacities, including research director of his 1988 presidential campaign and in the Majority Leader's Office. Ms. Bair received her B.A. degree from the University of Kansas in 1975 and her J.D. from the University of Kansas School of Law in 1978. She has published numerous papers on derivative instruments.

Tanya Styblo Beder is a principal and founder of Capital Market Risk Advisors, Inc., which specializes in strategic and risk-management issues for dealers, end-users, regulators, and others. Previously, she was a vice president of The First Boston Corporation, where she worked in mergers and acquisitions, capital markets, derivative products, and fixed-income research. Ms. Beder has also worked as a consultant in the financial institutions practice at McKinsey & Company. She is on the board of directors of the International Association of Financial Engineers and is a management fellow at the Yale School of Management. Ms. Beder received a B.A. in mathematics from Yale University and an M.B.A. from the Harvard Business School.

Gregory C. Beier is a vice president of Global Finance at Hanmi Securities, a Los Angeles-based investment banking and fund management firm specializing in Korea. Previously, Mr. Beier spent his career producing institutional research as a vice president for Harmonic Research, a principal of Caldwell & Co., and an analyst at Cowen & Co.

Jeffrey P. Burns is an associate with Morgan, Lewis & Bockius of Philadelphia. Previously, he was an attorney in the Branch of Derivatives Regulation, Office of Self-Regulatory Oversight, Division of Market Regulation at the Securities and Exchange Commission. Mr. Burns is a graduate of John Carroll University (B.S. Economics), Cleveland–

Marshall College of Law (J.D.), Cleveland State University (M.B.A.), and Georgetown University Law Center (L.LM. Securities Regulation).

Peter J. Connors is a tax partner at the Baker & McKenzie office in New York City. Previously, he was the director of International Capital Markets Tax Services for Ernst & Young L.L.P. Mr. Connors specializes in the taxation of U.S. capital markets transactions and international tax planning. He received his LL.M. (Taxation), from the New York University School of Law; his J.D. from the University of Richmond; and his B.A. from Catholic University in Washington, D.C. Mr. Connors has authored and co-authored nearly 100 articles for leading industry periodicals and has served as chairman of the American Bar Association's Tax Section Committee on Financial Transactions.

Anthony G. Cornyn is the director of the Risk Management Division of the Office of Thrift Supervision, which is responsible for interest-rate-risk analysis. Previously, he was the head of the Federal Reserve Board's Financial Analysis and Special Studies Section. In 1984, Mr. Cornyn was appointed assistant director in the Division of Banking Supervision and Regulation by Chairman Volker. Mr. Cornyn received a B.S. from Villanova University and an M.B.A. from the University of Pittsburgh. He is a graduate of the Stonier Graduate School of Banking at Rutgers University.

Christopher L. Culp is a senior fellow in financial regulation for the Competitive Enterprise Institute, and an independent financial-risk-management consultant. Previously, Mr. Culp served as senior examiner of the Federal Reserve Bank of Chicago, an economist at G.T. Management (Asia) Ltd., a desk trader for TradeLink LLC, and a research associate for Friedberg Commodity Management, Inc. Mr. Culp expects to complete his Ph.D. in corporation finance at the University of Chicago Graduate School of Business by the end of 1995. He has been widely published and has given many lectures on derivatives, risk management, and corporation finance.

David Dixon is business development manager at Midas-Kapiti International, a U.K.-based financial software house, where he is responsible for the future development strategy for Midas-Kapiti's derivative products. He has over 15 years experience in the financial software industry. Prior to Midas-Kapiti, Mr. Dixon worked for a U.K. merchant bank, where he was involved in the design, implementation and support of their systems. Mr. Dixon graduated from Cambridge University with a masters degree and post-graduate diploma in Computer Science.

Joel B. Finard is a senior manager in Deloitte & Touche's Financial Instruments and Strategies Group, where he consults on derivatives issues and financial risk management. Previously, he was a vice president in the treasury department of Hong Kong and Shanghai Bank. In addition, Mr. Finard spent several years managing multicurrency investment portfolios at Travelers Insurance Company, and served as an adjunct professor at Columbia Graduate School of Business and New York University for a number of years. Mr. Finard holds a M.Phil. and M.A. in Economics from Columbia University and is a chartered financial analyst.

Jeremy A. Gluck is a vice president in the Structured Derivative Products Group at Moody's Investors Service. His primary responsibility is the evaluation of the risks associated with derivative products activities, particularly the establishment and operation of Aaa-rated derivatives subsidiaries. Previously, Mr. Gluck was a vice president and money market economist at Mitsubishi Bank, and a senior economist at the Federal Reserve Bank of New York. Mr. Gluck holds a Ph.D. in economics from Stanford University and a B.A. degree in Economics and English from the University of California at Berkeley.

Esther Eckerling Goodman is the senior executive vice president of Kenmar Asset Allocation Inc., an asset management firm responsible for the design and active management of managed futures investments for large institutional and private clients throughout the world. Mrs. Goodman is responsible for the day-to-day management of the firm, and is actively involved in the research and analysis of traders as well as ongoing risk management activities. She has held postions with leading firms in the futures industry since 1974. Mrs. Goodman has served as director of the Managed Futures Trade Association and the Managed Futures Association. Mrs. Goodman graduated from Stanford University in 1974 with a B.A. degree.

L.G. "Chip" Harter is a tax partner in the Washington, D.C. office of Baker & McKenzie. Mr. Harter's practice emphasizes the tax treatment of financial transactions and international tax planning generally. A significant portion of his practice involves the taxation of derivative financial instruments. He regularly represents taxpayers in controversies involving the taxation of financial transactions. Mr. Harter is currently chairman of the Notional Principal Contracts Subcommittee of the Financial Transactions Committee of the American Bar Association Section of Taxation. Mr. Harter graduated from Harvard College *magna cum laude* in 1977 and the University of Chicago Law School in 1980, where he served as comments editor of the *University of Chicago Law Review*.

Thomas S.Y. Ho, a pioneer in the field of fixed-income research, is founder and president of Global Advanced Technology (GAT), a firm which provides software, research, and consulting services to the fixed-income market. GAT's software products include GAT Precision, a CMO analytical tool, and the Integrative Bond System, a portfolio management product. Dr. Ho has published dozens of articles in professional journals, including the "Ho-Lee" interest-rate movement model, the first arbitrage-free approach to pricing bond options. He is a former professor of finance at New York Universitys Stern School of Business. Dr. Ho received his undergraduate education in England and his Ph.D. in mathematics from the University of Pennsylvania in 1978.

R. McFall (Mac) Lamm, Jr. is vice president, Global Economic Research with Bankers Trust. Previously, he was chief economist at both the Commodity Exchange and the Coffee, Sugar & Cocoa Exchange. Dr. Lamm has also served as group general manager of International Operations with Pepsico, Inc., and director of Business and Economic Research at the Pillsbury Company. His areas of expertise include commodity markets, derivatives, global economics and investing, international business strategy, and quantitative analysis. Dr. Lamm received a Ph.D. degree from Virginia Polytechnic Institute, and M.A. and B.A. degrees from North Carolina State University. He has published more than a hundred articles and reports and has carried out projects in countries throughout the world.

Robert J. Mackay is professor of finance and director of the Center for Study of Futures & Options Markets in the R.B. Pamplin College of Business at Virginia Polytechnic Institute and State University. He is a co-founder of the Financial Innnovation Study Committee, an interdisciplinary group examining the economics, accounting, regulation, and taxation of innovative derivative products. Previously, Dr. Mackay served as chief of staff of the U.S. Commodity Futures Trading Commission and as a member of the senior staff of the President's Working Group on Financial Markets. He has also served as a member of the CFTC's Regulatory Coordination Advisory Committee and as a project advisor to the Group of Thirty's Study Group on Global Derivatives Risk. Dr. Mackay received his Ph.D. in economics from the University of North Carolina at Chapel Hill.

David Madigan is an institutional tax-advantaged portfolio manager for Bankers Trust Companys Global Investment Management, which manages $160 billion in assets for institutions and high net-worth individuals. He joined Bankers Trust in 1994 from Merrill Lynch, where he was the Municipal Strategist named to *Institutional Investors* All-American Team in 1993. Mr. Madigan earned an M.B.A. from the University of Chicago and a B.B.A. from the University of Notre Dame.

Robert M. Mark is an executive vice president at the Canadian Imperial Bank of Commerce, responsible for the Treasury and Market Risk Management Group, which covers all market, contingent credit, and operating risks. Previously, he was the partner in charge of the Financial Risk Management Consulting practice at Coopers & Lybrand. Earlier, Dr. Mark served as a managing director in the Asia, Europe, and Capital Markets Group at Chemical Bank, and as a senior officer at Marine Midland Bank/ Hong Kong Shanghai Bank Group. Dr. Mark earned his Ph.D. with a dissertation in options pricing from New York University's Graduate School of Engineering and Science. He subsequently received an Advanced Professional Certificate in accounting from NYU's Stern Graduate School of Business.

Dr. Jeffrey L. McIver, director of financial engineering for Infinity Financial Technology, Inc., is active in the research and development of financial analytic tools for Infinity's object-oriented class library, Fin++. Dr. McIver worked at Bank of America, where he contributed to the development of an advanced probabilistic credit evaluation system, and at the Federal Home Loan Bank in San Francisco, where he was engaged in all aspects of the U.S. mortgage market. Dr. McIver holds a Ph.D in Mathematics from the University of California at Berkeley. He is a member of the FMA and the AMA.

William J. McSherry, Jr. is a partner with Battle Fowler LLP, where he is chairman of the Litigation Department. Mr. McSherry is a member of the American Bar Association, where he is vice chair, General Practice Section Subcommittee on Alternative Dispute Resolution. Mr. McSherry earned his B.A. from Fordham College and graduated from the Harvard Law School.

Susan M. Milligan is counsel to Commissioner Sheila C. Bair of the Commodity Futures Trading Commission. She provides legal and policy advice on proposed regulations, enforcement actions, and opinions. Previously, Ms. Milligan was acting counsel to the chairman and worked in the Office of General Counsel as an attorney drafting briefs and pleadings for proceedings before the federal courts. Ms. Milligan received her B.A. degree from Dickinson College, *magna cum laude,* in 1980 and her J.D. from American University in 1984. She is a member of the Maryland and District of Columbia Bars.

Israel (Izzy) Nelken is the founder of Super Computing Consulting Corporation, which provides services to the financial community. He has developed new methodologies and software for pricing and evaluating exotic options, convertible bonds, option-embedded securities, and structured notes. Previously, Dr. Nelken served on the faculty of the Department of Computer Science at the University of Toronto. Dr. Nelken received his B.Sc. in mathematics and computer science from Tel Aviv University, and his Ph.D. in computer science from Rutgers University. He has published numerous articles, and is a frequent lecturer on topics such as credit derivatives, exotic options, and equity swaps.

Michael K. Ong is head of the Market Risk Analysis Unit of First Chicago Bank, where he is involved in global risk-management, assessment of trading models and hedging strategies, and oversight of the corporation's overall involvement in market risk, among many other activies. He also serves as Chair of the Research Council of First Chicago, and as Adjunct Professor at the Stuart School of Business of the Illinois Institute of Technology. Previously, Dr. Ong was responsible for quantitative research at Chicago Research and Trading Group (now NationsBanc-CRT), and served as assistant professor of Mathematics at Bowdoin Colledge, with research specialty in mathematical physics. Dr. Ong holds a B.S. in Physics from the University of the Philippines, an M.A. in

Physics, and both M.S. and Ph.D. degrees in Applied Math from the State University of New York at Stony Brook.

Raj Patel is senior vice president, sales and marketing for INSSINC, where he also has responsibility for new products. He specializes in systems for the risk management and derivatives marketplace. Previously, Mr. Patel worked for a software house dedicated to providing real-time systems to wholesale banks, initially as a product manager and then as business/marketing manager working in the U.S., the U.K., and the Far East. Earlier, he gained experience developing, project managing, and integrating systems for a major computer manufacturer.

A. Robert Pietrzak is a partner in the law firm of Brown & Wood. He is a member of the New York and federal bars and the American Law Institute and has been appointed by the Commodity Futures Trading Commission to its Financial Products Advisory Committee. Mr. Pietrzak is on the Editorial Advisory Board of the *Fordham International Law Journal* and the CLE faculty of the Fordham University School of Law. Mr. Pietrzak received his B.A. from Fordham University and his J.D. from Columbia Law School. He has lectured extensively on derivative products, futures, securities, and litigation.

Antonino Piscitello is responsible for Operations at Société Générale, where he has overseen the restructuring that has included development of the professional back office, and implementation of derivatives and capital market back-office systems and controls. Mr. Piscitello was part of the team that launched the bank's wholesale operations, and has also served as manager of the Information Services Group. Previously, he worked in systems management for Republic National Bank and Delta Resources. Mr. Piscitello holds a B.S. in Physics from City College, an M.A. in Physics from the State University of New York and an M.B.A. in Finance from Long Island University. He has completed Columbia University's Executive Program in International Management and is a certified cash manager.

Caroline Poplawski is a senior research analyst with Kenmar Asset Allocation, Inc., where her responsibilities include the evaluation of Commodity Trading Advisors, the markets they trade as well as the risk monitoring and management of managed futures investments. One of her focuses has been in researching and developing tools for risk analysis. Previously, she held positions with Mocatta Futures Corporation, a futures commission merchant, Shearson Lehman Hutton, and Prudential Bache Securities. Ms. Poplawski graduated from New York University with honors in 1987, with degrees in both Economics and Finance.

Lisa M. Raiti is a managing director at Centre Financial Products Limited. Her responsibilities include marketing a turnkey product—the creation of AAA-rated derivative subsidiaries for banks, insurance companies, and brokerage houses. Ms. Raiti also focuses her efforts on the development and securitization of credit-enhanced securities that bridge the gap between insurance and the capital markets. Previously, Ms. Raiti was director of the Derivative Product Companies Group at Standard & Poor's Corporation. She spearheaded the development of criteria for rating these innovative companies, and has lectured extensively on this topic. Ms. Raiti holds an M.B.A. in Finance and Accounting from New York University and a B.S. in Civil Engineering from Columbia University.

Joseph Rosen is a managing director of Enterprise Technology Corporation, a pioneer in technology consulting and custom software development services to the financial community. He is an authority on the strategic use of information techology for competitive advantage in financial services. Previously, Mr. Rosen was chief information officer of Dubin & Swieca Capital Management, and a founding partner of Rosen Kupperman Associates, where he advised executives of leading techology users and suppliers on three continents. He is an authority on risk management and technology who has published numerous articles in international financial and technology publications and speaks frequently at industry conferences and seminars. Mr. Rosen is an alumnus of Columbia University, with M.B.A. degrees in Finance, International Business, and Marketing. He also holds M.A. and A.B.D. degrees in International Politics and Quantitative Methods from the State University of New York at Stony Brook.

Michael Rulle is managing director and head of CIBC Wood Gundy's Financial Products. Based in New York, he directs the activities of approximately 225 employees who work out of offices in New York, Toronto, Montreal, London, Singapore, Hong Kong, and Tokyo. Mr. Rulle is the chairman of the firm's Transaction Committee and a member of the Risk Committee. Previously, he served as head of derivatives worldwide from 1990 to 1992 for Lehman Brothers and head of global equity derivatives from 1992 to June 1994. Mr. Rulle is a 1972 graduate of Hobart College and has graduate degrees from the College of William and Mary and Columbia University.

Michael S. Sackheim is counsel to the law firm of Brown & Wood. He is the chairman of the International Derivative Transactions Subcommittee of the American Bar Association and is on the editorial board of the *Futures International Law Letter.* Mr. Sackheim received his B.A. from Queens College, his M.A. from the New School for Social Research, his J.D. from Brooklyn Law School and his LL.M. from New York University School of Law.

Jeffrey L. Seltzer is a managing director of CIBC Wood Gundy Financial Products. He has global responsibility for the Advisory Group which provides technical product development and transaction structuring expertise with a special focus on the credit, legal, regulatory, tax, and accounting aspects of swaps, options and structured securities across all markets. Previously, Mr. Seltzer was a managing director of the Lehman Brothers Derivatives Department and a securities lawyer in private practice in New York City. Mr. Seltzer graduated from The Wharton School of the University of Pennsylvania in 1978 and the Georgetown University Law Center in 1981.

Colin Southall is a senior consultant with the Commercial and Investment Banking Group within Ernst & Young's London Financial Services consulting practice. He has specialized in the selection and implementation of trading and risk management systems and the use of object-oriented methodologies to define architectures and identify migration strategies for systems in the derivatives area. Previously, Mr. Southall worked for an independent City consultancy focused on dealing room system selection and implementation, and the development of system architectures to support migration planning within banks.

Richard M. Steinberg is a senior partner in Coopers & Lybrand L.L.P.'s In-Control Services unit. He served as partner on the Coopers & Lybrand team that conducted the landmark study and wrote the report, *Internal Control—Integrated Framework,* published by the Committee of Sponsoring Organizations of the Treadway Commission. As chairman of the firm's International Internal Controls Task Force, Mr. Steinberg oversees development of the firm's client service capabilities around the world and is called on as a senior consulting resource on international engagements. Mr. Steinberg, a CPA, is a graduate of the University of Pennsylvania Wharton School and holds an M.B.A. from New York University's Graduate School of Business. He is a member of the AICPA and New York State Society of CPAs, and is recognized in *Who's Who in Finance and Industry.*

Mary Ellen Stocks is a senior manager at Deloitte & Touche LLP and a member of the Financial Instruments and Strategies Group, where she specializes in Treasury and Financial Risk Management consulting. Previously, Ms. Stocks was a manager of Corporate Finance at a Fortune 10 corporation, focusing on capital markets and international treasury, and a Derivatives Product Specialist at a major Wall Street firm. Ms. Stocks holds an M.A. in International Finance and Economics from Columbia University.

Paul A. Straus is an associate with Battle Fowler, LLP. He received a B.A. from Cornell University and a J.D. from New York University School of Law.

Jordan E. Yarett is a partner at Battle Fowler, LLP. Previously, he served with Ballard, Spahr, Andrews & Ingersoll. Mr. Yarett received his B.A. from Yale University and his J.D. from the University of Pennsylvania. He is the author of numerous articles and book chapters on the municipal market and tax-exempt derivatives, and frequently speaks at industry conferences and seminars.

Ezra Zask is president of Ezra Zask Associates, Inc., a Connecticut-based funds management and financial advisory firm. He trades a diverse basket of of foreign currencies based on optimization and modern portfolio-theory techniques, and consults in the areas of international portfolio management, currency exposure management, and the use of derivatives in risk management. Previously, he served in senior treasury management positions with major international banking institutions and as an adjunct professor of finance at Carnegie-Mellon University. Mr. Zask earned a B.A. degree from Princeton University and M.A. and M. Phil. degrees from Columbia University in International Affairs. He has written numerous articles and lectured extensively.

Contents

MANAGEMENT

Chapter One

A View for the Top
The Role of the Board of Directors and Senior Management in the Derivatives Business*

Jeffrey L. Seltzer
Managing Director, Financial Products
CIBC Wood Gundy

INTRODUCTION

Imagine that one of the three major television networks announces it is canceling all of its current programming, to be replaced by 24-hour-a-day coverage of the activity taking place in an ant farm.

Or let's say a famous beer maker believes the next craze in beer drinking will be mud-flavored beer and throws all of its resources into this new product.

We can easily predict that both decisions would be disastrous and result in significant losses to shareholders of these two companies. Most people may feel there ought to be a law against this kind of addled thinking, but intellectually we all know that it is up to the board of directors to punish unwise management behavior. And it is up to the shareholders to punish the board.

---

*The views expressed herein are the views of the author and may not express the views of Canadian Imperial Bank of Commerce, Wood Gundy, or their affiliates (including any of their officers, directors, employees, or agents).

To think that the government should actually intervene and dictate with some specificity the role of the board of directors and senior management of corporations, either through legislative or regulatory action, would seem to be the most extreme hypothetical of them all.

Yet some people believe that it is not extreme to suggest that government intervene in corporate use of derivatives by setting standards for behavior that go beyond the norms of business judgment. Others argue that derivatives activities by regulated financial institutions should be subject to more stringent rules than other types of trading activities. How can this be?

The Issues

Gerald Corrigan, former president of the Federal Reserve Bank of New York, in a speech in early 1992, gave the derivatives industry a harsh wake-up call urging senior management of firms engaged in the business to learn, understand, and manage the attendant risks.

Corrigan's speech raised some serious questions on the regulation of derivatives and the role of senior management. It caused many firms to take a closer look at how they manage derivatives and how derivatives fit into their overall business strategy. In the aftermath of that speech, many regulators now regularly examine the role of senior management in this business and freely render views on what the role should be.

Recommendations have been made by regulatory bodies such as the Federal Reserve Bank and the Office of the Comptroller of the Currency with respect to those institutions they regulate. Similar recommendations have been made by the Group of Thirty, the American Institute of Certified Public Accountants, and trade associations such as the Investment Company Institute. The latter do not carry the weight of law but rather help to set best practices against which a company's derivatives activities can be benchmarked.

These recommendations, although directed at derivatives, encompass principles of effective management that can be applicable to running any business in a responsible manner. The recommendations have two major themes: knowledge and accountability.

Regulatory Framework

Let's take a look at what regulators and other experts believe is the appropriate role for senior management and boards of directors with respect to the derivatives business.

1. Derivatives activities must be subject to effective senior-management supervision and oversight by the board of directors. The board doesn't need operating expertise in derivatives, but must have sufficient understanding of the products and risks to (a) approve the bank's derivatives business strategy, (b) limit the amount of earnings and capital at risk, and (c) review periodically the results of derivatives activity.

2. The board must approve comprehensive written policies and procedures to govern the use of derivatives that should be consistent with the organization's (a) broader business strategies, (b) capital expertise, and (c) risk tolerance. Magnitude and complexity of risks of derivatives activities should be commensurate with the institution's overall objectives.

3. The board and senior management must establish an independent unit for measuring and regularly reporting risk exposures to the board and senior management. Such reports should accurately present the nature and levels of risk taken and compliance with approved policies and limits. They must be easily read and understood, and they should be based on a common conceptual framework for measuring and limiting risks.

4. Senior-management must ensure that appropriate risk-management procedures are implemented and reviewed at least annually in light of activity and market conditions.

5. Senior-management approval should be sought for new products or risk types and/or products for which the institution has no relevant experience or for which liquidity is uncertain. Unusual types of transactions may require specific approvals.

6. The board and senior management must ensure that derivatives activities are allocated sufficient staff so that risks are adequately managed and controlled.

7. The board and senior management must provide for audit coverage to ensure timely identification of internal control weaknesses and/or system deficiencies. They must also establish mechanisms for the effective assessment of capital, accounting, and legal exposures.

8. The board must conduct and encourage discussions between itself and senior management, and between senior management and others in the institution regarding the risk-management process

and risk exposures (see Appendix A for a summary of practices recommended by regulators and trade associations).

Legal Liability

Now what do U.S. corporate lawyers think about the role (i.e., liability) of directors in setting derivatives policy? There is, of course, the long-standing legal precedent surrounding the general level of a director's duty of care and reasonable action. Throw into that mix a recent Indiana Court of Appeals case, which held against the directors of a grain cooperative for their manager's failure to hedge price changes, which resulted in significant losses. The court found the board breached its duty of care by failing to supervise the manager and by not becoming aware of the essentials of hedging so that it could effectively monitor the business.

In a similar action, shareholders sued a major manufacturer of computers for its failure to hedge its foreign currency exposures. The case was dismissed on procedural grounds, but the manufacturer probably didn't need the aggravation.

The business judgment rules set by the courts protect directors from liability if their decision was an informed one. The duty of care is violated only by uninformed decisions, not merely by decisions that have negative consequences.

Business executives must learn how to apply these standards to their institutions now that they know that directors are fair game for a share-holders' suit. Clearly, directors need to understand the risks and set up proper mechanisms to address those risks, including delegation of authority to qualified employees. There may be a higher standard of care for financial institutions that are dealers in derivatives or for those institutions whose financial performance is significantly impacted by changes in interest rates, foreign exchange, commodity prices, etc. This includes banks, insurance companies, transportation companies (fuel use), and those companies with extensive foreign operations (foreign exchange). And occasional users of derivatives also will need to evaluate their board's level of knowledge against the types of risks they take on a limited basis.

The Perception

When regulators aggressively pursue the risk-management standards cited above, it seems as if they don't believe that derivatives dealers follow these general practices. The perception problem that plagues the derivatives industry seems to be that management teams don't understand the products and their inherent risks, don't even want to know about them, and don't have the means to control them. Distinctions have been made between people in the trenches, who understand the business, and less-informed senior management, who may not.

One could then wonder whether management is out of touch generally or just out of touch with derivatives? I think it is the latter. Hence the need for some form of "best practice."

Most financial institutions with major derivatives activities are generally acknowledged to be successful in their cash and loan businesses through effective management of credit/market/legal/operational/settlement/liquidity risks. Derivatives are sophisticated and may bundle certain risks—but major derivatives dealers clearly have the management expertise necessary to do the job. If they didn't, they could not be successful in other businesses which require similar risk management techniques.

A recent study by the Group of Thirty on the derivatives market supports this view. Its report states: "[D]erivatives by their nature do not introduce risks of a fundamentally different kind or of a greater scale than those already present in the financial markets. Hence, systemic risks are not appreciably aggravated; and supervisory concerns can be addressed within present regulatory structures and approaches."

The reality is that current analyses should cover all trading activities. Derivatives should not be treated in isolation from other capital market endeavors. However, in looking at the wide range of customized products in the market today, one can begin to understand why some critics think the business is too complex for management to know what's going on and why there is a feeling that derivatives are somehow different from other businesses. I submit that the underlying techniques remain the same, and the question "why are derivatives different from all other financial instruments" is unwarranted.

However, management should recognize that this is a dynamic business that will require a dynamic approach to effective senior management. We must, however, continue to work to overcome the notion that derivatives are different and be vigilant with respect to *all* trading activities. The experience of Kidder Peabody with respect to alleged accounting irregularities related to government bond trading and of Barings with respect to alleged unauthorized futures trading are vivid examples of this point.

The General Focus

So how do a board and senior management understand all of these products? Well, of course, they don't, as a group, know the details of everything. But does the chairman of a car company really need to know in detail how a catalytic converter works to be able to run his company? It is important to analyze the management of the business in this context.

The role of any board and senior management is to shape overall strategy and be comfortable that such strategy is being successfully implemented. They determine if the organization should be in the derivatives business and allocate the necessary resources—people, technology, credit lines, and capital. They also analyze how the business fits in with other businesses. Because derivatives combine aspects of many other businesses—debt, equity, credit, and market risk—most members of senior management do bring general technical knowledge to the table and all bring management expertise that works well in other businesses. In this way, they coordinate the overall risk parameters for the business. Senior management chooses the business heads and senior line managers for the business and leaves the mechanics—the detailed technical understanding of each product and function—to the specialists.

But that isn't the end of it—senior managers don't operate in a vacuum and they are *not* complacent. They don't shrug their shoulders and hope "the experts" know what they're doing on the trading floor.

As a firm, you put in place controls to maintain a watch and report on each area of risk; and it's part of the job of senior management to continually carry out reality checks on the controls' effectiveness, so that they can be comfortable that those on the trading floor or treasury area are protecting the firm. The independent risk-management function—as well as internal audit, financial control, and the legal division—play key roles in this process by performing comprehensive and independent reviews of the control procedures. This is an ongoing process. It is performed formally, with regular reviews, and informally with day-to-day contact.

Others can write in depth about the specifics of the basic approaches to market, credit, operational, and legal risks. These are the constants that the financial services industry faces every day and, I think, handles well. I will mention, however, that where senior management should be vigilant is in the variations caused by the constant customization of meeting clients' needs. This translates into the development of lots of new products. Serving customers through tailored product delivery is the heart of the derivatives business and the reason for its success. This is what I mean by dynamic management.

The key to success in risk management is to have line managers in place who will always be reviewing the business in general, as well as the specifics of risk management, transaction execution, and product development. These people must have the expertise to detect the variations and quickly assess the impact. These are the managers who will also "bubble up" the problems related to the variations and glitches. Derivatives dealers must have managers who can be trusted to run the business and who will immediately raise critical issues to the next level on the managerial ladder.

Recent Events

A great deal has been written of late about the misfortunes of a few end-users of derivatives. I emphasize the word "few," and add that the resulting losses seem to be the by-products of weak procedures and controls and not of any particular financial instrument. I should also point out that the number of problems of end users is extremely limited when compared to the large number of transactions executed globally.

Some legislators and regulators have called for corporate end-users of derivatives to be regulated in some manner to prevent losses. As a matter of policy, I find such notions suspect.

If corporations make mistakes, as did some over the last year, so be it. As Carter Beese, former commissioner of the Securities and Exchange Commission, has said, "We must keep intact the inalienable right for corporations and individuals to lose money. If we ever lose the right, making money will become very hard indeed."

The Federal Deposit Insurance Corporation examination memorandum on derivatives use by nondealer banks states, "It is not the intent to discourage the taking of reasonable risks by appropriately capitalized, well-managed institutions, but to ensure that acceptable capital limits, suitable expertise and sufficient management controls are maintained for all such activities." Jerry Johnson, president of the Federal Reserve Bank of Cleveland, observed that regulators and lawmakers can't prevent all losses. He states, "There is a lack of appreciation that the capitalist system is a profit and loss system. Losses are educational and attention getting." Recent events show us that Mr. Johnson's theory is correct as many derivatives users tightened up their controls as a result of the publicized misfortunes of a very limited number of end users of derivatives.

Recommendations

I'd like to close by citing the story of a new president at a financial institution with a large derivatives dealing operation. As he was about to begin his first day on the job he was handed three envelopes by his predecessor. "Open these," he said, "in the event of a crisis in your derivatives unit." The new president put the envelopes in his desk and forgot about them.

A few months later a crisis hit. The president scurried to his office in a panic and remembered the envelopes. He opened the one marked Number 1, which read "blame the accountants." He did and the crisis ended.

A few months after that the second crisis of his administration occurred. He ran to his office again and ripped open the envelope marked Number 2. "Blame the markets," it said. Once again, the problem went away.

Not long thereafter, a third crisis entered the scene. Feeling confident, he walked into his office and opened the envelope marked Number 3. This message read, "Prepare three envelopes."

I'd now like to give you my embellishments of the recommendations for senior management that may prove more useful in the long run than the three envelopes:

- Don't treat derivatives in isolation. Sound risk-management principles should apply to the trading of *all* financial instruments.

- Recognize that derivatives dealing is a dynamic business that requires a dynamic approach to management.

- Create a process to understand the product lines and generally identify and review the risks on a regular basis. Encourage product education at all levels of the organization.

- Ensure that information is timely and of high quality for its intended purpose. Make sure that everyone uses standardized terminology. There is a potential for problems when people use jargon. If the traders can't explain the transaction to senior management, senior management shouldn't approve the transaction.

- Value your positions regularly against the market and compare to the hedged positions regardless of your accounting method. That way you will always know where you stand.

- The more complex the activity, the greater the level of in-house expertise that will be required. So, place experienced senior line managers that you trust in the key positions. Challenge their assumptions about the business and their ability to perform under pressure. The human factor is the most critical factor of this business. Pilot error, as opposed to systems error, will be the most likely cause of a problem.

- Create a "bubble-up" process in which people are comfortable discussing issues with you. If they're scared of your reaction, they won't seek it.

- Stay close to the business. Come out of the ivory tower frequently and spend time on the trading floor.

- Remember that you cannot prevent all losses. However, with appropriate controls in place, both surprises and losses will be minimized.

CONCLUSION

The derivatives business is going to continue doing what it has done since its inception, which is to grow at a significant pace because of its ability to meet risk-management needs in a more optimal manner than any other product. The difference between now and the early days is that derivatives are now in the glare of the public spotlight. The best way to assure the public that we're running the business well is by operating in a prudent manner. This will require the education, involvement, and support of senior management and directors. Hopefully, this chapter sets out a framework for their involvement in this business.

Chapter Two

The Derivatives Risk-Management Audit

Ezra Zask
Ezra Zask Associates

PLAYING WITH FIRE: THE GROWTH OF A DERIVATIVES CULTURE

Catastrophic losses from failed derivatives strategies have been documented with alarming frequency over the last few years; the more recent headline-grabbing debacles include the collapse of a major international bank and the bankruptcy of a wealthy California municipality. Even the "conservative" corporate world now appears as vulnerable to derivatives-related financial disasters as the more risk-tolerant hedge funds. Indeed, nearly every bout of financial market turbulence since the stock market crash of 1987 has been blamed on the proliferation of increasingly complex and highly leveraged derivatives.

Despite voluminous studies undertaken by respected financial market institutions that categorically deny that derivatives are inherently destabilizing, they remain among the most controversial and least-understood areas in finance. A recent *60 Minutes* television program featuring a well-known economist proclaimed to the world that even the pros have difficulty understanding derivatives.

While derivatives' media spotlight may have enhanced the mystique of finance practitioners, it has also heightened the regulatory zeal of government bodies worldwide. Corporations are now required to disclose to

FIGURE 2–1

Factors Driving Demand for Derivatives

• The ongoing **globalization of capital markets** and ever expanding trade in goods and services virtually guarantees that market risk will continue to grow for many firms. Derivatives will be used to manage that risk.

• **Increased capital mobility** and the resulting rise in currency, interest rate, and commodities market volatility suggests that it will become costlier for companies not to hedge.

• In an increasingly **competitive global business environment,** corporations will find further inducement to seek profits from market movements in the course of their normal hedging and debt-management operations.

---

shareholders their purpose in using derivatives and what derivatives are being used; further regulations by a variety of public institutions may not be far behind. Private entities such as corporations, financial institutions, and banks are responding to the regulatory threat by undertaking a massive self-policing effort to measure and control derivatives risk in their own operations.

Public clamor surrounding recent derivatives blow-ups, coupled with the new disclosure rules, has prompted some end users to ban derivatives use completely. Nevertheless, there is little doubt that over the longer term, an increasing number of corporations will turn to derivatives to help manage exposures and reduce financing costs (see Figure 2–1).

TYPOLOGY OF DERIVATIVES LOSSES: UNDERSTANDING WHAT WENT WRONG

The large number of derivatives-related financial catastrophes over the last few years has revealed an underlying pattern of mistakes and mispractices that can be classified into broad categories. Before initiating an approach for derivatives risk-management for corporations and financial institu-

FIGURE 2–2
Typology of Derivatives Risk-Management Disaster

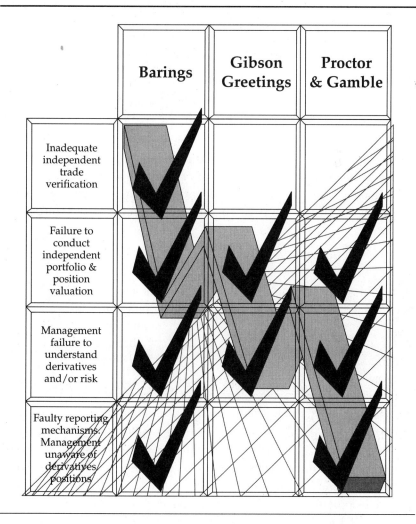

tions, it is worthwhile developing a topology of the phenomena under observation (see Figure 2–2). Each of the components of potential derivatives disaster discussed below highlights the critical issues that an effective derivatives risk-management program needs to address.

"Ticket in the drawer"

"Ticket in the drawer" is an old trading phrase referring to a deliberate effort by a trader to hide either the size of his position or the full extent of his losses, typically because he has exceeded the position size or loss limits set by management or has used unauthorized instruments.

"You mean it goes down too?"

Another common source of derivatives losses results from excessively large positions undertaken by an institution *with the knowledge of its management*. Often these large positions are linked to high-leverage instruments or positions that magnify the firm's exposure to market movements. Unlike the previous scenario, the firm's management is fully aware of the size of the position, but does not recognize its risks.

"Ignorance is bliss"

In this case, the firm does not know its position or the risk caused by this position due to inadequate operations and management information systems. Here, the management is misled only by their own faulty controls process.

MANAGING DERIVATIVES RISK: THE BASICS

No derivatives risk-management plan can ever be completely foolproof given the human component: the same ingenuity that develops control mechanisms can also outwit them. Nor can any derivatives risk-management system be prepared for all possible permutations of market activity. There is a series of measures, however, that if rigorously implemented, can reduce both the human element and intrinsic derivatives risk to an acceptable level.

Consider that all derivatives losses, no matter how seemingly complex, stem from market movements that negatively affect the value of the position. Thus, the root components of derivatives risk are:

1. The sensitivity of the position's value to market movement (a function of the instruments and leverage used).
2. Market movement.

The first step in managing derivatives risk is correctly measuring it; that is, valuing the position based on current market prices and conducting sensitivity analysis to determine future risk. The *manner* in which derivatives risk-management is conducted is critical to the process itself; a hierarchy of overseers including traders, the control functions (operations/ back office, audit/accounting, and risk control), and management (the board of directors, president/chairman, and treasury finance officials) all play key roles in the proper utilization, monitoring, valuation, and control of derivatives.

THE DERIVATIVES RISK-MANAGEMENT AUDIT

Creating the Right Framework

One of the most glaring paradoxes in the spate of recent derivatives crises is the fact that both internal and external auditors *consistently* proved unable to expose the flaws in the policies and procedures that led to the losses. Whether a lack of independent trade verification or failure to ensure that the position was correctly marked-to-market was at the root of the derivatives' runaway loss, one thing is clear: the breach in security almost always escaped normal audit and accounting reviews.

It is for this reason that a derivatives risk-management audit independent of the normal accounting and internal audit function is the critical starting point for any derivatives risk-management program. At minimum, the audit must make the following basic assessments:

1. The firm's exposures and its use of derivatives to manage them.
2. The appropriateness and adequacy of the firm's policies and procedures regarding derivatives.
3. The explicit mandate for the treasury department regarding hedging and speculative trading.
4. The knowledge and awareness of derivatives use by senior company officials and the board of directors.
5. Treasury's understanding of the derivatives it is utilizing.
6. The extent to which the firm is kept aware of its positions and risks through management reporting and risk sensitivity analysis.
7. How adequately the firm monitors its trading activities in relation to its stated policies and procedures.

8. The firm's ability to mark derivatives positions to market and independently verify all its trades.

DERIVATIVES RISK-MANAGEMENT: CORPORATIONS

New transparency rules that reveal to shareholders the true market value (and present profit or loss) of certain highly leveraged derivatives transactions and require that corporations state their purpose for using derivatives in annual reports have, at least momentarily, caused some firms to ban derivatives use outright. Nevertheless, the legitimacy, indeed the necessity, of derivatives utilization by corporations in risk and debt management is well established, and companies neglecting these tools will find themselves at a competitive disadvantage. As such, corporate exposure to derivatives is likely to resume its upward trend.

Even with stricter rules for derivatives accountability to shareholders and a rising awareness of the risks that improperly managed derivatives present, the corporate world most likely remains the most fertile breeding ground for derivatives disaster today (see Figure 2–3). The reason? The blurry line between hedging and speculation, and risk-management controls that fail to differentiate between the two, or that are simply inadequate.

Speculation, after all, is an intrinsic part of risk management: While a "pure" hedge, for example, will result in no net gain or loss (aside from transaction costs), the vast majority of hedges remain bets on the future direction of prices. A company that, at its own discretion, only partially hedges its foreign-exchange exposure, adjusts its hedge ratio frequently, or selectively chooses not to hedge certain exposures at all is, in effect, *speculating* in currencies. Many corporations engage in such "selective hedging" without the extensive systems controls and procedures required in banks and financial institutions that conduct transactions with a clearer understanding of their speculative nature. Under the guise of "selective hedging," many corporations aim to make a profit on their "risk-management" activities. Those companies using derivatives more aggressively by explicitly establishing a profit center in their treasury operation or by selectively hedging (or managing debt) without adequate safeguards may well carry the seeds of the next derivatives-related news headline.

The only way to reconcile the potential dangers of derivatives and their proven usefulness for corporate risk-management and finance is through a well-designed, carefully implemented program that applies the use of

FIGURE 2–3

> ### Gibson Greetings: In Over Its Head
>
> The 1994 Gibson Greetings case underscores the critical role of independent derivative valuations, but it also raises the equally important imperative that corporations *fully understand* the instruments they are using and the risk associated with them. Gibson's losses (ultimately valued at $20 million) grew from their stated $3 million tolerance for loss because Banker's Trust deliberately understated the red ink in the hope that the market would turn around, thereby saving Gibson from discovering the true magnitude of risk intrinsic to the derivative securities that Bankers Trust had sold them. Had Gibson (a) truly understood the derivatives they were buying—and their associated leverage and risks, and (b) known exactly how much money the position was losing, the losses would have been minimized, or never sustained at all. Even though Bankers Trust was censured for deceptive practices and fined, an adequate derivatives risk-management program at Gibson Greetings would have saved them the $6.2 million share of the hit they ultimately had to make good on.

---

derivatives in a manner consistent with an individual company's exposure to risk and tolerance for it. Corporations need to create control frameworks involving *every* level of the corporate hierarchy, but most importantly, beginning at the top (see Figure 2–4).

DERIVATIVES RISK-MANAGEMENT AT THE BOARD LEVEL

One of the most notable aspects of some recent derivative mishaps in the corporate world is the complete lack of awareness by board members and senior company officials of the true nature of the risks they were incurring. Indeed, management guru Warren Buffet recently suggested that if every CEO affirmed to shareholders that he understands every derivative contract and transaction entered into by his company, "you'll fix up just about every problem that exists."

Clearly, top corporate management participation is critical to the derivatives risk-management function. At the outset, the board of directors must explicitly define corporate policy on hedging and speculation: does

FIGURE 2–4
Derivatives Risk-Management Control Hierarchy

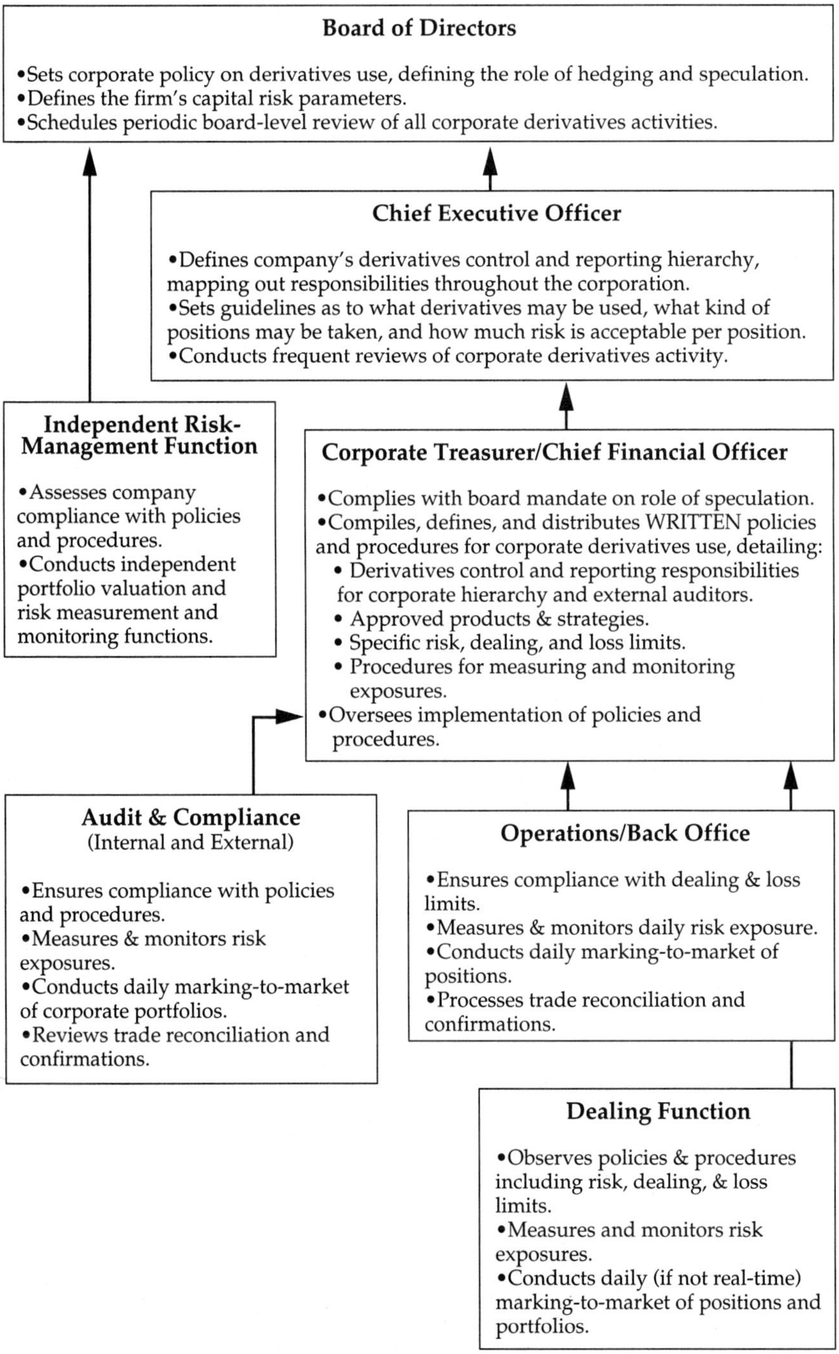

Board of Directors

• Sets corporate policy on derivatives use, defining the role of hedging and speculation.
• Defines the firm's capital risk parameters.
• Schedules periodic board-level review of all corporate derivatives activities.

Chief Executive Officer

• Defines company's derivatives control and reporting hierarchy, mapping out responsibilities throughout the corporation.
• Sets guidelines as to what derivatives may be used, what kind of positions may be taken, and how much risk is acceptable per position.
• Conducts frequent reviews of corporate derivatives activity.

Independent Risk-Management Function

• Assesses company compliance with policies and procedures.
• Conducts independent portfolio valuation and risk measurement and monitoring functions.

Corporate Treasurer/Chief Financial Officer

• Complies with board mandate on role of speculation.
• Compiles, defines, and distributes WRITTEN policies and procedures for corporate derivatives use, detailing:
  • Derivatives control and reporting responsibilities for corporate hierarchy and external auditors.
  • Approved products & strategies.
  • Specific risk, dealing, and loss limits.
  • Procedures for measuring and monitoring exposures.
• Oversees implementation of policies and procedures.

Audit & Compliance
(Internal and External)

• Ensures compliance with policies and procedures.
• Measures & monitors risk exposures.
• Conducts daily marking-to-market of corporate portfolios.
• Reviews trade reconciliation and confirmations.

Operations/Back Office

• Ensures compliance with dealing & loss limits.
• Measures & monitors daily risk exposure.
• Conducts daily marking-to-market of positions.
• Processes trade reconciliation and confirmations.

Dealing Function

• Observes policies & procedures including risk, dealing, & loss limits.
• Measures and monitors risk exposures.
• Conducts daily (if not real-time) marking-to-market of positions and portfolios.

the treasury function have the mandate to operate as a profit center, or not. Since this distinction must now be divulged in the annual reports of publicly held companies, the treasury mandate must be accompanied by a strict set of parameters for their firm's derivatives use, establishing how much of the company's capital can be put at risk, what types of positions should be taken, and what risks associated with these positions are acceptable. Provisions that are not seen as consistent with the treasury mandate will leave the corporation vulnerable to regulatory censure and shareholder litigation.

To ensure the rigid implementation of its derivatives-use policies, senior management must map out the relative roles, responsibilities, and reporting lines of various parts of the corporation. Treasury managers, operations and accounting staff, and the traders themselves are necessarily included in the derivatives control process. And, as a general principle, no derivative instrument should be used without prior approval of senior management.

WRITTEN POLICIES AND PROCEDURES

The treasurer and the CFO, more intimate with the logistical details of corporate finance, are best suited to the task of setting down corporate policies and procedures for derivatives use. This written set of guidelines must be unambiguous in setting limits, controls, and responsibilities. At a minimum, they must address the goals of corporate derivatives use; define the approved products and strategies; provide specific authorization to commit the company to what type and size of trade; detail the responsibilities of the board, the CFO, and the treasury staff; establish counterparty credit-limits and procedures for measuring and monitoring exposure; lay out the frequency and methodology of portfolio valuation and stress testing (scenario analysis, simulation); define the responsibility of internal auditors; and establish sensitivity and concentration limits such as maximum allowable dealing levels and loss limits.

ALLOCATION OF RESPONSIBILITIES AND OVERSIGHT

A critical focal point of effective risk-management practice is the proper allocation of responsibilities among the trading, operations, and accounting areas. It is axiomatic that most derivatives disasters could have been prevented had these three groups adequately performed their checks and balances (see Figure 2–5). Traders are responsible for maintaining the dealing guidelines as set out in the policies and procedures. While it is impossible to prevent an unauthorized trade, an operations group that takes care of trade reconciliation and confirmation can ensure that a trade is closed in a timely fashion. There must be a separation between the dealing function and the exchange of confirmations between trading parties.

AUDIT AND COMPLIANCE

The audit and accounting departments (both internal and external) are in charge of all audit and compliance reports. The key element here is *independent* marking-to-market of portfolios and instruments by a group reporting to a different line of management than the traders. The frequency of market-based portfolio valuation should depend on the volatility, size, and complexity of the portfolio.

An independent risk-management function should be established. This group should report directly to the board of directors, and be charged with the following responsibilities:

1. Assessing company compliance with policies and procedures.
2. Conducting sensitivity analyses.
3. Marking company portfolios to market.

DERIVATIVES RISK-MANAGEMENT: BANKS

While the essential derivatives risk-management framework for corporations and banks is the same, banking's far greater exposure to derivatives demands a more sensitive and timely system of internal controls and audits, including more-sophisticated information systems for risk-measurement, derivatives pricing, portfolio valuation, and management reporting.

Despite the magnitude of banks' exposure to derivatives risk (the notional value of outstanding derivatives contracts held by U.S. commer-

FIGURE 2–5

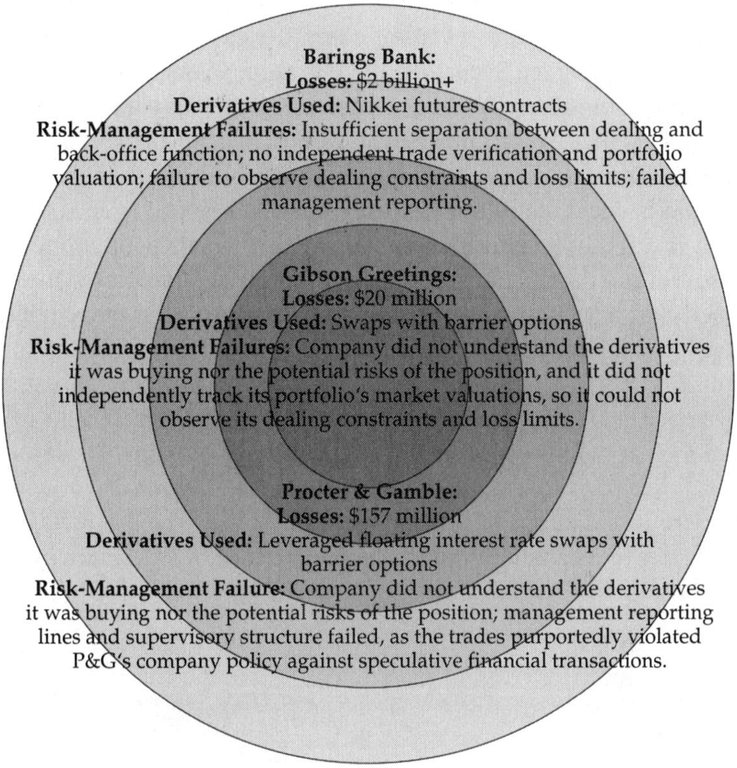

Barings Bank:
Losses: $2 billion+
Derivatives Used: Nikkei futures contracts
Risk-Management Failures: Insufficient separation between dealing and back-office function; no independent trade verification and portfolio valuation; failure to observe dealing constraints and loss limits; failed management reporting.

Gibson Greetings:
Losses: $20 million
Derivatives Used: Swaps with barrier options
Risk-Management Failures: Company did not understand the derivatives it was buying nor the potential risks of the position, and it did not independently track its portfolio's market valuations, so it could not observe its dealing constraints and loss limits.

Procter & Gamble:
Losses: $157 million
Derivatives Used: Leveraged floating interest rate swaps with barrier options
Risk-Management Failure: Company did not understand the derivatives it was buying nor the potential risks of the position; management reporting lines and supervisory structure failed, as the trades purportedly violated P&G's company policy against speculative financial transactions.

cial banks reached upwards of $15 trillion in 1994), the Office of the Comptroller of the Currency (OCC) recently noted that many banks lack written or adequate derivatives risk-management policies and have lapses in their valuation systems.

Additionally, banks have much greater exposure to counterparty risk than their corporate counterparts, and need to utilize master agreements, net exposure, collateralize transactions, and employ third-party credit enhancement, including letters of credit and guarantees.

PERIPHERAL ISSUES IN DERIVATIVES RISK-MANAGEMENT FOR BANKS

The Bankers Trust censure by the Federal Reserve Board and the $10 million fine levied by the Securities and Exchange Commission (SEC) and the Commodity Futures Trading Commission (CFTC) has highlighted what may become a more prominent area of risk to banks engaged in derivatives trading. Though the problem of the misconduct of derivatives salespeople is not directly related to the management of derivatives risk per se, it is directly related to a breakdown in management controls and can pose a significant financial liability to derivatives dealers. Moreover, while Fed chairman Alan Greenspan specifically noted that the regulations imposed on Bankers Trust should not be construed as setting the guidelines for all derivatives dealers, the tendency toward stricter regulation—and increased customer scrutiny—in this area should compel banks to take a harder look at their derivatives dealings with corporations. Dealer banks are already required to assess whether a transaction is consistent with the counterparty's policies and procedures; real or perceived lapses in this regard can leave a bank holding the bag in the case of a derivatives blow-up by a customer.

Chapter Three

Understanding the Difference Between Hedging and Speculating

Greg Beier
Vice President
Hanmi Securities

INTRODUCTION

Understanding the difference between hedging and speculating is a critical skill for those responsible for derivatives risk, such as a director, a portfolio manager, or a treasurer. Without it, these individuals run a greater risk of losing a substantial amount of money, like those listed in Table 3–1 below, entitled "Body Count." Each firm lost money through a hedging program. The Body Count strongly suggests that there is a significant misunderstanding of the term "hedging."

TABLE 3–1
"Body Count"

Firm	Dollar Loss*	Source of Loss
Mead	$12.1 million	Leveraged interest-rate swaps
Gibson Greetings	$16.7 million	Leveraged interest-rate swaps
Dell Computer	$35 million	Leveraged interest-rate swaps
Olympia & York	$65 million	Interest-rate swaps

TABLE 3–1 *(concluded)*

Firm	Dollar Loss*	Source of Loss
Air Products	$113 million	Interest-rate and currency swaps
Procter & Gamble	$157 million	Leveraged currency swaps
Codelco	$207 million	Metal derivatives
Granite Fund Mgmt.	$600 million	Mortgage derivatives
Metallgesellschaft	$1.34 billion	Oil futures
Kashima Oil	$1.53 billion	Currency forwards
Showa Shell Sekiyu	$1.66 billion	Currency forwards
Total	$5.736 billion	

*These figures have been taken from media sources. Actual final losses may vary.

At first blush, it would seem that understanding the difference between hedging and speculating is quite simple. Speculation is a plain old simple bet; the assumption of risk. Hedging, on the other hand, is taking action to reduce risk. In the real world, though, things are more complicated than this, as the Body Count can attest. Hedging with derivatives does not implicitly mean risk reduction. The intention may be risk reduction but in reality what happens is that the bet is shifted from the performance of the asset to the performance of the hedge (the underlying asset and the derivative hedge-instrument together). When a hedge is entered, one is speculating on the risks of hedging, not on the direction of a price or a volatility.

DISTORTED TERMS

The term "hedge" by itself does not have meaning today. The term has become distorted to serve the needs of promoters. Salespeople have learned that it is easier to sell a hedge product than a speculative one, since the customer is always looking for a "sure thing," a chance to get a big gain with little risk. The evolution of the term "hedge fund" is a good example. When hedge funds first appeared about 30 years ago, they originally pursued a strategy of being long and short stocks. Hence, the logic went, these funds were hedged. Before long, hedge funds were taking long and short positions in practically anything. New funds that were brought to market that were using the same investment policy were also called hedge funds. The term became more commonplace and desirable to use. Now, hedge funds generally engage in leveraged speculation and have nothing to do with hedging. The original meaning is practically irrelevant.

The term "hedge" followed a similar pattern of distortion as the derivatives markets developed. Initially, hedging meant balancing gains and losses. With the introduction of viable options exchanges, the complexity of hedging jumped, since options provided so many new ways of addressing specific risks that the definition of hedging was significantly stretched. Eventually, a whole menagerie of other derivatives were developed. Hedging began to cover any kind of risk that was changed through using a derivative; very often this is not necessarily risk reduction.

DERIVATIVES GROWTH

At this point, it may be useful to look at how and why the derivatives markets developed. Exploring the primary trends that established derivatives provides a framework for approaching current issues. The forces behind the growth of the derivatives marketplace also supported the change in the meaning of the word "hedge." Since the equity bear market of 1974, the rise of derivatives use has been chiefly driven by the end of fixed commissions, the information technology (IT) effect, and a favorable derivatives growth environment. The end of fixed commissions allowed bets to be changed at a low cost. The IT effect made it possible to easily identify previously unseen risks. The favorable growth environment encouraged the use of derivatives to change bets to fit specific needs.

Fixed Commissions

The end of fixed commissions in 1975 prompted brokerages to do principal (over-the-counter, or OTC) transactions, develop new products, and increase agency (client) volume as revenues slid from declining commission rates. Derivatives fit the new needs of Wall Street in every respect.

In the past, good client relationships were the franchises that brought business into most investment banks. As competition increased—much of it precipitated by the end of fixed commissions—new products like derivatives became crucial to the growth of many Wall Street firms, since they offered a means to establish a franchise. Firms have been willing to take the investment risk of creating derivatives franchises because good new products always command a high premium. As always, competition drove down fees, but brokerage firms had a chance to retain market share by adding different spins to the same product concept and by creating an air of authority from being the originator that attracted business. The sheer difference in the number and kinds of financial products available between 1975 and today is simple proof of this trend.

New kinds of derivatives usually require the originating firm to make a market in the product. Brokerage firms have been willing to take the risk of making markets since it can be a lucrative business. The often large and undisclosed fee to clients has made principal trading a core business activity of most large firms. The growth of the NASDAQ market, which rose from its humble origins to challenge the New York Stock Exchange, is a reflection of this trend. A widely recognized symbol of this change has been the growth of the market capitalization of Microsoft relative to the decline of IBM.

New derivative products often required other transactions to be done as part of a broader strategy, thereby satisfying the need of firms to increase client volume. For example, dynamic hedging requires one to regularly re-balance the hedge instruments through buying and selling. Though a valid idea, dynamic hedging is also a commission generator. Volume also gets driven up by clients, who can now take much larger positions and hedge specific risks. Additionally, block trading greatly increased the rate of growth in equities volume after 1975.

The Information Technology Effect

The Information Technology (IT) effect is the impact of declining costs amid the rising power and reliability of information technology (hardware, software, and telecommunications) on finance. The IT effect has benefited brokerages by creating price models, speeding up new product development, and increasing transaction volume.

The IT effect made real-time price models a reality. Cheap computing power allowed investors to quickly process large amounts of information, which was previously not possible. For example, the idea of duration (a common measure of a bond's volatility) has been around since 1938 but did not gain widespread acceptance until the 1980s, when the platforms were so broadly available that everyone could calculate it. The faith of the derivatives marketplace rests on these models. The IT effect also made OTC markets fast enough to compete with the organized exchanges.

The IT effect has led to increased liquidity for the derivative markets. Since the inputs that make up the prices of a derivatives market are widely available, market participants can calculate values for themselves to check the dealer or exchange quotes. As mentioned, this increases the investors' confidence and the transparency of prices. The IT effect also enhances liquidity by pooling a global base of investors through worldwide real-time quote systems. By tying together markets from around the world and across asset classes, the IT effect has created demand for new products too.

New product development has also been driven by the IT effect. Derivatives developers create pictures of previously unseen risk through crunching vast amounts of data. Developers then securitize the solution into a derivative product or strategy to sell. This process of isolation, analysis, and securitization has been at the heart of the derivative product cycle.

Favorable Development Climate

The conditions for derivatives product development have been very favorable. After the 1974 bear market, fixed commissions died, the options exchanges started to grow, and the inflation scare of the late 1970s and early 1980s motivated the financial community to devise a means to hedge risk. Additionally, investors have been confident to try out new products because the bond and equity markets have performed well since 1982. The huge interest-rate decline in 1993 pushed many bond fund managers to the edge of risk to capture extra yield, which drove demand for fixed-income derivative products to the extreme. Moreover, the regulatory environment loosened considerably under Republican administrations, allowing financial innovation to flourish.

THREE KINDS OF HEDGING

The following sections will explore three new ways of breaking down hedging activities, as well as the different risks of each. The main point to bear in mind is that a hedge is merely a shift in the kinds of bets one is making.

The Straight Hedge

A straight hedge is the most common form of hedging. Normally, someone has an asset, called the underlying in derivatives parlance, and develops the opinion that the price of it will go down. Through using a

FIGURE 3–1

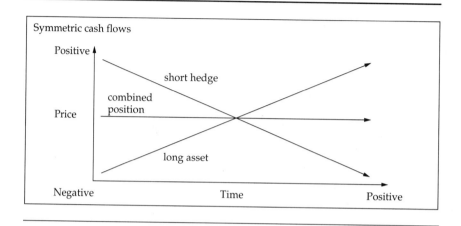

derivative of the underlying asset, such as a bond future for a bond, one can sell short to hedge the value of the underlying. The goal, therefore, is to freeze the value of the asset. Any price rise or decline of the underlying asset is offset by the derivative hedge. In fancier terms, a straight hedge is an attempt to make the cash flows between the asset and the hedge instrument symmetric so that the losses and gains cancel each other out. Normally, the hedge instrument is a derivative substitute or other close proxy to the asset being hedged, so a change in the value of one is closely balanced by the other, and the price of the asset remains stable at around where the hedge was initiated.

Examples of strait hedges are numerous and easy to see. A farmer, who has a field full of wheat, sells wheat futures to lock in the price of his crop prior to harvest. A portfolio manager, who owns a lot of bonds, sells bond futures to freeze the value of her portfolio. A company, expecting to buy $100 million worth of yen, enters into currency forwards to lock in a dollar-yen exchange rate.

In Figure 3–1, the prices of a short hedge, a long asset, and the combined positions of the long asset and short hedge have been plotted over time.

The risks of straight hedging are as follows:

Correlation risk is the most common risk in all hedging. Correlation risk is the risk that the value of the hedge instrument will change unequally to the value of the asset as the asset changes value in the marketplace. Correlation risk always increases when the hedge instrument is not a direct derivative of the underlying, such as a Treasury bond future being used to hedge corporate bonds.

Ratio risk is the risk of using the correct amount and combination of hedge instruments. Ratio risk always increases when the hedge ratio changes with price changes.

Execution risk is the risk that a hedge may be improperly initiated or liquidated. Execution risk is always higher when strategies like dynamic hedging require hedge positions to be changed regularly.

Liquidity risk is the risk that the hedge instrument cannot be purchased or liquidated at the correct price. It is pointless to enter a hedge if one cannot get out of it. The simplest test of liquidity involves a knowledge of the number of firms that make a market in the hedge instrument, the daily volume, and the conditions that will change the volume. The riskiest hedge instrument to use is illiquid and leveraged.

Model risk is the risk that the derivatives pricing model may be incorrect. Particular attention must be paid to see if the assumptions that are being used to determine the structure of a hedge are sound; models are only as good as their assumptions. There is no one standard model and there are many different ways of estimating prices. Other model risk issues are frequency of pricing, margins for error, and even the data used if the instrument is not priced on an exchange market (since there are many different market-makers in an OTC market). Many models use short data-sets that work well with small fluctuations but often produce incorrect analysis when large trends change. Subsequently, hedges are least likely to work as expected when the markets are at extremes in price, volatility, or a trend's length.

Options hedge

An options hedge is like buying insurance. The goal is to pay a price for protection from specific events. It is an attempt to keep a value above, below, within a range, or outside of a price range for a finite period of time. The goal is to purchase the possibility of exposure without having to assume it unless it is needed, which is like insurance. Again, to use fancier terms, the result is an asymmetric cash flow. This means that the value of the underlying asset remains unchanged by the option (less the cost of the option) unless the option is elected (see Figure 3–2).

FIGURE 3–2

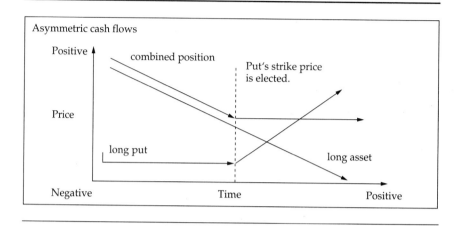

Examples of options hedges are a bit vaguer. A money manager, worried about a decline in the stock market, purchases a portfolio put (a put specifically tailored to protect his portfolio). If the stock market goes up or stays sideways until his put expires, then he has lost the money he paid for his put. If, though, the stock market sinks below the strike of his put, then the put will help to protect him by increasing in value as the market goes down.

Option risk is a complex combination of the aforementioned risks. In fact, options can behave in ways that even the best traders do not understand at times. Questions arise such as: Will the option be properly valued in the marketplace? Will its valuation respond to changes in the underlying market? How often will the hedge ratio have to be changed? Options also add additional risks such as interest-rate risk and volatility risk. Liquidity risk is always another important consideration with options hedging. There is an old comparison of illiquid options to roach motels, "You can get in but you cannot get out," that is helpful to bear in mind when considering whether to enter a potentially illiquid option position.

Speculative hedge

A speculative hedge is an attempt to protect the value of an asset by using a proxy when the hedge instrument is not a derivative of the asset or when

FIGURE 3–3

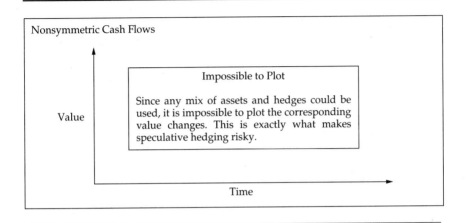

the historical relationship between the hedge instrument and the underlying has been volatile beyond what one considers stable enough for a hedge. This is where judgment risk increases (see Figure 3–3).

JUDGMENT RISK

Judgment risk is the core risk of speculative hedging. It is also the most important risk in any kind of market operation. Judgment is the ability to make good decisions. Poor judgment causes most financial disasters by letting one of the aforementioned risks get out of control.

Generally speaking, experienced professionals just do not wake up one morning and decide to put on a trade that could end up losing a billion plus dollars. They lure themselves into it. The loss of judgment occurs slowly, normally with the acceptance of market trends as facts. Therefore, the biggest losses normally follow the biggest successes. A big win gives people the courage to make huge bets. Big bets are easy to make (and hide) with derivatives. Big bets cause disasters. Any of the risks so far described apply here and can cause a disaster if a big bet is made.

As trends progress in markets, judgment decreases. The proof of this is in financial history. Over the years, there have been many examples of

FIGURE 3–4

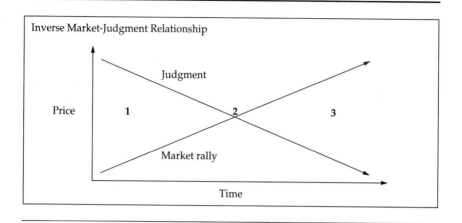

Inverse Market-Judgment Relationship

competent professionals making tremendous bets near the extreme tops and bottoms of markets, resulting in large losses. A large loss almost never happens without a trend being in effect.

The effect of trends on judgment can be graphed with two lines (see Figure 3–4). The first represents the time and size of the move and the second is a generalization of a person's judgment quality going down as the market rallies. At point one, the trend has just started and everyone's judgment is as its sharpest. At point two, everyone relaxes, relieved that things are working out as expected. They may even increase their bets here. At point three, everyone is ecstatic and caution is thrown to the wind. Judgment almost ceases to exist.

EXAMPLES OF DERIVATIVES DISASTERS

Metallgesellschaft AG

MG Corp., the U.S. subsidiary of the German concern Metallgesellschaft, lost roughly $1.34 billion in oil futures. MG quickly grew an oil supply business through offering 5- to 10-year petroleum supply delivery deals. These contracts are the same as making short sales. They hedged their short exposure by going long oil futures. As the business continued to increase, so did their oil positions, until eventually they held more than 20 percent of the long positions in the first three months of crude-oil futures.

Their strategy was dependent on the front months of crude-oil trading at a premium to the back months. If MG could sell the front months at a 10-cent premium to the back months, then rolling over their oil-futures hedge would work. MG made an enormous bet that the front months would stay at a premium for the life of the oil delivery contracts. The only problem is that oil back-months can trade at a premium to the front months and sometimes do. This is exactly what happened.

In November 1993, the November gasoline futures were trading 3.15 cents over the spot (cash market) month. MG had 40,000 gasoline futures contracts to roll over, which at that premium required $53 million. To put this figure into perspective, the U.S. subsidiary needed more than two times the parent company's 1992 net profits of $26.7 million to cover a hedge that was failing to work. As the losses began to mount, the parent company reported that they did not know what was happening at their U.S. unit. They said they were misled.

This is a good example of how a hedge can be deceptively complicated. If MG had been hedging oil-supply deals of the same length as the their oil futures, then they would have been engaging in a straight hedge. But because they entered into long-dated short sales and could only hedge with a short-term instrument, MG entered into a speculative hedge. They were speculating on the correlation risk between the underlying and the cash market. MG made a bet on the price relationship between the front months and back months of energy futures to offset the risk of their long-term obligations. This is a good example of a speculative hedge, since it is well-known that the relationship between the front and back months can change with supply/demand shifts.

The Carry Trade

Many banks got involved in the carry trade as the economy went into a recession. Their rationale was that loan demand would decline as business activity slowed, and this would produce lower interest rates. Therefore, in order to hedge their earnings against weak loan demand, aggressive banks entered into swaps, where they received a fixed long-term rate and paid a short-term rate. If, for example, the 5-year rate was 8 percent and the 1-year rate was 4 percent, the bank gained a positive carry of 4 percent, a hefty gain without having to take any credit risk if the bonds are

U.S. governments. Ironically, several of the entities that were hurt the worst by the carry trades were nonbanks, such as Orange County and Procter & Gamble. These organizations were engaged in leveraged carry trades that backfired when rates rose in 1994.

Granite Partners

Granite Partners was a New York hedge fund that lost $600 million in mortgage derivatives. Granite is a good example of distorting the term "hedge" for marketing needs and of problems with models. Granite sold itself to prospective clients by claiming in its sales literature "to use a great deal of leverage when trading CMO derivatives." They went on to claim that a client's risk is "very little when investing through Granite, [since] when market conditions are not favorable, Granite has the option to wait it out until conditions improve." These marketing statements were a warning to investors, since leverage means that price moves magnify losses and gains. A leveraged portfolio always has less staying power than an unleveraged portfolio. Eventually, the bond market went against their positions and they started losing money. Granite believed that the dealer quotes were incorrect, so they began marking their positions to their in-house models, which offered more favorable prices than the brokerage firms. In the end, Granite had to report large losses to their clients and the firm was shut.

THE THREE FAILURES

Derivatives are likely to continue to cause more problems, since the knowledge, accountability, and judgment failures that caused the previous disasters still persist, according to surveys of derivatives users. Until these failures are corrected, terrible losses will continue. Eventually, some mega-event (e.g., a nuclear strike, an assassination, a major default, war) will quickly move the markets far outside their normal ranges and likely bankrupt the derivatives users that are unprepared. Given the amount of leverage in many derivatives, a "blow-out" scenario from massive market moves against expectations is a real probability for the future. The only question is when? In one year? Five years? Ten years?

This bold forecast is not without precedent. Before 1929, stocks were widely considered to be extremely speculative while bonds were for the prudent investor. The Great Crash and events since have taught the financial community how to manage a stock market, and equities are now core holdings of pension funds and trusts. Like stocks were then, derivatives are still in their youth and are likely to cause trouble until the regulations and training are implemented so that the marketplace can understand and manage these products. The first step in avoiding a derivatives disaster is to ensure that the three kinds of failures that cause large losses are being dealt with.

The first failure that can cause a derivatives disaster is a knowledge failure. It is the easiest to correct. In order for an organization to use derivatives, the people involved in the decision-making process should know what they are doing. Given the technical nature of derivatives and the desire by busy executives to delegate, the top management of many organizations do not understand the risks that they are taking. This can be easily remedied by training, reading, and gradual experience. According to a survey conducted by Record Treasury Management in England, nearly three-quarters of all treasurers in the Financial Times 100 companies marked their positions to market on a monthly basis. Since it is widely accepted that derivatives positions should be marked-to-market on a daily basis (or at a minimum on a weekly basis), it is apparent that knowledge failure is still widespread.

An accountability failure is the second failure. Accountability failure means that the controls are not in place to have derivatives used in an organization. The two primary controls needed are a policy statement and an evaluation procedure. A policy statement defines what derivatives are supposed to do, what kinds of risks can be managed if there is hedging, how much a firm is willing to lose if things go wrong, how derivatives are valued, and what kinds of instruments can be used. The evaluation procedure is the way that the policy statement is enforced and updated. It is also the way the organization learns what strategies are best for them to use and what are not. The evaluation procedure specifically defines who is responsible for what and how tasks are supposed to get done. Markets move in real time, and an organization must be prepared to do so as well.

The third failure is the most devastating. It is a judgment failure. The biggest derivatives risk in an organization is not in the markets, as is commonly thought, but in the individuals making the decisions and implementing them. A large bet made outside the mandate of the policy statement and unchecked by the evaluation procedure can bring an organization down. Companies listed on the Body Count (Table 3–1) learned this.

CONCLUSION

Some day, markets will move violently. It is a fact of life. Those who are ill-prepared and are holding risky positions could get wiped out. It is in the interest of everyone who uses derivatives to understand the kinds of bets that they are making and to determine if these bets are appropriate for what they are supposed to be doing. Large losses, especially if they are outside the mandate of the risks to be hedged, could permanently destroy the careers of those who have responsibility for derivatives risk.

Appendix 3A

Signs of Judgment Failure

INTRODUCTION

The following discussion of judgment failure can be applied to any kind of business where success or failure depends primarily on decision-making skills. For derivatives, judgment (the ability to make good decisions) is paramount.

Grasping the risk picture of any business is always a challenging task. The job becomes even more difficult when reviewing risks that derivatives present. It is probably impossible for many with responsibility for derivatives risk to be able to determine for themselves what their actual risk level is from derivatives. Most executives do not have the time to study the derivatives positions until it is too late.

The biggest derivatives risk an executive has does not come from the markets but from the people working with derivatives. Therefore, the simplest solution to this problem is for an executive not to put his or her energy into gaining a deep understanding of derivatives but to leverage the existing base of people-skills by carefully observing those handling derivatives on a daily basis. People are the "markets" an executive must scrutinize for risk. The key is to determine when people are likely to be involved or get involved in exorbitant risk and then intervene. There are many signs of judgment failure, but they can be distilled down to two classes: overconfidence and hypertension.

Overconfidence

Overconfidence in one's abilities can lead to making big bets, which are the cause of all disasters. Overconfidence is most apparent in the way people spend money both on themselves and on their business overhead.

The signs of an employee's personal spending getting out of control are:

- New custom-made clothes, especially if the person did not wear them before—this is almost always a dead giveaway.
- Expensive sports cars, especially Porsches.

- Always going to expensive restaurants.
- Costly jewelry, watches, and cuff links.
- A big house.
- Excessive dating.

A large expansion in business overhead expenses is the other reliable sign of overconfidence taking root. Overhead normally balloons in two ways. The first is a hiring binge. An investment bank, for example, went from one derivatives specialist to 70 in a single year before the derivatives business went into a severe decline the next year. The other way derivatives professionals raise fixed expenses is through substantially increasing the amount of quote terminals and sophisticated computers. If a department suddenly has several times the amount of equipment that they previously had and their needs have not changed much, a problem may be brewing.

Hypertension

Hypertension, or extreme stress, causes people to not think through situations in a clear and rational manner. They are also more likely to make simple mistakes and disrupt teamwork. The signs of hypertension in an employee include

- Extreme irritability.
- A need to watch every quote, since he or she is afraid of missing something.
- Long-standing business and personal relationships end.
- Divorce.
- Always working and unable to take a vacation, even if asked to.
- Gaining or losing a lot of weight.

Combined Result

Taken together, overconfidence and hypertension tend to create two changes in an employee. The first is that he is likely to stop doing what made him successful in the first place. There are many ways this can happen, but the most common is for an employee to start spending a lot of time in the evenings going out to restaurants and clubs when he did not do so previously. Another way would be for him to "discover" some new way of doing things that is a "sure thing." These "discoveries" tend to lead to problems, since his judgment is already skewed.

The second change is that an employee cannot admit he is wrong. He can see only what he wants to see. The danger is that he will not take a loss when a position starts losing a lot of money or a trade does not work out as expected. This behavior is at the heart of every single derivatives disaster. If a manager sees this problem in any shape, he must act.

Fraud

There is one other important advantage of looking for judgment failures. Many executives claimed that they were lied to by their own employees about the size of the losses. Since a manager is relying on herself to check the judgment quality of her derivatives staff, she is more likely to detect a situation that creates strange changes in their behavior. If the profit-and-loss statement does not show a change but the situation still seems amiss, then a manager can order an audit of the positions by an outside consultant, thus protecting herself from fraud.

Good Judgment

Good judgment comes from a commitment to deal with reality—to see things as they are. An employee who shows good judgment will avoid prolonged periods of extreme optimism or pessimism. He will stick with getting all of the facts and then make a decision based on those facts. Risk of judgment failure declines if these qualities are evident.

CONCLUSION

If a careful eye looks out for overconfidence and hypertension to develop, especially when there is a big price trend in the markets, then the probability of catching a problem before it happens increases.

Chapter Four

New Products, Old Mistakes
*Putting the Derivatives Business
into Context**

Michael S. Rulle
Managing Director and Business Head
CIBC Wood Gundy Financial Products

There was a great deal of turmoil in the financial markets in the mid-1990s. Wide interest-rate swings, currency gyrations and devaluation were visible parts of the everyday scene. Mexico's equity market declined over 50 percent in the first quarter of 1995. The U.S. and Canadian dollars accelerated their secular decline relative to the deutsche mark and yen that began in 1983.

The U.S. dollar dropped 5 percent relative to the yen in the first week of March 1995, the largest percentage decline ever in one week. It had dropped 25 percent in the two years since Bill Clinton took office. The U.S. bond market was almost 20 percent lower than it was one year prior. In yen terms, the U.S. bond market declined almost 40 percent in 12 months.

A lot of value has surely changed hands around the globe. This means that many people, businesses, and governments had huge gains or losses, and we will continue to see further asset shifts of similar size. However, within this turbulent sea of change nothing seems to capture the imagination of market watchers more than activity in the so-called derivatives markets.

---

*The views expressed herein are the views of the author and may not express the views of Canadian Imperial Bank of Commerce, Wood Gundy, or their affiliates (including any of their officers, directors, employees, or agents).

A loss involving derivatives is trumpeted throughout the media as if we had just discovered the concept of financial losses. Losses that cannot be attributed to derivatives are downplayed or given a "so what else is new" response. As Michael Lewis, author of *Liar's Poker* wrote in a recent *Manchester Guardian* editorial: "It is as if the general hysteria about derivatives has created a demand for evidence that we all should be hysterical."

This is not to say that the devaluation of the Mexican peso, major layoffs, or other financial events won't get attention. Clearly, however, a need has arisen to reorder the balance between reactions to bad news with and without the appearance of "derivatives" in the initial paragraph.

For example, in February 1995, rumors abounded in the market about losses at a venerable European financial institution. Trading of shares was suspended and speculation had the firm losing over $1 billion. The company issued a statement that it would make an announcement by the end of the day. Dealers pulled their lines and other firms scrambled to see if they had any exposure. At the end of that day the financial institution called a press conference and announced a $1.3 billion loss. Of course the reader knows to whom I am referring . . . Barings PLC ("Barings"), right?

Wrong! The firm in question was Banque Indosuez, the French banking conglomerate.

Banque Indosuez took $1.3 billion in French real estate write-offs. Most of the loans were to developers, and the losses reflected a severe deterioration in the commercial real estate market in France, particularly in the Paris region. Due to its real estate exposure, the market value of Banque Indosuez declined 25 percent in less than half a year, and shareholders lost over $1 billion.

I find the comparison with the Barings situation to be intriguing. So, too, is the way journalists and legislators reacted to each incident. The glaring differences reflect a peculiar sensibility.

In each case, both the institution and its shareholders suffered $1 billion in losses. In the case of Banque Indosuez, losses were suffered by a diverse group of shareholders. In Barings' case, equity losses were suffered by one shareholder—the Barings family, with a diverse set of shareholdings. Banque Indosuez was downgraded by the rating agencies; Barings was put into receivership.

Despite being put into receivership, Barings did not disappear. Nor did Banque Indosuez. Barings' business was acquired by Internationale Nederlander Greop (ING) after an active bidding process.

My point here is that in both instances, losses were suffered in areas where other institutions have lost money before—and in decades long before the turbulent 1990s. Barings was victimized by a large proprietary trading position in financial futures, the most widely used and understood of financial products. Banque Indosuez was hurt by real estate lending, an activity that has plagued financial institutions on every part of this planet. Virtually all Japanese banks, many Canadian banks, the entire U.S. savings and loan industry, and now the French banking system have had reason to regret some or all of their real estate lending endeavors.

In the mid-1980s, real estate lending helped take down almost the entire Texas banking system in the U.S. The largest of the Texas banks, Texas Commerce Bancshares, was at one time the only bank in America rated AAA by both S&P and Moody's. However, the Texas institution went bankrupt, due in large part to extensive lending to the real estate, oil, and oil services industries.

Both Banque Indosuez and Barings had been profitable in recent years in the activities that ultimately did them harm. What is different is that, in the days following their losses, Banque Indosuez was *not* in the press under headlines castigating a rogue real estate lender. In fact, despite the real estate losses, Banque Indosuez actually released a statement that its Singapore operation was not involved with the Barings derivatives trading loss!

However, do not think for a minute that there will not be an extensive internal due-diligence process based on how Banque Indosuez got itself into such a situation and how it can be avoided in the future. Certainly, individuals' jobs and reputations are at stake.

What I find remarkable in the comparison of the two events, is not that there was absolutely no hue and cry about real estate lending, but rather that there *was* great hue and cry about so-called derivatives activity. The lack of congruence in the amount of attention brought to these two events is paradoxical and in my opinion fundamentally irrational. Other examples of this exist.

The state of West Virginia successfully sued six Wall Street firms because these firms, in its view, convinced the state treasurer to invest in securities whose value characteristics were not fully understood. The securities declined in value, and the state sued and won some significant out-of-court settlements. The securities? Government bonds.

My favorite nonderivative loss that did not raise any hue and cry from regulators, legislators, or the press occurred in 1993. It was the largest shareholder loss ever: $53 billion to be exact. Tens of thousands of people lost their jobs. Seventy percent of the security's value disappeared in 24 months! The investment? IBM common stock.

IBM shares were trading at $130 per share in 1991. The company had a market capitalization of $76 billion. By July of 1993 the stock was at $40 per share with a market capitalization of $23 billion. No editorials were written on the horrors of the stock market. There were no grim warnings or proposed legislation limiting the risks of investing in securities.

A recent op-ed page article in *The New York Times* illustrates what I consider to be typical of the confused reactions to losses in the so-called derivatives market. In an essay about Barings' recent losses, entitled "Singapore Sling," William Safire implores us to "stop the derivatives binge."

Mr. Safire is a former speech writer for Richard Nixon, a political conservative, and a free marketeer. He is considered to be one of the most measured and intelligent observers of the political and economic market-place. Mr. Safire is one of my favorite columnists, and he typically has a perspective that sheds a different and illuminating light on an issue. However, in this instance, I believe he is wrong.

Mr. Safire accuses the Singapore International Monetary Exchange of "looking the other way." He tells us that he has had his ear bent about how swaps and hedges can help in the sharing of risk, but after the Barings episode he concludes that our "financial sages are being a little too cool and comfortable."

What swaps have to do with the Barings situation is very unclear, but Mr. Safire has made this link, somehow.

Let's look at what Barings did. It went long $7 billion in the Japanese stock market using Nikkei futures. Swaps, on the other hand, are bilateral financial contracts on interest rates, primarily G-10 currencies. The only link Nikkei futures and interest-rate and currency swaps have with each other is that they both have been grouped together under the all-inclusive term "derivatives." But this comparison makes no sense. This is like telling the world that we have been too "cool and comfortable" about the benefits of owning U.S. government bonds because IBM shareholders lost $53 billion owning IBM common stock. After all, they both happen to be called "securities," and everyone knows "securities" are risky. Stop the securities binge!

Mr. Safire further writes ominously about dangers "we can sense but do not comprehend"; "that too many old guys don't know what the young guys are doing or how to stop them before one huge loss gets computer driven into a chain reaction that wipes out wealth, reputation and jobs." However, there was nothing computer-driven about what happened at Barings nor anything difficult to comprehend. Is going long or short the market difficult to understand?

Mr. Safire concludes from the Barings' events, not that management had lost control of its internal processes, but that "global exchanges and national regulators need to draw a line between legitimate risk and reckless endangerment." He urges the G-10 financial superpowers to act now to avert a world financial crisis. And yet the only financial crisis that occurred was in the Barings family.

Perhaps because it reads Mr. Safire's columns—or more likely on its own—Barings claimed victim status. However, it appears that the trader executing these strategies had been given a great amount of de facto authority and freedom by management and a line of almost $1 billion. It is unusual that management should give so much authority to one individual, especially one without much experience.

As unfortunate as such an absence of careful risk management is, it certainly does not portend a global financial crisis. Imagine the government being the determinant of what each individual firm's appropriate risk profile should be. Only crude and blunt controls or instruments could be applied to such an endeavor. This would result in limiting the activities of the overwhelming majority of the market, which does not need protection, in the vain hope of protecting the occasional stumbling actor. Even more importantly, how would a government choose which of the economy's infinite number of risky financial activities to regulate?

What if we were to apply the same sensibility Mr. Safire applies in analyzing derivatives and Barings to either the Banque Indosuez or the IBM situation? For example, we might proclaim that we should stop the real estate binge or, as in the case of IBM, we should stop the new technology binge. Certainly, more money has been lost in real estate lending or in IBM stock than in any derivatives activity. Can we, for example, pretend to understand the enormous amount of "creative destruction" (to use a term coined by the economist Joseph Schumpeter) that has occurred in the technology industry for the past 15 years and not understand how a trader can lose money going long in the market?

IBM was a giant mainframe manufacturer who thought the personal computer (PC) (a term that it coined) was a clever little sidebar with no industry significance. It poured billions of dollars into propping up its mainframe business while not paying enough attention to the activities of the PC and related software industries. One of the great events in the history of the technology industry was when Bill Gates convinced IBM to use his operating software in their new PC line. The story goes that he did not even own the software when he completed the deal with IBM, but was soon to buy it from another Seattle software company. IBM agreed to market it and use it in its PC line, but did not demand to have exclusive rights to the system.

A dominant IBM could never imagine that a cloning industry composed of companies like Compaq, Dell, and NEC could take 90 percent of the market. Nor could it imagine that the PC market itself would have strategic significance relative to the mainframe. It failed to understand the possibilities of the very technology that had given IBM its leadership role.

When early victors became later casualties (Appollo, Wang, Digital, IBM) did we call for government regulation because wrong decisions and wrong implementations were made by the management of these firms? When IBM continued to invest billions in "going long" the mainframe did we call for new bureaucracies or for the Securities and Exchange Commission to step in and "draw the line between legitimate investment and reckless endangerment"? Of course not. In fact, it seems ridiculous to even suggest it. Nonetheless, because Barings made a bad decision and a worse implementation, Commentators on derivatives would have us severely limit a multinational, multiasset and multicurrency global market. Worse, they would have us ignore the countless ways derivatives have enabled companies to manage risk and retain capital—capital that was put to use in building better mousetraps and creating jobs.

So why the great concern and interest regarding the dangers of derivatives? Why all the media attention—e.g., cover stories in leading news and business magazines, and a quasi-hysterical airing of the subject on the television program *60 Minutes*? What are the legitimate issues?

The main issue is that derivatives *are* fascinating, and they are in the process of changing our financial environment. This is because of what they represent in the marketplace, a "third wave," to use a cliche, in the recent history of financial markets. As the capitalist system continues to cut its creative/destructive path through history, the need to have an ever increasing efficient capital-allocation mechanism is required. Derivatives have become a key component of that mechanism.

The twentieth century is characterized by unprecedented and almost mind-numbing financial growth. We take this for granted because we are right in the middle of it. When you have lived only in a storm you don't recognize the significance of the wind and rain. The rate of change in the lives of people and the globalism of the twentieth century has to fascinate, humble, and perhaps frighten any historian.

At the end of the nineteenth century, the leading industrial country in the world, the United States, had over 90 percent of its people earning their living from farming or related agrarian activity. There were no cars, no planes, no phones, no radios, no TVs, no electricity; just great expanses of land. Today, less than 5 percent of Americans are employed in farming.

It is barely 90 years since each person was basically responsible for growing their own food for self-survival. If society at large were willing to accept the same living standards as 90 years ago, only 5 percent of the populace would need to work at any one time!

Imagine a work-life of one to two days a month! In fact, this is not a new concept. Herbert Marcuse, the New Left intellectual and heir to Hegel and Marx, wrote in the 1950s and 1960s that technology would free human beings from work.

Of course, the United States is just the tip of the iceberg. The population of the G-10 financial superpowers is approximately 800 million people, representing just 15 percent of the world's population but two-thirds of the world's gross production. That percentage difference represents the amount of slack that exists between the potential and the actual. If the G-10 stood still and grew no further, the rest of the world would have to increase production by a multiple of 15 for there to be proportionality between population and production. That means, just given the *known* technology, there is, objectively or materially speaking, the potential for the global economy to grow that much further relative to today.

The absolute rate of change in the economy, and therefore society, is stunning. Just the *increase* in the GDP in the United States in 1994 represented the total output of the U.S. economy in 1910 and almost 10 percent of the U.S. *total* output in Reagan's first year in office. Despite this remarkable growth, the World Bank released a study last year that showed that at the current differing rates of growth between China and the United States, China will be the largest economy in the world by the year 2030! Yet, at the current rate of growth, the U.S. economy will be four to five times its current size. Now, I am not about to forecast the future; the past is mind-boggling enough. My point is that there has been an enormous surge in the growth of the global economy and the requirement for capital.

Also, as fast as the world's economies are growing, the capital markets that support them are growing at an even faster rate. The U.S. economy is approximately twice the size it was when Reagan first took office. However, the U.S. equity, bond, and money markets are five times as large! It is likely that as the emerging economies reach a certain critical mass, they too will experience comparable growth in their capital markets. Japan is a perfect example of this.

So what does any of this have to do with derivatives? I suggested that derivatives represent a third wave in the financial markets in the latter half of the twentieth century. But what were the other two waves?

The first was the loan market. The large commercial or money center banks were the financial engines of growth. But soon the mechanism of lending and the banking system generally became inadequate to fund all the growth the economy required. It became a financial bottleneck. Loans had little or no liquidity, the risk/reward payoff for the banks became skewed against them, and risk could not be shared efficiently across the broad spectrum of the marketplace. Decisions could not be made fast enough and risk could not be distributed fast enough to account for investors' changes in outlook.

The great period of so-called disintermediation occurred in the 1970s and 1980s, and debt became more freely traded in the global marketplace rather than frozen on banks' books. This period of disintermediation created new instruments and put the money center banks in jeopardy. However, it did not create new risks. Those risks were merely distributed in a more efficient manner. The SEC and other regulators globally changed their rules to permit instant access to the capital markets. This expanding securities market represents the second wave.

A look at the equity markets reveals a similar pattern. After World War II, the U.S. public equity market functioned primarily as a new issue "buy and hold" market. In the 1960s, 1-million-share days were not unusual; now we routinely have 300-million-share days. The equity markets needed to distribute risk more freely as a result of each participant's changing risk/reward outlook. This was difficult because the high fixed-rate commission system in the U.S. equity markets created large negative incentives to buy and sell.

The two most significant regulatory changes that marked the end of this first wave were "May Day" 1975, which ended the fixed-commission system in the U.S. equity markets, and the introduction in 1982 of Rule 415, which permitted issuers real-time access to debt markets. Each event caused both great disruption and benefits.

May Day led to a huge merger and consolidation wave within the investment banking industry. Every equity research firm either merged or went out of business. There were dozens, if not more, that were affected. Rule 415 accelerated this trend as retail firms rushed to enter the origination business and vice-versa. The industry adapted and changed from being advisory-based. The intermediation of capital in the form of securities market-making became its primary function. Banks were disintermediated because they were prohibited by law from engaging in this activity. Large securities firms went out of business. I wonder if there were articles in the 1970s and 1980s bemoaning the casualties of change? The form may have been different, but the effects were the same. Change is both destructive and creative.

The most recent financial wave is in response to the capital markets' need to further distribute risk. Just as the banking system became a bottleneck and gave birth to disintermediation, the capital markets became a bottleneck and in turn gave birth to a new kind of disintermediation—derivatives.

Rather then capital being traded in the form of securities, which was how the banking system was disintermediated, the *characteristics* of capital are being traded in the form of derivatives, and that is how the securities market is being disintermediated. These derivatives—in the form of swaps, options, futures, etc.—are traded on exchanges and over-the-counter, just as stocks and bonds are traded on exchanges and over-the-counter. Just as the growth of the fixed-income and equity markets caused great change, the growth of the derivatives markets has caused change as well. In fact, derivatives gave the big money-center banks the opportunity to return to the front and center of financial market flows.

To expand the parallel to the aforementioned waves, derivatives have allowed institutions to take broader views of the market. This activity brings more capital into play, thus producing a quantum leap in how much risk the capital market can absorb. That's good for corporations and governments because it allows them to expand and enter into new ventures. In other words, derivatives help accelerate economic growth.

Just as the growth of the securities markets helped distribute risk more efficiently in the marketplace relative to the loan market, the growth of derivatives has helped distribute risk more efficiently relative to the securities market. Financial institutions now act as risk holding-tanks. For example, they hold risk transferred to them by issuers and investors until they can find a safe place to transfer the risk themselves.

What is the next wave? Some have said it will be virtual money, sort of a high-tech barter system on the Internet in which economic entities in effect issue their own currency, undertake to trade with each other, and bypass the financial markets altogether—the financial markets and a shadow economy as the ultimate bottleneck!

Whatever is coming, there is one thing that I'm sure will happen: There will be virtual-money adventurers like the Barings' rogue trader and there will be old derivatives hacks who will write articles that harken back to the "better, more comprehensible" good old days.

As this third wave brings back pieces of the first two waves, albeit in a slightly different version, I'm reminded that the noted lawyer Clarence Darrow once said, "History keeps repeating itself and that's one of the things that is wrong with History." Well, in this case, the revivals are good, and derivatives are critical catalysts in the revitalization process.

So what does the Barings incident teach us?

I think my views are obvious. It is no different from what we can learn from Banque Indosuez and from IBM. Ultimately, management has to take responsibility for its own actions and shareholders must hold management accountable. When shareholders and management are the same people, as in the case of Barings, it is truly a case of "we have met the enemy and it is us."

IBM made a bad decision by not recognizing the declining role of the mainframe and the growing role of the personal computer. Because of that, it lost $50 billion for its shareholders. This was a financial disaster of significant proportions, but investors did not panic. Instead, they responded by changing management. They didn't demand new legislation to protect them from the decisions of management. The capital markets didn't blink, the investors didn't flee the technology sector, and IBM was responsive enough to re-emerge as a leader in its industry.

Banque Indosuez will likely learn yet another lesson about concentration of risk and will reassess how it makes loans. I predict that banks will continue to extend loans and that there will not be dire warnings against the evils of lending money.

Barings continues to exist, and ownership was transferred to ING as neatly as the $1 billion was so neatly transferred from the buyers of the futures contracts to the sellers of those contracts.

Here is what I take away from the Barings fiasco: Never give anyone access to a billion dollars without first asking what he or she is going to do with the money. Also, have mechanisms in place so that if you don't like the answer you needn't worry. He or she wouldn't be able to get into mischief anyway.

Chapter Five

Lessons from Derivatives Losses*

Tanya Styblo Beder
Principal
Capital Market Risk Advisors, Inc.

INTRODUCTION

Losses are not new in the capital markets. But for many, *derivatives* losses are. Perhaps you as a manager, board member, or trustee of a dealer, financial institution, corporation, municipality, or fund that might be executing derivatives have asked the question, Should I be worried? You will probably not be surprised to learn that the answer is, It depends. Not all derivatives pose the same risks. Some are inherently riskier than others. Risk also depends a great deal on how the derivatives are used.

A few anxiety-ridden directors, trustees, and supervisors have take the extreme step of placing a moratorium on derivatives activity or purging *all* derivatives from their firms or portfolios. Others have made the mistake of assuming that without derivatives, risk is under control. Sadly, not only do many purged asset- or liability-portfolios have greater residual risk, but they are likely to produce noncompetitive returns or higher costs of borrowings. And, eliminating derivatives places a huge, permanent sector of the capital markets off-limits. This chapter surveys recent losses for

*Reprinted by permission of the publisher, from Tanya Styblo Beder, "Updating Risk Management to Control Losses," in *Financial Engineering with Derivatives,* Jess Lederman and Robert A. Klein, eds. (Chicago: Irwin Professional Publishing, 1995), pp. 167–182.

FIGURE 5–1
Publicly Disclosed Derivatives Losses
(As of December 1994)

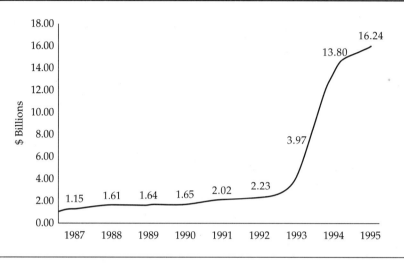

© Capital Market Risk Advisors.

lessons to be learned and discusses ways to reduce the risk of loss in the future. The past 18 months offer lessons for dealers and end users alike. While 1994 became known as the year of the self-risk assessment, 1995 was the year of infrastructure-building in order to maximize benefits while containing loss. Value at risk will continue to be a central theme. The goal for managers, board members, trustees, and supervisors is to update systems, policies, controls, risk-management procedures, and knowledge in order to benefit from the advantages of derivatives.

DERIVATIVES LOSSES

Figure 5–1 illustrates the huge increase in the pace of losses during 1994 and the first quarter of 1995. Since the market's inception, publicly disclosed derivatives losses total over $16 billion. The vast majority of losses occurred between 1993 and 1995. Funds barely present during the first 10 years of derivatives losses racked up almost $5 billion in losses

FIGURE 5–2
Overview of All Publicly Disclosed Derivatives Losses

- All sectors: $12.3 billion in losses since January 1994
- All funds: $4.6 billion in losses since January 1994
- All dealers: $2.3 billion in losses since January 1994

© Capital Market Risk Advisors.

since January of 1994. Dealers who experienced a high degree of loss prior to 1994 re-emerged as losers again in 1995. A list of familiar fund and dealer losses blamed on derivatives appears in Figure 5–2. The most common culprits in losses fall into six categories:

- Insufficient management oversight.
- Mark-to-model risk.
- Improper hedging techniques.
- Unexpected market moves.
- Too much risk relative to capital.
- Fraud.

It is important to observe that these factors are not specific to derivatives. They are the primary culprits that cause losses in *most* financial markets. Only recently emerging is one common culprit in other financial market losses: credit risk, or default risk. During the past 12 years, the financial demise of companies such as Drexel, Bank of New England, Olympia & York, Confederation Life, and other derivatives players has not caused significant counterparty default losses. However, this may change. Recently, both Bankers Trust and Chase announced losses due to the nonperformance of certain counterparties on OTC derivatives transactions. Derivatives credit losses are a clear possibility in situations such as the Chapter 9 bankruptcy filing by Orange County and the failure of many counterparties to pay on complex transactions pending resolution of claims regarding "unsuitability."

How significant is the $16 billion in losses? The answer depends on how the market is sized. One major source, The International Swaps and Derivatives Association, includes primarily OTC derivatives in its estimates. Other sources include exchange-traded derivatives and financially

FIGURE 5–3
Derivatives Universe

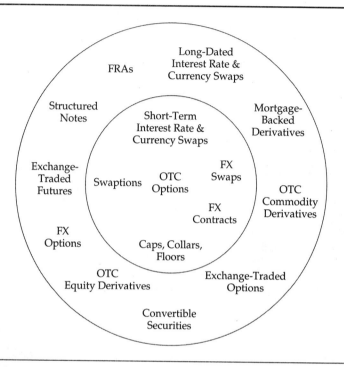

engineered securities. Using this wider definition for the derivatives universe, Capital Market Risk Advisors sizes the derivatives market at an estimated $37 trillion in face amount. Of this, $22 trillion is estimated to be OTC derivatives such as swaps, caps, floors, forwards, and options on such derivatives. Another $3 trillion is estimated to be derivatives-linked securities such as structured notes and engineered mortgage securities. The wider universe of derivatives is illustrated in Figure 5–3. Based on the notional amount outstanding, losses aggregate 0.04 percent. On a mark-to-market basis, losses aggregate 2 percent. Compared with the overall drop of 8 percent in value in the $3.1 trillion U.S. Treasury securities market ($250 billion) from January 1, 1994, to January 1, 1995, the derivatives losses are small. Of huge importance to the market will be the results of the Bank for International Settlement's (BIS) study of the derivatives market as of March 31, 1995. The study will be the most comprehensive survey of OTC and exchange-traded derivatives activity to date. Note that a similar study by the BIS of the foreign-exchange market revealed that while volume estimates were $650 billion daily at the time that the study was commenced, the actual volume was $1 trillion daily, indicating an error factor of over one-third. A similar finding is possible in the case of the derivatives market.

MORTGAGE DERIVATIVES AND STRUCTURED NOTES

Mortgage derivatives and structured notes accounted for a high proportion of losses during 1994 and the first quarter of 1995. During the last two years, an estimated $1.5 trillion in engineered mortgage securities were issued and structured notes grew to over 25 percent of new medium-term note issuance. Many purchasers of the derivative-embedded securities are pension funds, mutual funds, municipal funds, and foundations that are not frequent direct participants in the OTC market for derivatives. Financially engineered mortgage securities began a dramatic period of growth with the introduction of the first collateralized mortgage obligation (CMO) in 1986. In 1986, there were about 500 CMO tranches outstanding. Today there are over 50,000 CMO tranches outstanding.

Structured notes, first issued in the Japanese market in the late 1980s, began a dramatic period of growth in 1991. Most are issued by high-quality credits, including agencies, sovereigns, and global corporations. As with engineered mortgage securities, there is an abundance of unique structures. The spectacular growth of both markets was fueled by yield-hungry investors during a period of falling rates, and by investors who desired customized risk/reward products unavailable in the traditional marketplace. While the engineered structures facilitated the investor's desire to exploit a bull market outlook, without reengineering the embedded rate outlook, there is little surprise that the same structures caused losses as the markets turned bearish.

Many investors discovered that their mortgage investments, purchased with an expectation of a 2- to 5-year life, extended to 10 years or more as interest rates rose and prepayments slowed. Other investors discovered that their structured notes, after providing supernormal returns, not only

FIGURE 5–4
Mortgage-Backed Derivatives

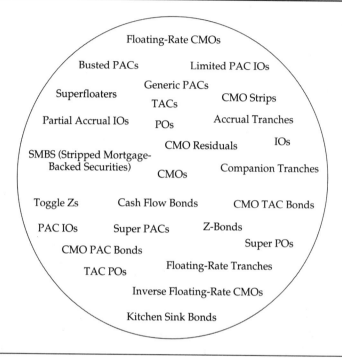

Floating-Rate CMOs
Busted PACs   Limited PAC IOs
Generic PACs
Superfloaters   CMO Strips
TACs
Partial Accrual IOs   POs   Accrual Tranches
CMO Residuals   IOs
SMBS (Stripped Mortgage-
Backed Securities)   Companion Tranches
CMOs
Toggle Zs   Cash Flow Bonds   CMO TAC Bonds
PAC IOs   Super PACs   Z-Bonds
Super POs
CMO PAC Bonds
TAC POs   Floating-Rate Tranches
Inverse Floating-Rate CMOs
Kitchen Sink Bonds

lost value at two or three times the rate of the market at large, but also reset to yield submarket or zero rates of return.

Figure 5–4 illustrates the vast array of engineered mortgage securities. (Note that the galaxy is only a partial listing of what has been invented over the past few years.) Significantly, many of the engineered mortgage securities were created to exploit demand driven by a bullish market outlook. Also, many engineered tranches offered little price transparency, leaving investors dependent on a single dealer to provide a price for mark-to-market purposes. While one should not be surprised that such investments produced losses as the Federal Reserve raised the discount rate during the first and second quarters of 1994, one should be surprised that many investors failed to conduct "what if" analysis to determine *how far* portfolio values would fall with such changes in interest or prepayment rates. One should also be surprised by the failure of many investors to establish limits and procedures for the portion of the portfolio that was single-dealer dependent.

As the mortgage market dislocated subsequent to the downfall of Askin's funds in April 1994, many owners of engineered mortgage securities found that prices were no longer available from their single-dealer source. As a result, owners of such securities were forced to turn to theoretical prices created by mathematical models, with little ability to conduct price verification. Dealers suffered as well. Many lawsuits and arbitration cases pending suggest that dealers may be held to a fiduciary standard in single-price quote situations. There is little doubt that greater transparency in price formulation and greater disclosure regarding the value of derivatives transactions under a wide variety of market scenarios will improve the positions of both dealers and end users. Recently, regulators and dealer associations have stated that end users should obtain valuations from a source independent of the selling dealers.

The galaxy of structured notes is also quite extensive. According to a recent study performed by the Investment Company Institute, the most common derivatives owned by mutual funds are forward foreign-exchange contracts, inverse floating-rate securities (mortgage and nonmortgage based), interest-only mortgage derivatives, principal-only mortgage derivatives, and structured notes. The structured notes are based on numerous underlyings, including interest rates, currencies, equities, commodities, and emerging markets. Two versions of the leveraged inverse floater, one of the most popular types of structured notes held by pension funds, mutual funds, and municipalities, are illustrated in Figure 5–5. Note that while the illustration includes one mildly leveraged structure, namely 30 percent minus three times LIBOR, much more exotic and leveraged structures exist. In our review of several fund portfolios, we have encountered structured note returns such as:

- The Swedish krona rate minus the Paris interbank offered rate cubed (i.e., raised to the third power).
- 19,000% minus 1,900 times LIBOR.
- Twelve times the difference between DM LIBOR and U.S.-dollar LIBOR, denominated in yen.
- The average of swap spreads in Japan, Spain, and Italy times a function of the 10-year constant maturity Treasury rate.

FIGURE 5–5
A Comparison of Returns
(LIBOR Floater versus Structured Note)

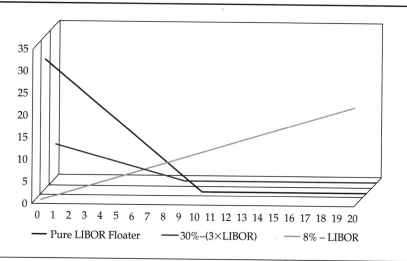

© Capital Market Risk Advisors.

- A coupon based on the formula:

$$15\% \times [1 + Dur_1 \times (7.10\% - CAD\ 5\text{-yr}\ CMS)]$$
$$+ 15\% \times [1 + Dur_2 \times (7.38\% - CAD\ 7\text{-yr}\ CMS)]$$
$$+ 15\% \times [1 + Dur_3 \times (7.11\% - AUD\ 5\text{-yr}\ CMS)]$$
$$+ 15\% \times [1 + Dur_4 \times (7.35\% - AUD\ 10\text{-yr}\ CMS)]$$
$$+ 40\% \times [1 + Dur_5 \times (4.27\% - 7\text{-yr}\ CMS)]$$

where

$Dur_1 = (1/CAD\ 5\text{-yr}\ CMS)$
$\quad \times [1 - (1 + CAD\ 5\text{-yr}\ CMS/2)^{-10}]$
$Dur_2 = (1/CAD\ 7\text{-yr}\ CMS)$
$\quad \times [1 - (1 + CAD\ 7\text{-yr}\ CMS/2)^{-14}]$
$Dur_3 = (1/AUD\ 5\text{-yr}\ CMS)$
$\quad \times [1 - (1 + AUD\ \text{-yr}\ CMS/2)^{-10}]$
$Dur_4 = (1/AUD\ 10\text{-yr}\ CMS)$
$\quad \times [1 - (1 + (AUD\ 10\text{-yr}\ CMS/2)^{-20}]$
$Dur_5 = (1/¥\ 7\text{-yr}\ CMS \times [1 - (1 + ¥\ 7\text{-yr}\ CMS/2)^{-14}]$

To manage such investments, it is vital that dealers and end users be able to reverse-engineer the structure, as well as analyze expected performance under a broad range of probable scenarios. In many situations, reverse engineering produces a better economic result than outright sale. In other situations, it is the *only* alternative—for example, in periods of market dislocation. The failure of many investors to establish limits and procedures for the portion of the portfolio that was single-dealer dependent for pricing and market-making—and the losses that resulted—should be a significant lesson to directors, trustees, and supervisors. A review of the percentage of an investor's portfolio not able to be readily priced by the custodian provides a useful starting point in the pricing arena.

Derivatives losses disclosed by investment portfolios have involved not only exotic or highly leveraged securities in the mortgage market or structured note market, but common structures as well. Some of the investments are simple to value, are liquid, and have no greater volatility than cash-market instruments, whereas others require sophisticated mathematical models. The latter type of investment creates the risk that the model's value may be different than that ultimately obtained in the market. In several situations we reviewed recently, inadequate models existed for the valuation of many mortgage-market and structured-note market investments held in the portfolios. These riskier derivatives, model risk, dealer dependence, and the lack of adequate systems deserve significant focus by managers, directors, supervisors, and trustees to ensure that capital is protected to the desired degree. But the clear challenge is to implement risk management that reflects the reality that in most cases it is the *application* of the derivative or the *overleveraging* of the derivative, *not* the derivative itself, that is likely to cause losses.

LACK OF OVERSIGHT

The demise of Barings as the result of a single individual's actions does not provide new lessons, but reinforces the need for adequate checks and balances plus diligent oversight of all risk-taking activities. The creation of an independent risk oversight (IRO) function is vital to capital preservation within a dealer's or end user's risk appetite. Rating agencies and regulators concur that the IRO function is necessary for firms to comply with minimum standards for risk management in today's markets.

UPDATING RISK MANAGEMENT
FOR DERIVATIVES

How can management, directors, trustees, and supervisors update risk management? Answering this begins with the observation that most derivatives possess no greater risk than other capital market instruments. Capital market instruments may be liquid and be simple to value, such as newly issued U.S. Treasury notes, or they may be illiquid and be complex to value, such as the bonds of a bankrupt company. So it is with derivatives. For example, plain-vanilla interest-rate swaps are simple to value and are liquid, whereas leveraged, path-dependent options on a basket of emerging-market stocks are complex and are likely to be illiquid. In other words, both traditional capital market instruments and derivatives may be more or less volatile in their likelihood to change value. Both offer great risk or small risk, depending on how they are used.

All dealers and end users need to dynamically update policies, controls, and procedures to benefit from developments in risk management. Ideally, the IRO function is designed to encompass all financial risks, not just derivatives and financial engineering. The need to upgrade risk practices not only is apparent from recent losses, but is one of the major points of consensus across regulatory bodies, who agree that the primary safeguards against derivatives losses are adequate authorization, authority levels that increase with the size of capital committed, written and approved investment guidelines, and independent risk oversight. In need of urgent attention are fund guidelines that measure performance based solely on reward dimensions (for example, relative to the Russell 2000 or an S&P index). The need to implement risk dimensions is vital to keep risk within acceptable parameters. A review of several common loopholes created by "old" risk management policies is helpful in illustrating this need:

- A structured note may be linked to a market exposure for which no limits have been set. For example, a fund may have no established limits for a foreign market or commodity but may take on such exposure embedded in a structured note.
- An OTC derivative may involve counterparties below the desired credit level of cash instruments. For example, a AAA requirement may pertain to cash market investments but may not be in force for an interest-rate swap transaction. Alternatively, the swap may be with an unrated, nonguaranteed affiliate.

- The "seven-day sale" definition or other definition for assessing liquidity may be difficult to apply in the case of many derivatives and engineered securities.
- A structured note, while maturing in less than two years, may have the price behavior and volatility of a 20- or 30-year security. For example, a leveraged inverse floater issued by a AAA agency that matures in 18 months may have a 22-year duration.
- Swaps may be permitted, and options may not, but a fund may execute a swap with an embedded option.

The most common level of control for mutual funds is the prospectus. The most common level of control for pension funds, corporate portfolios, foundations, and municipalities is the statement of investment philosophy. While prospectuses and philosophies worked well to control most risks for many years, the fact that they are necessarily broad made them less effective for controlling risk as investment alternatives grew exponentially. Reflecting this fact, a number of funds have implemented specific internal and external guidelines to plug risk-management gaps. In addition, more-detailed information and predefined risk-reports are being required from outside fund managers as well as from custodians.

Current best practice in risk management for dealers and end users includes implementation of a value-at-risk (VAR) measure. VAR is a measure of potential loss over a specific time period, given particular market moves. It is based on statistical analysis and probability theory, with assumptions defined by the user. Numerous VAR calculations have been published, ranging from single-factor to multifactor models. Some VAR models are based on historical data, while others are based on implied market data. Note that a calculation such as VAR is *necessary* but not *sufficient* for controlling risk. Appropriate policies, procedures, limits, controls, and stress testing are necessary, *in addition to* the checks and balances of an IRO function. Rating agencies, the Financial Accounting Standards Board, and numerous regulators have announced their support for VAR.

Sixteen specific steps will help you to bring risk-management policies up-to-date to control losses:

1. Provide in-depth training in derivatives, financial engineering, and risk management for senior management, the board of directors, trustees, and supervisors.
2. Conduct a self-risk audit against widely accepted benchmarks

such as the Group of 30 risk recommendations, CMRA minimum risk standards, guidelines for fund managers in municipalities, or other appropriate risk recommendations.

3. Establish specific, written policies and controls for all financial instruments including derivatives and engineered securities, such as structured notes and engineered mortgage securities.

4. Ensure that risk policies are consistent across cash markets, derivatives, engineered securities, and hybrids.

5. Establish an independent risk oversight function with authority that reports separately from the line investment or hedging function.

6. Ensure that requisite knowledge and systems are in place to manage cash-market instruments, derivatives, engineered securities, and hybrids.

7. Institute stress testing and simulation that cover movements in underlying markets (for example, interest rates, currency rates, commodity rates) *as well as* movements in model assumptions (for example, Hull and White options models versus Black-Scholes, and spline versus linear interpolation).

8. Mark-to-market regularly. This risk measure should be implemented *regardless* of the accounting methodology utilized. For example, firms that utilize accrual accounting should calculate a shadow mark-to-market as part of the risk-management process. Note that for most firms this requires at least a daily mark-to-market.

9. Limit what portion of the portfolio is permitted to be dependent on theoretical models, whether a single dealer's model or your own internal model.

10. Establish adequate reserves to be charged against the mark-to-market values stated in risk reports. These should include, at a minimum, reserves for credit risk, liquidity risk, and operations risk. Model reserves should be implemented for portfolios with significant assets dependent on theoretical pricing models to determine value. Dealers may wish to implement legal reserves for complex or exotic transactions.

11. Require that all transactions be presented in their deleveraged equivalent not only for approvals but also for ongoing measurement vis-a-vis limits. This should include both the leverage em-

bedded in engineered structures and additional leverage via borrowings, reverse repurchase agreements, and so on.

12. Define clearly the relevant roles and responsibilities of asset managers, liability managers, risk managers, senior management, audit, control, and independent risk oversight.

13. Establish clear policies and action for violation of policies, limits, and authorities.

14. Do not allow, or severely limit the amount of, capital at risk in transactions that you do not have the expertise to reverse-engineer and/or the systems to value.

15. Establish early warning systems for risk gone awry and for all variables that can produce a loss beyond acceptable levels.

16. Implement a value-at-risk (VAR) measure and ensure that all assumptions have been stress-tested to determine their impact on capital.

CONCLUSION

Derivatives are a powerful tool for dealers and end users. They are also vital to the competitiveness of many firms.

The responsibility facing managers, directors, trustees, and supervisors is immense. The Office of the Comptroller of the Currency, the Securities and Exchange Commission, the General Accounting Office, and others have made it clear that regulators are looking to the board and senior management to understand, manage, and control the use of powerful but risky derivatives. Updating your risk management practices, including the 16 steps above, can help to ensure that you reap the benefits of this valuable sector of the capital markets while limiting the risk of loss.

Chapter Six

A Framework for Corporate Financial Risk Management

Joel B. Finard

Mary Ellen Stocks
Deloitte & Touche LLP

INTRODUCTION

What is corporate financial risk management? If you're looking for a consensus, you may find yourself walking a tightrope stretched between the treasurer, the CFO, and the board of directors—all likely to have dramatically different answers to the question. The board may be concerned about negative earnings while the CFO concentrates on earnings stability and the treasurer focuses on minimizing the cost of managing commodity, foreign-exchange (FX), and interest-rate exposure. These diverse views and perspectives should not be mutually exclusive, but an agreement on overall strategy, definition of priorities, and a conceptual framework for managing financial risks is essential if the corporation wishes to remain balanced on the highwire of a competitive global marketplace.

A starting point for achieving a coherent and unified financial-risk-management strategy is to ask the following questions:

- What financial risks should be managed?
- What are the goals?
- How will these be accomplished?

- What is the risk tolerance of the institution?
- How will success or failure be defined?

Establishing a successful framework begins with these basics: articulating objectives, strategies and tactics, and defining how performance will be measured. The process requires understanding and commitment throughout the organization to attain these central goals.

Using a mythical company as an example, we will achieve the following three objectives: first, create an integrated financial-risk-management (IFRM) framework, including setting objectives, strategies, and tactics; second, quantify the amount of the company's financial risk; and third, discuss performance measurement techniques to assess the company's ability to achieve its goals.

THE BREAKFAST COMPANY

The Breakfast Company (TBC) is a public corporation comprised of two operating subsidiaries: Sunny Ray's Orange Juice and Gourmet Mountain Coffee. TBC sources orange juice from domestic distributors and purchases coffee from Colombia; these transactions are both denominated in U.S. dollars (USD). In addition to the subsidiaries' domestic sales, Gourmet Mountain Coffee exports coffee to a Paris-based distributor with sales denominated in French francs (FRF). TBC funds itself through the issuance of commercial paper (CP), primarily with 90-day maturities. Senior management of TBC historically has allowed each of the subsidiaries to manage its financial exposures on a completely decentralized basis. Operating performance of the subsidiaries incorporates Sunny Ray's and Gourmet Mountain Coffee's commodity purchasing performance and Gourmet Mountain Coffee's ability to manage foreign-exchange exposure. The treasurer's office of TBC is responsible for managing CP issuance, based on funding requirements. Table 6–1 summarizes TBC's financial requirements/exposures, the company's profitability, and market conditions for its last profitable fiscal year (prices quoted are market averages).

TBC had been profitable every year since its inception; its decentralized approach to managing financial risk appeared to be effective. However, last year the price of coffee and orange juice rose 44 percent and 56 percent, respectively. In addition, short-term interest rates increased 125 basis points, raising TBC's interest expense while the FRF depreciated

TABLE 6–1 *TBC's Most Recent Profitable* **Year**

Market Conditions

Financial Exposure	Commodity Price	Foreign Exchange	Interest Rate
Coffee	$1.60/ pound	FRF 4.25 /USD	
Orange Juice	$0.90/ pound		
Commercial Paper	5.00%		

TBC's Raw Materials, Foreign Exchange, and Funding Requirements

Financial Exposure	Commodity Requirements	Foreign Exchange	Interest Rates
Coffee	225.0 MM pounds	FRF 765.0 MM/ $180 MM Coffee Exports	
Orange Juice	150.0 MM pounds		
Commercial Paper			$200 MM Principal $10 MM Interest Expense

TBC's Income Statement

Income Statement (in $ Millions)

Operating Revenues	**$742**
Cost of Sales	495
Interest Expense	10
Other Costs, Taxes, Charges	75
Net Earnings	**$162**

nearly 20 percent against the USD, making FRF earnings less valuable in USD terms. To make matters worse, demand for coffee and orange juice declined domestically, and to hold on to its current market share TBC was forced to maintain the prior year's retail prices in spite of the dramatic increase in commodity prices. These market conditions caused the first operating loss in TBC's 35-five year history, as Table 6–2 illustrates.

After this painful experience, TBC's board of directors questioned

TABLE 6–2   TBC's Most Recent Year

Market Conditions

Financial Exposure	Commodity Price	Foreign Exchange	Interest Rate
Coffee	$2.30/ pound	FRF 5.25 /USD	
Orange Juice	$1.40/ pound		
Commercial Paper			6.25%

TBC's Raw Materials, Foreign Exchange, and Funding Requirements

Financial Exposure	Commodity Requirements	Foreign Exchange	Interest Rates
Coffee	225.0 MM pounds	FRF 765.0 MM/ $146 MM Coffee Exports	
Orange Juice	150.0 MM pounds		
Commercial Paper			$200 MM Principal $12.5 MM Interest Expense

TBC's Income Statement

Income Statement (in $ Millions)		
Operating Revenues	**$708***	
	Cost of Sales	727.5
	Interest Expense	12.5
	Other Costs, Taxes, Charges	12.5
		75
	Net Earnings	**$(107)**

*Operating revenue falls by $34 million because the FRF depreciated against the USD.

the company's approach to financial risk management. The decentralized nature of financial risk management had prevented the board and senior management from understanding the magnitude of aggregated exposures. In the future, an alternative approach was needed to prevent the unforeseen losses that resulted in a negative earnings report. TBC's management decided to adopt an integrated financial-risk-management (IFRM) framework.[1]

FRAMEWORK—INTEGRATED FINANCIAL RISK MANAGEMENT

Objectives

The first step in effective financial risk management is to clearly define the objectives. In creating a framework to consistently measure, monitor, and manage financial risks on a timely basis, TBC's management decided to focus on the following three objectives:

- Prevent negative earnings.
- Maximize earnings stability.
- Minimize the cost of managing financial exposures.

Strategy

Defining the objectives for financial risk management must be followed by agreement on a strategy for achieving them. Financial risk management can be approached in several ways:

- Decentralized, with operating subsidiaries responsible for managing each exposure with an appropriate hedge.
- A decentralized approach modified by a corporate overlay program, which allows subsidiaries to manage exposures but provides a centralized oversight and hedge adjustment process to ensure consistency of positions.
- A centralized financial risk management process, which limits the role of subsidiaries to providing financial risk exposure information.

TBC's senior management determined that, based on their recent operating loss, a centralized approach to risk management was needed. The strategy proposed by TBC to accomplish their objectives is to:

---

[1]All information contained in this chapter has been created for illustrative purposes and is not a representation of historical market prices or standards. Any similarity to a real corporation is purely coincidental.

Manage the financial exposures centrally, as an integrated portfolio, using concepts of portfolio theory to measure, monitor, and manage risks within acceptable parameters.

A portfolio approach to risk management requires that financial exposures be identified by and then extracted from the operating subsidiaries. Once exposures are aggregated, they can be centrally managed by financial specialists rather than being viewed as separate risks. In TBC's case, and in the case of many corporations, the financial specialists are located in the treasury department, which already manages TBC's interest-rate risk through CP issuance. Centralization of risk will allow TBC's treasury to focus on a broader range of financial-risk-management issues, while portfolio theory provides a mechanism to manage these risks on a systematic basis. Portfolio theory provides a formal methodology for understanding the relationships between exposures, a critical element in minimizing the cost of financial risk management. Additional advantages of this strategy will be discussed in the section "Benefits of Integrated Financial Risk Management."

Tactics

Centralize Management—Treasury Department. For TBC, as with many corporations, the treasury is the logical location for the management of all financial exposures. Since the company's inception, TBC's treasury has historically managed many of the corporation's financial risks, including access to liquidity and interest-rate risk. Although the treasury department has not played the role of an active financial risk manager, it has experience with derivatives instruments, hedge strategies, and the complexities of the financial markets. In assuming a centralized position, the treasury will effectively become TBC's "front line" risk manager, responsible for implementing IFRM strategy and achieving the company's risk-management objectives. Sunny Ray's Orange Juice and Gourmet Mountain Coffee will be responsible only for managing business risk (such as a new product introduction)—a realignment of responsibilities that will have profit-and-loss implications for the subsidiaries. Like each subsidiary, the treasury will have to quantify the value it adds to the corporation; the "value created" will be the treasury's performance as measured against appropriate benchmarks established by the board of directors.

Financial Risk Management Style. TBC must also determine its risk-management style. Will the company decide to hedge each identified exposure, a "pure hedging" style that is the most conservative method of managing financial risks, or will it choose an active style, managing risk on an opportunistic basis by using a variety of hedge products and considering the cost of hedges, market conditions, and trends? Another approach, the speculative risk-management style, allows risks to be traded with a profit objective. This alternative encompasses assuming other exposures than those generated by normal business operations.

TBC has determined that an active risk-management style will most closely fit the business objectives and character of the organization.

Financial Exposure Identification and Measurement. TBC's financial exposures are those encountered in the normal course of business and should be understood as separate and distinct from the business risks that arise from the manufacturing and marketing of products. Unlike business risks, which cannot be readily traded, financial risks have typically been standardized. For example, the nature of the financial risk in rising orange juice prices is the same for all companies that market orange juice. However, changes (or expected changes) in the price of orange juice affect businesses that depend on buying juice one way and those that rely on selling juice in an opposite direction. For example, while Sunny Ray's Orange Juice profits are threatened by an increase in juice prices, a Florida grower fears prices may fall as the result of a bountiful crop and, in anticipation of a market drop, wishes to lock in the current high price for a crop that will soon come to market. The standard definition of orange juice exposure allows each counterparty to exchange risks by entering into a financial contract to achieve their strategic objectives. The grower wishes to lock in the current price to ensure a profit, while TBC needs to be certain of a profit if orange juice prices rise above the current market.

Corporations face many types of financial risks, including interest-rate fluctuations, volatile commodity prices, and erratic foreign-exchange rates. Financial exposures are also categorized by their probability of occurrence, i.e., whether the exposures are firm in nature or anticipated. Once identified, financial exposures can be broken down into risk components that can be traded in over-the-counter (OTC) or exchange-traded financial markets. Derivative instruments such as futures, options, and swaps are common tools that serve as the means for trading away or recharacterizing financial exposures.

TABLE 6–3   *TBC's Financial Exposures Forecast ($ in Millions)*

Financial Exposure	Commodities	Foreign Exchange	Interest-Rate Expense
Coffee	$517.5	$146	
Orange Juice	$210.0		
Commercial Paper			$12.5

From our knowledge of TBC's business and an analysis of their financial statements, we can see that the company's primary exposures are to rising commodity prices, interest rates, and the potential strengthening of the USD against the French franc.

Measurement of Financial Exposures.   Once identified, financial exposures must be quantified. TBC's next step is to forecast types of exposures and the time frame in which they are expected to occur. After reviewing previous years' funding requirements, commodity purchases, and projected sales, TBC has estimated its total financial exposures for the upcoming year to be very similar to those of the prior year. These are shown in Table 6–3.

For complex corporations, the process of measuring and forecasting financial exposures can be lengthy. Forecasting future exposures requires an examination of operating plans and economic conditions in prior years. Most corporations find it useful to implement an exposure capture system that permits subsidiaries to forecast raw-materials purchases, sourcing assumptions, anticipated sales, and financing costs. Forecasting also requires the subsidiaries to categorize firm and anticipated commitments in order to devise an appropriate hedging strategy. The frequency of forecasting will depend on the nature, complexity, and predictability of exposures as well as a continual reassessment of the competitive environment for sourcing and sales alternatives.

Measure Price Volatility.   To effectively estimate and aggregate total corporate exposure, different indexes must be compared. Volatility, or the statistical term "standard deviation," provides the necessary theoretical framework to permit the comparison of different types of exposures on an "apples to apples" basis. Volatility is a measure of the range of

TABLE 6–4   *Financial Exposure Volatility*

	Coffee	Orange Juice	CP	FRF
Standard Deviation	28%	35%	15%	10%

observations around the mean of a set of observations for a specified period of time. It translates historical observations into meaningful information that explains how much and how often a price has risen above or fallen below its average. The typical market methodology for estimating volatility is to use empirical or historical information for a specific index. Calculating volatility assumes a statistical distribution. The most common distribution assumption is a normal distribution,[2] often referred to as a bell-shaped curve. In our example we use a yearly estimate of volatility for the four indexes we are examining—coffee, orange juice, commercial paper, and the French franc. These are shown in Table 6–4. Calculating a historic volatility can be done by using an add-in function on most spreadsheet software.

Confidence Interval.   A confidence interval is a probability measure of the likelihood of a specific occurrence. The board of directors must decide how "confident" they need to be (95 percent, 97.5 percent, or 99 percent) to achieve their objectives. The standard deviation of a normal distribution simply communicates the width or range of possible outcomes in a normal "bell-shaped" distribution. A standard deviation can then be translated into a confidence interval by determining the appropriate percentage probability of an event occurring. In our example we will use two standard deviations,[3] a 97.5 percent confidence interval, that prices will not fall outside a specific level. This means that the company can be 97.5

---

[2] Actually, log-normal distributions are used but the subtle difference is not important for explanatory purposes.

[3] Two standard deviations represent a 97.5 percent confidence interval when one tail of the normal distribution is observed. The rationale for using only one tail of the normal distribution is that only one side of the distribution represents the loss due to price movements. The other side of the normal distribution would represent a gain to earnings due to an opposite movement in prices.

percent confident that the market price of each index will not rise by more than a certain dollar amount in one year's time. For coffee, a 97.5 percent confidence interval translates into a price that will not rise above (0.56 × 1.60 = $0.896) $2.496 per pound. This figure is calculated by multiplying the standard deviation x 2 for a 97.5 percent confidence interval, a figure then multiplied by the current price of coffee at $1.60 per pound, and lastly adding the starting price of coffee. For coffee, a 97.5 percent confidence interval translates into an expected price that will not increase by more than $.896 in 97.5 out of 100 observations. A higher confidence interval will increase the potential exposure and require additional hedging. There is a positive relationship between a higher confidence interval and increased hedging costs.

Measure Exposure Correlations. Correlation measures the strength of the relationship between two variables. Some relationships are stronger than others. For example, the color of your right eye is highly correlated to the color of your left. Other relationships, like the one between the movement of coffee prices and commercial-paper interest rates, may be weak or nonexistent. Correlation shows how different indexes are related. It is important to TBC because it helps to trace the connections between orange juice, coffee, commercial-paper rates, and the French franc (see Table 6–5).[4]

---

[4]For example, when coffee prices rise, people may drink less coffee in the morning and increase their consumption of orange juice. The demand for coffee falls and the demand for orange juice rises. These indexes, as well as their prices, are inversely related. The correlation matrix in Table 6–5 estimates how the price of coffee will move in relation to the price of orange juice. This is indicated in the correlation matrix by the two having a −.25 correlation. This correlation should be based on a historical analysis of the price movements. This means that as coffee prices rise, there is an approximately 25 percent confidence that orange juice prices will fall. The correlation does not explain the magnitude of the move. To estimate the magnitude of the move an analysis of standard deviation must be performed. Combined in a portfolio, these two indexes represent diversity. Portfolio risk depends not only on the risk of the specific index such as coffee or orange juice but also on the degree to which diversification can reduce these risks. Correlation coefficients range from +1 to -1 with:

- + 1 = Perfect correlation; does not diversify risk
- 0 = No correlation; somewhat diversifies risk
- − 1 = Inverse correlation; maximum diversification of risk

Estimating correlation between different indexes requires a historical analysis of data of different indexes. A number of statistical software packages are available to perform this analysis.

TABLE 6–5   *Correlation Matrix*

	Coffee Price	Orange Juice Price	CP Rates	French Franc
Coffee Price	1.00	−.25	.10	−.20
OJ Price	−.25	1.00	.30	−.40
CP Rates	.10	.30	1.00	−.50
French Franc	−.20	−.40	−.50	1.00

Aggregate Exposures

The theoretical foundation for understanding volatility, confidence intervals, and correlation matrixes shown in Table 6–5 will facilitate the aggregation of financial exposure and reduce overall exposure by offsetting different indexes. Once centralized, the treasury may simplify risk management through the use of offsets. A more robust method for managing risks across exposure groups would involve the portfolio diversification methodology established above. This would require the aggregation of the information presented above by using matrix algebra or commercially available software packages. The process is relatively straightforward and is shown in Table 6–6. First, enter the projected revenue, then multiply it by the required standard deviations for a given confidence interval. The total of exposures for different indexes is significantly greater than when correlation or diversification benefits are utilized. The benefits of diversification are substantial and can be seen in Table 6–7. Diversified exposure now allows for a considerably smaller hedging program because it takes advantage of the natural hedges, i.e., the correlations, that exist in the total portfolio.

TBC can reduce the cost of its hedging program by hedging with third-party banks only when an exposure offset does not exist within the company's own portfolio. Centralized exposure management will provide for more efficient hedging for the corporation's overall exposures than was possible when the subsidiaries operated independently.

Portfolio Aggregation

Integrated financial risk management takes advantage of the principles of diversification. TBC has a diversified set of exposures that represent a

TABLE 6–6 *Financial Exposures' Confidence Intervals*
($ in Millions)

	Coffee	Orange Juice	CP	FRF
Total Projected Exposure from Table 6–3	$517.5	$210	$12.5	$(146)
Multiply Two Std Devs	0.56	0.70	0.30	0.20
97.5% Conf Inter				
Potential Additional Exposure	$289.8	$147	$3.75	$(29.2)

variety of risks. To avoid undue concentration of risk, each exposure should be analyzed within the context of the overall portfolio. The basic principle of diversification is that the risks of any set of exposures are not necessarily additive. This is because specific risks are diversifiable and portfolio risks reduce overall exposures. A simple addition of business risk will overstate the true risk of a portfolio of exposures. The "true risk" of a business is the change in the entire portfolio as a result of additional exposure.

Monitoring Exposure

With the above steps completed, the corporation now has compiled a "financial risk map," which will permit the frontline risk managers of the corporation to monitor exposures on an ongoing basis. TBC's financial risk map will provide the basis for designing an appropriate hedge strategy for the "undiversified" risk that remains for the corporation.

Tools for Implementing the Hedge Strategy

Traditional Tools. Having identified, forecasted, and aggregated financial exposures, the corporation must begin to develop a hedge strategy. Some traditional tools for managing commodity-based exposures include vertical integration or entering into a cost-sharing arrangement with the supplier. Foreign-exchange exposure risks can be mitigated by generating payables in the same currency in which the corporation has receivables. Alternatives include denominating all business flows (e.g., payables or receivables) in the corporation's home currency, or changing the sales or sourcing practices of the corporation. TBC's senior manage-

TABLE 6–7 *Benefits of Diversification ($ in Millions)*

Total Exposure 97.5%	$411
Confidence Interval without Diversification	
Total Exposure 97.5%	$273
Confidence Interval with Diversification	
Benefits of Diversification	$138

ment has determined that traditional tools will not be sufficient to manage its financial exposures.

Derivative Instruments.   Both OTC and exchange-traded derivative instruments are used to manage and hedge interest expense, currency exposure, and commodity costs. Because of the ability to match or customize the derivative to the needs of the corporation, these instruments offer a corporation unparalleled flexibility in the capital markets. Exchange-traded and customized derivatives can allow a corporation to unbundle financial risk into its component parts.

Interest-rate swaps and options are effective tools for managing interest-rate risk and permitting a corporation to unbundle its risk into two separate components: liquidity risk and interest-rate risk. In the case of TBC, the company's funding decision was driven by its objective to secure funds at the lowest possible cost. In an upward-sloping-yield-curve environment, the decision was, quite logically, to fund with very short maturities by issuing CP. Although this decision was correct in terms of interest cost, it meant exposure to liquidity risk, and TBC's access to a stable supply of funds has always been critical to the effective managing of its business. To better manage liquidity risk, while retaining exposure to short-term rates, TBC could have issued a 5-year, fixed-rate note and then changed its fixed coupon into CP-based interest expense through an interest-rate swap. Derivatives allow the funding decision to be separated from the term of the funding. If derivatives were not available, the company would have only two options: to issue a fixed-rate note or CP. Typically, by separating these two decisions the funding cost can be reduced.

To better manage foreign-exchange flows such as TBC's FRF exposure, a variety of derivatives tools are available. The most common is the forward sale or purchase of a currency to lock in the value of the future flow today. Foreign-exchange options such as purchased puts (the right to sell a currency) and calls (the right to buy a currency) are also frequently used. Combination options in which there is a simultaneous purchase and sale of options is a popular risk-management strategy because the corporation can reduce its option premium by sacrificing upside potential while still hedging downside risk.

The hedging of commodity exposures such as TBC's orange juice and coffee raw-material prices can be accomplished through the use of futures traded on, in TBC's case, the Coffee, Sugar & Cocoa Exchange and the New York Cotton Exchange. An alternative would be to manage commodity price volatility through the use of an OTC commodity swap, which would allow TBC to lock in its commodity costs by agreeing to pay a fixed price to the counterparty and receiving the "floating" (the price TBC would be charged by its suppliers) or current market cost of the commodity. The effect of entering into this type of swap is to insulate TBC from rising commodity prices; however, the swap also prevents TBC from taking advantage of the possibility of falling prices.

Implementation of Hedges

After determining the type of hedge instruments needed to manage exposures, the next decision involves a choice of which exposures to hedge and whether the positions should be fully or partially hedged. Using the IFRM, the company can devise an optimal hedge program based on the exposure correlations and the coverage exposures that senior management has determined to be appropriate.

Allocation of Exposure—Management's Profits/Losses

Once financial risks have been managed, TBC must allocate the hedge results to each of the operating subsidiaries in order to assess the performance of the overall business. Although the process of allocation is beyond the scope of this chapter, as TBC develops an allocation methodology it must view hedge allocation from an economic standpoint and comply with accounting and tax requirements that relate to exposures and hedges.

Performance Measurement

A critical element of the IFRM framework is the adoption of a performance-measurement methodology. Detailed performance measures are necessary to determine the amount of "value added" by the treasury department and provide the feedback needed to refine hedge strategies. There is clearly no one correct answer to the optimal performance measurement methodology. Performance measurement is a critical tool that must be used to guide the treasury in their pursuit of adding value. One critical element in establishing measurement criteria is understanding the corporate risk management objectives. The initial objectives were to

1. Prevent negative earnings
2. Maximize earnings stability
3. Minimize the cost of managing financial exposures

Therefore, a first step would be to measure if the corporation had negative earnings or not. The second criteria would be to measure the volatility of earnings over the year if no hedging positions had been transacted. This would be compared to the volatility of the earnings that were experienced with the chosen hedges. To measure the cost of managing financial exposures, as a first cut, hedge performance may be measured against a zero percent hedge position. This may answer the question of whether hedging has added any value to the corporation or minimized the cost of managing financial exposures but is probably too broad a performance measure. A better measure might be to compare hedge results against the average forward rate/price of the exposure for the hedge horizon. This will provide senior management with a better indication of treasury's ability to add value with respect to hedge implementation over and above simply placing hedge orders with brokers or banks. Another way to attack this same measurement criterion would be a comparison of hedge results against the rates/ prices that are used in the corporation's budget process in order to set profitability targets. The setting of appropriate performance benchmarks for financial-risk-exposure management is similar to the setting of hedge objectives: the right benchmark for a corporation is based on its particular goals and business attributes.

TBC has determined that its performance benchmarks will be based on three factors:

1. Did the company have negative earnings due to adverse commodity price movements that could have been hedged?
2. Did hedging decrease the volatility of earnings?
3. Was the cost of managing financial exposures minimized? To measure this third criterion, TBC's benchmark will be based on

the average forward rates/prices for each type of exposure for a one year horizon.[5]

TBC's senior management believes that these performance benchmarks are appropriate for several reasons: They are realistic benchmarks that are available in the financial markets and they fit with the active risk management style that TBC has adopted.

CONCLUSION—BENEFITS OF INTEGRATED FINANCIAL RISK MANAGEMENT

The key to managing financial risks within a corporation is to adopt and implement a financial-risk-management framework. To be successful, it is imperative that the board of directors and senior management of the corporation clearly articulate the objectives to be achieved and the strategy for achieving them. In this chapter, we have discussed a new approach to risk management based on the premise that risks are interrelated. The integrated financial-risk-management framework centralizes the responsibility for identifying and minimizing financial risks and permits active management of these risks, adjusting hedge decisions to changing market conditions. By taking advantage of the concept of risk diversification and permitting exposures to offset one another, this framework reduces the amount of hedging required and lowers the cost to the corporation.

Derivatives are powerful tools to manage the corporation's residual risk, i.e., risk remaining once correlations have been taken into account. Exchange-traded and OTC products to manage foreign-exchange, commodity, and interest-rate exposures are readily available in the financial markets. Allocation of results and performance measurement are the final two components of the integrated financial-risk-management framework. Both of these elements are critically important because they permit senior management to assess the overall performance of its businesses and the effectiveness of the corporation's hedge program. The integrated financial-risk-management framework is a powerful tool to increase shareholder value.

---

[5]TBC's average forward prices for coffee and orange juice are based on futures prices, the FRF benchmark is based on the monthly forward rates for one year, and the interest-rate benchmark is based on the average of one month forward CP rates, also for one year.

Chapter Seven

Views on Measuring the Risks of a Derivatives Trader*

Esther Eckerling Goodman
Senior Executive Vice President
Kenmar Asset Allocation Inc.

Caroline Poplawski
Senior Research Analyst
Kenmar Asset Allocation Inc.

Joseph Rosen
Managing Director
Enterprise Technology Corporation

INTRODUCTION

As the diligent reader should by now see very clearly, the terms and concepts of "risk," "risk measurement," and "risk management" in the financial trading arena have numerous and varied meanings and applications, depending on the context of the need as well as on the observer.

*Acknowledgments: Measurements of risk can most clearly be expressed in graphic formats. A special word of thanks is owed to Vicki Rabinowitz and Jean-Marc Merine of Kenmar, who provided assistance in the production of all visual aids. Their meticulous work and attention to detail supplied us with the nineteen illustrative graphs and charts the reader will find in this chapter. Thanks also to Jacquelyn Coffee, of Enterprise Technology Corporation, who carefully edited the manuscript.

Perhaps the importance of effective risk management—whatever that means—need not be pointed out again in times such as these, when a venerable institution like Barings can disappear almost in a flash due to poor or nonexistent risk management and controls.

One useful way of sorting through the various definitions of risk management is to look at it from the perspective of answers to four related, but still conceptually distinct, questions that in our estimation encompass nearly all of the generally accepted purposes of risk management. These questions include:

- What is?—How exposed and risky are our current positions?
- What if?—What could happen to our current exposures if various market parameters (e.g. interest rates, volatilities) change?
- What was?—How well did we perform, and what sorts of risks did we incur in the process?
- What do we want?—Which guidelines do we want to follow in our portfolio asset-allocation decisions—in particular, how much money do we give to which traders?

In this chapter we will focus, though not exclusively, on the retrospective view, or post mortem, of the risks that were assumed by a particular trader or portfolio, and to a lesser extent, on how these risks should be incorporated into the portfolio construction/asset allocation process. One of the benefits of this type of risk measurement is that it more easily lends itself to cross-market analysis and comparison, which is not always the case with the other questions, where you often have the problem of comparing apples to oranges because of the different instruments.

Themes

A number of complementary themes and messages are threaded throughout this book, and in this chapter in particular. Most important, no single measure or ratio, concept, or formula can by itself adequately express, let alone manage, financial risk in a portfolio of assets. In other words, there are no magic bullets available to slay the risk dragon.

One must not lose sight of the reality that all of these algorithms and systems are only tools, and can never substitute for human thought, judgment, and common sense. We confess that much of our discussion is basic common sense. Unfortunately, events of the last couple of years suggest that all too often common-sense rules are ignored. For example, even those organizations with the most sophisticated analytical systems are doomed to fail if they lack the other equally critical elements. Effective risk management requires and entails a holistic philosophy and a truly integrated set of components that must also include the requisite level of senior management involvement, organizational structure, and a culture that fosters cooperation. It also requires a compensation system that does not skew the risk-reward scale for traders so as to give them a "free option," which could encourage some to take untoward risks with the firm's capital.

Managed Futures as a Case Study

The various analyses and examples we present use real numbers from real traders from real Kenmar portfolios—though for obvious reasons trader anonymity is maintained. It is the authors' strongly held view—based on our combined track record of nearly half a century of successfully creating and utilizing risk-management systems to build and manage portfolios of external traders—that a great deal of risk-management technique can best be learned from practices within the managed futures industry.

The proof is in the pudding. As Figure 7–1 illustrates, this industry has experienced tremendous exponential growth over the last decade, increasing in assets under management by a factor of more than 25, to some $26 billion, with approximately one thousand commodity trading advisors (CTAs)—the analogue to the registered investment advisors (RIAs) of the "traditional" money management world—trading mostly futures and options on global exchanges. Kenmar is in the class of industry firm called a CTA and trading manager—although affiliates are registered as an RIA and commodity pool operator (CPO)—whose primary business is the construction and management of multi-advisor, multisector portfolios of external traders for global institutions and large private investors.

Organization of the Chapter

This chapter comprises four additional sections. Following this introduction, we review a number of methods traditionally used to measure risk by both the RIA and CTA worlds, briefly describing for each the underlying

FIGURE 7–1
Growth of the Managed Futures Industry

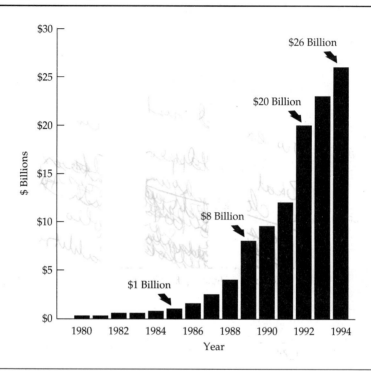

Source: Managed Account Reports, New York, NY.

concept and algorithm, plus key advantages and drawbacks. Next, we broaden the readers' horizons with more creative and innovative approaches to risk-adjusted performance measurement, and pay special attention to the use of graphical views for illustration of the concepts presented. This section also touches on a microlevel review of trade-by-trade risk and real-time exposure analysis, as well as the more qualitative—but still equally important—elements of monitoring and managing traders' risks and performance. The next section puts it all together and examines the portfolio approach to risk management in action. We conclude with a summary of our major points, and a reference list for those interested in additional research and readings.

FIGURE 7–2
Various Views of Standard Deviation—Trader A

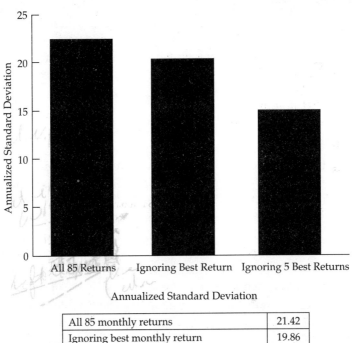

Annualized Standard Deviation	
All 85 monthly returns	21.42
Ignoring best monthly return	19.86
Ignoring five best monthly returns	14.38

Source: Kenmar Asset Allocation Inc.

LIES, DAMN LIES, AND STATISTICS

Many measures used for years to rate money managers are nothing short of woefully inadequate and irrelevant, even when applied with some thought. They are especially misleading when utilized blindly. The analysis of "Trader A's" annualized standard deviation presented in Figure 7–2 (we will have a lot more to say about standard deviation as a measure of risk further on) is a case in point. This trader is clearly penalized by extremely positive returns; note that if the five months with *highest* returns are excluded from the calculation, the trader's standard deviation actually *declines* by about *one-third*.

One-Dimensional Views and the Herd Mentality

Seven discrete statistics that purport to measure either risk, return, or both are described below. Some have clearly become industry "standards" for measuring trader/manager risk—especially by pension fund consultants. In fairness, we must admit that with all their defects noted below, these measures are still a step up from what is unfortunately the rule at many a major bank and trading house, where the only measure of risk and return is that of pure P&L in straight dollar terms.

Average Monthly Return   This sums all of a trader's monthly returns and divides by the total number of months traded to produce the "mean" or "arithmetic average" monthly return. This measure's major advantage is its intuitive appeal as well as its wide acceptance, often on an annualized basis, which is computed by simply multiplying by 12. It is also easy to obtain this information. In the managed futures industry, the Commodity Futures Trading Commission (CFTC) mandates that this data be provided directly by the trader, and in a format dictated by CFTC regulations. The big drawback, shared with other "return only" measures, is that there is little sense of the type and magnitude of risk borne to achieve the return. Furthermore, this figure may be very deceptive when it comes to total return because it does not take into account the effects of compounding.

Standard Deviation (of Monthly Return)   Standard deviation is simply the square root of the variance. This in turn is computed by taking the difference between each monthly return and the mean (see above), squaring this difference, summing the squares, and dividing the sum by the number of months. This measure represents how on average any month's return will vary from the mean (or "expected return" in statistical parlance), and shows the dispersion, or volatility, of monthly returns around the average. Standard deviation describes the riskiness of a trader's or portfolio's returns in the sense of consistency, or how likely you are to actually achieve the average monthly return in any given month. This measure is often annualized by multiplying by the square root of 12. As with the average monthly return described above, this measure can also be computed for differing periods, for example, daily returns and the standard deviation of daily returns (which in turn would be annualized by multiplying by 260 [the approximate number of trading days in a year] and the square root of 260, respectively).

Criticism of this measure is prevalent; we will limit ours to its most annoying features. First of all, in common with other "risk only" performance measures, standard deviation provides no clue to the returns associated with the risk. In addition, this measure does not distinguish between intermittent and consecutive losses, and it therefore does not accurately portray the actual risk of drawdowns, or losses in equity. But most frustrating to those who are still amazed by its pervasive use is the plain fact that it does not focus at all on the risk of loss, but rather includes both upside and downside volatility. In other words, returns that are "too high"—i.e., way above the mean—are by definition as "risky" as those that are way below the mean (see Figure 7–2).

Having said this, however, it is easy to believe that if a trader's mean monthly return is 3 percent and he or she is up 30 percent in a month, even if the worst drawdown has never been as great as −5 percent, more risk *must* exist. Intuitively, you can't make 30 percent in a month without taking risks. In other words, although upside volatility is not as "bad" as the downside variety, it still is risky, albeit in a different sense. This is just another way of looking at the basic relationship between risk and reward as taught in Finance 101.

Now that we have spoken a bit in defense of standard deviation, let's go back to pointing out its shortcomings. Another example will even more clearly illustrate the ludicrousness of this measure. Let's say that Trader 1 has 12 monthly returns, each of which is exactly equal to −2 percent (i.e., ignoring compounding, the trader has lost about 24 percent of your equity). Trader 2, by contrast, has incurred no losing months during the year, with monthly returns ranging between 2 and 5 percent. Well, guess what? In standard deviation terms, Trader 1 is preferred, because he or she has no risk (the standard deviation in this case is zero). To call this counterintuitive is an understatement; "perverse" seems more descriptive.

Sharpe Ratio   The Sharpe Ratio—named after economics Nobel Prize winner William Sharpe—is computed by simply dividing the average monthly return by its standard deviation, with purists first subtracting the monthly risk-free rate from the numerator (the monthly return). While an improvement on return-only or risk-only measures, it is still tainted by the deficiencies inherent in its denominator—monthly standard deviation.

Sterling Ratio   The Sterling Ratio is calculated by computing the average annual return over the last three years, and then dividing by the sum of 10 percent and the average of each of the last three years' drawdowns (we dwell at greater length on the subject of drawdown analyses in the next section). On the one hand this measure has the same benefit as the Sharpe Ratio: that of synthesizing both risk and return. However, this measure has its criticisms as well. First of all it may be unrepresentative of the true downside risk because it only measures the depth, but not the frequency or duration, of drawdowns. Likewise, regarding both return and drawdown, it somewhat arbitrarily restricts the analysis to three years of a trader's track record. Another problem with the Sterling Ratio is its arbitrary use of the 10 percent figure in the denominator. Finally, this measure may also omit larger drawdowns that span *calendar years* (more on this issue below).

MAR Ratio   One computes the MAR Ratio by dividing the average annual return by the maximum peak-to-valley decline (drawdown). While the return component is more representative than that of the Sterling Ratio, specifically for traders with more than three years of history, the reverse is the case with the risk component, because only one figure is used.

Compounded Annual Return and Unit Value   Unit (asset) value is how much an initial $1,000 investment in a trader or portfolio is worth today (this is sometimes called Value Added Monthly Index [VAMI]). As a simple example, assume that after three years of trading the initial value of $1,000 has grown to $1,953. In this case, the compounded annual return is exactly 25 percent: $(1 + 0.25)^3 = 1.953$. The total return for the three-year period is then 95.3 percent (rounded to the nearest tenth).

While compounded return is usually viewed as the "truest" of "average" return measures, it is still lacking an explicit measure of risk; likewise with the unit value figure. However, as we shall see in our discussion of drawdown analyses below, a time-series presentation of unit values by period—especially as a line graph—is information rich indeed, and clearly illustrates downside risk via the peaks and valleys associated with each drawdown and recovery.

Percentage/Number of Months Profitable   Finally, while useful as an indicator of trader consistency, this measure lacks magnitude of risk as well as return.

This short list of statistical measures is just a sampling. There are, of course, many more measures that can be employed to analyze trading performance.

GRAPHICAL AND OTHER VIEWS OF RISK/ RETURN IN TANDEM

In this section, we discuss a number of different but complementary approaches to analyzing risk, which, together with some graphics, facilitate cross-trader comparisons.

Windows Analysis

As we all well know, numbers, especially those describing investment performance, can quite often mislead more than they inform. Let's consider again the "standard" measure: average annual return. Figure 7–3 depicts seven years of trading history for Trader A, with the average annual return equal to approximately 30 percent.

Clearly, this number does not tell the whole story about "expected return," nor about what is going on during the year. For example, what would happen if an investor either exited or entered the trader's program in the middle of a calendar year? A basic problem is that the measure is based on a calendar year—a constraint that is not usually imposed on investors.

A truer and more realistic picture of expected return, as well as risk, can be presented by using a "windows," or "rolling returns," analysis. This analysis focuses on a particular length of time—typically 12 months—and then computes the total return for each consecutive 12-month period in a trader's history. It then calculates a series of statistics based on the entire set of rolling, or window, periods.

Some of these derived statistics include (1) average 12-month rolling return, (2) last 12-month rolling return, (3) best and worst of all rolling returns, and (4) the percentage and number of all 12-month periods profitable. These analyses clearly tend to dampen the exaggerated influence of freak periods of unusually high or low returns. In addition, they are tailor-made for graphical displays. One drawback, or more precisely a complicating factor, is the need for relatively more data to make it meaningful, since you have only N-11 rolling 12-month periods, where N

FIGURE 7–3
Annual Returns (1988–1994)—Trader A

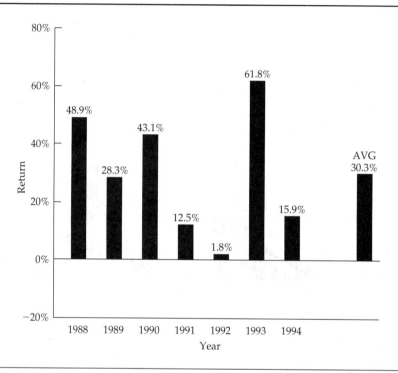

Source: Kenmar Asset Allocation Inc.

is the number of months of history for the trader in question. For example, a trader with a track record of 15 months will only have 4 rolling 12-month periods available to analyze.

Many experts consider this to be one of the best syntheses of risk and reward, as it combines in one set of measures the consistency, magnitude, and riskiness of a trader's performance over time. It also overcomes the calendar year problem, and therefore enables one to specify precisely what the maximum annual gain or loss would have been for any 12-month period. Figure 7–4 illustrates this concept for the same Trader A, over the same period in question. Note that the average 12-month rolling return is substantially greater than the average annual return.

FIGURE 7–4
12-Month Rolling Returns (1988–1994)—Trader A

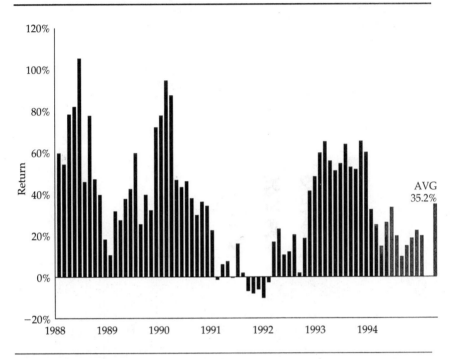

Source: Kenmar Asset Allocation Inc.

A Picture Is Worth a Thousand Words

The above adage is especially true when it comes to measuring, analyzing, and managing financial trading risk. As we never hesitate to point out, numbers alone are usually necessary, but certainly not sufficient, for proper risk management. Figures 7–5 to 7–8 illustrate the explanatory power of "raw" rates of return numbers when combined with graphical displays.

The time-series graphs in Figures 7–5 and 7–6 depict the actual daily percentage changes in account equity, overlaid with a Unit Asset Value Growth Line, for two traders over the same time period. While the performance numbers themselves are clearly material—obviously given your druthers you'd prefer to see stable performance that results in a

FIGURE 7–5
Daily Rates of Return—Trader A

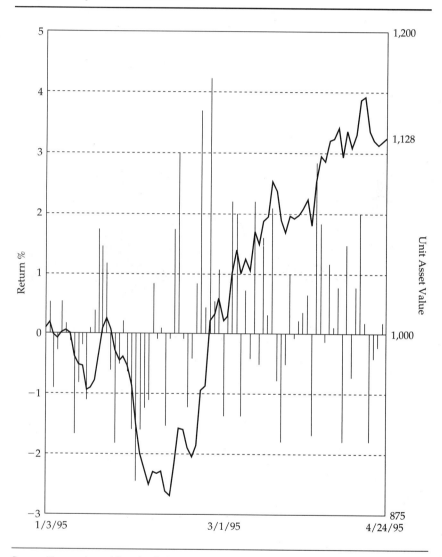

Source: Kenmar Asset Allocation Inc.

FIGURE 7–6
Daily Rates of Return—Trader B

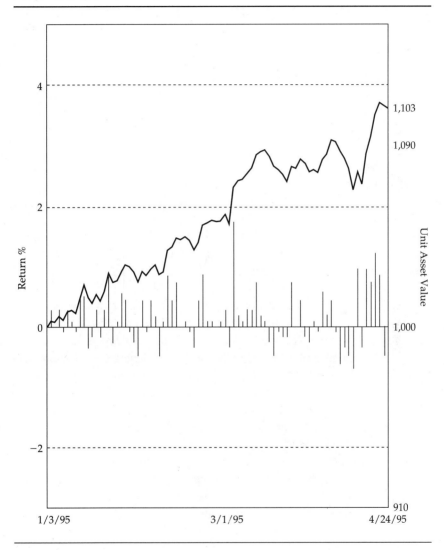

Source: Kenmar Asset Allocation Inc.

smooth capital growth curve over time, as opposed to extremely volatile moves, especially on the downside—it is the pattern, however, that is most instructive. What may be perfectly acceptable and "normal" for one trader and style may not be for a trader with a different style. Here, again, we touch on the qualitative aspect, which we will discuss at length below. Some of this is not easily quantifiable, but with enough experience and knowledge of both the markets traded and the individual traders involved, it is possible to "sense and feel" that something is wrong, and actually see it when the pattern of returns changes dramatically without justifiable reason.

Looking back at Figures 7–5 and 7–6, we see that Trader A is more volatile than Trader B—on both the upside and the downside. This is not inherently an undesirable characteristic. In fact, Trader A outperforms Trader B over this time period. The relevant aspect of these two figures lies in understanding the "why" of the volatility of each of these traders and in particular, any outliers. It is just as important to understand these answers for the less volatile trader as it is for the more volatile trader. In general, recouping a large outlying loss is more challenging for a less aggressive trader than for a very aggressive trader.

Notice how we have used words and concepts like "experience," "due diligence," "judgment," and "knowing your traders," for which numbers are just no substitute. It is one thing to read statistics about daily trading activity, but quite another to actually have it presented before your eyes and see how far off the "outliers" really are. While this is obviously not "rocket science," it is every bit as dependent on advanced information technology as is crunching numbers for the latest algorithms and models.

In fact, a reasonably good argument can be made that not only is it "easier" in some sense to look at the data pictorially, but that in this age of information overload, visual scanning will allow the seasoned observer to quickly discern anomalies that might otherwise be missed. In other words, it can help to both see and "feel" what is normal and abnormal for a given trader and a given market/environment.

Once again, we feel obliged to point out to readers how so much of this is basic common sense. With this in mind, it is nothing short of amazing how few firms actually use these relatively simple yet extremely powerful tools to help manage their traders' performances and associated risks.

Assuming adequate computer horsepower—which we believe to be a given in our industry, when a recent survey estimates that U.S. banks will spend some $17 billion on technology in 1995 (USBanker [1995])—it is

FIGURE 7–7

Distribution of Monthly Returns (1993–1994)—Trader A

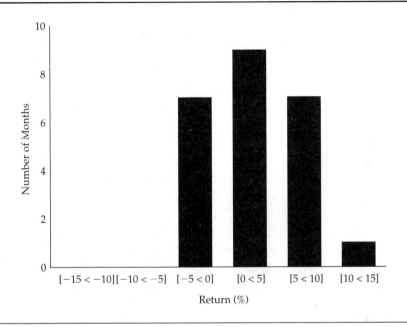

Source: Kenmar Asset Allocation Inc.

just a matter of creativity to decide how best to convert the data into graphical views and what time periods to use.

For example, the simple histogram shown in Figure 7–7 speaks volumes on what are reasonable expectations for this trader's monthly returns, and what outliers should signal "red flags" that demand more-detailed investigations of the trader's positions and overall trading strategy. Perhaps the trader has totally changed his or her methodology and style without bothering to fill you in.

Flexibility is another key factor in successfully monitoring and managing trading risks. Do not be dogmatic or unidimensional in your approach and analysis. For example, even though your specific time frame is an important element in how you do your analysis, you should not arbitrarily restrict yourself to only one particular period and interval of time. Figure 7–8 depicts the same trader's distribution of returns, but this time on a

FIGURE 7–8
Distribution of Daily Returns (1993–1994)—Trader A

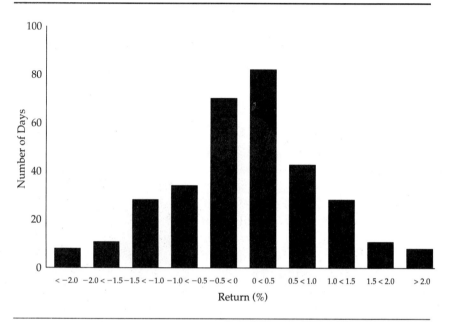

Source: Kenmar Asset Allocation Inc.

daily basis. Clearly, both views are important to prevent the "forest and trees" problem.

Let us also return for a moment to one of our major messages; that there is no one right number or measure or tool appropriate by itself and in all instances. You must have both macro and micro views on various levels and across different time periods and intervals. This could include anything from the percentage of trades in gold futures that were profitable and their average gain, to the trader's best and worst ever 12-month rolling (window) return. You must be able to go back and forth, and especially drill down when necessary. The trick is knowing which technique is most suitable when, and likewise, what are or are not acceptable numbers in a given environment. And once again, for better or worse, this to some extent comes only with experience.

We should also reiterate that basically all of the analytical techniques in our toolkit can and should be used to select traders for inclusion in a portfolio as well as to monitor their continued suitability on an ongoing basis.

Drawdown Analysis

Another deceptively simple, but nevertheless powerful, concept is that of "drawdown," or decline in equity. The unit asset-value graph in Figure 7–9 illustrates this approach to measuring risk. Note the various highs/lows and peaks/valleys in this trader's performance, and—equally important—the respective time intervals in getting from one to the other.

This type of analysis is viewed by many as the truest and most comprehensive measure of downside risk in the classical sense, the risk of losing significant amounts of equity. A drawdown is typically defined as a peak-to-trough percentage drop in equity (as measured by unit value). The time period involved may be one or more months before the previous high (peak) is achieved or surpassed.

Conceptually, drawdown analysis presents, among other perspectives, that of the worst case. In other words, if you were unfortunate enough to have invested with a particular trader at the start of his or her worst-ever period of performance, then how bad would it have been? And how long would it have lasted?

While the graphical display of unit value—particularly when it is labeled with drawdown start-and-end periods—is very useful, when it is combined with a number of derived measures it is unsurpassed in utility. In addition to magnitude, measures of drawdown frequency and duration are also of prime interest. These measures would usually include:

• Worst percentage drawdown ever.
• Recovery period from worst drawdown (to previous peak or more).
• Longest recovery period from any drawdown.
• Average drawdown in magnitude, duration, and recovery period.
• Total number of drawdowns.

Figures 7–10 and 7–11 display graphically and list in a table format, respectively, some of these derived statistics.

FIGURE 7–9
Unit Asset-Value (1988–1994)—Trader A

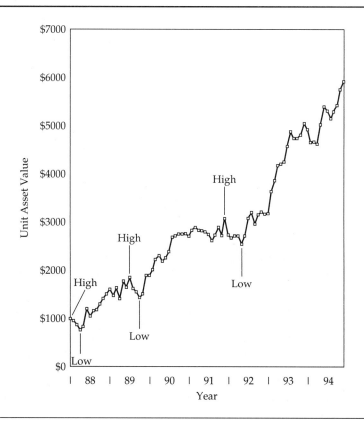

Source: Kenmar Asset Allocation Inc.

Replacing Standard Deviation

It appears that slowly but surely the tide is turning away from standard deviation as *the* measure of investment risk, notwithstanding its relatively long tenure. In fact, a growing literature—both of the scholarly variety (i.e., a lot of equations in academic journals) and in the more mainstream business and financial press—has sprouted to suggest a number of very attractive alternative methodologies that capture the useful aspects of standard deviation without its flaws.

FIGURE 7–10
Drawdown & Recovery Analysis—Trader A

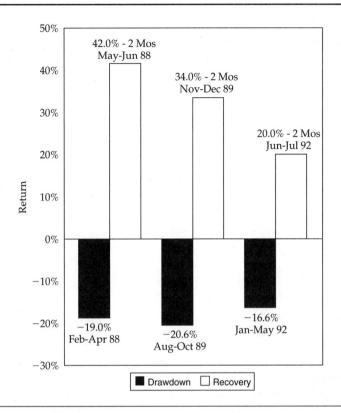

Source: Kenmar Asset Allocation Inc.

These measures go by various names, from "semivariance" and "semideviation" to "downside risk" and "downside probability" or "shortfall risk." What they all have in common is that they do not penalize a trader or portfolio for volatility on the upside, usually defined as returns that are above the mean, or at least positive. In other words they distinguish between "good and bad" volatility. The more sophisticated ones allow the user to specify a target return to use in the analysis, which could be the risk-free rate, or perhaps an actuarially significant rate of return for a pension fund. These measures are also very important when optimizing the allocation of a portfolio's assets via efficient-frontier analysis (using the tools of Modern Portfolio Theory).

Rather than cause readers' eyes to glaze over with mathematics beyond

FIGURE 7–11
Additional Drawdown/Recovery Analysis
February 1988 through March 1995

	Percent Decline	# of Months to Decline	# of Months to Recovery*	% Return During Recovery*
Peak-Valley Drawdowns				
Largest	−20.6%	3	2	34%
Second	−19.0%	3	2	42%
Third	−16.6%	5	2	20%
Consecutive Losses				
Largest	−20.6%	3	2	34%
Second	−19.0%	3	2	42%
Third	−13.5%	2	5	16%
Single Losses				
Largest	−11.8%	1	4	20%
Second	−11.0%	1	6	13%
Third	−10.7%	1	2	42%

Source: Kenmar Asset Allocation Inc.

*Recovery is defined as the period from a valley to a new peak equity (or unit asset-value) level.

the scope of this chapter, we have provided references to a number of useful sources (see especially Markowitz [1959], Rom and Ferguson [1993], and Balzer [1994]).

Analyzing the Trades

As we noted above, in our view both macro and micro analyses of a trader's performance are essential. The sample report in Figure 7–12 illustrates one way of looking at the details of trading profitability by market. While raw dollar figures are clearly not sufficient by themselves, they still are necessary. For example, it is very useful to know where (and when, for that matter) a trader is earning the bulk of profits, and with what degree of consistency. These figures also lend themselves very readily to bar chart and similar graphical views.

FIGURE 7-12
Analysis of Trades by Market (1993–1994)

Market	$ Profit	$ Loss	Net	Ratio	Average Trade Size	Largest Single-Traded Profit	Contracts Traded (#)	Largest Single-Traded Loss	Contracts Traded (#)	# of Trades Profit	# of Trades Loss	% of Trades Profit	% of Trades Loss	Average Net Profit ($)	Average Net Loss ($)
German Bund	376,167	272,607	103,560	1.38	17	126,963	39	(48,120)	26	15	15	50	50	25,078	(18,174)
Aussie Bill	124,608	142,023	−17,419	0.88	41	69,327	30	(22,341)	52	13	27	33	68	9,585	(5,260)
Eurodollar	136,658	154,594	−17,936	0.88	26	88,119	77	(27,125)	49	7	20	26	74	19,523	(7,730)
EuroYen	219,747	308,012	−88,265	0.17	50	67,303	104	(61,391)	147	16	21	43	57	13,734	(14,667)
EuroSwiss	34,815	35,507	−692	0.98	9	23,447	24	(6,192)	24	11	22	33	67	3,165	(1,614)
Long Gilt	367,909	221,481	146,428	1.66	13	86,064	33	(46,967)	20	13	22	37	63	28,301	(10,067)
Italian Bond	336,611	138,104	198,507	2.44	6	70,373	15	(20,264)	10	17	16	52	48	19,804	(8,632)
JapaneseBond	719,555	417,644	301,911	1.44	3	102,426	8	(57,323)	4	15	16	48	52	47,970	(26,103)
Short Sterling	35,692	158,147	−132,455	0.16	13	17,170	39	(11,565)	14	8	49	14	86	3,212	(3,227)
Notional Bond	1,152,669	542,512	610,157	2.12	30	261,936	78	(144,792)	78	17	17	50	50	67,804	(31,912)
Pibor	286,440	201,667	84,773	1.42	27	67,401	80	(31,590)	50	17	20	46	54	16,849	(10,083)
Aussie Bond	547,537	391,314	156,223	1.40	13	221,692	42	(64,319)	42	19	26	42	58	28,818	(15,051)
Aussie 3yr	181,033	158,189	22,844	1.14	21	5,124	18	(17,366)	30	2	4	33	67	5,059	(10,972)
Euro/DM	76,616	80,373	−3,757	0.95	23	47,413	88	(13,229)	8	11	28	28	72	6,965	(2,870)
Tbonds	390,844	483,817	−92,973	0.81	14	115,154	18	(72,773)	28	16	21	43	57	24,428	(23,039)
Tnotes	10,177	43,886	−33,769	0.23	7	47,175	14	(26,324)	14	16	17	48	52	11,315	(9,305)
Interest rates	**4,987,018**	**3,749,877**	**1,237,141**	**1.33**	**20**	**261,936**	**Notional**	**(144,792)**	**Notional**	**213**	**341**	**38**	**62**	**23,413**	**(10,997)**

Source: Kenmar Asset Allocation Inc.

If you are considering hiring a trader for specific market expertise, it might not be a bad idea to review this level of detail. In addition, it is imperative that this analysis be continual, to ensure that the trader remains "true" to his or her trading style and philosophy.

Ongoing Monitoring of Traders

Even more important than the initial analysis of a trader is the ongoing monitoring. It is vital to continually reassess a decision to use a trader. You must keep monitoring the risk exposure of each trader—and of course, of the portfolio as a whole.

The daily monitoring of trading activity for each trader should attempt to ensure consistency with expectations in areas such as:

- Volatility (both upside and downside).
- Trading size (e.g., number of contracts).
- Margin usage (i.e., leverage or gearing).
- Velocity (transaction turnover).
- Performance per market environment.
- Overall adherence to trading strategy.

In cases where the trader has multiple accounts, due diligence dictates that one checks for parallel performance across accounts. In other words, make sure that all the good or bad trades are not going into one account. Likewise, it is important to periodically talk with the traders, find out what they are thinking, and keep tabs on their emotional stability. For example, during losing periods it is important to ensure that the trader is taking the losses in stride, that he or she is not altering the trading strategy and risk-management rules that made that trader successful (successful enough to have been selected to manage money for you). You certainly don't want a trader to *increase* exposure during losing periods in order to more quickly recover.

It is important to ensure that your traders employ their trading and risk-management strategies *consistently* over time. That doesn't mean they shouldn't modify their strategies over time as a result of ongoing research. It means that modifications should not be hastily made as an emotional response to excessive profits or losses.

Portfolio Monitoring

There is no substitute for knowing where your traders and portfolios are now, including their positions, latest market prices, and change from the previous close. Figure 7–13 is a subset of a sample report that shows this information updated on-screen in real time.

The overall portfolio must also be monitored for risk exposures in each market and market sector. This is important, since even if each trader is meticulously and successfully following his or her strategy, you could very well end up with too much exposure in a market on the portfolio level.

One must also constantly monitor portfolio exposure relative to market environment and opportunity. You can alter exposure by removing traders, adding or taking some money away from one or more traders, and by adding new traders who may concentrate in those sectors to which you want greater exposure.

Another view of portfolio diversification by market sector is presented in Figure 7–14. Note how the exposure changes over time to reflect expected relative market opportunities.

The most important message here is that, like it or not, the monitoring function is enormously time- and labor-intensive for all, and must involve everyone in the firm from the "lowest-level" clerk on up to the portfolio manager. It cannot be done part-time nor halfheartedly. Knowledge and experience are indispensable. You might get away without it for years, but the one time that you miss something, there may be no second chance to correct the error.

Qualitative Side

Qualitative input and evaluation is just as important as quantitative input, if not more so. In fact, the two must often be used in tandem for best effect. You must know which statistical measures are most meaningful for different types of traders, and what is "normal" for each. For example, it is vital to understand the rebound/recovery capabilities (from a draw-down) for technical trend-followers, since their downside can be more extreme. Their ability to recover quickly is critical in making them good traders. One should also know that these types of traders usually lose on a

FIGURE 7–13
Real-Time Analysis of Exposure

Today's Performance: 0.6459%		*Last Month's Ending Equity: $142,452,177.42*		
Commodity	*Equity Change*	*Current Position*	*Previous Settlement*	*Current Price*
Financial Instruments				
Aussie 3-yr bond	0.0110%	198	90.2900	90.3300
Aussie 10-yr bond	−0.0302%	156	89.9650	89.9100
Aussie 90-day bill	−0.0003%	−5	91.0300	91.1300
German Bund	0.5495%	493	91.1200	92.0000
Canadian 3-mth bill	−0.0009%	37	92.1400	92.1200
Canadian govt bond	−0.0023%	47	102.8100	102.7100
Metals				
Interbank lead	0.0000%	29	619.2500	625.0000
Interbank nickel	−0.0000%	−8	7,300.4000	7,460.0000
Gold, comex	−0.0793%	706	387.2000	385.6000
Platinum	−0.0004%	6	423.6000	421.7000
Silver, comex	−0.0030%	433	476.2000	476.0000
Currencies				
Interbank b-pound	0.0100%	34	1,613.2680	1,618.3680
British pound option	0.0263%	200	2.5000	2.8000
British pound	−0.0055%	14	159.5800	158.6800
Canadian dollar	0.0154%	−274	70.4300	70.3500
Interbank deutsche	−0.0386%	157	7,194.2450	7,166.2450
Softs				
LDN cocoa	0.0203%	−200	99.2000	98.3000
Coffee	−0.3521%	176	178.2000	171.2000
Coffee option	0.0000%	20	13.0000	13.0000
Cocoa	−0.0007%	8	13.5800	13.4600
Cocoa options	−0.0000%	−27	0.1200	0.1200
Agriculturals				
Corn	−0.0485%	922	248.5000	247.0000
Corn options	0.0175%	−995	6.7500	6.2500
Cotton	−0.0089%	283	109.0900	109.0000
Cotton options	0.0000%	40	1.8600	1.8600
Soybeans	−0.0243%	198	585.7500	582.2500

Source: Kenmar Asset Allocation Inc.

FIGURE 7–14 *Portfolio Diversification by Market Exposure over Time*

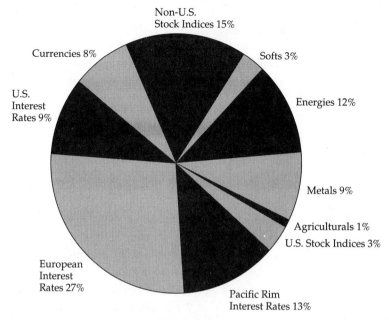

September 1994

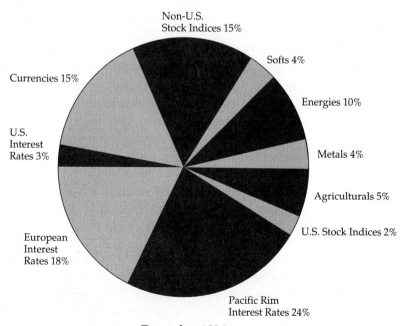

December 1994

Source: Kenmar Asset Allocation Inc.

majority of their trades, as opposed to discretionary traders, whose percentage of winning trades is generally much higher.

It is important for an analyst to have the judgment to know how and when to go from absolute and quantitative measures of performance to relative measures and analyses. For example, in evaluating a bond trader, it is key for an analyst to understand the market's past movement and to have an idea of the potential future movement in that market. Have there been opportunities in the bond market that the trader's style should have captured? Have others with similar styles captured additional profits or controlled risks more effectively? In addition, when comparing this bond trader against benchmarks and other traders, it is more relevant to compare the results against a benchmark that either consists of bond traders or the bond market.

A trader who is up 5 percent for a month may appear to be performing well. However, if the markets have been strongly trending, perhaps he or she should be doing two or three times better, based on our assessment of the trader's strategy and analysis of how and when he or she makes money.

Reliance on pure quantitative analysis alone will not help you here. Likewise, it can't tell you that a U.S. bond trader, for example, who made 50 percent per year between 1991 and 1993 was in the middle of a bull market of unprecedented proportions. What will or should happen to this trader's performance when interest rates start to climb? What happens if the interest-rate markets are volatile and trendless? Can this trader still make money? It is qualitative assessment and judgment that gives rise to these sorts of questions—as well as helping to find some of the answers.

Part of risk assessment and management can be called human risk. Due diligence warrants knowing your trader! There is no excuse for not fully investigating his or her educational and professional background, as well as outside interests. In addition, you should look into his or her moral character, emotional stability, and relationships with other people.

Knowing your traders means also investigating their administrative/ operational/back-office capabilities. This is obviously especially important for external traders. You must visit their office, since one cannot measure a trader's ability to administer and operate a business with performance statistics. And as we all know too well, a failure to manage operational risk could just as easily be a trader's downfall as any trading loss.

The chart of trader attributes listed in Figure 7–15 illustrates another type of portfolio diversification that is very much qualitative in nature. Note that the nine traders in this portfolio are diversified not only by markets traded, but also by trading style and methodology.

FIGURE 7–15
Qualitative Factors in Portfolio Diversification

		Trader A	Trader B	Trader C	Trader D	Trader E	Trader F	Trader G	Trader H	Trader I
Style	Discretionary	✔		✔				✔		✔
	Computerized				✔	✔				
	Systematized		✔				✔		✔	
	Discretionary Overlay		✔				✔			
Analytical Tools	Technical	✔	✔	✔	✔	✔	✔		✔	✔
	Fundamental	✔		✔				✔		
	Diversified	✔	✔		✔		✔			
	Specialized			✔		✔		✔	✔	✔
Markets Traded	U.S. Markets	✔	✔		✔		✔	✔		✔
	Non-U.S. Markets	✔	✔	✔	✔	✔	✔		✔	

Source: Kenmar Asset Allocation Inc.

MANAGING THE RISKS IN A PORTFOLIO OF TRADERS

In this section we put the various concepts and methodologies discussed in this chapter to work in a portfolio context. Much of the discussion that follows involves Modern Portfolio Theory (MPT) and its offshoots. For those readers desiring some brushup we recommend either Elton and Gruber [1991] or Markowitz [1959]. The essence though, is how and why to manage portfolio performance and risk via diversification, using an analytical technique called efficient frontiers (which we touch on below).

We start with a number of illustrations that show a high-level, more-theoretical view of MPT and the role of derivatives traders. Following

FIGURE 7–16
Portfolio Optimization—Managed Futures with Stocks and Bonds

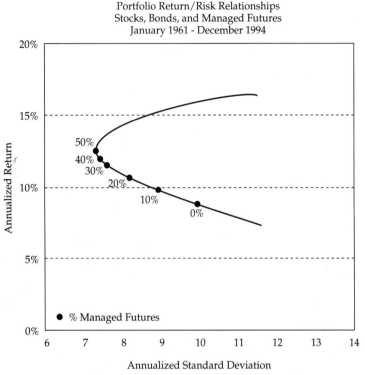

Portfolio Return/Risk Relationships
Stocks, Bonds, and Managed Futures
January 1961 - December 1994

Annualized Standard Deviation

Past performance is not necessarily indicative of future results.

Managed Futures: BARRA/MLM Index
Stocks: S&P 500 with dividends reinvested
Bonds: U.S. long-term bond

Source: Kenmar Asset Allocation Inc.

this, we drill down to *real* examples of MPT in action, and how its concepts can be (and are) applied profitably via multiadvisor, multisector portfolios of external traders. It is hoped that this analysis will also help to ameliorate the concern among some readers over the utility of using derivatives traders for their portfolio.

FIGURE 7–17
Effect of Introducing Managed Futures

Balanced Portfolio (50% Stocks/50% Bonds) Optimized with Managed Futures (1/61–12/94)

Portfolio %MF	Annualized Return	Annualized Standard Deviation	Return/ Std.Dev. Ratio	Total Return	Maximum Drawdown
0%	8.7%	10.0	0.87	1609.6%	−25.6%
10%	9.6%	9.0	1.07	2188.9%	−17.3%
20%	10.5%	8.3	1.26	2896.6%	−14.3%
30%	11.3%	7.6	1.48	3758.9%	−12.9%
40%	12.1%	7.3	1.66	4788.6%	−12.3%
50%	12.9%	7.3	1.77	6013.5%	−11.8%

Past performance is not necessarily indicative of future results.

Managed Futures: BARRA/MLM Index
Stocks: S&P 500 with dividends reinvested
Bonds: U.S. long-term bond

Source: Kenmar Asset Allocation Inc.

MPT in Theory

Figures 7–16 through 7–18 help demonstrate the raison d'etre for managed futures and the whole concept of using derivatives traders, such as CTAs. Figures 7–16 and 7–17 illustrate graphically and via table, respectively, how a representative portfolio comprised of 50 percent stocks and 50 percent bonds benefits from both increased returns and lower risk as varying allocations to managed futures are added. The efficient frontier depicted in Figure 7–16 plots annualized return on the Y axis and annualized standard deviation on the X axis.

For example, going from a zero allocation of managed futures to 50 percent not only raises the return by nearly half—from 8.7 percent to 12.9 percent—but also decreases the portfolio risk as measured in a number of ways. We should also point out that replacing standard deviation with "better" risk measures, such as downside risk, does not change this effect.

Next, Figure 7–18 illustrates in a real-world context, and graphically, the heart of MPT as it pertains to derivatives and the really simple

FIGURE 7–18
Analysis of Bear Equity Markets

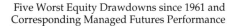

Five Worst Equity Drawdowns since 1961 and
Corresponding Managed Futures Performance

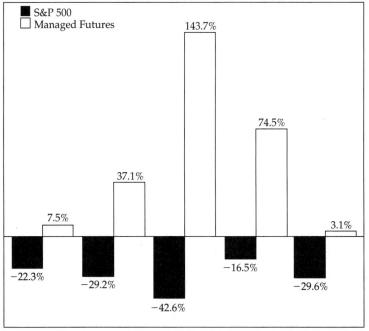

[1/62 – 6/62] [12/68 – 6/70] [1/73 – 9/74] [12/80 – 7/82] [9/87 – 11/87]

Past performance is not necessarily indicative of future results.

Source: Kenmar Asset Allocation Inc.

meaning of diversification. It shows the noncorrelation of derivatives in general and managed futures in particular to the equity market.

As the numbers and charts show, during the five worst periods for equities over the last three decades—as measured by the S&P 500—managed futures indeed provided a very attractive and positive return.

MPT for Real

Now that we have set the stage with some real-world, but still general, examples, we can proceed to illustrate a specific portfolio application of

FIGURE 7–19
Portfolio Gain/Loss by Market Sector (February 1995)

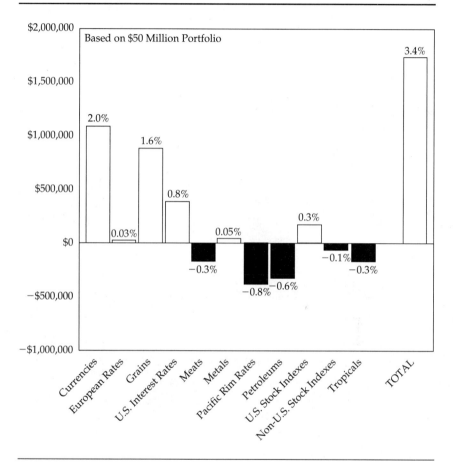

Source: Kenmar Asset Allocation Inc.

MPT for derivatives-trading risk management. Our last figure is based on real data from a Kenmar portfolio and shows diversification from various perspectives.

The various market sector returns depicted in Figure 7–19 clearly demonstrate the benefits of portfolio diversification—the tendency for some markets to be up while others are down. Sounds easy in theory, doesn't it?

SUMMARY

Effective measurement and management of risk in a derivative trader's and portfolio's performance have both quantitative as well as qualitative components, which must work together. You must know your traders in every sense, continue to monitor them, and understand what they are thinking about and how they tick.

It is critical to know how to use which measures and when, and to whom they should be compared—to which "like-style" traders and/or market benchmarks/indices. You must also realize that there does not exist a single, perfect measure with which to slay the risk dragon. Rather, what is called for is a series of complementary approaches and techniques, a number of which we have tried to illustrate in this chapter.

Finally, one must always keep in mind that these are *only tools*, and cannot replace human thought, judgment, and a good dose of common sense.

ADDITIONAL READINGS*

Derivatives

"A Risky Old World: Financial "Derivatives" Can Make It Safer, But the Word Itself Is a Suitable Candidate for Banning." *The Economist*, October 1st 1994.

"Derivatives." *Financial Times Survey*, November 16, 1994.

Figlewski, Stephen. "Innovations: How to Lose Money in Derivatives." *The Journal of Derivatives*, Winter 1994.

Loomis, Carol J. "Cracking the Derivatives Case." *Fortune*, March 20, 1995.

Monroe, Ann. "Derivatives Disclosure: What the SEC Really Wants." *CFO*, March 1995.

Pfabe, Peter K. "Making America's Derivative Markets Work." *Investor's Business Daily*, April 24, 1995.

"Using Derivatives: What Senior Managers Must Know." *Harvard Business Review*, January-February 1995.

---

*For those readers interested in any of these publications and unable to locate them, please feel free to contact the authors.

Managed Futures

Baratz, Morton S. *The Investor's Guide To Futures Money Management* (Columbia, MD: LJR Communications, 1989).

Chance, Don M. *Managed Futures Investing for Institutional Portfolios* (Charlottesville, VA: The Research Foundation of the Institute of Chartered Financial Analysts, 1994).

Lapper, Richard. "Appeal of Derivatives Widens: There Is Growing Interest in Managed Futures Funds in Europe." *Financial Times*, April 18, 1995.

Lintner, John. "The Potential Role of Managed Commodity-Financial Futures Accounts and Funds in Portfolios of Stocks and Bonds." *Financial Analysts Federation Annual Conference*, May 16, 1983.

Peters, Carl C. *Managed Futures—Performance, Evaluation and Analysis of Commodity Funds, Pools and Accounts* (Chicago: Probus Publishing Company, 1992).

Rock, Mitchell S., and Joseph Rosen. "Does Money 'Barrier' Alter Trading Style, Returns?" *Futures*, April 1990.

Managing Traders

Acker, Bill. "Another Fine Mess." *The Banker*, April 1995.

Eichenwald, Kurt. "Learning the Hard Way How to Monitor Traders." *The New York Times*, March 9, 1995.

"Footloose Traders." *Financial Times*, April 26, 1995.

Gallo, Donald D. "How to Succeed in Business Without Betting the Bank." *The New York Times*, April 9, 1995.

Goodhart, Charles. "Why Bonus Payments Are Dangerous." *Financial Times*, March 23, 1995.

Krantz, Matt. "Brokers Find Reforming Traders' Pay to Be a Difficult Proposition." *Investor's Business Daily*, April 24, 1995.

"Pay and Performance: Bonus Points." *The Economist*, April 15, 1995.

"Rethinking Remuneration." *Financial Times*, April 11, 1995.

"Taming the Masters of the Universe." *The Economist*, July 23, 1994.

Modern Portfolio Theory

Elton, Edwin J., and Martin J. Gruber. *Modern Portfolio Theory and Investment Analysis* (New York: John Wiley & Sons, 1991).

Markowitz, Harry M. *Portfolio Selection* (New Haven, CT: Yale University Press, 1959).

Rom, Brian, and Kathleen W. Ferguson. "Post-Modern Portfolio Theory Comes of Age." *Journal of Investing*, Winter 1993.

Rock, Mitchell, Joseph Rosen, et al. "The Right Multi-Advisor Mix or How Much Is Too Much?" *Futures*, April 1991.

Sortino, F., and R. vander Meer. "Downside Risk." *Journal of Portfolio Management*, Summer 1991.

Performance Measurement

Balzer, Leslie A. "Measuring Investment Risk: A Review." *Journal of Investing*, Fall 1994.

Essinger, James, and Joseph Rosen. *Advanced Computer Applications for Investment Managers* (Oxford, England: Elsevier Science Publishers, 1989).

"Pension Fund Investment." *Financial Times Survey*, April 27, 1995.

Sortino, F., and L. Price. "Performance Measurement in a Downside Risk Framework." *Journal of Investing*, Fall 1994.

Risk Management

Arterian, Susan. "Lessons of Barings: Understanding Your Broker's Appetite for Risk Is Not Enough." *Plan Sponsor*, April 1995.

Carey, David. "Getting Risk's Number." *Institutional Investor*, February 1995.

Davis, Stephen. "It's 4:15. Do You Know Where Your Risks Are?" *Institutional Investor*, December 1994.

Essinger, James, and Joseph Rosen. *Using Technology for Risk Management* (Cambridge, England: Simon Schuster International, 1991).

MacRae, Desmond. "In Search of Risk Sensitivity." *FW's Corporate Finance*, Winter 1994.

"Risk Management: Contracting Out." *The Economist*, October 1, 1994.

Rosen, Joseph. "Managing Risk Through Multi-Advisor, Multi-Sector Portfolios." Computers in The City 8 (Proceedings of the conference held in London, November 1989, Blenheim Online Publications).

Technology

"Information Technology." *Financial Times Review*, April 5, 1995.

"Waste Not, want Not." *USBanker*, March 1995.

PART

II

INNOVATIVE STRATEGIES AND TECHNIQUES

Chapter Eight

Measuring and Controlling the Credit Risk of Derivatives*

Jeremy A. Gluck
Vice President
Moody's Investors Service

INTRODUCTION

On one level, coping with the credit risk inherent in a derivatives portfolio is not very different from managing the credit risk associated with any book of fixed-income assets. The risk depends on the exposures to various entities, the likelihood that those entities will default, and any recovery of what is owed upon default. But even in a conventional fixed-income portfolio, measuring credit risk is a nontrivial exercise. Nominal exposures may not vary over time, but their market values generally will. Defaults, particularly by highly rated firms, are never easy to predict. Correlations among default rates for a group of firms are very difficult to measure and manipulate. Moreover, recovery rates and, for that matter, the promptness of recovery, are inherently unpredictable.

In the derivatives context, the problem of variable nominal exposures is layered on top of the usual fixed-income concerns. Perhaps uniquely

---

*The opinions expressed herein are those of the author and may not represent the views of Moody's Investors Service.

among financial assets, a swap can be an asset one day and a liability the next. Such changes in nominal exposures may not be fundamentally different from the changes in market value that affect any fixed-income portfolio, but they must certainly be taken into account when modeling the credit risk of a derivatives book.

Apart from the problem of predicting exposures, managing the credit risk of a derivatives book poses special problems. Unlike bond contracts, (nonoption) derivative transactions are at least partially symmetric in that they may pose credit risk to either party. The pricing of credit risk will reflect this bilateral perspective. Of potentially greater concern is the failure of many derivatives tracking-systems to accurately and comprehensively reflect the full set of exposures with respect to individual or groups of counterparties.

Despite these obstacles, the credit risk that resides in a derivatives portfolio can and should be modeled. It cannot be modeled precisely, but that does not give the credit analyst license to pull a potential credit-loss figure out of thin air, nor to ignore the resources required to offset credit risk. Rather, the difficulty in getting a firm grasp on the extent of credit risk argues for a conservative approach to measuring risk—one that will result in an allocation of financial resources that is at least as large as the "true" figure, but also one that is not so extravagant that it borders on paranoia. The danger of overestimating and overpricing credit risk is that the practice may discourage the use of derivatives to prudently hedge market risk.

Over the balance of this chapter, we will review the components of credit risk that must be captured by any model of risk—counterparty default rates, transaction exposures, and diversification effects among counterparties and among transactions. We will also cite some of the sources of risk that cannot be sensibly modeled, but which may nonetheless be important. Finally, we will consider some of the means available for minimizing credit risk.

THE LIKELIHOOD OF COUNTERPARTY DEFAULT

Evaluating the risk of counterparty default is akin to evaluating the risk of earthquakes: they rarely happen, but the consequences are so severe that the possibility can't be ignored. Fortunately, there is some guidance with respect to the probability of a counterparty default over a relevant span of

FIGURE 8–1
Historical Cumulative Default Rates by Moody's Credit Rating

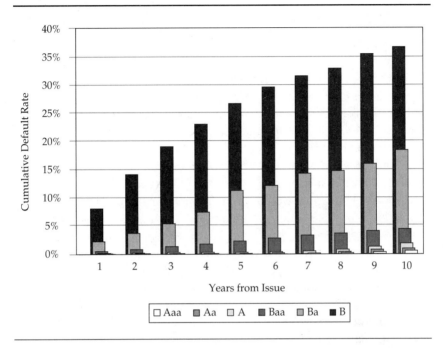

time. One obvious source of information is the various credit-rating agencies. A second possibility is to infer default probabilities from market data. Finally, one might directly analyze pertinent financial ratios, management capacity, and environmental factors to assess creditworthiness.

Relying on Credit Rating Agencies

Credit rating agencies such as Moody's Investors Service have extensively studied the default behavior of firms (see Carty, et al.). As depicted in Figure 8–1, these studies have yielded historical relationships between credit ratings and default rates over various horizons. Each column in the figure represents the average incidence of defaults over the period 1970–1994 for U.S. corporate bonds initially rated at the indicated levels. (Downgrades typically occurred prior to actual default.)

The notable feature of Figure 8–1 is not simply that, as expected, cumulative default rates are higher for lower-rated issues, but that they rise dramatically in moving from the A or better range to the Baa category, and especially to the non-investment-grade (below Baa) ranks. Of course, virtually all derivatives dealers fall within the investment-grade tiers, and most are rated A or better.

How does one apply such rating-default relationships to potential swap counterparties? For the most part, it is appropriate to treat a counterparty's senior unsecured-debt rating as its counterparty rating. This reflects a strong likelihood that swap counterparties will rank equally with other unsecured senior creditors should the firm become insolvent (May and Curry). In certain other cases, where a senior unsecured-debt rating may not be available or suitable, adjustments to other types of ratings may be in order. For example, one would generally infer a counterparty rating from an insurance firm's financial-strength rating by making a one-rating-notch adjustment downward (e.g., moving from A1 to A2). In some cases, a similar adjustment to a bank's long-term deposit rating might be called for. To resolve any doubts about how to derive a counterparty rating from another type of rating, both Moody's and Standard and Poor's have explicitly assigned counterparty ratings to several hundred entities and will continue to broaden the scope of their counterparty-rating coverage.

Of course, there is no guarantee that these historical relationships will hold up in the future. In fact, there is some evidence that for any given rating and a chosen horizon, the associated probability of default has increased over time. This upward drift suggests that it may be appropriately conservative to adjust the average historical default rates upward when looking ahead. Moreover, the historical results reflect the experience of a very large number of rated issues. Substantial deviations from this record are possible in dealing with the inevitably smaller number of counterparties that comprise a typical derivatives book.

Inferring Default Probabilities from Market Data

Since fixed-income market participants routinely place bets on the likelihood that a borrower will make good on an obligation, it stands to reason that one can infer something about the probability of default from market data. Such inferences typically rely on the assumption that markets are efficient, that transaction costs are low and, usually, that investors are "risk neutral." In this context, "market efficiency" implies that current market prices (yields) incorporate all currently available, relevant information about the instrument being evaluated. The absence of significant transaction costs makes it possible for market participants to respond quickly and fully to new information. The concept of "risk neutrality" may be somewhat confusing. The notion certainly does not suggest that investors are indifferent to default risk. Rather, it implies that investors focus only on their expected return, without regard for the distribution of possible returns. For example, a risk-neutral investor would be indifferent between an investment that offers a 10 percent return with absolute certainty, and another that promises either a 5 percent or a 15 percent return with equal probability.[1]

The most straightforward way to infer default probabilities from market rates is from yield data. Specifically, one can compare the yield on debt that bears credit risk with the yield on default-risk-free Treasury debt. Given the assumptions above, one might anticipate the same return, on average, from an investment in Treasury debt as one would from the purchase of risky debt, providing that the duration of the two instruments is similar. The simplest case applies to zero-coupon instruments (since we need not worry about defaults occurring between cash flows). The zero-coupon instrument promises to pay $100 at maturity. In this instance,

$$Z_T = (1 - P_d) \times Z_R + P_d \times (R \times 100 - P_R)/P_R \qquad (1)$$

where:

Z_T = yield on the zero-coupon Treasury instrument

Z_R = yield on the risky zero-coupon instrument

P_d = the probability of default

P_R = the price of risky debt (= $100/[1 + Z_R]$)

R = the recovery rate (as a percentage of face value) upon default

Equation (1) indicates that the Treasury zero-coupon yield Z_T equals an average of the yields on the risky instrument in the nondefault and default

---

[1] Alternatively, if risks can be perfectly hedged, it makes no difference whether investors are risk neutral or risk averse. Market prices will be determined as if investors were risk neutral. However, it appears unlikely that investors can fully hedge credit risk. The developing market for credit derivatives may help in this respect.

cases, weighted by the likelihoods of nondefault and default. We can rewrite (1) to solve for the default probability P_d:

$$P_d = (Z_R - Z_T) / [(1 + Z_R) \times (1 - R)] \tag{2}$$

While simple in concept, the yield-spread approach may not be easy to implement. First, and most obviously, many prospective counterparties don't have public debt outstanding. For those that have issued debt, the yield spreads over Treasuries may embody more than a premium for credit risk; for example, it is likely that a fraction of the spread can be attributed to a liquidity premium. Of course, if the issuer's debt is callable or carries other embedded derivatives, the spread will reflect the value of the those features. Even where the firm in question issues a suitably "plain vanilla" note, the maturity may differ substantially from the horizon that is relevant for a contemplated swap transaction. Finally, bond price/yield data are very poor, often reflecting "indicative" rather than traded levels, and often subject to "matrix pricing" through which a uniform spread over Treasury yields is assumed for an entire class of risky debt.

If none of the above issues presents a major problem, there is still the matter of disentangling the probability of default from the recovery upon default. One cannot infer the default probability P_d from equation (2) without knowing the recovery rate R. Some guidance comes from historical studies conducted by the rating agencies (Carty, et al.). The seniority of the debt is naturally a key determinant of the recovery rate, but even given the seniority, the extent and timing of recovery are difficult to project. To the degree that one is interested in "expected loss" (discussed more fully below), rather than the pure probability that a counterparty will default, the need to separate the impacts on the credit spread of the default probability from the expected recovery rate may be diminished. A more careful analysis would also take account of variations in marginal default probabilities over time (for example, see Hull and White).

A relatively sophisticated approach stems from the observation that the value of a firm's debt equals the value of its assets, minus the value of a call on the firms assets "issued" to the firm's stockholders by its debt holders (as suggested in Merton). The price of the "call" is simply the value of the firm's common stock. The market value of the (solvent) firm's assets is equal to the value of its equity plus the value of debt. Using an option-pricing formula, one can infer from these relationships the probability that the value of the firm will fall short of its debt. Unfortunately, this is quite difficult to apply in practice. Firms don't simply issue one form of debt. Instead, most firms offer a variety of public and private debt instruments with varying maturities and different degrees of seniority.

Examining Financial and Operating Ratios

A third option for evaluating the credit risk associated with a potential counterparty is to carefully evaluate publicly or—if the counterparty is cooperative—privately available financial records. In so doing, one would duplicate the efforts of rating agency or bank credit analysts. Naturally, this is not a cost-effective approach for a typical derivatives end user. Only if the cost of maintaining a credit department can be defrayed over a large number of derivatives and nonderivatives transactions is the approach practical. To the extent that an end user transacts primarily with well-known, rated dealers, an analysis of financial data may be redundant.

The task of evaluating a counterparty's financial data may be complemented by applying statistically based methods. That is, one can associate the likelihood that a particular firm will fail by applying appropriate weights to various financial ratios (Altman, et al.). The danger here is that the weights derived from a study of, say, industrial firms will be completely inappropriate for financial counterparties. Even if estimated parameters come from an appropriate sample, the parameters may well shift over time.

CALCULATING POTENTIAL EXPOSURES ASSOCIATED WITH DERIVATIVES TRANSACTIONS

To determine the current exposure to a derivatives counterparty, one needs to price each of the transactions entered into with that counterparty under a single contract, such as an International Swaps and Derivatives Association (ISDA) Master Agreement, and aggregate receivables in a way that is consistent with the netting status of the counterparty. Thus, the exposure to a counterparty will be determined by:

$$\text{Exposure} = \max (0, \Sigma V_i) \qquad \text{(netting), or} \qquad (3a)$$

$$\text{Exposure} = \Sigma \max (0, V_i) \qquad \text{(nonnetting)} \qquad (3b)$$

where V_i is the value of the ith transaction with the particular counterparty. Of course, one might enter into multiple ISDA agreements with a single counterparty, in which case the properly calculated exposure under each master would be aggregated in a gross fashion.

It is worth highlighting a point that may appear self-evident: One cannot hope to address credit risk adequately without implementing the systems that are required to track current transaction values with all counterparties, and to aggregate such values in a meaningful way. Transaction data must therefore be globally integrated, and valuation techniques must be sufficiently accurate to at least calculate near-market values for all trades. (A dealer must do better than near-market when quoting prices.) It makes little sense to focus on the details of modeling credit risk before such a comprehensive system is in place.

Monte Carlo Simulations

A particularly useful tool for examining potential derivative transaction exposures is the "Monte Carlo" simulation. These simulation exercises entail the generation of many paths for market rates by applying random shocks to previous (or anticipated) values of each rate. The application of the shocks reflects assumptions about the distributions of market rates, including volatility and correlation parameters. For example, if one wanted to assess the potential exposure associated with an interest-rate swap on a quarterly basis over a 5-year period, one might generate a series of 20 yield curves at quarterly intervals. Using the yields generated for each quarter along a particular path, one would reprice the swap at each of the 20 quarters. The exercise could then be repeated for another set of random shocks. After generating many such paths—typically, thousands—one would gain a sense of the distribution of possible swap values each quarter.

Monte Carlo simulations have drawbacks, perhaps the greatest of which is the computational burden that they impose. Various methods may be applied to run simulations in a relatively efficient manner, or one can take other numerical approaches. Like any modeling technique, Monte Carlo simulations rely on simplifying assumptions, which may be inappropriate. For example, the parameters or distributional assumptions used to model the random shocks that are applied to market rates may be inaccurate. An attractive means of addressing this issue is to randomly sample percentage changes in market rates from historical data, rather than by generating random shocks via a model. While this method may avoid the use of arbitrary simplifying assumptions, it too is valid only if the future resembles the past. The frequently invoked assumption that default events are uncorrelated with exposures, or with each other, is also subject to question.[2] Nonetheless, Monte Carlo simulations provide a valuable insight into the potential behavior of a derivatives book and are therefore widely used to model both market and credit risk.

Exposure Profiles

We now apply the simulation technique to a 5-year, plain-vanilla interest-rate swap. Figure 8–2 illustrates the 98 percent confidence level and expected value[3] for exposures (as a percentage of notional) at quarterly intervals.[4] Note that these figures provide summary information about the distribution of potential swap exposures in the future, considered at the swap's inception. It is a different exercise to examine the potential value of the swap over a short interval, beginning at various points in the life of the swap (e.g., for a quarterly interval beginning one year out, two years out, etc.). The latter is more relevant for assessing pure market risk.

   The exposure profiles first rise and then fall, reflecting two factors. The first, often described as the "diffusion effect," is the tendency for rates to diverge more widely from initial values as time passes. As rates vary more widely, so does the value of the swap. The diffusion effect is offset by the "amortization effect," which refers to the decreasing sensitivity of remaining cash flows to changes in rates as the swap approaches maturity. Ultimately, the amortization effect dominates.

---

   [2]For a discussion of many of these issues, see Duffee [1994]. Note that alternative methods of evaluating risk are likely to be subject to the same objections, such as the use of potentially outdated historical parameters to model future market behavior.

   [3]The expected value of the exposure differs from zero for two reasons. First, though rates and swap values may rise or fall, exposure can never be negative. The average of positive numbers and zeroes must always be positive. Second, a positively (negatively) sloped yield curve implies that rates will have a tendency to rise (fall).

   [4]To generate market paths, we rely on the historical sampling approach. Specifically, we calculate (detrended) percentage changes for each point on the yield curve, as well as exchange rates, for 40 quarters over the past 10 years, using end-of-quarter data. After interpolating for missing points on the yield curve, we sample from these percentage-change figures to evaluate the value of swaps at six-month intervals. That is, we randomly select two quarterly changes in relative rates to infer a semiannual relative change. That semiannual change is applied to the yield curve implied by the yield curve estimated 6 months earlier. Because we reprice semiannual pay swaps on a semiannual basis, the exposure patterns are fairly smooth. More frequent evaluation would produce a more jagged exposure pattern.

FIGURE 8–2
Exposure Patterns for 5-Year Interest-Rate Swaps

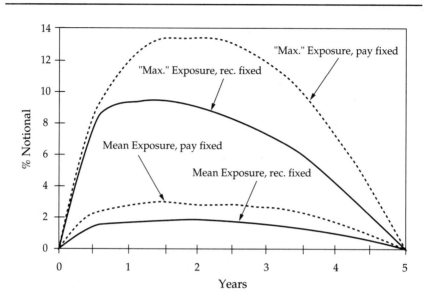

Even among plain-vanilla swaps, potential exposure patterns may vary. If, as is most typical, the yield curve slopes upward, then expected future short-term rates (implied forward LIBOR rates) will tend to lie above the current short-term rate. In this environment, the current 5-year swap rate, which is effectively an average of current and expected future short-term rates, will exceed current LIBOR. Hence, in the early years of a 5-year swap, the fixed-rate payer will normally make a net payment to the floating-rate payer. The market expects LIBOR to exceed the swap rate later in the life of the transaction, so that the fixed-rate payer will ultimately recoup its money. In a sense, the fixed-rate payer is making a loan to the other party, thereby incurring credit risk. The greater exposure of the fixed-rate payer, both in an expected value sense and at the 98 percent confidence level, is shown in Figure 8–2.

The pattern is very different for a cross-currency swap (Figure 8–3). In this case, both interest rates and foreign-exchange rates affect the value of the swap, and both sets of rates will tend to become more diffuse over

FIGURE 8–3
Exposure Patterns for 5-Year Cross-Currency Swaps

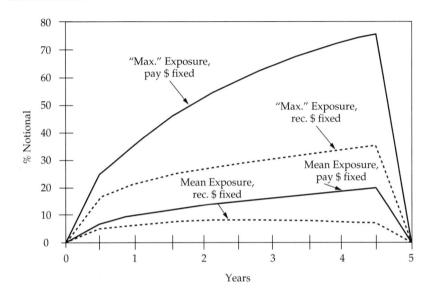

time. The amortization effect is still relevant, but less potent because the stream of cash flows tends to be dominated by the value of the final exchange of principal, the local currency value of which is uncertain. The net effect is that the range of potential values for the cross-currency swap becomes ever wider, until the swap matures.

Here too, it makes a difference which side of the swap one finds oneself on. Suppose, for example, that one enters into a swap to pay a fixed $US rate, and receive yen LIBOR, based on an initial notional of $100 million (assumed equal to 10 billion yen). Suppose further that both $US and yen yield curves are upward sloping, but that the $US curve lies uniformly above the yen curve. Initially, the net $US value of reset payments will be negative (an outflow). The $US fixed-rate payer builds up an exposure to his or her counterparty that will only be offset by the time the final exchange of $100 million for 10 billion yen occurs, a time when the dollar value of the yen payment is likely to exceed $100 million. Hence, the exposure is greater for the $US fixed-rate payer.

FIGURE 8–4
Exposure Patterns for 5-Year Caps

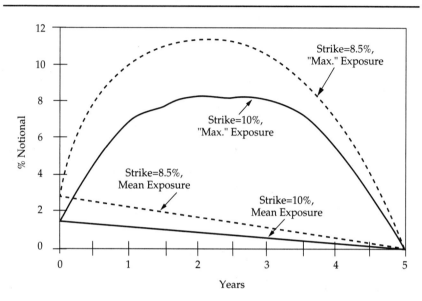

Perhaps the most widely traded OTC option product is the cap. As with any option, only the buyer incurs exposure. Figure 8–4 presents the exposure profiles for caps.

The profile resembles that of an interest-rate swap. Here too, the amortization effect ultimately brings potential exposures back toward zero. Note that the lower the strike rate—the more the cap is "in the money"—the greater the value the cap and the greater the potential exposure.

Beyond Fixed Income

So far, we have only considered the potential exposures associated with certain fixed-income derivatives. While the range of possible indexes to which derivatives may be linked is almost limitless, the primary classes of non-fixed-income derivatives are equity- and commodity-linked trans-actions. In general, both equity and commodity indexes tend to be more volatile than interest rates; however, broad indexes, such as the S&P 500, are considerably less volatile than, say, individual stock prices. Some commodity indexes, such as those related to energy product prices, tend to be quite volatile, while precious metal prices are far less so.

The volatility of the underlying index(es) is, however, only one determinant of the variability of potential exposures. The structure of the derivative trade itself is also critical. For example, one can take a relatively innocuous index, such as LIBOR, and create a very risky swap via leverage. Leverage might take the form, for example, of a swap in which the fixed rate is set at twice the current 5-year swap rate, in return for payments equal to the notional multiplied by twice LIBOR. The effect is to double the notional volume of the swap, but the doubling would not be picked up in a report covering notional portfolio size. Various other exotic and semi-exotic structures can be imagined in which potential exposures could be formidable, though the trade is tied to a conventional interest-rate index.[5]

PRICING FOR CREDIT RISK

Having considered the likelihood that a counterparty will default, and the potential exposure one might face at the time of default, we can address the question of measuring and pricing for potential loss. A particularly useful measure of loss is expected loss. Here, "expected" has a particular technical meaning; it refers to the mathematical expectation of the loss that might arise from a counterparty default. Put differently, the expected loss is the probability-weighted loss associated with the transaction(s) conducted with a particular counterparty. The notion can best be illustrated through a simple example. Suppose that we are considering an investment in a one-year zero-coupon instrument. The security returns the principal value of $100 with 90 percent probability, and $95 with 10 percent probability. Hence, we expect to lose nothing nine times out of ten, and expect to lose $5 one time out of ten. In this instance, the expected loss equals:

$$\text{Expected Loss} = 90\% \times \$0 + 10\% \times \$5 = \$0.50 \qquad (4)$$

---

[5]For a discussion of the risks posed by various derivatives embedded in structured notes, see Pimbley and Curry.

Relative to the face value of $100, the loss equals 0.50 percent.

The expected loss of 0.50 percent ought to be reflected in the price of this risky security. If, for example, the risk-free rate for a zero-coupon security at a one-year maturity is 10 percent and investors are risk-neutral, then from Equation (1), the yield on the risky security should be 10.55 percent and the price $90.45. If there were no credit risk, the price would instead be somewhat higher, at $90.91. The difference of $0.46 is precisely what is needed to offset the 0.50 percent expected loss associated with the risky offering.

We can make the same sort of adjustment for a derivative instrument. Consider again the case of the 5-year, plain-vanilla, pay-fixed swap. We can again calculate the expected loss by applying appropriate default probabilities to the losses that might occur at each point in the life of the swap. The task is greatly simplified if we make a further assumption: The probability of default and the exposure are uncorrelated at any point in time. The assumption is generally reasonable, but one can think of at least two circumstances where it might be called into question:

• The exposure arising from a swap, or, more correctly, a set of swaps entered into under a single master agreement, could become significant relative to the resources of the counterparty. In most cases, this will not occur. A typical corporate counterparty, and certainly any prudent dealer, will conduct a range of transactions with numerous different counterparties. It is unlikely that the exposure to a single counterparty would become large relative to the counterparty's total obligations for swaps and conventional borrowings. Exceptions will occur where a counterparty's borrowings are poorly diversified, or where there is no excess cash flow to meet unexpected contingencies. The latter is particularly important for municipalities. It could certainly be argued that the notorious Hammersmith and Fulham debacle demonstrated a tight relationship between the exposure of derivatives dealers to those London boroughs and the willingness or ability of the municipalities to meet their obligations.

• Swap exposures and default probabilities may be linked by business risk. One might easily imagine that entering into a pay-fixed swap with a financial firm could be hazardous if rising interest rates not only produced positive exposures, but also damaged the financial health of the counterparty. Similarly, entering into commodity swaps with a commodity producer could also prove unexpectedly risky. However, most firms that are heavily exposed to movements in a widely traded index will hedge some or all of that risk. In fact, if one entered into, say, an oil swap with an oil producer that owns substantial oil reserves, the energy firm would most likely use that swap to hedge itself (by making payments positively linked to the price of oil), so that the exposure and the default likelihood would be *negatively* correlated. In such cases, the danger of assuming independence of exposures and default probability would be to overstate risk.

If we adopt the view that default events and exposures are largely uncorrelated, then calculating the expected loss is straightforward. We need only weight the exposure in each period by the marginal probability of default in that period. Taking the present value of the incremental loss expected for each period, and dividing by the notional value of the swap, we can calculate the number of basis points by which the swap rate should be raised to offset credit risk. The adjustment is quite small in the case of the interest-rate swap; for example, a 5-year interest-rate swap with an A2-rated counterparty would only entail about a one-basis-point adjustment. However for the cross-currency swap, which is characterized both by relatively high exposures and a tendency for the highest exposures to correspond to higher marginal default rates, the appropriate adjustment is around 4 basis points for the same maturity and counterparty rating.

Table 8–1 reports the necessary adjustment for counterparty credit risk for the interest-rate and cross-currency swaps across a range of potential counterparty ratings. It is clear that the adjustment will tend to be small when one enters into an interest-rate swap with investment-grade counterparties. This may explain the observation that dealers do not always appear to charge a premium for credit risk. The premium may, however, be significant for non-investment-grade counterparties (those rated below Baa3), or for nearly any counterparty with whom one transacts a cross-currency swap.

These credit premiums would be lower still if we were to assume that some recovery would occur upon default by a counterparty. For U.S. corporate bonds, Moody's historical default studies have typically produced recovery rates of roughly 40 to 50 percent of face value. There is insufficient evidence to draw any conclusions about recoveries following defaults on derivative obligations. To the extent that derivatives contracts are accorded equal treatment by bankruptcy courts (where relevant), one might anticipate similar recovery rates. However, one should keep in mind that any recovery that does occur could take months, or even years, to realize.

We have, as yet, taken a one-sided view of credit risk by putting ourselves in the place of an entity that is concerned that its counterparties

TABLE 8–1
Swap Rate Adjustments for Various Counterparty Credit Ratings[6]

Swap Type	Aaa	Aa2	A2	Baa2	Ba2	B2
Interest-Rate	0	0	1	3	17	38
Cross-Currency	0	1	4	13	62	125

[6]These figures, which come from simulations, are appropriate for "typical" interest-rate and currency swaps. Since swap structures and market conditions vary, they should be seen as illustrative, rather than precise adjustments.

might default.[7] These figures, which come from simulations, are appropriate for "typical" interest-rate and currency swaps. Since swap structures and market conditions vary, they should be seen as illustrative, rather than precise adjustments. But the situation is symmetric; both counterparties will normally worry about the creditworthiness of the firms with which they transact. It's true that if we are rated Aaa, other firms may tend to ignore the counterparty risk that they incur by transacting with us. In general though, they will be as enthusiastic about charging us a credit premium as we are about charging them. The result may be that only a differential spread is charged. That is, if we believe that it is appropriate to add 3 basis points to the swap rate to adjust for our counterparty's credit risk, while our counterparty believes it appropriate to charge 2 basis points, then we may wind up getting an additional basis point tacked on to the swap rate. The outcome could also be the result of a negotiated process, and may be dominated by other considerations, such as long-term relationships, current market conditions, or, as we are about to discuss, portfolio effects.

An Option-Pricing Alternative

An alternative approach to pricing for credit risk is to rely on options theory. At each reset date, a counterparty has the "option" to default. The resulting loss to the nondefaulting counterparty would be the exposure to

[7]For a full discussion of this issue, see Sorenson and Bollier.

FIGURE 8–5
Loss Resulting from a Counterparty Default

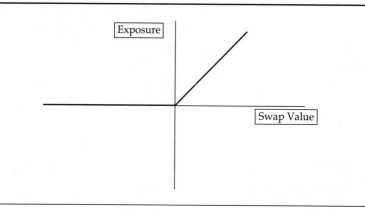

the defaulting firm. Since exposures must be nonnegative, the loss profile resembles the familiar option payoff diagram (Figure 8–5).

The default resembles the cancellation of the remaining life of the swap, which is economically equivalent to exercising a swaption. It is possible to price the value of this swaption by applying a standard pricing formula (such as in Hull). The price adjustment calculated via this method will generally be quite similar to the adjustment suggested by a Monte Carlo simulation.

The advantage of the option approach is that it requires very little computation. The disadvantage is that it is difficult to apply to a swap that depends on more than one index, such as a cross-currency swap. It is also not clear how to use the option technique to evaluate credit risk within a portfolio. Here, simulation may be the only viable approach.

A "BIS-like" Alternative

We have argued that credit risk can be reasonably measured via simulation techniques. If, however, the simulation technique appears daunting, one can always fall back on an approach that resembles the Bank for International Settlements (BIS) methodology. Under the BIS guidelines proposed for banks in 1988, credit risk is assessed on a transaction-by-transaction

TABLE 8–2
BIS Add-on Factors for Swaps

Swap Type	Factor for tenor < 1 year	Factor for tenor > 1 year
Interest Rate	0%	0.5%
Cross Currency	1%	5.0%

basis. For swaps, potential exposure is measured as current exposure plus an add-on factor that depends on the tenor and type of swap. Current exposure is equal to the mark-to-market value of the swap, if that value is positive, or zero otherwise. The add-on factors, as a percentage of notional, are shown in Table 8–2.

The percentages applied to remaining exposures are themselves derived from simulations. With these potential exposures in hand, one could apply default probabilities suitable for each counterparty to the exposure for the transaction under consideration, leading to an expected loss figure for the trade. (The BIS, by contrast, did not distinguish between counterparties of different credit ratings; instead, the BIS assigned risk weights to potential exposures that vary with the type of counterparty. For example, OECD sovereign entities are viewed as essentially riskless and OECD-area banks are given relatively favorable treatment.) The sum of the expected loss figures for each trade would represent a conservative estimate of portfolio expected loss.

The initial BIS approach was perhaps overly conservative in that it ignored the benefits of netting. That was partially rectified in 1993, when the BIS advocated the application of netting to calculate current exposure where a signed master agreement that provided for netting was in place, and in jurisdictions for which netting enforceability opinions could be obtained. The BIS has since proposed applying netting, after a fashion, to the add-on for potential exposure as well. The adjusted add-on would be calculated by averaging the current gross add-on with the gross add-on multiplied by the ratio of net to gross replacement value. A firm that wanted to adapt the BIS methodology for its own purposes might move further toward full netting for potential exposure by multiplying the gross add-on by the net-to-gross ratio. The danger is that the ratio itself might change as market values shift. This is more likely to occur for an end user than a dealer, since dealer net-to-gross ratios are more likely to be stable within a well-diversified book (Heldring).

Nonetheless, the BIS methodology continues to neglect the potential for diversification to reduce risk. Furthermore, a negative current exposure is "reset" to zero; for internal credit-risk management, one might instead use the true value of current exposure, even if negative. On the other hand, the simulations on which the BIS figures are based could be out of date, and would not be appropriate for all swaps. One could adjust the BIS add-on figures by running simulations for generic transaction types, extending beyond plain-vanilla interest-rate and foreign-exchange contracts. Within a product type, it would also be appropriate to distinguish several maturity classes. Modified in this way, a BIS-like approach, occasionally updated to reflect a changing market environment, may be an attractive substitute for running complicated and resource-intensive simulations. Again, the size of one's derivatives book may determine the most practical choice. It is interesting to note that some regulators have come around to the idea that it is appropriate to rely on dealers' own simulations to best measure credit risk, provided that the computations are sensible.

PORTFOLIO EFFECTS

We have focused our discussion on the credit risk associated with individual transactions. That may appear to be sufficient, since trades are entered into one at a time. However, even for an end user, portfolio effects are important and should not be ignored. Such effects occur along two dimensions: across transactions, and across counterparties.

Transaction Diversification

It should be apparent that in considering an incremental transaction with a given counterparty, it is inappropriate to ignore any existing transactions with that counterparty. An extreme, but instructive, case is the "mirror" swap. If one were to enter into a swap with a counterparty that precisely offset an existing swap—for example, a swap with identical terms to the first transaction, but with the direction of the cash flows reversed—and, if it were appropriate to net with the counterparty, then the second swap would actually eliminate the credit risk to the counterparty. In this case, it would be appropriate to charge the counterparty a *negative* credit premium for the mirror swap! While obviously an extreme case, the mirror swap example demonstrates that assessing credit risk on a trade-by-trade basis can be very misleading.

More realistically, suppose Counterparty A enters into a series of transactions with Counterparty B. (We ignore Counterparty B's adjustment for the credit risk that Counterparty A presents.) Counterparty A may choose to impose (or try to impose) a credit charge for each incremental transaction. This strategy will lead to some odd results. For example, the charge for a particular transaction will depend on the order in which it is introduced to the portfolio. If a particular transaction tends to hedge an earlier trade, it will entail a low, or even negative, credit premium. As the number of trades grows, incremental credit charges will tend to flatten out.

In a competitive market, this approach to pricing for credit risk is unlikely to work. One cannot expect Counterparty A to pay a premium to enter into a swap that happens to pose unusual risk to Counterparty B, unless Counterparty A's participation in the swap would impose similar risks on other counterparties (for example, because Counterparty A has a very low credit rating). As a general proposition, one would expect market pricing to reflect nondiversifiable (or nonhedgeable) risk, rather than "idiosyncratic" risk. Similarly, it would be unnecessary for Counterparty A to pay a premium to enter into a transaction with Counterparty B that is particularly attractive to Counterparty A, simply because the trade reduces Counterparty A's own credit risk.

Nonetheless, measuring the credit risk associated with each transaction, or rather, with the portfolio following each transaction, is useful. The expected loss calculation provides guidance as to the appropriate size of any reserve that is present to offset credit risk. By calculating the size of the reserve, one can then assess whether the credit premiums that are inherent in dealer bids are consistent with the risk-adjusted value of the transaction.

Counterparty Diversification

Just as a particular transaction with a counterparty may appear less risky in the context of the full set of transactions with that counterparty, the set of transactions with a counterparty are generally less risky in the context of a portfolio of transactions with many counterparties. To concentrate on the issue of counterparty diversification, suppose that we have a fixed $1 billion, 5-year exposure divided among between one and ten counterpar-

FIGURE 8–6

Expected Loss: Impact of Varying Number of Counterparties ($100mm Capital)

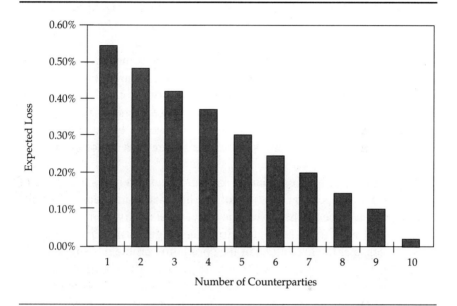

ties. (Hence, the exposure to each counterparty is $1 billion/the number of counterparties.) If each counterparty is rated A2, and counterparty default rates are assumed to be uncorrelated, we can calculate the expected loss that is associated with each number of counterparties for a given level of capital set aside to offset credit risk (Figure 8–6).[8] Diversification gains are initially substantial, but tail off after the first several counterparties. When the book consists of relatively few counterparties, diversification among additional investment-grade counterparties, given total exposure, almost inevitably reduces expected loss.

---

[8]If there were no capital (or other resources) backing the portfolio, diversification would not reduce expected loss because the *average* default experience would be the same for a group of A2 counterparties as for a single A2 counterparty. But if capital is positive, expected loss will fall, because the likelihood of an *extreme* loss outcome (in excess of capital) is reduced by diversification.

A critical assumption here is that default rates are uncorrelated. That assumption is sometimes difficult to justify. An end user, for instance, will tend to trade with dealers. The fortunes of dealers may be linked by the competitive environment, the regulatory infrastructure, etc. More broadly, within a given country, national economic forces will imply some correlation among counterparty defaults. Furthermore, there is some chance, however small, that a systemic crisis will produce some sort of "domino effect," forcing a number of financial institutions to fail at the same time because illiquidity at one firm inhibits the ability of other firms to meet their obligations in a timely fashion. The last case is one in which default correlation may be low in most states of the world, but suddenly rises following some critical event, such as the failure of a major derivatives dealer.

Arguing against high correlation among default events is the effect of intra-industry competition. The loss of one firm within an industry benefits its competitors. One might expect this effect to be relatively important in a concentrated industry, where each firm has a significant market share.

Some sense of the magnitude of the correlation problem is suggested in Figure 8–7. In this case, we assume a fixed exposure of $100 million to each of ten counterparties and investigate the change in expected loss as the correlation between each pair of such counterparties varies.[9]

In practice, such correlations are extremely difficult to measure. Actual defaults among highly rated counterparties are far too rare to yield useful correlation estimates. One might attempt to infer default probability correlations from market data, using the approach suggested earlier in this chapter. It is not, however, clear that such estimates would be useful (or stable) in a world where matrix pricing produces spurious correlations in yield spreads. The problem is even more acute in the presence of systemic risk, which suggests that some event could suddenly disrupt the financial environment in a way that the market failed to anticipate.

Whatever the extent of the problem, correlated default risk can certainly be mitigated by dealing with a variety of unrelated firms and imposing exposure limits by, for example, country of counterparty domicile. If

---

[9]These calculations are based on simulations. Specifically, correlated defaults are simulated by generating correlated uniform variables. Defaults occur whenever the uniform variable falls below a threshold that corresponds to the probability of default.

FIGURE 8–7
Impact of Default Correlation on Expected Loss

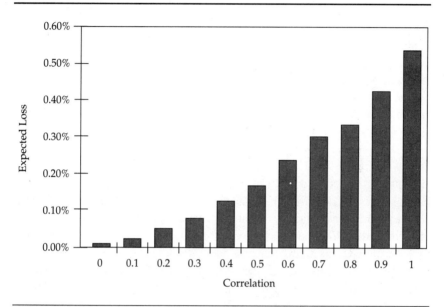

nothing else, the concern argues for providing an ample margin in calculating the resources that should be set aside to offset credit risk.

NONQUANTIFIABLE RISKS

The risks that we have so far addressed are, at least conceptually, measurable. However, a firm that trades derivatives must grapple not only with measurable risks, but with those less easily quantified as well. This includes all the things that are excluded from the model, such as correlation among default rates, the possibility that the particular processes chosen to model market rates differ from the "true" processes, the use of nonrepresentative periods to establish volatility parameters, and so forth.

Beyond these, one cannot ignore the risk for human error. No model can cope with data input errors, such as the failure to correctly book or price trades. Even more troublesome is negligence or outright fraud. It may be argued that no amount of capital can offset losses imposed by a trader determined to take extraordinary risks (perhaps to cover earlier losses), but that does not justify the absence of a reserve for operational errors. It is the duty of each firm to make an honest assessment of its internal controls, including its derivatives systems, front- and back-office procedures, and degree of management supervision. Based on that self-assessment, the firm will make its best guess as to the potential for losses associated with operational failures.

COPING WITH CREDIT RISK

We have argued that credit risk is measurable, if only imperfectly. But having measured credit risk, what do we do about it? There are several choices. One can certainly attempt to reduce credit risk by dealing with highly rated counterparties, by exploiting netting and diversification, or by entering into contracts that provide for collateral posting or termination that is linked to a credit rating downgrade. One can also set aside resources to offset credit risk by building an appropriately sized credit reserve.

Dealing with Highly Rated Counterparties

Perhaps the most obvious means of reducing credit risk, short of refraining from derivatives transactions altogether, is to deal only with Aaa-rated counterparties. The number of Aaa-rated counterparties has dwindled in the last decade, but a few Aaa-rated bank dealers remain. Beyond these, a number of potential counterparties have been established as fully guaranteed affiliates of Aaa-rated insurance firms.

An interesting development in the past few years has been the establishment of several "structured" derivative product companies (DPCs) (Clarkson and Gluck). These DPCs have been set up by various investment and commercial banks seeking to capture the business of very credit-sensitive counterparties. The subsidiaries typically operate within a narrow set of operating guidelines and are closely monitored by major accounting firms. However, the creditworthiness of DPCs is often more difficult to directly assess than that of a conventional dealer, leading potential DPC counterparties to rely on the credit rating agencies for guidance.

Of course, there may be some cost associated with dealing with Aaa-rated counterparties. If top-tier firms price rationally, they will tend to add a basis point, or perhaps a few basis points, to the pricing to reflect their creditworthiness. This cost may be thought of as an insurance premium against the event of counterparty default.

Exposure Limits

Rather than restricting oneself to Aaa-rated counterparties, one might decide to transact with firms across the credit spectrum, but only up to a point. Meaningful exposure limits should reflect the creditworthiness of the counterparty, measured by rating or some other criterion. One might, for example, set up exposure limits in such a way that the maximum loss associated with each counterparty is the same. If, for example, a single-A credit was three times as likely to default as a double-A credit, one might set the double-A exposure limit at three times the single-A level. Such simple rules tend to ignore portfolio effects, but can greatly limit the potential damage from counterparty defaults.

Exposure limits are useful only if they are enforced. If limits are routinely extended when the exposure to a counterparty reaches the initial threshold, then the limits will have little value. Rather, limits should be set at sensible levels, and enforced through collateral posting or the renegotiation of existing positions when a change in market rates threatens to breech the limit with a particular counterparty.

Taking Full Advantage of Netting and Diversification

We have noted that both netting and diversification can substantially reduce credit risk. While one should naturally take advantage of these, there is a tension between the two. Netting can be exploited by dealing with relatively few counterparties in jurisdictions where close-out netting (netting upon bankruptcy) is valid,[10] under master agreements that explicitly incorporate netting. Diversification, however, entails the spreading of transactions across a wide range of counterparties.

---

[10]To date, Moody's is only comfortable that netting works with Aaa certainty in the U.S., the U.K., Australia, and with French banks. However, most market professionals, bolstered by opinions solicited by ISDA, accept netting in a wider range of countries.

While there's no easy means to determine the optimal number of counterparties, a few considerations are likely to dominate. If one tends to transact with relatively low-rated counterparties, diversification becomes even more critical. If business tends to be "one-way"—for example, if one tends to enter into pay-fixed interest-rate swaps—then netting will not be particularly useful, and diversification is attractive. If, by contrast, one enters into a wide range of transactions that have a tendency to hedge each other, it may be desirable to transact with relatively few nettable counterparties. In any case, incremental diversification gains are likely to be small beyond five to ten counterparties, at least within a single currency book.

Collateralization

The posting of collateral is an increasingly popular means of reducing the credit risk that would otherwise arise from derivative transactions. Collateralization may take various forms:

- Bilateral or unilateral posting.
- Posting with or without a "threshold" amount.
- Collateral transfers with or without a "nuisance" amount.
- Posting only after a rating trigger is hit.
- Use of a conventional collateral custodian or a "full service" collateral intermediary.

Collateral posting arrangements need not be symmetric. Only one counterparty, almost inevitably the lower-rated counterparty, may be required to post. Some highly rated counterparties will only transact on this basis. Typically, posting will only be required once an exposure exceeds some threshold amount, such as $10 million. Even then, collateral transfers may only be required when the change in required collateral exceeds some "nuisance" level, usually well below $1 million. In many cases, collateralization will only be needed if one counterparty is downgraded below some predetermined level, such as A3 or Baa3, and even then, after a threshold exposure level is exceeded. Finally, collateral is normally held with some sort of custodian, typically a bank. The bank will sometimes perform the task of valuing collateral, even ensuring that collateral is of a permissible type. Indeed, some banks will send out call notices whenever additional collateral is due, or return excess collateral, as needed. The Chicago Mercantile Exchange plans to introduce a "Swaps Collateral Depository," in which the exchange will serve as a collateral intermediary for dealers, who can then post collateral on a pooled, rather than bilateral, basis.

Collateral posting is an effective means of reducing risk. It is, however, inconvenient and may lead to liquidity problems if a collateral "call" suddenly and unexpectedly arises (particularly following a rating downgrade). One must therefore balance the reduction in risk against the cost of entering into collateralization agreements. Bilateral posting is also inefficient in that the resources can only be used to offset credit risk posed by a single counterparty. Indeed, DPCs exist, in part, as a relatively efficient means of applying capital and collateral to risks on a multilateral basis. Ultimately, "swaps clearinghouses" may be formed for the same purpose.

Termination Contracts

Termination contracts are similar to those in which collateral is posted when one party is downgraded below a threshold rating.[11] In most, the (still) highly rated counterparty (Party A) will have the option to terminate the transaction if the other counterparty (Party B) is downgraded below a rating such as A3 or Baa3. Party A will typically not exercise this option if termination would force it to pay the market value of the transaction to Party B; in addition to the liquidity drain, Party A would have no current exposure to Party B, so that Party A will be in no immediate danger of a loss upon a default. A firm that enters into such agreements should be aware that if it winds up as the downgraded party, it may face a substantial liquidity drain following a descent below the threshold rating. That may be a particular concern if the firm, which may now be deemed as posing a serious credit risk, is unable to borrow to make the termination payments or to recontract with a third counterparty to step into the shoes of the counterparty that exercised the termination option.

---

[11]Economically, the termination option may be thought of as a "credit swaption." It gives the highly rated counterparty the right to exit a swap in which the swap rate is "off-market" in two senses: (1) Because rates will have changed since inception, the swap will have value to one of the counterparties. That value is addressed by the termination payment. (2) Because one of the counterparties has seen its creditworthiness deteriorate, the swap will have less value for the still highly rated counterparty than would otherwise be the case. The option allows the highly rated counterparty to recover this value.

Coupon Resets

Still another means of reducing credit risk is the practice of resetting the swap coupon to market on normal reset dates. The new rate is the swap rate that corresponds to the remaining tenor of the transactions. This is a form of marking-to-market, similar in its credit-risk-reducing effect to collateral posting, or, for that matter, to margin posting for exchange-traded contracts.

Providing a Credit Reserve

No matter how carefully one chooses derivatives counterparties, a degree of credit risk will inevitably remain. It is appropriate to set aside resources to offset such risk. As we have suggested, Monte Carlo simulations can be used to provide a probability distribution for potential losses. A BIS-like approach can offer a cruder measure of potential loss. The choice of a confidence level—95 percent, 98 percent, 99 percent, etc.—for potential losses depends, in part, on one's aversion to risk. It may also depend on the size of the derivatives book. An unexpected loss may not be particularly damaging to a firm that uses derivatives sparingly and tends to transact interest-rate swaps. To a dealer, a loss in excess of the confidence level could be disastrous.

One should certainly avoid false precision. A 99 percent confidence level does not necessarily imply true 99 percent confidence that losses will not exceed this level. Only if the modeling assumptions are exactly correct (which will never be the case), will an alleged 99 percent comfort level imply 99 percent confidence. All of the nonquantifiable sources of risk that we discussed earlier, whether part of or distinct from the modeling process, are relevant here. Such unmodelable contingencies could be addressed by choosing a higher confidence level than appears warranted, or by explicitly allocating a buffer of additional resources to offset such risks.

CONCLUSION

Like many facets of the derivatives market, the state of derivatives credit-risk management is rapidly evolving. Most dealers are moving toward a relatively rigorous approach in which simulations are used to capture a wide range of default and market-rate outcomes. But even if a full-blown simulation approach is beyond the capacity of some end users, much can be accomplished by taking intermediate steps to assess credit risk. The first and arguably the most important step is to capture all information about the derivative trades that a firm has entered into in a single system. For that matter, and precisely because derivatives are often used to hedge other financial exposures, the system should integrate derivative and conventional financial transactions. Once the data reside in a single system, either simulations or a BIS-like methodology may be employed to calculate potential losses. Such losses can be mitigated through risk-reducing practices, or offset via the setting aside of financial resources.

REFERENCES

Altman, Edward I., Robert B. Avery, Robert B. Eisenbeis, and Joseph F. Sinkey, Jr., *Application of Classification Techniques in Business, Banking and Finance,* Chapter 5 (Greenwich, CT: JAI Press Inc., 1981).

Carty, Lea, Dana Lieberman, and Jerome S. Fons, "Corporate Bond Defaults and Default Rates 1970–1994," Moody's *Special Report,* January 1995.

Clarkson, Brian, and Jeremy A. Gluck, "Moody's Approach to Rating Derivative Product Subsidiaries," Moody's *Special Report,* October 1993.

Duffee, Gregory R., "On Measuring Credit Risks of Derivative Instruments, *Finance and Economics Discussion Series* 94–27, Federal Reserve Board, September 1994.

Duffee, Gregory R., "The Variation of Default Risk with Treasury Yields," Working Paper, Federal Reserve Board, January 1995.

Heldring, Ottho, "Alpha Plus," *Risk Magazine,* January 1995.

Hull, John, *Options, Futures and Other Derivative Securities,* 2d ed. (Englewood Cliffs, NJ: Prentice Hall, 1993).

Hull, John, and Alan White, "The Price of Default," *Risk Magazine,* September 1992.

May, William L., and Daniel A. Curry, "The Status of Swap Agreements Under the U.S. Bankruptcy Code," Moody's *Special Report,* June 1994.

Merton, Robert, "On the Pricing of Corporate Debt: The Risky Structure of Interest Rates," *Journal of Finance,* Vol. 29 (May 1974), pp. 449–470.

Pimbley, Joseph M., and Daniel A. Curry, "Structured Notes and the Investor's Risk," Moody's *Special Comment,* February 1995.

Sorenson, Eric H., and Thierry F. Bollier, "Pricing Swap Default Risk," *Financial Analysts Journal,* May-June 1994, pp. 23–33.

Chapter Nine

Assessing Risk Exposures in Complex Derivatives*

Michael K. Ong
Vice President/Head of Market Risk Analysis Unit
First Chicago Corporation

INTRODUCTION

Customized derivative products come in all shapes and sizes, differing basically only in the complexities of their underlying structures. While it is not practical to enumerate the various structures in detail, it is quite feasible, however, to analyze all of the embedded complexities. The term "complex derivatives" is used in the context of second-generation derivative products, a step away from the familiar vanilla options and futures contracts representing first generation derivatives. In today's market, complex structures are usually associated with structured notes and other customized products embedded with at least one kind of non-standard optionality. Depending on the nature of the embedding, the risk exposures can vary from the very transparent to the most opaque.

Structured notes, being fixed-income debentures linked to derivatives, necessarily contain exotic-type payoffs. Furthermore, the added flexibility needed to provide customization to fit the unique requirements of individ-

*Acknowledgement: The author wishes to thank Mark Kolas and Chris Hansen for their very helpful critique of the manuscript. Outstanding graphics work by Art Porton is also greatly appreciated.

ual investors inevitably leads to a myriad of possible combinations of exotic payoffs. Finally, since the structures normally provide investors with above-market yields if certain market conditions were to materialize, the embedded optionalities in the structures are inevitably of the "betting" variety, e.g., digitals and barriers.

This chapter is primarily concerned with the assessment of risk exposures in complex derivatives. Through simple examples, we demonstrate that once a complicated structure has been decomposed, each of the individual risk exposures can then be analyzed separately. In most cases, the total risk exposure of the structure is a simple arithmetic sum of the individual exposures. We list some exotic options commonly embedded in complex structures and discuss their unique features like path-dependency, singularity in payoffs, co-dependency due to correlation effects, and their curvilinear payoffs, all of which contribute to hedgeability concerns.

In practice, it is not only the precision of the model that matters. Often times, as in the case of options with abrupt jumps in their payoffs, we are faced with the dilemma of concocting an approximation, which then lends itself to better risk management. The question "What is the correct model to use?" we argue, needs to be answered in conjunction with how one chooses to manage the position. Finally, we present a hierarchy of methods used to measure the value-at-risk of complex derivatives. In particular, we present three general methods, one based on gross exaggerated estimates (the simple strategy method), another based on taking increasingly higher-ordered corrections (the price sensitivities method), and finally a full-blown scenario-based or simulation method, which may be particularly useful when confronted with unknown conditions and uncertainties in the market.

DECOMPOSING COMPLEX STRUCTURES

The key to deciphering the behavior of complex structures lies in the knowledge of the optionality embedded in a given structure. Embedded optionality can generally be categorized into two kinds: *explicit* and *implicit*. Here are two simple examples.

Explicit: A *Floating Range Note,* which pays above market rates only if the index falls within a predetermined range, is a very

FIGURE 9–1
Range Note with Embedded Digitals

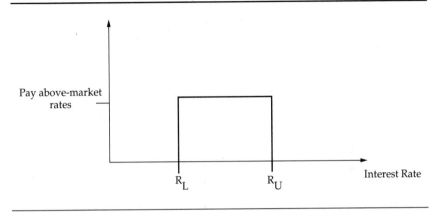

common example of an explicitly embedded optionality. In this example, there are two *explicitly* embedded digital options on either end of the range. Digital options pay either something or nothing, and they constitute a kind of "bet" that the index will remain within the chosen range. The digital options embedded in the range notes can be analyzed separately and the risk exposures of the notes understood. Figure 9–1 illustrates the embedded digital options when betting on the range of interest rates between R_L and R_U.

Implicit: *Index Principal Swaps* also have a payoff contingent on some floating index falling within a range. Depending on a predetermined schedule, the notional amount amortizes accordingly. For example, in a steadily decreasing interest-rate environment, the principal amount could gradually amortize away according to the schedule. This is an example of an implicitly embedded optionality, since there is no "real" option in the swap although the payoff behaves in a curvilinear fashion, just like an ordinary option. The embedded optionality described above is akin to the prepayment optionality embedded in mortgage-backed securities. Being *implicitly* embedded in the swap, the prepayment option is, for the most part, difficult to isolate. Nevertheless, an estimate can be made, and therefore the risk exposure of the amortizing swap can also be

TABLE 9–1
Index Principal Swap Schedule

Notional Amount:	US$100MM
Fixed Rate:	5.50% (2-yr US treasury @4.50% + 100bp).
Maturity:	5 years
Index:	3-month LIBOR
Initial Base Rate:	5.60% (to be set by customer).
Lock-out:	No paydown of principal for the first 2 years.
Amortization Schedule:	

Index Change (bp)	Index (%)	Annual Amortization Rate (%)
−300 or lower	2.60	0
−200	3.60	25
−100	4.60	50
0	5.60	100
+ 100	6.60	100
+ 200	7.60	100
+ 300 or higher	8.60	100

Clean-up Provision: The swap matures if the outstanding notional amount reaches 10% or less of the original notional amount.

conveniently analyzed. It is important to point out, however, that there are marked differences in the embedded prepayment optionality between amortizing swaps and mortgage-backed securities, the most prominent of which is the certainty of the amortization schedule in the amortizing swaps. In Table 9–1, we present a typical amortization schedule.

To understand the risk exposures embedded in a complicated structure, one needs to decompose a given structure into its constituent parts. Each individual part can then be analyzed separately. In many cases, the total of the risk exposures is simply the arithmetic sum of the exposures in each part. The following example illustrates the point.

Example 1: A Complex Structure Dissected

A 5½-year structured note that pays fixed rates for the first three years and turns into an inverse floater with a floor for the last two years. It also becomes callable when it turns into an inverse floater. The details of the note are as follows:

Instrument:	Agency Structured Note
Principal Amount:	US$100MM
Issue Date:	13 January 1994
Settle Date:	13 January 1994
Maturity Date:	27 July 1999
Coupons:	from settlement to 27 January 1995: 4.250%
	from 27 January 1995 to 27 January 1996: 6.125%
	from 27 January 1996 to 27 January 1997: 7.625%
	from 27 January 1997 to maturity: 11.00%–6m LIBOR
	where 6m LIBOR is the USD LIBOR rate posted on Telerate 3750 two business days prior to the beginning of each semiannual interest payment period
Floor Provision:	Coupon payments can never be less than zero.
Call Provision:	Note may be called in whole by the issuer effective any coupon date commencing 27 January 1997, with at least 30 days notice.
Payment Frequency:	semiannual
Calculation Basis:	30/360

The most intuitive way to analyze the risk exposure of this complex structure is via *decomposition*. We can dissect this structure by considering each leg of the fixed-coupon payments and then analyzing the embedded optionalities, if any, for the remaining two years of the note.

First Three Years:

The first three years of cash flows, being fixed in nature, are trivial to value. Since the payment frequency is semiannual, there are six semiannual cash flows. The value of these six cash flows is simply the sum of the present values of the six fixed semiannual coupon payments. This is synthetically a *3-year bond* with incrementally increasing coupon rates for each year, but without principal repayment at maturity.

Last Two Years:

Assuming that we are long the note, there are four parts to analyze in this period, namely: a swap, a cap, a swaption, and the principal repayment.

Swap: The cash flows for this period, consisting of five coupon payments, are similar to a swap wherein we receive a fixed rate of 11 percent and pay a floating 6-month LIBOR rate, semiannually, based on a notional amount of $100MM. This part is essentially a *2½-year swap* paying floating and receiving fixed.

Cap: Because of the floor provision that (11 percent − 6m LIBOR) > 0, we can never pay more than we receive. Mathematically, the payoff function is

max [11% − 6m LIBOR, 0]

which looks like an option's payoff function. Indeed, this is like being long a cap on 6-month LIBOR with a strike of 11 percent.

Swaption: The call provision allows the issuer to call away the note from us, therefore from our perspective of being the holder of the note, we are short this call option. The underlying of this short call option is the swap for the remaining two and a half years, hence, the embedded optionality is a swaption. Furthermore, the call feature also provides for the callability to be effective any coupon date commencing 27 January 1997, with at least 30 days prior notice, so that there is an element of early exercise (i.e., *American*-style option). The early exercise is restricted, however, to 30 days prior to each coupon date so that the early exercise has a *Bermudan* feature. Effectively, the embedded optionality translates into a Bermuda-style American swaption.

Principal: The principal repayment of $100MM, payable at the maturity date of 27 July 1999, has to be discounted to today. This is effectively a zero-coupon bond.

FIGURE 9–2
Call Payoff Function

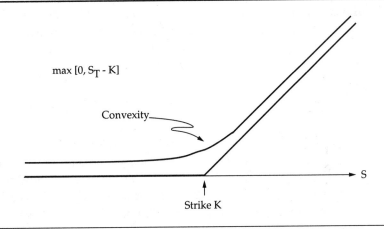

max [0, S_T - K]

Convexity

Strike K

S

Piecing the structure together, we have (from our perspective of owning the note), the following decomposition:

long 5½-year note = long 3-year incremental coupon bond
+ 2½-year fixed receiver/float payer swap
+ long a 3-year forward-starting 2½-year cap struck at 11%
+ short a forward-starting 2½-year Bermuda swaption
+ zero-coupon bond

Once the decomposition is established and the embedded optionalities determined, the risk exposure of the complex structure can now be analyzed quite easily.

The risks associated with options are dictated by their terminal payoffs. For instance, a vanilla call has terminal payoff, max[0, $S_T - K$], which is the largest of either zero or the difference between the stock price S_T (at expiration time T) and the strike price K. Figure 9–2 shows that there is a potential for price distortion in the vicinity of the corner as defined by the strike price. The curvature (or *convexity*) is greatest in the vicinity of the strike K.

Similar intuitions arise when examining the terminal payoff functions of more exotic options. In most cases, the risk exposures can be quickly determined by simply inspecting the payoff of the option at maturity. Below we list the payoffs of some common exotic options.

1. **Digital Options:** (also known as *all-or-nothing, binary,* and *bet* options): This option pays \$1 if the underlying price at expiry, S_T, is greater than the strike price K or it pays nothing otherwise. Mathematically, the payoff function is

   1, if $S_T > K$

   0, otherwise

2. **Barrier Options:** These options either come into existence (knock-in) or get extinguished (knock-out) if, at any time t prior to maturity T, the underlying price touches upon a threshold price or barrier H. Sometimes there is a provision of receiving a cash rebate when the barrier H is breached. For example, a *down-and-out call* has a payoff function of

   $\max [0, S_T - K]$, *if* $S_t > H$, *for all time* $t \leq T$

   rebate, if $S_t \leq H$, *for some* $t \leq T$

   There are 16 different possible combinations of puts and calls.

3. **Average Rate:** The payoff is based on the arithmetic average of the underlying asset, given by $\sum_i S_i$, over a given period of time. The payoff function for a call option is therefore

$$\max [0, \frac{1}{n} \sum_i^n S_i - K]$$

   Average Strike: In contrast to the average rate, it is the strike that is replaced by the average of the underlying asset, viz.,

$$\max [0, S_T - \frac{1}{n} \sum_i^n S_i]$$

4. **Basket Option:** The underlying is replaced by the weighted sum of all the assets in the basket. Suppose there are n different assets labeled $A_1, A_2, A_3, \ldots, A_n$ with corresponding weights (or percentage of the basket's composition) $\omega_1, \omega_2, \omega_3, \ldots, \omega_n$, then

the payoff function for a call option on the basket, with strike K, is

$$\max \left[0, \sum_{i=1}^{n} \omega_i A_i - K\right]$$

5. **Rainbow Options:** Rainbow options are a large class of options whose payoffs depend on several underlying assets, say, A, B, C. . . . The fundamental payoff function is based on a portfolio (or linear combination) of all the underlying assets, weighted by some constants $c_1, c_2, c_3, \ldots$, viz.,

$$\max \left[0, c_1 + c_2 \times A + c_3 \times C + c_4 \times D + \ldots \right]$$

We then have a variety of possible combinations, such as
spread (exchange): max $[0, A - B]$
min/max: max $[0, \max (A, B, C, \ldots) - K]$
$\qquad\qquad\quad$ max $[0, \min (A, B, C, \ldots) - K]$

6. **FX-linked Options:**

Quantos: the underlying is denominated in the same currency as the strike price, but the payoff will be paid out in a different currency. Using X as the symbol for exchange rate, we have a quanto call

$$X \times \max [0, S - K]$$

Compos: the underlying is denominated in a currency unit different from the strike price and, therefore, has to be converted first. The payoff function for a compo call is

$$\max [0, X \times S - K]$$

7. **Power or Leveraged Options:** Power options have highly leveraged payoffs, which depend on both the multiplicity ω_i and the polynomial growth of the underlying S. A power call has payoff function given by

$$\max \left[0, \sum_{i=1}^{n} \omega_i S^i - K\right], n = 2, 3, 4, \ldots$$

The case when $n = 1$ reduces to a vanilla call.

RISK PROFILES OF EXOTIC OPTIONS:

Based on their taxonomy, the risk exposures presented by exotic options
are mainly attributable to their:

a) path-dependency,
b) singularity in payoffs,
c) co-dependency due to correlation effects,
d) leveraged or curvilinear payoffs, and
e) hedgeability concerns.

Path-Dependency and Singularity

Path-dependent options, unlike the vanilla variety, have payoff structures
that depend on the movement of the underlying asset over the entire life of
the option—between the time the option is struck and its maturity date.
Consequently, due to their dynamic behavior, path-dependent options are
inherently difficult to hedge using the conventional wisdom employed in
managing the risks in vanilla options. Some of these structures—e.g.,
ladders, lookbacks, and barriers—have abrupt payoffs that change from
one level to another. Mathematically, this introduces sharp changes in the
premium, resulting in exaggerated "greeks," particularly delta and
gamma. Complex structures that are therefore embedded with one or more
of these exotic options require a more dynamic monitoring of the embedded risk exposures. In some cases, using the digitals as an example, where
the payoff exhibits a more severe discontinuity that jumps from a payoff of
one to nothing, the structure becomes inherently unhedgeable.

Co-Dependency

When the contingent claim is on more than one underlying asset, co-
dependency between the assets immediately kicks in. The pricing of the
claim therefore depends on the *correlations* among the different underlying assets. Correlation risk is an important component in the pricing of a
multivariate structure, since the correlation coefficients must be priced
into the structure just as volatility is. The *spread option*, whose payoff is
the difference between two indexes, is classified as a *first-order correlation product* because the payout of the option depends explicitly on the
correlation coefficient. The quanto/compo option or the differential swap

are *second-order correlation products,* since there is only one underlying asset. However, the price of the structure is greatly affected by the co-movement of the foreign-exchange rate with the underlying asset, although the foreign-exchange component of the structure is not the subject of the contingent claim. From a conservative perspective and in normal market practice, one assumes that there is no positive correlation among the different assets. The risk exposures for each individual component can therefore be added together, resulting in a maximum risk exposure for the entire transaction.

Leverage and Curvilinearity

Among complex structures with *leveraged or curvilinear* payoffs, the most common are embedded with power caps, inverse floaters (also known as reverse swaps), or leveraged swaps. All of these have payoffs that are a function of a multiple of the underlying asset or index. The effects of the leverage can oftentimes be very substantial. A wrong bet in a directional play on the indexes is almost always costly, since the leverage factor has a compounding effect on the directional view, thereby exacerbating the risk exposures of the structure. In almost all cases, hedging costs for leveraged transactions can be expensive and these transactions are therefore either partially hedged or left unhedged in naked positions. In Figure 9–3, we demonstrate the effect of leverage using a "squared" power option as an example.

VALUATION AND MODELING: CHOOSING THE "CORRECT" MODEL

All of the attributes mentioned above contribute not only to hedgeability concerns but also to the issue of how the embedded option should be modeled. For instance, in the case of a digital option where the payoff is extremely abrupt, paying either one or zero, the trading desk needs to make a decision on how "accurately" to model the option. While it is mathematically trivial to come up with an *exact* closed-form formula for the digital option using Black-Scholes type assumptions, the singularity in the transition from a payoff of one to zero makes it extremely difficult to perform normal delta and gamma hedging. In practice, instead of using a

FIGURE 9–3
"Squared" Power Option

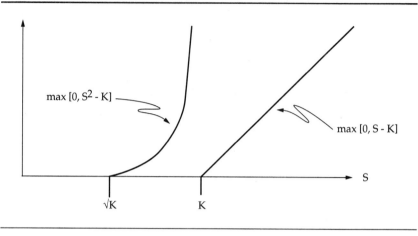

precise mathematical description of the "step function" in the digital option, the digital option is *approximated* by the decomposition,

digital with strike K $\approx$ long a call with strike K $-$ ϵ
+ short a call with strike K $+$ ϵ

where ϵ is some small positive number. Observe in Figure 9–4 that as ϵ approaches zero, the payoff approaches the step function of the digital option.

Figure 9–4 clearly shows that the payoff is now less abrupt and the approximation for the digital option can now be risk-managed more easily. Of course, the choice of how small ϵ is depends on the intuition and experience of the trader. Similar approximations using spreads of two or more vanilla options can be applied to barrier options that either knock out or knock in at some prescribed level H. The barrier H is an instance of a singularity resulting from an abrupt jump in the payoff function, and the barrier is, therefore, embedded with a digital feature.

The simple example above illustrates how a digital option could be effectively risk-managed by a clever approximation wherein the user decides on the level of accuracy. It also points to the important decision-

FIGURE 9–4
Decomposing a Digital as a Call Spread

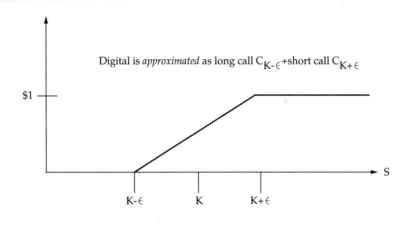

Digital is *approximated* as long call $C_{K-\epsilon}$ +short call $C_{K+\epsilon}$

$1

K-ϵ K   K+ϵ

S

Payoff

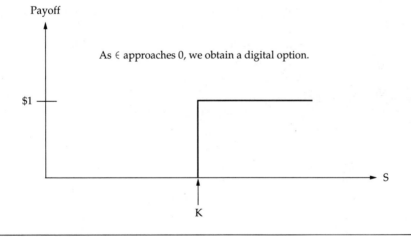

As ϵ approaches 0, we obtain a digital option.

$1

K

S

making process in the choice of a *suitable* model to use. In essence, what we have demonstrated is the close relationship between modeling and the actual valuation of a complex structure and the preceding decisions that have to be made during the modeling process. To answer the question "What is the correct model to use?" requires the answer to the query "How can the structure be risk-managed effectively?" Very often, elegant and exact solutions do not address the issues of practicality and common sense—elegance versus parsimony; precision versus common sense.

RISK EXPOSURES IN OPTIONS

Like most other financial instruments, options entail both credit risk and market risk. Both types of risk, however, are driven by the *same* process, namely, market movements in the form of changes in different market rates, prices, volatility, liquidity, etc. Options also have a variety of unique risk characteristics. Since options have *curvilinear payoffs*, i.e., payoffs which are not flat, the values of option contracts can change very quickly, given some relatively small change in market conditions.

To a great degree, options are most profoundly impacted by the movements of the underlying rates or prices and are, therefore, normally classified as market-risk products. Prior to this section, earlier discussions in the chapter focused strictly on the assessment of risk exposure in complex derivatives embedded with either standard or nonstandard options. From a market-risk perspective, while it is true that options can be a two-edged sword capable of slicing either buyer or seller, the credit exposure of options is very one-sided.

This brings us to the second point: risk exposure in options is one-sided—only the buyer is exposed to credit risk. The seller of the option earns a premium in exchange for providing a payoff to the buyer. Once the premium is received, the seller is no longer dependent on the buyer for the future performance of the option. Consequently, the seller has no exposure to the buyer.

Third, the buyer's payoff is subject to market risk, since this payoff is dependent on market movements. In the event that the seller defaults, the buyer immediately experiences

1. loss of premium paid to seller (if the premium was paid up-front at the inception of the transaction), and
2. loss of economic gain from the performance of the option if the market moves in the buyer's favor.

MEASURING RISK EXPOSURES IN OPTIONS FOR CAPITAL REQUIREMENTS

Translating risk measures into capital requirements can be a complex task. This task is made even more difficult since there is no uniform method for calculating capital set forth by the regulatory bodies. Consequently, the methods used to calculate capital requirements can range from the ultra-conservative, rendering no benefit to the trading desks, to a haphazardly concocted number that has no relevance to the risk factors involved in the complex structure. For a relatively large trading book, the speed with which the capital calculation is performed is crucial. In this section, we present a hierarchy of measurement methods with increasing accuracy and robustness. All of these measures entail two basic steps:

1. Make assumptions about the potential movement of risk factors over a defined holding period and at a prescribed confidence level.
2. Measure the sensitivities of the option positions to assumed potential movements in risk factors and arrive at a profit/loss summary.

The risk factors may be in the form of market rates, volatility, term to maturity, and liquidity, among other things.

EXPOSURE MEASUREMENTS

There are a variety of techniques to measure the risk exposures embedded in a complex structure. For risk-assessment and capital-requirement purposes, we can name three methods that are easy to understand and relatively simple to implement.

1. **Simple-Strategy Methods:** Simple methods offer very quick estimates of possible exposure to counterparties. They usually assume a "worst-case" scenario, i.e., immediately after a transaction, the counterparty goes into default. The estimate is calculated at the inception of the transaction, and therefore does not take future price changes of the underlying into account. The calculations are static in nature and normally provide a *maximum* exposure calculation.

2. **Price-Sensitivities Method:** This method is based on a simple ap-proximation of an option's price sensitivities to changes in the un-derlying price, interest rates, volatility, and other parameters. Since an option's basic price-sensitivities—e.g., delta, gamma, and vega—are used to approximate the option's risk exposure, this method is dependent on the model used to value the option. Fur-thermore, while higher-order corrections may be included as de-sired, the calculated sensitivities tend to be *localized* effects and hence inappropriate for large movements in market parameters.

3. **Scenario/Simulation Analyses:** The scenario approach and Monte Carlo simulation analysis are interrelated and complemen-tary methods. The scenario approach prescribes a desired level of standard deviation about the means of the appropriate market pa-rameters. On the other hand, the Monte Carlo approach simulates the movement of market parameters, given today's market infor-mation and a prescribed level of confidence. Regardless of how the movements in market parameters are obtained, the option is then revalued using the generated paths. Based on some conser-vative percentile of the losses, the risk exposure of the option can finally be determined.

All three methods mentioned above are equally applicable for single transactions or for a conglomeration of transactions in a portfolio context, taking into account correlations among market parameters and natural or legal offsets.

MARKET RISK

When discussing complex derivatives, there is a plethora of risks to consider, e.g., operational risk, model risk, delivery risk, among many other things. The focus here will be on credit risk and market risk. Fortunately, these two types of risk are both driven by the *same* underlying market movements, therefore by ignoring default probabilities, we can simply focus on market risk. *Market risk* can be defined generically as the risk of loss due to movements in market prices or rates. It arises primarily because the intermediary value of a structure is sensitive to market prices or rates. There are two important distinctions that can be made concerning market risk:

1. **Potential Market Risk (PMR)** Potential market risk is the risk exposure an entity must allocate today against a counterparty's credit limit, at the inception of a transaction.
2. **Actual Market Risk (AMR)** Actual market risk is the true value of risk exposure once a trade is underway. It is the actual credit loss sustained by the entity in unsecured transactions if the counterparty defaults. It can be measured by mark-to-market valuation or by the replacement-value method.

At the inception of a trade, the potential market risk is positive, which then decreases over the life of the transaction, until it diminishes to zero at the maturity of the trade. In contrast, the actual market risk is zero at inception, since the market parameters have not yet changed. As soon as market conditions move away from conditions at inception, the actual mark-to-market value of the trade can remain unchanged, decrease or increase. At maturity, the actual market risk can therefore be zero, negative, or positive. Since the actual market risk is quantified by the mark-to-market values, there is nothing much to do about AMR, and our focus should therefore be on PMR.

RISK EQUIVALENCY

Not all complex structures are created equal. They differ in notional amounts, number of contracts, varying degrees of complexity in the embedded optionality, frequency of payments, market parameters at inception, and maturity. Whenever possible, all of these characteristics somehow need to be incorporated into a single coherent measure of risk exposure. This measure is called *risk equivalency*. In light of the different characteristics of a complex structure, one can adjust the notional amount so that the actual and the anticipated (or potential) risks are appropriately quantified.

An effective measurement of risk requires at least three major components:

1. Movements of underlying rates and prices
2. Time to maturity
3. Desired level of confidence

We will justify this argument later when we discuss simulation methods in the final section of this chapter.

For simplicity and for the purpose of this exposition, it is sufficient to represent movements of rates or prices by volatility and represent the time element by the square root of remaining time to maturity (as in a Black-Scholes environment). These three components—namely, volatility, term to maturity, and confidence level—collectively define the quantity called *risk factor* (*RF*). We then have

RF = market movements $\oplus$ maturity $\oplus$ confidence level,

or equivalently,

$$RF = \sigma \times \sqrt{T} \times z$$

where

σ is annualized volatility

T is tenor of the transaction (i.e., time to maturity)

z is desired confidence level (e.g., 1 standard deviation, 2, etc.)

The annualized volatility number may be estimated from history or implied from the market. The square root of the tenor is an artificial correction for the dynamic behavior of volatility. As T gets longer, the time element becomes more meaningless. A more appropriate method is to replace $\sigma\sqrt{T}$ by some in-house proprietary term structure of volatility.

We are now ready to do some simple calculations of risk exposures using the three methods outlined earlier: *simple strategy, price sensitivities,* and *simulation.*

SIMPLE-STRATEGY METHOD

As mentioned earlier, this is a rather crude and simple method and would, therefore, tend to overestimate or underestimate the risk exposure. It is an attempt to come up with a quick estimate of the *maximum* risk exposure, over the life of the transaction, measured *at the inception* of the transaction. The basic underlying premise of this method lies in recognizing the payoff function of the structure. For a simple call option with underlying price S and strike price K, the payoff function is max[0, S – K]. In the event of a default, the risk incurred by the buyer of the option has three components:

1. Loss of the premium paid to the seller

2. Further fluctuation in the underlying price away from current market price

3. Loss of the *potential* payoff of the option

The risk exposure for a vanilla call can, therefore, be crudely quantified by the *risk equivalent exposure* (REE), viz.,

$$\text{REE} = \text{premium} + \max\ [0, \text{potential market risk}]$$
$$= \text{premium} + \max\ [0,\ N \times \{(RF \times S) + (S - K)\}]$$

The second equation can also be expressed in terms of the notional amount as follows:

$$\text{premium} + \max\ [0,\ (\text{Notional}/K) \times \{(RF \times S) + (S - K)\}]$$

where

N is number of contracts

K is strike price

S is current underlying price

RF is the risk factor of the underlying price

Explanation: The term (RF^*S) represents the *potential* fluctuation in the current underlying price, in either upward or downward direction. The risk factor RF represents the desired level of confidence of the deviation of the underlying price from the current market price. Multiplying the current price S with the risk factor RF, therefore, provides us with a *maximum* upward or downward deviation from the current market price over the life of the transaction. The term $(S - K)$ is the payoff (or intrinsic value) of the call option. For a vanilla put option, the payoff function is $\max[0, K - S]$, hence the risk equivalent exposure requires one slight change to the intrinsic part of the put, $K - S$, i.e.,

$$\text{premium} + \max\ [0,\ (\text{Notional}/K) \times \{(RF \times S) + (K - S)\}]$$

Here are two simple examples to clarify how the calculations can be performed.

Example 2: Exposure of a Vanilla Put

Bank A buys 100 put contracts on the German mark, struck at 0.5800 $/DM with a spot price of 0.5893 $/DM and a time to maturity of eight months. A premium of $2.36 is paid to the seller, Bank B. At the inception of the trade, the $/DM annualized volatility is 12.5 percent. Calculate the risk exposure given a 3-standard-deviation level of confidence.

The *risk factor* RF is

$$RF = \sigma \times \sqrt{T} \times z$$
$$= 0.125 \times \sqrt{8/12} \times 3$$
$$= 0.30619$$

The *risk equivalency exposure* REE is

$$REE = \text{premium} + \max\ [0,\ N \times \{(RF \times S) + (K - S)\}]$$
$$= \$2.36 + \max\ [0,\ 100 \times \{(0.30619 \times 0.5893) +$$
$$(0.5800 - 0.5893)\}]$$
$$= \$2.36 + \max\ [0,\ 17.1138]$$
$$= \$19.47$$

This means that over the next eight months, in the event that Bank B defaults, the buyer (Bank A) is exposed to $19.47 worth of risk, consisting of the premium paid ($2.36) and the loss of *potential* performance of the put option ($17.11). The latter is, of course, unrealized paper money. This number is an overestimation of the true risk exposure, since the calculation tacitly assumes that the counterparty immediately goes into default upon completion of the transaction. This is also exacerbated by the fact that the calculations are performed at the "peak" of the underlying price movement as expressed by the risk factor RF.

Remarks:

1. A sharper estimate would be to consider a risk factor that adjusts itself continually through time. In particular, the risk factor could take into account the *volatility term structure* for $\sigma(t)$, so that the volatility now depends on time t, and the sloping nature of volatility through time could be incorporated.

2. The risk exposure is directly related to the tenor of the transaction. If the time to maturity of the option were shorter, the risk factor would be smaller, thereby reducing the impact of the second part of the REE calculation to the overall risk exposure.

Let's consider another calculation of risk exposure with a longer maturity using a 5-year call equity-swap as an example. The following is an example of an "embeddo," i.e., a structure embedded with exotic options.

Example 3: Dissecting an Equity Swap Embedded with Exotic Options

Suppose Bank A buys a 5-year call equity-swap from Bank B, with a notional of ¥1.3BB (or $10MM at the current exchange rate). Bank A agrees to pay Bank B 12-month Yen-LIBOR plus 25 basis points each year beginning at inception, in exchange for the appreciation in the Nikkei Index over 20,000. In order to lower the cost to Bank A, Bank B further agrees to lower the annual floating payment to simply 12-month Yen-LIBOR *flat*, provided that the embedded call on the index knocks out at the 17,000 level. Furthermore, Bank A wants the payoff denominated in yen to be brought back to U.S. dollars. What is the risk exposure to Bank A if Bank B defaults?

The structure consists of three major components. Two of these components are *embedded* options, namely:

1. *Down-and-out call*, struck at K = 20,000 with knock-out barrier H = 17,000
2. *Quanto* from yen to U.S. dollar

The third component arises from a stream of annual cash flows based on the 12-month yen-LIBOR interest rates. All of these components have to be taken care of separately. See Figure 9–5 for a diagram of the structure and Figure 9–6 for the embedded knock-out call.

Suppose the current market parameters are as follows:

current Nikkei index = 19,000

FX exchange rate = 130 ¥/$

current 12-month yen-LIBOR = 4.5%

annualized volatilities are

$\sigma_{Nikkei} = 23\%$

$\sigma_{¥/\$} = 18\%$

$\sigma_{¥\text{-LIBOR}} = 12\%$

FIGURE 9–5
Equity Swap with Embeddos

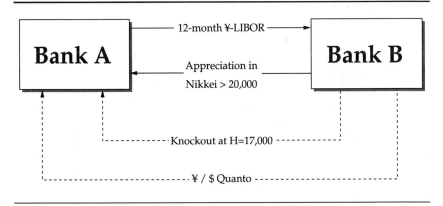

Using the information given above, we have the risk factors:

5-year Nikkei RF: $RF_{Nikkei} = 0.23 \times \sqrt{5} = 0.51$
5-year ¥/$ RF: $RF_{¥\$} = 0.18 \times \sqrt{5} = 0.40$

The annual Yen-LIBOR rates for the next five years are *projected* as follows:

Trade date : 4.50%
Start year 1: 5.04% (4.50% × 1.12)
2: 5.64% (5.04% × 1.12)
3: 6.32% (5.64% × 1.12)
4: 7.08% (6.32% × 1.12)

Note: Using the knowledge that the annualized yen-LIBOR volatility is 12 percent, we projected the maximum growth for the yen-LIBOR curve. In other words, the yen-LIBOR rate is assumed to grow by 12 percent each year for the next five years.

FIGURE 9–6
Down-and-Out Call

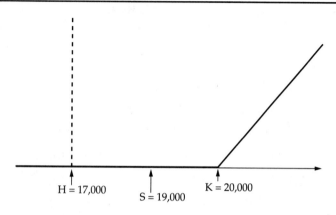

H = 17,000   S = 19,000   K = 20,000

Strike : K
Barrier : H
Current Index : S

The risk equivalent factor for the swap and the knock-out call is calculated as

$$REE = Notional \times RF_{Nikkei} + (Notional/K) \times (S - K) +$$

$$\sum_i Notional(i) \times LIBOR(i)$$

= ¥1.3BB × 0.51 + (¥1.3BB/19,000)
× (19,000 − 20,000) + ¥1.3BB ×
(0.045 + 0.0504 + 0.0564 + 0.0632 + 0.0708)

= ¥ 663MM + ¥303MM

= ¥ 966MM (or $7.43MM using today's ¥/$ exchange rate)

Explanation: Each component in the REE is self-evident. The first term, Notional × RF_{Nikkei}, represents the *mark-to-market* value of the equity swap that Bank A will be forced to reckon with if Bank B defaults. The second term, (Notional/K) × (S − K), corresponds to the *call option*. To be more precise, since the embedded call option is of the knock-out type, as the Nikkei Index falls toward the barrier H, not only does the probability of knocking out becomes greater, the call option also goes further out-of-the-money. Once the call is knocked out, there is no more risk exposure for Bank A. The last term, Σi Notional (i) $\times$ LIBOR(i), is the loss of receipt of the *LIBOR-based cash flows* for each period if the counterparty defaults.

In addition, we need to incorporate the FX portion of the swap. The "quanto" component has a risk-equivalent exposure of

$$REE_{quanto} = (REE_{orig} - \text{premium paid to Bank B}) \times RF_{\yen/\$}$$
$$= (\yen 966MM - \yen 303MM) \times 0.40$$
$$= \yen 265.2MM \text{ (or \$2.04MM using today's exchange rate)}$$

Finally, the total risk equivalent exposure for this structure is

$$REE_{total} = \text{original risk exposure} + \text{quanto}$$
$$= \yen\ 966MM + \yen\ 265.2MM$$
$$= \yen 1.2312BB \text{ (or \$9.47MM)}$$

Since Bank A is long the call option, it is exposed to Bank B's credit. In addition, Bank A also has to make periodic LIBOR-based payments to Bank B in exchange for the appreciation in the Nikkei. The calculations above show that the risk exposure could be substantial even when the option started initially out-of-the money. The real culprit lies in the projection of the yen-LIBOR rates for the next 5 years. This is a fairly long time to consider. By assuming a 12 percent annual volatility, we have naively projected an increasing term structure of interest rates. This need not be true. As long as the interest-rate curve is positively sloped throughout the life of the transaction, Bank A's risk exposure will necessarily be large. The best way to get out of this dilemma is clearly pointing toward simulating the interest-rate curve using many different possible paths, including downward-sloping and flat scenarios. This will be touched upon in the next section.

SOME REMARKS ON THE SIMPLE-STRATEGY METHOD:

1. The method is very simple. It provides a quick assessment of risk-exposure measurement at the inception of a transaction. While the method tends to provide an estimate of exposure based on a worst-case scenario—i.e., the counterparty immediately de-

faults right after the trade is structured—the risk factor RF (which naturally declines through time) can continually be adjusted through time to give a more realistic estimate. Furthermore, the intrinsic part of the REE acts as a surrogate for the actual-market-risk contribution to the total risk exposure, completing our earlier argument that total risk exposure is made up of two distinct components, namely, potential market risk (PMR) and actual market risk (AMR). In our crude approximation of risk exposure, we have effectively taken total risk = PMR + AMR.

2. The main reason why the simple method tends to represent a worst-case scenario at inception is that there is no knowledge of the timing of counterparty default. The current framework does not allow for the *probability of default*. The higher the rating of the counterparty, the lower the probability of default, and therefore a lower assignment of potential risk exposure is warranted. The actual market risk as measured by mark-to-market, however, remains the same.

PRICE-SENSITIVITIES METHOD

The price-sensitivities method is based on the changes in the price of an option resulting from small changes in the parameters that determine the option's value. This is nothing but a simple Taylor series expansion of an option's price function with respect to some chosen parameters, e.g., the underlying price, volatility, and interest rates. The approximation results in the well-known sensitivity measures like delta, vega, rho, and so on. A second-order correction to the linear approximation can be complemented by incorporating higher-order sensitivities like gamma and omega (second-order vega).

The delta term, by itself, is the slope of the value function about the current parameters. Any large deviation about the given parameters introduces significant errors, particularly if the function has a high level of convexity. For options, there is high convexity about the at-the-money point. The addition of higher-order terms in a Taylor series expansion therefore allows a better approximation. Figure 9–7 illustrates the point. As an example, suppose the only parameter of interest is the underlying

FIGURE 9–7
Taylor Series Expansion

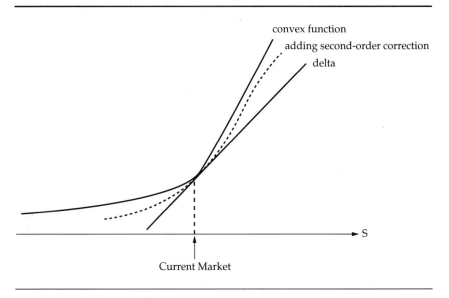

price. Then, the change in the value V of an option, with respect to a
change in the underlying price u, is given by

$$\Delta V = V(u + \Delta u) - V(u)$$

$$= \frac{\partial V}{\partial u} \Delta u + \frac{1}{2} \frac{\partial^2 V}{\partial u^2} \Delta u^2 + \ldots$$

$$\rightarrow \frac{\partial V}{\partial u} (z\sigma) + \frac{1}{2} \frac{\partial^2 V}{\partial u^2} (z\sigma)^2 + \ldots$$

In the last line of the equation above, we replace u by z to indicate the
number of standard deviation z, given the current volatility or standard
deviation σ. The number z is effectively the desired confidence level. The
partial derivatives in the equation above are the delta and the gamma,
respectively, of the option, viz.,

$$\Delta V \rightarrow delta \times (z\sigma) + \frac{1}{2} \times gamma \times (z\sigma)^2 + \ldots$$

From a larger perspective, when V is an options portfolio, the delta and the gamma in the expression above would consist of the weighted sums of all the individual deltas and gammas in the portfolio. For a hedged portfolio, if the magnitude of the changes in the underlying price and price volatility of the underlying asset is sufficiently small, the approximation for ΔV up until the second-order term is sufficient to capture the change in value of the portfolio. To incorporate volatility risk, one normally includes a correction of the following form,

$$\Delta V = V(\sigma + \Delta\sigma) - V(\sigma)$$

$$= \frac{\partial V}{\partial \sigma} \Delta\sigma$$

$$= (vega)\Delta\sigma$$

The risk exposure due to changes in volatility (i.e., vega) can be an add-on factor to the change in value of the portfolio due to delta and gamma. In practice, a second-order correction to vega is not necessary since, for most options, the relationship tends to be almost linear in nature and the order of magnitude is insignificant.

For capital requirements, the rules can be formulated as follows:

$$\mid \min [\, 0 \, , \frac{\partial V}{\partial u}(z\sigma) + \frac{1}{2}\frac{\partial^2 V}{\partial u^2}(z\sigma)^2 \, , \frac{\partial V}{\partial u}(-z\sigma) + \frac{1}{2}\frac{\partial^2 V}{\partial u^2}(-z\sigma)^2] \mid$$

Option payoffs are curvilinear in nature and are therefore *not symmetric* about the current underlying price u. To take into account the difference in either a price increase or a price decrease, a minus sign was introduced in the capital requirement above.

A *more conservative* rule is to take the sum of the absolute value of each individual terms in the expansion, i.e.,

$$\max [\, \mid \frac{\partial V}{\partial u}(z\sigma) \mid + \mid \frac{1}{2}\frac{\partial^2 V}{\partial u^2}(z\sigma)^2 \mid \, , \, \mid \frac{\partial V}{\partial u}(-z\sigma) \mid + \mid \frac{1}{2}\frac{\partial^2 V}{\partial u^2}(-z\sigma)^2 \mid \,]$$

The following example uses only delta to assess risk exposures. The extension to include gamma is trivial.

Example 4:

Consider a hedged portfolio containing a long call on $100 of the underlying asset hedged by a short position in $100 of the underlying asset. The portfolio is equally weighted in the call and the hedge. The current deltas of the option and the hedge are 0.38 and −1.00, respectively, giving a total delta of

portfolio delta = option delta + hedge delta

$\qquad$ = 0.38 + (−1.00)

$\qquad$ = −0.62

Suppose the current annualized volatility of the portfolio is 25 percent and the analysis horizon is 0.5 years. (Assume that both the option and the underlying asset are trading at 25 percent volatility, otherwise a weighted sum is required.) Then given a three-standard-deviation move, the risk factor is

$RF = 3 \times \sigma \times \sqrt{T}$

$\qquad = 3 \times 0.25 \times \sqrt{0.5}$

$\qquad = 0.53033$

and the total risk exposure is

delta × RF

$\qquad$ = −0.62 × 0.53033

$\qquad$ = −0.32880

This indicates that the portfolio stands to lose $0.33 per $1 move in the underlying asset, over the half-year horizon with about 99.8 percent confidence level (or three standard deviations). From a capital-requirement perspective, the credit officer should levy a charge of $33 on the transaction (since the notional amount is $100 and we have calculated the absolute value of −0.3288 × 100).

Remarks: In the example above we simplify matters by assuming that the option and the underlying asset have the same implied volatility and that the option's payoff is symmetric. For payoffs that differ significantly for either an increase or decrease in volatility, the delta of the option should be calculated using both $+\sigma$ and $-\sigma$. The total exposure will be the larger of the absolute values of the exposures calculated using $-\sigma$ and $+\sigma$, as outlined in the discussion above.

In the next example, we incorporate the gamma effects.

Example 5:

Let's now examine the case using the example above when the gamma of the option is 0.23. The portfolio's gamma is also 0.23, since the hedge, being the underlying asset itself, has a gamma of zero. The correction due to gamma is therefore given by

$$\frac{1}{2} \times (gamma)^2 \times (\text{RF})^2$$

$$= 0.5 \times (0.23)^2 \times (0.53033)^2$$

$$= 0.00744$$

The total risk exposure is simply the sum of the contributions from the delta calculated earlier and from the gamma term calculated above:

Total risk exposure $= |-0.32880| + |0.00744| = 0.33624$

The gamma in this example does not contribute significantly to the overall risk exposure of the portfolio.

Remarks:

1. Observe that we took the absolute value of the delta term, since we were applying the *conservative rule* of summing, in absolute terms, all the contributions to the risk exposure.
2. Notice that the gamma contribution is always squared, therefore contribution due to gamma always has a positive effect.

MORE GENERAL PRICE-SENSITIVITIES

In general, to make the approximation of the change in portfolio value more robust, one needs to consider a *multivariate* Taylor-series expansion of $V(u,r,\sigma,t)$ as a function of the underlying price u, interest rate r, volatility σ, time t, among other things, viz.,

$$\Delta V(u,r,\sigma,t) = V(u + \Delta u,\ r + \Delta r,\ \sigma + \Delta\sigma,\ t + \Delta t) - V(u,r,\sigma,t)$$

$$= \frac{\partial V}{\partial u}\Delta u + \frac{\partial V}{\partial r}\Delta r + \frac{\partial V}{\partial \sigma}\Delta\sigma + \frac{\partial V}{\partial t}\Delta t + higher\ order\ terms$$

$$= (delta)\Delta u + (rho)\Delta r + (vega)\Delta\sigma + (theta)\Delta t + \ \ldots$$

The respective changes Δu, Δr, $\Delta \sigma$, and Δt can now be easily replaced by their own prescribed levels of confidence and calculated historical (or implied) standard deviation. There are now two new additions, namely, rho and theta. The *rho* term takes into account the sensitivity to interest-rate movements, while *theta* takes into account the time decay of the options position in the portfolio. It is clear from the expansion above that the contribution to the total change in the value of the portfolio is *additive* in nature.

SCENARIO/SIMULATION ANALYSES

The scenario-based methods and the Monte Carlo simulation methods are complementary analyses that can be used to enhance each other. Both methods begin with today's market rates and attempt to project the behavior of these rates at the end of a chosen horizon, given some levels of confidence. In the *scenario-based* case, a carefully chosen set of possible scenarios is decided upon, and then a transaction is repriced as many times as there are scenarios. The chosen scenarios are invaria-bly derived from historical movements to arrive at an estimate of where future movements might be. Based on historical data, the possible scenarios could range from one extreme, e.g., a negative three-standard-deviation move from today's rates, to the other extreme, e.g., a positive three-standard-deviation move from today's base rates, or anything in between. After a transaction is repriced, the largest possible loss resulting from all the chosen scenarios is then determined to be the risk exposure of the transaction, given say, a three-standard-deviation confidence level.

Instead of using scenarios derived from observed historical movements, another viable alternative is to conduct an experiment using random numbers and simulating potential future outcomes. This is called the *simulation analysis*. There are many ways to perform simulation analyses, the most common of which is the Monte Carlo simulation technique. The Monte Carlo simulation employs random numbers to generate future market rates. The future outcomes all originate from using today's base rates. The main idea is to allow the market rates to follow a random process, starting from today's base rates. Given a sufficiently large number of simulations, the performance (and hence the risk exposure) of a transaction can be ascertained. The common statistics, e.g., standard error and variance, associated with the simulation can also be calculated to give an assessment of how accurate the simulation is.

Monte Carlo simulation analysis is analytically tractable but computationally intensive to perform. Nevertheless, in an environment where things are either uncertain or unknown, the Monte Carlo simulation method has proven to be a very powerful and viable tool in the financial industry.

The simulation normally starts with an assumption of the behavior of the underlying random variable. The assumption, for the most part, is purely mathematical and can be quite subjective. For instance, we can begin with an assumption of a random-walk process for say, interest rate r, viz.,

$$\frac{dr}{r} = \mu dt + \sigma dz$$

The equation above tells us that we have assumed interest rate r to increase with a mean growth rate of μ, over a small increment of time dt. The term dz tells us that, due to uncertainty in the way interest rate r behaves over time, there is a noise component given by the standard deviation σ. This is a so-called *stochastic differential equation* and can easily be solved to yield,

$$r + \Delta r = r \exp[(\mu - 0.5\sigma^2)\Delta t + \sigma\sqrt{\Delta t}\ \epsilon]$$

The number represents a random number sampled from a normal distribution with mean 0 and standard deviation 1. Armed with this, we can now simply iterate from one step in time to the next, or equivalently from one point on the interest curve, r_i, to the next, r_{i+1}. The iteration is

$$r_{i+1} = r_i \exp[\mu_i\Delta t_i + \sigma\sqrt{\Delta t}\ \epsilon_i]$$

where the mean growth rate μ is calculated as the future growth rate of the interest rate between the periods i and i + 1, adjusted by the volatility within the period. One can show that

$$\mu_i = m_i - m_{i-1}$$

where

$$m_i = [\ln(r_i / r_{init}) - 0.5\sigma^2\Delta t]/\Delta t$$

The quantity r_{init} is the interest rate today and t is the period length (measured in years).

FIGURE 9–8
Simulation of Interest Rates

By performing the iteration from one period to the next, over the entire horizon being analyzed, one obtains a *single path* taken by the interest rate *r*. Using different sets of normal random numbers ϵ_i, many other paths can be generated.

Figure 9–8 is an example of five such paths. We started with an initial rate of r_{init} = 15 percent, assuming a growth rate of μ = 12 percent per annum and an annualized volatility of σ = 35 percent. In practice, thousands of such paths need to be generated.

The assumption we have chosen above for interest rates is not very realistic. There is a fairly large class of possible assumptions to choose from. Suppose one feels that the "mean-reverting" feature of interest rates is important, then alternatively, one could assume a random process like,

$$dr = k \, (\hat{r} - r)dt + \sigma dz$$

where over time the interest rate r is assumed to revert to some mean rate $\hat{r}$, with some speed of mean reversion k. The parameters k and $\hat{r}$ are usually *calibrated* to match today's term structure of interest rates. The process for the short rate presented above is known as the Vasicek model.

In principle, if there were more than one interest rate and they are mutually correlated in some fashion, a more complicated multidimensional simulation could also be performed. Furthermore, the underlying assets need not be limited to interest rates. The assets could be stock prices, prices of crude oil, interest-rate swaps, etc., and they could all be simulated in a similar manner, albeit utilizing different assumptions about their underlying stochastic processes.

For example, suppose one were analyzing the risk exposure of a vanilla option on a stock using the Monte Carlo method described above. The steps outlined below could be followed.

1. Make an assumption about the lognormal stochastic process of the underlying stock price, consistent with the Black-Scholes formulation, i.e.,

$$\frac{dS}{S} = \mu dt + \sigma dz$$

2. Specify today's stock price, S_{init}, and choose a suitable step size (say, one day) for time, Δt.

3. Specify the confidence level z (i.e., the number of standard deviations from the mean) for the diffusion of the stock price by replacing σ with $z\sigma$, where z can be 2, 3, etc. Notice the choice of $z = 1$ is conspicuously absent.

4. Perform the iteration from today until the end of the horizon (i.e., the option's expiry) using the equation

$$S_{i+1} = S_i \, \exp \, [\mu_i \Delta t_i + z\sigma \sqrt{\Delta t} \, \epsilon_i]$$

where μ_i is given above.

5. The result from Steps 1–3 is one possible path that the stock price could travel from today's price S_{init} until the option expiry.

6. Value the option using this path generated from Step 4.

7. Choose another sequence of normal random numbers ϵ_i and perform Steps 4–6. Do this tens of thousands of times.

8. The average value of the thousands of values generated in Step 7 represents the value of the option calculated with z number of standard deviations.

9. The difference between the option value using today's known market parameters and the option value obtained in Step 8 is the risk exposure of the option.

The steps briefly outlined above convey the essence of using simulation analysis to assess the risk exposure of an option. Depending on the underlying instrument or the complexity of the structure, some of the steps could easily be modified. In particular, Step 6 could be modified to model the payoff of the complex structure.

The key to a simulation approach is that by knowing today's market conditions and by making reasonable assumptions about the statistical distribution of the parameters in question, future paths can be artificially generated with the help of random numbers. The average of the tens of thousands of potential future realizations can then statistically represent today's expected outcome of the future behavior of the underlying asset.

Finally, we point out one interesting connection between our definition of the risk factor RF introduced earlier in the chapter, viz.,

$$RF = \sigma \times \sqrt{T} \times z$$

and the evolution of the stock price from one step in time to the next. This definition actually arises from the stochastic component of the evolution of the stock-price equation presented in Step 4 above. It is this random component that determines, with confidence level z, the probabilistic evolution of the stock price from today's observed price until the termination time of the transaction.

SUMMARY

In this chapter, we learned how a complex structure is decomposed into its constituent parts. Once each of the individual parts is analyzed and understood, the risk exposure of the entire complex structure could easily be determined. The embedded optionalities are not all created equal; therefore, different methods have to be used to understand the underlying risk exposures. In all cases, however, the terminal payoffs of the options provide many insights into how the options could behave, so we listed a taxonomy of some common exotic options to illustrate their terminal payoff functions. For capital-requirements purposes, we introduced a hierarchy of three methods, namely, the simple-strategy method, price-sensitivities methods, and scenario-based or simulation methods. Collectively, these three methods constitute a very broad class of analytical tools needed to measure both market risk and credit risk, the primary risk-exposures embedded in complex derivatives.

REFERENCES:

Banks, E., *Complex Derivatives* (Chicago: Probus Publishing, 1994).

Estrella, A., D. Hendricks, and J. Kambhu, "The Price Risk of Options Positions: Measurement and Capital Requirements," *Fed. Res. Bank of NY Quarterly Review*, Summer/Fall 1994, pp. 27–43.

Smithson, C., C. Smith, and D. S. Wilford, *Managing Financial Risk*, (Burr Ridge, IL: Irwin, 1994).

Chapter Ten

Strategic Commodity Risk Management
Why and When to Use Derivatives

R. McFall Lamm, Jr.[1]
Vice President
Bankers Trust Corp.

INTRODUCTION

In recent years, derivatives have received an extraordinary amount of attention. The press reported numerous derivatives "disasters" in which corporations lost significant amounts of money. In the majority of these cases, managers blatantly speculated in financial markets, gambling to obtain high returns using financial derivative products. In several instances, firms had only a limited understanding of the instruments that they had purchased. In others, treasurers knew what they were doing and were operating the treasury function as a profit center without informing senior management fully of the risks involved.

With one exception, none of the derivatives headlines in 1994 and early 1995 involved commodities, despite the fact that billions of dollars in commodity derivatives are traded annually. This is largely because firms that deal in commodities primarily hedge and have engaged in hedging

---

[1]Opinions are those of the author and do not necessarily represent those of Bankers Trust.

activities for decades.[2] They understand the risks, the strategies, and the necessity of hedging, and they typically avoid direct speculative activity. The one commodity problem that did surface—Metallgesellschaft's massive failure—came about not as a consequence of speculation, but was primarily due to a failed hedging strategy.

The major reason most commodity producers and processors have hedged for decades is that hedging is essential for the survival of companies that purchase or sell commodities. For example, a huge decline in commodity prices that results in drastically lower sales, or a surge in commodity costs that cannot be passed through to customers, can cause bankruptcy if sufficient cash is not on hand to cover losses. Commodity price fluctuations destabilize revenue flows for producers, who typically face relatively fixed costs. And for commodity buyers, price explosions destabilize costs for firms that normally face relatively fixed revenues. For both commodity producers and buyers, commodity price fluctuations make planning difficult, if not impossible, unless a reliable hedging program is in place. And without an adequate risk-management or hedging strategy, significant management effort is expended while managing erratic revenue flows (in the case of producers) or uncertain costs (in the case of commodity buyers).

This chapter surveys commodity risk management and hedging. The major focus is on why hedging is necessary and when commodity derivatives should be used. The principal topics covered include (1) the extraordinary nature of commodity price-risk versus that of financial products, currencies, and stocks; (2) hedging in general and its distinction from speculation in corporate business activities; (3) hedging strategies and hedging implementation risks; (4) the corporate risk-management function; and (5) new tools and approaches to commodity risk management.

COMMODITIES ARE RISKIER THAN STOCKS, CURRENCIES, AND BONDS

Commodity prices have been and remain among the most volatile of any asset class, including common stocks, currencies, and interest-rate instruments. This makes the management of commodity risk by hedging physi-

---

[2]This applies primarily to agricultural commodities and base metals. Gold hedging started in the 1970s following the decoupling of the U.S. dollar from gold, and energy hedging evolved in the 1980s following the deregulation of energy prices.

TABLE 10–1
Historical Market Volatilities for Selected Commodities

Group	Commodity	Years	Volatility
Energy	WTI crude oil, near futures, NYMEX	1982–94	30%
	No. 2 heating oil, NY harbor	1980–94	31%
Metals	Aluminum, NY	1984–94	18%
	Copper cathode, NY	1986–94	23%
	Lead, cash, London	1983–94	27%
	Nickel, cash, London	1980–94	26%
	Silver, Handy & Harman, NY	1980–94	30%
	Zinc, cash, London	1989–94	24%
Agricultural	Live cattle, Midwest	1982–94	14%
	Cotton, Memphis	1980–94	24%
	Live hogs, Omaha	1982–94	26%
	Corn, near futures, CBOT	1979–94	22%
	Soybeans, no. 2, Decatur	1980–94	21%
	Sugar, world, cash	1980–94	42%
	Coffee, near futures, CSCE	1980–94	31%
	Minneapolis wheat	1982–94	21%
	Wheat, hard, no. 2	1980–94	19%
	Wheat, soft, no. 2	1984–94	25%
Currency	German mark vs. dollar	1986–94	11%
	Japanese yen vs. dollar	1986–94	10%
Financial	U.S. 5-year Treasury bond	1983–94	16%
	U.S. 10-year Treasury bond	1983–94	14%
Stocks	FTSE 100 stock index	1980–94	16%
	S&P 500 stock index	1980–94	15%
	Nikkei 225 stock average	1980–94	17%

Source: Datastream and BT Global Economic Research. Based on six-month weekly historical volatilities.

cal and trade positions much more imperative than managing most other corporate risks and explains why most commodity processors and buyers have hedged for decades.

The extraordinary riskiness of commodities is illustrated by their long-run price volatilities. Most commodities have a price volatility of at least 20 percent, whereas the major reserve currencies average closer to 10 percent; U.S. financial instruments average near 15 percent; and key international stock indexes average a little more than 15 percent (see Table 10–1 and Figure 10–1). Over the long run, commodity price volatilities range from an average in the upper teens for some domestically traded

FIGURE 10–1
Price Volatilities of Selected Commodities and the S&P 500, 1980 to 1994

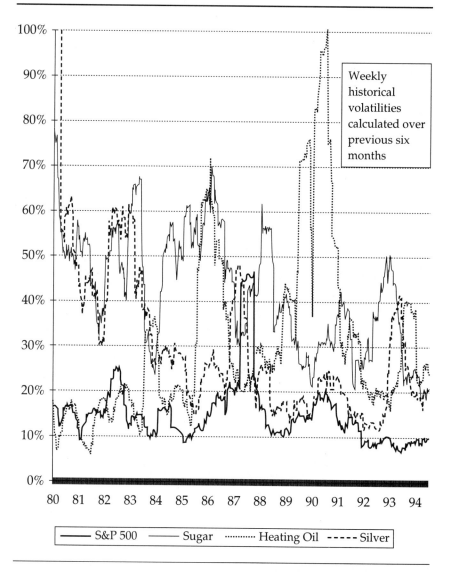

agricultural products to 42 percent for sugar. Energy products average 30 percent price volatility, while industrial metals and silver are almost as high. Clearly, it is fair to say that commodities are significantly riskier than stocks, bonds, and currencies.

The higher average volatilities of commodities reflect a tendency for explosive market breaks and bursts of extraordinary fluctuation due to the unique characteristics of the market.[3] For example, last year coffee prices tripled and volatility surged to more than 100 percent as a consequence of dual freezes in Brazil. Energy markets exhibited a similar surge in 1991 when the Kuwait-Iraqi war broke out. And in years of drought or floods in the Midwest, U.S. grain prices move dramatically.

Besides being more volatile, commodities are also subject to extreme seasonal fluctuations that play virtually no role in financial-product markets. The most obvious examples are grain products where price volatilities often double during the growing season. In addition, heating oil, gasoline, and natural gas exhibit seasonal patterns, as do tropical commodities such as coffee.

THE PURPOSE OF CORPORATE COMMODITY-HEDGING

Conceptually, hedging is defined as executing financial transactions to "lock in" known forward cash sales or purchases. It is the creation of offsetting forward or future transactions against future cash-market commitments such that the gain (loss) in the futures position equals the loss (gain) in the cash position. By effectively locking in a contractual price on a specific product volume, hedging assures that a sharp price increase or decrease, which would drastically affect sales or costs, is protected by an equal and opposite transaction.

The purpose of hedging in commodity markets is most obviously to protect the firm from exploding or plunging prices. Hedging is indispens-

---

[3]The market for most commodities is extremely demand-and-supply inelastic. For example, an increase in price does not reduce the amount of energy or food consumed significantly—people must still travel to work and eat. Similarly, an increase in price does not have an immediate effect on the supply of energy (it takes years to find new petroleum reserves and bring them into production) or food (crops can only be planted and harvested once a year). Consequently, small shifts in supply or demand have dramatic effects on price.

TABLE 10–2
The Consequences of Hedging—The Case of a Mill Producing 100,000 Tons of Sugar Annually

Item	With Hedging*		Without Hedging	
	-$million-	-cts/lb-	-$million-	-cts/lb-
Cash sales	19.8	9	19.8	9
Futures gains (losses)	6.7	3	NA	NA
Total revenue	26.5	12	19.8	9
Raw material costs	24.2	6	24.2	6
Other operating costs	4.4	2	4.4	2
General and administrative	2.2	1	2.2	1
Interest expense	4.4	2	4.4	2
Total costs	24.2	11	24.2	11
Profit (loss)	2.3	1	(4.4)	(2)

*Hedged results assume that sugar prices are locked in for the year at 12 cents per pound and that prices subsequently fall and average 9 cents per pound.

able for producers who pay predetermined prices for their inputs and receive a varying market price for their output—if market prices plunge before costs are covered, bankruptcy can result. Similarly, processors who pay a floating market price for their inputs and receive fixed product prices can incur huge losses if commodity input prices soar.

A good illustration of the direct consequences of failing to hedge is Pan American World Airways (PanAm). PanAm was forced into bankruptcy in part because of unhedged positions in jet fuel at the outbreak of the Kuwait-Iraqi war. At that time, jet fuel prices tripled and passenger fares could not be raised to compensate—especially in a competitive environment where other firms, such as British Airways, had already hedged to lock in lower fuel costs.

Alternatively, consider the case of a sugar mill producing 100,000 tons of sugar annually (Table 10–2). At the beginning of the year, sugar is selling at 12 cents per pound and the firm can sell forward raw sugar at this price using futures contracts, ensuring itself an adequate profit. If the firm does not sell forward, it assumes market risk and must be prepared to accept whatever price is available in the cash market as its sugar cane is crushed and processed into raw sugar. In this latter case, the firm is purely speculating on sugar prices that it will receive. There is an upside—sugar prices may rise above 12 cents per pound, increasing profit. But there is also downside risk in that sugar prices may crash. Because the firm's processing costs are fairly constant, it faces tremendous exposure to the vagaries of the market.

Suppose immediately following the beginning of the year, sugar prices decline to 9 cents per pound and remain at this level on balance for the rest of the year. If processing costs are 11 cents per pound, then the firm will lose 2 cents per pound, or $4.4 million for the year. In contrast, if the firm had hedged by locking in a price at 12 cents per pound, then it would earn $2.3 million in profit. It would still receive an average cash price of 9 cents per pound, but it would book futures- or forward-contract profits of 3 cents per pound. The lower cash price received is exactly offset by the profit on futures or forward contracts.

In this illustration, the firm's annual interest expense is $4.4 million. Because most of its other costs vary with output and must be paid as sugar cane is processed, the firm can continue to operate, but it cannot cover its interest expense. It will be forced to default or reschedule its loans, and possibly be forced into bankruptcy, unless it has $4.4 million in cash reserves. Although extreme, this clearly shows the risks of not hedging.

Hedging is often compared to insurance. Its role is to protect against a catastrophe—a dramatic price movement—that could cripple a firm if it did not have protection. In many ways this is an appropriate analogy. But beyond insurance, hedging has a number of other benefits. One is to allow the firm to focus on managing its core business. If a firm is unhedged, it is constantly exposed to commodity price risk, either on the revenue or cost side. Management will spend its time reacting to a continuously changing commodities market. Either there will be an emergency, when commodity prices move unfavorably and there is a mad scramble for cash, or when commodity prices move in the "right" direction, the firm will be flush with transitory funds. In this latter situation, an illusion of false prosperity often emerges, which sometimes leads to ill-advised decisions concerning capital investment, funding options, and dividend payouts.

In addition, it is often argued that hedging enhances the value of the firm by stabilizing its cash flows. The stock market rewards companies with steady and stable earnings and punishes companies that often have earnings surprises that result from an unexpected explosion or dive in commodity prices. Consequently, firms that hedge should normally have a higher stock price relative to earnings.

In summary, hedging eliminates a major source of firm uncertainty and allows management to focus on the business instead of managing external commodity price volatility. The corporation obtains economies from hedging with obvious benefits. Hedging stabilizes cash flow, allowing the firm to expand its businesses to meet corporate return targets on investment, assets, or equity. Hedging allows the careful planning of capital expenditures and research/development spending over a multiyear horizon. And finally, hedging facilitates the management of the firm strategically rather than operating in a "fire-fighting" mode.

CORPORATE HEDGING AND SPECULATION

If future commodity costs or revenues are absolutely assured, there is no price risk and there is no reason to hedge. For example, if a petroleum refiner is offered an effective price of $20 per barrel for crude products at year-end, and the firm's cost of crude is now a constant $18 per barrel, there is nothing to hedge because uncertainty is not present. The refiner could make a profit simply by selling forward. However, if the refiner must buy crude on the open market at year-end to meet this commitment, then it makes no sense to sell products for $20 per barrel because crude costs could be $15 per barrel or they could be $25. If the refiner agrees to the forward product sale without simultaneously fixing its crude price, this would represent a gamble that crude costs would be low enough to yield a profit. In this latter case, the firm is *speculating* on its crude cost. In this sense, the portion of unhedged firm exposure subject to uncertainty represents a speculative "bet" by the firm that prices will attain some expected level.

Because no one can predict commodity prices in the future with accuracy because of all the random elements that affect markets (weather, political events, wars, plagues, strikes, etc.), uncertainty always exists. In contrast, rent, labor costs, capital equipment, and many noncommodity material prices are stable and are known in advance with reasonable certainty. There is no need to hedge these costs.

In commodity markets the need to hedge is obvious, but what companies actually do varies widely. Many firms do not hedge 100 percent of their commodity sales or costs. This is in part because they have their own view about commodity prices that is at variance with the market, or they may feel comfortable with some market exposure. For example, a corn miller in a short crop year could be faced with year-end corn futures prices at $3.25 per bushel, yet feel that the market price will be only $2.75 per bushel. As a result, the company might hedge only a small portion of requirements—perhaps as little as 20 percent to 30 percent—knowing that the risk of higher prices can be tolerated. The firm then is partially hedged and partly speculating on prices for the unhedged portion of its requirements. In this way, many firms both speculate and hedge in commodity markets.

Characteristically, companies that partially hedge can tolerate higher risk, but this varies across industry and by a firm's upstream or downstream position. For example, start-up firms with sizeable debt or established companies with high leverage cannot afford the luxury of speculating that commodity prices will not move against them—an adverse break could easily cause bankruptcy by reducing cash flow to the point that loans could not be repaid. They must hedge if they are prudent. In contrast, a firm with no debt can tolerate more risk—a commodity price shock could be absorbed from capital this year and any deficit balanced by favorable commodity prices in subsequent years.

Banks financing new farmers with high leverage often require them to hedge everything, whereas established farmers who own their own land and have no debt will often hedge nothing. Similarly, some leveraged gold-mining companies hedge virtually all their production and even finance mine development through gold loans based on forward selling. Other gold companies with little debt hedge nothing.

Notably, it is not so much commodity producers and processors who hedge all their market risk, but commodity firm intermediaries. For example, petroleum refiners, metal dealers, grain merchandisers, cattle feedlot operators, sugar refiners, soybean processors, and commodity traders all hedge virtually 100 percent of their commodity risk. This is because margins are thin and there is commodity risk on both the buy and sell side of their business. A purchase on one side of the market must be balanced by a sale on the other side to ensure profitability. Not hedging could be devastating because commodity input costs could rise at the same time that commodity product prices decline, thereby yielding losses.

Raw commodity suppliers and finished product manufacturers often have more latitude and are more risk-tolerant. For example, only a small percentage of farmers hedge, because their debt is low (family-owned farms are passed from one generation to the next). Similarly, for food manufacturers, ingredient costs may be only 5 percent of total costs and an ingredient cost-surge is damaging but not catastrophic. In contrast, the petroleum refiner who buys crude today at $16 per barrel must sell products forward immediately or risk negative net margins if product prices fall before the crude is processed into heating oil, gasoline, and other products that are sold.

WHO USES COMMODITY HEDGING PROGRAMS?

The major traditional users of commodity hedging programs are (for more than a hundred years) agricultural commodity buyers and sellers. Flour millers buy wheat futures to hedge their costs; corn wet- and dry-millers purchase corn futures to lock in prices; soybean crushers buy soybean futures and sell soybean oil and meal futures to lock in their margins; livestock producers buy corn and soybean meal futures and sell live cattle or hog futures to guarantee returns; and food companies purchase a diverse array of forward or future contracts to lock in their ingredient costs: soybean oil, orange juice, sugar, cocoa, coffee, pork bellies, etc. (see Table 10–3).

With respect to metals, much the same is true. Fabricators have for decades used futures contracts to secure or lock in their metal costs. Aluminum, tin, lead, zinc, and nickel buyers (and sellers) have long operated hedge programs. Precious metals are somewhat different due to the important role of government in these markets. Gold futures trading really evolved only in the late 1970s after fixed exchange rates were abandoned.

More recently, with the deregulation of the energy sector, crude oil, gasoline, and heating-oil futures emerged, as well as futures contracts on natural gas. Futures on crude oil, gasoline, and heating-oil offered independent refiners a way to lock in their margins while presenting crude producers with a way of selling forward. And for users of energy products such as heating-oil distributors, independent gasoline distributors, airlines (who use heating-oil futures to hedge jet fuel prices), and trade intermediaries, energy futures offered a method for mitigating their commodity price risk.

Based on the past, it is easy to anticipate the likely evolution of hedging

TABLE 10–3
Primary Users of Commodity Derivatives for Hedging

Commodity group	Commodity	Natural buyers	Natural sellers
Grains	Wheat	Flour millers	Food grain merchandisers
	Corn	Corn millers, livestock feeders, dairy operators	Feed grain merchandisers
Oilseeds	Soybeans	Soybean crushers	Merchandisers
	Soybean meal	Livestock feeders, dairies	Soybean crushers
	Soybean oil	Food processors	Soybean crushers
Livestock	Live cattle	Meat producers	Feedlot operators
Energy	Crude oil	Petroleum refiners	Crude producers
	Heating oil	Heating oil distributors	Petroleum refiners
	Gasoline	Independent distributors	Petroleum refiners
	Natural gas	Utilities, manufacturers	Natural gas producers
Metals	Gold	Jewelry manufacturers	Mining companies
	Silver	Photographic film makers	Mining companies
	Base metals (aluminum, copper, nickel, *etc.*)	Fabricators	Mining companies
Tropical products	Sugar	Refiners, food processors	Producers and traders
	Coffee	Coffee roasters	Coffee producers/ suppliers
	Cocoa	Cocoa processors, candy producers	Cocoa bean distributors, producers

over the rest of the decade. Because deregulation or changes in regulation have typically driven the development of futures or forward markets in the past, the forthcoming deregulation of the electricity market may unleash a new wave of market volatility. This will create the need for hedging, and in the near future, corporations may well be hedging electricity costs while utilities are hedging their revenues. Similarly, with new farm legislation coming this year and a freeing of agricultural markets, price volatility will increase. This will likely stimulate the creation of new futures or forward markets, or at minimum, the expansion of existing agricultural derivatives markets.

THE DESIGN OF CORPORATE HEDGING PROGRAMS

Most companies maintain an explicit and comprehensive policy on hedging. For example, commodity intermediaries such as trading companies require that all transactions be hedged or offset with a physical trade. In addition, firms such as petroleum refiners, metals dealers and distributors, and soybean crushers generally will hedge all transactions. They buy forward on the input side of the trade and simultaneously sell forward a matched volume of product on the sell side. This is regarded as standard operating procedure and is a critical responsibility of management. The corporate oversight role in this case is to absolutely assure that lower-level managers comply with policy.

For other firms, particularly manufacturers who produce goods that require the purchase of commodity raw materials, hedging and the degree of hedging is often delegated to the business unit manager. The manager presents a plan for the year with expected commodity costs and then is expected to deliver on the plan. This may involve hedging all commodity costs, or in the case of experienced management, the discretionary hedging of some costs and the paying of market price (speculating) on others. In this instance, if management feels that current commodity prices are high and likely will fall, it might opt to hedge only a small percentage of requirements. In contrast, if the company expects that prices will rise, management could opt to lock in or cover 100 percent of requirements.

As already discussed, the degree of outright market risk taken is a function of the nature of the business. If raw material costs are small then a speculative position is less risky. For example, for a food manufacturer with commodity ingredient costs of 10 percent, hedging only a quarter or a third of requirements could be tolerated if a decrease in prices is very likely. Whether this is done or not depends on the firm, the independence of management, and the depth of experience. In many cases, management will have years of purchasing experience and be able to fairly assess the probabilities of higher or lower prices. In this case, management can bring dollars to the bottom line, although there will always be the occasional negative surprise when management guesses wrong.

In instances where management is not experienced or where there is strong risk aversion, the corporation will often insist on 100 percent coverage of commodity costs—that is, complete hedging. In other cases, companies with experienced corporate management will require the business unit manager to present the hedging strategy as part of the business plan. It may then approve lower or higher levels of coverage, depending on its comfort with the strategy and the current market situation.

In all circumstances, it is imperative that the corporation monitor the risk exposure of the business unit and understand total corporate exposure. Especially when a business is given discretion to hedge relatively little of its requirements, corporate management must know at all times the amount of the exposure and the effects on the company of any adverse price move. This procedure is the most critical part of the corporate risk-management function and many companies assign a corporate risk officer specifically to this task.[4]

CLASSICAL CORPORATE COMMODITY-HEDGING METHODS

Static hedging.   Generally, hedging commodities requires establishing futures or forward positions in equal volume to the forward buy or sell commitment. As long as basis risk is minimal (or averages to zero in the long run) and the futures position can be liquidated at approximately the same time as the cash transaction being hedged, such one-to-one hedging works well. Problems sometimes arise if futures contracts are used for hedging and expire in subsequent months following the cash transaction. In this case, the futures contract volatility may be less than the spot cash volatility and the hedge may not work well. This is a classic

---

[4]The risk-management function involves not just commodities but financing and currency hedging as well. In many firms there is a distinction between management of commodity risks (a purchasing function), which is often embedded in the individual business units, and the management of financing and currency risk, which is part of the corporate treasurer's responsibility. Trade houses are more progressive in managing all these risks collectively.

problem in commodity hedging with futures—contracts are usually available only at two- or three-month intervals. In these situations forward
contracts offer a distinct advantage.

The hedge ratio.   One solution is to put on the hedge at a ratio to
the required physical volume. Such hedge ratios are a direct function of
the correlation between the futures and spot market price changes and the
ratio of the standard deviation of the spot to futures price changes.
Generally, such ratios are 90 percent or more although in some instances
they can be less. It is straightforward to estimate hedge ratios by regress-
ing spot on futures market price changes.

Dynamic hedging.   A better approach is to use dynamic hedging,
in which the size of the hedge is adjusted over time as the transactions
commitment-date approaches. This allows adjustments to be made as
volatilities or correlations change and results in superior risk management.[5] Its disadvantage is that dynamic hedging requires constant staff
monitoring and adjustment.

Rolling hedges versus matched expiration.   Another issue is
whether to use the nearest contract month or months to establish the
hedge, and then to roll over the necessary number of contracts into the next
nearest future when the near contract expires, and continuing rollovers
sequentially until the cash transaction date, at which time the futures
positions are liquidated. This approach is often referred to as "stacking"
futures and is advantageous if the cash transaction is in a distant month
and the corresponding futures are illiquid. It does subject the firm to
rollover risk, however, since the futures contracts rolled into may differ in
price (above or below the expiring near futures contract).

Options.   Corporations with specific views on price often choose
to hedge or not hedge depending on the direction of price expectation. An
alternative method of partial hedging is available using options. If commodity buyers expect prices to fall, then obviously they should simply
wait and pay lower market prices. However, if buyers expect prices to rise,
they can buy call options (to lock in a maximum price that will be paid) or

---

[5] See Duffie (1989) for an example of dynamic hedging.

FIGURE 10–2
Simple Commodity-Hedging Strategies for Different Market Scenarios

	Price expectation		
	Prices rising	**Prices volatile**	**Prices falling**
Commodity buyers	Buy calls Sell puts	Buy futures	No action, pay lower price
Commodity sellers	No action, take higher price	Sell futures	Sell calls, Buy puts

sell put options (allowing another party to force them to buy at a specified contractual price). In the former case, insurance is purchased, while in the latter income is enhanced. Commodity sellers who expect prices to fall can sell calls (enhancing their income) or buy puts (to lock in a minimum price that they will receive). The obvious strategy for commodity sellers expecting prices to rise is to take no action (see Figure 10–2).

HEDGING PROGRAM IMPLEMENTATION RISKS

There are four major execution risks associated with futures hedging. These include basis risk, funding risk, rollover risk when a stacked futures strategy is used, and liquidity risk. Basis risk is more an issue in commodities than in financial products because financial contracts are usually cash-settled, or if not, are easily transferable geographically at minimal cost. In contrast, if a firm is hedging an agricultural transaction in the Southeast with a futures contract that settles basis the Midwest, then there is the possibility that spot prices in the Southeast are not well correlated with the futures delivery point. Over short time-intervals, such as several months, corn prices in one area may move up while declining in another region in response to regional demand and supply conditions. A regression of local market prices on cash market prices of the underlying futures contract normally reveals the magnitude of basis risk.

Funding risk is a notorious corporate problem that has long produced conflict between company treasurers and purchasing departments charged with implementing commodity hedging strategies. The issue emerges when futures positions begin to lose money. Of course, the offsetting cash obligations are gaining in equal value, but the mark-to-market of futures requires that cash be posted immediately with brokerage firms as future contract values decline. In a sharp decline, a company can be forced to post hundreds of thousands of dollars (or in the case of Metallgesellschaft, millions) if the position is large. Corporate treasurers are not typically prepared for such unplanned events and are sometimes resistant because it appears that the firm is losing money outright.

In extreme cases when there are large commodity-price movements, senior management will overreact to futures losses and will intercede to remove the hedge.[6] To prevent this, the company treasurer and management need to be brought into hedging strategy formulation and acquainted with the fact that in extreme situations, a substantial amount of cash can be required to post margin. Many firms use OTC forward agreements to avoid daily mark-to-market, but even here the issuer typically has the right to ask for margin under certain conditions.

Regarding rollover risk, it is most damaging when forward markets invert from contango to backwardation or vice versa. An excellent example is the experience in the crude-oil market. For years, crude oil generally traded in backwardation on the New York Mercantile Exchange. Then in 1994, the situation reversed (see Figure 10–3). A firm carrying large "stacked" positions in near futures as a hedge against oil prices several years out was immediately faced with a major problem—outright losses on each rollover in addition to higher margin. Prior to contango, firms actually earned profits on every rollover (the rollover yield).

Lastly, liquidity risk is normally a very minor concern and occurs only if a firm's futures positions are large or if the market is small. In either case, the firm's purchases or sales can move the market, forcing the company to pay more for hedging than it would in a deep, liquid market. Such risk can obviously be eliminated by avoiding less-liquid markets or in some cases simply using OTC forward agreements indexed to a public market price.

In summary, there are risks involved in establishing hedges once the

---

[6]This in part increased Metallgesellschaft's losses. See Culp and Miller (1994) for a review.

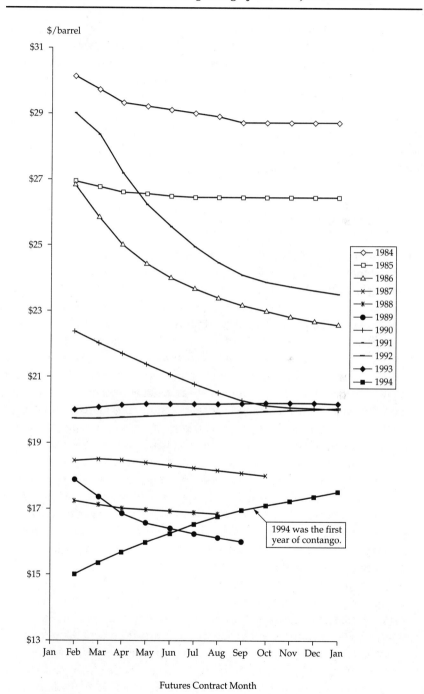

decision has been made to hedge. These are minor, however, given that management is informed and knowledgeable about the markets. Basis risk is usually a minor concern and will usually average to zero in the long run. Nonetheless, companies should be prepared for occasional basis gains or losses. Funding mark-to-market and margin calls are also problematic on occasion, but with an enlightened management it will be understood that this is part of hedging and costs will be offset by gains on cash sales. Rollover risk is easily contained by avoiding the strategy, using the forward market, or limiting exposure by keeping positions small.

THE RISK-MANAGEMENT FUNCTION

Corporate risk management typically involves the systematic aggregation of business unit risks into a total company picture, measurement of total corporate risk exposure, approval of business unit hedging strategies, and placing limits on positions held by business units. Often this system is "tight," with all businesses reporting transactions to a central office where the corporation instantaneously offsets open positions with hedges (in a trading company, for example). In other situations, the risk-management system is "loose," with business units reporting in net positions daily or even weekly, or not reporting at all if they are within preestablished tolerance limits (for example, a food processor with commodity ingredients).

In the most perfect case, in a corporation geared to steady, stable earnings growth, it would be reasonable to hedge all volatile commodity costs (or revenues if a commodity is sold as a product). At the beginning of the year, each division would develop their annual plan and then lock in their costs accordingly through the appropriate hedges. Management could then focus on the issues that really matter—improving productivity, research and development, developing new markets, and generally "growing" the company—knowing that hedge-execution risk was the only worry. This is perhaps the ideal risk-management system.

Unfortunately, it is not always possible to hedge all commodity risks because forward or futures markets may not exist, because there are execution risks, and because there are transaction costs. But in firms that primarily trade or refine intermediary products, 100-percent hedging is not only customary but essential and part of management's job. For example, as noted previously, crude-oil refiners, soybean crushers, livestock feeders, and grain millers must all hedge their production to lock in their margins. Otherwise they could be "whipsawed" by a price move either on the buy or sell side, and that could yield severe losses. The appropriate corporate oversight role then becomes "hedge everything" and the parent company must ensure that this is done consistently.

A critical element of risk management is the risk accounting system. Such a system should show all corporate commodity risk for the year, the amount hedged, and the net residual risk or market exposure at any time. This should be aggregated by commodity and a total should be derived for the firm. The firm will then know its "value at risk." The system should also be capable of simulating the effects of price shocks if there is a dramatic commodity price explosion or dive.

Although creating an adequate risk-management system might appear simple on the surface, it is really a complex task.[7] Options, futures, forward agreements, and swaps positions must all be combined into a common unit. This is possible since options can be delta-adjusted to an equivalent forward or futures position, and because a swap contract can be transformed into an equivalent basket of forwards or futures contracts. But it is not easy and few companies incorporate the amount of detail truly needed for an adequate system, except for trading companies, which live or die by adequately managing their risk.

THE ROLE OF SPECULATION IN CORPORATE ACTIVITIES

In some corporations, speculating on company commodity positions is viewed as a legitimate activity. And in some firms, not only do line businesses speculate on commodity prices, but some companies have business units committed solely to proprietary trading. Proprietary trading profits tend to be highly erratic and destabilize the firm's cash flow, however. For this reason, and because it is difficult to consistently beat the market, most commodity companies have relegated proprietary trading to a minor role, although this is less true for trade houses, where it can be a dominant business. Importantly, firms engaging in proprietary trading typically place position and capital risk limits on their traders to prevent catastrophe.

---

[7]See Dembo (1994) and Rutterford, et al. (1992) for a discussion of some of the complexities of risk management.

The justification for proprietary trading within a firm is that the corporate information base offers a competitive advantage in speculative activities. This may well be the case for some of the larger companies that have worldwide operations. Certainly having local offices in Asia or Africa that can report on local market conditions offers some insight into market dynamics.

For companies with proprietary trading units, it is critical that the trading units' net positions be aggregated with those of the rest of the company. This is part of having a comprehensive risk-management program and can prevent the proprietary trading unit from getting on the same side of the market as the major business units and concentrating commodity risk excessively. In many instances, the proprietary trading unit may take an opposite view, and its position can be netted internally against another business unit, reducing the firms transaction costs.

NEW APPROACHES TO COMMODITY RISK MANAGEMENT

The most important innovation to appear in the commodity derivatives market in the last decade is swaps. Swaps were first used in financial instruments and currencies, and then came to energy products in the 1980s. In the early 1990s, swaps came to be extensively used in metals, especially gold, and are now becoming more accepted for agricultural commodities.

Swaps offer food processors a less expensive hedging method. Instead of buying numerous staggered futures or forward contracts, managing margin flows and daily mark-to-market, and constantly monitoring positions, firms can execute a single swap-agreement to lock in ingredient costs for the year or quarter. Similarly, producers and intermediaries can hedge their revenues using swaps, thus saving significant transactions, execution, and management costs.

Swaps are particularly appealing to corporate treasurers accustomed to dealing with currency and financial swaps. They often dislike dealing with unexpected and unplanned margin calls arising from futures positions established by their purchasing departments. As the distinctions between traditional treasury functions and purchasing departments continue to blur, and companies look for less expensive ways to hedge, swaps will make further inroads in agricultural commodity markets.

OTC options and forward agreements are also being used increasingly for commodity hedging at the expense of established futures markets. OTC products can be tailored specifically to users' needs. Basis, timing, and liquidity risk can often be eliminated with OTC products, sometimes at a lower total cost. The only added complication is counterparty risk, but this can be minimized by restricting transactions to creditworthy firms.

Finally, it should be noted that in many cases the more sophisticated derivatives firms can bundle corporate risk management into a single package by combining currency, financial instrument, and commodity risk into one transaction. This has obvious appeal by greatly simplifying the corporation's total risk-management problem.

CONCLUSION

In summary, strategic commodity risk management has become a complex process as organizations and markets have become more heterogeneous. Commodity price volatility is not declining and likely will only increase in the future. This means that the importance of risk management will increase. Hedging has some minor risk but as corporations strive to enhance shareholders' value by maintaining stable cash flow, hedging and the role of risk management can only expand in the future. New instruments are evolving, such as commodity swaps and bundled transactions, to improve the efficiency of risk management.

REFERENCES

Culp, Christopher L., and Merton H. Miller, "Hedging a Flow of Commodity Deliveries with Futures: The Lessons from Metallgesellschaft," *Derivatives Quarterly* 1 (1994), pp. 7–15.

Dembo, Ron S., "Hedging in Markets That Gap," in *The Handbook of Derivatives and Synthetics*, Robert A. Klein and Jess Lederman, eds. (Chicago: Probus Publishing, 1994), pp. 423–442.

Duffie, Darrell. *Futures Markets* (Englewood Cliffs, NJ: Prentice Hall, 1989).

Fink, Robert E., and Robert B. Feduniak. *Futures Trading: Concepts and Strategies* (New York: NYIF Corp., 1988).

Froot, Kenneth A., David S. Scharfstein, and Jeremy C. Stein, "A Framework for Risk Management," *Harvard Business Review* 72 (November-December 1994), pp. 91–102.

Rutterford, Janette, A. Sher, and Desmond Fitzgerald. "Building Blocks" in *From Black-Scholes to Black Holes: New Frontiers in Options,* (London: Risk Magazine Ltd., 1992), pp. 75–78.

Weinberger, David, *et al.* "Using Derivatives: What Senior Managers Should Know," *Harvard Business Review* 73 (January-February 1995), pp. 33–41.

Chapter Eleven

Using Derivatives and Quantitative Techniques to Increase Portfolio Returns

David J. Madigan
Vice President
Bankers Trust Company

INTRODUCTION

Portfolio managers look at their portfolios in one of two ways. A bottom-up approach, or "value management," looks for individual securities that are mispriced by the market. This requires extensive credit research of securities and some risk-valuation method. A top-down approach looks at the portfolio as a bundle of risks. Each security has different risks included in the position. By breaking down the risks in the securities and summing the individual risks across the portfolio, the portfolio manager can evaluate what problems exist in the portfolio.

For bottom-up managers, credit and duration-management derivatives can leverage their research to identify mispricing in markets. These types of securities include credit swaps, leveraged bonds, and notes that adjust to credit ratings.

For top-down managers, derivatives allow the manager to hedge, alleviate, or eliminate unintentional risks taken in developing a portfolio. Derivatives have the unique quality of levering individual risks. If the appropriate derivative is added to a portfolio, the return is increased with reduced unintentional risk.

In this chapter, most of the discussion is directed at the evaluation of various portfolio risks as in the top-down management style. The application of generic and specialized derivatives is most appropriate in a risk-management environment. Portfolio management requires identifying and controlling risks to maintain a consistent return.

VALUATION OF CALLS AND PORTFOLIO MANAGEMENT

Evaluating portfolio risk with option-adjusted spread analysis is the key to the use of derivatives in a portfolio. Briefly, the option-adjustment process is used to identify the controllable risks in a portfolio.

Modified duration estimates the change in price for a change in yield on a series of cash flows. Simply, the duration of a bond is the slope of the price/yield relationship. As yields rise, the prices of bonds fall. By calculating the duration of a bond, the portfolio manager can estimate the price change of his or her portfolio for a given change in yields.

That estimate can then be used to evaluate the principal risk of the portfolio to yield-changes compared to other portfolios or indexes. Duration estimates the relationship as long as the yield curve shifts in a parallel fashion (all yields along the curve move in the same direction by the same increment). This consistent estimation is used to match liabilities and assets or to measure the relative risk of different portfolios. By controlling market exposure against a "bogey" duration, the portfolio manager has more control over the portfolio's sensitivity to interest-rate changes.

Convexity estimates the change in the price of the bond that is caused by the curvature of the duration/yield relationship. As yield levels change, the duration of a bond will change. The convexity estimates the difference between the duration estimate of the price change and the actual price change of the bond. Positive convexity means the bond's duration will lengthen when the yield falls, increasing the amount by which the price will rise for each basis point the yield drops. Negative convexity means the duration will shorten when interest rates drop, decreasing the amount by which the price will rise for each basis point the yield drops.

Among the bonds with the highest convexity are zero-coupon noncallable bonds. The lowest convexity is from bonds that have long maturities but short optional calls. The largest elements in determining convexity are embedded options and higher duration. Buying an option can be described as buying convexity. The key element in determining the price of an option is the volatility. Similarly, convexity is a measure of the portfolio's exposure to market volatility. To a lesser extent convexity also measures the bond's exposure to yield-curve twists by estimating the changing value of the optional redemption dates.

Together, duration and convexity describe the bond's exposure to changes in the yield curve. Duration measures the bond's exposure to parallel yield shifts. Convexity measures the bond's exposure to yield volatility and twists in the yield curve. A portfolio manager can use this information to adjust bond purchases to fit his or her current market outlook. After adjusting for the duration and convexity measures, option-adjusted spreads can then be used to compare the relative value of bonds.

USING OAS TO ESTIMATE RELATIVE VALUE

Briefly, the option-adjusted spreads (OAS) of various bonds can be compared to determine the relative value of bonds in the market. This tool is useful for determining which bonds should be bought, sold, or held when the portfolio manager is actively trading in the market. Comparing OASs in the municipal market is more difficult than in other markets. Generally, taxable markets measure the OAS of a bond as spread over the Treasury curve, either an estimate from all outstanding Treasuries or from an interpolated curve of current Treasuries. This makes comparing bonds easier because the Treasury curve represents a "risk-free" yield curve for dollar-denominated securities. However, the taxability and yield-curve shape differences between municipals and Treasuries make this base less reliable as a measure of a municipal risk-free yield curve. The goal is to pick a consistent market curve for comparison.

The relative value of bonds can be measured in two ways. A time series of the OAS of a bond can be calculated and the relative value at any point in time determined by the spread from the average OAS. The alternative is to price a great number of bonds in the market on a particular day, calculate a market matrix, and determine the relative value of a bond by its spread over the yield in the cell of the matrix in which the bond would fall. There are weaknesses to both methods.

Time-series analysis is dependent on a consistent yield curve. The underlying yield curve can change the OAS of the bonds on a particular day and give misleading relative values. However, the time-series method eliminates the need to price large numbers of bonds. The time series can be used on a limited number of active bonds. A market-matrix method requires large numbers of bonds, given the individual state-tax differences, credit types, and rating classes of bonds. The pricing sources for large numbers of municipal bonds generally use a matrix to price the bonds. The calculation of a daily matrix would simply reveal the inefficiencies of matrix pricing without revealing the underlying market.

Consistency in modeling the underlying yield curve is important to yield-curve analysis. Calculating the OAS is a time-consuming process. Consistent modeling of benchmark issues across the market allows for quicker evaluation and fewer lost opportunities on mispriced bonds.

USING FUTURES TO HEDGE MAIN PORTFOLIO RISKS: YIELD SHIFTS, YIELD-CURVE SHAPE, VOLATILITY

As with most markets, the municipal bond market has focused most bond research efforts on the credit risk of a bond. This approach means that most portfolio managers are trained to look at their portfolio as a series of individual credits rather than as a portfolio. However, over the last 15 years the default rate of municipal bonds has been extremely low and the market yield risk has been very high. By breaking out the yield-curve risks and measuring them, a portfolio manager can have a more profound impact on his or her returns than through the evaluation of credit risk.

In the 1980s, the most important element in the fixed-income markets was the drop in yields from 1983 to 1993. Long Treasury yields fell from over 13 percent to under 6 percent. The swift changes in yields sensitized managers to the duration of their portfolio. The returns from this movement of rates are estimated through duration management. The first of the widely used portfolio derivatives was a duration hedge—the Chicago Board of Trade financial index futures contracts. The goal was to allow portfolio managers to use a derivative to extend or shorten duration cheaply by buying or selling the price movement of a synthetic bond or index.

In using the futures contracts to hedge a portfolio, the portfolio manager must first calculate a weighted-average option-adjusted duration for the portfolio and then calculate a weighted-average option-adjusted duration for the futures contract. Using the portfolio's duration, the portfolio manager must decide on a target duration for the portfolio. This will depend on the index that the fund is compared to and on the portfolio manager's outlook on the direction of interest rates. Using the targeted duration, the portfolio manager must then decide whether to hedge the portfolio in the cash market or to use futures contracts.

The key element in deciding whether to use cash-market trades or futures contracts will be the relative total return to the portfolio if the manager's outlook is correct. The cash-market alternative involves trading bonds in a relatively inefficient market. The portfolio manager must sell into the secondary market and purchase bonds in the primary or secondary market. Typical sales spreads for off-the-run bonds (any bond that is not very current or actively traded) would be at least $2.50 a bond. The cost of purchasing bonds would vary from the average $5.00 a bond in the primary market, where portfolio managers have access to larger blocks of bonds, to $2.50 a bond in the secondary market. Given a relatively short-term outlook, these spreads can represent a major portion of the expected gains from executing the trades. However, the additional expense of dealing in the cash market can be compensated for by the additional control over the selection of bonds to which the portfolio has credit-risk exposure.

Futures contracts are much cheaper to trade, usually $14 to $30 a contract, depending on the volume of futures trading. Since a contract represents an underlying value of 100 bonds, the net cost of the transaction is reduced from $2.50 to $7.50 a bond to only $0.014 to $0.030 a bond. This allows the portfolio manager to take advantage of short-term strategies and outlooks more efficiently. Using the futures contract, though, reduces the portfolio manager's bond selection control and introduces a new basis risk. Basis risk is the risk that the cash portion of the portfolio will behave differently from the futures contract hedging the portfolio. Basis risk can be broken down into elements, and the most important element in the municipal contract is the relative mispricing of the contract. The contract is trading at "fair value" if the contract is priced so that the portfolio manager cannot benefit from the difference between buying the cash bonds and buying short-term bonds and futures contracts. The fair value of the municipal contract varies, depending on the funding method of the trader. For banks and securities dealers, the funding rate is LIBOR or a taxable funding rate at which the trader can borrow funds to purchase municipal bonds. Because the rate is taxable, the difference between the long municipal yield of the index and the short-term funding cost is lower;

typically, the threshold rate for these traders to break even is higher. For example, with the index at 94–00 (yielding 7 percent) and eight days to expiration, a dealer can either borrow at 5.75 percent for eight days and buy the index bonds and sell futures contracts, or he or she can do nothing. The break-even spread for the dealer to trade the bonds is the difference between the borrowing cost and the accrued interest on the bonds for eight days. This difference comes to 1/32 point for the period. The trader will do nothing or buy the futures contract if the spread between the index and the contract is more than 1/32, and will borrow to buy municipal bonds and sell the contract if the spread is less than 1/32. The arbitrage-free value for the contract is called fair value for dealers.

Portfolio managers have a different, lower hurdle for the fair value. This is because their alternative investments are money market instruments or Treasury bills. In the same case as above, the portfolio manager can fund his or her purchase of bonds at 4.65 percent. This lowers the hurdle spread to 2/32. So the portfolio manager will sell municipal contracts 1/32 cheaper than the dealer can for an eight-day hedge rather than selling bonds in the cash market.

The fair value of the index/futures spread is important because the portfolio manager will use this determination to decide if the portfolio duration change should be done with higher transaction costs and lower basis risk in the cash market, or whether the cheaper transaction costs and relative value of the futures contract compensate for the greater basis risk of the trade. The length of the trade and the marketability of the bonds in the portfolio have as great an impact on the decision as the relative value of the futures contract.

Large short-term changes in the duration of a portfolio are nearly always cheaper in the futures markets. The availability of bonds to unwind a cash-market trade and the transactions of the trade usually make the cash-market alternative too expensive. For longer-term changes in duration, the cash-market elimination of basis risk should make up for the higher transaction costs.

Yield-curve shifts and yield volatility can also be hedged, but less efficiently with the futures contract. Given a neutral outlook for duration but high expected volatility (a scenario where yields are expected to move but the direction is unknown), futures can be combined with options on futures to create a hedge for this scenario. The CBOT added options on the municipal futures contracts, but this market has traditionally been relatively inactive. The options allow the portfolio manager to purchase or write calls and puts on the municipal-bond futures contract. The options have the same basis-risk problems as the futures contracts, but offer the additional benefit of hedging volatility. In the given scenario, the portfolio manager would adjust his duration to a neutral position, either the average of the other funds or to the index he is comparing to. The portfolio manager would then evaluate the volatility implied in the option; then he can purchase options. This use of options is difficult or impossible to mimic in the cash market. The portfolio manager would have to employ a dynamic cash-market hedge, and as shown above, the transaction costs would eliminate most of the gain from this strategy.

Futures and options offer very little hedge for yield-curve shape changes. The BBI40 is made up of long bonds. The lack of shorter-average-maturity futures limits the amount of flexibility in trading the futures. However, since convexity plays a role in measuring the risk of a yield-curve shape-change, there are some strategies using futures and options to hedge the risk of yield-curve twists. The future's fair value is dependent on the spread between long- and short-term rates. If short-term rates are expected to rise or long-term rates are expected to fall, the portfolio manager should purchase futures contracts. As short-term rates rise, the fair discount of the futures versus the index will fall. As the discount falls, the futures' price rises and the portfolio manager would gain from holding futures versus holding long bonds. For an intermediate to long yield-curve flattening, the portfolio manager can gain by buying noncallable long bonds and creating a synthetic barbell by selling futures contracts. Since the futures contracts are based on an index of 10-year callable bonds, as long bonds rally, the futures contract will tend to trade to the calls, similar to an intermediate bond. These trades work, but are generally less profitable than the cash-market alternatives.

This same analysis holds for taxable futures. The difference between holding the futures and owning bonds is the cost of financing. Buying contracts along the curve leverages this short-term rate exposure. This risk must then be compared to the portfolio yield-curve exposure. The more futures that are held, the less cash-equivalent exposure the portfolio has. If short-term rates rise, the cost of financing rises and the value of the futures falls.

Yield-curve trades in derivatives can be much cheaper than cash trades. Synthetic barbells are typically cheaper from a cost-of-carry perspective and transaction costs are lower.

Futures can be used to adjust duration, as intended, or for yield-curve trades. The benefits to portfolios of illiquid bonds like corporates and municipals are obvious: transaction costs are low and "value" research is not overruled by other portfolio risks.

YIELD-CURVE TRADES USING DERIVATIVES

Exchange-traded futures are useful for duration management, but they also have the drawbacks described above. The futures are not specifically designed for a portfolio outlook. Many times a portfolio manager needs to look beyond futures to accomplish trades in the derivatives market. In response to this need, many different types of over-the-counter derivative bond structures have been introduced. In most cases these derivatives serve several purposes, but most are based on taking advantage of the yield curve.

Generally, the yield curve is upward-sloping. This condition persists even though the Treasury curve has flattened or inverted. Inverse floating-rate securities take advantage of a steep yield curve by paying the difference between a long- and short-term rate. In municipals, this is more important because the interest income from a bond is tax-exempt. An inverse floating-rate security pays a fixed interest-rate from an underlying bond plus the difference between a long interest rate and a short-term auction or swap rate. Since short-term municipal rates tend to be lower than the long-term rates, the inverse floating-rate securities tend to offer a higher tax-exempt income stream. Over the life of the bond this income stream will increase as rates fall and decrease as rates rise. This, in effect, will change capital gains into tax-exempt income over the life of the bond. The derivative lengthens the portfolio duration with the leverage. These derivatives generally produce higher income, something that portfolio managers need but that cannot easily be gained in the cash market without lowering credit quality.

In addition to increasing duration and income, the swap-based derivatives allow a portfolio manager to take advantage of yield-curve twists. For example, if the intermediate portion of the yield curve is particularly attractive, a derivative can be assembled to leverage that portion of the yield curve and maintain a neutral duration for a long bond fund. The strength of this trade lies in the fact that the yield curve has persistently been steeper from 1 to 15 years than it is from 15 to 30 years. By shortening maturity and extending duration with leverage, the portfolio can remain at a neutral duration but pay a higher dividend from a leveraged position in intermediate maturities.

These derivatives generally, but not always, come with calls or opt-puts. This option allows for liquidity in specialized derivatives. The specialized derivatives that do not have a liquidity option must be held to maturity or call, but can be hedged using other derivatives (which may be expensive) or by investing the cash portion of the portfolio, which may reduce or eliminate the benefit of holding an illiquid derivative. In general, specialized derivatives like structured notes serve a specific purpose for a portfolio. Generally, that specialization makes them illiquid because portfolios have individual needs. With a more generalized auction-based product, the liquidity is generally better because the security will fit more portfolios. Liquidity is a concern for most buyers of derivative products, but with opt-out clauses and market offsets, the portfolio manager can alleviate much of this concern.

TARGETING A PORTFOLIO

Much of the specialization done in a portfolio is to adjust the risk exposure to take advantage of the outlook or unrecognized value in the market. When the portfolio is reduced to risks from a collection of bonds, adjustments can be made to duration, convexity, and yield-curve risk through derivatives. Derivatives have been used to leverage or hedge other risks. For example, currency swaps and credit options have been embedded in structured notes to hedge risks or to take risks that are beyond yield risk.

Portfolios are generally run in an extremely competitive environment. The portfolio is sold to investors with an understanding that the returns will be slightly better than, but highly correlated to, an underlying index or risk measurement. Portfolio managers must choose how to model this underlying risk to generate a higher return. This is done with bond-selection and risk-management techniques. Derivatives often offer the most efficient methods of managing the unwanted risks. Since the portfolio is going to be evaluated against a benchmark, "conservative" risks like short duration, higher convexity, and higher quality will create a portfolio at risk. The lost yield and market volatility can be negatives, as they have been for most of the 1980s. Being too conservative is not a "safe" option.

As mentioned earlier, this chapter is focused on duration and yield-curve management. No derivatives can run a portfolio or make it a top-performing fund without a correct outlook. Derivatives can be a cheap and effective means of implementing an outlook, but they are not a substitute for an outlook. In particular, the derivatives currently available in the municipal market are directed to duration and convexity management. There are other risks that are embedded in these securities. Credit risk is leveraged along with the duration. Single-state funds may have trouble finding a diverse group of issuers for derivatives. When an investor buys a derivative product, he or she must be aware of the other risks that come along with the derivative. Generally, the problems of derivatives in a portfolio are not the risks that the derivatives are designed to have. The problem for a portfolio manager is not recognizing that the derivative is based on an issuer and has optional calls and other structural risks. These risks must be quantified and identified by the buyer.

SUMMARY

Derivatives offer a useful tool for the portfolio managers to adjust risk exposure. When the derivative offers opportunities that cannot be gained from the cash market, the tool can be invaluable. Generally, however, the derivative is a long-term portfolio management tool. The cost of structuring derivatives can be high, and if there is a cash market alternative, these costs need to be incorporated in the analysis.

Using derivatives to adjust a portfolio exposure to yields and yield curves is currently the widest use. As the market develops, credit swaps and similar tools will be applied to the market. Portfolio management is no more than selecting the appropriate risk/return balance and knowing how to achieve the balance in the least expensive way. A value-managed portfolio that is neutral to the benchmark will usually outperform more consistently. Derivatives allow the value manager to use top-down management techniques to eliminate the risks of targeting undervalued securities.

Chapter Twelve

Object-Oriented Strategies for Derivatives Risk Management

Dr. Jeffrey L. McIver
Director of Financial Engineering
Infinity Financial Technology, Inc.

INTRODUCTION

Risk management is a key concern in the derivatives markets today and promises to be a defining facet of the market's growth throughout the '90s. Ironically, risk assessment and management is by and large a solved theoretical problem, yet achieving these goals poses some of the biggest challenges faced by today's market participants. An effective risk-management capability necessarily relies on a firm's information systems and on their ability to deliver the scale and level of integration that a risk-management-systems solution requires; unfortunately, these systems are often not in place and are difficult to establish. One way to provide this required risk-management infrastructure is through the use of the innovative object-oriented design strategies which have been developed within the last 10 years. This chapter shares some of the insights and lessons in object-oriented design and development that one acquires in building systems for the derivatives marketplace. It is a discussion of lessons learned in addressing many of the systems challenges faced today.

A gentle introduction to an "object-oriented view" of software construction is as close as the nearest personal computer, where object-oriented concepts are already ubiquitous in many productivity programs. Many desktop business-presentation packages allow the user to create different graphical objects (text, lines, boxes, and so on) and treat them in similar ways. One can group, resize, move, rotate, copy, and paste all of the graphical objects even though each object has to do its individual task somewhat differently than every other. It is the application of this every-day software paradigm to derivatives' risk management that is the goal of object-oriented design.

While object-oriented software design is in one sense just a strategy for building systems, applied to financial systems it is also a technique that can cater directly to meeting today's requirements for better risk manage-ment and control. One of the most striking aspects of the way systems have always been built in the past is that they tended to be oriented toward single products. Disjoint single-product systems equaled decentralized analytic expertise and trade data and almost always produced a duplication of the system's efforts. Perhaps more pernicious, bankwide integration of the risk-management and control function was rendered almost impossi-ble, and even accessing data from the score of single-product systems was often an overwhelming task. At best, postscriptive consolidation and guestimation of firmwide risk, such as the J.P. Morgan RiskMetrics approach, was the only alternative left to financial institutions.

However, object-oriented design of financial systems offers a way out of this equation. Instead of accepting that each product line equals a separate system, building trading systems based on encapsulating instru-ments and valuation components as objects provides a paradigm that can lead to an integrated, bankwide system of risk assessment, management, and control. If all of a bank's trades—all of its bonds, swaps, caps, swaptions, futures, and FX—are carried in one system with integrated analytics and data management, this not only allows for maximum sys-tems integration, but also better business practices. With an integrated trading environment, you can assess and control your risk with much finer dexterity than with the swarm of different systems that is the current norm. More than just a way to build better systems, an object-orientation can also present a framework for this unified and consistent treatment of risk control across all desks. What I would like to discuss here are some of the issues to be considered in order to make this grand plan a practical reality.

This chapter first addresses the context and historical perspective of object-oriented design (OOD) applied to financial systems. While OOD lights a path toward an integrated approach to risk management, that path is strewn with obstacles and diversions. I will highlight some of the design issues that an OOD strategy must consider. Finally, I will try to give some tactical advice about applying object-oriented design to building advanced financial analytics.

THE CONTEXT OF OBJECT-ORIENTED DESIGN

Let's start with an overview of what OOD is, and why one would be interested in using it in developing systems for risk management. It is not so much a choice of a computer language, although some languages— such as C++, Smalltalk, or Objective C—are conducive to an object-orientation (OO), languages like Fortran might be considered antagonistic to it. While most large-scale, Unix-based, object-oriented development today is done using C++, much of what we will discuss is not related to any particular computer language. OOD and object-oriented development are perhaps best introduced by saying why they came about.

In the old days, when one wrote a C or Fortran program to do a financial calculation or to capture a trade, there would be data, and there would be subprograms that processed the data. There was nothing in the language to encourage the coupling of these two disparate program components. The design technique called Data Flow Diagrams was meant to organize a program with this view in mind; data was a passive construct that was meant to be passed (or flowed) between processes that acted on it. In financial applications, a financial instrument would be described by perhaps several large sets of isolated data, but this or that financial calculation on the instrument may only use a maturity here or a coupon there and would accept these as function arguments. Systems were built, and some systems were quite successful, but people realized that life did not end when the first version of a program was completed. A purgatory called systems maintenance began, and it was here that the deficiencies of software as "data plus functions" began to show.

For instance, in the financial arena, maintaining consistency between an instrument's data and the financial analytic functions (which needed to operate on that instrument through the inevitable changes that a maintenance cycle introduces) ultimately produced a legacy system that stubbornly refused to easily accommodate enhancements. Adding an additional attribute to an instrument definition and a function call often meant changes that diffused throughout the whole body of software. Separate trading systems, often doing very similar calculations on roughly similar instruments, would sit side by side on adjacent trading desks unable to talk to each other or reuse the other's analytics. More subtle but perhaps more detrimental in the long run, separate systems meant separate risk-management activities and the inability to centralize the bank's risk under one umbrella.

On the maintenance issue, it was observed that many of the problems would disappear if programs were reoriented to a worldview less incongruent with the worldview that the program was trying to service. In a financial application, instead of having different data structures store different aspects of an instrument in isolation, the approach would be to bring all the instrument's data into one package. Instead of, for instance, storing a bond's cash flows and call provisions in separate arrays that are only logically connected, one would unite the different aspects of the bond in one package, maybe called BOND. Likewise, functions that are logically tied to an instrument and which process that instrument's data—for instance, a yield-to-worst-call calculation—would be similarly tied to the BOND package. This reorientation has the effect of casting off the ideas of passive data and functions that process the data; instead, one thinks of this data and function "package" as an active *object* (the BOND object) that encapsulates the real world *entity* (in this case, a tradable security with its related functionality). The object internalizes the representation of the entity and provides a place for the functionality of the entity to live in computer code.

Another key idea for making OOD work is the concept of *inheritance*. In the same way that children inherit characteristics from their parents, "child" objects can be *derived* from other classes and inherit both functions and data from their "parent" object. For example, an object representing a bond is one particular example of an abstract notion of an instrument. Yet, just as there are other instruments (swaps, caps, swaptions, and so on) there could be other objects (SWAPS, CAPS, SWAPTIONS) that model them in computer code. All of these objects that represent individual instruments could be viewed as a child of, or *instances* of, an object called INSTRUMENT, which models the abstract notion of instrument. Unlike the BOND case, however, there is no tangible entity corresponding to the notion of "instrument," only a logical entity.

There are two reasons why an object that represents only a logical entity would be useful, the first of which is related to the distribution of functionality among parent and children objects. Since an object is both data and function, an INSTRUMENT object provides a convenient and parsimonious way to provide functionality that is common to ALL instruments. For instance, if every instrument object had an associated counterparty, retrieval of the counterparty could be implemented as a function associated with INSTRUMENT instead of rewriting the same function again and again on every (real) instrument object. This reuse of functionality can, under the right circumstances, be substantial, and reusability of code is one of the marquis buzzwords associated with OOD.

INSTRUMENT may also provide a placeholder for common functionality, without actually doing any work itself, which each child could service in its own individual way. For example, INSTRUMENT may "declare" a VALUE function without doing any calculation; each child instance of INSTRUMENT that represents an actual tradable instrument would service the VALUE function in that instrument's characteristic fashion. The benefit of this mechanism is that one can invoke the VALUE function on an INSTRUMENT without having to know what particular child instrument object is actually doing the calculation. This faculty to implement the "same" functionality (here, the VALUE function) in different ways is called *polymorphism* and is an important tactical benefit of OOD and development.

The second reason an abstraction like INSTRUMENT would be useful is related to the logical indirection it provides. To see why polymorphism and the viewpoint it fosters are important to the risk management of derivatives, imagine that every question a risk-management system might want to ask of an instrument could be answered by this polymorphic function paradigm. Assume the risk-management system has a list of INSTRUMENT objects in a portfolio that in fact are BONDs or SWAPs or some other type of real instrument object. Without knowing the true identity of the INSTRUMENT objects, the risk-management system could ask each abstract instrument for its risk characteristics (like a valuation via a call to the INSTRUMENT's VALUE function) with the expectation that the correct calculation will be carried out for each type of instrument. All the risk-management system would have to do is aggregate and sort the answers and produce a report. The risk system would work with instruments *anonymously*, or abstractly, to carry out this functionality.

The capability to work with objects anonymously, a capability that is strongly aided by polymorphic functions, has always seemed to me to be the main strength of inheritance in OOD. In the context of our hypothetical risk-management system, which can work with any child object derived from INSTRUMENT, its key benefit comes during the maintenance phase of the risk system's life. To add a new traded instrument to the system, one would structure a new object, making it a child of INSTRUMENT, and reflect all the relevant characteristics and functionality of the new instrument. Then, the OOD magic happens. As the risk-management system only knows about INSTRUMENT, coupled with the fact that the new object is a child and therefore, an instance of INSTRUMENT, the risk system would be able to include the new instrument in its analysis seamlessly, *without change*. This seamless extension without changing existing code is perhaps the most important goal of OOD applied to financial systems.

Of course, the corollary to Murphy's Law that says, "Something that is much too good to be true, isn't" is applicable here. The problems associated with getting risk management to work with anonymous instruments are not overcome simply, as we will discuss below. Nonetheless, the goals and benefits of OOD are real and attainable. They include code reuse through inheritance and other techniques, easier life-cycle systems maintenance, and the promise of painless (less painful) extendibility. These are worthy goals, and despite the care and forethought that they require, goals that I believe are achievable using OOD approaches to creating risk-management systems for derivatives.

THE SIREN SONG OF INHERITANCE

Inheritance of children objects from parents is one of the most useful facets of OOD because it provides encapsulated anonymity and gives a mechanism to reuse data and functionality. The data-reuse mechanism is clear: The parent defines a set of attributes to which the child might add some distinguishing additions. Reuse of functionality comes about by having a parent object implement a piece of functionality (e.g., a yield calculation, a database load operation) that is common to all its children instead of having each one reimplement the same functionality. The children are "reusing" the functionality of the parent.

Object inheritance is based on the notion that a child is an instance of the parent. The child object "is a" (ISA) parent object, but may also be more specialized than the parent. However, as an instance of the parent object and as a result of the ISA relationship between parent and child, a child cannot do less than the parent in terms of supported functionality. A child cannot legitimately take the attitude that "the parent says I can do this, but actually I cannot" because that breaks down the meaning of being a parent object. Turning this around, a parent should not announce a capability that cannot be meaningfully performed by each and every one of its children. For example, say a base INSTRUMENT object announced that it could return a COUPON rate. This could be serviced by the BOND child of INSTRUMENT, since bonds have meaningful notions of coupons. Even if the exact definition of COUPON differed from one bond to the next, an answer could be returned by all bonds. On the other hand, an interest-rate cap object, CAP, has no meaningful way to provide a COUPON rate and would not (could not) comfortably be considered a child of this base INSTRUMENT object. The implication is that a less provincial INSTRUMENT object should not announce a functionality to return a COUPON rate since not all of its children can service it.

While important, object inheritance does not solve all problems, especially those associated with financial applications. The discussion above hints at the analysis with which a hierarchy needs to be scrutinized. Very often, the first notion as to how to model the universe of financial instruments with a hierarchy, basing relationships on casual or nomenclatural market practices, often proves to be a very inconvenient way to structure the hierarchy. Instead of a solid and extensible foundation, a design mistake in an instrument hierarchy can lead to years of application patches and difficulty in achieving the gains that OOD promises.

Let's illustrate with an example. Say we begin to build a risk-management system to support only derivatives trading and try to follow market practice by dividing all instruments into either exchange-traded instruments, derived from EXCHANGE, which in turn is derived from INSTRUMENT, and over-the-counter instruments, which derive from OTC, which itself is another child of INSTRUMENT. Children objects derived from EXCHANGE would include money market futures (MM\FUTURES), while for the trading we are initially supporting, almost everything else would be derived from OTC. A swap (SWAP), for example, would be considered an OTC child and in turn a (grand) child of INSTRUMENT. As exchange-traded instruments are defined once but can be traded multiple times, we may build mechanisms into our EXCHANGE object to take advantage of that aspect of exchange instruments. All seems well, and the design is rooted in apparent market practice.

Now, lets say that right after we deliver our risk-management system, we're asked to integrate bond trading. The problem is, there is no place in our hierarchy for a BOND object to live comfortably. Certainly, bonds are traded as OTC instruments and have none of the attributes that one would associate with an exchange-traded instrument, indicating BOND should probably be a child of the OTC parent. On the other hand, bonds share the "defined once but traded many times" attribute of exchange-traded instruments, so to allow them to use that faculty we would want BOND to be a child of EXCHANGE. We come to the conclusion that there is no home for BOND in the hierarchy because we never allowed for a non-EXCHANGE "defined once but traded many times" instrument. Barring major surgery to the hierarchy some type of ad hoc compromise must be made. This inflexibility of our hierarchical design is referred to as the hierarchy being *brittle* to additions or enhancements.

This example, albeit a simple-minded one, is a common pitfall in OOD applied to financial applications. A statement of the problem is, "How does one hierarchically model instruments in an OOD setting so that future additions to the suite of instruments do not produce a design crisis?" It is not enough to say, "Well, the hierarchy should have been designed for all instruments, including bonds" since (1) ALL instruments means, literally, all instruments, and just gathering information will be exhausting and time-consuming, and (2) no matter how diligent your initial analysis of the financial arena is, you will not be able to anticipate future market developments and instruments. On the one hand, one must take care not to fall into an unproductive "analysis paralysis" characterized by being stuck in the design phase of a project for eternity. Perhaps more unproductive, however, is to create a design that provides no evolution path and becomes a legacy system overnight.

A somewhat radical approach, but by no means the only one, to meet the challenge of trying to make a hierarchy immunized from a design crisis is to not have a hierarchy at all, or at least, a hierarchy deeper than one level. A rule of thumb in object design is: the deeper the hierarchy, the more brittle the hierarchy. If the natural problem-domain hierarchies are based on logical principles or true ISA relationships, deep hierarchies are not a problem because the relationships are apparent, natural, and unchanging. In a problem domain like financial instruments where relationships are not apparent, and are man-made, and ever changing, deep hierarchies are simply not a prudent design strategy. Just like a tall, brittle, glass sculpture, a deep and brittle hierarchy will easily break when stressed in an unforeseen way. In this minimalist approach, one still has a base INSTRUMENT object, because the whole point of OOD applied to risk management is to treat all instruments in the same way at some level. However, in this approach, all instruments would be directly derived from INSTRUMENT including SWAP, BOND, and MM\FUTURE. With no hierarchy decisions to make, there will be no potential hierarchy crises to face.

One must keep in mind that traded instruments in the derivatives industry have come about through market forces and traditions and were not "designed" with hierarchical relationships in mind. Future derivative instruments will not be developed with a backward compatibility condition imposed based on anyone's hierarchical model. Often the market "relationships" that may form the basis of a hierarchy are spurious on closer examination. For example, many would derive a CAP object from an OPTION object even though cap is not really an option (there is no choice involved) while a corporate bond with real embedded options is derived from BOND, not OPTION. While many instruments worldwide are called "futures," this does not imply that their software representations should inherit some qualities from a common root. For instance, the functional similarities between a U.S. bond future and an oil future, although both are "futures," are arguably much less than between a fixed-rate loan and a bond. A hierarchy that tries to place all bond futures in one object branch and money market futures in another would find that Australian bond futures might be considered more akin to money market futures. The point would be that the traditional classifications used in the market are not necessarily useful in modeling these instruments in software.

With few or no hierarchy relationships in our modeling of instruments, however, it is certainly a valid concern as to what we have given up. While we have given up functionality reuse via inheritance, we have not given up functionality reuse altogether. An alternate approach to functionality reuse is through the fashioning of reusable object components that have a focused and limited purpose, like cash-flow objects or, even more focused, business-day-roll convention objects. If there is any unifying theme to the financial markets, it may be the recombination and repackaging of traditional market practices, like rolling business days based on calendars and forming cash flows, in order to form new instruments. To the extent that this recombination view of instruments is correct, an OOD effort that parallels this structure through the creation of component objects should better match both the current and future instrument spectrum. Instruments would not be related solely because they derive from a common parent, but instead because they share many similar structural components. As an example, whereas one reason to have all instruments derive from an OPTION class is for them to inherit an analytic capability, one might instead just package the analytic capability into an OPTIONMODEL object and include it as a component in whatever instrument might need it.

While object inheritance is a powerful and extremely useful concept, it is susceptible to being misused, especially when applied to modeling the derivatives market. One thing that the financial engineer should keep in mind is that an object hierarchy will not impose order on an otherwise disordered jumble of real-world entities. If one concludes, "All we need to do is survey all the instruments in the so-and-so market to come up with a hierarchy design," that should signal a red flag concerning the robustness of the resulting hierarchy. Any foundational object design that depends on the market's conventional view of instrument relationships, and that further relies on it being a consistent picture, now and in the future, will almost invariably result in the hierarchy destined for a design crisis. The rule of thumb is: Do not rely on the market to provide a hierarchical view of instruments.

THE INSTRUMENT, MODEL, AND DATA TRIANGLE

At the analytic core of most derivatives risk-management and trading systems is the need to value instruments accurately and flexibly. Some models are very simple, such as valuing a particular seasoned bond with a particular spread off the on-the-run U.S. Treasury curve. The usual forecast models used for swap valuation require, in general, several interest-rate curves that distinguish between the forecasting of index values and the discounting of cash flows. More complicated models such as interest-rate term structure models may make large systems-demands and require several interest and volatility curves and a score of configuration options. Each model, in turn, may have different market-data requirements even for the same instrument. And market data itself is a heterogeneous collection of forecast rates, benchmark prices, implied volatility rates, historical correlations, and myriad other quantities. Valuation on a system-wide basis, which involves bringing the right market-data to the right model for the appropriate instrument, is complicated just from the object and data marshaling point of view.

Possibly the biggest challenge faced today in building financial systems is to facilitate, or at least not complicate, the goal of creating an integrated risk-assessment functionality in the bank. In order for the goals of an extensible, object-oriented risk-management system development to be realized, this linking of market data, instruments, and models needs to be abstracted and carried out anonymously at some level in the risk-management machine. Whether the objective of a risk-measurement system is hedging and tactical positioning in the market, or risk reporting and control, it is desirable to apply a consistent system's approach to a portfolio of instruments. A consistent approach minimizes the overhedging that more product-oriented risk-management systems deliver and maximizes the information content that a risk analysis provides, since it allows a more global, portfoliowide statement of risk. ("Consistent" in this sense does not mean "the same" analysis for every instrument; instead it means the ability to produce comparable results that can be integrated across product lines.)

Probably the chief logical obstacle to overcome in building an integrated risk-management system is the management of the model, data, and instrument triangle. The first approach that is often taken is in some ways the simplest, and in some respects, the most "object-oriented." Laying aside the question of feeding the appropriate market data to an instrument valuation, the most obvious approach is to associate the valuation functionality with the instrument as an intrinsic attribute of that instrument. As in our example, the object INSTRUMENT could have a nonactive VALUE functionality, which is filled in via the polymorphism mechanism. This would seem to be a clear and useful application of the inherited functionality.However, for financial applications, it may in retrospect turn out to be inconvenient to place valuation functionality on the INSTRUMENT objects themselves. While by no means obvious, in practice, and especially for more complicated instruments, the analytics component of valuation is the most malleable part of the instrument. The instrument definition, in contrast, is almost static or unchanging. As a distinct feature of the modeled instrument, valuation is usually the most demanding of maintenance. Over the life cycle of the actual instrument, new models are often developed to replace existing ones, and this requires changing existing code if the valuation functionality is part of the child INSTRUMENT object. In addition, different models may need to be invoked for the same instrument as it gets processed from the front office through to the back office. Both of these considerations, likely life-cycle maintenance and the requirement to support run-time choice of valuation model, imply that valuation is less an intrinsic part of the instrument and more an outside analysis to be performed on the instrument. The INSTRUMENT object is still an active object, but valuation is not one of its activities.

Taking this recommendation to heart, the implication is that there should be some indirection and flexibility built into the invocation of a valuation model for a particular instrument. This is not an abandonment of object-oriented principles, it is simply a recognition that what appeared at first sight as an intrinsic attribute of the INSTRUMENT object, appears on second look as a functionality distinct from the INSTRUMENT. In fact, the picture that emerges is one of the parallelism between instruments, for which we want a parent INSTRUMENT object so that we may work with them abstractly, and models, which we also now need to work with abstractly. The conclusion of this analysis is that, just as with instruments, there should be a MODEL object that can be associated with instruments at run-time.

However, a parent MODEL object must live within the same guidelines as we discussed for INSTRUMENT at the beginning of the previous section. In other words, the parent MODEL object can only advertise functionality that every child model can fulfill. This is a stiff requirement considering that the intersection of inputs and outputs of all the various ways to value derivative instruments is practically nil, at least at the detail level. On the other hand, there is an abstract notion of "models" that is worthwhile, and this is illustrated by the very fact that we can even talk about the conception of an entity called a MODEL. Certainly, there is an appealing notion of a risk manager associating an instance of an anonymous INSTRUMENT with an instance of an anonymous MODEL and calling on the model to value its assigned instrument. It need not be the only value that is returned; the model could return some stylized collection or packet of risk measurements, which is perhaps the child object of some parent (say RISKVAL) in its own right.

Another implication of having a MODEL object is that every child model, from bond valuation to cap valuation to IAS valuation, must resemble every other child model in the sense that if all a risk system had was an instance of a MODEL object, it could invoke that object's functionality. This is an extraordinary requirement given the wide range of curves, volatilities, correlations, and myriad other market data packets that are used in valuation in the derivatives market. As fits the pattern we have developed, the way out of this seeming impossibility is to abstract the notion of model inputs into some object MARKETDATA. Every child of MODEL, then, takes an appropriate child of INSTRUMENT and an appropriate child of MARKETDATA and calculates various instrument and model specific results, returning them in a child of a RISKVAL object. Risk management consists of brokering the right models and data to the right instruments, and collecting, sorting, and reporting the calculated results.

In truth, there may be no system like this currently available. We have mentally carried a hypothetical design specification that would allow abstracted risk-management and seamless extensibility.

THE OBJECT IMPERATIVE: THE TRIUMPH OF FORM OVER CONTENT

We have discussed an approach to building risk-management systems using object-oriented design techniques that emphasizes anonymity through restrained and extensible hierarchical relationships, flexible and indirect linking of static instruments with analytics, and risk management as the conductor or choreographer of the pieces. Working together, these constitute a risk-management system. This is a good occasion to summarize this attitude toward OOD and relate it to the goal of creating an integrated risk-management system.

What our hypothetical risk-management system design did was encapsulate the knowledge of details and keep that knowledge at the lowest possible level. These details are items like the precise cash flows of swaps or the notional amount on FX options; from a risk-management standpoint these are essential pieces of information but are too detailed for any system to manage directly. Instead, we have created an object-design where instrument details are encapsulated in INSTRUMENT children, model details are encapsulated in MODEL children, and data is fed into and obtained out of these models as abstracted packets. At this highest design level, we have repressed details and concentrated on how the abstract pieces could best work with one another. This is the imperative that object design forces on the system builder. The result is that the form or pattern to which an object conforms is more important from a design perspective than the content of the object.

Concentration on the form of high-level interaction and deference of content and details to a lower level of analysis are exactly what must be achieved if one wishes to create an integrated trading and risk-management system. OOD supports and encourages this viewpoint. As such, using the OOD paradigm in building systems can cultivate a view of the business as pieces or as objects in an integrated whole, which in turn can lead to improved management of business risks.

To point to an analogy borrowed from mathematics, there is a construct in differential geometry called a tensor. Many classical references to the subject actually define a tensor, not so much with intrinsic properties, but rather as a quantity that transforms or behaves in a certain way. Like defining a tensor by how it behaves and not by a particular representation, a high-level object design seeks a behavioral context first instead of the intrinsic or low-level properties. The goal often is to seek those abstractions that fit a pattern or set of behaviors that, if satisfied, achieve the overall intent of the design. Once these behaviors are obtained, filling in the rest of the design presents fewer surprises because the global scope of the design is done. Only the details needs to be completed.

Of course, the details are almost all of the work. Even had we taken the risk-management design above as something other than a hypothetical, somewhere there would be curve-generation algorithms, the Black model, forecasting of floating-rate indexes, and all the other analytic tasks that a risk-management machine must deliver. However, by considering form first, before actual financial content, we might avoid the rapid slide into the usual maintenance difficulties so characteristic of many risk-management systems.

OBJECT-ORIENTED DESIGN IN ADVANCED FINANCIAL ANALYTICS

I have often heard that while object-oriented design techniques are helpful in data management and even in general system-development and maintenance, analytics have little to gain from the OOD. Object-oriented design techniques, it is said, are either inappropriate or too slow to support efficient computation and that procedural languages like C or Fortran are the languages of choice for "serious" financial models. In this view, the object-oriented risk-management system becomes a large funnel to collect and embed data in static procedural language constructs and to call the appropriate Fortran model. As my interest is in the construction of just these sorts of analytics, I would like to take the remaining space in this chapter to advance the use of OOD techniques and languages for advanced financial modeling.

Certainly, one of the main reasons that financial models are written in procedural languages is inertia. Traditionally, the quants who write the esoteric financial models—including exotic option models, term structure models, and Monte Carlo simulation capabilities—usually come from a scientific background where Fortran is still the prevalent computation language. Even if these models were written in something other than Fortran, the something was almost invariably C, not an object-oriented language. I attribute this reluctance to switch to a more object-oriented approach for three main reasons: The people who write these models are not acquainted with the OOD approach; they have concerns about the performance of the resulting analytics; and they do not see any potential benefit.

The first reason, that the people who build the advanced valuation models are unfamiliar with OOD and the languages that support them, will simply disappear in time. While the scientific community may take its time in utilizing the latest developments in computational science, the financial community, where systems maintenance and fast development time are critical issues, simply cannot afford to disregard the advantages of the new techniques. There are real obstacles in the beginning steps of using OOD languages; the concepts are unfamiliar and the language itself simply is difficult to learn. However, as it becomes clear that OOD techniques are useful in developing analytics, the supply of OOD-aware quants will undoubtedly rise to the demand.

The second reservation that is often expressed about OOD in advanced financial analytics is that the resulting software implementation of the analytics is too slow compared to its procedural language counterpart. Certainly, a poorly written model in an OO language like C++ can be a spectacular time waster. The point is, however, that it need not waste time, and that a slow C++ implementation is more a reflection on the implementor's progress up the learning curve than anything else. It is worthwhile to view carefully claims like "I learned C++ to see whether it could be as fast as my C library" since very often the answer is reassuringly (to the C library owner) negative. When all is said and done, because some of the implementational tactics to support inheritance and polymorphism, one could expect that a model written in C++ might be a few percent slower than the comparable C program on any given machine. The same

C++ model running on next year's machine will beat, hands down, the C program running on this year's machine.

The real gain in using object-oriented design and development is in the flexibility that can be achieved, coupled with the reduction in time to create, debug, and maintain complicated financial models. This is really the place where the gains of OOD can be capitalized. For instance, one often needs to interpolate a value within a series of knot points, such as how one might model a zero curve. The OOD prescription would be to form an object that encapsulates the interpolation data and the functionality so that anywhere the model builder may subsequently need interpolation functionality, he would simply use the debugged component object. Maintenance, such as adding more interpolation techniques, and debugging, need only be concerned with the one object in isolation. The same can be said of matrix classes, iterative solvers, and option models. Even more financially oriented utilities can be encapsulated into objects for placement anywhere in code. Examples of this type of financial utility object would include a day-counting convention object and business-day-roll convention objects. Prepackaged, pre-debugged utility component objects allow real gains in productivity.

The gains in using OOD in developing advanced analytics are real. For example, I have been involved in developing a commercially available, sophisticated term-structure model which includes functionality to handle many path-dependent securities, using the OOD approach. This approach enhanced the maintainability of the model and cut the development time to a fraction of what an implementation in a procedural language would have taken. However, perhaps one of the biggest gains in using OOD for model development is one of the most intangible; the realization that a design can be realized as individually encapsulated pieces able to interact with one another aids not only in the execution of these models, but also in the design process. Knowing that local algorithm components translate directly into implementation objects, one is less apt to make preemptive design compromises based on implementational inconveniences. It may turn out that this is the biggest advantage in using OOD for sophisticated analytics.

Chapter Thirteen

Innovative Strategies and Techniques for Pricing Contingent Credit Risk

Robert M. Mark
Executive Vice President
Canadian Imperial Bank of Commerce

OVERVIEW

Introduction

The pricing methodologies used by an institution must be based on a comprehensive framework that encompasses all types of risk. The framework needs to facilitate a directionally correct and integrated approach toward quantifying, managing, and pricing counterparty credit risk. For example, one should ensure that one's credit-risk-measurement approach is fully integrated with one's market-risk-measurement approach. The assumptions used to compute credit and market risk exposure must be consistent. This is essential, since the two concepts of market risk and credit risk are related. One's pricing approach also needs to include consideration of the risks that may occur in normal as well as abnormal markets. Accordingly, scenario and stress testing are particularly important parts of that framework.

Institutions require an integrated risk-management capability, as illustrated in Figure 13–1, to help them identify where the returns outweigh the risks (credit risk, market risk, etc.). Institutions also need to look at and

FIGURE 13–1
Return vs. Risk

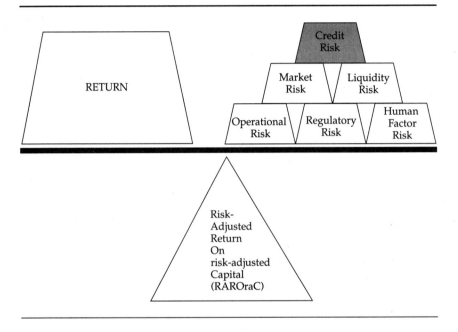

balance the return-to-risk ratios within the context of a Risk-Adjusted Return[1] On risk-adjusted Capital (RAROraC) framework. The RAROraC framework allows one to appropriately price in derivatives credit risk as well as measure risk-adjusted performance. The RAROraC techniques discussed in this chapter are consistent with the underpinnings of the Capital Asset Pricing Model (CAPM).

Leading-edge institutions are currently making the necessary methodological (e.g., risk tools) and infrastructural (e.g., risk-application software) investments to measure and appropriately price risk. The failure to measure and price credit risk, market risk (consisting of trading and gap risk components), and other key risks (as indicated in Figure 13–2) in an accurate and integrated manner can seriously threaten a financial institution's stability. A clear articulation of the risks incurred in managing a derivatives business

---

[1] A business unit's projected risk-adjusted return refers to subtracting a business unit's expected losses from its projected net profitability (= projected revenue–projected expense).

FIGURE 13–2
Key Risks

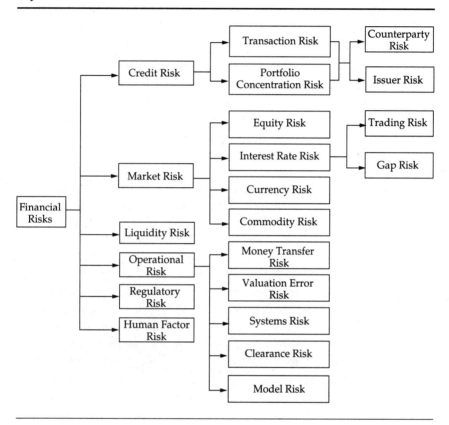

should be a prerequisite for participation in the business. For example, from a pricing perspective one needs to develop sophisticated techniques to price projected credit losses. However, in the past, many institutions did not invest in building the tools required to measure and price credit risk comprehensively. This often led to flawed risk-measurement methodologies that failed to facilitate a consistent pricing of credit risk.

Credit-Risk Exposure, Default, and Recovery Rates

One needs to differentiate between credit-risk *exposure* and *loss*. Low probabilities of default and high recovery amounts, combined with netting—as well as the intelligent use of collateral and termination agree-ments—can all contribute to reducing high credit-risk exposure levels to a very low level of real losses. Pricing in the potential for credit loss can be estimated through an analysis of credit-risk exposures, default rates, and recovery rates. For example, one approach is to determine an expected replacement cost. The expected replacement cost is the expected credit-risk exposure in the event that the counterparty defaults at a particular point in the future. The average expected credit-risk exposure is the average of the expected credit-risk exposures over the life of a transaction. The credit-risk exposure can never be less than zero, since the credit-risk exposure of negatively valued positions is zero.

The *default rate* is typically defined as the expected percentage of defaults associated with a particular credit counterparty class (e.g., BBB), which defaults at a particular point in the life cycle. Similarly, the *recovery rate* is typically defined as the expected percentage of an exposure amount associated with a particular credit counterparty class that can be recovered in the event of default at a particular point in the life cycle. As with credit-risk exposure, the default and recovery rate probability distributions need to be constructed. Ultimately, one needs to combine the default and recovery rate probability distributions with the credit-risk exposure proba-bility distribution to produce a credit-loss probability distribution. Clearly, the credit loss probability distribution depends on the *quality* of the counterparty and the *tenor* of the loan. For example, a derivatives transac-tion with a AAA-rated counterparty has a lower credit-loss probability than a derivative transaction with a BBB-rated counterparty. Similarly, a 10-year derivatives transaction with a BBB-rated counterparty has a higher credit-loss probability than a 1-year derivatives transaction with the same BBB-rated counterparty. The credit-loss probability distribution is utilized to derive the expected and unexpected credit loss. Once this has been determined, the necessary provision and economic capital required to support a transaction can be computed and priced into one's transaction.

Establishing a Best-Practice Risk-Management Framework

Financial institutions need to accelerate their efforts toward establishing a more uniform and sophisticated framework (an integrated set of princi-ples) for pricing credit risk. The framework can be benchmarked in terms of policies, methodologies, and infrastructure. These provide the neces-sary foundation to perform a first-class active management of risk.

Clearly, establishing a first-class risk-management framework is a prerequisite for implementing a best-practice approach to pricing credit risk. Today many institutions have a structure that can manage their current level of trading activities only to the bare minimum standard. The framework for a first-class risk-management function needs to include establishing a risk-management function that is independent of direct risk takers. The framework also needs to include establishing an environment that is philosophically and culturally attuned to promote best-practice risk management. One needs to develop best-practice policies (e.g., trading authorities) and best-practice methodologies (e.g., value-at-risk measures) that protect against loss while supporting a profitable business. One also has to create a best-practice infrastructure. As indicated in Figure 13–3, a first-class active management of risk includes the capability to appropriately price risk and to actively manage the portfolio of residual risks.

Establishing the appropriate policies, methodologies, and infrastructure, as illustrated in Figure 13–4, are the necessary three legs for building a first-class risk-management function. However, the function is only as strong as its weakest leg. One also needs to ensure that management has a healthy respect for working in *partnership,* promotes an efficient risk-management *process,* and provides *perspective* (the three P's). Obtaining management commitment toward building a first-class risk-management function provides the sufficient condition required for success. Clearly, a first-class risk-management function should be capable of creating the necessary tools to price in risk.

Best-practice policies.   One needs to create best-practice policies, as illustrated in Figure 13–5, that follow directly from *business strategies.* From a risk perspective one needs to set reasonable *risk tolerances* regarding how much risk one is willing to assume. Unambiguous and measurable *authorities* need to be set within the risk tolerances established by policy. One also needs to review the internal and external *disclosure* of a business unit's risk profile.

Best-practice methodologies.   The best-practice methodologies, as illustrated in Figure 13–6, refer to applying the appropriate formulas to measure and price risk (such as *market risk, credit risk, operational risk,* and so on). The objective is not solely to measure risk but also to ensure that the *pricing* and *valuation* methodologies are appropriate. For example, the Group of 30 (G-30) recommended that dealers and end users of derivatives should value derivatives at market prices. Further,

FIGURE 13–3
Risk-Management Framework

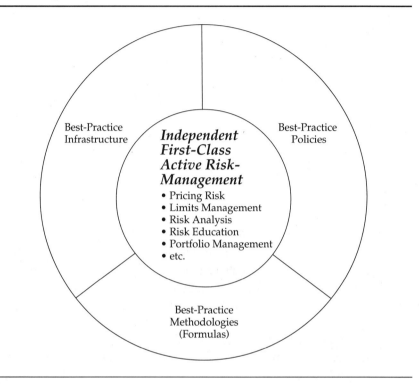

they recommend that one should quantify market and credit risk based on a value-at-risk framework. Specifically, the G-30 recommends that credit-risk exposure should be measured based on current plus potential exposure. Finally, one must develop risk-measurement tools to ensure that one is on the efficient frontier of the risk/reward trade-off. Toward this end, implementing a RAROraC approach is a particularly important pricing priority. Simply put, what you can't measure well, you can't price well.

Valuation. A valuation adjustment refers to the degree to which one fails to properly adjust the valuation of a position for going-forward risk. The G-30 recommends that one should take the mid-market price of the trade, less the sum of the expected credit loss and the going-forward

FIGURE 13–4
Necessary Three Legs

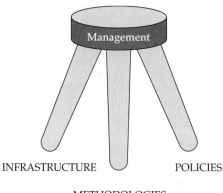

INFRASTRUCTURE   POLICIES

METHODOLOGIES

administrative cost (when valuing a perfectly matched derivatives transaction). Accordingly, one needs to analyze the reasonableness of one's approach to estimating an expected credit loss. The G-30 also suggests additional adjustments for close-out costs (i.e., "eliminating" market risk) as well as investing and funding costs.

One needs to develop the appropriate techniques to value derivatives in a highly illiquid market. In other words, one needs to differentiate valuing a transaction where one has only limited price-discovery from valuing a transaction where one has reasonable price-discovery. For example, one would observe limited price discovery for long tenor (e.g., a 10-year option on a 20-year swap) and highly structured derivative transactions. This necessitates assumption-driven valuation methodologies (e.g., constructing the term structure of interest rates beyond 10 years) that normally require use of mark-to-model techniques. The need to make assumptions for illiquid transactions typically forces one to accept a wider range of reasonable valuations. The attributes of the selected model become highly important in terms of the ultimate value placed on an illiquid derivatives position. A wider range of values impacts the calculation of the average expected and average unexpected credit-risk exposure levels (which in turn is utilized to establish the projected level of loss).

FIGURE 13–5
Best-Practice Policies

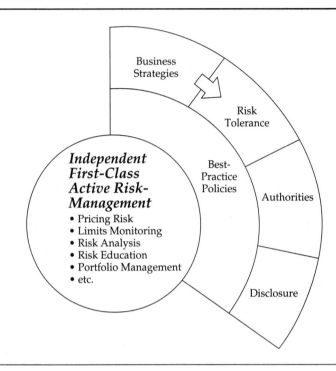

Best-practice infrastructure. The importance of infrastructure can be appreciated by considering a situation where best-practice policies and methodology have been developed but there is no infrastructure to make them work. Infrastructure is expensive and time-consuming to construct. The first and most important component of one's infrastructure, as illustrated in Figure 13–7, is *people*. One needs people with great skills, rewarded with fair and reasonable compensation, who have to be trained (or recruited) and motivated. Given the right environment and support, it is people who will make everything else happen. Pricing decisions will not be derived solely from a complex analytical black box—management judgment will always be a significant input. *Data* integrity is an important competitive advantage. One needs to translate market data into risk-management information for both transaction makers and policy makers.

FIGURE 13–6
Best-Practice Methodologies

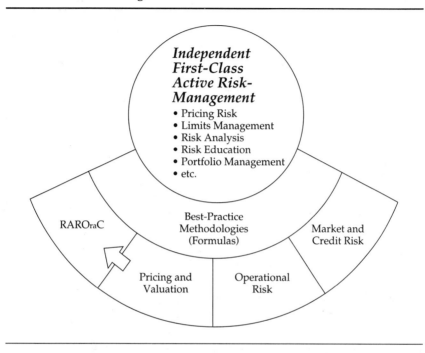

Finally, a key goal (critical to the successful management of risk) is to integrate one's risk-management *operations* and *technology*.

       Integrated goal-congruent risk-management process.   An integrated goal-congruent risk-management process that puts all the elements together, as illustrated in Figure 13–8, is the key that opens the door to a best-practice pricing of risk. "Integrated" refers to the need to ensure that one avoids having a fragmented approach to risk management. Risk management is only as strong as the weakest link. "Goal congruent" refers to the need to ensure that one's policies and methodologies are consistent with one another. For example, one goal is to have an apple-to-apple risk-measurement scheme so that one can compare risk across all products and aggregate risk at any level. The end product is a best-practice pricing of risk, whose efforts are consistent with one's business strategies.

FIGURE 13–7
Best-Practice Infrastructure

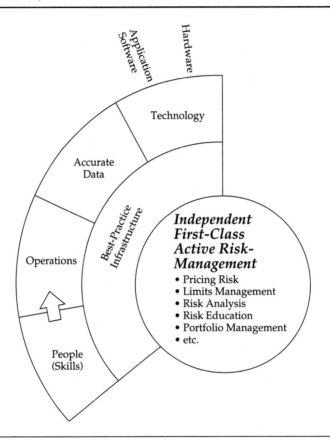

This is a "one firm, one view" approach, which also recognizes the specific risk dynamics of each business.

Portfolio Effects

One should be aware that if one prices risk at the transaction level (without considering portfolio effects across the entire organization), then one would price in more risk than is necessary. Accordingly, one needs to consider the practical difficulties of the more complicated task of pricing in risk at the

FIGURE 13–8
Integrated Goal-Congruent Risk-Management Process

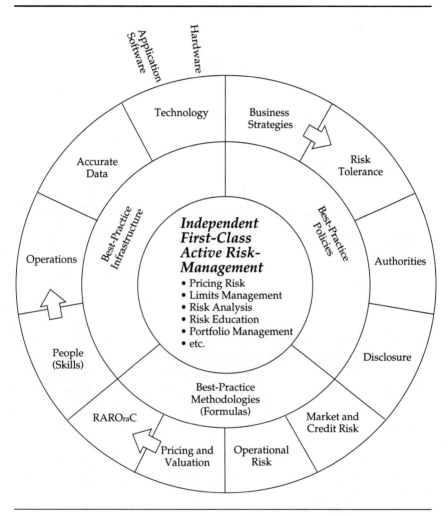

portfolio level (versus the relatively simpler task of pricing in risk at the transaction level). If portfolio effects are taken into account, then one can calculate the required economic capital for the entire organization. Economic capital is attributed as a function of risk and is sometimes referred to as risk capital. The economic capital required at higher organizational levels

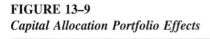

FIGURE 13–9
Capital Allocation Portfolio Effects

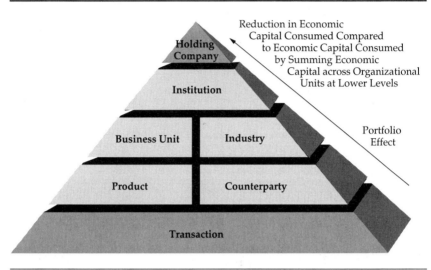

(e.g., the institution), as illustrated in Figure 13–9, is less than the sum of the economic capital required across organizational units at lower levels (e.g., across business units within an institution). Economic capital should be compared across organizational levels and within each level (e.g., across products within a business unit). A portfolio-based risk-measurement system incorporating correlations can assist an organization in understanding its risk profile not only by counterparty but also for the organization as a whole. For example, a well-designed portfolio-risk-measurement approach enables one to "slice and dice" risk vertically and horizontally across an organization to facilitate the pricing of risk.

Focus of Chapter

This chapter focuses primarily on pricing contingent credit risk (as shaded in Figure 13–1). Specifically, the chapter provides a broad-based analytical framework for pricing credit risk as a function of the credit exposure, default rates, and recovery rates to generate an expected credit loss (e.g., provision), and an unexpected credit loss (e.g., economic capital). An analytical approach is provided to illustrate one of several best-practice methods that can be used to price derivatives transactions. The analytical approach discussed assumes, for illustrative purposes, that default rates are independent of exposure values and that the recovery rate is negligible. One can also use empirical (sometimes called historical) or simulation approaches (in lieu of or in combination with analytical approaches) to price a derivatives transaction. For example, a Monte Carlo simulation approach is particularly useful, since it allows one to construct a full range of loss-distribution values so that a worst-case percentile can be constructed (e.g., 2.5 percentile).

An introduction to pricing basics is provided in the second section of this chapter. In particular, one needs to price a transaction's projected expected-loss as well as the cost of risk capital. Accordingly, the calculation of credit-grade-specific expected and unexpected default factors is provided in the third section of this chapter. The unexpected default factor is often referred to as a default risk capital factor. The methodology to combine credit-risk exposure with default and recovery rates to produce future credit-loss probability distributions is provided in the fourth section of this chapter. The methodologies for translating a future credit-loss probability distribution into provision and capital is provided in the chapter's final section.

INTRODUCTION TO PRICING BASICS

Overview

Establishing a best-practice RAROraC methodology is at the core of enabling one to appropriately price in credit risk. The sophistication of performance measures has risen to meet the increase in risks taken by financial institutions. Specifically, one needs to think in terms of return versus risk while simultaneously shaping and capping risk at an appropriate level. The evolution of risk-adjusted performance measurement and with it RAROraC is depicted in Figure 13–10. Revenues should be judged on a risk-adjusted basis, rather than in the context of return on assets or return on cash equity. Clearly, one needs to build a credit-loss probability distribution in order to quantify the amount of credit risk. For example, the calculation of a transaction's expected credit loss and unexpected credit loss can be derived directly from the transaction's probability distribution of future credit loss.

FIGURE 13–10
Evolution of Performance Measures

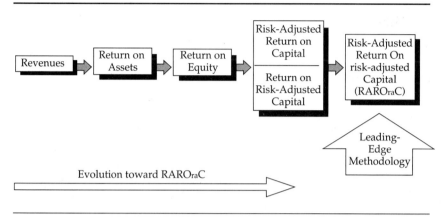

The relationship between projected returns and projected risk is central to the RAROraC approach. One can analytically illustrate the relationship between required returns and the projected risks associated with those returns. Calculating performance based on RAROraC is a function of several key factors, as illustrated in Figure 13–11. The risk factors (i.e., credit risk, market risk, and other risks) include consideration of the risk associated with both normal risk and special risk (e.g., caused by concentration risk).

One can look to and gain from CAPM for some key lessons for pricing in credit risk. If we assume for illustrative purposes that CAPM approximates reality, then it can be utilized to determine a transaction's expected return. More important, one can manipulate CAPM to show how it can be utilized to determine a transaction's required return. Pricing needs to be a function of one's required return (not one's expected return). A transaction's required return can be viewed as the return associated with a "naive efficient portfolio" which has the same risk as the transaction. One can also benchmark a transaction's return against the market portfolio. One should recognize that the lessons gained from CAPM (or other more advanced theoretical models) need to be adjusted for the realities of the marketplace (e.g., the CAPM is equivalent to the one-factor Arbritrage Pricing Theory [APT] model. Accordingly, ATP enables a more complete specification of market reality than CAPM.).

FIGURE 13–11
RAROraC Factors

$$RAROraC = f\left(\begin{array}{l} \bullet \text{ Direct \& Indirect Revenues} \\ \bullet \text{ Direct \& Indirect Expenses} \\ \bullet \text{ Credit-Risk Factors} \\ \bullet \text{ Market-Risk Factors} \\ \bullet \text{ Other Risk Factors} \\ \bullet \text{ Correlation Effects} \end{array}\right)$$

CAPM Basics

According to CAPM, the expected return of security S (ER_S) can be represented as a function of S's beta (β_S) against the returns of a market portfolio (M). The "market premium" is defined as the expected return of the market portfolio (ER_M) minus the risk-free return (R_F.). CAPM states that

$$E\ R_S = R_F + \beta_S\ (E\ R_M - R_F)$$

where

$$\beta_S = \frac{\text{Cov}(R_S,\ R_M)}{\sigma_M^2}$$

or

$$E\ R_S - R_F = \beta_S\ (E\ R_M - R_F)$$

which says that expected excess returns of security S is β_S-proportional to the market premium. These equations describe the capital markets line (in risk-return space), which is a key concept within the CAPM framework.

From the definition of correlation

$$\rho_{S,M} = \frac{\text{Cov}(R_S, R_M)}{\sigma_M \sigma_S}$$

it is clear that

$$\beta_S = \frac{\text{Cov}(R_S, R_M)}{\sigma_M^2} = \frac{\sigma_S}{\sigma_M}\frac{\text{Cov}(R_S, R_M)}{\sigma_M \sigma_S} = \frac{\sigma_S}{\sigma_M}\rho_{S,M}$$

which says that the beta of a security can be decomposed into three statistics: (1) risk of the security, (2) risk of the market portfolio, and (3) correlation of the security to the market portfolio. This relates beta and correlation as a simple proportion. Plugging this relationship back into the basic CAPM equation gives

$$\text{E } R_S = R_F + \frac{\sigma_S}{\sigma_M} \rho_{S,M} \,(\text{E } R_M - R_F)$$

and a slight rearrangement of terms gives

$$\text{E } R_S = R_F + \sigma_S \rho_{S,M} \, \frac{(\text{E } R_M - R_F)}{\sigma_M}$$

The term $\dfrac{(\text{E } R_M - R_F)}{\sigma_M}$, which is the market premium divided by market risk, is called "the market price of risk." Hence CAPM represents the expected return of a security in terms of the risk-free rate (whose maturity corresponds to the holding period of the investment) plus a portfolio-dependent proportion of the market price of risk.

Separating Good Risk from Bad Risk

The expected return of S (as indicated above) is directly linked to $\sigma_S \times \rho_{S,M}$. One can define good risk as the risk of S (σ_S) multiplied by the correlation of S with the market portfolio (i.e. $\rho_{S,M}$). According to CAPM, an efficient market only pays (rewards) one for good risk. Good risk is the risk that can't be diversified away and can be called systematic risk. One could say that systematic risk is rewardable.

If the market only rewards (pays) one for good risk, then the corollary is that the market does not reward (pay) one for bad risk.[2] One can use a simple example of a golf cart and umbrella company to illustrate the concept of bad (i.e., specific) versus good (i.e., systematic) risk. Observe that the profitability of a business that rents golf carts is negatively correlated with a business that rents umbrellas. The *specific risk* of both businesses is the weather. The specific portfolio-risk of the combined

---

[2]One should be aware that the literature uses many terms synonymous with "good risk" such as systematic risk, nondiversifiable risk, market portfolio risk, etc. Similarly, one has many terms synonymous with "bad risk" such as nonsystematic risk, unsystematic risk, diversifiable risk, nonmarket portfolio risk, specific risk, etc.

portfolio of the two businesses is not eliminated. For example, the profitabilities of the two businesses are not perfectly negatively correlated (i.e., correlation equals -1), as there will always be someone who likes to play golf in the rain. The *systematic risk* cannot be eliminated. If a recession (the systematic risk) comes, then people do not play golf even on sunny days and cannot afford umbrellas when it rains. For example, it is likely that the stocks for both the golf cart and umbrella manufacturers went down during the October 1987 crash. One needs to consider both the portfolio interrelationships, as well as the external factors (systematic risks) that affects business and portfolio profitability.

The amount of good risk contained in security S can be separated from the amount of bad risk in security S by decomposing the variance σ_S^2 as *follows:*

$$(\text{good risk})^2 = \sigma_S^2 \, \rho_{S,M}^2 = \beta_S^2 \sigma_M^2 \quad \text{i.e., } \textit{systematic } \text{variance}$$

$$(\text{bad risk})^2 = \sigma_S^2 \left(1 - \rho_{S,M}^2\right) \quad \text{i.e., } \textit{specific } \text{variance}$$

from which it is immediately clear that

$$\sigma_S^2 = (\text{total risk})^2 = (\text{good risk})^2 + (\text{bad risk})^2 = \sigma_S^2 \, \rho_{S,M}^2 + \sigma_S^2 \left(1 - \rho_{S,M}^2\right)$$

Pricing in the Required Return

Transactions need to be priced to achieve a required return. One can twist CAPM to reveal the degree to which a security adds value (beyond the required return). The required return of S can be measured against a naive efficient portfolio (on the CAPM line), which contains the same risk as S. This has important implications for how one should price in risk.

The naive efficient portfolio (*NP*) is a portfolio consisting of combinations of owning the market portfolio and a risk-free investment (or a risk-free borrowing) for which $\rho_{NP,M} = 1$, so that

$$\mathsf{E}\, R_{NP} = R_F + \sigma_{NP} \frac{(\mathsf{E}\, R_M - R_F)}{\sigma_M}$$

The required return of S (in excess of the risk-free rate) can be determined from the beta of a naive efficient portfolio NP (β_{NP}) chosen such that $\sigma_{NP} = \sigma_S$.

$$\mathsf{E}\, R_{NP} - R_F = \beta_{NP}(\mathsf{E}R_M - R_F)$$

where

$$\beta_{NP} = \frac{\sigma_{NP}}{\sigma_M} \rho_{NP,M} = \frac{\sigma_S}{\sigma_M}$$

In other words, the beta of the naive portfolio (β_{NP}), which has the same risk of S ($\sigma_{NP} = \sigma_S$) can be determined from dividing the risk of S (σ_S) by the risk of the market portfolio (σ_M). Specifically, if one believes CAPM, then one must price in risk to meet a required excess return of $\sigma_S \times$ the market price of risk.

Example 1: Security (S)   Assume that S and M are such that

$\sigma_S = 10\%$

$\sigma_M = 5\%$

$\rho_{S,M} = 0.5$

$R_F = 10\%$

$ER_M = 15\%$

To derive ER_S, we first calculate β_S as follows

$$\beta_S = \frac{\sigma_S}{\sigma_M} \rho_{S,M} = \frac{.10}{.05} \times .5 = 1$$

Then $ER_S = R_F + \beta_S(ER_M - R_F) = 10\% + 1 \times 5\% = 15\%$

One can now compute the good risk and bad risk components of the risk of S.

(good risk)^2 = $\sigma_S^2 \times \rho_{S,M}^2 = (0.1)^2 \times (.5)^2 = .0025 = 25$ basis points

(bad risk)^2 = $\sigma_S^2 \times (1 - \rho_{S,M}^2) = (.1)^2 \times (1-.5^2) = .0075 = 75$ basis points

One should observe that the (total risk)^2 of S (σ_S^2) equals = $(.1)^2 = .01 = 100$ basis points, which agrees with the fact that

(total risk)^2 = (good risk)^2 + (bad risk)^2

which is analogous to the Pythagorean theorem, but for risk. Observe that the beta of S, in our example, can equal 1 and not be the market portfolio.

Example 2: Market portfolio (M)   Assume that one owns the market portfolio and therefore $ER_M = 15\%$ (as assumed above). Observe also that (by construction) CAPM states that $ER_M = R_F + \beta_M(ER_M - R_F)$ which (after plugging in numbers) equals $10\% + 1 \times 5\% = 15\%$. Again, one can compute

$$\text{(good risk)}^2 = \sigma^2_M \times \rho_{S,M}^2 = (.05)^2 \times (1)^2 = .0025 = 25 \text{ basis points}$$
$$\text{(bad risk)}^2 = \sigma^2_M \times (1-\rho_{S,M}^2) = (.1)^2 \times (1-1)^2 = 0 \text{ basis points}$$

Observe that the (total risk)^2 of the market portfolio (σ^2_M) consists entirely of good risk and equals 25 basis points.

Example 3: Naive efficient portfolio (NP)   Assume that one is looking for a naive efficient portfolio with the same risk as S, such that

$$\sigma_{NP} = \sigma_S = 10\%$$

Observe that the β_{NP} with the same risk as S equals σ_S / σ_M. Accordingly,

$$\beta_{NP} = \frac{10\%}{5\%} = 2$$

Also, observe that we can compute the expected return of the naive efficient portfolio as

$$ER_{NP} = R_F + \beta_{NP}(ER_M - R_F)$$
$$= 10\% + 2 \times 5\% \ (= .15 - .10) = 20\%$$

Benchmark Perspective

The returns from an institution's ability to select S (sometimes referred to as selectivity) can be subdivided into returns achievable from net selectivity and returns achievable from diversification. For example, assume that the actual return on the S cited above equals 25 percent. The required return of the naive efficient portfolio (which has the same risk as S) was seen to be 20 percent. The return from selectivity is

$$R_S - ER_S = 25\% - 15\% = 10\%$$

Observe that the net selectivity component of S is

$$R_S - ER_{NP} = 25\% - 20\% = 5\%$$

The diversification component is

$$ER_{NP} - ER_S = 20\% - 15\% = 5\%$$

The return from selectivity is equivalent to the Jensen Measure. Observe that the return from selectivity (i.e., 10 percent) is equal to the net selectivity component (i.e., 5 percent) plus the diversification component (i.e., 5 percent). One should observe that the expected shortfall of S measured against the return required by the naive portfolio is $\mathsf{ER}_{NP} - \mathsf{ER}_S = 20\% - 15\% = 5\%$.

One can also price in risk to achieve a certain risk-adjusted benchmark performance. For example, one can analyze the comparison between the expected return of S benchmarked against the expected return of the market portfolio (where $\beta_M = 1$). Observe that

$$
\begin{aligned}
\mathsf{E}\ R_S - \mathsf{ER}_M &= \mathsf{E}\ R_S - R_F - (\mathsf{E}\ R_M - R_F) \\
&= \beta_{S,M}\ (\mathsf{E}\ R_M - R_F) - (\mathsf{E}\ R_M - R_F) \\
&= (\beta_{S,M} - 1)\ (\mathsf{E}\ R_M - R_F) \\
&= \left(\frac{\sigma_S}{\sigma_M}\ \rho_{S,M} - 1 \right) (\mathsf{E}\ R_M - R_F) \\
&= (\sigma_S \rho_{S,M} - \sigma_M) \left(\frac{\mathsf{E}\ R_M - R_F}{\sigma_M} \right)
\end{aligned}
$$

Accordingly, one can conclude that the expected performance of S benchmarked against the returns of the market portfolio can be expressed as a hurdle rate $\left(\dfrac{\mathsf{E}\ R_M - R_F}{\sigma_M} \right)$ multiplied by $(\sigma_S \rho_{S,M} - \sigma_M)$, where the hurdle rate is the market price of risk. This can be summarized as shown in Table 13–1.

Hedging Effectiveness

If one's goal is to price marginal risk, then one needs to consider the risk transformation properties of any incremental transaction. For example, one should be aware of the degree to which a hedge reduces (or unintentionally increases) risk. Consider a portfolio S consisting of a long position of amount N_X of Security X and a long position of amount N_Y of Security Y. The portfolio volatility (σ_s) is such that

$$
\sigma_S^2 = N_X^2 \sigma_X^2 + N_Y^2 \sigma_Y^2 + 2\rho_{X,Y} N_X N_Y \sigma_X \sigma_Y \ ^3
$$

---

[3] If one defines a Risk Measurement Unit (RMU) in terms of $k\sigma$ (where k represents the number of standard deviations associated with a desired statistical confidence level) then the portfolio RMU, calculated as $\sqrt{RMU_X^2 + RMU_Y^2 + 2\rho_{X,Y} RMU_X RMU_Y}$, can be used to measure market risk (where $RMU_X = N_X\ k\ \sigma_X$ and $RMU_y = N_Y\ k\ \sigma_Y$) to any desired level of statistical confidence. Further, observe that σ_P in Table 13–1 is calculated as $\sqrt{\sigma_S^2 + \sigma_M^2 - 2\rho_{S,M}\sigma_S\ \sigma_M}$.

TABLE 13–1
Risk-Adjusted Benchmark Performance

				Return on Equity	
Portfolio	Actual Excess Return	Expected Excess Return	Volatility	Actual	Expected
Security (S)	$R_S\text{-}R_F$	$ER_S\text{-}R_F$	σ_S	$\dfrac{R_S - R_F}{\sigma_S}$	$P_{M,S}\left[\dfrac{ER_M - R_F}{\sigma_M}\right]$
Market (M)	$R_M\text{-}R_F$	$ER_M\text{-}R_F$	σ_M	$\dfrac{R_M - R_F}{\sigma_M}$	$\dfrac{ER_M - R_F}{\sigma_M}$
S-M	$R_S\text{-}R_M$	$ER_S\text{-}ER_M$	σ_P	$\dfrac{R_S - R_M}{\sigma_P}$	$\left[\dfrac{P_{S,M}\,\sigma_S - \sigma_M}{\sigma_P}\right]\left[\dfrac{ER_M - R_F}{\sigma_M}\right]$

Assume for illustrative purposes that both N_X and N_Y equal 1. The variance would then be

$$\sigma_S^2 = \sigma_X^2 + \sigma_Y^2 + 2\rho_{X,Y}\sigma_X\sigma_Y$$
$$= (\sigma_Y + \rho_{X,Y}\sigma_X)^2 + \sigma_X^2\left(1 - \rho_{X,Y}^2\right)$$

where the last line is just a rearrangement of terms from the line preceding.

One can make this more concrete by plugging in numbers. For example, if σ_X equals 4 percent and σ_Y equals 3 percent then (plugging in numbers) one has σ_S equal to $16 + 9 + 24\,\rho_{X,Y}$, [which can also be expressed as $(3 + 4\,\rho_{X,Y})^2 + 16\,(1 - \rho_{X,Y}^2)$]. Observe that if $\rho_{X,Y}$ equals 1 then the risk is additive (i.e., σ_S equals σ_X plus $\sigma_Y = 7\%$). If $\rho_{X,Y}$ equals -1 then one can take the difference in risks (i.e., σ_S equals σ_X minus $\sigma_Y = 1\%$). Also, observe that if $\rho_{X,Y}$ equals 0 then ρ_S equals 5.

If one uses an amount N_Y of product Y to hedge N_X of product X then one would adjust the $\sigma^2{}_S$ equation described immediately above by inserting a negative sign in front of N_Y. It can be shown (by solving for the value of N_Y such that $\delta\,\sigma_S = 0$) that the optimal hedge ratio N_Y/N_X which minimizes σ_S is
$$\sigma N_Y$$

$$\frac{N_Y}{N_X} = \frac{\sigma_X}{\sigma_Y}\rho_{X,Y}$$

Plugging this ratio into the equation for variance gives

$$\sigma_S^2 = N_X^2\sigma_X^2 + N_X^2\sigma_X^2\rho_{X,Y}^2 - 2\rho_{X,Y}^2 N_X^2\sigma_X^2$$
$$= N_X^2\sigma_X^2\left(1 + \rho_{X,Y}^2 - 2\rho_{X,Y}^2\right)$$
$$= N_X^2\sigma_X^2\left(1 - \rho_{X,Y}^2\right)$$

One can also express the residual risk of the hedge as

$$\sigma_S^2 = (N_Y\sigma_Y - \rho_{X,Y}N_X\sigma_X)^2 + N_X^2\sigma_X^2(1 - \rho_{X,Y}^2)$$

Observe that if one plugs the optimal hedge into the equation then the first term equals zero. The risk-reduction effectiveness can be defined in terms of the percentage change in the square of risk. Accordingly, the risk-reduction effectiveness can be defined as

$$\text{one minus } \frac{\text{square of the risk after the hedge is put on}}{\text{square of the risk before the hedge is put on}}$$

$$= 1 - \frac{N_X^2\sigma_X^2\left(1 - \rho_{X,Y}^2\right)}{N_X^2\sigma_X^2} = \rho_{X,Y}^2$$

Observe that the hedge ratio N_Y/N_X increases as σ_Y declines relative to σ_X. Further, observe that the hedge ratio increases as an increasing function of $\rho_{X,Y}$. Clearly, the degree to which Y is a good hedge for X is a function of $\rho_{X,Y}$. For example, observe that if one suboptimally used one unit of Y to hedge one unit of X then one may actually increase risk unless $\rho_{X,Y}$ is sufficiently large. Specifically, if $\rho_{X,Y} \leq \sigma_Y/2\sigma_X$, then the one-for-one hedge would increase risk (since $\sigma_X^2 + \sigma_Y^2 - 2\rho_{X,Y}\sigma_X\sigma_Y \geq \sigma_X^2$). For example, if σ_X equals σ_Y then $\rho_{X,Y}$ needs to be greater than one-half in order for the one-for-one hedge to be risk reducing. Observe that, to be more precise, if the absolute value of $P_{X,Y}$ is greater than one-half, then the one-for-one hedge would be risk reducing.

Capital Attribution

One needs to initially determine the amount of economic capital and then subsequently price in the cost of economic capital. The cost of economic capital, as pointed out earlier, needs to be factored into one's pricing equation. One can calculate the required amount of economic capital necessary to achieve specific rating-agency ratings (e.g., AAA). The amount of economic capital required for credit risk is typically attributed

FIGURE 13–12
Credit-Loss Probability Distribution

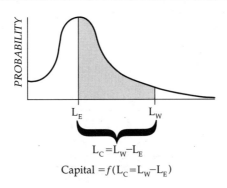

as a function of the unexpected credit loss. For example, one can use a credit-loss probability distribution, as illustrated in Figure 13–12, to determine the amount of economic capital required for credit risk such that the probability of exceeding the sum of the expected credit loss (denoted by L_E) plus the unexpected credit loss (denoted by L_C) is less than a preset probability (e.g., 2.5 percent). The shaded area in Figure 13–12 indicates the probability that the amount of credit loss is within the region between L_W and L_E. The worst-case credit loss denoted by L_W, equals $L_E + L_C$. Observe that this approach is consistent with a philosophy where economic capital is assigned as a function of risk at a preset statistical confidence level.

Regulatory Approach

One should be aware of and contrast the regulator's approach to arriving at regulatory capital with best-practice approaches of arriving at economic capital. On-balance-sheet assets and off-balance-sheet amounts are risk-weighted according to various percentages set by BIS. For example, at the Canadian Imperial Bank of Commerce (CIBC), as illustrated in Table 13–2, the risk-weighted amount (as of October 31, 1994) totals $113 billion. The risk-weighted amount can be broken down into $91 billion for on-balance-sheet assets and $22 billion for off-balance-sheet items. Ob-

TABLE 13–2
CIBC Risk-Weighted Amount on October 31, 1994
(CAN $ Billions)

Category	Assets (Notional)	Risk-weighted Amount	Risk-Weighted Amount as a Percentage of Assets
On Balance Sheet	151	91	60.0%
Off Balance Sheet	895	22	2.5%
Credit-related arrangements	90*	19	21.0%
Derivatives	805**	3	0.4%
Total Risk-Weighted Amount		113	

*Composed of lines of credit (75.8), guarantees and letters of credit (13), and other items (1.2)
**Composed of interest-rate products (510), foreign-exchange products (284), and other items (11)

serve that the $3 billion derivatives risk-weighted amount is only 2.9 percent of the $113 billion risk-weighted amount and 4 percent as a percentage of the notional. The $3 billion risk-weighted amount for derivatives can be decomposed into its three counterparty risk-weighted constituent parts (i.e. 0 percent, 20 percent and 50 percent weightings). For example, the total $3 billion risk-weighted amount for derivatives equals 0 percent × 0.8 billion + 20% × 8.4 billion + 50% × 3 billion.

Observe that CIBC's regulatory capital ratios are well in excess of those ratios established by BIS. For example, Tier 1 and total capital at CIBC (as of October 31, 1994) were respectively $8.1 billion and $11.3 billion. The regulatory capital ratios are calculated by dividing Tier 1 and total capital by the risk-weighted amount of $113.3. For example, the Tier 1 capital ratio is 7.1 percent, derived from dividing $8.1 by $113.3. The required Tier 1 and total capital are respectively 4 percent and 8 percent. The methodology to calculate the risk-weighted amount is described over the next several pages.

Calculation steps. A detailed calculation of the interest-rate derivatives risk-weighted amount requires a two-step process. The first

FIGURE 13–13
BIS Credit Equivalent Calculation

Current Replacement Cost	+	Add-on Factor	=	Credit Equivalent

step requires one to compute a credit-equivalent amount and the second step requires one to compute a risk-weighted amount. The risk-weighted amount results from applying counterparty risk weights (similar to weights for on-balance-sheet amounts) to reflect the credit quality of the counterparty. One needs to first calculate the current replacement cost. Second, one needs to calculate an add-on factor to project the future replacement cost. Finally, as illustrated in Figure 13–13, one sums the two calculations to produce the credit equivalent amount.

One utilizes only the positive amount of the mark-to-market value of the contract to determine the current replacement cost. For example, if one had a 5-year fixed/floating interest-rate swap, then the current replacement cost is typically found within the shaded region of Figure 13–14.

The add-on factor is arrived at by multiplying the notional amount of the derivatives transaction by the BIS required add-on percentage as partially reproduced in Table 13–3 (for interest-rate products). The add-on factor is used to estimate the future replacement cost. The credit-equivalent amount for derivatives is then determined by summing the current replacement cost and the add-on factor. The credit-equivalent amount is equivalent to an on-balance-sheet amount for regulatory risk purposes.

The second step, as illustrated in Figure 13–15, requires one to multiply the credit-equivalent amount by a counterparty risk weighting in order to compute the risk-weighted amount. The counterparty risk weightings are: 0% percent for OECD governments, Canadian Provinces, and their agencies; 20 percent for OECD incorporated banks and public sector entities; and 50 percent for corporate and other counterparties.

In summary, if we combine Figure 13–13 and Table 13–3, then the detailed calculation of a risk-weighted amount for derivatives can be depicted as shown in Figure 13–16.

Let's take an example transaction to illustrate how one performs a detailed calculation of the risk-weighted amount for a 5-year interest-rate swap with a Canadian corporate counterparty. Assume the notional

FIGURE 13–14
Replacement-Cost Curve

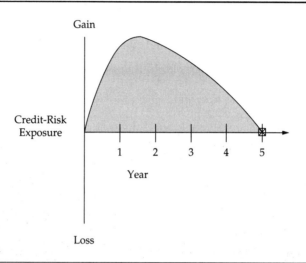

TABLE 13–3
BIS Interest-Rate "Add-On" Percent

	Add-On Percentage	
Product Type	*Less than 1 year*	*Greater than 1 year*
Interest Rate	*0%*	*0.5%*

amount of the interest-rate swap is $100 million and the mark-to-market (current replacement cost) is $2 million. The add-on factor is $0.5MM (= 0.5% × $100MM), since the remaining maturity of the swap is more than one year. The credit equivalent is the sum of $2 million plus $0.5 million, which equals $2.5 million. One uses a 50 percent weighting since the counterparty is a corporation. The risk-weighted amount for our derivative example is $1.25MM, obtained from multiplying $2.5MM × 50 percent. Observe that the $1.25MM is 1.25 percent of the notional amount.

FIGURE 13–15
BIS Risk-Weighted Amount Calculation

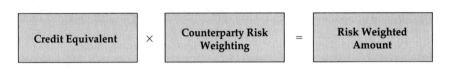

FIGURE 13–16
Summary of the Two-Step BIS Risk-Weighted Amount Calculation

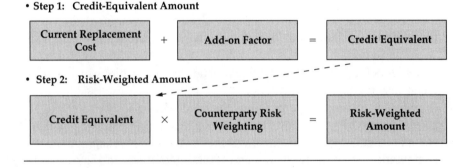

ESTABLISHING CREDIT-GRADE-SPECIFIC PROVISION AND ECONOMIC CAPITAL FACTORS

Overview

An institution needs to calculate the expected and unexpected credit loss for each derivatives transaction. The expected credit loss is utilized as an input to calculate the projected provision, and the unexpected credit loss is utilized to establish the amount of required economic capital. Clearly, the projected provision and economic capital are two vital factors in pricing and managing credit risk in an integrated manner. An institution can attribute the expected and unexpected credit losses to a derivatives transaction as a function of its assigned credit grade. As we will describe later,

FIGURE 13–17

Calculating Provision and Economic Capital

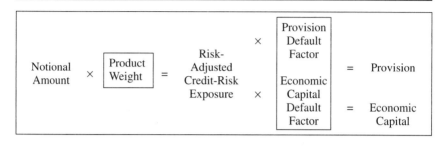

the assignment of a credit grade implies that a unique default- and recovery-rate probability distribution has been determined. The institution needs to combine the projected credit-risk exposure probability distribution with default- and recovery-rate probability distributions to produce a credit-loss probability distribution.

Assume for illustrative purposes that one takes a loan-equivalent approach to calculating credit provision and economic capital. The basic chain of calculations (associated with the loan-equivalent approach) in the computation of credit provision and capital is outlined in Figure 13–17. First, the notional amount is multiplied by a product weight to create a risk-adjusted credit-risk exposure. The risk-adjusted credit-risk exposure is utilized to ensure that all credit-risk exposures are expressed in a common credit-risk framework (i.e., a loan equivalent). Assume for simplicity that the default factors are net of recovery. The risk-adjusted credit-risk exposure is multiplied by a credit-grade-specific provision default factor to arrive at the required provision. Similarly, the risk-adjusted credit-risk exposure is multiplied by a credit-grade-specific capital default factor to arrive at the required economic capital.

The risk-adjusted credit-risk exposure is designed to estimate the projected average expected credit-risk exposure over the life of the transaction. For example, assume that the product weight for a 3X6 forward rate agreement (FRA) is 4.8 basis points. Accordingly, the risk-adjusted credit-risk exposure for a 1 million 3X6 FRA would equal 480. Observe that 480 is calculated by multiplying 1 million by 0.00048. One would overstate the value of the risk-adjusted credit-risk exposure by a factor of five if the product weight for the 3X6 FRA were based on an estimate of an average worst-case credit-risk exposure. The average worst-case credit-risk exposure can be called a fractional exposure (FE), since the credit-risk exposure is a fraction of the nominal amount. The FE for the 3X6 FRA is 2,400 and therefore five times the average expected credit-risk exposure. Clearly, a 100-million loan outstanding involves a different degree of risk-adjusted exposure than a 100-million commercial letter of credit, a 100-million unused facility, or a 100-million fixed/floating interest-rate swap.

The credit-grade-specific expected and unexpected default factors are expressed as a percentage (of the risk-adjusted credit-risk exposure). The expected default factor is sometimes referred to as the projected-provision default factor and the unexpected default factor is sometimes referred to as the projected economic-capital default factor. Percentages assigned to the provision and economic capital default factors will vary with the credit-worthiness of the counterparty and the tenor of the transaction. Typically, an estimate of the projected expected and unexpected credit loss for a counterparty is calculated based on a standardized, institution-specific credit grading system. One would assign percentages for provision and economic capital as an increasing function of the lower credit quality of the counterparty. Clearly, bigger annual loss provisions are needed for transactions that have a higher projected probability of default. Similarly, one would observe that transactions with a lower credit quality would exhibit a greater volatility in loss patterns than transactions with a higher credit quality. Accordingly, the capital cushion is an increasing function of the declining credit quality of the counterparty. That is why best-practice pricing methodologies are based on the amounts of the credit-grade-specific provision and capital that are required to support a transaction.

Each year one must set aside enough premium to cover the average of the yearly expected credit losses (an average credit loss over time). The aggregate credit-risk premiums (on a portfolio of transactions) must therefore (over time) equal or exceed credit losses. Credit quality, however, changes over time. One needs a process to project the credit-grade (CG) migration path over the life of the asset. In other words, one needs to determine the probabilities that the counterparty will stay at the same credit grade, improve to a higher grade, or worsen to a lower grade. The CG migration path ultimately affects the amount of average expected and unexpected credit losses that need to be priced into a transaction.

If actual losses rise above the average for a sustained period of time, then one could easily consume the accumulated reserve. One needs a capital cushion sufficient to cover these peak loss periods. These peaks, and the underlying volatility, are the basis behind the term "unexpected loss." The size of the capital cushion is a function of the pattern of the losses. Clearly, a more volatile credit-loss pattern would require a bigger capital cushion. The size of the capital cushion also depends on a desired level of confidence (such as 97.5 percent) that the cushion will be sufficient.

A key principle within this measurement system is to separate the upcoming year's projected risk from the average future risk over the life of the transaction required for pricing. Clearly, the amount of projected risk for a multiperiod transaction (say, four years) is not the same as the projected risk of a one-year transaction. In other words, the ratio of the projected risk to a one-year risk factor rises as an increasing function of the maturity of a transaction. This ratio is greater than one for multiyear transactions, since in the past there has been a tendency for downward credit-grade migration due to generic declining credit quality for longer-tenor assets and the holder's right to prepayment (which generally will be exercised should credit quality improve). For example, a four-year swap (or loan) for a customer should be priced differently from a one-year swap (or loan) to that same customer.

Credit-Grade-Specific Default Factors

One needs to exercise considerable judgment along with best-practice methodologies to arrive at the credit-grade-specific default factors. The expected and unexpected default data for each credit-grade bucket can be derived based on analyzing bond-credit spreads as well as internal and external data. For example, rating agencies publish studies based on corporate bond cohort default data (e.g., Moody's). A bond-credit spread typically refers to the spread above duration-matched Treasuries that investors require as compensation for credit risk. One can also use external services that provide expected default data (e.g., KMV provides one-year expected default frequency [EDF] data). One needs to choose a statistical sample of bonds (which are deemed equivalent in terms of internal risk buckets) in order to arrive at credit-grade-specific expected and unexpected default factors. Publicly listed corporate bonds provide important information because sufficiently broad, unbiased data on loans is unavailable. One would need to adjust default data obtained from corporate bonds to reflect the practical dynamics of a corporate loan book. Internal risk buckets could be structured so that CG10 is assigned for a portfolio of

AAA to AA, CG20 for a portfolio of AA to A, CG30 for a portfolio of A+ to BBB+, CG40 for portfolio of BBB+ to BBB, and so on through CG100. These credit grades, which map to overlapping bond ratings, could be further subdivided into ten finer divisions (for example, the CG10 could be subdivided into CG10 to CG19 buckets) for a total of 100 credit-grade categories. In practice, one would find it impractical to establish as many as 100 credit-grade categories. One would need only 10 credit-grade categories. One may want to subdivide the middle credit-grades, such as credit grades 50, 60, and 70, in order to obtain finer gradations within a very broad band of credit risk. The average expected and unexpected default statistics form the basis for each bucket.

One needs to adjust the credit-grade-specific unexpected default factors to incorporate the specific risk of any individual risk-adjusted exposure within a common credit grade (since the unexpected default factors are typically derived from analyzing a portfolio of risk-adjusted exposures within a credit grade). For example, if one utilizes Moody's cohort default data then the individual default factors implicitly benefit from the portfolio effect. One must make adjustments to account for the fact that the unexpected default factors for any credit grade mostly reflect systematic risk. For example, typically the economic capital (arrived at by multiplying the risk-adjusted credit-risk exposure by the credit- grade-specific economic capital default factor) in most institutions would erroneously be the same for a single 100 million CG30 risk-adjusted credit-risk exposure versus ten different CG30 counterparties whose total risk-adjusted credit-risk exposure is also 100 million. A portfolio of risk-adjusted credit-risk exposures should benefit from the effects of diversification (e.g., 10 different CG30 counterparties) when compared to an equivalent-size risk-adjusted credit-risk exposure to a single counterparty. Accordingly, one should attribute less economic capital to a portfolio of exposures than the sum of the economic capital assigned to each exposure. The economic capital required can be calculated by examining the portfolio effect between the various counterparties (e.g., through analyzing default correlations between industry classes within a credit grade class).

Provision and economic capital default factors typically apply to the principal amount of a loan. One also needs to consider other factors such as the loss of net interest income. For example, revenue should be set aside to cover the cost of carrying nonaccrual assets. Further, revenue should also be set aside for liquidity charges to cover the cost of maintaining adequate access to funding throughout the life of the asset. One needs also to consider administration and opportunity costs.

TABLE 13–4

Credit-Grade-Specific Economic Capital Default Factors

Credit grade	Asset Type	Weighted-Average Life				
		1	2	3	4	10
10		C10.1	C10.2	—	—	C10.10
20		C20.1	C20.2	—	—	C20.10
30	Amortizing	C30.1	C30.2	—	—	C30.10
40	Asset	C40.1	C40.2	3.00%	3.19%	C40.10
50		C50.1	C50.2	—	—	C50.10
60		C60.1	C60.2	—	—	C60.10
70	Capital	C70.1	C70.2	—	—	C70.10
80	Default	C80.1	C80.2	—	—	C80.10
90	Factors	C90.1	C90.2	—	—	C90.10
100	(%)	C100.1	C100.2	—	—	C100.10
		Tenor				
10		C10.1	C10.2	—	—	C10.10
20	Non-	C20.1	C20.2	—	—	C20.10
30	amortizing	C30.1	C30.2	—	—	C30.10
40	Asset	C40.1	C40.2	2.82%	2.91%	C40.10
50		C50.1	C50.2	—	—	C50.10
60	Economic	C60.1	C60.2	—	—	C60.10
70	Capital	C70.1	C70.2	—	—	C70.10
80	Default	C80.1	C80.2	—	—	C80.10
90	Factors	C90.1	C90.2	—	—	C90.10
100	(%)	C100.1	C100.2	—	—	C100.10

One cannot simply add the economic capital for individual positions within a portfolio of exposures across credit grades. This results in more economic capital than is necessary, since adding economic capital across credit-grade classes assumes a perfect correlation between each credit grade (which is highly unlikely). For example, if one simply added 3 million of economic capital for a CG30 exposure with 4 million of economic capital for a CG40 exposure (e.g., whose credit risk is uncorrelated) then the economic capital would be overstated (e.g., by 2 million).

Assume the economic capital default factors for pricing nonamortizing assets are as shown in Table 13–4. For example, pricing in economic capital for a three-year risk-adjusted nonamortizing credit grade 40 asset is assumed to utilize 2.82 percent of the risk-adjusted exposure per year (Reference C(40, 3)). Pricing in economic capital for the same risk-adjusted nonamortizing asset with a credit grade 40 for four years is assumed to use 2.91 percent per year (Reference C(40, 4)).

Most credit-grading systems only provide a single set of provision and capital factors for each credit grade. The charges for pricing amortizing assets are different from nonamortizing assets. The economic capital default factors for amortizing assets in Table 13–4 are provided as a function of a weighted-average life, whereas the economic capital factors for nonamortizing assets are provided as a function of tenor. For example, pricing in economic capital for a comparable amortizing asset would be 3.00 percent for a three-year weighted-average life and 3.19 percent for a four-year weighted-average life. Similar tables can be generated for credit-grade provision default factors. One should note that the weighted-average life of an amortizing asset is typically derived by present value tenor-weighting the declining principal amounts. One can create a matrix of provision (P) default factors (e.g., P[i,j] factors; for credit grade $i = 10$, $20, \ldots, 100$ and tenor $j = 1, 2, \ldots, 10$), which are analogous to the C(i,j) economic capital default factors shown in Table 13–4.

Credit-Grade Migration

Default studies are typically conducted in a cohort fashion, where corporate bonds are tracked over time by the corporate bonds' initial credit quality in order to arrive at default factors as a function of tenor. Default cohort studies implicitly contain a credit-grade migration matrix. One could explicitly build a credit-grade migration matrix that contains the probabilities (conditional on the current credit grade) of migrating from one credit grade to another. One could next apply the conditional probabilities over the life of the asset to an initial set of default factors (say one year) in order to arrive at a set of default factors (expected default and unexpected default factors) to be applied as a function of tenor.

Reserves (say for the expected credit loss) need to be adjusted as the credit quality changes. One can define this approach as a "pay-as-you-go philosophy." The pay-as-you-go philosophy captures the appropriate charge over the life of the asset and is similar to marking-to-market one's reserves. As pointed out earlier, the default factors are applied to risk-adjusted credit-risk exposures in a portfolio to estimate the required provision and capital cushion. If the risk grade of a credit-risk exposure in

TABLE 13–5
Credit-Grade Risk-Migration Utility

From Risk Grade	To Risk Grade after One Year						
	20	30	40	50	60	70	Total
30	2%	91%	5%	2%	0%	0%	100%
40	0	3%	89%	6%	2%	0%	100%
50	0	0	4%	87%	7%	2%	100%

the portfolio changes, then different provision and capital default factors are applied to that credit-risk exposure. For example, a credit-risk exposure under a pay-as-you-go system that changes from a credit grade 30 in the first year to a credit grade 40 in the second year would be charged higher provision and economic capital. Such a pay-as-you-go method is suited to the valuation of portfolios and the evaluation of business units. The adjustment is necessary because there is a significant probability that any individual credit will migrate from the initial credit risk to other credit-risk grades.

The credit-grade migration path that a particular transaction will take is unknown. However, one can derive probabilities of the various paths, and use those probabilities to construct a credit-grade risk-migration utility (CGRMU). The CGRMU is a matrix of "from-to" credit-risk grade probabilities. Assume for illustrative purposes that the credit quality of a transaction changes at yearly intervals and that the CGRMU matrix is stable over time. For example, as illustrated in Table 13–5, the CGRMU reveals the probability (e.g., 91 percent) that a credit starting from risk grade (e.g., CG30) in the far left column will be in a grade in the top row (e.g., CG30) after one year.

One can use the CGRMU to derive a default probability for any multiyear transaction. The yearly CGRMU can be applied repeatedly to derive the probability of the credit being in different grades during each year of the transaction. For example, there is an 83 percent (i.e., 91 percent × 91 percent) probability that a CG30 today will stay a CG30 two years from today (throughout the third year). In other words, the CGRMU can be utilized to provide probabilities of a credit being in a given risk bucket

FIGURE 13–18
Probability of a Credit-Grade Changing

First Year	Second Year	Third Year
	2% chance of being a CG20	4% chance of being a CG20
Credit Grade 30	91% chance of being CG30	83% chance of being CG30
	5% chance of being a CG40	9% chance of being a CG40
	2% chance of being CG50	4% chance of being CG50

(or grade) during a particular year of a multiyear transaction. Pricing factors would be adjusted in direct proportion to confidence interval bands (around the conditional probabilities) used to describe the credit-grade migration.[4]

Blended Default Factors

One can derive a blended default provision factor, similar to a provision default factor directly obtained from a cohort study, by taking the weighted sum of the pay-as-you-go credit-grade-specific provision default factors by the corresponding probability for each credit grade. For example, if an institution does a derivatives transaction with a CG30 counterparty, as illustrated in Figure 13–18, then in the second year there is a 2 percent chance of being a CG20, a 91 percent chance of being a CG30, a 5 percent chance of being a CG40, and a 2 percent chance of being a CG50.

If one applies the respective pay-as-you-go credit-grade provision

---

[4]The confidence interval of a conditional probability (Q) is proportional to the square root of $Q - Q^2$. The largest confidence interval or poorest predictive quality occurs when Q equals 50 percent.

TABLE 13–6
Blended Provision Default Factor

YEAR	Risk-adjusted credit-risk exposure	Blended yearly provision default factor (%)	Projected yearly expected credit loss*
First Year	10,000	0.12	12.00
Second Year	8,000	0.14	11.20
Third Year	6,000	0.19	11.40
Blended Provision Default Factor	—	0.14	—

*The blended yearly provision default factor in the second column multiplied by the risk-adjusted credit-risk exposure in the first column yields the projected yearly expected credit loss.

factors (say A percent for CG20, B percent for CG30, C percent for CG40, and D percent for CG50, then the weighted factors of A × 2 percent plus B × 91 percent plus C × 5 percent plus D × 2 percent provide a blended provision default factor for the second year of K percent (say K = 0.14 percent).

The blended provision default factor each year multiplied by the risk-adjusted credit-risk exposure for that year yields the projected expected loss amount for that year. The weighted sum of the multiplications is the estimated provision necessary to cover the expected losses over the life of the transaction, given the migration probabilities. For example, in Table 13–6, assume the risk-adjusted credit-risk exposures are 10,000 in the first year, 8,000 in the second year, and 6,000 in the third year. Furthermore, assume the blended yearly provision default factors are 0.12 percent, 0.14 percent, and 0.19 percent, respectively. One then performs the appropriate multiplication to arrive at an estimated provision of 12, 11.2, and 11.4 in each year, respectively.

One needs to price the projected average provision (expected loss) into each transaction. As shown in Table 13–6, the weighted average of the blended yearly provision default factors (ignoring present value considerations) is the appropriate provision (i.e., 0.14 percent in this case). One also needs to price the projected cost of capital (unexpected loss) into each transaction.

COMBINING CREDIT-RISK EXPOSURE WITH DEFAULT AND RECOVERY RATES TO PRODUCE FUTURE CREDIT LOSS PROBABILITY DISTRIBUTIONS

Overview

Expected and unexpected credit losses, as illustrated in Figure 13–19, are estimated through analyses of the future distributions of three credit-risk factors. Specifically, one needs to combine a transaction's credit-risk exposure with default and recovery rates to produce an estimate of future credit loss.

Credit-Risk Exposure (CE)

The expected credit-risk exposure is greater over time than the expected market-risk exposure. The logic behind this relationship is straight-forward: both movements up and down in market value are relevant for determining market risk, while only positive mark-to-market values are relevant for credit-risk exposure. In other words, a single transaction does not have credit-risk exposure for negative mark-to-market values. For example, as illustrated in Figure 13–20, assume the percentage change in price is described by a normal probability density distribution. If one assumes the expected percentage change in price is zero, then it is consistent with this assumption that one will have an expected credit-risk exposure that is positive. One should note that negative mark-to-market values may be used to offset positive mark-to-market values with a counterparty where one is allowed to net.

An expected average credit-risk exposure is the first input necessary to calculate counterparty credit loss. Assume, as illustrated in Figure 13–21, that the credit-risk exposure grows as a function of time (e.g., for a FRA). The credit-risk exposure can be separated into a worst-case peak credit-risk exposure, a cumulative average worst-case credit-risk exposure, an expected peak credit-risk exposure, and a cumulative average expected credit-risk exposure.

One can use either the worst-case peak (the peak exposure for an FRA occurs at the maturity of the transaction and can be called a worst-case terminal credit-risk exposure) or average worst-case credit-risk exposure as a measure when setting limits on credit-risk exposure—one simply needs to be consistent. For example, if one uses the worst-case peak credit-

FIGURE 13–19
Credit-Loss Function

risk exposure to measure credit risk, then limits should be set in terms of a worst-case peak credit-risk exposure (not average worst-case credit-risk exposure). As pointed out earlier, the average worst-case credit-risk exposure is sometimes called the fractional exposure. The dynamic credit-risk exposure for limit purposes is often calculated as the sum of the current replacement cost plus the projected average worst-case credit-risk exposure.

So how do we derive the average worst-case credit-risk exposure? Assume for illustrative purposes that the "worst-case" credit-risk exposure at time t (W_t) is equal to $K \times \sigma \times t^{1/2}$, where K is a function of the desired confidence interval, σ is the overnight volatility of the position's percentage change in price, and t varies from 0 to T. Observe that the standard deviation is assumed for simplicity to come from a stable stochastic process where the risk grows as a function of the square root of time. For illustrative purposes we will also assume that the probability of default is uniformly distributed over the time period.[5] If we integrate (from 0 to T) the worst-case credit-risk exposure over the entire time period (and divide this result by the time period (T)) then this provides us with the average worst-case credit-risk exposure.

---

[5]In other words, for simplicity, we will assume that there is an equal probability of a default at any point over the life of the transaction (i.e., from initiation of the transaction until termination of the exposure at time period T). Further, we will assume for illustrative purposes that default rates are independent of the severity of the credit-risk exposure.

FIGURE 13–20
Credit-Risk Exposure Probability Distribution

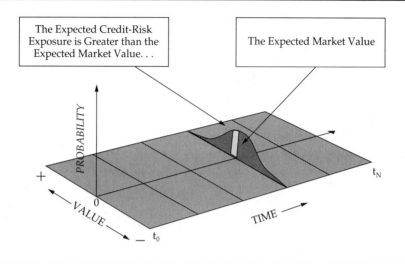

Thus the FE equals

$$(\int_0^T K \times \sigma \times t^{1/2}dt)/T) = (K \times \sigma \times T^{3/2})/(3/2) \times (1/T) =$$
$$2/3 \times [K \times \sigma \times T^{1/2}] = 2/3 \times W_T$$

One can conceptually view the terminal expected credit-risk replace-ment cost at time T ($E[R_T]$) from an options-pricing framework. Assume that the distribution of returns (x) is normally distributed (with a zero mean and a standard deviation that grows as a function of the square root of time) then (ignoring present value considerations) one need only perform the following integration:

$$E\left[R^*_T\right] = \int_{-\infty}^{\infty} \max(o,x)f(x)dx = \int_0^{\infty} xf(x)dx$$

where

$$f(x) = \frac{1}{\sqrt{2\pi}\,\sigma^*} \exp\left(-\frac{x^2}{2\sigma^{*2}}\right)$$

is the univariate normal probability density function and $\sigma^* = \sigma\sqrt{T}$. Accordingly,

FIGURE 13–21
Credit-Risk Exposure Curves

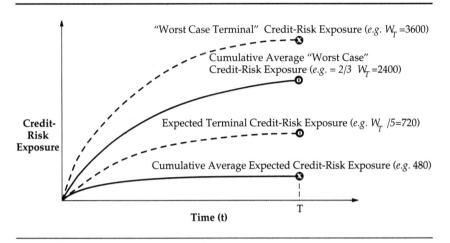

$$E[R_T^*] = \frac{1}{\sqrt{2\pi}\,\sigma^*}\left[-\int_0^\infty \frac{d}{dx}\left(\exp\left(\frac{-x^2}{2\sigma^{*2}} \right) \right)dx \right][\sigma^{*2}]$$

$$E[R_T^*] = \frac{\sigma^*}{\sqrt{2\pi}}\left[-\exp\left(\frac{-x^2}{2\sigma^{*2}} \right)\Big|_0^\infty \right]$$

$$E[R_T^*] = \frac{\sigma^*}{\sqrt{2\pi}} = \frac{2\sigma^*}{2\sqrt{2\pi}} = \frac{1\sigma^*}{2\sqrt{2\pi}}[2\sigma\sqrt{T}]$$

If one sets the worst-case terminal credit-risk exposure at a 97.5 percent confidence level (or a 2σ, one-sided level of confidence) then

$$W_T^* = 2\sigma\sqrt{T}$$

Accordingly,

$$E[R_T^*] = \frac{1}{2\sqrt{2\pi}} \times W_T^*$$

Further, if the notional amount (N) is then multiplied by $E[R_T^*]$ and $W_T = W_T^* \times N,$, then

$$E[R_T] = \text{Expected terminal replacement cost} = E[R^*_T] \times N \cong \frac{W^*_T}{5} \times N = \frac{W_T}{5}\,^6$$

$$E\!\left[R_T\right] \cong \frac{FE}{3.33} \text{ since FE, called Fractional Exposure, is defined in this}$$

application as $\frac{2}{3}\,W_T\,^7$

Default Rates (DR)

Default rates are a critical second factor needed to calculate counterparty projected credit losses. Specifically, one needs to develop techniques to calculate the expected default-rate path and the probability distribution around the default-rate path (estimated by examining the probability distributions at specific points in the future). The family of default-rate probability distributions at specific points over the life of a transaction can be modeled through analyses of S&P or Moody's default-rate data. As pointed out earlier, one normally combines information gathered from agency data (e.g., corporate bond data) with an institution's proprietary default-rate data (e.g., loan data). One also analyzes credit spreads of securities (e.g., yields of specific securities over duration-equivalent risk-free securities) to generate a default-rate probability distribution.

These estimates of future default-rate probability distributions are calculated for each credit grade. The probability distribution of future default rates can be characterized by both an expected default rate (e.g., 0.05 percent) and a "worst-case" default rate (e.g., 1.05 percent). The difference between the worst-case default rate and the expected default rate is the unexpected default rate (i.e., 1 percent = 1.05 percent − 0.05 percent). Typically, as illustrated in Figure 13–22, the probability distribution is highly asymmetric. A worst-case default rate (e.g., the aforementioned 1.05 percent) would be structured so that one could say there is a prespecified probability (e.g., 2.5 percent) of exceeding the "worst-case" default rate. The probability density function, which describes the probability of default, varies over time. Clearly, the longer the maturity of the

---

[6] $5 \cong 2\sqrt{2\pi} = 5.013$

$$[7]\ \frac{W_T \times N}{5} = \frac{\dfrac{3}{2} \times \left[\dfrac{2}{3}\,W^*_T \times N\right]}{5} = \frac{\dfrac{3}{2} \times FE}{5} = \frac{FE}{(10/3)} \cong \frac{FE}{3.33}$$

FIGURE 13–22
Family of Default-Rate Probability Distributions

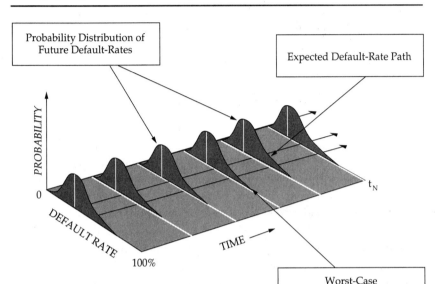

financial instrument, the greater the worst-case default rate. One needs the
marginal probability of default to calculate the projected year-by-year
expected loss. One can calculate the cumulative default probabilities
through appropriate perturbation of the CGRMU. As described earlier, if
one uses a CGRMU, then it can be shown that the results of repeated
perturbation of the CGRMU are consistent with published rating-agency
cumulative cohort default probabilities.

Recovery Rates (RR)

The third factor needed to calculate counterparty credit loss is the expected recovery-rate path (given default) and the probability distribution
around the expected recovery-rate path (estimated by examining the
probability distributions at specific points in the future). The family of
recovery-rate probability distributions may also be modeled through S&P

FIGURE 13–23
Family of Recovery-Rate Probability Distributions

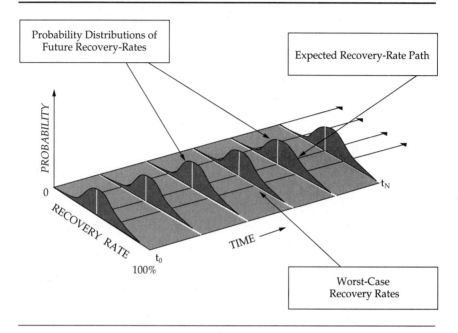

or Moody's recovery-rate data. Surveys on the recovery rate of senior corporate bonds that have defaulted indicate that they vary as a function of the pecking order (e.g., lien position) of the debt. For example, senior debt has a higher probability of recovery than junior (subordinated) debt.

As in the process for default data, one normally combines information gathered from agency recovery-rate data with an institution's proprietary recovery-rate data. One also obtains input from specialized legal counsel (or insolvency practitioners) in order to provide a recovery-rate probability distribution for each credit grade. These analyses, as illustrated in Figure 13–23, produce estimates of future recovery-rate probability distributions that vary as a function of time. Recovery-rate probability distributions, similar to default-rate probability distributions, do not typically follow a normal probability density function. One can use the recovery-rate probability distribution to determine an expected recovery, as well as worst-case recovery rates.

FIGURE 13–24
Credit-Loss Probability Distributions

CREDIT-RISK FACTORS   *TO PRODUCE COMBINED PROBABILITY*
MAY BE COMBINED...   *DISTRIBUTIONS OF FUTURE CREDIT-LOSSES*

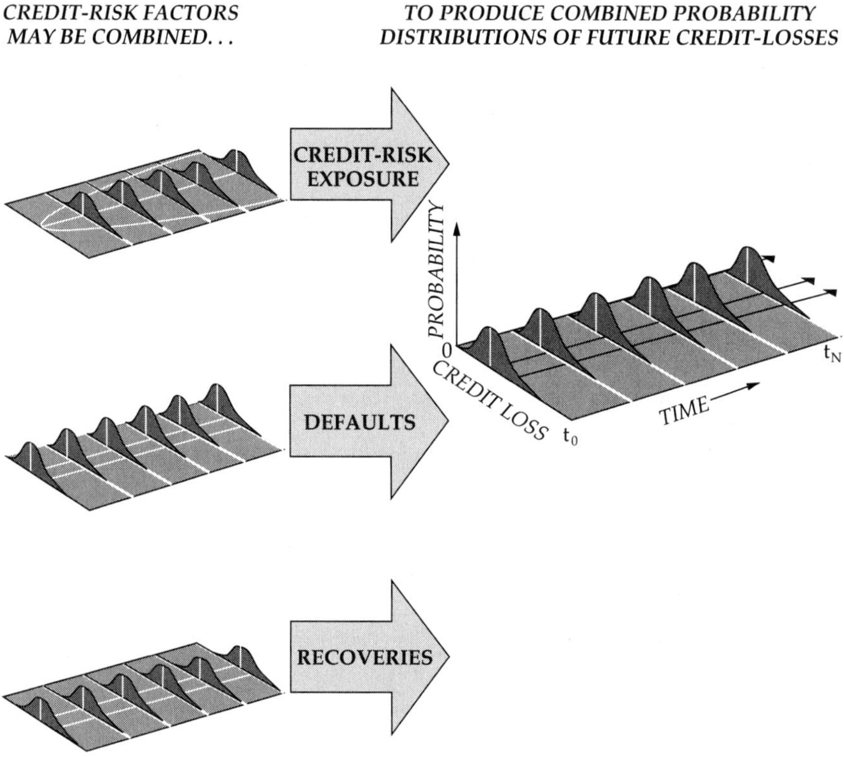

Combining The Three Factors (CE, DR, and RR)

The probability distributions of credit-risk factors (i.e., credit-risk exposure, default-rate, and recovery-rate data) can be combined, as illustrated in Figure 13–24, to produce a future credit-loss probability distribution. Observe that the combined probability distribution is asymmetric. Theoretically, one combines these three probability distributions to produce key components of the combined multivariate probability distribution by integrating across the combined function. For example, the expected credit loss at a given point in time equals

$$\iiint CE \times DR \times (1-RR) \times f(CE, DR, RR) \; dCE \; dDR \; dRR$$

(where CE denotes credit-risk exposure, DR the default rate, RR the recovery rate, and $\int$ (CE, DR, RR) the multivariate probability density function). In other words, one could calculate the expected credit loss from a multivariate options pricing framework (similar to the univariate expected credit-risk exposure calculation). Nevertheless, if one assumes (for illustrative purposes) statistical independence between CE and DR (as well as a zero-percent recovery rate) then one can multiply the average expected credit-risk exposure by the expected default rate to determine an expected loss. Furthermore, if one assumes that a certain percentage of the expected loss can be recovered (as well as statistical independence between RR, CE, and DR), then one can multiply this by 1 minus the expected recovery rate to obtain the expected loss.

If one utilizes a Monte Carlo simulation approach, then one first simulates an exposure from a credit-risk exposure probability distribution (given a default at a particular point in time). Second, one simulates from a default probability distribution (typically a binomial probability function with a single probability of default) whether or not the counterparty defaulted. Finally, assuming negligible recovery rates, one then summarizes the credit losses that occur across all points in time in the appropriate fashion.

TRANSLATING A FUTURE CREDIT LOSS PROBABILITY DISTRIBUTION INTO PROVISION AND ECONOMIC CAPITAL

Summary Credit-Loss Probability Distribution

One needs to combine probability distributions of future credit loss at various points over the life of a transaction, as illustrated in Figure 13–25, to produce a single summary credit loss probability distribution.

The single summary credit-loss probability distribution, as pointed out earlier, can be characterized by an average expected credit loss (L_E) and an average "worst-case" credit loss (L_W). The economic capital, defined as the difference between L_W and L_E ($L_c = L_W - L_E$), is equal to the average unexpected credit loss. Ideally, as discussed earlier, one needs to construct a cumulative probability density credit-loss distribution through integrating the multivariate probability density function such that the worst-case

FIGURE 13–25
Summary Credit-Loss Probability Distribution

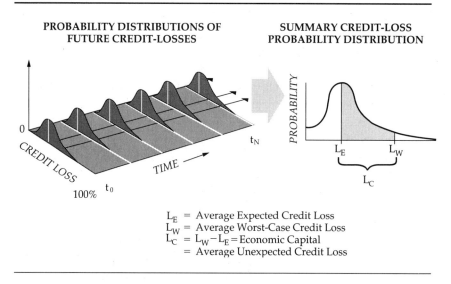

PROBABILITY DISTRIBUTIONS OF
FUTURE CREDIT-LOSSES

SUMMARY CREDIT-LOSS
PROBABILITY DISTRIBUTION

L_E = Average Expected Credit Loss
L_W = Average Worst-Case Credit Loss
L_C = $L_W - L_E$ = Economic Capital
    = Average Unexpected Credit Loss

credit loss over the time period is set to a desired worst-case probability of loss.

Combining the credit-risk exposure probability distribution with the probability distribution of default rates (net of recovery) yields the probability distribution of credit-risk loss. The probability distribution of credit loss can be manipulated to arrive at an expected loss and unexpected loss. For example, as illustrated in Figure 13–26, assume that the average expected credit-risk exposure for a derivative transaction is 100 million and that the expected probability of default is 1 percent. In our example, the expected credit loss of 1 million is calculated by multiplying the 1 percent expected probability of default (net of recoveries) by the average expected credit-risk exposure of 100 million to arrive at an expected credit loss of 1 million. Further, since the worst-case probability of default is 3 percent, then one can say that the worst-case credit loss is 3 million and therefore one would assign an unexpected loss (economic capital) of 2 million derived from the difference between the worst-case credit loss and the expected credit loss.

The probability of the potential unexpected credit loss (and the associ-

FIGURE 13–26
Calculating Economic Capital

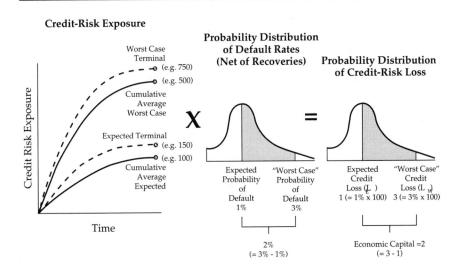

Note: Assumes Capital = Unexpected Loss

ated economic capital), as illustrated within the shaded region of Figure 13–27, is clearly a function of the confidence level set by policy. For example, a confidence level of 97.5 percent would call for less economic capital than a confidence level of 99 percent.

Let us return to the 1 million 3X6 FRA example. The analytical approach described herein utilizes the average expected credit-risk exposure (e.g., 480) multiplied by the difference between the worst-case default probability (e.g., 1.05 percent) and expected default probability (e.g., 0.05 percent) to arrive at L_C (e.g., 4.8).

The loan-equivalent approach of calculating the average expected credit-risk exposure and utilizing two default probabilities per credit grade is a proxy for utilizing more sophisticated approaches and has the virtue of facilitating the comparison to a loan product whose credit-risk exposure is assumed known. A more rigorous, though time-consuming approach would be to directly generate (through analytical, empirical, or simulation

FIGURE 13–27
Unexpected Credit Loss

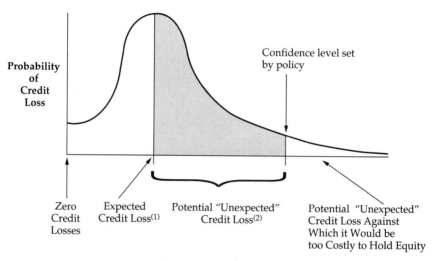

Note: (1) For which reserves should be held
      (2) For which capital should be held

techniques) the full distribution of credit losses, and then one can select the appropriate confidence interval percentile.

A third alternative approach would be to multiply a binary probability of default by the difference between the average worst-case credit-risk exposure and the average expected exposure to compute L_C. The third approach may not provide the same answer as the prior two approaches. For example, one can utilize the expected probability of default (e.g., 0.05 percent) multiplied by the difference between the 3X6 FRA's average worst-case credit-risk exposure (e.g., 2,400) and the average expected credit-risk exposure (e.g., 480) to arrive at the appropriate L_C calculation (e.g., 0.96). In any event, the basic idea of the best-practice approach is to ensure that the amount of economic capital is established based on a preset confidence level (e.g., 97.5 percent). The amount of unexpected credit loss (L_C) should be used to establish the projected amount of economic capital associated with the derivatives transaction.

The credit-grade-specific probability distributions of credit-risk loss for

FIGURE 13–28
Portfolio Effects

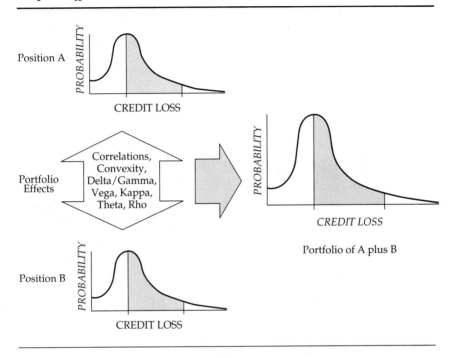

several positions may be combined into one overall probability distribution for the entire portfolio. Observe, as illustrated in Figure 13–28, that the credit-loss probability distribution for position A has been combined with the credit-loss probability distribution of position B to produce one combined credit-loss probability distribution for the portfolio consisting of positions A and B.

Stress Testing

One needs to relate the amount of economic capital not only to the risk determined from normal markets, but also to a portion of the risk derived from abnormal markets. If one allocates economic capital as a function of risk in normal markets, then one is assuming that economic capital is required only to cover the normal amount at risk. Distributions of credit-

FIGURE 13–29
Credit-Risk Stress Testing

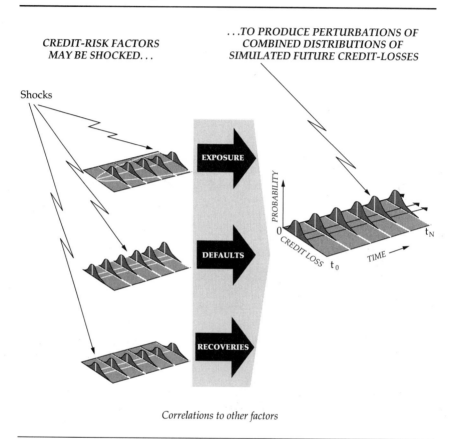

Correlations to other factors

risk factors, as illustrated in Figure 13–29, should be individually stressed (i.e., perform a series of "what if" analyses) to find boundaries of risk.

Further, as part of one's stress-testing approach, one should apply shocks (as illustrated in Figure 13–30) to the relationships between the default probabilities and other factors. For example, one should stress test the impact of a declining credit-grade risk rating.

FIGURE 13–30
Default-Rate Stress Testing

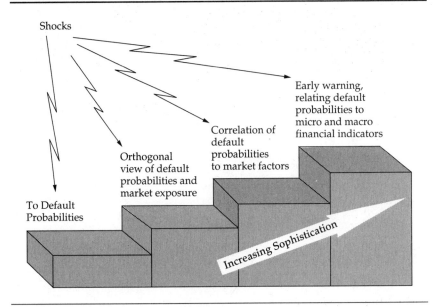

Pricing In Concentration Risk

Let's now turn to the important topic of how one prices in concentration risk. A typical derivatives dealer, as previously illustrated in Figure 13–2, has the potential for credit risk, market risk, liquidity risk, operational risk, regulatory risk, and human factor risk. Pricing risk becomes more complex as one manages risk simultaneously on a portfolio basis. One should not be concerned about taking on a prudent amount of any risk. Pricing these risks is part of the business. However one should establish a policy regarding overloading on any one risk as one manages more and more risk simultaneously.

For derivatives, as for most business, one also needs to consider the effect that economic risk, firm-specific, and systemic risks have on pricing a product. For example, as illustrated in Figure 13–31, the combination of recession and poor internal policies may induce a business failure. The domino effect of any business failing may in turn cause other businesses to

FIGURE 13–31
Domino Effects

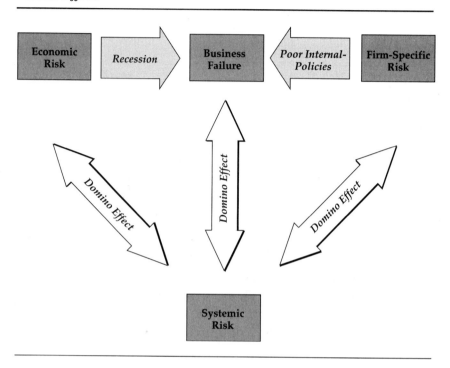

fail, which in turn may magnify any macro or firm-specific concentration risks.

      Market risk. Let us first turn our attention to loading up on market risk. Analyzing the degree of correlation between various derivative products is one key to limiting market risk concentration for a portfolio of derivatives. In order to manage and price a portfolio of derivatives one must pay close attention to the correlations between the risks. For example, it is self-evident that the worst-case market risk of two perfectly positively correlated swaps is the sum of the worst-case market risk of the two swaps. Conversely, if one swap has a perfect negative correlation with the other swap, then the worst-case market risks offset one another. In this case, the total portfolio worst-case market risk is zero. This would be the case when the cash flows of a fixed-rate receive swap were completely offset by those of a fixed-rate pay swap. If the worst-case market risk of one swap (e.g., say 4 million) is independent of the worst-case market risk of a second swap (e.g., say 3 million) then the worst-case market risk of the portfolio (e.g., say 5 million) is higher than any individual swap in the portfolio but less than the worst-case market risk of the sum of the two.[8]

Credit risk.   Now let us turn our attention to loading up on credit risk. The principles for derivative products are similar to the principles for loan products. Namely, one needs to avoid concentration to specific market sectors (e.g., real estate). Derivatives can over time diversify credit exposure through introduction of new high-quality counterparties such as governments, other financial institutions, and asset managers. Further, similar to market risk, one can explicitly measure the impact of correlation (between the credit-risk exposure of two products) on a portfolio of credit-risk exposures.[9]

Liquidity risk.   One also needs to consider concentration risk arising from liquidity risk. In this case, we are talking about market liquidity, which refers to the ease with which a position can be closed out or wound down (as opposed to funding liquidity, which refers to having sufficient cash flow to meet one's obligations). For example, one needs to avoid overloading on highly profitable but illiquid derivatives, such as swaps beyond 10 years. Swaps beyond 10 years are certainly appropriate. Nevertheless, one simply needs to avoid concentrating too much of one's swap book beyond 10 years.

Operation risk.   One very important aspect of operational risk is the risk arising from inappropriate mathematical models. Clearly, one needs to avoid using the wrong mathematical model. One also needs to avoid an excessive reliance on mathematical models that incorporate too

---

[8]Recall that if one defines the portfolio $RMU = K\sigma$ (where K represents the number of standard deviations associated with a desired statistical confidence level), then the RMU used to measure market risk for a portfolio is $RMU = \sqrt{RMU_X^2 + RMU_X^2 + 2\rho_{X,Y}RMU_XRMU_Y}$ (where $RMU_X = N_Xk\sigma_X$ and $RMU_Y = N_Yk\sigma_Y$). Accordingly $5 = \sqrt{4^2 + 3^2}$

[9]If one appropriately defines a transaction's credit-risk exposure in terms of a Credit-Risk Measurement Unit (CRMU), then one can measure credit-risk exposure for a portfolio by substituting CRMU terms for RMU terms in Footnote 8.

many complex and not well understood assumptions about market behavior. For example, certain markets—such as a portfolio of spot currency positions—do not require the use of complex models for either pricing or managing the risk. Other markets, however—such as a portfolio of long-dated options on long-dated interest-rate swaps (a derivative on a derivative)—make heavy use of mathematical models. Further, one needs to ensure that the required input parameters to any mathematical model are properly estimated.

Legal, regulatory, and human factor risk.   Next, let's turn to legal and regulatory risk. In many countries laws have not caught up with financial market developments. Derivatives have unique enforceability issues and in some countries those issues have not been resolved by either legislation or validation through the courts. Finally, let's turn to the human risk factor. Human factor risks may arise from an outright failure to acquire skilled personnel, but the more subtle point here is that hiring too few skilled people may lead to overreliance on the contribution of key individuals and increase the opportunity for breakdowns in the management of risk. Management can also pose human-factor risk. It's an age-old problem . . . when management gets gung-ho in a product or business they tend to take on bigger and bigger positions.

One can control the risk for which concentrations can arise on a one-by-one basis, but in summary, these risks are themselves very interdependent and must be managed and priced from an institution-wide perspective.

SUMMARY

One needs to develop best-practice methodologies for measuring credit risk and then prudently pricing the credit risk. One also needs to use these methodologies to set up appropriate reserves and to allocate economic capital as a function of risk.

As described earlier, best-practice policies, methodologies, and infrastructure, as illustrated in Figure 13–32, are the necessary three legs for building a first-class risk-management function. One should introduce measures of risk that can be used not only at the firmwide level but also at the deal level for both control and pricing purposes. RAROraC methodologies can be used to determine the price one should charge for taking a specific amount of risk. A RAROraC approach, as illustrated in Figure

FIGURE 13–32
Necessary Three Legs

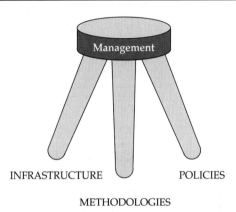

INFRASTRUCTURE   POLICIES

METHODOLOGIES

13–33, will ensure that different transactions can be analyzed on a comparable basis and will give the business manager an effective tool for obtaining the largest risk-adjusted return for a given level of risk. The risk-adjusted return, in the numerator of the RAROraC ratio, is calculated by subtracting the average expected credit loss from the projected net profit. The projected net profit is calculated by subtracting the projected net direct and indirect expenses from the direct and indirect revenues. The risk-adjusted capital in the denominator of the RAROraC ratio is calculated as a portfolio sum of the credit-risk economic capital plus market-risk economic capital (needed to support unexpected losses) plus economic capital attributed other risks. The economic capital attributed to other risks includes economic capital attributed to liquidity risk, operations risk, regulatory risk, human factor risk, and so on.

One must develop an institution-wide risk-management pricing framework, which includes having a common language of risk.[10] The language

---

[10]It is startling that there has not been a more aggressive push by the derivatives industry as a whole to develop what I call "Generally Accepted Risk Principles" (GARP). Establishing GARP could move us beyond the accounting focus of Generally Accepted Accounting Principles (GAAP) and the regulatory focus of "Regulatory Accounting Principles" (RAP) toward a common language reflecting a deeper economic reality. GAAP and RAP are no substitutes for GARP.

FIGURE 13–33
Components of RAROraC

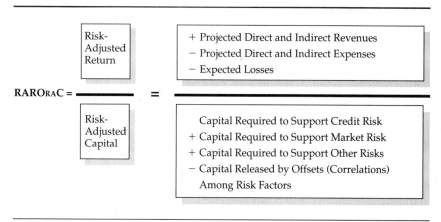

must accurately describe the multiple dimensions of risk, as illustrated in the front panel of Figure 13–34, as well as accommodate the complexity inherent in restructuring and repackaging risk. The institution also needs to ensure that its policies, methodologies, and infrastructure (as illustrated in the top panel of Figure 13–34) follow from and are compatible with the business strategies of direct risk-takers. The risk-management function needs to be independent but work in partnership with direct risk-takers. For example, as illustrated in the side panel of Figure 13–34, one needs to appreciate the impact that the measurement of risk will have on the ability of a direct risk-taker to compete on price. Direct risk-takers are responsible for understanding and pricing the risk they assume in pursuing their business activity. Direct risk-takers will only use measures of risk for pricing if they are based on best-practice methodologies with a low "ivory tower" content.

Derivatives is a client-driven business, which can increase an institution's long-term competitiveness and profitability, as well as expand and enhance its client relationships. Nevertheless, the derivatives business can expose one to the potential of a large loss. The risk-management function and the business need to work in partnership to implement best-practice pricing methodologies. One needs to ensure that these risks are not only priced, but also understood and controlled. These best-practice pricing methodologies need to measure risk in terms of a worst-case loss. Also,

FIGURE 13–34
Risk-Management Framework

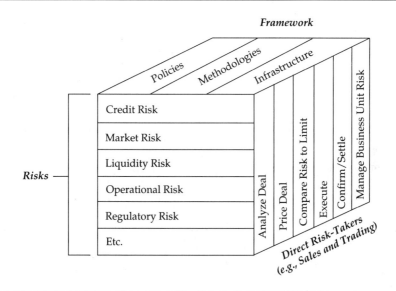

one needs to keep senior management informed of the overall pricing strategy. One needs to increase the level of understanding of the risks by senior management and the board through presentations and workshops.

The risk-management and business functions need to ensure that their pricing capabilities stay ahead of business expansion plans in order to ensure that the financial institution stays in control. There is little that can be done to guarantee absolutely against a loss, but one can price in risk so as to ensure that one considers the potential size of a loss. Ultimately, as illustrated in Figure 13–34, risks are interdependent and must be actively priced from a portfolio perspective.

As described earlier, one can look to and gain from CAPM for some key lessons for pricing in risk. For example, if one believes CAPM, then it follows that the market only pays (rewards) for "good risk." Accordingly, a reward-to-risk measurement framework can be designed based on the idea that the expected payoff (reward) can be determined (predicted) based on the degree to which one's portfolio generates good risk. The amount of good risk contained in the total risk can be separated from the

FIGURE 13–35
Integrated Risk-Management Process

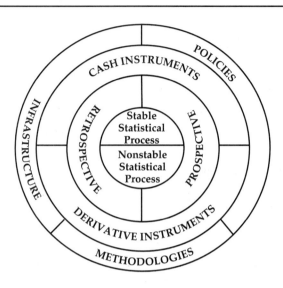

amount of "bad risk." The degree to which a portfolio adds value can be measured against a naive efficient portfolio that has the same risk as one's portfolio. Accordingly, a portfolio's required return can be determined by multiplying the portfolio's risk (σ_S) by the market price of the risk $[(R_M - R_S)/\sigma_M]$.

An institution should ensure that its incentive compensation system is tied in with its approach to recovering the cost of economic capital. One should solely price in the cost of economic capital as opposed to pricing in the cost of regulatory capital. Nevertheless, one should be aware of the difference between the cost of economic capital and regulatory capital. If one first allocates economic capital as a function of risk and then generates the cost of economic capital (by multiplying the economic capital by a desired hurdle rate) then one has implemented a pricing methodology that is broadly consistent with CAPM. Further, if one prices in the cost of economic capital as described above, then one is consistent with a RAROraC approach.

This chapter focused on the pricing of prospective (going forward) view of risk. Nevertheless, one also needs to analyze risk, as illustrated in

FIGURE 13–36
Pricing Epistemology

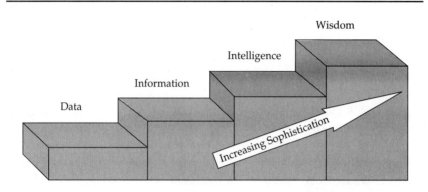

Figure 13–35 from a retrospective (going backward) point of view. Similarly, while the chapter focused on pricing derivatives risk, one needs to build up the capability of pricing risk for both cash and derivative instruments. One also needs to consider the impact of pricing in risk as a function of both stable and nonstable statistical processes.

Clearly, an institution needs to keep in mind that pricing in credit risk requires one to follow more than a blind, purely analytical pricing approach. For example, as illustrated in Figure 13–36, one would always need to translate raw market data into meaningful information necessary to have a well-rounded view of the competitive supply and demand factors that drive pricing decisions. Further, the information obtained from market data needs to be intelligently sorted so as to provide the appropriate interpretation of the insights gained from the facts contained in the information. Finally, one needs the wisdom to synthesize one's intelligence with the appropriate "gut feel" of an analytically derived optimal pricing strategy.

SUGGESTED READING

Allen, S. L., and A. D. Kleinstein. *Valuing Fixed Income Investments and Derivative Securities: Cash Flow Analysis and Calculations* (New York: Simon and Schuster, 1991).

Fabozzi, F. J. *Fixed Income Mathematics* (Chicago, IL: Probus Publishing Company, 1993).

Hull, J. C. *Options, Futures and Other Derivative Securities* (Englewood Cliffs, NJ: Prentice Hall International, Inc., 1993).

Marshall, J. F., and K. R. Kapner. *Understanding Swaps* (New York: John Wiley and Sons, Inc., 1993).

Ray, C. *The Bond Market: Trading and Risk Management* (Homewood, IL: Business One Irwin, 1993).

Schwartz, R. J., and C. W. Smith, Jr. *The Handbook of Currency and Interest Rate Risk Management* (New York: New York Institute of Finance, 1990).

Schwartz, R. J., and C. W. Smith, Jr. *Advanced Strategies in Financial Risk Management* (Englewood Cliffs, NJ: New York Institute of Finance, 1993).

Smith, C. W., and C. W. Smithson. *The Handbook of Financial Engineering* (New York: Harper and Row, 1990).

Weston, J. F., and T. E. Copeland. *Managerial Finance* (Orlando, FL: The Dryden Press, 1989).

Wunnicke, D., D. Wilson, and B. Wunnicke. *Corporate Financial Risk Management: Practical Techniques of Financial Engineering* (New York: John Wiley and Sons, Inc., 1992).

Chapter Fourteen

Structured Notes:
Mechanics, Benefits, and Risks

Christopher L. Culp
Competitive Enterprise Institute

Robert J. Mackay
Center for Study of Futures and Options Markets
Virginia Tech

INTRODUCTION

The widely publicized derivatives-related losses of Barings PLC, Orange County, Gibson Greetings, Procter & Gamble, Metallgesellschaft AG, and other corporations have been largely responsible for the definition of "derivatives" by the popular press as any seemingly complex financial transaction that has recently lost a lot of money. The result has been an unfortunate confusion about what derivatives are and how they differ from other financial transactions. Structured notes are one type of financial instrument tossed into this definitional stew. While structured notes do share some similarities with derivatives contracts—their value, in part, is indexed to some underlying asset, reference rate, or index—they are, in fact, fundamentally different products providing unique advantages to issuers and investors. The purpose of this chapter is to demystify structured notes by explaining in straightforward terms their mechanics, benefits, and risks.

The second section of this chapter defines structured notes—or, more generally, structured securities—and gives several specific examples to show the variety of structures embedded in these debt instruments. Next,

we present and evaluate the two principal advantages of structured securities to investors: improved management of financial risk and enhanced
yields. The following section, in turn, presents and evaluates the principal
advantages of structured securities to issuers: lower funding costs, diminished credit constraints, reduced agency costs, and favorable tax and
regulatory treatment. The next section presents some of the prudential
risk-management policies and procedures that should accompany either
the issue or purchase of structured products. The chapter's final section
offers some concluding observations.

THE MECHANICS OF STRUCTURED NOTES

What Are Structured Notes?

A structured note can be defined as a traditional debt instrument whose
coupon payments and/or principal value is linked to the value of some
underlying asset, reference rate, or index. Structured notes are also called
"hybrid debt instruments"[1] and "derivative securities."[2]

Structured securities are often confused with derivatives contracts, or
privately negotiated bilateral contracts deriving their value from some
underlying asset, reference rate, or reference. Some of the confusion
results because structured debt can actually be viewed from a cash-flow
perspective as a *combination* of a traditional debt instrument with a
derivatives contract. Indeed, issuers of structured securities often have the
alternative of simultaneously entering into a straight derivatives contract
and issuing a straight debt instrument rather than issuing the structured
security.[3]

There are at least three important distinctions, nonetheless, between
derivatives and structured securities. First, common derivatives contracts
such as swaps and forwards are typically off-balance-sheet contracts.
Structured securities, by contrast, are on-balance-sheet items. Second,
most structured securities are *securities* as defined by laws such as the

[1]Charles W. Smithson and Donald H. Chew, Jr., "The Uses of Hybrid Debt in Managing Corporate Risk," *Journal of Applied Corporate Finance* Vol. 4, No. 4 (Winter 1992).

[2]Global Derivatives Study Group, *Derivatives: Practices and Principles* (Washington, DC:
The Group of Thirty, 1993).

[3]For an explanation, see Christopher L. Culp, Dean Furbush, and Barbara T. Kavanagh,
"Structured Debt and Corporate Risk Management," *Journal of Applied Corporate Finance*, Vol.
7, No. 3 (Fall 1994).

1934 Securities Exchange Act. This legal classification implies that structured securities are often regulated quite differently from derivatives contracts, which are *not* securities. Examples of such regulatory differences will be discussed later.

Finally, structured securities can be viewed as a combination of a debt instrument and an embedded derivatives contract, with the debt serving to "collateralize" the derivatives. A derivatives transaction, by contrast, typically involves collateral only some of the time. Even then, because the credit exposure on derivatives is two-sided, collateral may be required by one *or both* counterparties. Structured notes, by contrast, involve an up-front purchase of a debt instrument by the investor, which is in effect pledged as collateral to cover losses, if any, on the embedded derivatives component of the structured note. These instruments, in other words, bundle capital-raising and risk-management functions in a single instrument and are thus fundamentally distinct from pure derivatives transactions.

The Components of Structured Notes

That structured debt instruments can be viewed, from a cash-flow perspective, as equivalent to straight debt plus a combination of derivatives contracts should be a concept already familiar to corporate finance practitioners. A typical convertible bond, for example, allows its holder to convert the bond into a specified number of common stock shares at a particular price if the stock price of the firm rises above some preset level. Convertible bonds can thus be viewed as a combination of straight bonds and an embedded derivatives contract called an "equity warrant."[4] While structured debt instruments are usually issued as single financial instruments, this example illustrates how they can be conceptually decomposed into two components: debt and derivatives.

Before proceeding with the analysis of structured debt, a brief review of the general types of debt instruments and derivatives contracts is a necessary first step.

Debt instruments. A loan is an obligation of a borrower to repay a fixed amount, called principal, to a lender on some later date. The principal may be fixed, as in a traditional commercial loan, or it may

---

[4]E. Philip Jones and Scott P. Mason, "Equity-Linked Debt," *Midland Corporate Finance Journal,* Vol. 3, No. 4 (Winter 1986); and John D. Finnerty, "The Case for Issuing Synthetic Convertible Bonds," *Midland Corporate Finance Journal,* Vol. 4, No. 3 (Fall 1986).

amortize at some agreed-upon rate or at the lender's discretion, as with typical mortgage loans. Some loans also require the borrower to make periodic interest payments before the principal is repaid. For fixed-rate loans, those interest payments are based on a fixed interest rate on which the borrower and lender agree.

For a traditional loan, the borrower and lender negotiate all the terms individually. Loans are therefore nonfungible—that is, they are bilateral contracts, which usually cannot be transferred by borrower or lender to another party without the counterparty's consent. A secondary market in loans, nonetheless, does exist in the form of the loan resale market.

A debt instrument is just a fungible loan. Rather than borrower and lender negotiating the terms, a borrower predefines the loan terms and issues the securities for investors to purchase. Because the terms of debt contracts within a particular issue are standardized, they can be more readily transferred or resold to another investor. Securities issued by institutions of high credit quality generally trade in relatively liquid secondary markets.

There are four general types of debt securities: principal-only or zero-coupon debt, level-coupon debt, amortizing debt, and floating-rate debt. The first type, a zero-coupon bond, has only a face value that is returned to investors at maturity.[5] The price paid by investors for zero-coupon securities is less than (i.e., at a discount to) the face value of the instrument. The second type, a level-coupon bond, pays agreed-upon amounts to investors at periodic dates called coupon dates *before* the instrument matures. The principal is returned to the purchaser of the security at maturity. The third type, an amortizing bond, has an agreed-upon schedule of generally level payments throughout the life of the securities. The level payments include scheduled payments of both interest and principal. The fourth type, a floating-rate bond, has variable coupon payments that are indexed to some reference rate, asset price, or index.

Cash-flow time lines for each of the types of bonds are shown in Figure 14–1. In this figure, FV is the face value, C is the level-coupon payment, A is the level-annuity payment, and $\tilde{R}_t$ is the floating-rate payment. P_B, P_{CB}, P_{AB}, and P_{FRB} represent the prices of the zero-coupon bond, the level-coupon bond, the amortizing bond, and the floating-rate bond, respec-

---

[5] The face value of a security corresponds to the principal of a loan, and in fact is often referred to as such.

FIGURE 14–1

Cash-Flow Time Lines for Types of Debt Instruments

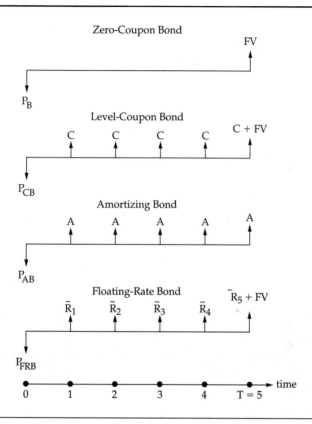

tively. T is the maturity date of the instrument. The cash-flow time lines are drawn from the perspective of the investor, since arrows pointing down indicate outflows of cash at particular points in time, while arrows pointing up indicate inflows of cash.

Borrowing can be on either unsecured or secured terms. In unsecured borrowing, firms issue debt securities, which are backed by nothing other than the ability of the issuing corporation to repay the loan. Secured borrowing, by contrast, involves debt instruments whose principal and interest payments are backed by some underlying pool of assets or receivables on which the lender has a claim if the issuer goes bankrupt.

Asset-backed securities may repay fixed principal and interest amounts based on the interest and principal received on an underlying pool of assets ranging from mortgages to credit-card receivables.[6] Secured lenders thus rely on both the creditworthiness of the borrower and the quality of assets underlying the debt security.[7]

Debt securities also differ in name and characteristics according to the type of issuer.

Corporate-issued debt securities. Commercial paper is unsecured short-maturity debt issued by corporations to finance expenditures on current operations or physical assets (e.g., plants and equipment). Most commercial paper matures roughly 30 days after it is issued, and firms rarely issue commercial paper beyond 270 days to maturity.[8]

Many corporate-issued debt securities (especially structured debt securities) are medium-term notes (MTNs or notes, for short).[9] MTNs initially arose as an outgrowth of the commercial paper market, with the exception being that firms went through the shelf registration process to register MTNs with the Securities and Exchange Commission (SEC) before issuance. At present, many MTNs extend from 9 months through 2–5 years to maturity. Longer-dated MTNs also exist, however, sometimes extending as far as 30 or more years to maturity. MTNs are also issued through the private placement process, in which buyers for the securities are pre-arranged, usually by an investment bank, before the security is issued.

---

[6]Charles Stone, Anne Zissu, and Jess Lederman, eds., *The Global Asset Backed Securities Market* (Chicago: Probus, 1993); and Barbara Kavanagh, Thomas Boemio, and Gerald A. Edwards, "Asset-Backed Commercial Paper Programs," *Federal Reserve Bulletin,* Vol. 78, No. 2 (February 1992).

[7]Other forms of borrowing are distinguished based on the priority the lender receives should the firm declare bankruptcy. Secured lenders always receive the highest priority, as specific assets have been pledged to back the loans. Senior debt provides lenders "me-first" treatment in the event the assets of a corporation not already pledged as collateral are liquidated to pay off the firm's creditors. Finally, subordinated debt provides lenders a *pro rata* share of the cash proceeds from liquidated assets after secured and senior lenders have been paid off.

[8]If an issue has a maturity of greater than 270 days, firms must register the issue with the Securities and Exchange Commission.

[9]Some interesting, albeit now dated, aggregate statistics of the MTN market are presented in Leland Crabbe, "Corporate Medium-Term Notes," *Journal of Applied Corporate Finance,* Vol. 4, No. 4 (Winter 1992). Comparable data for the structured note market is presented in Leland Crabbe and Joseph Argilagos, "Anatomy of the Structured Note Market," *Journal of Applied Corporate Finance,* Vol. 7, No. 3 (Fall 1994).

Corporate debt securities may be "callable"—i.e., redeemable by the borrower after the occurrence of a specific event, such as an interest-rate decrease, at a particular price. Noncallable securities, by contrast, have absolutely fixed terms to maturity. Some debt securities are also "putable,"—i.e., can be redeemed at the lender's discretion after a specific event such as an interest-rate increase.

Bank-issued retail debt securities. Commercial banks and thrifts frequently issue debt securities as well. But beyond simply issuing commercial paper and MTNs to finance their business operations, a variety of depository instruments have been developed and marketed as *retail* debt securities. Certificates of deposit (CDs) are fixed-maturity loans that individuals and corporations make to commercial banks and thrifts for a repayment of interest and principal. Unlike some debt instruments, interest is accrued over the life of the CD and repaid to the investor with principal at maturity, which can range from two weeks to five years or longer.[10] Similar to CDs, banks also borrow using deposit notes and bank notes. These securities are essentially term deposits or portfolios of term deposits with generally greater maturities and face values than typical CDs. Deposit notes and bank notes generally do not require the payment of deposit-insurance premiums or adherence to reserve requirements.

U.S. banks also offer Eurodollar deposits, or deposits issued by foreign branches of U.S. banks denominated in U.S. dollars. An important interest-rate index, frequently referred to below, is the London Interbank Offered Rate (LIBOR). That rate represents the rate at which banks borrow from one another on wholesale terms using Eurodollar deposits.

U.S. treasury debt securities. Debt securities are issued by the Department of the Treasury of the United States government for public finance. Since their distinguishing characteristics include relatively high liquidity and very high credit quality, Treasuries generally are the benchmark from which other debt securities are priced. The price of a corporate note on the secondary market, for example, may be quoted as a spread over the same-maturity Treasury security, where the spread is primarily a function of credit and liquidity risk differences. All Treasury securities have nonamortizing.

---

[10]CDs are term deposits with a fixed maturity, whereas a demand deposit is a loan to a bank for an amount of time determined by the lender.

Treasury bills are zero-coupon Treasury securities that are generally issued with 3, 6, or 12 months to maturity. By convention, Treasury notes are level-coupon debt securities issued by the Treasury with 2 to 10 years to maturity, while Treasury bonds are level-coupon debt securities with more than 10 years to maturity.

In the early 1980s, major broker-dealers initiated programs in which they purchased Treasury notes and bonds, posted them as collateral for a trust, and issued debt securities from the trust based *separately* on the interest and principal received on the underlying Treasury securities. These debt securities quickly became known as "zeros," because they represented claims on the principal-only components of the decomposed Treasury securities. Interest-only Treasury securities also arose, leading the Treasury department to classify these securities as part of the STRIPS program, or Separate Trading of Registered Interest and Principal of Securities, in 1984. The zero-coupon component of STRIPS ultimately became controlled by the Federal Reserve Board, and zeros are now considered standard Treasury securities even though they are not actually issued directly by the Treasury department.

Agency and municipal securities. A variety of other governmental entities issue debt securities. Agency securities include debt securities issued by a group of government-sponsored enterprises (GSEs). GSEs generally arise from decisions by the federal government that the volume or terms of credit allocated to a particular sector of the economy is too low.[11]

The Federal Home Loan Bank (FHLB) system, for example, is the system of 12 regional federally sponsored banks that stand behind the savings and loan and thrift industry and now banks and credit unions. The primary debt securities issued by the FHLB are discount notes, with maturities of up to one year, and bonds that have maturities of one year or more. Both types of instruments are issued as a joint obligation by the 12 member banks of the system.

The Federal National Mortgage Association (FNMA), called Fannie Mae, was set up in 1938 by Congress to facilitate mortgage lending.

---

[11]A variety of GSEs, not discussed in this chapter, such as the Farm Credit Administration, also issue structured notes to finance their operations.

Fannie Mae issues various debt securities, including discount notes and debentures. The notes are debt securities with from 30 days up to a year to maturity, are noncallable, and are zero-coupon securities. The debentures are long-dated securities that pay interest periodically.

The Student Loan Market Association (SLMA), or Sallie Mae, serves a function similar to the FHLB system and to Fannie Mae, facilitating capital flows to a particular sector of the economy. For Sallie Mae's case, facilitating educational loans to students is the objective. Sallie Mae issues securities, including structured notes, primarily to finance its operations.

The Government National Mortgage Association (GNMA), or Ginnie Mae, is another GSE designed to facilitate mortgage lending. GNMA actually issues few securities to finance its own operations. Instead, GNMA issues securities called "pass-through" securities, which represent securitized claims on underlying mortgage pools. These securities are intended to promote mortgage lending by transforming mortgages into fungible and more-liquid assets through the securitization process; they are *not* mechanisms by which GNMA finances itself as a GSE. As a result, they are not analyzed in this chapter.

Another GSE that does issue securities to finance itself is the Federal Home Loan Mortgage Corporation (FHLMC), or Freddie Mac. Freddie Mac issues a variety of debt securities, many of which are similar to those issued by Fannie Mae for financing purposes. Other securities issued by Freddie Mac include pass-through securities similar to those issued by GNMA to liquefy the market for securitized mortgage obligations.

The credit quality of securities issued by GSEs is relatively high, as they are implicitly backed by the U.S. government. These securities, however, are called as a group "agency securities" because GSE credit ratings are, in fact, technically independent of the U.S. Treasury.

In addition to securities issued by federally sponsored GSEs, municipalities also issue debt securities of their own.

Derivatives contracts. Derivatives contracts come in many shapes, sizes, and flavors. Just as structured debt can be decomposed into debt and derivatives components, so, too, can derivatives be broken down into basic elements: forwards and options. A forward contract is an agreement between two parties to exchange an asset at a future date for a prespecified price or settle the difference in value with cash. Forward contracts can thus take two basic forms: physically settled and cash-settled.[12] In a physically settled gold forward contract, for example, a buyer (the "long") might contract with a seller (the "short") for the future purchase of 100 troy ounces of gold at $400/oz. If the price of gold is above $400/oz when the forward contract matures, the long or forward purchaser makes a profit, whereas a decline in the spot price of gold will force the forward purchaser to buy gold at the higher, pre-agreed amount, leading to a loss. The payoff to the short or seller is the opposite of the long's payoff.

In a cash-settled forward, two counterparties merely agree to exchange cash flows on a future date. The cash flows, in fact, may be netted with one party paying the difference. A forward-rate agreement (FRA), for example, obligates one counterparty—the fixed-rate payor—to make a cash payment at a prespecified settlement date based on an agreed-upon fixed rate of interest and receive a cash payment based on a floating rate of interest, such as 6-month LIBOR. The floating rate is set on an agreed date in the future (e.g., three months from contract initiation). The principal of the FRA serves only as a basis for calculating the interest-based cash flow actually exchanged and is not itself exchanged between the parties. As a result, the principal is referred to as "notional."

Cash-flow time lines for various types of forward contracts—foreign-exchange, commodity, and interest-rate forwards—are shown in Figure 14–2. In these transactions, as in most derivatives contracts, no cash is exchanged at initiation of the contract. Performance is thus deferred until contract maturity. In Figure 14–2, for example, $Y are exchanged for £X at maturity of the foreign exchange forward; $Y is exchanged for X barrels of oil at maturity of the commodity forward; and a payment based on a fixed rate, $\overline{R}$, is exchanged for a payment based on a floating rate, $\tilde{R}$, at maturity of the interest-rate forward. As a result of deferred performance, credit risk is two-sided, meaning that the contract can be either an asset or a liability for a particular counterparty, depending on the movement in the

---

[12]Related to the forward contract is a futures contract. Because futures are exchange-traded, they cannot be directly combined with debt to make structured securities. Futures are therefore not addressed in this chapter. Futures and options contracts can nevertheless be used to hedge and synthetically create structured notes. They also play an important role in the relative valuation of certain structured notes. For good discussions of futures, see Todd E. Petzel, *Financial Futures and Options* (New York: Quorum, 1989); and Charles W. Smithson and Clifford W. Smith, Jr., *Managing Financial Risk* (Chicago: Irwin Professional Publishing, 1995).

FIGURE 14–2
Cash-Flow Time Lines for Currency-, Commodity-, and Interest-Rate Forwards

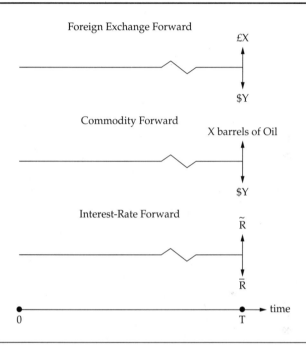

underlying. The payoff profile for a long forward contract is shown in Figure 14–3.

The other elemental building block of derivatives is an option—i.e., a derivatives contract that gives its buyer the right *but not the obligation* to purchase or sell an asset or cash flow for a specified price on or before a specified date. In return for agreeing to honor the buyer's option, an option seller or "writer" collects an up-front premium. A call option is an option to buy an asset, whereas a put option is an option to sell an asset. European options allow their holder to exercise their right to purchase or sell the underlying asset only on the specific date when the contract matures, whereas American options can be exercised at any time before or at maturity. As with forwards, options can be physically settled or cash-

FIGURE 14–3
Payoff Profiles for a Long Forward Contract

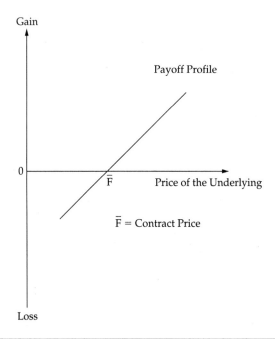

A Long Forward Contract

settled. The payoff profile at expiration for a long call option is shown in Figure 14–4 as an example.

Because all derivatives can be decomposed into combinations of forwards and options, Smithson has aptly dubbed these elemental derivatives "LEGOs®," or the building blocks of derivatives.[13] A swap contract, for example, is a popular type of derivatives contract (marketed as a single

---

[13]Charles W. Smithson, "A LEGO® Approach to Financial Engineering: An Introduction to Forwards, Futures, Swaps, and Options," *Midland Corporate Finance Journal,* Vol. 4, No. 4 (Winter 1987). See also Clifford W. Smith, Jr., and Charles W. Smithson, "Financial Engineering: An Overview," in *The Handbook of Financial Engineering*, ed. by Clifford W. Smith, Jr., and Charles W. Smithson (New York: Harper Business, 1990); and Smithson and Smith (1995), *op. cit.*

FIGURE 14–4
Payoff Profile at Expiration for a Long Call Option

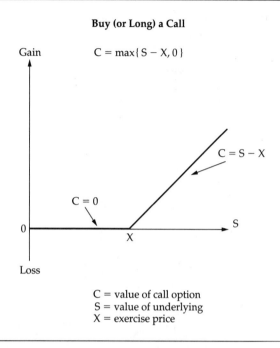

Buy (or Long) a Call

Gain $C = \max\{S - X, 0\}$

$C = S - X$

$C = 0$

0
          X

                                S

Loss

C = value of call option
S = value of underlying
X = exercise price

financial contract) between two counterparties that agree to exchange cash flows on future settlement dates. A fixed-for-floating interest-rate swap is an agreement in which one party agrees to make fixed interest payments based on some notional principal in return for receiving floating payments (based, say, on LIBOR) from the swap counterparty. In terms of net cash flows, a swap can thus be viewed as a portfolio of FRAs, with each settlement date in the swap corresponding to the settlement date of each component FRA. Figure 14–5 shows how an interest-rate swap's cash flows can be decomposed into the cash flows defined by a bundle of FRAs. The cash flows for the "receive floating/pay fixed" counterparty to an interest-rate swap are shown by cash-flow time line A. The swap's fixed payments at each settlement date, $t = 1, 2, \ldots, T$, are based on $\overline{R}$ while the floating receipts are based on the corresponding floating $\tilde{R}_t$. The cash

FIGURE 14–5
An Interest-Rate Swap As a Portfolio of Forward Rate Agreements

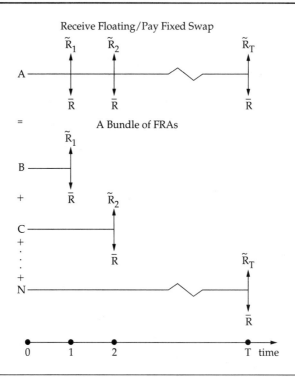

flows from the swaps (i.e., A) are replicated by the cash flows from the bundle of FRAs (i.e., B + C + ... + N).

Because of the focus here on structured securities, it is worth noting that many derivatives contracts (e.g., swaps) can also be decomposed into a portfolio of debt securities that replicates the net cash flows. A receive floating/pay fixed interest-rate swap, for example, is equivalent to a securities portfolio that involves lending at a floating rate while borrowing at a fixed rate. This relation is depicted in Figure 14–6. As before, cash-flow time line A represents the receive floating/pay fixed swap. Time line B shows the cash flows from a floating-rate loan issued at par—i.e., with a price at issue equal to the face value, FV, of the loan. Time line C shows the cash flows from a fixed-rate borrowing issued at par. The prices or face

FIGURE 14–6
An Interest-Rate Swap as a Portfolio of Loans

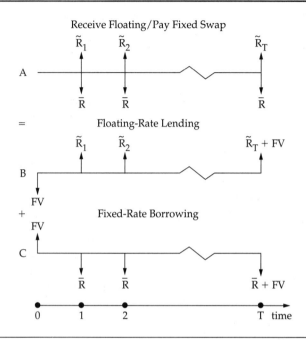

values of the two bonds cancel at origination of an at-the-money swap. The cash-flow equivalence between a swap and a portfolio of loans has important implications for the pricing and hedging of both swaps and structured notes.

An example of an option composed of these derivatives building blocks is a LIBOR cap. A cap is an option marketed as a single financial product, which pays its holder the excess of LIBOR over a fixed interest rate (i.e., the cap) on several settlement dates in the future. A cap can thus be viewed as a portfolio of caplets—i.e., a portfolio of individual interest-rate options. Similarly, a swaption (i.e., an option on a swap) can be viewed as an option on a bundle of forwards.

With these building blocks in hand, the analysis can now turn to the construction of structured notes. For purposes of exposition, structured notes are divided into interest-rate-indexed notes and notes indexed to currency, commodity, or equity prices and indices.

Interest-Rate-Indexed Structured Notes

Most structured notes are issued by corporations and GSEs, such as the Federal Home Loan Bank System, Fannie Mae, and Sallie Mae. The Federal Home Loan Bank System, in particular, is the largest issuer of structured notes in the world. Structured notes issued by these entities generally fall into the MTN category, with more than a year to maturity.[14] They are usually coupon-bearing instruments, and most structured notes have their coupon payments indexed to some underlying asset price or reference rate. Some notes also involve principal-indexing. The most important types of interest-rate-indexed structured notes are analyzed in this section.[15]

Floating rate notes (FRNs).   A floating-rate note (FRN) is a structured note in which the borrower's interest payments are indexed or linked to a floating reference interest rate or index of interest rates. FRNs have coupon payments (usually semiannual) that are unknown when the security is first issued; the rate resets on each coupon date according to some specified formula involving the reference rate or rates. A typical FRN has coupon payments based on a spread over LIBOR, such as 6-month LIBOR + 25 basis points (bp).

The cash flows from an FRN can be replicated by a portfolio of other financial instruments—a fixed-rate coupon bond plus an interest-rate swap. Consider two possible financing strategies. First, suppose a firm issues a 2-year FRN with coupon payments equal to 6-month LIBOR + 25 bp. Alternatively, suppose the firm issues a two-year bond with face value FV and fixed semiannual coupons of C, and then enters into a two-year interest-rate swap contract with notional principal FV. In the swap, the issuer of the bonds agrees to pay 6-month LIBOR + 25 bp semiannually, in return for receiving semiannual fixed interest payments

---

[14]Occasionally reference is made to corporate *bonds*, as distinct from corporate notes. This is a terminological difference alone for corporate and agency issues, however, and the terms can be considered functionally equivalent.

[15]The list of instruments included is far from exhaustive. For discussions of other innovative structured notes, see John D. Finnerty, "An Overview of Corporate Securities Innovation," *Journal of Applied Corporate Finance,* Vol. 4, No. 4 (Winter 1992); Gary L. Gastineau, *Dictionary of Financial Risk Management* (Chicago: Swiss Bank Corporation and Probus, 1992); and Vol. 4, No. 4 (Winter 1992) of the *Journal of Applied Corporate Finance.* Gastineau, in particular, provides a useful road map for navigating the confusing terminology of structured debt issues.

FIGURE 14–7
A Floating-Rate Note As a Fixed-Rate Note and an Interest-Rate Swap

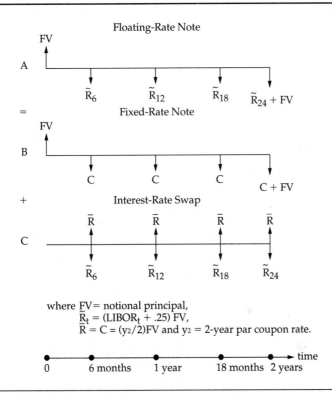

where FV = notional principal,
$\tilde{R}_t = (LIBOR_t + .25)\ FV$,
$\bar{R} = C = (y_2/2)FV$ and y_2 = 2-year par coupon rate.

C. The fixed interest payments C made in the swap cancel with the coupons received on the fixed-rate bond, and the resulting payments made by the bond issuer are simply LIBOR + 25 bp as a percent of FV.[16] The cash flows from the fixed-coupon bond and the swap replicate the FRN. (See Figure 14–7.)

The equivalence between issuing an FRN and issuing a fixed-rate note while entering into a receive fixed/pay floating swap has important implications for the valuation and hedging of structured notes. First, arbitrage

---

[16]The fixed interest payments C cancel because both the level-coupon bond and the fixed rate in the swap are priced off the 2-year par coupon yield curve.

opportunities will be available if the price of the FRN is out of line with the pricing of the fixed-rate note and the swap. To achieve floating-rate financing, in other words, it may be less costly to issue fixed-rate debt and swap into floating. Second, the availability of swaps (or derivatives more generally) means that the issuer can issue the type of debt most preferred by investors, or a particular investor, and then enter into a swap to achieve the desired form of financing. Put another way, issuing an FRN and entering into a pay fixed/receive floating interest-rate swap results in "synthetic" fixed-rate funding.[17]

Inverse FRNs.   Inverse floating-rate notes were first issued in 1986 by Sallie Mae under the name yield-curve notes.[18] A summary announcement for a more recent offering by Sallie Mae is shown below. Those securities are also called "bull floaters," because of their appeal to investors bullish on bond prices (i.e., expecting bond prices to rise, hence interest rates to fall).[19] The floating coupon payment at any time t on an inverse FRN, or "inverse floater," can be expressed as

$$C_t = \text{Max} \; [\overline{K} - \tilde{R}_t, \; 0]$$

where $\overline{K}$ is a fixed percent times the face value and $\tilde{R}_t$ is the floating reference rate at time t times the face value. The minimum coupon is generally zero, although structures involving a positive minimum coupon are also offered. In the announcement shown below, $\overline{K}$ equals 15.10% times the FV and $\tilde{R}_t$ equals 6-month LIBOR times the FV. The minimum coupon is zero.

For valuation (or price comparison) and hedging purposes, an inverse FRN can be viewed as a combination of an FRN with face value FV, *two* interest-rate swaps, each with notional principal FV, and an interest-rate cap. Suppose Sallie Mae issues an FRN with face value FV and semiannual coupon payments equal to $\tilde{R}_t$. Sallie Mae might then combine the

---

[17]This can be demonstrated with some simple financial arithmetic. In terms of using Figure 14–7, subtracting C (i.e., the interest-rate swap) from both sides of the equation results in A – C = B, where –C is the interest-rate swap with the cash flows reversed, a pay fixed/receive floating swap. See Donald C. Smith, "The Arithmetic of Financial Engineering," *Journal of Applied Corporate Finance*, Vol. 1., No. 4, 1989.

[18]J. Ogden, "An Analysis of Yield Curve Notes," *Journal of Finance* (March 1987).

[19]Donald C. Smith, "The Pricing of Bull and Bear Floating Rate Notes: An Application of Financial Engineering," *Financial Management*, Vol. 17, No. 4 (1988).

$150,000,000

SallieMae

Student Loan Marketing Association

Yield Curve Notes Due 1990

Interest on the Yield Curve Notes due 1990 will accrue from April 11, 1986 and is
payable semi-annually in arrears on each April 11 and October 11, commencing
October 11, 1986, at a rate for the Initial Interest Period of 3.50% per annum and
thereafter at a floating rate of 15.10% per annum minus the arithmetic mean of the
London interbank offered rates for six-month Eurodollar deposits ("LIBOR")
prevailing two Business Days before the beginning of each Interest Period. Interest
will be computed on the basis of a 365- or 366-day year, as the case may be, and
the actual number of days in the applicable Interest Period.

FRN with *two* interest-rate swaps, each of which requires it to pay $\overline{R}$ while
receiving $\tilde{R}_t$ on a notional principal value of FV.[20] Again, $\overline{R}$ is determined
by the par coupon yield for the maturity of the swaps. The resulting
coupon payment Sallie Mae makes is $\overline{K} - \tilde{R}_t$ equal to $2\overline{R} - \tilde{R}_t$ semiannually. If interest rates fall (rise), the actual coupon paid rises (falls). Because
the minimum coupon is zero, Sallie Mae has also sold the investors an out-
of-the-money interest-rate cap struck at $2\overline{R}$. The equivalence between
issuing an inverse FRN and issuing an FRN while entering into two swaps
and selling a cap is illustrated in Figure 14–8.

As mentioned in the case of the FRN, these types of equivalence
relations are useful for both valuation and hedging (or financing)
purposes.[21] By issuing an inverse FRN and then entering into two
receive fixed/pay floating swaps and buying a cap, for example, Sallie
Mae can create a "synthetic" FRN. In some situations, several of
which will be discussed below, the "synthetic" FRN can provide a
lower funding cost.

---

[20]The issuer might also have entered into a single swap with notional principal 2FV.

[21]Jacob Navon, "Structured MTN's: Adding Value Using Embedded Derivatives" in *Advanced
Interest Rate and Currency Swaps*, Ravi Dattatreya and Kensuke Hotta, eds. (Chicago, IL: Probus
Publishing Company, 1994) for an analysis of how this relationship can be used by investors to
analyze how competitively the note is priced.

FIGURE 14–8

An Inverse FRN as an FRN, a Swap, and a Cap

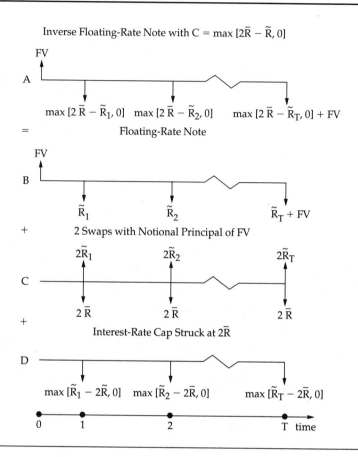

Inverse Floating-Rate Note with C = max [2$\bar{R}$ − $\tilde{R}$, 0]

Levered floaters and levered inverse floaters. Levered FRNs and inverse FRNs are structured so that the coupon payment changes more rapidly than the underlying interest rate changes. "Bear floaters" are an example of levered FRNs. A bear floater is so named because investors with a bearish sentiment about bond prices (i.e., expectation of falling bond prices, hence, rising interest rates) find them appealing. The first issuer of bear floaters is unknown, but at least one source suggests these instruments were first offered by Mellon Bank in 1986, just after the first

Sallie Mae issue of an inverse floater. Mellon Bank's bear floater was a three-year floating-rate CD with a coupon formula that paid investors twice LIBOR less a fixed 9.12 percent.[22] Although a bear floater resembles a simple FRN in that the coupon payments rise with market rates, the coupon payments rise *faster* than LIBOR. In the Mellon Bank issue, for example, the "leverage" factor was 2, so coupon payments increased twice as rapidly as LIBOR.

In principle, a levered inverse floater is similar to a levered floater. The issuer simply chooses a leverage factor and multiplies the floating portion of the coupon payment by that factor. A levered inverse floater with a leverage factor of 2 and a minimum coupon of zero would pay a coupon at time t equal to

$$C_t = \text{Max } [\overline{K} - 2\tilde{R}_t, \, 0]$$

where $\overline{K}$ is a fixed percent times the face value and $\tilde{R}_t$ is the floating reference rate at time t times the face value.

That levered floaters and levered inverse floaters can be decomposed into straight debt plus a bundle of derivatives contracts is evident from an example. Suppose an issuer offers an inverse floater that pays investors a coupon that declines twice as fast as LIBOR and has a minimum coupon of zero. Alternatively, the firm could issue FRNs with face value FV and enter into *three* interest-rate swaps, paying a fixed rate of $\overline{R}$ and receiving a floating rate of $\tilde{R}_t$ on a notional principal of FV. (Equivalently, it could enter into a single fixed-for-floating swap with notional value 3FV.) Because the minimum coupon on the levered inverse FRN being replicated is zero, the issuer would also sell an interest-rate cap struck at $3\overline{R}$. The issuer's net payments from the FRN, swaps, and cap are given by

$$\text{Max } [3\overline{R} - 2\tilde{R}_t, \, 0]$$

This portfolio then results in a "synthetic" levered inverse FRN with the same stream of coupon payments as the structured note.

Range notes/accrual notes/corridor notes. A range note is a structured note that pays an above-market interest rate when a reference rate, such as LIBOR, falls within a specified band and pays zero otherwise. Also known as corridor notes or accrual notes, these innovative debt

---

[22]D. Smith (1988), *op. cit.*

TABLE 14-1
Paribas Capital Markets' 2-Year Range MTN

Reference Ranges		Coupon Payment	
Coupon Period	LIBOR (%)	Time in Range (% days)	Spread Over 2-yr Treasury (%)
1	3.25–4.00	100	1.35
2	3.50–4.5625	95	1.08
3	3.75–5.00	90	0.80
4	3.75–5.3125	85	0.53
		80	0.25
		75	−0.02
		70	−0.30

instruments have been issued by the Kingdom of Sweden, Landesbank Hessen-Thuringen, Swedish Export Credit Corporation, the World Bank, and numerous commercial and merchant banks.[23]

To take a specific example, consider a two-year accrual MTN issued by Paribas Capital Markets in 1993.[24] The Paribas MTN paid a semiannual coupon whose amount was determined not just by LIBOR, but specifically by the *number of days* in the six-month period in which LIBOR fell within a prescribed range. If LIBOR fell within the prescribed range every day during any one of the four coupon-periods, the note paid a coupon of 1.35 percent over the 2-year constant-maturity Treasury (CMT) rate, where the two-year CMT rate is the rate on a Treasury note with exactly two years to maturity. The coupon payments on the Paribas MTN are shown in the extract from the offering announcement shown in Table 14-1.

Even though the coupon payments are based on a spread over the 2-year CMT rate, the level of *LIBOR* determines whether or not the note pays a coupon. Range notes are also often indexed to a CMT rate instead.[25]

---

[23]Charles W. Smithson, *Managing Financial Risk: 1995 Yearbook* (Princeton, NJ: Chase Manhattan Bank, 1995); and William Falloon, "Fairway to Heaven," *Risk,* Vol. 6, No. 12 (December 1993).

[24]Falloon, *op. cit.,* and Culp, Furbush, and Kavanagh, *op. cit.*

[25]Falloon, *op. cit.*

The cash flow of a range note can be replicated by a portfolio of zero-coupon bonds and "digital options"—i.e., call (put) options, which pay either nothing or a fixed amount when the underlying interest rate is above (below) the strike rate. The payout on an in-the-money digital call option, for example, does not change as the underlying interest rate rises, whereas the payout on a standard call option would rise with the underlying interest rate.

Investors in range notes are effectively writing the issuer digital options on the underlying reference rate, as the first coupon period in the Paribas accrual note illustrates. Supposing that there are 180 days in that period and the investor has written Paribas Capital Markets 180 digital put-options on LIBOR with a strike rate of 3.25 percent. If LIBOR is above 3.25 percent, the investor receives a fixed 1.35 percent over the 2-year CMT rate. If LIBOR is below 3.25 percent, the investor receives nothing. The investor has also written 180 call options on LIBOR to Paribas with a strike rate of 4 percent, receiving payments of 1.35 percent over the 2-year CMT rate only if LIBOR falls below the strike rate of the options.

Step-up bonds. A step-up bond is a structured note with two types of contractually specified fixed coupon rates: a low rate during an initial period and one or more higher "stepped-up" rates during subsequent periods. Step-up bonds are noncallable by the issuer during the initial, low-coupon period but callable during later periods.

Step-up bonds can be viewed as traditional fixed-rate bonds with embedded call options written on the reference index rate. Suppose, for example, that a step-up bond pays an initial coupon of C_1 during the noncallable period and a higher coupon C_2 during the callable step-up period. Consider an issuer who can borrow at LIBOR. An investor in this issuer's step-up bond effectively writes the issuer a European-style call option on LIBOR with a strike price of C_2, and a maturity or expiration date equal to the end of the noncall period. The investor receives C_1 during the initial period, and also receives a higher (but less than market) yield if the bond is not called. If the bond issues at par, the investor thus typically earns an above-market yield during the noncall period. This above market yield is the *de facto* premium the investor collects from selling the embedded call option to the issuer.

Dual-indexed FRNs. A dual-indexed FRN is a structured note whose coupon payments are based on two reference interest rates. The reference rates underlying many dual-indexed notes are LIBOR and a CMT rate. An example of a dual-indexed bond is shown in the summary offering notice for the Federal Home Loan Bank's (FHLB) "Dual Indexed Consolidated Bonds." The FHLB's bonds pay investors the *difference* between the 10-year CMT rate plus a spread and 6-month LIBOR. The spread increases over time according to specified schedules.

OFFERING NOTICE

FEDERAL HOME LOAN BANKS
$100,000,000 DUAL INDEXED CONSOLIDATED BONDS

Non-Callable
Date of Issue September 30, 1993   Series E-2005
Maturity September 30, 2005
Interest payable March 30 and September 30
Interest rate based on 10-Year CMT Index and LIBOR Index

The Bonds are Joint and Several Obligations of the
Federal Home Loan Banks and are not obligations of the
United States and are not guaranteed
by the United States.
Minimum amount of $100,000 with integral multiples of $5,000

The interest rate of 9.80% per annum for the period September 30, 1993 through September 29, 1994 and the formula for subsequent interest rates (Indexing Formula) were established on Wednesday, September 1, 1993, to be effective September 30, 1993. Subsequent Interest rates (Interest Reset Rates) will be based on the Indexing Formula for the interest rate on the Bonds set forth below and will be adjusted on March 30 and September 30 (Reset Dates).

Commencing September 30, 1994, for each Interest Period the interest rate per annum will be equal to a rate determined according to the following Indexing Formula:

Interest Reset Rate
September 30, 1994 through September 29, 1999   10-Year CMT + 2.75%–6 month LIBOR
September 30, 1999 through September 29, 2002   10-Year CMT + 4.00%–6 month LIBOR
September 30, 2002 through September 29, 2004   10-Year CMT + 6.00%–6 month LIBOR
September 30, 2004 through September 29, 2005   10-Year CMT + 9.00%–6 month LIBOR
provided, however, that the interest rate per annum will not be less than 0% nor greater than 24%.

The cash flows of a dual-indexed note can be replicated by an FRN combined with a floating-for-floating interest-rate swap (referred to as a "basis" or "diff" swap) where the payments on the swap are indexed to two different reference rates. Consider a firm that issues FRNs with face value FV paying LIBOR semiannually and that enters into a basis swap with notional principal FV to pay LIBOR and receive the 10-year CMT rate. The issuer has thus ensured a net semiannual coupon payment of the 10-year CMT rate *less* LIBOR. Interest-rate caps or floors may also be needed to limit the minimum and maximum coupon payments.[26]

Principal-indexed debt securities.   All of the examples of structured notes discussed so far involved only coupon indexing. Structured notes can also include instruments whose *principal* repayment is indexed to a reference rate through a principal redemption formula.

Perhaps the most common structured notes whose principal is indexed to an interest rate are "index amortizing notes" (IANs). IANs repay principal based on an amortization rate that is fully prespecified in an amortization schedule as a function of an underlying reference rate, such as LIBOR. An increase in the reference rate results in an increase in the effective maturity of the IAN. The reference rate chosen is generally correlated with prepayments on mortgage obligations or receivables of the issuer. As rates increase and the prepayments on the associated mortgages decline, the IAN maturity rises.

IANs can be replicated by combining a fixed-rate coupon bond or FRN with an "index amortizing rate" (IAR) swap with the same amortization schedule as the IAN.[27] IARs, in turn, can usually be decomposed (depending on the amortization schedule) into an interest-rate swap with an embedded portfolio of LIBOR caps and floors (i.e., calls and puts, respectively, on LIBOR).

---

[26]These rates provide a cash-flow stream correlated with the slope of the yield curve between any two points. This "multifactor" indexing distinguishes dual-indexed notes from the yield-curve notes, or inverse floaters, discussed earlier.

[27]For an interesting discussion of Banc One Corporation's uses of IAR swaps, see Ben Esty, Peter Tufano, and Jonathan Headley, "Banc One Corporation: Asset and Liability Management," *Journal of Applied Corporate Finance*, Vol. 7, No. 3 (Fall 1994); the comments on that article by Robert Albertson, Christopher James, Ethan Heisler, and Edward J. Kane; and the reply by Ben Esty and Peter Tufano.

Currency-, Commodity-, and Equity-Indexed Structured Notes

This section briefly examines a sampling of some specific structured notes that derive a portion of their value from foreign exchange, commodity, or equity prices or index levels. As with interest-rate-indexed structured notes, these structured securities can be decomposed into a debt component and a derivatives component.

Dual-currency bonds. A dual-currency bond is a structured note that pays interest in one currency and repays principal in another. The coupon payments are usually denominated in the currency of the investors, and the principal is typically paid in the currency of the issuer.[28] An announcement for a dual currency bond issued by Philip Morris Credit Corporation is shown below. The bond calls for interest payments in Swiss francs (SFr) of 7.25 percent on a subscription price of SFr 123,000,000 with a principal payment of U.S. $57,810,000.

New Issue   *This announcement appears as a matter of record only*

September 1985

PHILIP MORRIS CREDIT CORPORATION

Dual Currency Bonds Due 1993

U.S. $57,810,000

Interest Payable in SFr At 7 1/4%
on the Aggregate Subscription Price of
SFr 123,000,000

The straight-debt component of a dual currency bond can be viewed from either the issuer's or investors' standpoint as a fixed-rate coupon-bearing bond. From the investors' standpoint, the derivatives component of a dual-currency bond is simply a forward sale of Swiss francs for

---

[28]Gastineau, *op. cit.*

FIGURE 14–9

A Dual-Currency Bond as a Level-Coupon Bond and a Forward Foreign-Exchange Contract

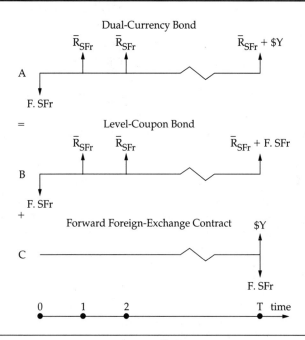

U.S. dollars. This decomposition, shown *from the perspective of the investor,* appears in Figure 14–9. The subscription price in Swiss francs is denoted by F.SFr, the principal redemption in U.S. dollars is denoted by $Y, and the fixed interest payments in Swiss francs are denoted by $\bar{R}_{SFr}$.

From the issuer's standpoint (e.g., U.S.-dollar-based Philip Morris Credit Corporation), the dual-currency bond's derivatives component can be viewed as a portfolio of forward contracts to sell Swiss francs for U.S. dollars, with the maturity date of each forward corresponding to the coupon dates and the principal value of each forward contract equal to the SFr coupon payment. The straight-debt component to the issuer looks like a U.S.-dollar-denominated fixed-rate bond.

PERLS and reverse PERLS. Principal exchange-rate linked securities (PERLS) are similar to dual-currency bonds, but unlike dual-currency bonds, both coupon and principal payments are paid in a single currency. The debt instrument in a PERLS is a coupon-bearing bond that pays interest and principal in the same currency. The principal repayment, however, is indexed to the foreign currency value of the face value of the bond at maturity. If the foreign currency appreciates relative to the currency in which the coupon and interest payments are denominated, the investor receives as principal redemption more than the face value of the security. If the foreign currency depreciates, the investor receives less than the face value at principal redemption. The entire face amount, in other words, is exposed to currency fluctuations.

Consider, for example, the summary announcement shown below for the PERLS issued by Sallie Mae in 1987. The PERLS paid both coupons *and* principal in U.S. dollars, but the principal repayment was indexed to the value of the Australian dollar. The coupon payments were 12 1/8 percent and the principal redemption was the U.S. dollar equivalent of A$1,452 per US$1,000 face amount. From the investors' perspective, the PERLS was equivalent to a straight bond selling at a premium because of

---

OFFERING CIRCULAR
U.S. $100,000,000
(Face Amount)
Principal Repayable at Maturity in the U.S. Dollar
Equivalent of Australian Dollars 145,200,000
Student Loan Marketing Association

SallieMae

12 1/8% Principal Exchange Rate Linked Securities ("PERLS")
Due March 20, 1990

Interest on the Principal Exchange Rate Linked Securities ("PERLS") offered hereby (the "Notes") will be payable in U.S. dollars based on the face amount of the Notes, semiannually in arrears on each March 20 and September 20, commencing September 20, 1987. The Notes will mature and be payable on March 20, 1990 (the "Maturity Date"). The principal amount of each U.S. $1,000 face amount of the Notes will be payable at maturity in the U.S. dollar equivalent of A $1,452, as determined by the average of the exchange rate quotations of three reference dealers on the second business day prior to the Maturity Date.

the higher-than-market coupons plus an out-of-the-money long forward contract to buy Australian dollars with U.S. dollars.

A reverse PERLS is a structured note whose principal repayment *declines* with exchange-rate appreciations. A summary announcement for a reverse PERLS issued by the Ford Motor Credit Corporation in 1987 is shown below. The principal redemption is indexed to the dollar/yen exchange rate. From the investors' perspective, the reverse PERLS was equivalent to a straight bond selling at a premium because of the above-market coupon plus an in-the-money short forward to sell yen for dollars and a long call option to put a floor of zero under the potential loss of principal.

PROSPECTUS SUPPLEMENT

(To Prospectus dated May 6, 1987)

U.S. $100,000,000
(Face Amount)
Principal Repayable at Maturity is an Amount Equal to
U.S. $200,000,000 Minus the U.S. Dollar Equivalent of
Yen 13,920,000,000

Ford Motor Credit Company

11% Reverse Principal Exchange Rate Linked Securities
(Reverse PERLS™) Due May 19, 1992

Interest on the Reverse Principal Exchange Rate Linked Securities™ (Reverse PERLS™) offered hereby (the "Notes") will be payable in U.S. dollars based on the face amount of the Notes, semiannually in arrears on each May 19 and November 19 commencing on November 19, 1987. The Notes will mature and be payable on May 19, 1992. Principal in respect of each U.S. $1,000 face amount of the Notes will be payable at Maturity in an amount equal to U.S. $2,000 minus the U.S. dollar equivalent of Y 139,200 as determined by the average of the exchange rate quotations of three reference dealers on the second business day prior to the date of Maturity. Accordingly, as more fully described herein, Holders will receive an amount of principal greater than the face amount of the Notes if, at Maturity, the U.S. dollar has appreciated against the Yen and a lesser amount of principal (to a minimum of zero) if, at Maturity, the U.S. dollar has depreciated against the Yen.

FIGURE 14–10

A Reverse PERLS as a Straight Coupon Bond, an in-the-Money Short Forward, and a Call Option

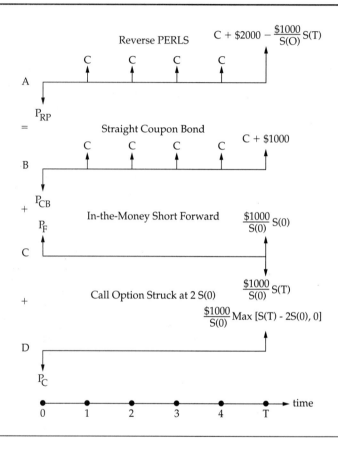

This decomposition *from the perspective of the investor* appears in Figure 14–10. In this figure, C denotes the above-market coupons on the reverse PERLS and the replicating straight bond, S(0) is the U.S. dollar/ Japanese Yen exchange rate at the issuance of the note, and S(T) is the exchange rate at maturity. P_{RP}, P_{CB}, P_F, and P_C represent the prices of the reverse PERLS, the straight coupon bond, the in-the-money short forward, and the call option, respectively.

The structure of a reverse PERLS is similar to an inverse floater and bear floater in that the minimum repayment (of principal) is guaranteed not to fall below zero or some other specified amount. To assure this, the forward contract embedded in the reverse PERLS is coupled with a call option on yen with a strike price of twice the spot exchange rate when the security was issued. That puts a floor of zero on the principal redemption value at maturity.

Gold-indexed bonds. In 1986, the Pegasus Gold Corporation issued bonds with gold warrants. Unlike most structured notes, which are sold as a single product, the Pegasus bonds were actually a bundle of two *distinct* securities sold together. Pegasus sold fixed-rate coupon-bearing bonds that repaid a fixed principal at maturity and bundled a *detachable* gold warrant (i.e., a long-dated, European, cash-settled call option on gold).

When the price of gold went up, Pegasus's revenues rose. Investors could exercise their gold warrants when the bonds matured and receive a higher effective principal repayment, thereby directly participating in the firm's higher revenues. In turn, Pegasus was able to offer the straight bonds to investors with a lower coupon rate.

Investors also had the alternative of *selling* their gold warrants to other investors while keeping the straight bonds. If the price of gold increased substantially, even though investors could not directly exercise the options, they could sell the detachable gold warrants and capture some of the price increase while still remaining lenders to Pegasus.

Copper-indexed notes. In 1988, Magma Copper Company issued 10-year notes with their value linked to the price of copper. A summary announcement is shown below. Unlike the Pegasus gold bonds with warrants, the Magma Copper notes indexed the *coupon* payments (rather than the principal repayment) to the price of copper. Investors could not sell their copper options without also selling their notes.

The Magma Copper notes paid coupons to investors quarterly, based on the *average* price of copper during the quarter of the coupon payment. The schedule of interest rates that investors were paid for a given average copper price is shown below in the extract from the prospectus.

PROSPECTUS

$200,000,000
MAGMA
COPPER COMPANY
Copper Interest-Indexed Senior Subordinated Notes due 1998

The Copper Notes will pay interest on each February 15, May 15, August 15 and November 15, commencing on February 15, 1989 and will bear interest from November 30, 1988 through May 15, 1989 at the rate of 18% per annum. The Copper Notes will pay interest during each quarterly period thereafter at the Indexed Interest Rate determined by the Average Copper Price during the immediately preceding quarterly period. The Indexed Interest Rate will range from 21% per annum at Average Copper Prices of $2.00 per pound and above to 12% per annum at Average Copper Prices of $.80 per pound and below. The "Average Copper Price" is the average closing settlement price on the Comex of the contract for delivery in the near month of high-grade copper cathode for each trading day during the relevant period. If the Average Copper Price applicable to an interest payment is $.80 per pound or less, the Company may elect, under certain circumstances, to pay 50% of such interest by delivery of additional Copper Notes

("Pay-in-Kind Notes") in principal amount equal to the amount of such interest.

The cash flows from the Magma Copper notes can be replicated with a portfolio of a 10-year fixed-rate coupon bond and 40 embedded call options on copper, each maturing on the 40 respective quarterly coupon dates. But the options were not ordinary call options. The exercise value of the options was based on the *average* copper price from the previous coupon date less the fixed strike price. These types of options are called average-price or Asian options.[29]

Equity-indexed notes. Numerous MTNs and debt instruments have been issued in which the coupon and/or principal value of the note is indexed to an equity index or equity share price.[30] To take a specific example, consider the SIGNs issued recently by the Republic of Austria.

---

[29] William C. Hunter and David W. Stowe, "Path-Dependent Options," and "Path-Dependent Options: Valuation and Applications," in *Financial Derivatives: New Instruments and Their Uses* (Federal Reserve Bank of Atlanta, December 1993).

[30] Some of the trade names of these equity-indexed notes include Equity Participation Notes (EPNs), Guaranteed Return Index Participations (GRIPs), Guaranteed Return on Investment Cer-

---

PROSPECTUS

$200,000,000

MAGMA
COPPER COMPANY
Copper Interest-Indexed Senior Subordinated Notes due 1998

Average Copper Price Per Pound	Indexed Interest Rate Per Annum
$2.00 or above	21.0%
1.80	20.0
1.60	19.0
1.40	18.0
1.30	17.0
1.20	16.0
1.10	15.0
1.00	14.0
0.90	13.0
0.80 or below	12.0

A summary announcement is shown below. Those securities are 5-year MTNs whose single interest payment at maturity is linked to the S&P 500 index. The notes thus pay to investors either the face value of the note or the face value plus interest based on the percentage appreciation in the S&P 500 over the preceding five years.

From the investors' perspective, the Republic of Austria SIGNs can be viewed as a combination of a zero-coupon bond plus an embedded long, at-the-money call option on the S&P 500. If the S&P 500 declines in value over the five years, the call expires worthless and the investors would be repaid only the face value of the bond. Investors would, however, participate fully in any S&P 500 appreciation over that time span through the payoff on the call option. This decomposition is shown in Figure 14–11.

---

tificates (GROIs), Index Growth-Linked Units (IGUs), Index Participation Certifications (IPCs), Market Index Target Term Securities (MITTS), Protected Equity Notes (PENs), Protected Equity Participations (PEPs), Protected Index Participations (PIPs), Stock Index Growth Notes (SIGNs), and Stock Market Annual Reset Terms (SMARTs). *See, for example,* Gastineau, *op. cit.,* and Charles Baubonis, Gary Gastineau, and David Purcell, "The Banker's Guide to Equity-Linked Certificates of Deposit," *Journal of Derivatives* Vol. 1, No. 2 (Winter 1993).

SUBJECT TO COMPLETION, DATED JANUARY 8, 1991
Prospectus Supplement to Prospectus Dated January , 1996
$100,000,000
REPUBLIC OF AUSTRIA
Stock Index Growth Notes™ ("SIGNs") due , 1996

*Stock index Growth Notes™ due , 1996 offered hereby will mature on , 1996.
At maturity, a holder of a Note will be entitled to receive, with respect to each $10
principal amount thereof, $10 plus an interest payment based upon 100% of the
appreciation (as described below), if any, in the S&P 500 Composite Stock Price index
from the date of this Prospectus Supplement to the maturity date of the Note, if there is
no increase in the S&P 500 index at the maturity date, or if there has been a decrease in
such index, a holder will be repaid the principal amount of the Note, without interest.*

*With respect to each $10 principal amount of a Note, the interest payment will be equal
to the product of (A) the excess, if any, of the "Final Value" over the "Initial Value"
divided by the "Initial Value" and (B) $10. The "Final Value" is the unweighted
arithmetic average of the closing values of the S&P 500 Index (such values as
calculated by Standard & Poor's Corporation) at the market close for the 30 Business
Days immediately preceding the second Business Day prior to the maturity date of the
Notes.™*

*The Notes are not redeemable prior to maturity.
Application will be made to list the Notes on the New York Stock Exchange, Inc.*

S(0) is the level of the S&P 500 index at issuance where S(T) is its level at
maturity of the note. P_{SIGN}, P_B, and P_C represent the prices of the SIGNs,
the zero-coupon bond, and the long "at-the-money" call, respectively.

Equity-indexed CDs. Similar to the equity-indexed notes discussed in the previous section, equity-indexed certificates of deposit have
exploded in popularity since early 1993. Equity-indexed CDs have been
issued by Citicorp, Bankers Trust, Republic Bank of New York, Bank of
America, and numerous other banking institutions of all sizes.

To take a specific example, consider Citicorp's Stock Index Insured
Account. This five-year CD pays no coupons but at maturity returns the
greater of the face value of the CD or the face value of the CD plus twice
the average increase in the S&P 500 over the preceding five years. The
cash flows on the Citicorp CD can be replicated by a portfolio of a 5-year
zero-coupon bond and two Asian options on the S&P 500 with strike
prices set at the level of the S&P 500 when the CD is purchased. The

FIGURE 14–11

A SIGN-Type Instrument as a Zero-Coupon Bond and a Long Call Option

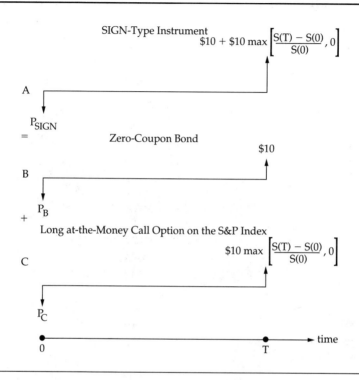

SIGN-Type Instrument
$$\$10 + \$10 \max\left[\frac{S(T) - S(0)}{S(0)}, 0\right]$$

A

P_{SIGN}

=

Zero-Coupon Bond $10

B

P_B

+

Long at-the-Money Call Option on the S&P Index
$$\$10 \max\left[\frac{S(T) - S(0)}{S(0)}, 0\right]$$

C

P_C

0   T   time

investor effectively pays for these options by foregoing the interest that would be earned on a traditional CD. Most equity-indexed CDs are insured by the Federal Deposit Insurance Corporation and hence can typically be issued at lower cost than equity-indexed notes.[31]

THE BENEFITS OF STRUCTURED NOTES TO INVESTORS

Institutions of various types may find it beneficial to purchase structured notes, thereby becoming lenders to the issuers in the process. Investors in

---

[31]Baubonis, Gastineau, and Purcell, *op. cit.*

FIGURE 14–12
Investors in Structured Notes

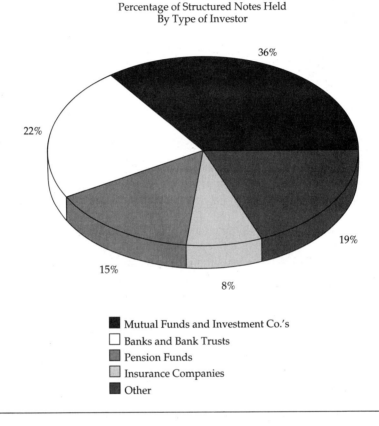

Percentage of Structured Notes Held
By Type of Investor

■ Mutual Funds and Investment Co.'s
□ Banks and Bank Trusts
▨ Pension Funds
▨ Insurance Companies
■ Other

structured notes include corporations, institutional and individual investors, municipalities, and governmental enterprises. Figure 14–12 shows
the estimated breakdown of investors in structured notes by type in 1994.[32]

The reasons for investing in structured notes are many and diverse. As
with all financial activities, any particular investor may choose to purchase
structured notes for reasons quite different from another, otherwise similar
investor. In general, however, the reasons for investing in structured notes

---

[32]This table appeared in Crabbe and Argilagos, *op. cit.*

can be separated into two main categories: managing financial risks and enhancing yields.

Managing Financial Risks

A primary attraction of structured notes is to manage existing or anticipated financial risks.[33] The relevant financial risks are summarized briefly below:

- *Interconnection*: the risk that the correlation between the values of assets and liabilities in a portfolio change unexpectedly;
- *Systematic:* undiversifiable risks that systematically affect all asset values;[34]
- *Market:* the risk that changes in market prices will adversely affect the value of an asset, liability, or portfolio;
- *Operational:* the risk that human error, poor personnel-quality, and the inherent complexity of certain business strategies make financial losses more likely;
- *Regulatory*: the risk that ill-informed examiners or poorly constructed regulations or statutes may result in regulatory actions that lead to financial losses;
- *Credit:* the risk that a counterparty may default on an obligation;
- *Intellectual:* the risk that traders with highly specialized knowledge may leave a firm unexpectedly;
- *Liquidity:* the risk that cash or funding shortfalls may create financial losses or inhibit servicing existing liabilities; and
- *Legal:* the risk that a contract may be deemed unenforceable.[35]

---

[33]This chapter does not discuss why a firm might want to manage financial risk in the first place, although the answer to that question is more subtle than some suspect. See, for example, David Fite and Paul Pfleiderer, "Should Firms Use Derivatives to Manage Risk?" in *Risk Management: Problems and Solutions*, William H. Beaver and George Parker, eds. (New York: McGraw-Hill, 1995).

[34]For a discussion of systematic versus diversifiable risk, see Sudipto Bhattacharya and George M. Constantinides, eds. *Theory of Valuation* (New Jersey: Rowman & Littlefield, 1989).

[35]Richard A. Miller, "Risk in a Nutshell: IS MORC ILL," *Futures International Law Letter,* Vol. 14, Nos. 5–6 (July/August 1994). For a discussion of the risks as presented here compared to Miller's original list, see Christopher L. Culp, *A Primer on Derivatives: Their Mechanics, Uses, Risks, and Regulation* (Washington, D.C.: Competitive Enterprise Institute, 1995).

Most of these risks can be managed with structured notes. These applications are discussed below.

Interconnection risk. Interconnection risk is the risk that the correlations between assets and liabilities in a portfolio or balance sheet change unexpectedly. If a firm, for example, hedges future purchases of Swiss francs with U.S. dollars by using deutsche mark/U.S. dollar forward-sale contracts, unexpected changes in the Swiss franc/D-mark exchange rate could impose losses on the firm. In other words, a break-down in the correlation of the D-mark/U.S. dollar exchange-rate with the franc/U.S. dollar exchange-rate could cause unexpected losses.

Interconnection risk typically arises from combinations of assets and liabilities whose values are determined by imperfectly correlated underlying market-risk factors. Investing in structured notes can offer a low-cost way of managing such correlation risks with a *single* financial product. Dual-index bonds, for example, pay coupons based on the relationship between two indexes. An institution with an existing exposure to changes in the correlation of those indexes thus might reduce its risk by purchasing dual-indexed structured notes.

To take an example, suppose an institution borrows semiannually at 6-month LIBOR + 50 bp and lends to the U.S. government by purchasing 10-year Treasuries for its investment portfolio. If changes in 6-month LIBOR and the 10-year CMT rate are perfectly correlated, the two rates will rise or decline together, thus ensuring that the firm always earns the positive spread between the two. If the 10-year CMT rate falls as 6-month LIBOR rises, by contrast, the institution's borrowing costs will rise while its investment portfolio return declines. It thus might opt to purchase structured notes that pay semiannually the difference between 6-month LIBOR and the 10-year CMT rate, thereby protecting itself, at least in part, from unexpected changes in the correlation between the two indexes.

Market risk. One of the most popular risk-management uses of structured notes is for reducing market risk.[36] An investor who either

---

[36]The decision by investors to use structured notes for managing market risk may be affected by accounting considerations. Under the recently adopted FAS 115, securities that are designated as "being held to maturity" may be accounted for at cost. Those designated as "available for sale" must be marked-to-market regularly. Expressing an interest-rate view through a structured

desires or is willing to act as a lender to a structured-note issuer can often simultaneously manage some aspect of its market risk. To take a simple example, suppose an investor, such as a pension or mutual fund, has investments that leave it exposed to decreases in LIBOR. If the investor becomes concerned that rates could fall, it may wish to neutralize its exposure to LIBOR. One way to do this without selling any of its existing securities is to purchase inverse FRNs, or securities that increase in value as LIBOR falls.

Structured notes can also be used to manage more-complex types of market risk than exposures to directional changes in interest rates and prices. Consider, for example, a finance company that earns a flat fee for financing receivables up to a specific interest rate and earns a proportionally higher fee for rates above the guaranteed financing level. Higher interest rates result in higher fee-income for the firm, but because the firm is effectively purchasing call options on interest rates, it also benefits from increases in interest-rate *volatility*. If the finance company wants to neutralize its exposure to rate volatility, it could purchase step-up bonds. If the coupon dates on the bonds match the effective expiration dates of its options, the written calls in the bond will neutralize the long volatility-exposure of the firm on the receivable financings.

Operational and intellectual risks. Complex hedging and investment programs can be difficult to both manage and administer, creating the possibility for mistakes to be made. The more complex the strategy, the more a firm faces operational risk. The developer and implementer of an innovative and complex strategy, for example, may leave the firm without providing an adequate understanding of the requirements of the particular investment program to her successor. At the extreme, operational and control difficulties may altogether prohibit certain types of strategies involving outright derivatives. Structured notes offer institutional investors and firms an often-simpler alternative that circumvents many of the operational and intellectual risks associated with actively managing a portfolio of outright derivatives.

Consider an investment manager with multiple customer accounts.[37] If

---

note that is designated as being held to maturity rather than through an outright derivative may allow the investor to defer recognition of losses if the view proves incorrect.

[37]This example was provided by Crabbe and Argilagos, *op. cit.*

the investment manager expects interest rates to rise and the associated mortgage prepayments to decline, IANs could be purchased and allocated among the customer accounts. A single IAR swap, on the other hand, could *not* be allocated across customer accounts; the fund manager would have to enter separate IAR swaps for each account, creating higher transaction costs and a greater opportunity for mistakes.

Exchange-traded futures contracts require margin to be posted up-front and accounts settled daily (or more often) through variation margin payments. Swaps may call for collateral after an adverse credit event, or at some predetermined credit exposure interval. Suppose, for example, a finance company enters into short Eurodollar futures contracts, so it is long LIBOR. Each day the futures contracts are marked-to-market and settled. As a result, the firm must periodically forecast and make provisions for potential liquidity requirements. Purchasing an FRN, by contrast, gives the firm the same long-term economic exposure to LIBOR without imposing any of the operational complications on the investor.[38]

Credit risk. The purchaser of a structured note bears the full risk that the issuer of the note will default on interest and/or principal payments. In many cases, however, the alternative to the structured note is to enter into separate debt and derivatives transactions. Structured notes may offer investors two advantages over this debt-plus-derivatives alternative.

First, a structured note requires only one credit-risk evaluation, whereas debt-plus-derivatives may require several evaluations. If a firm purchases a structured note, the full credit-risk is a function of the risk that the issuer defaults. By contrast, a purchaser of straight debt that also enters into a derivatives contract with a counterparty other than the note-issuer, in order to create the desired risk profile, must evaluate the probability of default of both counterparties.[39]

Second, structured notes pose no liquidity risk to purchasers due to declines in their *own* credit rating. As noted earlier, the coupon payments received on inverse FRNs can be replicated by the purchaser buying floating-rate debt and simultaneously entering into two pay-floating/

---

[38]The firm could also enter an FRA.

[39]Crabbe and Argilagos, *op. cit.*

receive-fixed LIBOR swaps. If the investor receives a credit downgrade after entering into the swaps, however, swap counterparties may demand collateral or some other form of credit enhancement. The inverse FRN, by contrast, is self-collateralized because the investor has made a loan to the borrower *up-front* that subsumes potential collateral concerns. On the other side, the investor faces no credit-related liquidity risk due to changes in its credit status.[40]

Liquidity risk. Structured notes can help investors manage liquidity risks in various ways. First, some structured notes are specifically designed to help firms manage the liquidity risks of their borrowings. Wholesale-funded banks, for example, fund their short-term operations using interbank and other wholesale borrowings rather than with retail liabilities. As another wholesale alternative, a bank may purchase range notes, such as the Paribas issue described above, which pay interest regularly based on *daily* interest-rate changes. Second, most structured notes can be traded on the secondary market. As a result, they may be easier to trade, transfer, and liquidate than the replicating portfolio of derivatives transactions, which must be "unwound" by negotiating with the original counterparty (or counterparties) or "offset" by putting on new derivatives positions.

Yield Enhancement

Many underwriters, issuers, and investors in structured notes argue that the notes are attractive because they frequently offer opportunities for enhanced yields when compared to traditional debt securities.[41] Equity-indexed CDs are often used as an example, since they appear to offer *retail* investors the chance to improve on the relatively low yields of traditional CDs by giving them low-cost access to the upside of equity participation.

In some cases, however, so-called yield enhancements may be illusory. They may simply represent a return for embedded written options or other aspects of the note that have not been adequately accounted for. Real yield-enhancements, nevertheless, can occur when there are imperfections or disequilibria in the capital markets.

---

[40]Culp, Furbush, and Kavanagh, *op. cit.*

[41]Smithson and Chew, *op cit.,* and Navon, *op. cit.*

An important consideration in this regard is that structured notes do offer some capital market participants access to markets from which they would otherwise be excluded, thereby expanding their opportunities and *effectively* enhancing their yields. In these cases, yields are enhanced because structured notes allow some market participants to circumvent legal, regulatory, or other restrictions that inhibited their access to national or global capital markets before.[42] Until recently, commercial banks and many institutional investors were prohibited from engaging in commodity futures transactions. Holding a commodity-indexed bond, such as the Pegasus gold bonds or Magma Copper notes, would allow these institutions to obtain exposure to commodity markets through a *debt* instrument. These banks could then earn an enhanced, risk-adjusted return that would have been impossible to earn without the notes.

Many institutional investors, such as pension funds, are also prevented from using swaps and forwards outright either because of credit considerations or institutional restrictions. Structured notes offer these investors access to the same risk exposure through a *security* rather than derivatives contract.[43]

THE BENEFITS OF STRUCTURED NOTES TO ISSUERS

Judged solely by the volume of structured note offerings, issuers appear to have found these notes quite advantageous. Figure 14–13 shows as an example the volume and types of bonds issued by the Federal Home Loan Bank (FHLB) System in 1993 and 1994. The FHLB is the single largest issuer of structured products, issuing $62.2 billion and $44.6 billion in 1994 and 1993, respectively. The types of structures issued vary from year to year. As Figure 14–13 shows, the predominant types of structured notes issued by the FHLB in 1994 were bullet bonds and step-up bonds, respectively representing $17.7 billion and $16 billion. In 1993, by

---

[42] In this sense, structured notes can also be used to manage regulatory or legal risk. See Culp, Furbush, and Kavanagh, *op. cit.*

[43] A firm facing institutional prohibitions on the use of derivatives could replicate an outright derivatives position by issuing a structured note and then *lending* or *buying back* its own non-structured debt, thereby leaving its capital structure unchanged.

FIGURE 14–13
Bonds Issued by Federal Home Loan Banks

By Type, 1993–1994

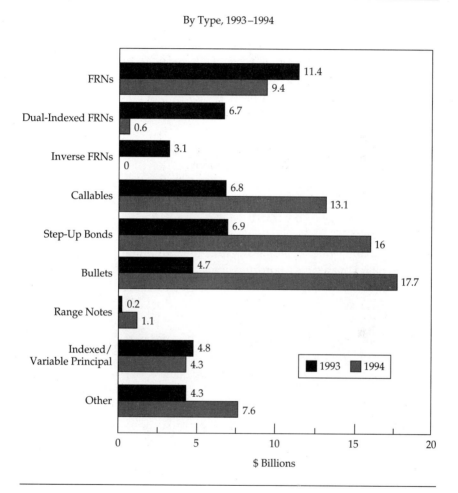

contrast, the predominant types were FRNs and step-up bonds, respectively representing $11.4 billion and $6.9 billion.

Once the decision to borrow has been made by a firm, structured notes can benefit an issuer in four principal ways relative to issuing straight debt: lowering funding costs, relaxing credit or borrowing constraints, reducing agency costs, and exploiting institutional frictions.

Lowering Funding Costs

Perhaps the most common benefit of borrowing with structured notes is reducing the costs of financing for corporations and government sponsored entities (GSEs). Indeed, Fannie Mae, Freddie Mac, Sallie Mae, and the Federal Home Loan Banks have drastically reduced their funding costs by borrowing using structured notes. One estimate suggests that many firms will simply decline to issue structured notes unless borrowing costs are reduced by at least 5 to 15 basis points.[44]

An attribute common to most structured note issues is the "laying off of the embedded market risk" by the issuer. As discussed earlier, structured notes can be viewed from a net cash-flow perspective as a combination of straight-debt security plus a combination of derivatives transactions.[45] Issuers of structured notes, therefore, can eliminate the embedded market risk of the issue by reversing the implicit derivatives component with a stand-alone derivatives contract.

Consider a GSE, such as Sallie Mae, that has issued an inverse FRN and yet wants floating-rate financing. As illustrated in Figure 14–8, an inverse FRN can be replicated by a portfolio composed of an FRN, two swaps, and an interest-rate cap. The arithmetic of financial engineering implies that the GSE can issue the inverse FRN with a principal of F and then create a synthetic FRN by entering into two receive-fixed/pay-floating swaps, each with notional principal of F, and then buying an interest-rate cap.[46]

The explanation for how firms can reduce their funding costs by issuing structured notes and then hedging the embedded exposure must lie in some capital market imperfections, frictions, or disequilibrium. If a firm has trouble accessing foreign capital markets and diversifying its sources of funding across currencies, it may issue a security like a PERLS or reverse PERLS and then enter into a currency or cross-currency swap

---

[44]Crabbe and Argilagos, *op. cit.*

[45]When the latter two transactions are undertaken on their own, the firm is said to have issued a synthetic structured note.

[46]In terms of Figure 14–8, issuing the inverse FRN (i.e., A) equals issuing the FRN (i.e., B) plus entering into two receive floating/pay fixed swaps (i.e., C) plus selling an interest-rate cap (i.e., D). That is, A = B + C + D. This implies, though, that B = A − C − D. Issuing the inverse FRN (i.e., A) and reversing the implicit derivatives components with stand-alone derivatives (i.e., −C −D) results in a synthetic FRN (i.e., B). Similar calculations using the cash-flow time lines in Figures 14–7 to 14–11 reveal how the issuer can hedge the embedded exposures in each of these structured products. This exercise is left to the reader.

thereby creating synthetic foreign currency financing. The firm thus circumvents whatever friction inhibited its international diversification.

Consider another case of a retail-funded commercial bank with access to a large pool of federally insured deposits. The bank may exploit its subsidized deposit base by *cross*-subsidizing structured note issues. A retail-funded bank that borrows using equity-indexed CDs is likely to have lower funding costs than retail-financed institutions whose products are *not* insured. At least one analysis indicates that a retail-funded bank issuing FDIC-insured CDs can lower the bank's cost of funds by more than a noninsured equity-indexed note reduces a nonbank's funding costs, even including the deposit insurance premiums the bank must pay.[47]

Some issuers of structured notes are able to lower their costs of funding by exploiting comparative advantage in credit risk. GSEs typically have high credit-ratings because they are implicitly backed by the federal government. Even though structured notes issued by the GSEs are direct liabilities of the GSEs and not of the U.S. Treasury, the GSEs often have high credit-ratings because of their implicit federal backing. As such, issuing structured notes can allow GSEs to lower their funding costs by taking advantage of their enhanced credit rating.[48]

Loosening Binding Credit-Related Borrowing Constraints[49]

Another reason often cited for the popularity of structured note issues is to circumvent binding constraints on a firm's borrowing due to its credit risk. In late 1989, Sonatrach, the state-owned hydrocarbon producer of Algeria, was having difficulty servicing a conventional FRN issue held by a syndicate of banks. In 1990, the Chase Manhattan Bank led a restructuring

---

[47]Baubonis, Gastineau, and Purcell, *op. cit.*

[48]This should not be confused with some early explanations for swaps, which argued that swaps were used by some corporations to exploit "comparative advantage" in funding at either floating or fixed rates. Those arguments were not generally accepted as an explanation for widespread swap activity because they did not rely on a market friction, like the present statement, and hence should have been arbitraged away over time. For examples of this theory and its criticism, see, respectively, G.M.S. Hammond, "Recent Developments in the Swap Market," *Bank of England Quarterly Review* (1987); and Stuart M. Turnbull, "Swaps: A Zero Sum Game?" *Financial Management*, Vol. 16, No. 1 (Spring 1987).

[49]This section is drawn from Culp, Furbush, and Kavanagh, *op. cit.*. Smithson and Chew, *op. cit.*, originally discussed the Sonatrach issue.

in which Sonatrach's FRNs were retired with a series of inverse oil-indexed bonds. The transaction was structured as follows:

- Sonatrach issued FRNs at LIBOR + 100 bp to a syndicate of banks;
- Sonatrach sold two-year calls on oil at a strike price of $23 to Chase; and,
- Chase, in turn, sold 7-year calls on oil (strike $22) and 7-year puts on oil (strike $16) to the syndicate of banks.

In return for being granted the oil-price puts and calls by Chase, the syndicate accepted a significantly lower spread over LIBOR (by some estimates, several hundred basis-points lower) than what would otherwise have been Sonatrach's floating-rate cost of funds. This reduction in period-by-period interest costs in turn reduced the likelihood that Sonatrach would experience further financial distress. The options did not impose any new oil-risk on Sonatrach because the firm was committed to additional option payments only when the price of oil rose. The company's financing costs would therefore increase only when it could afford the additional interest payments.

The Sonatrach notes effectively allowed the company to circumvent what had become a binding credit constraint, obtaining additional funding at a lower cost. The syndicate included some of the original as well as new lenders. The original lenders, in particular, were willing to reduce their coupon rate in exchange for a higher probability of repayment.

Reducing Agency Costs

When a principal (e.g., creditor) explicitly or implicitly contracts with an agent or agents (e.g., managers of a firm) to take actions on the principal's behalf, an agency relationship is defined.[50] Agency relationships often necessitate careful monitoring by principals of the agents, who may have conflicting incentives. Corporate managers often choose to act mainly on behalf of shareholders, and sometimes at the expense of creditors. A problem known as asset substitution occurs if management reduces the value of outstanding debt by entering into riskier business lines. Or, in

---

[50]Clifford W. Smith, Jr., "Agency Costs," in *The New Palgrave: A Dictionary of Economics*, John Eatwell, Murray Milgate, and Peter Newman, eds. (London: Macmillan, 1987).

another form of managerial opportunism known as claims dilution, managers could add new debt to old without giving new debt holders a lower priority in bankruptcy. When facing a heavy enough debt load, a troubled management could go so far as to refuse projects with high net-present-values simply because the gains from the projects would accrue predominantly to creditors. This phenomenon is known as the underinvestment problem.[51]

Costly contracting usually results in agency costs, or costs that principals must incur to monitor the performance of their agents.[52] Structured debt can reduce the agency costs of lenders to corporations and GSEs by reducing the costs incurred by creditors in monitoring the borrower's hedging and investment activities. Structured debt reduces monitoring costs by forcing the borrower to precommit itself to a hedging policy *as a condition of borrowing*.

To illustrate this point, suppose that the creditors of an exporter insist that the firm hedge its exposure to foreign exchange depreciation. To hedge, the firm could enter into futures or forward contracts to sell foreign exchange forward. The creditors, however, would now have to continuously monitor the company's currency exposure to ensure that the exposure *remains* hedged. The exporter could instead issue foreign currency structured notes, such as PERLS or dual-currency bonds. This would ensure that the firm hedges its currency exposure, greatly reducing the creditors' monitoring costs and thus lowering the rate of return that they would require. At the same time, the structured-debt holders can (and typically do) include bond covenants that prohibit the firm from "undoing" its embedded hedge with derivatives transactions.[53]

Notice that firms issuing structured debt to reduce agency costs will usually have different risk profiles than firms issuing structured debt either to lower funding costs or to manage credit risk. Firms issuing structured

---

[51]For a discussion of the various sources of stockholder/creditor/management conflicts, see Stewart C. Myers, "Determinants of Corporate Borrowing," *Journal of Financial Economics,* Vol. 5 (1977); Michael C. Jensen and William H. Meckling, "Theory of the Firm: Managerial Behavior, Agency Costs, and Capital Structure," *Journal of Financial Economics,* Vol. 3 (1976); Clifford W. Smith, Jr., and Jerold B. Warner, "On Financial Contracting: An Analysis of Bond Covenants," *Journal of Financial Economics,* Vol. 7 (1979); and the readings reprinted in Clifford W. Smith, Jr., ed., *The Modern Theory of Corporate Finance* (New York: McGraw-Hill Publishing Company, 1990).

[52]Jensen and Meckling, *op. cit.,* and C. Smith (1987), *op. cit.*

[53]Smithson and Chew, *op. cit. See* more generally Smith and Warner, *op. cit.*

debt in order to reduce funding costs typically incur no new market-risk from the structured-debt issue because they combine the issue with derivatives contracts designed to neutralize the embedded market risk.

Firms issuing structured debt in order to manage credit risks, like Sonatrach, will typically issue structured notes whose payments to investors are positively correlated with the revenues of the firms. At the same time, because such issuers are credit-constrained, they will generally issue only structured notes with limited downside risk for investors, such as debt with embedded long options rather than embedded forwards. Credit-constrained issuers will typically not combine a structured note issue with a straight derivatives contract, as that would neutralize the benefits to investors of having their probability of repayment increased.

In the last category are firms that issue structured debt to reduce agency costs. Such firms will typically issue securities that *reduce* their *existing* market risks. Because the notes themselves act as a type of rate or risk hedge for the firm, these issues are not combined with straight derivatives transactions.

Institutional Frictions

Several institutional factors may account for firms' decisions to issue structured debt. The main institutional frictions affecting the decision of an organization to issue structured notes are taxes, accounting, and regulation.

Taxes.   Firms may choose to issue structured securities to reduce taxes. Merrill Lynch's Liquid Yield Option Notes (LYONs) are zero-coupon structured notes that are callable, putable, and convertible.[54] As with all OID bonds, the issuer may deduct *deferred* interest payments from *current* income, thus resulting in a reduction in current tax liabilities. The embedded options in LYONs make the tax benefit of issuing them particularly high.

The Internal Revenue Service, however, is generally quite aggressive and fast in closing tax loopholes, as their recent reaction to issuance of SIGNs-type notes indicates. Types of instruments that are issued initially at a tax advantage for the issuer usually have that tax advantage taken

---

[54]John J. McConnell and Eduardo S. Schwartz, "LYON Taming," *Journal of Finance,* Vol. 41, No. 3 (1986).

away not long after for later issues. Taxes do nonetheless explain the initial development of a variety of financial products.[55]

Accounting. Firms may choose to issue structured notes because of favorable accounting treatment.[56] Under compound instrument accounting, a structured note could be accounted for as a conventional debt instrument and carried at historical cost. With outright derivatives, by contrast, the firm would generally have to mark the positions to market regularly unless they were hedging a specific transaction. As a result, the historical cost-accounting treatment of structured notes could be attractive for firms hedging economic exposure.

Regulation. Structured-note issues are typically regulated by the SEC as securities. To avoid shelf-registration requirements, issuers may shorten the maturity of structured medium-term notes (MTNs) to commercial paper status, or they may issue MTNs by private placement.

Structured notes with embedded options or forwards on commodities also may be subject to regulation by the Commodity Futures Trading Commission (CFTC).[57] The Commodity Exchange Act requires that commodity futures and options be traded on a regulated commodity exchange

---

[55]Merton H. Miller, "Financial Innovation: The Last Twenty Years and the Next," *Journal of Financial and Quantitative Analysis,* Vol. 21 (December 1986); and M. Miller, "Financial Innovation: Achievements and Prospects," *Journal of Applied Corporate Finance,* Vol. 4, No. 4 (Winter 1992).

[56]Accounting treatment for structured notes, however, is ambiguous, uncertain, and potentially subject to substantial changes. FASB is considering (and reconsidering) major changes in the accounting treatment of derivatives (especially free-standing derivatives) including those used for hedging. For a presentation of FASB's recent proposal and critical commentary, see *Accounting for Hedges: Current Developments and Market Impacts,* Summary of Proceeding of a Conference Sponsored by Virginia Tech, Chase Manhattan Bank, and Arthur Andersen, L.L.P., Washington, D.C. (March 8, 1995). See also Halsey G. Bullen, Robert C. Wilkins, and Clifford C. Woods, III, "The Fundamental Financial Instruments Approach," *Journal of Accountancy,* Vol. 168, (1989); and J. Matthew Singleton, "Hedge Accounting: A State-of-the-Art Review," *Bank Accounting and Finance* (Fall 1991).

[57]James V. Jordan, Robert J. Mackay, and Eugene J. Moriarty, "The Regulation of Commodity-Linked Debt and Depository Instruments," in *Handbook of Financial Engineering,* Clifford W. Smith, Jr., and Charles W. Smithson, eds. (New York: Harper Business, 1990); Dean Furbush and Michael Sackheim, "U.S. Hybrid Instruments: Evolving Legal and Economic Issues," in *Advanced Strategies in Financial Risk Management,* Robert J. Schwartz and Clifford W. Smith, eds. (Englewood Cliffs, NJ: New York Institute of Finance, 1993); and Christopher L. Culp and Todd E. Petzel "Structured Notes and the Commodity Exchange Act: Financial Innovation, Regulation, and 'Functional Dynamics,' " Working Paper, (March 1994).

and not be offered (subject to certain exemptions) off-exchange or over-the-counter. A decision by the CFTC that a particular structured note constituted a "commodity futures or option" could render the note "illegal" unless its terms and conditions meet certain exemption criteria.

Under present CFTC rules, however, issuers of structured debt can gain an exemption from CFTC regulation and, in particular, the exchange-listing requirement, by structuring the security appropriately. Although there are four explicit criteria that must be satisfied to obtain such an exemption, the principal challenge is ensuring that the present value of the cash flows from the straight debt (or "commodity-independent") component of the notes exceeds the value of the "commodity-dependent" component, which attempts to measure the extent to which the instrument is a commodity play.[58]

If the issuer of structured debt chose to issue the commodity-linked component separately in a derivatives transaction, the separately issued instrument could potentially be deemed an illegal off-exchange futures or options contract. Whatever the benefits and costs of the criteria used by the CFTC to assess the legality of structured debt, it is certainly true that those criteria are *better and more explicitly defined* than for swaps and some other types of outright derivatives. Firms thus may be induced to issue structured debt to minimize legal risk and avoid regulatory uncertainty.

THE RISKS OF STRUCTURED NOTES

Much concern has been raised lately about the risks of issuing and purchasing structured securities.[59] The widely publicized losses of Orange County, California, for example, involved the purchase of structured notes that stepped up into inverse FRNs. In response to losses incurred from purchasing certain structured notes, preliminary guidance on investing in these issues has already been issued by most financial regulators in the United States.[60]

---

[58]Furbush and Sackheim, *op. cit.*

[59]The risks of mortgage-backed securities and derivatives are not addressed. For a good discussion, see Charles Austin Stone and Anne Zissu, "The Risks of Mortgage Backed Securities and Their Derivatives," *Journal of Applied Corporate Finance,* Vol. 7, No. 3 (Fall 1994).

[60]Federal Deposit Insurance Corporation, *Examination Guidance for Structured Notes*, FDIC Division of Supervision Memorandum 94–130 (August 31, 1994); Board of Governors of the Fed-

Despite all this attention, however, structured notes are no more inherently risky than other, more traditional financial products.[61] One of the more complex structured notes on the market—the IAN—has risks not fundamentally different from a mortgage loan. But it is true that structured notes can be very complex and difficult to understand. As with all financial activities, prudent risk-management policies and procedures are necessary before structured notes are either issued or purchased.[62]

Identification of Risks

The key to managing the risks of structured notes is identifying the risks to which the instrument is subject. A necessary first step is thus a precise understanding of the mechanics of the financial instrument.

In the popular press, a failure by investors to understand the risks of structured notes has generally been cited as the cause of the major publicized losses that occurred in 1994.[63] This assertion, however, should not be uncritically accepted. The investment and commercial banks that typically market and often underwrite the issue of structured notes face powerful economic and legal incentives to explain the risks of structured notes to purchasers.[64] Several recent lawsuits and regulatory actions against some large dealers for alleged fraud involving the marketing of derivatives have certainly increased the incentive of derivatives dealers and security underwriters to be forthright with investors about the risks of the products they are selling.[65]

---

eral Reserve System, *SR Letter 94–45* (August 5, 1994); Office of the Comptroller of the Currency, *OCC Advisory Letter AL 94-2* (July 21, 1994), and Securities and Exchange Commission, Letter from Barry P. Barbash to Paul Schott Stevens (June 30, 1994).

[61] In fact, most of the losses in the Orange County case can be attributed to the leveraging up through repos of a fairly straightforward government securities portfolio—i.e., the losses resulted from borrowing short and lending long in a rising-interest-rate environment.

[62] Our views on risk management are discussed in detail in Christopher L. Culp and Robert J. Mackay, "Managing Derivatives Risk: A Strategic Guide," in *1995 Handbook of Business Strategy* (New York: Faulkner & Gray, 1995).

[63] For an excellent discussion of these losses, see Stephen Figlewski, "How to Lose Money in Derivatives," *Journal of Derivatives*, Vol. 2, No. 2 (Winter 1994).

[64] "Review of the Sales Practices of the Largest National Bank Derivatives Dealers," Office of the Comptroller of the Currency (June 1995), for a survey of current sales practices and a list of "Best Practices."

[65] *Written Agreement by and among Bankers Trust New York Corp. et. al. and Federal Reserve Bank of New York,* before the Board of Governors of the Federal Reserve System (December 2,

There are nonetheless several items of which investors in structured notes should be especially aware.[66] First, low-probability events should not simply be ignored because they occur infrequently. Few investors would *deliberately* ignore catastrophic events, but there is a natural temptation to acknowledge the possibility of a catastrophe, dismiss it as highly unlikely, and subsequently ignore it. Catastrophic events do nonetheless occur, and structured-note purchasers should pay particular attention to identifying the extreme market movements that might affect the value of their investments.

Second, issuers and purchasers of structured notes alike should keep in mind that yield enhancement generally goes hand-in-hand with an increase in risk. Unless a true arbitrage opportunity is being exploited or a structured security is being issued or held to exploit capital market frictions, issuers and investors should be aware that turning a treasury function into a profit center simply cannot be done without incurring additional financial risks.

Finally, participants in structured-note markets should be careful to consider the full range of financial risks. Although it is tempting to treat market risk as the "biggest" risk of issuing or holding structured securities, the instruments are still principally securities and the other risks are quite real. Given the pace of innovation in the structured note market and the general rigidity and inflexibility of a financial regulatory scheme established in a prior era, legal risk must always be considered. And lest either liquidity or credit risk be treated dismissively, recall that The Drexel Burnham Lambert Group, Inc., ultimately filed for bankruptcy protection because it had insufficient liquidity to honor a commercial paper payment.[67]

Risk Measurement

Once the risks of issuing and holding structured securities have been isolated and identified, firms should utilize appropriate methods of quanti-

---

1994); *In re BT Securities Corp.,* before the Commodity Futures Trading Commission, Docket No. 95-8 (December 22, 1994); and *Gibson Greeting, Inc.* vs. *Bankers Trust Company, et. al.,* U.S.D.C. (So. District of Ohio, Western Div.) No. 94-620 (September 12, 1994).

[66]Most of this "check list" is discussed in Figlewski, *op. cit.*

[67]*In re The Drexel Burnham Lambert Group, Inc., et. al.,* U.S. Bankruptcy Court S.D.N.Y, Civ. 90-6954 (Chapter 11 Case No. 90-B-10421 (FGC), Jointly Amended) (January 3, 1992).

fying those risks. Market, credit, and liquidity risks are especially important to measure.

Market risk. To measure market risk, it is important that the issuer and investor carefully identify the underlying "risk factors" affecting the value of the financial instrument. The value of a dual-index bond whose coupon payments are indexed to the difference in the 10-year CMT rate and 6-month LIBOR might depend on the level of each interest-rate index as well as the *correlation* between the two indexes.

Because of their relative complexity, structured notes with embedded options necessitate particular attention. As with traditional options, the value of an option embedded in a structured note typically depends on the level of the asset price or reference rate underlying the option, the rate of change in the underlying price or rate, time to maturity, the interest rate, and the volatility of the underlying.

Once firms have identified the risks affecting the value of their structured notes, sensitivity analyses and stress testing should be used to measure the effects of changes in the underlying risk factors on the value of the instrument. Simple scenario analysis can be done in virtually any spreadsheet program. Where possible, firms should incorporate the risks of issuing (holding) structured notes into an aggregate measure of the "value at risk" for the firm's whole borrowing (lending or investment) portfolio. As an ideal objective, firms should include structured securities in calculations of the value at risk and stress tests of the entire consolidated value of the institution. The risks of most structured debt instruments can be incorporated into measures of aggregate values at risk for portfolios or firms relatively easily.

Beyond the fundamental risk factors, the firm should also evaluate how the structured security issue affects the interest-rate risk of the firm. Asset/liability committees should be apprised of how issuing or purchasing structured notes affects the duration, convexity, and effective maturity of their asset and liability portfolios.

Credit risk. It is important for the purchaser of a structured note to know how to evaluate and set credit limits on issuers of structured notes, especially if the purchaser has credit exposures with the issuer arising from other business lines. To measure the credit exposure of a structured note, firms should use scenario analysis and other statistical and

analytical techniques to quantify the possible amounts of future coupon
and principal repayments on which the issuer might default.[68]

Liquidity risk. For issuers of structured notes, liquidity risks
can be significant. Consider, for example, a retail-funded bank that finances its operations by issuing floating-rate CDs of 6-months to 5-years
to maturity and makes adjustable-rate mortgage loans with an average
effective maturity of 10 years. To manage the interest-rate risk associated
with nonparallel shifts in the term structure of interest rates, the firm might
issue dual-index bonds that pay coupons indexed to the 10-year CMT rate
less the 2-year CMT rate. If the yield curve inverts and the bank's assets
yield less than the cost of funding its liabilities, the lower coupon rate
required on the dual-index bonds may offset some of the adverse effects of
the term structure shift on the bank's net funding costs.

Now suppose that the inversion of the yield curve is accompanied by a
dramatic increase in interest rates of all maturities. Prepayments on the
bank's mortgage assets may decline, thus resulting in a substantial increase in the effective average maturity or duration of its assets. That
would not only affect the duration of the bank's portfolio, it would also
affect the *net interest income* of the bank. Although the structured notes
would have protected the bank somewhat against changes in the slope of
the yield curve, the bank still might face problems funding its short-term
liabilities.

As with market risk, firms should use scenario analysis to measure
potential changes to the firm's net cash flows. In most cases that funding
risk should be addressed by a corporation's asset/liability committee and/
or treasury function, making liquidity-risk management a natural complement to market-risk management for most structured debt instruments.

Risk Control

Identifying and measuring risks are not enough if the issuer or investor in
structured notes does not have in place the policies and procedures to
control risks. Firms should have policies and procedures in writing which
govern their issuance of and investments in structured notes. Risk limits—
notably on market, credit, and liquidity risks—should be set, monitored,

[68]Culp and Mackay (1995), *op. cit.*

and updated as appropriate to the firm's activities and exposures. Prudent risk-control should also include adequate risk reporting, internal and external audit, and oversight by senior managers and directors.[69]

CONCLUDING NOTE

Structured notes provide an innovative means by which firms—private corporations and government sponsored enterprises—can raise capital. Structured securities issued to date range from simple FRNs to more exotic securities with complex payoffs. The potential benefits to both investors in and issuers of structured notes are pronounced for both the simple and complex products. Structured notes do nevertheless pose risks to these issuers and investors, just like other more traditional liabilities and assets. With prudent risk-management policies and procedures, however, the risks of structured notes can be managed—measured, monitored, and controlled—quite adequately.

---

[69]For a more detailed discussion of risk control, see Global Derivatives Study Group (1983), *op. cit.*, and Culp and Mackay (1995), *op. cit.*

P A R T

III

ACCOUNTING, TAX, SYSTEMS, & CONTROL

Chapter Fifteen

Accounting, Financial Reporting, and Disclosure for Derivatives and Synthetics*

Robert H. Herz
Partner
Coopers & Lybrand L.L.P.

Accounting is a system that feeds back information to organizations and individuals, which they can use to reshape their environment.[1]

INTRODUCTION

The accounting and financial reporting environment plays a critical role in designing new derivative and synthetic products, in implementing new strategies with regard to these products, and in monitoring, controlling, and evaluating the results of using these products. While accounting rule makers have been hard pressed to keep pace with the rapid development of new products, a number of pronouncements covering accounting for forwards, futures, and options exist. However, the authoritative literature

---

*Reprinted with changes from Robert H. Herz "Accounting and Financial Reporting for Derivatives and Synthetics," *The Handbook of Derivatives and Synthetics,* Robert A. Klein and Jess Lederman, eds. (Chicago: Probus Publishing Company, 1994), pp. 821–865.

[1]Donald E. Kieso, and Jerry J. Weygandt, *Intermediate Accounting,* New York: John Wiley & Sons, 1989, p. 4.

represents a somewhat piecemeal, and often internally inconsistent, set of rules on the subject. Accordingly, the Financial Accounting Standards Board (FASB) continues to work on a major project on financial instruments[2] and off-balance-sheet financing, the goal of which is to develop a more comprehensive and consistent framework for accounting for all financial instruments, including derivatives and synthetics. Because of the complexity of the issues involved, specifically with regard to the recognition and measurement issues, the FASB decided that an interim step, improved disclosure about financial instruments, was necessary.

In this regard, three Statements of Financial Accounting Standards (SFAS)—Nos. 105, 107, and 119—have been issued. The application of these three pronouncements will be covered later. While these statements did not alter the existing accounting practices, they did mandate much more extensive disclosure regarding financial instruments in general, and derivatives in particular. Further, as discussed later in this chapter, during 1994, the staff of the Securities and Exchange Commission (SEC) performed extensive reviews on the adequacy of disclosures made by hundreds of public companies on their use of derivatives, often requiring these companies to significantly expand and enhance these disclosures.

The FASB has now turned in earnest to reexamining the whole area of accounting for derivatives. As discussed later in this chapter, the result of this effort could well be a dramatic change in the way derivatives are accounted for in the future, with a shift toward mark-to-market or fair-value accounting and away from the traditional hedge accounting model.

The primary goal of accounting is to produce relevant information that is reliable, neutral, and capable of being compared among different entities. Also, embedded in accounting theory is the belief that the costs of obtaining information should not exceed the benefits (broadly defined) of

---

[2]Financial instruments have been defined by the FASB in various pronouncements as follows: A financial instrument is cash, evidence of an ownership interest in an entity, or a contract that both

a. Imposes on one entity a contractual obligation (1) to deliver cash or another financial instrument to a second entity or (2) to exchange other financial instruments on potentially unfavorable terms with the second entity; and

b. Conveys to that second entity a contractual right (1) to receive cash or another financial instrument from the first entity or (2) to exchange other financial instruments on potentially unfavorable terms with the first entity.

It should also be noted that although the thrust of the FASB's project has been directed toward financial instruments as defined above, similar accounting generally applies in the case of contracts that can be settled by delivery of physical commodities.

such information.[3] The matching principle, under which gains and losses on related items should be recognized in the same period, is also important, as it underlies hedge accounting practices.

Accounting theory has traditionally been based on the notion of historical cost. Accountants have traditionally relied on arms-length transactions to report the value of assets and liabilities. Lately, however, with the perceived increased riskiness of the investment portfolios of many financial institutions, there has been increasing pressure from regulators and Congress toward the use of fair-value accounting for financial assets and liabilities, including derivatives. Moreover, advocates of mark-to-market or fair-value accounting for financial instruments argue that this is more relevant to users of financial statements than measurements based on historical cost. Such mark-to-market accounting for financial instruments has traditionally been followed by broker-dealers, swap dealers, investment companies, hedge funds, and pension funds, who generally report unrealized gains and losses on securities and financial instruments as part of the current period's earnings. Until recently, however, most other financial institutions—such as banks, thrifts, and insurance companies, as well as commercial and industrial companies—generally carried most of their securities on a historical cost or lower of cost or market basis. However, the issuance by the FASB of SFAS No. 115, *Accounting for Certain Investments in Debt and Equity Securities*, in May 1993, dramatically changed this. As discussed later in this chapter, starting in 1994, even these "non-mark-to-market" entities now have to carry significant portions of their debt securities and all of their marketable equity portfolios on a market or fair-value basis. This change has had an inevitable impact, particularly on banks, thrifts, and insurance companies, both in reported earnings and capital and in the way they invest in, trade, and hedge their securities portfolios. Moreover, it currently appears that the FASB is headed toward an approach that would extend market or fair-value accounting to all derivatives and for all entities.

This chapter will cover the existing accounting and disclosure rules and practices applicable to investors in and users of derivatives and synthetics, as well as the FASB's ongoing efforts in this area and current SEC views on derivatives. The rules applicable to mark-to-market entities such as pension funds, mutual funds, hedge funds, and broker-dealers; to financial

---

[3]For example, see the discussion on SFAS No. 107. Under that pronouncement, disclosures are to be made to the extent that the costs of computing "fair market value" are practicable, i.e., the costs do not exceed the benefits.

institutions such as banks, thrifts, and insurance companies; and to industrial and commercial enterprises will be covered.

Transactions that are entered into to hedge the risks associated with other transactions and that meet specific requirements qualify under the current rules for a special accounting treatment commonly referred to as hedge accounting. Hedge accounting will be discussed in detail later in this chapter; briefly, though, accounting for a transaction as a hedge generally means that the gains or losses from the hedge position are recognized in the same period as losses or gains on the hedged item.

Increasingly, companies are using derivatives in connection with cash market positions to produce so-called synthetic instruments that replicate the economic attributes of a single recognizable instrument. The key accounting issue is whether the individual instruments comprising the synthetic should be accounted for separately or as one combination based on the synthesis.

Another important issue that merits some discussion is the netting of positions. As swap webs become increasingly entangled, participants in the derivatives market are seeking to net-out their positions. For the accountant, a key issue emerges in presenting the financial statements and related footnote disclosures of the entity: should this netting of positions be done by product type, counterparty, duration, or otherwise, if at all?

The chapter will conclude with a discussion of the possible changes that loom on the horizon in the accounting and disclosure rules affecting derivatives and synthetics.

CURRENT AUTHORITATIVE GUIDELINES

Several sources of guidance on accounting for derivatives and synthetics exist. The Securities and Exchange Commission (SEC), under the authority of the Securities Act of 1933 and the Securities Exchange Act of 1934, has the power to set financial reporting guidelines for publicly traded companies. Although the SEC generally defers to the FASB and the Emerging Issues Task Force (EITF) of the FASB with regard to accounting treatment of new products, the SEC has taken a stand on certain hedging and disclosure issues related to derivatives and synthetics.

It is the FASB's mandate to narrow the range of alternative accounting principles and develop an underlying conceptual framework. As such, the Board has issued several pronouncements that apply to derivative products, the most important of which are shown in Table 15–1.

TABLE 15–1   Key FASB Documents

Document	Title	Application
SFAS No. 52	Foreign Currency Translation	Hedge accounting with regard to foreign currency transactions, including forwards and currency swaps
SFAS No. 80	Accounting for Futures Contracts	Establishes standards of accounting and reporting for futures contracts
SFAS No. 95	Statement of Cash Flows	Reporting of cash flows from hedging activities in the statement of cash flows
SFAS No. 104	Statement of Cash Flows–Net Reporting of Certain Cash Receipts and Cash Payments and Classification of Cash Flows From Hedging Transactions	
SFAS No. 105	Disclosure of Information About Financial Instruments with Off-Balance-Sheet Risk and Financial Instruments with Concentrations of Credit Risk	Disclosures relating to financial instruments with off-balance-sheet exposure and concentrations of credit risk
SFAS No. 107	Disclosures About Fair Value of Financial Instruments	Requires disclosure of fair value of financial instruments
SFAS No. 115	Accounting for Certain Investments in Debt and Equity Securities	Accounting for debt and marketable equity securities
SFAS No. 119	Disclosure About Derivative Financial Instruments	Requires specific disclosures on derivatives, distinguishing between derivatives held for trading purposes and those held for other than trading Encourages other disclosures on derivatives. Amends certain aspects of SFAS Nos. 105 and 107
FIN No. 39	Offsetting of Amounts Related to Certain Contracts	Right of offset with regard to derivatives transactions executed with the same counterparty

As previously noted, SFAS No. 115 covers the accounting for debt securities and marketable equity securities (other than those accounted for under the equity method or as investment in consolidated subsidiaries), for enterprises in industries that do not have specialized accounting practices for these items. Therefore, it covers most commercial and industrial companies and financial institutions such as banks, thrifts, and insurance companies, but it does not apply to broker-dealers, swap dealers, pension and hedge funds, or investment companies.

The major requirements of SFAS No. 115 are discussed in the next section, "Overview of Industry Practices," because they impact not only on the accounting by the affected entities for their debt and marketable equity securities, but also on the accounting for the derivatives used in connection with hedging or yield enhancement of these securities.

SFAS Nos. 52 and 80 are discussed in the section on hedging. FASB Interpretation No. 39 (FIN No. 39), on netting of positions in the balance sheet, is discussed later. The application of the three principal disclosure pronouncements—SFAS Nos. 105, 107, and 119—also is detailed later in the chapter.

The American Institute of Certified Public Accountants (AICPA) offers practical guidance, although not authoritative pronouncements, to the profession with regard to accounting and financial reporting. The AICPA issues Statements of Position (SOPs) and industry accounting guides, which assist in the planning of audit engagements, the application of FASB pronouncements, and the dissemination of generally accepted industry accounting practices. The AICPA also publishes issues papers on accounting topics, one of which, Issues Paper No. 86-2, *Accounting for Options,* which although not recognized as authoritative, is often relied upon with regard to accounting for options and option strategies.

Finally, a very important source of guidance is the consensus opinions reached by the Emerging Issues Task Force of the FASB. In June 1984, the FASB established the EITF as part of its plan to provide timely guidance on implementation questions and emerging accounting issues. The 13-member Task Force includes representatives of major public accounting firms, smaller public accounting firms, the Financial Executives Institute, the National Association of Accountants, and the Business Roundtable. The chief accountant of the SEC attends the task force meetings as an observer, and the FASB's director of research and technical activities is the task force's chairman. Consensus by the task force is intended to indicate that significant diversity in practice is not expected on a given issue (three dissenting votes precludes consensus on a given issue). Moreover, EITF consensuses are regarded as authoritative and as part of generally accepted accounting principles by auditors and by the staff of the SEC. It is noteworthy that over half of the issues dealt with by the EITF since its inception have related to financial instruments and new financial products, including many issues dealing specifically with derivatives and synthetics. See Table 15–2 for the most important EITF issues in this regard.

TABLE 15–2 *Key EITF Documents*

Document	Title	Application
EITF No. 84-36	*Interest-Rate Swap Transactions*	Provides guidance rather than authoritative rules on interest-rate swaps
EITF No. 85-6	*Futures Implementation Questions*	Discussion of a number of implementation questions relating to SFAS No. 80. Guidance on these issues was subsequently published in the June 1985 FASB "Status Report"
EITF No. 90-17	*Hedging Foreign Currency Risks with Purchased Options*	As described in title
EITF No. 91-1	*Hedging Intercompany Foreign Currency Lists*	As described in title
EITF No. 91-4	*Hedging Foreign Currency Risks with Complex Options and Similar Transactions*	As described in title
EITF No. 94-7	*Accounting for Financial Instruments Indexed to, and Potentially Settled in, a Company's Own Stock*	Accounting for forwards and purchased options settled in or linked to a company's own stock
EITF No. 95-2	*Determination of What Constitutes a Firm Commitment to Foreign Currency Transactions Not Involving a Third Party*	As described in title
EITF No. 95-11	*Accounting for Derivative Instruments Containing Both a Written Option-Based Component and a Forward-Based Component*	Accounting for mildly leveraged swaps and other derivatives containing embedded written options (Discussions only commenced in July 1995)

OVERVIEW OF INDUSTRY PRACTICES

The primary accounting distinction with regard to treatment of financial instruments, including derivatives and synthetics, is based on whether or not the entity utilizes market or fair value or historic cost when accounting for financial instruments. This varies by industry and, as discussed below for those entities covered by SFAS No. 115, it also depends on how a particular security is classified.

Brokers and dealers in securities, swap dealers, investment companies, hedge funds, and pension plans generally carry all of their investments at market or fair value. For the most part, the accounting treatment of financial instruments does not differ among these market-value entities.

Thus, the following excerpt from the *Audit of Brokers and Dealers in Securities* on accounting for options typifies the accounting by these market-value entities:

> [Market-value entities] carry all securities at market or fair value, and it is appropriate that options positions also be reflected at market or fair value. The cost or proceeds from sales of options are subsequently adjusted to the current market (marked-to-market) or fair value of the options, and as in the case of other securities, any gain or loss is included in the results of operations. The current market value of exchange-traded options generally should be based on the quoted bid and offer prices. The fair value of unlisted options should be determined by the broker's or dealer's management, which considers the price of the underlying securities, the liquidity of the market, and the time remaining to expiration date. The process of adjusting option positions to market or fair value gives appropriate accounting recognition to the option premium.[4]

This market/fair value applies to these entities whether the derivatives or synthetics are used for trading or speculative purposes, as part of a yield enhancement or arbitrage strategy, or even for longer-term investment purposes.

For most other entities, SFAS No. 115 is the key pronouncement covering the accounting for their financial assets. Some of the important requirements of this pronouncement include:

- Debt securities must be classified into three categories—held-to-maturity, trading, and available-for-sale—while marketable equity securities, including equity options, must be classified into two categories—trading and available-for-sale. Debt securities covered by SFAS No. 115 include mandatory redeemable preferred stocks, securitized loans, collateralized mortgage obligations (CMOs) and CMO residuals, interest-only and principal-only securities (I/Os and P/Os).

- Investments in debt securities classified as held-to-maturity are, consistent with prior practice, generally carried at amortized cost. However, the new rules under SFAS No. 115 make it more difficult to classify debt securities as held-to-maturity. Not only must the entity have the positive intent and ability to hold the debt

---

[4]*Audits of Brokers and Dealers in Securities* (New York: AICPA, 1985), pp. 84-5.

securities to maturity, but SFAS No. 115 explicitly prohibits an entity from classifying such securities as held-to-maturity if they might be sold in response to changes in market interest rates, prepayment risk, the enterprise's liquidity needs, foreign-exchange risk, tax-planning strategies, or other similar factors.

- Trading securities (both debt and equity) are carried at market value with unrealized gains and losses included currently in income.

- Any securities (both debt and equity) that are neither to be held to maturity nor acquired for trading purposes are classified as available-for-sale with unrealized gains and losses reported in a separate component of stockholders' equity until realized or until the security is judged to have suffered an "other-than-temporary" decline in value.

- If the decline in fair value is judged to be other than temporary, the cost basis of the individual security should be written down to fair value with a charge to earnings, i.e., the write-down is accounted for as a realized loss.

- Gains and losses, both realized and unrealized, on qualifying hedges of securities positions should follow the accounting for the related security. For example, gains and losses on hedges of trading securities are included currently in income, while those relating to hedges of securities in the available-for-sale category are included in stockholders' equity.

As a general rule, the accounting treatment of derivatives by commercial and industrial companies or by banks, thrifts, and insurance companies depends mainly on the purpose and designation of their use in a particular transaction. If specific criteria are met, hedge accounting treatment results. In other cases, primarily with regard to interest-rate swaps that are used to alter the interest flows on interest-bearing liabilities or assets, another form of accounting known by a variety of names such as *swap accounting, settlement accounting,* or *synthetic alteration accounting* results. In other, more complex situations, other forms of synthetic instrument accounting might apply. Failing these, the company would generally be presumed to be entering into a speculative transaction, and, therefore, mark-to-market accounting with recognition of all gains and losses in current period's earnings would result.

Valuation Sources

The determination of market or fair value[5] for accounting purposes warrants discussion, since for many entities it is their basis of accounting for investments in derivatives and synthetics, and, even for those entities that do not carry these items on this basis, fair value is now a required disclosure under SFAS No. 107. Fair value is considered by the FASB to be the dollar value for which a given instrument would be willingly exchanged in a situation other than forced sale or liquidation. For traditional financial instruments (equities and listed futures, for example) this is not a difficult concept to apply. However, for thinly traded, nontraded, and/or customized financial products, fair value is not as readily determined. At many organizations, the traders may be the only ones who know how to compute the value of a particular financial instrument; however, it is obvious that traders should not be the ones who are valuing their own portfolios for purposes of financial reporting. The following is a hierarchy of sources and methods for determining the value of a particular financial instrument (see Figure 15–1 for a graphic depiction of this information).

External valuation sources

Public exchange markets.   When available, the quoted price of an instrument on a public market generally provides the most reliable measure of fair value. Many equity and debt securities as well as certain derivative products, such as options and futures, trade in exchange markets. When a financial instrument is traded in an active market, its fair value is normally determined by reference to the last trade price.

Dealer markets or quotation services.   Dealers trade a plethora of financial instruments for their own account. Generally, these dealers provide the last bid and ask. The bid and asking prices should be used to estimate the fair value of assets (long positions) and liabilities (short positions), respectively.

Quotations services gather quotes from dealers and report them—either electronically or in hard-copy form—to other dealers and investors. Dealer prices and quotation services are generally available for most interest-rate swaps and related derivatives.

---

[5]Market value, one form of fair value, based upon published prices reported by public exchanges, is generally regarded as the best indicator of fair value for most purposes, including financial reporting.

FIGURE 15–1

Determining Fair Value of Selected Derivatives

	External sources					Internal sources			
	Public exchange markets	Dealer markets	Quotation services	Pricing services	Specialists/appraisers	Market comparables	Internal comparables	Present values	Option pricing models
Hedging Instruments									
Futures contracts	♦								
Swaps		♦	♦	♦	♦	♦		♦	
Options	♦	♦			♦	♦			♦
Forward exchange contracts		♦			♦	♦		♦	♦

Pricing services and other valuation specialists.   Pricing services and other valuation specialists use a variety of sources and techniques. Pricing models are often proprietary; therefore, it is necessary to gain comfort with the service providing the quote. These services value thinly traded products, such as warrants on foreign equity.

Market comparable.   This is an empirical pricing technique based on factors that can be objectively confirmed, such as yield curves and prices of similar securities for which quotes can be obtained. For example, a petroleum derivative future may not be actively traded on a public exchange. By developing a price relationship between a base commodity, such as West Texas Intermediate and the less widely traded Dubai, long-dated forward prices can be derived.

Internal valuation methods.

Internal comparable.   This technique utilizes prices currently charged by the entity for similar products. Recent sales of similar securities can provide a reasonable estimate of market value.

Present value of expected cash flows. Often, accountants must estimate the value of a given security by examining the expected cash flows, discounted by an appropriate rate. The discount rate used to calculate the present value should take into account both the current interest-rate levels and the creditworthiness of the counterparty. This technique has obvious applications with regard to swaps.

Pricing models. Most swap and derivative-products dealers have internal models, usually based on variations of the better-known option pricing models, such as Black-Scholes or the binomial model, to value many of their derivatives. This valuation approach, sometimes referred to as mark-to-model, is often necessary to value the more esoteric or customized instruments in a portfolio, for example, over-the-counter options with features different from those traded on public exchanges, knock-out options, and long-dated or highly structured interest-rate and currency swaps.

As noted in the July 1993 study by the Group of Thirty entitled *Derivatives: Practices and Principles*, the precise valuation techniques used by different dealers vary. The study recommends that derivatives portfolios of dealers be valued based either on midmarket price levels less specific adjustments, or on appropriate bid or offer levels. Where the midmarket approach is used, valuation adjustments should allow for expected future costs related to the portfolio, such as unearned credit spread to reflect credit risk, close-out costs associated with unmatched or unhedged instruments, investing and funding costs during the life of an instrument, and the administrative costs that will be incurred to administer the portfolio. Obviously, the combination of the use of often complex mathematical models to value the instruments, together with the adjustment of such values for some or all of the costs described above, can make the valuation of a swap dealer's portfolio of derivatives a very complex exercise.

By utilizing the above sources, those engaged in the preparation and audit of financial statements can determine appropriate values for most derivatives and synthetics. Figure 15–1 summarizes the alternative valuation methods for some common derivatives.

HEDGE ACCOUNTING

While, as previously noted, the U.S. accounting rules have developed over time in a somewhat piecemeal fashion and are currently in a state of flux, the following general principles apply:

- Derivatives used for trading or speculative purposes are "marked to market" with the resulting unrealized gains and losses included currently in income, whereas,
- Hedge accounting applies where certain specific criteria are met. As discussed below, these hedging criteria can differ depending on the particular derivative (e.g., foreign currency forwards or swaps vs. futures vs. options) being used to effect the hedge. Accordingly, an understanding of the various hedging criteria applicable to different types of derivatives is critical to those seeking to qualify for hedge accounting treatment.

In practice, whether a transaction qualifies for hedge accounting should be determined on a case-by-case basis. Before the appropriate accounting can be determined, however, the economics and purpose of the transaction must be fully understood.

Accounting for a transaction as a hedge generally means that the gains or losses from the hedge position are recognized in the same period as losses or gains on the hedged item. For example, if unrealized changes in the hedged item are included in income, the changes in the hedge will also be recognized in income as they occur. Alternatively, when the hedged item is an asset carried at lower of cost or market (for example, inventory), changes in the hedge should be recorded as an adjustment of the carrying amount of the hedged item (however, the hedge-accounting adjustment cannot result in the asset being carried at higher than market). The deferred gain or loss on the hedge becomes part of the carrying amount of the hedged item that will be recognized when the item being hedged is disposed of (e.g., when inventory is sold).

In other words, hedge accounting is an extension of the matching principle in the sense that since the hedge and the hedged item are economically linked, it is appropriate to recognize gains or losses on the hedge in the same accounting period that losses or gains on the hedged item are recognized.

Although there is no comprehensive authoritative pronouncement that addresses accounting for transactions involving hedges, there is general agreement that hedging transactions are frequently accounted for differently from transactions for other purposes and that certain criteria must be met to account for a transaction as a hedge. The authoritative pronouncements, SFAS Nos. 52 and 80, provide hedging criteria for foreign currency transactions and transactions involving non-foreign-currency futures contracts, respectively. In addition, EITF Issues 90-7, 91-1, and 91-4 address hedging of foreign currency risk with purchased options, intercompany foreign currency risks, and foreign currency risks with complex options, and similar types of instruments. Analogy to these pronouncements may be utilized for transactions not covered therein (including forwards, options, and swaps).

Hedge Accounting Criteria

Criteria for hedge accounting generally include the following:

- The item to be hedged exposes the enterprise (or separate entity for a foreign currency transaction) to price, currency, or interest-rate risk.
- The hedge position reduces the exposure (e.g., there is high correlation between changes in the market value of the hedge position and the inverse changes in market value of the hedged item).
- The hedge position is designated as a hedge.

There must be risk. The first criterion concerning exposure to risk means that hedge accounting cannot be applied to situations where there is deemed to be no risk. The purpose of hedging is to reduce risk, so without risk, hedge accounting is inappropriate. In situations without risk, gains or losses from positions in hedge-type instruments cannot be deferred.

In this regard, SFAS No. 80 describes risk as "the sensitivity of an enterprise's income for one or more future periods to changes in market prices or yields of existing assets, liabilities, firm commitments, or anticipated transactions." The Statement recognizes that the specific circumstances that create risk can and do vary significantly from company to company; the hedge recognition criteria for accounting purposes depend on whether the risk ultimately affects income. Not all situations expose an enterprise to price or interest-rate risk. A footnote to SFAS No. 80 cites the following example:

> An interest-bearing financial instrument that an enterprise will retain to maturity does not, in and of itself, create interest-rate risk if the instrument's interest rate is fixed. The amount of cash inflows or outflows is certain (assuming no default) and is not affected by changes in market interest rates. Notwithstanding that the cash flows associated with the instrument are fixed, the enterprise may be exposed to interest-rate risk if it has funded its assets with instruments having earlier maturities or repricing dates. Futures contracts may qualify as a hedge of a fixed-rate financial instrument the enterprise intends to hold to

maturity if the maturity or repricing characteristics of the instrument contribute to the enterprise's overall asset-liability mismatch.

Following this example, a financial institution that funds short-term variable-rate assets with floating-rate debt of similar maturity may not be exposed to interest-rate risk.

SFAS No. 80, dealing with futures contracts, and the consensus of EITF Issue 90-17, dealing with purchased options, differ from SFAS No. 52 as to how risk should be assessed. SFAS No. 80 and EITF Issue 90-17 generally require that for hedging instruments to be accounted for as a hedge, a risk condition must be present on an enterprise perspective. Determining whether a company's income is at risk requires evaluating whether a potential risk condition at one location or operating center is mitigated by conditions at another location or operating center. For example, a parent company with several subsidiaries should apply SFAS No. 80, using a total enterprise perspective if relevant information to assess risk on that basis is available. However, realizing that many large companies manage risk on a decentralized basis by business unit, SFAS No. 80 also permits risk assessment on that basis (i.e., by business unit). SFAS No. 52, in contrast, permits hedge accounting based on assessing risk on a transaction basis. For example, a U.S. parent may hedge a foreign currency commitment with a forward exchange contract even though a foreign subsidiary whose functional currency is the U.S. dollar may have a foreign currency balance equal and opposite to the commitment exposure of the parent and even though the parent itself may have offsetting exposures in the foreign currency.

Hedge position reduces exposure. The second criterion for hedge accounting concerns the correlation between the hedge position and changes in market value of the hedged item. This means that changes in the market value of the hedging instrument must track the changes in the market value of the hedged item. Under SFAS No. 52, this is not normally an issue, since that statement generally limits hedge accounting to hedges denominated in the same currency as the exposure being hedged (i.e., it does not generally permit cross-currency hedges). In contrast, SFAS No. 80 permits cross-hedging, and, therefore, demonstrating the effectiveness of a hedge is essential because it is the basis for entering into the hedge transaction in the first place (i.e., that the gain or loss on the hedged item will be offset by the loss or gain on the hedge). When determining whether high correlation is likely, an enterprise is required to consider such factors as historical correlation and variations in correlation that could be expected.

While companies may use a variety of approaches to evaluate expected future correlation, regression analysis is the statistical method most commonly used to measure this relationship. Regression analysis techniques examine historical data relevant to each variable and calculate the expected value of one variable based on the value of the other. The result is a measurement of the expected sensitivity of the movement in one variable to movement in another variable (this is referred to as the correlation coefficient). Once the correlation coefficient has been calculated, statistical analysis must be used to verify its strength, since knowing the strength of this coefficient is critical to a successful hedging program.

The strength of the correlation coefficient is indicated by the R-square statistic. An R-square statistic of 1 (its maximum value) means that 100 percent of a change in one variable can be explained by a change in the other variable. For example, if a 1 percent change in the value of item A triggers a 0.5 percent change in the value of item B and there is an R-square statistic of 0.90, there is a 90 percent assurance that if the value of item A moves 1 percent, the value of item B will move 0.5 percent. The price movements would then be said to be highly correlated. In this situation, selling futures contracts on item B that are twice the value of hedged item A will be highly effective in offsetting the effects of price changes on item A.

The assessment of correlation requires judgments that must be made on a case-by-case basis. Although measurement and analysis of correlation is an evolving process, and it is difficult to establish precise guidelines, a hedging instrument that is 80 percent or more correlated with the hedged item (i.e., that has an R-square statistic of 0.80 or higher) is generally considered to meet the test of high correlation.

Ongoing assessment of correlation. In addition to the requirement to assess high correlation at the inception of the hedge, SFAS No. 80 also requires an ongoing assessment of high correlation during the hedge period. While statistical techniques such as regression analysis may be used to assess probable future correlation at hedge inception, the test of actual past correlation (i.e., the ongoing correlation during the hedge period) should be generally measured based on the actual results of the hedge since inception. A common way of measuring the degree of ongoing correlation is to divide the cumulative price change for the hedging instrument, i.e., the futures contract, by the cumulative price change of the hedged item. Again, while precise guidelines are not available, in order to qualify for ongoing high correlation, the cumulative changes in the value of the futures contracts should be generally between 80 percent and 125 percent of the cumulative changes in the value of the hedged item. In addition to these percentage guidelines, the materiality of the absolute dollar amounts of net gains or losses to be deferred should also be considered to determine whether continuation of hedge accounting would be appropriate.

The assessment of ongoing high correlation should be made at least quarterly, i.e., as often as financial results are reported externally. SFAS No. 80 requires termination of hedge accounting if high correlation ceases to exist. However, an isolated incidence of inadequate correlation—e.g., the cumulative hedge ratio falling beyond the range of 80 percent and 125 percent—may not require termination of hedge accounting if there is sufficient basis for the conclusion that the incident was isolated and due to an identifiable, nonrecurring cause.

Indirectly related to the criterion regarding correlation is another difference between SFAS No. 80 and SFAS No. 52. Cross-hedging is a strategy where the hedging instrument's underlying item is different from the item being hedged. SFAS No. 80 permits cross-hedging as long as the high correlation requirement is met and there is a clear economic relationship between the item underlying the futures contract and the item being hedged. SFAS No. 52 permits cross-hedging only when it is not practical or feasible to hedge in a transaction denominated in the identical currency. So, for example, even if a company can demonstrate that it was economically hedged by entering into a forward exchange contract for Australian dollars to hedge its British-pound-denominated debt, SFAS No. 52 does not permit hedge accounting for the forward exchange contract because British pound forward-exchange contracts are available.

Designation as hedge. The third criterion for hedge accounting is the designation of the position, by the entity entering into the transaction, as a hedge of specific items. The hedge must be initially designated as such to recognize gains or losses from the hedging position in the same accounting period as the losses or gains of the hedged item. In other words, it is not appropriate to wait until it is determined that a loss has occurred in a position and then at that time decide to defer the loss—the hedge should be designated up front.

Indirectly relating to the designation criterion is another difference between SFAS No. 52 and SFAS No. 80. SFAS No. 80 permits hedging of firm commitments as well as anticipated transactions if the significant characteristics and expected terms of the anticipated transaction are identified and it is probable that the anticipated transaction will occur. SFAS No. 52 permits hedging of firm commitments but not of anticipated transactions. An example of an anticipatory hedge is a financial institution that purchases Treasury note futures-contracts to lock in the yield on a Treasury note it expects to purchase in three months when cash becomes available. The institution may be able to designate the futures contracts as a hedge and defer the gains and losses on the futures contract until the Treasury note is purchased (at which time the deferred gain or loss will become part of the carrying value of the Treasury note). However, if that same financial institution entered into a forward exchange contract to hedge an anticipated borrowing it had arranged in the European market, it would not qualify for hedge accounting (i.e., it could not defer the gains or losses on the forward exchange contract) because the anticipated borrowing would not be viewed as a firm commitment under SFAS No. 52 (e.g., usually a legally enforceable obligation).

The lack of authoritative literature and the differences between SFAS No. 52 and SFAS No. 80 make it difficult to apply specific criteria to many hedging transactions. As discussed later in this chapter, the FASB is currently reviewing all hedge accounting rules. However, in the meantime, companies entering into transactions involving hedging instruments, particularly those not specifically covered by SFAS No. 52 and SFAS No. 80, should consult with their accounting advisers to determine whether hedge accounting is appropriate in their particular circumstances.

Purchased Foreign-Currency Options

EITF Issue 90-17 permits hedge accounting for purchased foreign-currency options (with little or no intrinsic value at the date of purchase) used to hedge anticipated transactions, provided that the conditions in SFAS No. 80 are met.

In evaluating these conditions, SFAS No. 52 establishes the nature of foreign currency risk that may be hedged for accounting purposes—that is, risk associated with transactions and commitments in currencies other than the transacting entity's functional currency. In addition, the exposure to foreign currency risk from anticipated transactions should be evaluated on an enterprise basis, as defined in paragraph 4(a) of SFAS No. 80.

For a purchased option to qualify for hedge accounting, it must be probable that a high correlation will exist between the currency underlying the option contract and the currency in which the anticipated transaction is denominated. This correlation must exist at the time that the option is designated as a hedge and throughout the hedge period (or life of the option contract, if shorter). These criteria also permit hedge accounting using purchased options in highly correlated tandem currencies.

Guidance in paragraph 9 of SFAS No. 80 should be followed for purposes of identifying significant characteristics and expected terms of the anticipated transaction and assessing the probability that the anticipated transaction will occur. Judgment is required in determining if these conditions are met and that the likelihood of meeting such criteria diminishes the farther into the future the anticipated transaction is expected to occur.

In connection with Issue 90-17, the EITF also discussed the propriety of hedge accounting in certain specific situations using purchased foreign currency options with little or no intrinsic value.

One situation addressed an enterprise that estimated its minimum probable foreign sales for the next several years and would like to reduce its exposure to the related foreign-exchange risk. In this case, the propriety of hedge accounting depends on an assessment of the transactions using the SFAS No. 80 criteria described above.

Another situation addressed hedging by a U.S. parent of the net income of its foreign subsidiary. The foreign subsidiary generates revenues and incurs costs denominated in its functional currency. In this case, hedge accounting would not be appropriate because (1) the parent would not have foreign currency risk, as defined in SFAS No. 52, for its subsidiary's transactions denominated in the subsidiary's functional currency, and (2) future net income does not qualify as an anticipated transaction because it is the net result of many transactions and accounting allocations.

Hedge accounting would not be appropriate in situations where foreign currency options are purchased as a strategic or competitive hedge, where the gains on the options are intended to offset lost operating profits from increased competitive pressure associated with exchange-rate changes that benefit competitors. To qualify for hedge accounting, the options must be designated and effective as a hedge of a net investment in a foreign entity, a firm foreign currency commitment, or an anticipated foreign currency transaction.

Complex and Combination Foreign-Currency Options

EITF Issue 91-4, "Hedging Foreign Currency Risks with Complex Options and Similar Transactions," addresses the use of hedge accounting for

those option transactions that were specifically excluded from EITF Issue
90-17—such as deep-in-the-money purchased options, written options,
options purchased and written as a unit (combination options), and similar
transactions, including synthetic forwards, range forwards, and participating forwards. EITF Issue 90-17 addressed only foreign currency options
with little or no intrinsic value (the amount of advantage, if any, that would
be realized by exercise of an option equal to the difference between the
exercise price and the spot rate of the underlying currency). EITF Issue
91-4 is limited to combinations of foreign currency options that are
established as contemplated integral transactions, where the components
are entered into at or about the same time, are designated as a unit, and
have the same expiration date.

At the March 19, 1992, EITF meeting, the chief accountant of the SEC
indicated that the SEC will object to the deferral of gains and losses arising
from complex options and other similar transactions with respect to
anticipated foreign currency transactions. Additionally, the chief accountant noted that the SEC's staff will object to deferral of losses with respect
to written options because they believe they do not reduce but increase
risk. The SEC's staff will not, however, object to deferral of gains on
purchased options having little or no intrinsic value, as addressed in EITF
Issue 90-17. As a result of EITF Issues 90-17 and 91-4, combined with the
prohibition in SFAS No. 52 on hedging anticipated (but not firmly
committed) foreign currency transactions, those seeking to hedge such
anticipated transactions and receive hedge accounting are forced to use
simple purchased options, which are generally more expensive than
forwards or combination options.

Intercompany Foreign-Currency Risk

EITF Issue 91-1 provides that transactions or commitments among members of a consolidated group with different functional currencies (i.e.,
intercompany transactions) can present foreign currency risk that may be
hedged for accounting purposes. The appropriate accounting guidance
depends on the type of hedging instrument used. The provisions of SFAS
No. 52 must be applied to forward exchange contracts, foreign currency
futures, and agreements that are essentially the same as forward exchange
contracts. When hedging foreign currency commitments, SFAS No. 52
requires that both of the following conditions exist:

1. The foreign currency transaction must be designated as, and effective as, a hedge of a foreign currency commitment.
2. The foreign currency commitment must be firm.

In connection with the second condition, an intercompany foreign-currency commitment may be considered firm if there is a firm commitment to a third party obligating the affiliates to comply with the terms of the intercompany agreement.

In the event that a third-party commitment is not present, a firm commitment exists only if the agreement is legally enforceable and performance is probable due to sufficiently large disincentives for nonperformance. Examples of disincentives for nonperformance include minority interests, existing laws or regulations, and fiduciary responsibilities that result in significant economic penalties to the consolidated entity for nonperformance. In Issue No. 95-2, the EITF reached a consensus that the economic penalty must result from a condition imposed by an unrelated party. The specific facts and circumstances surrounding each transaction need to be assessed in determining whether disincentives for nonperformance arise from third-party imposed penalties and whether they are sufficiently large to ensure that performance of the intercompany transaction is probable.

The guidance set forth in EITF Issue 90-17, discussed above, is also appropriate for hedges of intercompany transactions using purchased foreign currency options.

Illustrations of Hedge Accounting

Assuming a transaction qualifies for hedge accounting, how are the hedge accounting concepts applied? The following illustrations and discussions apply the hedge accounting concepts to the basic hedging tools: futures, forwards, swaps, and options.

Futures Contracts

As discussed earlier, SFAS No. 80 describes the accounting for a futures contract. It requires all futures contracts to be marked to market and, if serving as a hedge, to defer the gain or loss until the loss or gain on the hedged item is recognized. Accounting for a futures contract that is hedging an anticipated borrowing is illustrated by the following hypothetical transaction.

Situation. On May 2, 19X1, a manufacturer expects to borrow $10 million on May 20, 19X1, for 90 days, with an interest rate tied to LIBOR (London Interbank Offered Rate), to finance the acquisition of inventory. The manufacturer expects to renew the loan for an additional 90 days, repay half the loan in November, and roll over the $5 million balance for another 90 days. Ninety days later, it will roll this $5 million over again. The manufacturer is exposed to risk because an increase in interest rates before the loan is incurred or rolled over will increase its financing costs.

Hedge strategy. To lock in the 9-percent interest rate in effect on May 2, 19X1, for a period of one year, the manufacturer sells a strip of Eurodollar futures contracts that coincide with the dates when it expects to borrow and roll over the debt:

- Ten* June** 19X1 Eurodollar contracts are sold to lock in the interest rate on the $10 million to be borrowed on May 20, 19X1.
- Ten* September** 19X1 Eurodollar contracts are sold to lock in the interest rate on the $10 million loan when it is rolled over on August 18, 19X1.
- Five* December** 19X1 Eurodollar contracts are sold to lock in the interest rate on the $5 million when it is rolled over on November 16, 19X1.
- Five* March** 19X2 Eurodollar contracts are sold to lock in the interest rate on the $5 million when it is rolled over on February 14, 19X2.

Contracts are closed as the debt is actually borrowed or rolled over. Eurodollar futures contracts are expected to reduce the manufacturer's risk of loss, since the price of these contracts and the interest expense associated with the loan are highly correlated.

Hedge results. The company's position in the futures contract is illustrated in Table 15–3.

---

*Eurodollar futures contracts are sold in units of $1 million, each of which represents a certificate of deposit with a major London bank maturing in 90 days. Therefore, 10 contracts are needed to cover each 90-day $10 million.

**These months represent the nearest relevant settlement months for which Eurodollar futures contracts are available.

TABLE 15–3
Hedge Results

Date	Cash Position	Futures Position	Margin Initial	Margin Variations[3]
May 2, 19X1		Sell 10 June 19X1 Eurodollar contracts @91.00[1]	$30,000[2]	
		Sell 10 Sept. 19X1 Eurodollar contracts @90.86		
		Sell 5 Dec. 19X1 Eurodollar contracts @90.62		
		Sell 5 Mar. 19X2 Eurodollar contracts @90.42		
May 20, 19X1	Borrow $10,000,000 @9.25%	Buy 10 June 19X1 Eurodollar contracts @90.64		$ 9,000
		Market values: • 10 Sept. contracts—90.39 • 5 Dec. contracts—90.18 • 5 Mar. contracts—89.94		11,750 5,500 6,000 $32,250
Aug. 18, 19X1	Roll $10,000,000 @10.18%	Buy 10 Sept. 19X1 Eurodollar contracts @89.59		$20,000
		Market values: • 5 Dec. contracts—89.18 • 5 Mar. contracts—88.92		12,500 12,750 $45,250
Nov. 16, 19X1	Roll $5,000,000 @9.87%	Buy 5 Dec. 19X1 Eurodollar contracts @89.94		($9,500)
		Market values: • 5 Mar. contracts—89.54		(7,750) ($17,250)
Feb. 14, 19X2	Roll $5,000,000 @10.00%	Buy 5 Mar. 19X2 Eurodollar contracts @89.84		($ 3,750)

[1]Eurodollar contracts are quoted using an index of 100 minus the annualized LIBOR for 90-day deposits. A quotation of 91.00 means the annualized LIBOR is 9.00 percent. A price change of one basis point (0.01 percent) equals $25.00 ($1,000,000 × 0.0001 × 90.360).

[2]A margin deposit of $1,000 per contract was deposited with the broker, as required by the futures exchange.

[3]Changes in market value of futures contracts will result in the requirement for increased (decreased) margin to be posted.

TABLE 15–4 Hedge Results

	June Contracts	Sept. Contracts	Dec. Contracts	Mar. Contracts
Market value on May 2	91.00	90.86	90.62	90.42
Market value on May 20	90.64	90.39	90.18	89.94
Market value change (in basis points)	36	47	44	48
Value per basis point	× $25	× $25	× $25	× $25
Market value decrease per contract	$900	$1,175	$1,100	1,200
Number of contracts sold	× 10	× 10	× 5	× 5
Total gain on contracts as of May 20	$9,000	$11,750	$5,500	$6,000

Calculating gains and losses on futures contracts. Because interest rates changed during the period covered by the futures contracts, the company incurs gains and losses equal to the increases and decreases in variation margin shown in the hedge results. The gains and losses on the futures contracts are the decreases or increases in their market value. For example, the gain of $32,250 as of May 20 is calculated as shown in Table 15–4.

Calculating hedge effectiveness. The basis gain or loss on a particular contract determines the overall effectiveness of that contract. The futures contract results are compared with the additional interest incurred because of rate changes. For example, the effectiveness of hedging the first rollover period is calculated as follows:

Additional interest cost:	
Principal	$10,000,000
Change in rate (9% to 10.18%)	× 1.18%
Cost for 360 days	$ 118,000
Cost for 90 days	$ 29,500
Gains on Sept. futures contracts:	
Gain through May 20	$ 11,750
Gain for May 20 through Aug. 18	20,000
	$ 31,750
Net basis gain	$ 2,250

This calculation shows that high correlation was achieved; the gain on the futures contracts offset 108 percent of the increased borrowing costs. The effective interest rate for this period as a result of the hedge can be calculated as follows:

Principal	$10,000,000
Target interest for 90 days (9%)	$ 225,000
Less basis gain	(2,250)
	$ 222,750

Effective rate for quarter:

$$\frac{\$222,750}{\$10,000,000 \times 90/360} = 8.91\%$$

Summary. The net futures-gains realized by the company reduced its overall borrowing cost from what would have resulted had the company not hedged. The impact of the hedge results can be summarized as shown in Table 15–5.

Forward Exchange Contracts

To illustrate the accounting for forward exchange contracts (see Table 15–6), assume a company enters into a forward exchange contract to hedge a 90-day currency risk on its foreign-denominated zero-coupon borrowing.

There may be different ways to apply SFAS No. 52 rules to the hypothetical transaction. The author believes that the method chosen should be one that best reflects the economics of the integrated nature of the borrowing and the forward contract. This objective is achieved by distinguishing between the two elements of the 90-day note, namely, the principal portion (representing the face amount less the unamortized discount) and the unamortized discount portion (representing the future commitment to pay interest expense), and by treating the corresponding amounts of the forward contract as hedges of each of the elements of the 90-day note.

Under this approach, the exchange gain or loss on the principal portion of the 90-day note (which results from a change in exchange rates between

TABLE 15–5 Impact of Hedge Results

	May 20– Aug. 18	Aug. 19– Nov. 16	Nov.17– Feb. 14	Feb. 15– May 6	Cumulative
Target interest (9%)	$225,000	$225,000	$112,500	$112,500	$675,000
Additional interest cost because of rate increases	6,250	29,500	10,875	12,500	59,125
Total interest paid	231,250	254,500	123,375	125,000	734,125
Gain on futures contracts	(9,000)	(31,750)	(8,500)	(7,250)	(56,500)
Net final interest cost	$222,250	$222,750	$114,875	$117,750	$677,625
Target rate on May 2	9.00%	9.00%	9.00%	9.00%	9.00%
Hedged rate	8.89%	8.91%	9.19%	9.42%	9.04%

the date of the borrowing and the intervening balance-sheet date or settlement date) is included in income. Offsetting this is the exchange loss or gain on the forward contract hedging the principal amount.

The interest expense relating to the FC$ discount is the U.S. dollar value of the current-period amortization determined on the effective interest method and translated at the average exchange rate for the period. The exchange gain or loss on the forward contract that hedges the unamortized discount portion (representing the future commitment to pay interest expense) is included in the measurement of the interest expense at the time of recording the amortization of the discount. As a result, the interest expense (the amortization of the discount on the note) is effectively fixed (based on the exchange rate at the date of issuance of the note) by the forward contract.

SFAS No. 52 also requires the premium or discount on a forward contract (i.e., the difference between the contract rate of the forward contract and the exchange rate at inception of the forward contract multiplied by the FC$ face amount of the forward contract) to be amortized over the life of the forward contract. Since the amortization method is not specified in SFAS No. 52, the straight-line method may be used. However, the author believes that the preferable method, given the

TABLE 15–6
Accounting Entries

	Debit	Credit
May 2, 19X1		
Amount due from broker	$30,000	
Cash		$30,000
(To record initial margin deposit)		
May 20, 19X1		
Cash	$10,000,000	
Loan payable		$10,000,000
(To record 90-day borrowing)		
May 2–May 20, 19X1		
Amount due from broker	$32,250	
Deferred gain on futures contracts		$32,250
(To record deferral of cumulative gain on futures contracts)		
May 21–Aug. 18, 19X1		
Interest expense	$222,250	
Deferred gain on futures contracts	9,000	
Cash		$231,250
(To amortize cumulative deferred gain on June contracts over the hedge period, and to record interest expense on the $10,000,000 borrowing)		
Amount due from broker	$45,250	
Deferred gain on futures contracts		$45,250
(To record deferral of gain on futures contracts since May 20, 19X1)		
Aug. 19–Nov. 16, 19X1		
Interest expense	$222,750	
Deferred gain on futures contracts	31,750	
Cash		$254,500
(To amortize cumulative deferred gain on Sept. contracts over the hedge period, and to record interest expense on the $10,000,000 borrowing that was rolled over on Aug. 18, 19X1)		
Deferred gain on futures contracts	$17,250	
Amount due from broker		$17,250
(To record loss on futures contracts since Aug. 18, 19X1, as a reduction of the deferred gain account)		

TABLE 15–6
(concluded)

	Debit	Credit
Nov. 16, 19X1		
Loan payable	$5,000,000	
Cash		$5,000,000
(To record repayment of half the loan)		
Nov. 17, 19X1–Feb. 14, 19X2		
Interest expense	$114,875	
Deferred gain on futures contracts	8,500	
Cash		$123,375
(To amortize cumulative deferred gain on Dec. contracts over the hedge period, and to record interest expense on the $5,000,000 borrowing when it was rolled over on Nov. 16, 19X1)		
Deferred gain on futures contracts	$3,750	
Amount due from broker		$3,750
(To record loss on futures contracts since Nov. 16, 19X1, as a reduction of the deferred gain account)		
Cash	$86,500	
Amount due from broker		$86,500
(To record receipt of margin deposit when hedge is terminated on Feb. 14, 19X2)		
Feb. 15–May 16, 19X2		
Interest expense	$117,750	
Deferred gain on futures contracts	7,250	
Cash		$125,000
(To amortize cumulative deferred gain on Mar. contracts over the hedge period, and to record interest expense on the $5,000,000 borrowing when it was rolled over on Feb. 14, 19X2)		
May 16, 19X2		
Loan payable	$5,000,000	
Cash		$5,000,000
(To record final principal payment due on the $10,000,000 loan)		

circumstances under which the discount on the note is amortized, is the effective interest method.

Further, SFAS No. 52 is silent as to the specific expense or income account in which the premium or discount should be included. The author believes it is appropriate, given the financing nature of the hypothetical transaction, to reflect it as an adjustment of interest expense.

With respect to the balance sheet of the issuer, the foreign currency dollar-face-amount and the unamortized discount of the note are translated at the reporting period's current exchange rate. Additionally, any receivable or payable relating to the forward contract is reflected on the balance sheet. To the extent the transaction is material to the financial statements of the issuer, a description of the transaction is required to be disclosed in the notes to the financial statements.

The accounting treatment described above is illustrated below:

- FC$ 90-Day Note:
  - Issued at a discount rate of 15 percent per annum
  - Face amount of FC$10,000,000
  - Proceeds received by issuer of FC$9,625,000
  - 90-day maturity
- Forward Contract:
  - Purchase FC$10,000,000
    - Hedge of principal of FC$9,625,000
    - Hedge of the commitment of FC$375,000 (interest)
  - Fixed contract price of FC$1/U.S.$0.63
  - Delivery date of the forward contract is the same as the maturity of the 90-day note
- FC$/U.S.$ Exchange Rates:
  - Inception date FC$1.00 = U.S.$0.65
  - Reporting date (i.e., end of fiscal year)
    - End FC$1.00 = U.S.$0.68
    - Average FC$1.00 = U.S.$0.66
  - Settlement date FC$1.00 = U.S.$0.70

The financial statement reporting date occurs 30 days into the term of the 90-day note.

The following represents the accounting journal entries (and related calculations) required to be made by the issuer of the 90-day note at the date of issuance and at the reporting date (Note: "BS" represents balance-sheet accounts, and "IS" represents income statement accounts):

Issuance of 90-Day Note
1. (BS) Cash (a) $6,256,250
   (BS) Discount on note payable   243,750
      (BS) Note payable (b) $6,500,000
   To record issuance of the note
2. No entry is required with respect to the
   forward contract.

(a) FC$9,625,000 × U.S. $0.65.
(b) FC$10,000,000 × U.S. $0.65.

Reporting Date—90-Day Note
1. (IS) Foreign currency transaction
   Loss (a) $292,500
   (BS) Discount on note payable (c)   7,500
      (BS) Note payable (b) $300,000
   To record the exchange loss on a foreign
   currency note

Calculation of Exchange Gain (Loss)—90-Day Note

(a) Outstanding principal, beginning of period:
    FC$9,625,000 × $0.65* =   U.S.$6,256,250

    Current period amortization:
    FC$125,000 × U.S.$0.65* =   U.S.$ 81,250
                                                              U.S.$6,337,500

    Outstanding principal, end of period:
    FC$9,750,000 × U.S.$0.68** =   U.S.$6,630,000
                                                              U.S.$ (292,500)

(b) FC$/U.S.$ exchange rate at inception date   U.S.$0.65
    FC$/U.S.$ exchange rate at reporting date   U.S.$0.68
    Difference   U.S.$0.03
    Multiplied by face amount   FC$ 10,000,000
                                                            U.S.$ 300,000

(c) FC$/U.S.$ exchange rate at inception date   U.S.$0.65
    FC$/U.S.$ exchange rate at reporting date   U.S.$0.68
    Difference   U.S.$0.03
    Multiplied by the unamortized discount***   FC $250,000
                                                              U.S.$ 7,500

---

* Exchange rate at inception.
** Exchange rate at reporting date.
***Beginning balance FC$375,000 less current period amortization FC$125,000.

Reporting Date—Forward Contract

1. (BS) Forward contract receivable $359,100
   (IS) Foreign currency transaction gain (a) $292,500
   (IS) Interest expense (b)   66,600
   To record the exchange gain and amortization of the
   discount

(a) Calculation of gain on the forward contract relating to the hedge of the principal amount:

FC$/U.S.$ exchange rate at reporting date	U.S.$0.68
FC$/U.S.$ exchange rate at inception date	U.S.$0.65
Difference	U.S.$0.03
Multiplied by the principal amount*	FC$9,750,000
	U.S.$ 292,500

(b) Calculation of discount on the forward contract:

FC$/U.S.$ exchange rate at inception date	U.S.$0.65
FC$/U.S.$ exchange rate at contract rate	U.S.$0.63
Difference	U.S.$0.02
Multiplied by the FC$ contract amount	FC$10,000,000
Discount amount	U.S.$200,000
Current period amortization (30 days)	U.S.$ 66,600

2. (BS) Discount on note payable $1,250
   (BS) Deferred gain (a) $1,250
   To record the transaction gain on the forward contract that
   hedges the commitment

3. (BS) Deferred gain $1,250
   (IS) Interest expense $1,250
   To include the transaction gain in the measurement of the
   commitment portion recognized

Reporting Date—Income Taxes

1. (BS) Income taxes receivable $5,860
   (IS) Provision for income taxes $5,860
   To record the income tax benefit of the interest deduction
   (40% blended rate × $14,650)

---

*Represents the hedge of the principal of FC$9,625,000 at inception plus the current period
amortization of the discount of FC$125,000.

(a) Calculation of transaction gain on recognized portion of forward contract:

Current period amortization	FC$125,000
Multiplied by the difference in FC$/U.S.$ exchange rates:	
Average rate	U.S.$0.66
Inception rate	U.S.$0.65
	U.S.$0.01
	U.S.$1,250

The net effect of these entries as of the reporting date is as follows:

Income Statement
Interest expense, comprised of:
- Amortization of discount on 90-day note $82,500*
- Adjustment relating to the hedged commitment   (1,250)
- Amortization of discount on the forward contract   (66,600)
                                                            $14,650**

Transaction (gain) loss, comprised of:
- Transaction loss on the 90-day note $292,500
- Transaction gain on the forward contract   (292,500)
                                                            $ –0–

Provision for income taxes   ($5,860)

---

* FC$125,000 x average rate 0.66 exchange rate.
**Interest expense for 30-day period approximates one-third of 90-day note fixed interest of $43,750.

Balance Sheet
Note payable, comprised of:
- Face amount*   ($6,800,000)
- Less the unamortized discount**   170,000
                                                           ($6,630,000)

Forward contract receivable, comprised of:
- Transaction gain on the forward contract $292,500
- Amortization of discount on the forward contract   66,600
                                                           $359,100

Income taxes receivable   5,860

---

* (FC$10,000,000 × U.S.$0.68).
**(FC$250,000 × U.S.$0.68).

Similar calculations would be made at each intervening reporting date and at the settlement date. In addition, at the settlement date the final entry to record the delivery of the forward contract and 90-day note would be made as follows:

(BS) Note payable (a)	$7,000,000	
(BS) Cash (b)		$6,300,000
(BS) Forward contract receivable		$ 700,000

The total net effect on income at maturity would be interest expense of $43,750 ($6,300,000 – $6,256,250), a transaction gain or loss of zero, and an income tax benefit of $17,500 (40% of $43,750).

(a) FC$10,000,000 × U.S.$0.70 (exchange rate at settlement date).
(b) FC$10,000,000 × U.S.$0.63 (forward contract rate).

Hedging Intercompany Foreign-Currency Risk with Forward Exchange Contracts

Economically, intercompany transactions denominated in foreign currencies do not expose an enterprise to currency risk. This is because the related cash flows remain with the enterprise. For instance, assume a U.S. enterprise has two subsidiaries: A and B. A's functional currency is the U.S. dollar and B's functional currency is a foreign currency (FC). A purchases goods from B for FC100 when the exchange rate is FC1.00 = U.S.$1.00. If at settlement date, the exchange rate is FC1.00 = U.S.$2.00, A needs to disburse U.S.$200 to buy FC100 on the spot market. A incurs a loss of U.S.$100. On the other hand, the value of the U.S. parent's net investment in B increases by U.S.$100 because the cash B received is now worth U.S.$200 (rather than U.S.$100). Therefore, on an enterprise basis, there is no economic gain or loss.

However, EITF Issue No. 91-1 provides that transactions or commitments among members of a consolidated group with different functional currencies can present foreign currency risk that may be hedged for accounting purposes. This is consistent with the functional currency approach in SFAS No. 52.

The appropriate accounting guidance depends on the type of hedging instrument used. The provisions of SFAS No. 52 must be applied to forward exchange contracts, foreign currency futures, and agreements that are essentially the same as forward exchange contracts. When hedging foreign currency commitments, SFAS No. 52 requires that both of the following conditions exist:

- The foreign currency transaction must be designated as, and effective as, a hedge of a foreign currency commitment.
- The foreign currency commitment must be firm.

In connection with the second condition, an intercompany foreign currency commitment may be considered firm if there is a firm commmitment to a third party obligating the affiliates to comply with the terms of the intercompany agreement.

In the event that a third-party commitment is not present, a firm commitment exists only if the agreement is legally enforceable and performance is probable because of sufficiently large disincentives for nonperformance. Examples of disincentives for nonperformance include minority interests, existing laws or regulations, and fiduciary responsibilities that result in significant economic penalties to the consolidated entity for nonperformance. In Issue No. 95-2, the EITF reached a consensus that a significant economic penalty to the consolidated entity exists under Issue No. 91-1 only when a penalty imposed by an unrelated party provides a sufficiently large disincentive for nonperformance such that performance under the intercompany foreign currency commitment is probable, even if the corresponding anticipated transactions do not occur.

However, as discussed earlier in this chapter, when hedging intercompany transactions with purchased foreign currency options, the more liberal provisions set forth in EITF Issue No. 90-17 apply.

Forwards Not Involving Foreign Currencies

As for forwards not involving foreign currencies, the FASB excluded forwards from SFAS No. 80; however, in paragraph 34, the Board states:

Exclusion of forward contracts from the statement should not be construed as either acceptance or rejection by the Board of current practice for such contracts, nor should the exclusion be interpreted as an indication that the general principles of this statement might not be appropriate in some circumstances for certain forward contracts, and it may address the conceptual aspects of accounting for executory contracts generally.

Accordingly, if it qualifies as a hedge, the forward would generally be carried at market value, and gains or losses would be deferred and included in the basis of the hedged item. In certain industries—for example, in the mining and other extractive industries—where commodity forwards are used to fix the price of future sales of production, common practice is to account for these as synthetic fixed-price sales at the time the sales are recorded without any intervening marking-to-market and hedge accounting for the forwards.

Interest-Rate Swaps

Currently, there is no U.S. authoritative literature that deals with accounting for interest-rate swaps. In general, the accounting treatment for interest-rate swaps should not be analogized to other situations because swap transactions have unique characteristics that may not be present in other transactions. However, accounting for plain-vanilla[6] interest-rate swap transactions has generally been as follows:

- Since most swaps are entered into either as an integral part of a borrowing arrangement or to hedge interest-rate exposure, it is generally inappropriate to recognize gain or loss related to changes in value of the swap contract except in instances in which the associated assets or liabilities are also being adjusted for changes in value (marked-to-market).
- Accordingly, interest expense should be adjusted for the net amount receivable or payable under the swap arrangement (i.e., interest expense should reflect the revised interest rate).
- The typical interest-rate swap transaction provides a legal right of offset for amounts due under the arrangement. Accordingly, any receivable or payable related to such a transaction should be presented net in the balance sheet (i.e., the swap should not be presented broad by recording a gross receivable and payable).
- With the exception of certain specialized industry practices, fees received or paid for entering into the swap should be amortized over the life of the swap as yield adjustments. However, fees

---

[6]In a plain-vanilla interest-rate swap, the parties agree to exchange streams of variable- and fixed-rate interest payments on a specified notional principal amount. Both the variable and fixed rates (or two variable rates, e.g., LIBOR vs. prime rate) in the contract are comparable to current interest rates on the date the contract is entered into, i.e., there is no significant premium or discount at the initiation of the contract. Also, there are no embedded options or leverage features in the swap.

received by an intermediary for arranging a swap when there is no
continuing involvement may be recognized in income.

• Unrealized gains and losses for changes in market value of speculative swaps should generally be recognized currently.

• Gains or losses on early termination of swaps accounted for as integral to a borrowing arrangement or as a hedge should be associated with the related debt and spread over the remaining original
life of the swap. (This is consistent with an EITF consensus on
accounting for termination of an interest-rate swap.)

Leveraged Interest-Rate Swaps

In a leveraged swap, the change in the base index rate (on which the
variable-rate interest payments are based) is multiplied by a factor (e.g.,
effectively five or ten times the increase or decrease in the index rate) or
the variable-rate payment is based on a formula that effectively includes a
written option so that the swap contract has the potential to generate very
large losses from relatively small increases in the variable index rate. To
compensate the variable-rate payer for accepting the leveraged risk, these
swaps pay a higher than normal fixed rate, which essentially is the
premium for the extra risk assumed.

Leveraged swaps that have embedded-written-option features are
asymmetrical—they have limited upside opportunity and significant or
unlimited downside risk, particularly when multiplied by the leveraged
feature. In addition, the downside risks of these swaps often are not offset
by upside opportunities from any designated on-balance-sheet instruments
(e.g., instruments with embedded purchased options).

The SEC staff has indicated that highly leveraged swaps or those that
include written option features should be marked to market. An alternative
approach that may be acceptable is to disaggregate the plain-vanilla
component and the leveraged component of the swap and only mark the
leveraged component to market. The SEC staff has indicated that they
would not object to such an approach provided it could be audited and the
plain-vanilla component is linked to an existing debt instrument. They
believe that it may be difficult to break the swap apart and obtain a market
value for only the leveraged component.

The following example illustrates a leveraged swap versus a plain-
vanilla swap, and the accounting for each.

	Receive Fixed	Pay Variable
Plain-Vanilla Swap	6%	LIBOR + 0.5%
Leveraged Swap	8%[2]	Formula[1]

Therefore, under the leveraged swap, if LIBOR increases to:

6%	8%	6.5%
7%	8%	12.5%
8%	8%	18.5%
9%	8%	24.5%

Notes:
(1) Example of a leverage formula:
   Pay variable = (a) + (b)
   (a) = LIBOR + 0.5%
   (b) = 5 (LIBOR − 6%)
(2) Receive 8% fixed instead of 6% fixed in the plain-vanilla swap represents the premium for agreeing to pay a leveraged, formula-based variable amount.

In the above example, a plain-vanilla swap, if linked with a fixed-rate borrowing, effectively converts the interest payments on the borrowing from fixed to floating and would be accounted for in this manner. In contrast, the leveraged swap really contains two separate financial instruments:

1. A plain-vanilla swap (receive 6% and pay LIBOR + 0.5%).
2. A written cap whereby the company agrees to receive an extra 2% (8% − 6%) in return for agreeing to pay 5 (LIBOR − 6%) as LIBOR increases above 6%.

Based on the SEC staff's views as noted above, the company could either mark to market the entire leveraged swap or alternatively could disaggregate the two components and account for the plain-vanilla swap component as a conversion of the interest expense on a related fixed-rate borrowing, thereby leaving only the embedded written cap to be accounted for on a mark-to-market basis, provided of course, that such market value can be reliably determined.

It is interesting to note that at its July 1995 meeting, the EITF began discussion on Issue No. 95-11 on the accounting for derivatives that contain both a forward element and a written option component. This may include mildly leveraged swaps like the one described above though the leverage in the above example would appear to be more than mild. At its September 1995 meeting, the majority of the EITF expressed support to bifurcate such an instrument into its written option and forward components. The EITF further agreed that if an instrument cannot be bifurcated, then it should be marked to market as a result of the written option component. The Task Force will continue its discussion at future meetings.

Index-Amortizing Interest-Rate Swaps

In index-amortizing swaps, the notional principal amount decreases, or amortizes over time. The swap, in effect, synthetically creates a situation akin to having a fixed-rate mortgage receivable that is financed by variable-rate debt. The rate of decrease in the notional principal amount of an index-amortizing swap varies with changes in interest rates, e.g., the rate of decrease speeds up when rates fall and slows down when rates rise in a similar fashion as prepayments on a pool of mortgages or mortgage-backed securities. A number of financial institutions have used index-amortizing swaps in their overall asset/liability and interest-sensitivity management strategies.

Some believe that a written interest-rate call option is, in effect, embedded in these swaps. To compensate the variable-rate payer for this written option, these swaps pay a higher than normal fixed rate, which essentially includes the premium for the written option. In the past, the SEC staff has not insisted that index-amortizing swaps be accounted for on a mark-to-market basis. Instead, the periodic-interest cash flows resulting from these swaps have been included in interest income or expense on an accrual basis. While it is possible that the SEC staff could change its stance on index-amortizing swaps and may in specific circumstances require a registrant that appears to be using such instruments for speculative purposes to use mark-to-market accounting, at present it appears that financial institutions can continue to use accrual accounting for index-amortizing swaps provided they can demonstrate that these are being used as part of their overall asset/liability management program and provided the details of the index-amortizing swaps and their impact on reported results and on the institution's interest-rate sensitivity are appropriately disclosed.

Currency Swaps

Currency swaps, on the other hand, are covered by authoritative literature. Paragraph 17 of SFAS No. 52 states: "Agreements that are, in substance, essentially the same as forward contracts, for example, currency swaps, shall be accounted for in a manner similar to the accounting for forward contracts."

> *Example.* Company A issues a £1,000,000 bullet note that matures in five years and bears interest at a rate of 10 percent a year. Company A hedges this transaction by entering into a currency swap. The currency swap consists of three elements: (1) an initial exchange, (2) the intervening payments, and (3) the maturity exchange. The payment dates of the swap are matched to those of the foreign currency debt.

Exchange rates and LIBOR rates for the next two years are as follows:

Year	Rate	LIBOR
0	1.60	—
1	1.65	11.0%
2	1.58	11.5%

Table 15–7 provides the pertinent cash-flow information. The journal entries for the first two years to record the transaction are shown in Table 15–8.

Options (Other Than Foreign Currency Options)

As described earlier, nonauthoritative guidance on accounting for options is provided by AICPA Issues Paper 86-2, *Accounting for Options*, dated March 6, 1986. Also, EITF Issues 90-17 and 91-14 address the accounting for options that are intended to hedge foreign currency risk.

Accounting

In general, the accounting recommended in the issues paper is similar to the accounting for futures, that is:

TABLE 15–7
Cash Flow Analysis for Currency Swap Example

	Debt		Currency Swap			
Year	Principal	Interest	Initial Exchange	Intervening Payments	Maturity Exchange	Total Cash Flow per Period
0	£1,000,000		£(1,000,000) $1,600,000			$1,600,000
1		£(100,000)		($LIBOR) £100,000		($LIBOR)
2		£(100,000)		($LIBOR) £100,000		($LIBOR)
3		£(100,000)		($LIBOR) £100,000		($LIBOR)
4		£(100,000)		($LIBOR) £100,000		($LIBOR)
5	£(1,000,000)	£(100,000)		($LIBOR) £100,000	$1,000,000 $(1,600,000)	($LIBOR) $(1,600,000)

- Options should generally be marked to market.
- For speculative options, the mark-to-market adjustment should be reflected immediately in income.
- For options that are hedges, the mark-to-market adjustment should be deferred and recorded as an adjustment of the carrying value of the item being hedged. As discussed below, hedge accounting is generally available for purchased options and certain combination option transactions, but generally not for written options.
- Consistent with SFAS No. 80 provisions covering futures contracts, the dollar amount of commodities underlying the futures contract (into which the option is exercisable) is not included in the entity's balance sheet.
- The requirements for an option to qualify as a hedge are the same—i.e., risk reduction, high correlation, and designation—with one important exception that in the case of options (except for foreign currency options where the risk assessment is on an enter-

TABLE 15–8   *Journal Entries*

Year	Description	Debit	Credit
0	Cash	$1,600,000	
	F/X debt		$1,600,000
	(To record the issuance of the £-denominated debt. Note: no entry is made to record the currency swap.)		
1	Interest expense	176,000	
	Accrued liability		176,000
	(To record the net swap payment and the interest due on the debt [$1,600,000 × 11%].)		
1	Transaction loss	50,000	
	F/X debt		50,000
	(To record the unrealized F/X loss on the debt [$1.65 − $1.60 × £1,000,000].)		
1	F/X contract receivable	50,000	
	Transaction gain		50,000
	(To record the unrealized transaction gain on the currency swap.)		
2	Interest expense	184,000	
	Accrued liability		184,000
	(To record the net swap payment and the interest due on the debt [$1,600,000 × 11.5%].)		
2	F/X debt	70,000	
	Transaction gain		70,000
	(To record the unrealized F/X gain on the F/X debt [£1,000,000 × 1.58 − 1,650,000].)		
2	Transaction loss	70,000	
	F/X contract receivable		50,000
	F/X contract payable		20,000
	(To record the unrealized transaction loss on the currency swap.)		

prise basis), the risk assessment can be made only on a transaction-by-transaction basis, and not on an overall enterprise basis as for futures contracts.

- When determining the probability of high correlation, the hedger should consider the correlation during relevant past periods *and also the correlation that could be expected at higher or lower*

price levels. The option may be for an item different from the
item to be hedged (i.e., a cross hedge) if there is a clear economic
relationship between their prices and high correlation is probable.

- Written (sold) options can qualify as a hedge only to the extent of
  the premium received.
- Combination or complex option transactions consisting of two or
  more options on the same item may qualify for hedge accounting
  provided that they meet all the other relevant hedging criteria, are
  entered into at or near the same time, and result in the payment of
  a net premium. Where a net premium is received, the combination
  is treated as a written option.
- Options can be used to hedge existing assets or liabilities, firm
  commitments, and anticipated transactions.

There are, however, some differences in the accounting that reflect the
economic differences between a futures contract and an option. An option
is a unilateral contract where the holder has a right, but no obligation, to
take (call) or make (put) delivery of the property underlying the option
contract, whereas a futures contract is two-sided. Since a futures contract
is a legally binding bilateral agreement, the holder of a futures contract
position will benefit or suffer 100 percent of the consequences of a change
in price of the underlying commodity. With a purchased option, however,
the holder has a right, not an obligation. Essentially, the long position pays
a price, the premium, to cover risk of adverse price (interest-rate,
exchange-rate) change.

Secondly, the accounting for that price, the premium, recognizes that it
may contain two elements:

- Intrinsic value, based on the degree to which the option is in-the-
  money.
- Time value, representing the market's estimation of how likely it
  is that the option will become valuable (in-the-money) before it
  lapses.

Only in-the-money options have intrinsic value; however, all options
may have time value. The deeper out-of-the-money they are, the less
likely they are to have any significant time value.

Recognizing that the premium paid for an option may include both
these elements, the options issues paper requires the two elements to be

separately accounted for by the option buyer in most cases. Essentially, it generally requires that the time value be amortized and recognized as expense over the life of the option since, in essence, the time value of an option is similar to an insurance premium. Any intrinsic value, however, is deferred and marked to market. This split accounting is illustrated in Example 1 below.

> *Example 1.* BankCo buys a June $89.00 U.S. Treasury bond call in February when June U.S. Treasury bond futures are trading at $90.00. BankCo pays a premium of $2,800. BankCo carries its investments in U.S. Treasuries at cost. The option is $1,000 in-the-money, so it has a $1,000 intrinsic value, and the remaining $1,800 paid must be time value. The intrinsic value would be recorded as an asset and marked to market at the end of each accounting period. The $1,800 time value would be amortized over the next four months—the life of the call option.

In certain situations, the time and intrinsic values of a purchased option would not be split or accounted for separately; for example, in the case of a purchased option that qualifies for hedge accounting and hedges an asset, liability, or firm commitment carried or to be carried at market and where gains and losses on the hedged item are included in income as they arise.

If the time and intrinsic values of an option are not split, changes in the entire value of the option should be included in income as they occur. Example 2 below illustrates this.

> *Example 2.* On September 1, Secure Securities (a broker-dealer) purchases 1,000 puts on Acme Manufacturing Corp. for a premium of $1,875 as hedge against a price decline on the 1,000 shares of Acme in its portfolio. The puts have a strike price of $22 and expire on December 31. As the current selling price of Acme stock equals $21, the option premium includes $1,000 of intrinsic value ([$22 − $21] × 1,000) and $875 of time value ($1,875 − $1,000). The broker-dealer follows mark-to-market accounting, and, therefore, daily changes in portfolio value are included in income, and the time and intrinsic values of the option premium are not split and accounted for separately.

At the purchase date of the options, the following journal entries would be made:

```
Options      1,875
    Cash              1,875
```

If the stock price rose to $23 and the market value of the options fell to $750, the following entries would be recorded:

Stock	2,000	
Gain on stock		2,000
Loss on options	1,125	
Options		1,125

If market prices were to rise, the entries similarly would record the change in value of both the options and the stock. This process continues until the options are exercised, closed out, or expire.[7]

As discussed earlier, an option that hedges a firm commitment or an anticipated transaction may qualify for hedge accounting. The portion of the time value of such an option that relates to the period before the related transaction occurs may be included in the measurement of the transaction or, alternatively, amortized to expense over that period.

When a purchased option that qualifies for hedge accounting is closed out, the difference between the unamortized balance of the time value and the time value received on closing out the option should be treated in the same manner as was the time value prior to the close-out. If the time value was being amortized to income, the difference should be recognized in income. If the time value was being deferred (e.g., in the case of a hedge of a firm commitment or anticipated transaction), the difference likewise should be deferred.

Written Options

The issues paper recognizes that written options can only provide an economic hedge to the extent of the premium received by the writer, and, therefore, any losses to the writer of an option beyond the amount of the premium he or she received must be charged to income.

Written options qualify as hedges if:

- The three criteria specified for purchased options are satisfied; and
- The option is so deep-in-the-money that it is reasonably assured that the option will remain in-the-money throughout its term.

---

[7]This example was adapted from *Accounting for Options,* Issues Paper 86-2 (New York: AICPA, 1986), pp. 177–78.

The last condition would be met, for example, when: (1) a call option with a one-year exercise period is written on a bond with a $900 strike price, when the market value of the bond is $1,000 (i.e., the option is $100 in-the-money); (2) over recent one-year periods the bond's market value has not changed by more than $100; and (3) the volatility of the bond's market value is not expected to change significantly in the future. The time and intrinsic values may not be split for a written option qualifying for hedge accounting.

While the Issues Paper allows for the limited hedge accounting for written options as discussed above, the SEC staff generally views written options as speculative and therefore requires mark-to-market accounting. For example, in stating its views on written foreign currency options in EITF Issue No. 91-4, the chief accountant noted:

> "The SEC staff also will object to deferral of losses with respect to written foreign currency options because they do not reduce but increase risk."

Members of the SEC staff have indicated that they have the same view for written options other than foreign currency options. These would include, for example, written caps, floors, and swaptions (i.e., options to enter into swaps).

Complex and Combination Options (Other Than Foreign Currency)

Combinations of options are sometimes used to achieve a desired hedging risk-management or risk-selection objective. For example:

- Buying a put and writing a call on the same underlying item at the same strike price and with the same expiration date to replicate the risks and rewards of a short futures position creates a synthetic futures contract.
- Buying an interest-rate cap and writing an interest-rate floor to create an interest-rate collar on a floating-rate debt.
- Creating a call bull spread (a purchased call option at a lower strike price than the written call option) to provide a range of protection against future increases in the market price related to a short securities position or in the price of a committed or anticipated future purchase of a commodity.

- Creating a put bear spread (a purchased put option at a higher strike price than the written put option) to provide a range of protection against future decreases in the market price of a long securities position or in the price of a committed or anticipated future sale of a commodity.
- Creating a participating forward in regard to the future sale price of an owned security or commodity by purchasing a put and simultaneously writing a call at the same strike price but on a lower quantity than the purchased put option in order to protect against future declines in the price of the hedged item while giving up some of the benefit of any future price increases.

The above are only some of the examples of the types of situations that can be created through a combination of two or more options. While the prior discussion of EITF Issue 91-4 covers complex and combination options involving foreign currencies, in the absence of any authoritative rules covering other options, financial statement preparers and auditors have generally looked to the guidance contained in the AICPA options issues paper when addressing the accounting for combination option techniques involving commodities, interest rates, or traded securities. In that regard the issues paper provides the following advisory conclusions:

- A synthetic future that otherwise qualifies for hedge accounting should be accounted for as a unit in the same way as a futures contract.
- A call bull spread or a put bear spread should be accounted for as a unit. Hedge accounting should be applied to the spread if the purchased option alone qualifies for hedge accounting and the spread should therefore be accounted for in accordance with the guidance for purchased options. Where a call bear spread or a put bull spread meets the criteria for a written option because it involves the receipt of net premium, the combination can only qualify for hedge accounting to the extent of the net premium received.
- Other option combinations should be accounted for as a unit as follows:
  — If the combination provides unlimited protection after a deductible, the criteria for a purchased option should be used to

determine whether the combination qualifies for hedge accounting.

— If the combination provides only limited protection, the criteria for a written option should be used to determine whether the combination qualifies for hedge accounting.

— If the combination qualifies for hedge accounting and:

  • the time value paid exceeds the time value received, the net time value should be accounted for in accordance with the guidance for purchased options.

  • the time value received exceeds the time value paid, the net time value should be accounted for in accordance with the guidance for written options.

Hedging Purchase Business Combinations

Companies sometimes enter into transactions intended to provide an economic hedge of a forthcoming business combination. For example, an acquiror that has agreed to issue a stipulated number of its shares to the target company's stockholders as part of the consideration in an acquisition, may want to lock in the value of the shares to be issued. Similarly, in an acquisition of a foreign company where all or part of the consideration is payable in the foreign currency, the acquiror may wish to protect itself against the effect of exchange movements between the date the terms of acquisition are negotiated and the closing date of the transaction.

In January 1995 at the Annual AICPA Conference on Current SEC Developments, the SEC staff addressed a number of situations regarding the propriety of using hedge accounting for economic hedges of business combinations accounted for under the purchase method. The following situations were specifically addressed:

Situation 1

A registrant would like to hedge the fixed purchase price of a purchase business combination so that the fixed price, when combined with gains and losses from designated hedging instruments, varies with certain changes in market conditions. The question is, can the purchase price of a purchase business combination be adjusted to reflect gains and losses from the hedging instruments?

The SEC staff responded that the purchase price could not be adjusted for the following reasons:

- Gains and losses from hedging instruments are not considered to be direct costs of an acquisition as required by APB Opinion No. 16, "Business Combinations."
- Since the hedging of the fixed purchase price is essentially the same as hedging changes in the value of goodwill, it would be difficult to determine objectively whether the hedging instrument was effective or highly correlated.

Situation 2

A registrant asked whether it is possible to hedge changes in the value of a target's assets and liabilities and account for gains and losses from the hedging instrument as an adjustment to the fair values of the acquired assets and liabilities.

The staff again noted that this would be inappropriate because any adjustments to the fair values of the assets and liabilities, including adjustments to reflect gains and losses from hedging instruments, would cause a conflict with the requirements of APB Opinion No. 16 because the initial carrying values of acquired assets and liabilities would be at a value other than their fair value as of the date of consummation.

Situation 3

A question was asked whether it is possible to hedge a purchase business combination if the number of shares to be issued is fixed and where the purchase price is not fixed (because of subsequent changes in the value of the issuer's stock) until consummation of the transaction.

The staff indicated that this would also be inappropriate for reasons similar to those discussed above.

Situation 4

A registrant asked whether the effects of a foreign currency hedge could be applied as a direct cost in a purchase business combination denominated in a currency other than the U.S. dollar.

The staff responded that they have not addressed this question before and stated that if such a transaction were contemplated, the registrant should discuss the situation with the staff. This answer seems somewhat surprising, since the use of hedge accounting in situations where the acquiror has entered into a firm commitment to pay for the target in whole or in part in a foreign currency seems not only appropriate but also well established in practice.

Finally, a question was posed as to when a target in a purchase business combination hedges its assets and liabilities at the initiation date of a combination, would such a hedge be considered appropriate in purchase accounting, i.e., would the hedging instrument be fair valued by the purchaser at the date of consummation.

The staff responded that yes, this would be considered in the purchase accounting.

As discussed in the next section below on derivatives related to a company's own stock, the current EITF discussions on Issue No. 94-7 could impact on the above.

Accounting for Derivatives and Other Financial Instruments Indexed to and Potentially Settled in a Company's Own Stock

There is, of course, a wide variety of financial instruments whose value is linked to the value of a company's own common stock. These include convertible debt, debt with common stock warrants, employee stock options and stock appreciation rights, exchange-traded equity options, and a variety of custom-tailored puts, calls, collars, and forwards. Depending on the terms of the particular instrument, settlement may be in shares of the company, cash, or in shares or cash at the option of either the issuer or the holder.

The authoritative accounting literature addresses a number of these instruments. For example, APB Opinion No. 14 addresses the accounting for convertible debt and debt issued with stock purchase warrants. APB Opinion 25 (which may soon be amended or replaced by a new FASB pronouncement on employee stock compensation), addresses the accounting for stock options and stock appreciation rights granted to employees. A detailed discussion of these areas is beyond the scope of this chapter, and the reader should therefore refer to the applicable pronouncements when addressing the accounting for these instruments. Also, APB Opinion No. 15, "Earnings per Share," and related interpretations address the treatment of these instruments in calculating earnings per share.

The EITF has also addressed the accounting for a number of other instruments linked to a company's own stock. For example, in Issue 87-31, the EITF discussed the accounting for put options issued by a publicly held company on its own common stock. The EITF reached a consensus that companies that sell put options, whether or not they are immediately exercisable or in-the-money on the date of issuance, should record the proceeds of the sale of the options in permanent equity and, in accordance with SEC Accounting Series Release No. 268 (ASR 268), should transfer from permanent equity to temporary equity an amount equal to the redemption price of the common stock. Subsequent changes in the market value of the options would not be recorded by the issuer. The equity section of the balance sheet would be adjusted only when the options are redeemed, are exercised, or expire. If the put options are in-the-money during the period being reported on, the potential dilutive effect on earnings-per-share should be computed using the reverse treasury stock method. Under that method, the incremental number of shares is computed as the excess of shares that will be issued for cash at the then current market price to obtain cash to satisfy the put obligation over the shares received from satisfying the puts.

As part of this issue, the EITF also discussed the adoption of a shareholder appreciation rights program (SHARP), in which a company distributes to its shareholders rights to put a specified number of common shares to the company. At date of issuance, the strike price is higher than the market price of the company's stock. The puts are publicly traded and expire shortly after issuance. The task force reached a consensus that for a public company, the fair value of the SHARP rights should be accounted for as a stock dividend and the provisions of ASR 268 provide guidance by analogy for such transactions.

In Issue 88-9, the EITF addressed a number of issues related to put warrants. Where a company issues put warrants on its own common stock, they entitle the holder to exercise (1) the warrant feature to acquire common stock of the issuer at a specified price, (2) the put option feature to put the instrument back to the issuer for a cash payment, or (3) in some cases, both the warrant feature to acquire common stock and the put option feature to put that stock back to the issuer for a cash payment. Put warrants are generally issued concurrently with debt securities of the issuer, are detachable from the debt, and may be exercisable only under specified conditions. The put feature of the instrument may expire under varying circumstances, for example, with the passage of time or if the issuer has a public stock offering. Under APB Opinion No. 14, a portion of the proceeds from the issuance of debt with detachable warrants must be allocated to those warrants.

The EITF addressed the following issues:

1. How the portion of the proceeds applicable to the put warrants should be classified in the balance sheet,
2. Whether the put warrants should be adjusted from the value assigned at the date of issuance to the put amount (redemption price), and
3. How the put warrant and any related adjustments should affect the earnings-per-share calculation.

On the first issue, the task force reached a consensus that the accounting approach for put warrants should be similar to that for mandatorily redeemable preferred stock and that the portion of the proceeds applicable to the put warrants should be classified as equity except in situations similar to those identified in EITF Issue 86-35, "Debentures with Detachable Stock Purchase Warrants," where the put price is substantially higher than the value of the warrant exclusive of the put at the time of issuance such that the put is economically more akin to a debt instrument. In those situations, the portion of the proceeds applicable to the put warrants should be classified as a liability. The SEC observer and task force members noted that publicly held companies should classify put warrants recorded as equity as temporary capital in accordance with ASR 268. Task force members agreed that the classification of the put warrant as of the date of issuance should not change subsequent to issuance.

On the second issue, the task force reached a consensus that adjustment of the put warrant from the value assigned at the date of issuance to the highest redemption price of the put warrant (the put feature adjustment) is appropriate. Put feature adjustments should be accrued over the period from the date of issuance to the earliest put date of the warrants. Changes in the highest redemption price after the date of issuance and before the earliest put date, including changes in interim periods, are considered to be changes in accounting estimate and should affect the put feature adjustment on a prospective basis. Changes in the highest redemption price after the earliest put date should be recognized in the current period. Classification of the adjustment should be consistent with the balance-sheet classification of the put warrant (that is, if the put warrant is classified as debt, then the adjustment should be reported as interest expense; if the put warrant is classified as equity, then the adjustment should be reported as a charge to retained earnings).

The task force reached a consensus on the third issue that for put warrants classified either as equity or as a liability, both primary and fully diluted earnings per share should be calculated on an equity basis or a debt basis, as follows, using the more dilutive of the two methods:

1. Equity basis assumes that the warrants will be exercised, which requires use of the "if-converted" method set forth in APB Opinion No. 15. For this computation, the effect of the put feature adjustment on earnings available to common shareholders should be reversed, and the number of additional shares of common stock that would be issued if the warrants were exercised, net of the Treasury shares that could be purchased from the proceeds from exercise of the warrants, should be included in shares outstanding.

2. Debt basis assumes that the put option feature will be exercised; thus, the put warrants are not considered common stock equivalents. For this computation, the effect of the put feature adjustment on earnings available to common shareholders should be retained, and no additional shares of common stock should be included in shares outstanding.

In Issue 90-19, the EITF discussed the accounting for convertible bonds that provide the issuer with a cash settlement option upon conversion. The task force discussed the following three variations of this kind of instrument:

Instrument A: Upon conversion, the issuer must satisfy the obligation entirely in cash based on the fixed number of shares multiplied by the stock price on the date of conversion (the conversion value).

Instrument B: Upon conversion, the issuer may satisfy the entire obligation in either stock or cash equivalent to the conversion value.

Instrument C: Upon conversion, the issuer must satisfy the accreted value of the obligation (the amount accrued to the benefit of the holder exclusive of the conversion value) in cash and may satisfy the conversion spread (the excess conversion value over the accreted value) in either cash or stock.

In all cases, if the holder does not exercise the conversion option, the issuer must repay the accreted value of the debt in cash at maturity.

The original scope of this issue addressed only zero-coupon convertible bonds. However, the task force agreed to broaden the scope and apply the consensuses reached on this issue to all convertible bonds with the characteristics described above.

The issues addressed by the EITF were:

1. Whether the initial balance-sheet treatment by the issuer should provide for separate or combined accounting for the conversion feature and debt obligation,
2. How the issuer should account for the excess conversion value over the accreted value, and
3. How each instrument should be treated in earnings-per-share computations.

The task force reached a consensus on issue 1 that combined accounting for the conversion feature and debt obligation is appropriate for instruments A, B, and C.

The task force reached a consensus on issue 2 that instruments A and C should be accounted for in a manner similar to the accounting for indexed debt obligations. The issuer should adjust the carrying amount of the instrument in each reporting period to reflect the current stock price, but not below the accreted value of the instrument. Adjustments to the carrying amount are included currently in income and not spread over future periods. Instrument B should be accounted for as conventional convertible debt. If the holder exercises the conversion option and the issuer satisfies the obligation in cash, the debt should be considered extinguished at that time and the issuer should follow the accounting prescribed by APB Opinion No. 26, which states, "A difference between the reacquisition price and the net carrying amount of the extinguished debt should be recognized currently in income of the period of extinguishment as losses or gains . . . " The gain or loss would be generally classified as an extraordinary item.

On issue 3, the task force reached a consensus that instrument A does not have an impact on primary or fully diluted earnings per share of the issuer other than the recognition of the conversion spread as a charge to income. Instrument B should be considered a common stock equivalent and included in the computation of primary earnings per share if, at the time of issuance, it meets the yield test set forth in FASB Statement No. 85. Instrument B would be included in the computation of fully diluted earnings per share (and in the computation of primary earnings per share if it is a common stock equivalent) using the if-converted method if the effect is dilutive. The earnings-per-share treatment is consistent with the accounting for instrument B as convertible debt. Instrument C should not have an impact on the computation of primary earnings per share of the issuer other than recognition of the conversion spread as a charge to income. This treatment is consistent with the accounting for an indexed debt obligation. For fully diluted earnings per share, the issuer should use the if-converted method prescribed by APB Opinion No. 15. Under the if-converted method, net income (loss) would be adjusted for the after-tax increase or decrease in the conversion spread to arrive at net income (loss) available to common shareholders. The incremental shares would be determined using the more dilutive of the average or end-of-period market prices for common stock. The consensuses on Issue 3 are subject to other provisions of APB Opinion No. 15 as well, such as the antidilutive provisions for fully diluted earnings per share.

The SEC has also issued Staff Accounting Bulletin No. 57 (SAB 57) regarding the accounting for contingent stock purchase warrants issued by a company to certain customers in connection with sales agreements. The contingent stock purchase warrants become exercisable only if specified amounts of products are purchased by the customers within a designated time period. Because the warrants are conditional, the staff believes that it is inappropriate to value such warrants at the date the agreements are executed. The staff's position is that the contingent warrants should be valued and accounted for when it is probable that the customers will make the requisite purchases in order to earn the warrants. Once the probable determination is made, a pro rata allocation of the ultimate cost of the warrants needs to be recorded as sales are made based on the quoted market price of the stock at the end of each reporting period.

In regard to other situations where the fact pattern differs from that described in SAB 57 but which involve the issuance by a company of equity options to nonemployees in exchange for goods or services or in exchange for a contract to provide goods or services, the SEC staff has indicated that it will accept either the mark-to-market approach in SAB 57 or an approach that measures the fair value of the options at the date of issuance.

Finally, it should be noted that at its January 1995 meeting the EITF began discussing a potentially far-reaching issue (Issue 94-7) on the accounting for a variety of purchased derivatives that are indexed to a company's own stock (e.g., purchased puts and calls and purchased forward contracts to sell or receive the stock) and which may be settled in stock, cash, or in a cash or stock at the option of the holder or the issuer. The principal issues to be addressed include whether such instruments should be classified as assets and liabilities or as equity transactions, whether the gains or losses on these contracts should be reported in earnings or in equity, and whether and under what circumstances hedge accounting may be appropriate.

Through its September 1995 meeting, the EITF has reached several tentative conclusions, as follows:

- Free-standing contracts that require net cash settlement should be accounted for as assets or liabilities and should be measured at fair value. Any gains or losses on those contracts should be included in earnings and disclosed in the financial statements.
- Free-standing contracts that require net share or physical settlement are equity instruments and should be measured initially at fair value. Subsequent changes in fair value should not be recognized. Any gains or losses on those contracts should be reported in shareholders' equity and not included in earnings.
- Task Force members observed that in EITF Issue No. 87-31, "Sale of Put Options on Issuer's Stock," the task force reached a consensus that the provisions of SEC ASR No. 268, Presentation in Financial Statements of "Redeemable Preferred Stocks," provide guidance by analogy to public companies for contracts that may require the company to redeem its stock at a future date.
- Free-standing contracts that give the company a choice of net cash settlement or settlement in its own shares should be classified as equity instruments and should be measured initially at fair value. Subsequent changes in fair value should be recorded in shareholders' equity. The task force agreed that if such contracts are ultimately settled in cash, accounting for the contracts as equity instruments should not change, that is, the amount of cash paid or received should be included in contributed capital. Free-standing contracts that give the counterparty a choice of net cash settlement or settlement in shares should be classified as assets or liabilities and should be measured at fair value. Any gains or losses on

those contracts should be included in earnings and disclosed in the financial statements. The task force agreed that if such contracts are ultimately settled in shares, the accounting for such contracts should not change, that is, any gains or losses on those contracts should continue to be included in earnings.

The EITF also agreed that the peripheral issues (i.e., written option accounting, EPS issues, pooling implications and embedded instrument issues) related to this Issue No. 94-7 that remain unresolved as a result of the above Consensuses would be taken to the EITF Agenda Committee for consideration to be included on the EITF's agenda. At the August 31, 1995 Agenda Committee meeting, the SEC observer stated that the SEC staff continue to be troubled by the direction of the task force's discussions on this Issue (No. 94-7) and the potential development of new criteria for hedge accounting. The SEC staff believes that EITF guidance should not expand existing hedge accounting practice at this time and await FASB's resolution of its derivatives and hedge accounting project.

SYNTHETIC INSTRUMENTS

The accounting method previously described for interest-rate swaps that are linked to borrowings or to interest-bearing assets is an example of what has become known as synthetic instrument accounting. While the topic of synthetic instrument accounting cannot be found in the current authoritative accounting literature, there have been a number of articles on the subject, and recent FASB discussion documents[8] acknowledging its existence. As applied in practice, synthetic instrument accounting involves treating two or more distinct financial instruments as having synthetically created a single recognizable instrument and, accordingly, accounting for those multiple instruments as the single instrument that was created. Thus, floating-rate debt, together with a swap of the floating interest payments into fixed payments, is treated as fixed-rate debt. The same holds true for the reverse, where fixed-rate debt is swapped into floating, to basis swaps that modify the interest-rate characteristics of debt, and to interest-rate

---

[8]For example, see Chapter 8 of the 1992 FASB Discussion Memorandum, *Recognition and Measurement of Financial Instruments,* and the FASB staff's June 1993 document on hedging and risk-adjusting activities, discussed later in this chapter.

swaps combined with interest-bearing assets. In all cases, the swap is not accounted for separately in either the income statement or balance sheet, and only the net payments under the swap and the related debt or asset are treated as periodic interest expense or income.

While this seems logical and appropriate because of the absence of authoritative standards or guidelines on the subject, questions can and have arisen in practice, even in the case of simple interest-rate swaps. For example, must the swap be entered into at the inception of the borrowing or lending transaction to be afforded the synthetic instrument accounting? Under current practice as it has evolved, the answer is generally no. The interest-rate swap can be entered into after the related borrowing or lending transaction and need not even be held through the maturity of the linked debt or asset to be afforded the synthetic treatment.

Other issues can arise in practice. For example, should synthetic treatment apply where either the debt or interest-bearing asset or the interest-rate swap (or both) are zero-coupon instruments? Moreover, the extension of synthetic instrument accounting to other kinds of transactions, for example, to currency swaps linked with a foreign currency borrowing, raises a host of accounting issues. For example, should a deutsche mark borrowing whose principal has been effectively converted into U.S. dollars via a currency swap be accounted for as a single-instrument U.S.-dollar debt? Here the answer under current accounting rules is no. Under SFAS No. 52 on foreign currency translation, both the deutsche mark debt and the currency swap are marked to market with the resulting gains and losses included in the current period's earnings. Thus, to the extent the loss or gain on the swap offsets the gain or loss on the debt, earnings are unaffected. However, for balance-sheet purposes the debt and the swap must be shown "broad," that is, in accordance with the consensus in EITF Issue 86-25, the current value of the swap must be shown separately and cannot be offset against the debt.[9] Accountants would argue that this treatment properly reflects the fact that the debt and the currency swap are with different counterparties. That notwithstanding, many accountants would acknowledge the synthesis and permit "as if" synthetic accounting for other purposes, for example, in the case of U.S.-dollar debt that has been swapped in deutsche marks, treating the combi-

---

[9]This assumes the debt and the swap are with different parties. When the debt and the swap are with the same party, balance-sheet netting would be permitted provided there is a legal right of offset.

nation as an effective hedge under SFAS No. 52 of a firm commitment to receive deutsche marks or of a net investment in a German subsidiary.

Synthetics involving options and swaptions raise additional accounting issues due to the one-sided nature of these instruments. Take the example of synthetic noncallable fixed-rate debt that arises from the combination of issuing callable fixed-rate debt and selling a swaption against the embedded call.

Assume the entity issues five-year callable (after three years) fixed-rate debt while simultaneously writing a swaption exercisable concurrently with the call date of debt. The swaption would be structured such that, if exercised, the issuer receives LIBOR and pays fixed during years four and five.

In this example, if interest rates have fallen at the call date in three years, the company will likely call the debt and refinance it short term with commercial paper. Similarly, the holder of the swaption will likely exercise it and enter into the two-year swap, paying the company LIBOR and receiving the fixed interest payment. If interest rates have risen, however, the company would not call the debt and the swaption holder would not exercise it. In either case, it is argued that the company has effectively created noncallable five-year fixed-rate debt, with the up-front premium received on the swaption providing a reduction of the effective financing cost. It would therefore seem logical to treat this transaction as a single instrument, synthetic five-year fixed-rate debt and amortize the premium received on the swaption as a reduction of interest expense over the five years. However, this presumes the intended synthesis will occur and will be effective, which in turn presumes symmetry between the company's decision whether or not to call the debt in three years and the swaption holder's decision whether or not to exercise the swaption at that date. Such symmetry might not always exist, for example, when a call premium is involved or when, as in the above example, different floating rates are involved (e.g., refinancing by the company at commercial-paper rates versus receipt of LIBOR on the swap), or when in three years, for whatever reason the company would be unable to refinance if it called the debt. Most accountants would therefore carefully assess the facts and circumstances surrounding a particular transaction of this kind before concluding on the propriety of using synthetic instrument accounting. Such facts and circumstances would include the company's financial condition and likely ability to refinance at the call date as well as the range of interest rates under which, given any call premium and/or differences in the floating-rate bases of the refinancing and the swap under the swaption, there might be asymmetry between the actions of the company and the swaption holder at the call date. Moreover, the longer the term of the debt and the farther out the call date—for example in the case of 20-year debt with a call at year 10—the more difficult it is to convince most accountants and auditors of the propriety of applying synthetic instrument accounting to this type of transaction.

In summary, at present there are no authoritative rules or guidelines governing the accounting for synthetics. In the absence of such guidance, accountants have generally only permitted synthetic instrument accounting in those cases where it is clear that the multiple instruments create another recognizable financial instrument and that there is a high probability that the company can achieve and maintain the intended synthesis. As discussed later in this chapter, however, the FASB has begun formally looking at the subject of synthetic instrument accounting and has reached certain tentative views on how and when it should be applied.

ACCOUNTING ISSUES RELATING TO INVESTMENTS IN MORTGAGE DERIVATIVES

For accounting purposes, mortgage derivatives—including CMO securities, CMO residuals, and mortgage-backed I/Os and P/Os—are generally considered to be debt securities. Thus, mark-to-market entities, such as broker-dealers, investment companies, and pension funds, generally carry investments in these securities at market or fair value, with any cash received and any changes in value reported as part of current-period income. For most other entities—including banks, thrifts, insurance companies, and commercial and industrial enterprises—SFAS No. 115 applies. Under SFAS No. 115, investments in these securities must be classified and accounted for as either held-to-maturity, available-for-sale, or trading in accordance with the previously discussed rules.

While the above accounting appears simple in concept, its application to some mortgage derivatives such as CMO residuals and I/Os is more complex and raises a number of issues. Many of these derivatives have little or no principal component, and their value is dependent not only on interest rates but also on the effect of changes in interest rates on prepayment levels. They are often referred to as high-risk mortgage securities both in the accounting literature and by financial institutions regulators because of the securities' often volatile nature and because they have the potential for loss of a significant portion of the original investment. A few of the important accounting issues raised for such securities include:

1. How to value them? If market or dealer quotations are available, they should be used to value these securities. If not, fair value should be estimated based on expected cash flows discounted at current market interest rates for similar securities. In estimating future cash flows, prepayment rates should be estimated based on current interest-rate levels.

2. Can such securities qualify as held-to-maturity under SFAS No. 115, and if so, how is amortized cost determined? SFAS No. 115 does not specifically address classification of debt securities with uncertain maturity; however, it does not proscribe held-to-maturity classification of such securities.

   The EITF discussed the issue of whether such securities can qualify as held-to-maturity under SFAS No. 115 at several meetings in 1993 and 1994. A key question raised related to mortgage securities that financial institution regulators could classify as high-risk and therefore possibly require sale of the securities by an institution. The FASB staff understood that regulators of financial institutions (e.g., banks, thrifts, credit unions) had the authority to require an institution to dispose of a security that was considered to be a high-risk security. Applying this understanding to the classification of securities under Statement 115, the FASB staff took the position that if a mortgage derivative product (e.g., I/Os, P/Os) purchased by an institution could become high-risk before maturity (e.g., when market rates change) and the institution's regulator could require the institution to dispose of the security, then the security should not be classified as held-to-maturity. The FASB staff formalized their position in an announcement at the November 1993 EITF meeting entitled, "Effect of Potential Designation as a High-Risk Mortgage Security." The announcement indicated that when an entity initially classifies a security as held-to-maturity (thereby asserting a positive intent and ability to hold to maturity), it must be cognizant of existing regulatory requirements that could affect its ability to hold the security to maturity.

In July 1994, the FASB staff received a memorandum clarifying the Federal Financial Institutions Examination Council (FFIEC) banking and thrift regulators' policy regarding high-risk mortgage securities. The memorandum included a sentence stating, "The mere existence of examiners' divestiture authority for high-risk mortgage securities should not preclude an institution from concluding it has the intent and ability to hold to maturity those securities that were non-high-risk when acquired." The FASB staff interpreted the clarification to mean that the regulators would only require divestiture in remote instances and therefore, determined that the announcement made at the November 1993 EITF meeting would not apply to financial institutions whose regulators have issued the aforementioned memorandum. Thus, such financial institutions would be permitted to classify a mortgage derivative product that is not a high-risk mortgage security at purchase as a held-to-maturity security under Statement 115. However, the November 1993 announcement would still apply to the other entities, such as credit unions, where the regulator has not issued such a memorandum.

In addition to the aforementioned issue, the EITF, in Issue 94-4, addressed the question of whether it is generally appropriate to classify mortgage-backed interest-only certificates as held-to-maturity. The EITF did not reach a consensus on this issue. However, the EITF did observe that due to the nature of interest-only securities, meeting the criteria under Statement 115 for classification as held-to-maturity would be rare. Further, as part of its current project on transfers of assets and extinguishment of liabilities, the FASB has been considering prohibiting held-for-maturity classification for high-risk mortgage securities.

In those rare cases where a high-risk mortgage security is classified as held-to-maturity, its amortized cost basis should be determined based on the guidance in EITF Issue 89-4. The investor should allocate total cash flows expected to be received over the estimated life of the investment between principal and interest, using the "prospective method" in the following manner. At the date of purchase, an effective yield is calculated based on the purchase price and anticipated future cash flows. In the initial accounting period, interest income is accrued using that rate. Cash received on the investment is first applied to accrued interest, with any excess reducing the recorded investment balance. At each reporting date, the effective yield is recalculated based on the amortized cost of the investment and the then current estimate of future cash flows. The recalculated yield is then used to accrue interest income on the investment balance in the subsequent accounting period. This procedure continues until all cash flows from the investment have been received. In this manner, the amortized balance of the investment at the end of the period will equal the present value of the estimated future cash flows discounted at the newly calculated effective yield.

3. If under SFAS No. 115 these securities are classified as either held-to-maturity or available-for-sale, when should such securities be considered to be impaired, thereby requiring a write-down to fair value via an immediate charge to earnings?

Prior to SFAS No. 115, EITF Issue 89-4 specified that investors in high-risk CMO instruments should evaluate each instrument separately to determine whether expected future cash flows are adequate to recover the recorded investment balance. However, under the EITF guidelines, an impairment write-down was not required, provided the recorded balance for each investment exceeded the *undiscounted* estimated future cash flows, i.e., the effective yield was not negative.

SFAS No. 115 changes the method of measuring impairment in Issue 89-4 from one based on undiscounted cash flows to one based on fair value. In Issue 93-18, the EITF agreed that a risk-free rate should be used to discount expected cash flows to measure fair value of these securities. The excess of the amortized cost basis over the present value so computed should be recognized as a realized loss in the income statement. The rate to be used to determine the present value amount should be the risk-free rate for instruments with a duration consistent with the security's estimated future cash flows at the time the impairment test is performed on the security.

Finally, as discussed later in this chapter, as part of its ongoing project on the accounting for derivatives, the FASB has recently tentatively concluded that certain other instruments with derivative-like characteristics, including I/Os and high-risk CMOs, should be accounted for in the same manner as derivatives, which based on the Board's current direction, would mean that all such instruments would be accounted for at fair value.

THE NETTING OF POSITIONS

The rules for netting of positions are contained in FASB Interpretation No. 39, *Offsetting of Amounts Related to Certain Contracts,* which although issued in 1991, was not mandated for most entities until 1994. These rules dictate when amounts due from the same counterparty may be offset in the reporting entity's balance sheet and related footnote disclosures such as those under SFAS No. 105. Accountants have relied primarily upon the legal definition of the right of offset in determining whether financial positions should be netted. As such, the right of offset is defined as a debtor's legal right, by contract or otherwise, to discharge all or a portion of the debt owed to another party by applying against the debt an amount that the other party owes the debtor. The following conditions generally must be met in order to net positions with the same counterparty:

- Each of the two parties owes the other determinable amounts.
- The reporting party has the right to set off the amount owed with the amount owed by the other party.
- The reporting party intends to set off.
- The right of offset is enforceable at law.

These four conditions were contained in an earlier FASB Technical Bulletin (No. 88-2) on the subject and carried forward by FIN No. 39. The conditions have proven troublesome, particularly to entities such as banks, investment banks, and derivatives product dealers who regularly have numerous open positions of varying durations with various counterparties and across various product lines (e.g., swaps, options, and forwards). While industry practice among such entities has not been uniform, many such dealers have reported their entire position as a single mark-to-market receivable or payable, arguing that the criteria for Technical Bulletin No. 88-2 should not apply to them. Recognizing the special nature of these entities' activities, FIN No. 39 permits offsetting of positions with the same counterparty (but only with the same counterparty) provided:

1. The positions are covered by a valid master netting agreement between the two parties, and
2. The reporting party carries the positions at market or fair value.

In effect, for the swap and derivatives product dealers, FIN No. 39 represents a compromise between the existing practice of netting positions across counterparties and the accounting rules that, if literally applied, would permit offsetting of only those positions that will actually be settled on a net basis with a particular counterparty. By putting in place valid master netting agreements with each counterparty, these entities will be permitted by FIN No. 39 to net open positions across product lines by counterparty in their balance sheet and related footnote disclosures. This same treatment presumably also applies to positions covered by master netting agreements held by mark-to-market investing entities such as pension funds, investment companies, and hedge funds.

Reporting of Cash Flows from Hedging Activities in the Statement of Cash Flows

SFAS No. 95, *Statement of Cash Flows*, provides that the statement of cash flows classify cash receipts and payments according to whether they stem from operating, investing, or financing activities. In Footnote 4, the FASB further stated,

> Each cash receipt or payment is to be classified according to its nature without regard to whether it stems from an item intended as a hedge of another item. For example, the proceeds of a borrowing are a financing cash inflow whether or not the debt is intended as a hedge of an investment, and the purchase or sale of a futures contract is an investing activity without regard to whether the contract is intended as a hedge of a firm commitment to purchase inventory.

Subsequent to the issuance of Statement No. 95 in 1987, the FASB received numerous requests to reconsider certain aspects of Statement No. 95, including the classification of cash flows from hedging transactions. Accordingly, in 1989, the Board issued SFAS No. 104, *Statement of Cash Flows—Net Reporting of Certain Cash Receipts and Cash Payments and Classification of Cash Flows From Hedging Transactions*, which amends Statement No. 95 to permit cash flows from futures, forwards, options, or swaps that are accounted for as hedges of identifiable transactions or events to be classified in the same category (i.e., operating, investing, or financing cash flows) as the cash flows from the items hedged, provided that accounting policy is disclosed.

Disclosure Requirements Relating to Derivatives and Synthetics

The current disclosure requirements relating to derivatives and their use are covered by a number of pronouncements including FASB Statements Nos. 52, 80, 105, 107, and 119.

SFAS No. 52 requires disclosure of gains and losses from hedges and SFAS No. 80 requires disclosure of "(a) the nature of the assets, liabilities, firm commitments, or anticipated transactions that are hedged with futures contracts and (b) the method of accounting for the futures contracts." The EITF reached a consensus in Issue 91-4 that when using currency options, option combinations, and similar instruments to hedge, the following should be disclosed in the notes to the financial statements:

- The method of accounting for those instruments, including a description of the events or transactions that result in recognition in income of changes in value.
- The nature of the anticipated transactions for which there is no firm commitment that are hedged by those instruments.
- The maximum number of years over which anticipated, but not firmly committed, foreign currency transactions are hedged by those instruments.
- The combined realized and unrealized net gain or loss deferred as of each balance-sheet date on those instruments that are designated as hedges of anticipated transactions for which there is no firm commitment.

SFAS No. 105

In March 1990, the FASB issued SFAS No. 105, *Disclosure of Information About Financial Instruments with Off-Balance-Sheet Risk and Financial Instruments with Concentrations of Credit Risk.* This Statement requires all entities to report the following information about financial instruments with off-balance-sheet risk of accounting loss:

- The face, contract, or notional principal amount.
- The nature and terms of the instruments and a discussion of their credit and market risk, cash requirements, and related accounting policies.
- An amount of the loss, at the balance-sheet date and ignoring any collateral the entity would incur if the counterparties to its off-balance-sheet financial instruments failed to perform.
- The entity's policy for requiring collateral or other security and a description of the collateral on instruments presently held.

The statement also requires disclosure of information about significant concentrations of credit risk from an individual counterparty or group of counterparties for all financial instruments.

SFAS No. 107

In December 1991, SFAS No. 107, *Disclosures About Fair Value of Financial Instruments,* was issued, requiring all entities to disclose, when *practicable,* the fair value of a variety of on- and off-balance-sheet financial instruments (see Table 15–2 for a decision flowchart useful for applying SFAS No. 107). These instruments include debt and equity securities, derivative products (e.g., swaps, options, forwards, and futures contracts), asset-backed securities, financial guarantees, letters of credit, and commitments to extend credit.

"Practicable" means that an estimate of fair value can be made without incurring excessive cost. This concept is dynamic—what is impracticable one year may be practicable the next. If management determines that it is not practicable to estimate the fair value of a financial instrument, then this fact should be documented. The meaning of the term fair value is precise:

> For purposes of this Statement, the fair value of a financial instrument is the amount at which the instrument could be exchanged in a current transaction between willing parties, other than in a forced or liquidation sale.[10]

Paragraph 10 of SFAS No. 107 requires that the method(s) and significant assumptions used to estimate the fair value of financial instruments be disclosed. Also, in some instances, an entity's management may decide to

---

[10]*Disclosures About Fair Value of Financial Instruments,* SFAS No. 107 (Norwalk, CT: FASB, 1991), ¶7.

provide further information about the fair value of financial instruments to avoid misleading inferences. If it is not practicable to estimate the fair value of a financial instrument, paragraph 14 requires the disclosure of the following:

- When it is not practicable, a statement in the notes to the financial statements that a reasonable estimate of fair value could not be made without excessive costs would generally be sufficient, and
- Information helpful in estimating the instrument's fair value (e.g., carrying amount, effective interest rate, maturity).

SFAS No. 119 and SEC Views on Derivatives Disclosures

The continued tremendous growth in the use of derivatives by entities of all types led during 1993 and 1994 to widespread calls to further improve financial statement disclosures in this area. In July 1993, the Group of Thirty, an international association of bankers and former government officials chaired by Paul Volcker, published a study entitled *Derivatives: Practices and Principles,* containing recommendations for the management of derivatives activity, including the need for improved and broader disclosures. Furthermore, in the wake of numerous highly publicized cases of significant losses reported by users of derivatives the business press, financial analysts, members of Congress, and various regulators—such as the Federal Reserve, the Comptroller of the Currency, the GAO, and the SEC—all expressed concerns regarding the risks associated with derivatives and with the perceived lack of adequate disclosures by companies on their use. Essentially, there was a consensus that the disclosures under Statements 105 and 107 are often ambiguous and did not clearly present the extent of an entity's involvement with derivatives, its sensitivity to interest-rate and other market risks, and the extent and effect of its hedging policies.

Against this backdrop, the FASB in December 1993 undertook a "rapid response" project to improve derivatives disclosures, which resulted in an exposure draft in April 1994 and in the issuance of a new standard, Statement No. 119, *Disclosures About Derivative Financial Instruments,* in October 1994. Statement 119 is effective for fiscal years ending after December 15, 1994, except that entities having total assets of less than $150 million may defer its implementation by one year.

Statement 119 requires disclosures for all derivatives held or issued by an entity of the accounting policies followed; of the nature, terms, and cash requirements of the instruments; and of the credit and market risk associated with the instruments, including the nature and impact of any inherent leverage features. Additional disclosures regarding derivatives held for trading are required for each class of instrument, business activity, or other category consistent with the management of the instruments. For each such category, companies must disclose: (a) at each balance sheet date, the carrying amount and the fair value of the instruments; and (b) for each period for which an income statement is presented, the average fair value of instruments held and the net gains or net losses recognized. For derivative instruments held for purposes other than trading, the standard requires disclosure of the company's objectives for holding or issuing derivatives and the related strategies. With respect to hedges of anticipated transactions, description of the nature and timing of the anticipated transactions, disclosure of the amount of explicitly deferred gain or loss under SFAS Nos. 52 and 80, and a description of the events leading to income statement recognition of the deferred gain or loss are required.

Statement 119 also contains a number of amendments to both Statements Nos. 105 and 107. With respect to Statement 105, it expands that Statement's disclosure requirements to a broader array of derivatives—including purchased options, caps, and floors—and to loan commitments and guarantees held and requires separating the disclosures between derivatives held for trading and derivatives held for purposes other than trading. With regard to the Statement 107 fair-value disclosures, Statement 119 requires that, in order to facilitate the financial statement user's understanding of the disclosures, all the fair-value amounts be included in a single footnote or table in the footnotes together with the related book-value amounts and that the fair value of any derivatives be disclosed separately from the fair value of any nonderivative financial instruments to which they relate.

Statement 119 also encourages but does not require disclosure of additional information about an entity's derivatives positions and activity, how it controls and manages its financial risks, and the role derivatives play in this process. Examples of these encouraged disclosures might include interest-rate gap and duration analyses and value-at-risk measures. It is also noteworthy that members of the SEC staff have, in several recent speeches, focused on the concept of value at risk and the potential benefits of value-at-risk disclosures by companies as a way to capture and portray the overall market risk profile inherent in their portfolio of derivatives and other financial instruments.

While the Statement 119 disclosures are broad and far-reaching, certain types of instruments that may be viewed by many as derivatives are specifically excluded from its scope. For example, it excludes commodity derivatives that require or permit settlement in the commodity even though they may be intended to be, and are actually, settled in cash. Thus, most commodity futures, options, forwards, and swaps would be excluded from the scope of Statement 119. Only those that must be cash settled are included. Statement 119 also only applies to freestanding derivatives. Thus, embedded derivatives such as those included in indexed and structured notes are excluded from the disclosure requirements.

SEC Views on Derivatives Disclosures

For public companies, it is important to note that the SEC has over the past year targeted derivatives disclosures by registrants for close scrutiny and monitoring. Chairman Levitt, the commissioners, and various members of the SEC staff have in numerous speeches urged registrants to expand and enhance their disclosures about their derivatives positions and activities, noting that registrants should disclose at least as much about their derivatives use as they disclose about on-balance-sheet financial instruments. Moreover, during 1994, in connection with its review of filings, the SEC sent comment letters to hundreds of registrants requesting detailed information on the companies' derivatives positions and activities and in many cases requiring registrants to enhance and expand their disclosures, both in the footnotes and in Management's Discussion and Analysis.

While Statement 119 now covers many of the disclosures considered appropriate by the SEC staff, the staff believes that a registrant's disclosures will often need to extend beyond those required by Statement 119. For example:

- With regard to the accounting policies followed by a registrant for its derivatives, the SEC staff believes that the types of instruments accounted for under each different method should be identified, and the income statement and balance-sheet classifications that include the effects of derivatives activities under each accounting

method should be identified. Registrants that use both the deferral
(hedge) method (e.g., for futures or foreign currency forwards)
and the accrual (settlement) method (e.g., for interest-rate swaps)
of accounting should discuss the pertinent features of those methods separately. The disclosure should also describe how an instrument's cash flows, changes in its market value, and fees and
termination gains and losses are accounted for under each method.

- While disclosure of terms and cash requirements is required by
  Statement 119 for *all* derivative instruments, a particular focus of
  the staff's reviews is on the adequacy of those disclosures with
  respect to derivatives accounted for using the accrual (settlement)
  method. The staff generally seeks a level of financial statement
  disclosure about those contracts that is at least as complete as the
  disclosure required for the related cash instrument. For example,
  a company holding an interest-rate swap for the purpose of modi-
  fying the interest expense of an outstanding debt obligation should
  disclose, as of the balance-sheet date, the material terms (interest
  rate, maturity, etc.) of *both* the debt and the swap. As with cash
  instruments, summarization of information about outstanding derivatives may be appropriate. For example, face, contract, or notional amounts, of derivative instruments having similar cash
  requirements may be aggregated, with material characteristics of
  aggregated contracts expressed in terms of reasonable ranges.
  However, fixed-rate contracts should be distinguished from variable-rate contracts; index-linked contracts should be grouped by
  significant index; significant currencies should be disaggregated. In
  certain cases the SEC staff has requested registrants to provide
  reconciliations, categorized by annual maturity, of the changes in
  notional or contractual amounts of interest-rate and currency
  swaps detailing the activity from new, terminated, and matured or
  expired contracts and distinguishing between fixed to floating,
  floating to fixed, and basis swaps in the case of interest-rate swaps
  and by currency for currency swaps. Registrants have also been
  asked to distinguish their exchange-traded derivatives from their
  OTC instruments.

- The SEC staff focuses on and continues to request registrants to
  provide complete descriptions of instruments having leverage
  features, written options, or other terms that are unusual or can

produce highly volatile changes in the instrument's market value in particular market scenarios. Management's assessment of whether disclosure about such instruments is appropriate should include consideration of the impact of market movements beyond the normal range.

• With regard to the kinds of disclosures that Statement 119 encourages but does not require, the SEC staff has requested registrants to discuss methods and disclose quantified parameters used to monitor and control risk-management strategies, including stress testing, sensitivity analyses, and any value-at-risk measurements. In addition, the staff has requested registrants to discuss the extent to which management's derivatives strategy is dynamic. Companies that more actively manage market exposures using derivative financial instruments are expected to discuss the nature of that activity, its purposes, and the extent to which management's strategy may entail alterations of previous positions in response to marginal changes or marginal anticipated changes in market conditions.

The staff of the SEC will no doubt continue to focus on these matters in its reviews of registrants' filings. Moreover, it is quite possible that the SEC will at some time in the near future publish formal rules or official guidance on this subject.

CONCLUDING COMMENTS ON DISCLOSURES

Clearly, there is an increasing and heightened focus on companies' derivatives activities and on the adequacy of their footnote and other disclosures related to these activities. Analysts, the business press, the SEC staff, and regulators will undoubtedly continue to focus on this area. Judgment is required to determine the extent of disclosures needed in a particular situation. Companies would be well served to inventory their derivatives activities and positions and discuss with their accounting advisors the effect these have on their present and future financial statement disclosures and their commentary in management's discussion and analysis.

The appendix to this chapter contains examples of the derivatives disclosures made by a major industrial corporation and a major banking institution in their 1994 financial statements.

WHAT'S AHEAD? THE FASB PROJECT ON ACCOUNTING FOR DERIVATIVES

As discussed at the outset of this chapter, the current set of accounting rules on derivatives were developed in a piecemeal fashion; they provide somewhat inconsistent guidance and do not explicitly cover a number of today's hedging instruments and techniques. As part of its broader project on financial instruments, the FASB has begun formally reviewing the current rules on hedge accounting and accounting for derivative instruments. In September 1991, it issued a lengthy Research Report, *Hedge Accounting: An Exploratory Study of the Underlying Issues.* This was followed in November 1991 by a Discussion Memorandum, *Recognition and Measurement of Financial Instruments,* which contains some 80 issues, many relating to various derivative instruments, hedge accounting, and synthetic instrument accounting. In June 1993, the Board circulated an informal document entitled "A Report on Deliberations, Including Tentative Conclusions on Certain Issues Related to Accounting for Hedging and Other Risk-Adjusting Activities" ("Report on Deliberations").

While certain of the tentative conclusions in the Report on Deliberations contemplated potentially significant changes in the rules on accounting for derivatives and synthetics, the Board, at that time, continued to embrace the concepts of hedge accounting and synthetic-instrument accounting. While it was proposed that all freestanding derivatives be carried at market or fair value, hedge accounting would have been permitted for qualifying hedges of existing assets and liabilities and for firm commitments. Whether or not hedge accounting should be permitted for hedges of anticipated or forecasted transactions was left undecided, with several Board members sharing the concerns voiced by the chief accountant of the SEC over both the conceptual propriety of permitting deferral of gains and losses on such transactions and the practical concern over the ability to develop workable rules that would prevent companies from deferring losses in situations where the expected transactions might never materialize. The tentative conclusions also proposed a new method of hedge accounting, termed the "partial effectiveness method." Under this method a hedge is considered effective to the extent that cumulative changes in the fair value of the hedging instrument do not exceed the (inverse) cumulative changes in the fair value of the item being hedged, with any excess change in the fair value of the hedging instrument over the (inverse) change in the fair value of the hedged item being recognized currently in earnings. For financial institutions and other entities that manage net interest-rate or currency risk of their overall asset/liability position, the Report on Deliberations proposed an elective mark-to-market pool approach under which all components of a dynamically managed portfolio (i.e., assets, liabilities, commitments, and related derivatives) be measured at market or fair value with the resulting gains and losses reported in current period earnings. Finally, with regard to synthetics, the Report on Deliberations described an approach under which a company would combine and initially measure the separate financial instruments used to create the synthetic as a single financial instrument based on the net proceeds received or paid. In subsequent financial reporting periods, the company would recognize in current period earnings any difference between the combined fair values of the separate instruments and the fair value of the prototype instrument that the company was trying to synthetically create.

Since June 1993, when the Report on Deliberations was issued the Board has continued its discussions on this topic. As evidenced by these discussions, the Report on Deliberations, though a noteworthy and interesting document, represented a very preliminary set of thoughts by the Board that since that time has changed direction several times. While this may be due, in part, to the fact that two of the seven FASB members at the time of the Report on Deliberations retired and were replaced by new Board members, the heightened focus on derivatives, in general, and on the accounting for derivatives in particular, by Congress, the GAO, the SEC, and others—together with the wave of reported losses and "busts" involving derivatives—has undoubtedly impacted on Board members' thinking. Critics of the current rules argue that not only are they incomplete and internally inconsistent, but moreover, that deferral accounting, whether it be in the guise of hedge accounting or synthetic-instrument accounting, is harmful because it often masks the extent of a company's involvement with derivatives as well as the potential losses the company may suffer from using these instruments. An accounting method is needed, it is argued, that is not only less complex and that leaves less room for subjective judgments, but that also gives great "visibility" to a company's use of derivatives by making sure they are captured on the balance sheet. Mark-to-market accounting, it is argued, will achieve all these objectives.

Thus it was that during 1994, while continuing to explore various hedge accounting methods, the Board also began to examine possible alternative mark-to-market approaches. As part of this effort, the Board considered a number of models that while measuring all freestanding derivatives at market or fair value, also attempted to provide some sort of special or hedge accounting for a broad array of hedging and risk management techniques, including dynamic portfolio management, hedging forecasted transactions, and managing exposures to changes in cash flows and market values. In each case, however, Board members found that the methods proposed were either too complex and/or yielded results that were conceptually difficult to justify. Accordingly, in November 1994 the Board, in an effort to move the project ahead, instructed the FASB staff to develop a model under which a company would classify all freestanding derivatives into two categories—trading and other than trading. Derivatives classified as trading (which would include derivatives used to manage risk in a trading portfolio) would be measured at market or fair value, with all gains and losses, realized and unrealized, recognized currently in earnings. Derivatives classified as other than trading would also be measured at market or fair value. However, the unrealized gains or losses would be included in a separate component of stockholders' equity until realized, at which point the realized gain or loss would be transferred from stockholders' equity and recognized in earnings. The Board also tentatively decided that commodity futures and other commodity-based derivatives that entitle the holder to settle in cash or by receipt or delivering of the commodity, and that certain other instruments that have derivative-like characteristics such as interest-only strips and some structured notes, should also be encompassed by this proposed accounting approach. It also tentatively decided that with regard to regulated futures, the daily settlement for changes in value via variation margin should be treated as an event of realization requiring recognition of the value change in earnings.

This approach is somewhat similar to the one adopted by the Board for debt and marketable equity securities in Statement No. 115. Arguments in support of the approach included that it captures all derivatives on the balance sheet and that it was comprehensive, easy to understand, and simple to implement. Critics argued that by effectively eliminating hedge accounting, the approach would result in an inappropriate and potentially misleading portrayal of a company's hedging and risk management activities in its income statement. Many, particularly banks and other depository institutions, pointed out that this approach could greatly increase the volatility of stockholders' equity because unrealized gains and losses on derivatives used to hedge assets and liabilities carried at historical cost would be included in stockholders' equity while the offsetting change in value of the item being hedged would not. Finally, the futures industry complained that by treating the daily settlement of regulated futures and options as realized gains and losses to be immediately included in income, the approach might drive many end users to increasingly turn to (potentially riskier) over-the-counter instruments.

In response to these criticisms, the Board has been exploring various other potential approaches including a possible three category approach that would account for some derivatives as trading, some as items to be accounted for through stockholders' equity, and others under an approach akin to hedge accounting whereby gains and losses on the derivatives would adjust the basis of the items being hedged. However, to date (September 1995), the Board has not definitively decided whether it should try to pursue developing such an approach further and in the iterim has asked its staff to explore a model that would mark all financial instruments to market and would provide for traditional deferral hedge accounting for nonfinancial instrument exposures with the potential to accommodate hedges of forecasted transactions by permitting unrealized gains and losses on a financial instrument to be recorded in equity until realized. Thus, at this point it's difficult to tell how and when the current rules may change.

CONCLUSION

This chapter provided an overview of the current accounting and financial reporting rules and practices for derivatives and synthetics. As explained, these are incomplete and often inconsistent. However, the FASB is now focusing on this area in earnest and has arrived at certain tentative views that would significantly change the current rules. Further, Statement 119 introduced expanded disclosure requirements relating to derivatives and their use and the SEC, regulators, and analysts continue to focus on how a company utilizes, manages, and controls its use of derivatives as part of its financial-risk-management programs. Clearly, those involved in using derivative instruments should be conversant with the current rules and should exercise care before initiating new transactions involving derivative instruments to ensure that the intended accounting, financial reporting, and disclosure ramifications are understood, and should consult with their accounting professionals on both the current rules and the FASB's progress on developing new rules.

Appendix to Chapter Fifteen
Examples of Derivatives Disclosures

This appendix contains the following examples of derivatives disclosures from 1994 annual reports:

1. Exxon Corporation
   - Footnote 1 on accounting policies on financial instruments, including the accounting policies for derivatives
   - Footnote 13 on Fair Value of Financial Instruments (SFAS No. 107), and Footnote 14 on Interest Rate Swap, Currency Exchange and Commodity Contracts (SFAS Nos. 105 and 119)
2. Chemical Banking Corporation
   - Extracts from Management's Discussion and Analysis covering derivatives and risk management
   - Footnote 1 on accounting policies on Risk Management Instruments and on Off-Balance-Sheet Instruments Used in Asset/Liability Management Activities
   - Footnotes 3, 19, 20, 21, and 22 covering the disclosures under SFAS Nos. 105, 107 and 119.

EXXON CORPORATION: NOTES TO CONSOLIDATED FINANCIAL STATEMENTS

Note 1: Summary of Accounting Policies

Financial instruments. Interests rate swap agreements are used to modify the interest rates on certain debt obligations. The interest differentials to be paid or received under such swaps are recognized over the life of the agreements as adjustments to interest expense. Currency exchange contracts are used to reduce the risk of adverse foreign currency movements related to certain foreign currency debt obligations. The gains or losses arising from currency exchange contracts offset foreign exchange gains or losses on the underlying assets or liabilities and are recognized as offsetting adjustments to the carrying amounts. Commodity swap and futures contracts are used to mitigate the risk of unfavorable price movements on certain crude and petroleum product purchases and sales. Gains or losses on these contracts are recognized as adjustments to purchase costs or to sales revenue.

Investments in marketable debt securities are expected to be held to maturity and are stated at amortized cost.

The fair value of financial instruments in determined by reference to various market data and other valuation techniques as appropriate.

Note 13: Fair Value of Financial Instruments

The fair value of financial instruments is determined by reference to various market data and other valuation techniques as appropriate. Long-term debt is the only category of financial instruments whose fair value has differed materially from the recorded book value. The estimated fair value of total long-term debt, including capitalized lease obligations, at December 31, 1994 and 1993 was $8.9 billion and $9.5 billion, respectively, and compared to recorded book values of $8.8 billion and $8.5 billion.

Note 14: Interest Rate Swap, Currency Exchange and Commodity Contracts

The corporation uses certain financial derivative instruments in its risk management activities. Derivative instruments are matched to existing assets, liabilities or transactions with the objective of mitigating the impact of adverse movements in interest rates, currency exchange rates or commodity prices. These instruments normally equal the amount of the underlying assets, liabilities or transactions and are held to maturity. The corporation does not hold or issue financial derivative instruments for trading purposes nor does it use financial derivatives with leveraged features. Instruments are either exchange-traded or are with counterparties of high credit standing. As a result of the above factors, the corporation's exposure to market and credit risks from financial derivative instruments is considered to be negligible.

Interest rate swap agreements are used to adjust the ratio of fixed and floating rates in the corporation's debt portfolio. Interest rate swap agreements, maturing 1995–1999, had an aggregate notional principal amount of $604 million and $705 million at year-end 1994 and 1993, respectively. Currency exchange contracts are used to reduce the risk of adverse foreign currency movements related to certain foreign currency debt obligations. Currency exchange contracts, maturing 1995–2005, totaled $2,998 million at year-end 1994 and $3,041 million at year-end 1993. In each year, over $2 billion of these amounts where contracts in which affiliates held positions which were effectively offsetting. Excluding these, the remaining currency exchange contracts totaled $789 million and $874 million at year-end 1994 and 1993, respectively.

The corporation makes limited use of commodity swap and futures contracts of short duration to mitigate the risk of unfavorable price movements on certain crude and petroleum product purchases and sales. These contracts had an aggregate notional amount of $37 million at year-end 1994 and will mature during 1995.

CHEMICAL BANKING CORPORATION AND SUBSIDIARIES

Management's Discussion and Analysis of Derivative and Foreign-Exchange Financial Instruments

In the normal course of its business, the Corporation utilizes various derivative and foreign exchange financial instruments to meet the financing needs of its customers, to generate revenues through its trading activities, and to manage its exposure to fluctuations in interest and currency rates.

Derivative and foreign exchange instruments represent contracts with counterparties where payments are made to or from the counterparty based upon specific interest rates, currency levels, other market rates, or on terms predetermined by the contract. These instruments can provide a cost-effective alternative to assuming and mitigating risk associated with traditional on-balance sheet instruments. Derivative and foreign exchange transactions involve, to varying degrees, credit risk (i.e., the possibility that a loss may occur because a party to a transaction fails to perform according to the terms of a contract) and market risk (i.e., the possibility that a change in interest or currency rates will cause the value of a financial instrument to decrease or become more costly to settle).

The effective management of credit and market risk is vital to the success of the Corporation's trading activities and asset/liability management. Because of the changing market environment, the monitoring and managing of these risks is a continual process. For a further discussion, see the Risk Management section.

The Corporation does not deal, to any material extent, in derivatives which dealers of derivatives (such as other banks and financial institutions) consider to be "complex" (i.e., exotic and/or leveraged). As a result, the notional amount of such derivatives were immaterial at December 31, 1994.

Trading activities. The Corporation has four fundamental trading activities which generate revenue. The Corporation seeks generally stable businesses of market-making, sales and arbitrage, while placing less emphasis on the potentially less-stable business of positioning.

Market-making: The Corporation trades with the intention of making a profit based on the spread between bid and ask prices. Market-making, compared with other trading activities, is considered to be a relatively stable business by the Corporation because revenue is related principally to market volumes, rather than to anticipating correctly material changes in the prices of various financial instruments. The Corporation considers market-making to be a key trading activity in its nonexchange traded businesses, particularly in its derivative, foreign exchange, and government markets businesses.

Sales: The Corporation provides products for its clients at competitive prices. The Corporation believes this to be a relatively stable business because revenue is related principally to the volume of products sold to the Corporations's worldwide client base.

Arbitrage: The Corporation enters into a risk position and offsets that risk in different but closely related markets or instruments. Because of the nature of trading markets, where there are numerous instruments that relate to one another, the Corporation believes it can effectively utilize this strategy. The Corporation considers arbitrage to be a key fundamental of its trading business.

Positioning: The Corporation takes certain positions in the market with the intention of generating revenue. This strategy has the lowest stability of all four trading activities and the Corporation's emphasis in this area is less than in the other trading activities.

The Corporation manages the market risk associated with these trading activities on an aggregate basis at the business unit level. For a discussion regarding the Corporation's market risk management process, see the Market Risk Management—Trading Activities section of Risk Management.

For a discussion of the derivative and foreign exchange financial instruments with respect to the Corporation's asset/liability management, see the Asset/ Liability Management section of Risk Management.

Risk Management

Credit-risk management. Credit risk for both lending-related products and derivative and foreign exchange products represents the possibility that a loss may occur if a borrower or counterparty fails to honor fully the terms of a contract. Under the direction of the chief credit officer, risk policies are formulated, approved and communicated throughout the Corporation. The credit risk management committee, chaired by the chief credit officer, is responsible for maintaining a sound credit process, addressing risk issues, and reviewing the portfolio.

The Corporation's credit-risk management is an integrated process operating concurrently at the transaction and portfolio levels. For credit origination, business units formulate strategies, target markets, and determine acceptable levels of risk. Credit officers work with client managers and, when appropriate, the syndications group during the underwriting process.

Lending-related products: The consumer and commercial segments of the portfolio have different risk characteristics and different techniques are utilized to measure and manage their respective credit risks. The consumer loan risk management process utilizes sophisticated credit scoring and other analytical methods to differentiate risk characteristics. Risk-management procedures include monitoring both loan origination credit standards and loan performance quality indicators. The consumer portfolio review process also includes evaluating product-line performance, geographic diversity and consumer economic trends. Within the commercial segment, each credit facility is risk graded. Facilities are subject to hold targets based on risk, and are often syndicated in order to lower potential concentration risks. Credits not syndicated remain on the balance sheet and are carefully monitored and analyzed. The loan review process includes industry specialists and country risk managers who provide independent expert insight into the portfolio. Industries and countries are also graded in a process which is incorporated into credit-risk decisions through the facility-risk grading system and by direct consultation with originating officers. In addition, real estate problem assets are managed in special units staffed for restructuring, workout and collection. The Corporation reassesses the market value of real estate owned for possible impairment on a continual basis.

Derivative and foreign-exchange products: The Corporation seeks to control the credit-risk arising from derivative and foreign-exchange transactions through its credit approval process and the use of risk control limits and monitoring procedures. The Corporation uses the same credit procedures when entering into derivative and foreign exchange transactions as it does for traditional lending products. The credit approval process involves, first, evaluating each counterparty's creditworthiness, then, where appropriate, assessing the applicability of off-balance sheet instruments to the risks the counterparty is attempting to manage, and determining if there are specific transaction characteristics which alter the risk profile. Credit limits are calculated and monitored on the basis of potential exposure which takes into consideration current market value and estimates of potential future movements in market values. If collateral is deemed necessary to reduce credit risk, the amount and nature of the collateral obtained is based on management's credit evaluation of the customer. Collateral held varies but may include cash, investment securities, accounts receivable, inventory, property, plant and equipment, and real estate.

The Corporation believes the true measure of credit-risk exposure is the replacement cost of the derivative or foreign-exchange product (i.e., the cost to replace the contract at current market rates should the counterparty default prior to the settlement date). This is also referred to as repayment risk or the mark-to-market exposure amount. The notional principal of derivative and foreign exchange instruments is the amount on which interest and other payments in a transaction are based. For derivative transactions, the notional principal typically does not change hands; it is simply a quantity that is used to calculate payments. While notional principal is the most commonly used volume measure in the derivative and foreign exchange market, it is not a measure of credit or market risk. The notional principal of the Corporation's derivative and foreign-exchange products greatly exceeds the possible credit and market loss that could arise from such transactions. As a result, the Corporation does not consider the notional principal to the indicative of its credit or market risk exposure.

Mark-to-market exposure is a measure, at a point in time, of the value of a derivative or foreign-exchange contract in the open market. When the mark-to-market is positive, indicates the counterparty owes the Corporation and, therefore, creates a repayment risk for the Corporation. When the mark-to-market is negative, the Corporation owes the counterparty. In this situation, the Corporation does not have repayment risk.

When the Corporation has more than one transaction outstanding with a counterparty, and there exists a master netting agreement with the counterparty, the net mark-to-market exposure represents the netting of the positive and negative exposures with the same counterparty. If there is a net negative number, the Corporation's exposure to the counterparty is considered zero. Net mark-to-market is, in the Corporation's view, the best measure of credit risk when there is a legally enforceable master netting agreement between the Corporation and the counterparty.

The Corporation routinely enters into derivative and foreign exchange product transactions with regulated financial institutions, which the Corporation believes have relatively low credit risk. At December 31, 1994, approximately 95% of the mark-to-market exposure of such activities were with commercial bank and financial institution counterparties most of which are dealers in these products. Nonfinancial institutions only accounted for approximately 5% of the Corporation's derivative and foreign exchange mark-to-market exposure.

Many of the Corporation's contracts are short term, which mitigates the credit risk as transactions settle quickly. The following table provides the remaining maturities of derivative and foreign exchange contracts outstanding at December 31, 1994. Percentages are based upon remaining contract life of mark-to-market exposure amounts.

At December 31, 1994	Interest Rate Contracts	Foreign Exchange Contracts
Less than 3 months	11%	57%
3 to 6 months	8	24
6 to 12 months	12	12
1 to 3 years	35	6
Over 3 years	34	1
Total	100%	100%

Allowance for credit losses: The allowance for credit losses is available to absorb potential credit losses from the entire loan portfolio, as well as from other balance sheet and off-balance-sheet credit-related transactions. The Corporation deems its allowance for credit losses at December 31, 1994 to be adequate. Although the Corporation considers that it has sufficient reserves to absorb losses that may currently exist in the portfolio, but are not yet identifiable, the precise loss content from the loan portfolio, as well as from other balance sheet and off-balance-sheet credit-related instruments, is subject continuing review based on quality indicators, industry and geographic concentrations, changes in business conditions, and other external factors such as competition, legal and regulatory requirements. The Corporation will continue to reassess the adequacy of the allowance for credit losses.

During 1994, 1993 and 1992, the Corporation's actual credit losses arising from derivative and foreign exchange transactions were immaterial. Additionally, at December 31, 1994 and 1993, nonperforming derivatives contracts were immaterial.

The following table reflects the activity in the allowance for credit losses for the years ended December 31, 1994 and 1993.

Year Ended December 31, (in millions)	1994	1993
Non-LDC Allowance:		
Balance at Beginning of Year	**$2,423**	$2,206
Provision for Losses	**550**	1,259[a]
Net Charge-Offs	**(650)**	(1,259)[a]
Charge for Assets Transferred to Held for Accelerated Dispostion	**(148)**	—

| | | *(concluded)* |
Year Ended December 31, *(in millions)*	*1994*	*1993*
Transfer from LDC Allowance	**300**	200
Allowance Related to Purchased Assets of the First City Banks	—	19
Other	**5**	(2)
Balance at End of Year	**2,480**	2,423
LDC Allowance:		
Balance at Beginning of Year	**597**	819
Provision for Losses	—	—
Net (Charge-Offs) Recoveries	**(239)**	130
Losses on Sales and Swaps	**(58)**	(152)
Transfer to Non-LDC Allowance	**(300)**	(200)
Balance at End of Year	—	597
Total Allowance for Credit Losses	**$2,480**	$3,020

(a) Includes $55 million related to the decision to accelerate the disposition of certain nonperforming residential mortgages.

Completion of the Brazilian refinancing package during 1994 brought to a close the broad rescheduling programs begun in the mid-1980s. In connection with the completion of the Brazilian refinancing program, the Corporation performed a final valuation of its LDC portfolio and adjusted its medium- and long-term outstandings to the various LDC countries in that portfolio to amounts that management believed to be the estimated net recoverable values of each of such loans. The final valuation resulted in a $291 million charge in the 1994 second quarter. The remaining LDC allowance of $300 million was transferred to the general allowance for credit losses.

Market-risk management—trading activities.   Risk limits originate with the chairman of the market risk committee who determines instrument authorities and exposure levels of individual business units. Criteria for risk limit determination include, among other factors, relevant market analysis, market liquidity, prior track record, business strategy, and management experience and depth. Procedures and policies specify authorized instruments and exposure levels. Critical risk limits that are designated as primary are centrally tracked and reported on a daily basis, while less-critical risk limits are independently monitored and centrally reported on a periodic basis. Individual business units often set additional internal limits.

The market risk management group (the Group) performs independent analysis of instrument authority, limit requests, and limit utilization. In addition, the Group tracks market risk-related revenue and compares it to the actual market risk incurred to produce such revenue and assesses risk levels and related tropics. Other focuses include measurement and calculation of value-at-risk, criteria for official volatility and correlation statistics, and formulas for determination of market-related credit exposure. Additionally, the Group reviews the market risk related to new products (as one element of the Corporation's new-product process) and provides independent review of the mathematical and simulation models utilized by business units. The Group combines efforts with other functional units to assess cross-discipline risks in business units having significant market risk.

The Corporation's business strategy seeks to manage the market risks associated with its trading activities through geographic, product and functional diversification. The Corporation's trading activities are geographically diverse. Trading activities are undertaken in more than 20 countries, with a majority of the Corporation's transactions in the United States, Japan, Singapore, United Kingdom and Western Europe. The Corporation trades in a wide range of products which include not only foreign exchange and derivatives but also securities, including emerging markets debt instruments.

The effects of market gains or losses on the Corporation's trading activities have been reflected in trading revenue, as the trading instruments are marked-to-market on a daily basis. For the impact of any unrealized market gains or losses on the Corporation's asset/liability management portfolio, see Note 22 of the Consolidated Financial Statements.

Measuring market risk: The Corporation's overall risk-management process utilizes a limit system incorporating three types of risk control: value-at-risk, non-statistical limits, and stop loss advisories. Value-at-risk is defined as the potential overnight dollar loss from adverse market movements that would cover 97.5% of likely market movements, which are determined by using two years of historical price and rate data. The value-at-risk calculations employ nearly 1,500 volatilities and 400,000 correlations (updated semiannually) of various market instruments. The Corporation monitors value-at-risk figures for major business units on a daily basis to ensure the potential for market loss is properly reflected. The methodology generally used to offset positions within a business unit is deemed by the Corporation to be conservative. Only partial credit for correlation between instruments within each business unit is incorporated since correlations can exhibit instability during volatile market environments. Aggregating across business units with no correlation offset resulted in an aggregated daily average value-at-risk figure of $29 million in 1994. Based on actual 1994 trading results, which capture the historical correlation among business units, the Corporation's daily average value-at-risk was reduced to approximately $121 million with 97.5% confidence.

Value-at-risk is an important concept, but it is not the sole control measure used in the risk management process. Nonstatistical limits include net open positions, basis point values, position concentrations, and position ages. These non-statistical measures are accorded the same importance as value-at-risk. Stop loss advisories also are used to advise senior management when losses of a certain threshold are sustained from a business activity. The use of nonstatistical measures and stop loss advisories to complement value-at-risk limits reduces the likelihood that potential trading losses will reach the daily average value-at-risk amount.

HISTOGRAM OF DAILY MARKET RISK-RELATED TRADING REVENUE FOR 1994

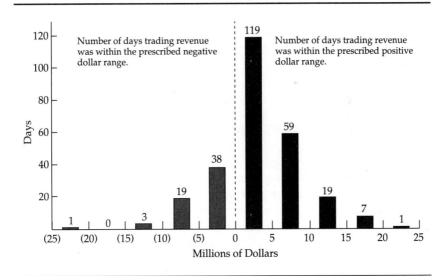

The above chart contains a histogram of the Corporation's daily market risk-related revenue for 1994. Market-risk-related revenue is defined as the daily change in value in marked-to-market trading portfolios plus any trading-related net interest income or other revenue. Net interest income related to funding and investment activity is excluded. The histogram covers the Corporation's major trading units (including Texas Commerce) which constitute approximately 98% of its trading activity. The histogram does not include the $70 million loss from unauthorized foreign exchange transactions related to the Mexican peso, as management considers this loss to be indicative of operating risk rather than market risk. As shown by the histogram, the Corporation posted positive daily market risk-related revenue far more often than negative results (approximately 77% of all days). The large number of results centered around the $0 million to $5 million range is representative of the Corporation's emphasis on market-making and sales activities. The low number of outlier results exemplifies the Corporation's diversified approach to market risk management as a business strategy.

Operating-risk management. The Corporation, like all financial institutions, is subject to the risk of fraud and to the risk of unauthorized activities by employees. The Corporation maintains a comprehensive system of internal controls designed to manage such risks.

Asset/liability management. The objective of the asset/liability management process is to manage and control the sensitivity of the Corporation's income to changes in market interest rates. The process operates under the authority and direction of the asset and liability policy committee (Committee), comprised of the office of the chairman and senior business and finance executives. The Committee seeks to maximize earnings—particularly revenues associated with net interest income—while ensuring that the risks to those earnings from adverse movements in interest rates are kept within specified limits deemed acceptable by the Corporation.

The Corporation's net interest income is affected by changes in the level of market interest rates based upon mismatches between the repricing of its assets and liabilities. Interest rate sensitivity arises in the ordinary course of the Corporation's banking business as the repricing characteristics of its loans do not necessarily match those of its deposits and other borrowings. This sensitivity can be altered by adjusting the Corporation's investments and the maturities of its wholesale funding activities, and with the use of off-balance sheet derivative instruments.

The Corporation, as part of its asset/liability management process, employs a variety of off-balance sheet instruments in managing its exposure to fluctuations in market interest rates and foreign exchange rates. These instruments include interest rate swaps, futures, forward rate agreements, options and foreign currency contracts (see Note One of the Consolidated Financial Statements for a discussion of the Corporation's accounting policy relative to off-balance sheet instruments used for asset/liability management and Note 19 of the Consolidated

Financial Statements for the aggregate notional principal of off-balance sheet instruments). Foreign currency instruments are used to hedge the exposure to changes in currency values. For example, the legal capital invested in the Corporation's foreign branches and subsidiaries is usually recorded in their respective local currencies, while the related funding by the Corporation is in U.S. dollars. The resulting market risk is generally hedged using foreign exchange forward contracts.

Risk managements and control: A key element of the Corporation's asset/liability process is that it allows the assumption of interest sensitivity at a decentralized level by authorized units with close contacts to the markets. These units are subject to individual authorities and limits administered centrally which limit the size of exposures by currency and the instruments that can be used to manage the sensitivities.

The Asset and Liability Policy Committee has ultimate responsibility for the Corporation's consolidated interest rate exposure. In addition to the individual limits placed on the decentralized risk management units, the Committee has established "global" limits for consolidated exposures along several dimensions of risk, including net gap exposure and earnings at risk.

Measuring interest-rate sensitivity: Management uses a variety of techniques to measure its interest rate sensitivity. One such tool is aggregate net gap analysis, and example of which is presented below. Assets and liabilities are placed in maturity ladders based on their contractual maturities or repricing dates. Assets and liabilities for which no specific contractual maturity or repricing dates exist are placed in ladders based on management's judgments concerning their most likely repricing behaviors.

Derivatives used in interest rate sensitivity management are also included in the maturity ladders. The aggregate notional amounts of derivatives are netted when the repricing of the receive-side and pay-side of two swaps occur within the same gap interval. Such net amount represents the repricing mismatch of the Corporation's derivatives during the particular gap interval. It is the amount of the net repricing mismatch, rather than the aggregate notional principal of the derivatives repricing during the period, that is included in the gap analysis, because it is the amount of the mismatch that reflects the impact of the Corporation's derivatives in altering the repricing profile of the Corporation.

A net gap for each time period is calculated by subtracting the liabilities repricing in that interval from the assets repricing. A negative gap—more liabilities repricing than assets—will benefit net interest income in a declining interest rate environment and will detract form net interest income in a rising interest rate environment. Conversely, a positive gap—more assets repricing than liabilities—will benefit net interest income in a falling rate environment.

INTEREST-SENSITIVITY TABLE

At December 31, 1994 (in millions)	1-3 Months	4-6 Months	7-12 Months	1-5 Years	Over 5 Years	Total
Assets						
Deposits With Banks	$ 5,458	$ 182	$ 9	$ —	$ —	$ 5,649
Federal Funds Sold and Securities Purchased Under Resale Agreements	12,660	137	—	—	—	12,797
Trading Account Assets	28,802	—	—	—	—	28,802
Securities	3,489	775	1,386	12,207	9,140	26,997
Loans, Net	49,835	7,906	3,461	9,843	5,242	76,287
Noninterest Earning Assets	12,378	367	649	4,451	3,046	20,891
Total Assets	$112,622	$ 9,367	$5,505	$26,501	$17,428	$171,423
Liabilities and Stockholders' Equity						
Deposits	$ 64,356	$ 4,031	$4,803	$16,348	$ 6,968	$ 96,506
Short-Term and Other Borrowings	34,734	35	37	76	59	34,941
Long-Term Debt	3,784	462	—	977	2,768	7,991
Other Liabilities	21,106	9	15	68	75	21,273
Stockholders' Equity	171	437	475	4,763	4,866	10,712
Total Liabilities and Stockholders' Equity	$124,151	$ 4,974	$5,330	$22,232	$14,736	$171,423
Balance Sheet	(11,529)	4,393	175	4,269	2,692	—
Off-Balance Sheet Items Affecting Interest-Rate Sensitivity[a]	1,622	(4,366)	587	1,581	576	—
Interest-Rate-Sensitivity Gap	(9,907)	27	762	5,850	3,268	—
Cumulative Interest-Rate Sensitivity Gap	(9,907)	(9,880)	(9,118)	(3,268)	—	—

INTEREST-SENSITIVITY TABLE

At December 31, 1994 (in millions)	1-3 Months	4-6 Months	7-12 Months	1-5 Years	Over 5 Years	Total
% of Total Assets	(6)%	(6)%	(5)%	(2)%	—	—
At December 31, 1993						
Interest-Rate-Sensitivity Gap	$ (12,523)	$ 2,311	$2,300	$10,795	$ (2,883)	—
Cumulative Interest-Rate Sensitivity Gap	(12,523)	(10,212)	(7,912)	2,883	—	—
% of Total Assets	(8)%	(7)%	(5)%	2%	—	—
At December 31, 1992						
Interest-Rate-Sensitivity Gap	$ (11,501)	$ 1,730	$2,516	$ 8,963	$ (1,708)	—
Cumulative Interest-Rate Sensitivity Gap	(11,501)	(9,771)	(7,255)	1,708	—	—
% of Total Assets	(8)%	(7)%	(5)%	1%	—	—

(a) Represents repricing effect of off-balance sheet positions, which include interest rate swaps and options, financial futures, and similar agreements that are used as part of the Corporation's overall asset and liability management activities.

At December 31, 1994, the Corporation had $9,118 million more liabilities than assets repricing within one year, amounting to 5.3% of total assets. This compares with $7,912 million, or 5.3% of total assets, at December 31, 1993. The consolidated gaps include exposure to U.S. dollar interest rates as well as exposure to non-U.S. dollar rates in currency markets in which the Corporation does business. Since U.S. interest rates and non-U.S. interest rates do not move in tandem, the overall cumulative gaps will tend to overstate the exposures of the Corporation to U.S. interest rates.

Gap analysis is the simplest representation of the Corporation's interest rate sensitivity. It cannot reveal the impact of factors such as administered rates (e.g., the prime lending rate), pricing strategies on its consumer and business deposits, changes in balance sheet mix, or various options embedded in the balance sheet. Accordingly, the Asset and Liability Policy Committee conducts comprehensive simulations of the interest income under a variety of market interest rate scenarios. These simulations provide the Committee with an estimate of earnings at risk for given changes in interest rates.

The simulations are based on a static balance sheet, reflecting the Corporation's then-current business mix and interest rate exposures. The simulations take explicit account of pricing strategies and deposit responses and the behavior of embedded options. Net interest income is then projected assuming stable interest rates and under a variety of other scenarios. The difference between these projections of net interest income after taxes, as a percentage of projected net income after taxes, represent earnings at risk to changes in interest rates.

At December 31, 1994, based on these simulations, earnings at risk to a gradual 150-basis-point rise in market interest rates over the course of 1995 was estimated to be less than three percent of projected 1995 after-tax net income. The gradual 150-basis-point rise in interest rates is a hypothetical rate scenario, used to calibrate risk, and does not necessarily represent management's current view of future market interest rate movements.

Simulation analysis fails to capture interest rate exposures beyond the simulation period. To capture these exposures, the Asset and Liability Policy Committee has constructed models to estimate the sensitivity in value of the Corporation's financial assets and liabilities which result from hypothetical, instantaneous shifts in the level of market interest rates. This sensitivity is calculated by comparing the net present value of net interest income-related cash flows under current market conditions to the net present values under different rate environments. In addition to gap exposures and earnings at risk, the Asset and Liability Policy Committee continuously monitors the longer-run sensitivity.

All the measurements of risk described above are based upon the Corporation's business mix and interest rate exposures at a particular point in time. The exposures change continuously as a result of the Corporation's ongoing business and its risk management initiatives. During 1994, the Corporation's net cumulative gap exposure at the one-year point ranged between 3.2% and 7.2% of total assets. Earnings at risk to a gradual, one-year 150-basis-point increase in interest rates varied between 2% and 4% of projected after-tax net income.

While management believes these measures provide a meaningful representation of the Corporation's interest rate sensitivity, they do not necessarily take into account all business developments which have an effect on net income, such as changes in credit quality or the size and composition of the balance sheet.

Interest-rate swaps: Interest-rate swaps are one of the various financial instruments used in the Corporation's asset/liability management activities. Although the Corporation believes the results of its asset/liability management activities should be evaluated on an integrated basis, taking into consideration all on- and related off-balance sheet instruments and not a specific financial instrument, the interest rate swap maturity table, which follows, provides an indication of the Corporation's interest rate swap activity.

The table summarizes the expected maturities and weighted-average interest rates to be received and paid on domestic and international interest-rate swaps utilized in the Corporation's asset/liability management at December 31, 1994. The table was prepared under the assumption that variable interest rates remain constant at December 31, 1994 levels and, accordingly, the actual interest rates to be received or paid will be different to the extent that such variable rates fluctuate from December 31, 1994 levels. Variable rates presented are generally based on the short-term interest rates for the relevant currencies (e.g., London Interbank Offered Rate (LIBOR)). Basic swaps are interest-rate swaps based on two floating rate indices (e.g., LIBOR and prime). Forward-starting swaps are interest-rate swap contracts that become effective at a future time.

NOTES TO CONSOLIDATED FINANCIAL STATEMENTS

Note 1: Summary of Significant Accounting Policies

Risk-management instruments: The Corporation primarily deals in interest-rate, foreign-exchange, and commodity contracts to generate trading revenues. Such contracts include futures, forwards, swaps, and options and are carried at market value with realized and unrealized gains and losses reported on the income statement as trading revenue. A portion of the market valuation

INTEREST-RATE-SWAP MATURITY TABLE

By expected maturities
At December 31, 1994 (in millions)

	1995	1996	1997	1998	1999	After 1999	Total
Receive fixed swaps							
Notional amount	$11,193	$ 5,297	$ 4,551	$ 1,316	$ 638	$ 2,057	$25,052
Weighted-average:							
Receive rate	6.10%	6.38%	6.53%	5.88%	5.93%	6.89%	6.29%
Pay rate	5.36	5.13	5.73	5.96	6.10	5.80	5.47
Pay fixed swaps							
Notional amount	$ 7,462	$ 5,891	$ 2,102	$ 599	$ 978	$ 1,366	$18,398
Weighted-average:							
Receive rate	5.60%	5.25%	5.29%	5.84%	5.79%	5.84%	5.49%
Pay rate	5.72	6.13	6.66	5.80	7.10	7.04	6.13
Basis swaps							
Notional amount	$ 4,955	$ 1,109	$ 415	$ 342	$ 405	$ 145	$ 6,471
Weighted-average:							
Receive rate	6.13%	6.28%	6.06%	6.34%	6.54%	5.83%	6.18%
Pay rate	6.10	6.02	5.95	6.24	6.57	5.95	6.11
Forward starting							
Notional amount	$ 46	$ 492	$ 68	$ —	$ —	$ 155	$ 761
Weighted-average:							
Receive rate	6.84%	5.76%	6.19%	—%	—%	4.64%	5.63%
Pay rate	7.11	6.23	7.83	—	—	5.78	6.33
Total notional amount[a]	$22,756	$12,789	$ 7,136	$ 2,257	$ 2,021	$ 3,723	$50,682

(a) At December 31, 1994, approximately $30.8 billion of notional amounts are interest rate swaps that, as part of the Corporation's asset/liability management, are used in place of cash market instruments. Of this amount, $15.7 billion is expected to mature in 1995, $8.2 billion in 1996 and $4.2 billion in 1997 with the remaining $2.7 billion in 1998 and thereafter. The unrecognized net gain related to these positions was approximately $80 million. See Note One to the Consolidated Financial Statements for a discussion of the Corporation's accounting policy relative to off-balance sheet instruments used for asset/liability management.

relating to certain contracts is deferred and accreted to income over the life of the contracts to match ongoing servicing costs and credit risks, as appropriate.

On January 1, 1994, the Corporation adopted Financial Accounting Standards Board ("FASB") Interpretation No. 39, "Offsetting of Amounts Related to Certain Contracts" ("FASI 39") which changed the reporting of unrealized gains and losses on interest-rate, foreign-exchange, and commodity contracts on the balance sheet. FASI 39 requires that gross unrealized gains be reported as assets and gross unrealized losses be reported as liabilities; however, FASI 39 permits netting of such unrealized gains and losses with the same counterparty when master netting agreements that are enforceable through bankruptcy have been executed. With the adoption of FASI 39, unrealized gains are reported as trading assets-risk management instruments and unrealized losses are reported as trading liabilities-risk management instruments, which is included in other liabilities. Prior to the adoption of FASI 39, unrealized gains and losses were reported net in other assets.

Off-balance-sheet instruments used in asset/liability management activities.   As part of its asset/liability management activities, the Corporation may enter into interest-rate futures, forwards, swaps and options contracts. Futures contracts are designated as hedges when they reduce risk and there is high correlation between the futures contract and the item being hedged, both at inception and throughout the hedge period. Interest-rate forwards, swaps and options contracts are linked to specific assets or groups of similar assets, specific liabilities or groups of similar liabilities. Additionally, the Corporation uses interest-rate swaps in place of cash market instruments. Asset/liability management instruments are accounted for on an accrual basis. Realized gains and losses on futures and forward contracts are deferred and amortized over the period for which the related assets or liabilities exposure is managed and are included as adjustments to interest income or interest expense. Settlements on interest-rate swaps and options contracts are recognized as adjustments to interest income or interest expense over the lives of the agreements.

Interest rate contracts used in connection with the securities portfolio that is designated as available-for-sale are carried at fair value with gains and losses, net of applicable taxes, reported in a separate component of stockholders' equity, consistent with the reporting of unrealized gains and losses on such securities.

Effective January 1, 1995, as part of its asset/liability management process, the Corporation discontinued the use of interest-rate swaps in place of cash market instruments. Accordingly, interest-rate contracts entered into subsequent to January 1, 1995 that do not meet the hedge or linkage criteria described above will be designated as trading activities-risk management instruments.

Note 3: Trading Activities

The Corporation uses its trading assets, such as debt and equity instruments and risk management instruments, to meet the financing needs of its customers and to generate revenues through its trading activities. The Corporation generates such trading revenue through market-making, sales, arbitrage and, to a lesser degree, positioning. A description of the classes of derivative and foreign exchange instruments used in the Corporation's trading activities as well as the credit-risk and market-risk factors involved in such activities are disclosed in Note 19.

Debt and equity instruments. Trading assets-debt and equity instruments at December 31, 1994 and 1993, which are carried at fair value, are presented in the following table.

December 31, (in millions)	1994	1993
U.S. Government and Federal Agencies	$ 2,548	$ 2,792
Obligations of State and Political Subdivisions	327	604
Certificates of Deposit, Bankers' Acceptances, and Commercial Paper	1,644	1,794
Debt Securities Issued by Foreign Governments	1,983	4,025
Foreign Financial Institutions	3,119	1,496
Other[a]	1,472	968
Total Trading Assets-Debt and Equity Instruments[b]	$11,093	$11,679

(a) Primarily includes corporate debt and eurodollar bonds.

(b) Includes emerging markets instruments of $544 million in 1994 and $426 million in 1993.

Risk-management instruments. On January 1, 1994, the Corporation adopted FASI 39, which changed the reporting on the balance sheet of unrealized gains and losses on interest-rate, foreign-exchange, and commodity contracts. See Note One for a further discussion with respect to FASI 39.

Trading assets-risk management instruments totaled $17.7 billion at December 31, 1994, and represents unrealized gains on interest-rate contracts of $7.9 billion, foreign exchange contract of $9.5 billion, and stock index options and commodity contracts of $0.3 billion.

Trading liabilities-risk management instruments, which totaled $16.0 billion at December 31, 1994, represents unrealized losses on interest-rate contracts of $7.0

billion, foreign exchange contracts of $8.9 billion, and stock index options and commodity contracts of $0.1 billion.

Trading revenue.   The following table sets forth the components of trading revenue.

Year Ended December 31, (in millions)	1994	1993	1992
Trading Revenue:			
Interest-Rate Contracts[a]	**$391**	$ 453	$333
Foreign-Exchange Revenues[b]	**152**[d]	302	363
Debt Instruments and Other[c]	**102**	318	157
Total Trading Revenue	**$645**	$1,073	$853

(a) Includes interest-rate swaps, currency swaps, foreign-exchange forward contracts, interest-rate futures, and forward-rate agreements and related hedges.

(b) Includes foreign-exchange spot and option contracts.

(c) Includes U.S. government and foreign-government agency and corporate debt securities, emerging-markets debt instruments, debt-related derivatives, equity securities, equity derivatives, and commodity derivatives.

(d) Includes $70 million of losses sustained from unauthorized foreign-exchange transactions involving the Mexican peso.

Note 19: Derivative and Foreign-Exchange Financial Instruments

The Corporation utilizes various derivative and foreign-exchange financial instruments for trading purposes and for purposes other than trading, such as asset/liability management. These financial instruments represent contracts with counterparties where payments are made to or from the counterparty based on specific interest rates, currency levels, other market rates or on terms predetermined by the contract. Such derivative and foreign exchange transactions involve, to varying degrees, credit risk and market risk.

Derivative and foreign-exchange instruments used for trading purposes: The financial instruments used for the Corporation's trading activities are disclosed in Note Three.

The credit risk associated with the Corporation's trading activities is disclosed on the balance sheet as a result of the Corporation's adoption of FASI 39. The effects of any market risk (gains or losses) on the Corporation's trading activities have been reflected in trading revenue, as the trading instruments are marked-to-market on a daily basis. See Note 1 for a discussion of FASI 39 and Note 3 for the categories of these trading instruments.

Derivative and foreign-exchange instruments used for purposes other than trading: The Corporation's principal objective in using off-balance sheet instruments for purposes other than trading is for its asset/liability management.

The majority of the Corporation's derivatives used for asset/liability management are transacted through its trading units.

For the disclosure of the fair value associated with the Corporation's asset/liability management activities, see Note 22, Fair Value of Financial Instruments.

At December 31, 1994, gross deferred gains and gross deferred losses relating to closed financial futures contracts used in asset/liability management activities were $23 million and $9 million, respectively. Deferred gains and losses on closed financial futures contracts are generally amortized over periods ranging from six to nine months depending upon when the contract is closed and the period of time over which the liability is being hedged. The Corporation does not generally terminate its interest rate swaps. As of December 31, 1994, the Corporation did not have any deferred gains or losses related to terminated interest rate swap contracts.

The Corporation generally does not use derivative financial instruments to hedge anticipated transactions. Accordingly, at December 31, 1994, deferred gains and losses associated with such transactions were insignificant.

The following table summarizes the aggregate notional amounts of interest-rate and foreign-exchange contracts as well as the credit exposure related to these instruments (after taking into account the effects of master netting agreements) for the dates indicated below. The table should be read in conjunction with the preceding narrative as well as the descriptions of these products and their risks immediately following.

December 31, (in billions)	Notional Amounts 1994	1993	Credit Exposure 1994	1993
Interest-Rate Contracts				
Futures and Forward-Rate Agreements				
Trading	$ 938.1	$ 780.4	$ 0.8	
Asset and Liability Management	32.8	14.0	—	
Interest-Rate Swaps				
Trading	1,107.9	630.5	6.9	

December 31, (in billions)	Notional Amounts		Credit Exposure	
	1994	1993	1994	1993
Asset and Liability Management	**50.7**	37.4	**0.2**	
Purchased Options				
Trading	**60.5**	87.5	**0.2**	
Asset and liability Management	**13.7**	26.3	—	
Written Options				
Trading	**69.5**	146.0	—	
Asset and Liability Management	**3.3**	19.3	—	
Total Interest-Rate Contracts	**$2,276.5**	$1,741.4	**$ 8.1**	$ 8.6
Foreign-Exchange Contracts				
Spot, Forward and Futures Contracts				
Trading	**$ 794.0**	$ 657.0	**$ 7.3**	
Asset and Liability Management	**12.3**	11.0	—	
Other Foreign-Exchange Contracts[(a)]				
Trading	**94.5**	63.8	**2.2**	
Asset and Liability Management	**0.3**	0.4	—	
Total Foreign-Exchange Contracts	**$ 901.1**	$ 732.2	**$ 9.5**	$ 8.1
Stock Index Options and Commodity Contracts				
Trading	**$ 4.5**	$ 5.7	**$ 0.3**	
Total Stock Index Options and Commodity Contracts	**$ 4.5**	$ 5.7	**$ 0.3**	$ 0.2
Total Credit Exposure			**$17.9**	$16.9
Less: Amounts Recorded as Assets on the Balance Sheet			**$17.9**	$ 3.3
Credit Exposure Not Recorded on the Balance Sheet			**$ —**	$13.6

(a) Includes purchased options, written options and cross-currency interest rate swaps of $34.2 billion, $38.4 billion and $22.2 billion, respectively, at December 31, 1994, compared with $21.9 billion, $23.7 billion and $18.6 billion, respectively, at December 31, 1993.

Classes of derivative and foreign-exchange instruments: The following classes of derivative and foreign exchange instruments refer to instruments that are used by the Corporation for purposes of both trading and asset/liability management.

Interest-rate futures and forwards are contracts for the delayed delivery of securities or money market instruments in which the seller agrees to deliver on a specified future date, a specified instrument, at a specified price or yield. The credit risk inherent in futures and forwards is the risk that the exchange party may default. Futures contracts settle in cash daily and, therefore, there is minimal credit risk to the Corporation. The credit risk inherent in forwards arises from the potential inability of counterparties to meet the terms of their contracts. Both futures and forwards are also subject to the risk of movements in interest rates or the value of the underlying securities or instruments.

Forward-rate agreements are contracts to exchange payments on a certain future date, based on a market change in interest rates from trade date to contract maturity date. The maturity of these agreements is typically less than two years.

Interest-rate swaps are contracts in which a series of interest-rate flows in a single currency are exchanged over a prescribed period. The notional amount on which the interest payments are based is not exchanged. Most interest-rate swaps involve the exchange of fixed and floating interest payments. Cross-currency interest-rate swaps are contracts that involve the exchange of both interest and principal amounts in two different currencies. The risks inherent in interest-rate and cross-currency swap contracts are the potential inability of a counterparty to meet the terms of its contract and the risk associated with changes in the market values of the underlying interest rates.

Interest-rate options, which include caps and floors, are contracts which transfer, modify, or reduce interest-rate risk in exchange for the payment of a premium when the contract is initiated. As a writer of interest-rate caps, floors, and other options, the Corporation receives a premium in exchange for bearing the risk of unfavorable changes in interest rates. Conversely, as a purchaser of an option, the Corporation pays a premium for the right, but not the obligation, to buy or sell a financial instrument or currency at predetermined terms in the future. Foreign-currency options are similar to interest rate option contracts, except that they are based on currencies instead of interest rates.

Foreign-exchange contracts are contracts for the future receipt or delivery of foreign currency at previously agreed-upon terms. The risks inherent in these contracts are the potential inability of a counterparty to meet the terms of its contract and the risk associated with changes in the market values of the underlying currencies.

Stock index option contracts are contracts to pay or receive cash flows from counterparties based upon the increase on decrease in the underlying index. Commodity contracts include swaps, caps and floors and are similar to interest rate contracts, except that they are based on commodity indices instead of interest rates.

To reduce its exposure to market risk related to the above-mentioned classes of derivative and foreign exchange instruments, the Corporation may enter into offsetting positions.

To reduce credit risk, management may deem it necessary to obtain collateral. The amount and nature of the collateral obtained is based on management's credit evaluation of the customer. Collateral held varies but may include cash, investment securities, accounts receivable, inventory, property, plant and equipment, and real estate.

Derivatives and foreign exchange products are generally either negotiated over-the-counter (OTC) contracts or standardized contracts executed on a recognized exchange (such as the Chicago Board of Options Exchange). Standardized exchange-traded derivatives primarily include futures and options. Negotiated over-the-counter derivatives are generally entered into between two counterparties that negotiate specific agreement terms, including the underlying instrument, amount, exercise price and maturity.

All the Corporation's interest-rate swaps and forwards are OTC-traded and all of the Corporation's financial futures contracts are exchange-traded. As of December 31, 1994 approximately 19% of the Corporation's options activity was exchange-traded, with the balance being OTC-traded. As of December 31, 1993, approximately 53% of the Corporation's options activity was exchange-traded, with the balance being OTC-traded. The percentage of options activity that is exchange-traded versus OTC-traded will vary depending upon conditions in the market place.

In addition to the financial instruments presented in the preceding notional table, the Corporation also enters into transactions involving "when-issued securities" primarily as part of its trading activities. When-issued securities are commitments to purchase or sell securities authorized for issuance, but not yet actually issued. Accordingly, they are not recorded on the balance sheet until issued. At December 31, 1994 and 1993, commitments to purchase when-issued securities were $6,289 million and $2,194 million, respectively, and commitments to sell when-issued securities were $6,658 million and $1,790 million, respectively.

Note 20: Off-Balance-Sheet Lending-Related Financial Instruments

In addition to using derivative and foreign-exchange financial instruments, the Corporation also utilizes lending-related financial instruments in order to meet the financing needs of its customers. The Corporation issues commitments to extend credit, standby and other letters of credit and guarantees, and also provides securities-lending services. For these instruments, the contractual amount of the financial instrument represents the maximum potential credit risk if the counterparty does not perform according to the terms of the contract. A large majority of these commitments expire without being drawn upon. As a result, total contractual amounts is not representative of the Corporation's actual future credit exposure or liquidity requirements for such commitments.

The following table summarizes the Corporation's maximum credit risk, which is represented by contract amounts relating to these financial instruments at December 31, 1994 and 1993.

OFF-BALANCE-SHEET LENDING-RELATED FINANCIAL INSTRUMENTS

December 31, (in millions)	1994	1993
Commitments to Extend Credit	$49,266[a]	$47,540[a]
Standby Letters of Credit and Guarantees (Net of Risk Participations of $5,218 and $1,285)	12,451	11,224
Other Letters of Credit	2,860	2,325
Customers' Securities Lent	18,979	14,530

(a) Extends credit card commitments of $19 billion and $18 billion at December 31, 1994 and 1993, respectively.

Unfunded commitments to extend credit are agreements to lend to a customer who has complied with predetermined contractual conditions. Commitments generally have fixed expiration dates.

Standby letters of credit and guarantees are conditional commitments issued by the Corporation generally to guarantee the performance of a customer to a third party in borrowing arrangements, such as commercial paper, bond financing, construction and similar transactions. The credit risk involved in issuing standby letters of credit is essentially the same as that involved in extending loan facilities to customers and may be reduced by participations to third parties. The Corporation holds collateral to support those standby letters of credit and guarantees written for which collateral is deemed necessary. At December 31, 1994, all of the Corporation's standby letters of credit and guarantees written expire in less than five years.

Customers' securities lent are customers' securities held by the Corporation which are lent to third parties. The Corporation obtains collateral, with a market value exceeding 100% of the contract amount, for all such customers' securities lent, which is used to indemnify customers against possible losses resulting from third-party defaults.

Note 21: Concentrations of Credit Risk

Concentrations of credit risk arise when a number of customers are engaged in similar business activities, or activities in the same geograhic region, or have similar economic features that would cause their ability to meet contractual obligations to be similarly affected by changes in economic conditions.

Concentrations of credit risk indicate the relative sensitivity of the Corporation's performance to both positive and negative developments affecting a particular industry. Based on the nature of the banking business, management does not believe that any of these concentrations are unusual.

The accompanying table presents the Corporation's significant concentrations of credit risk for all financial instruments, including both on-balance sheet as well as off-balance-sheet instruments (which include derivative and foreign-exchange financial instruments as well as lending-related financial instruments). The Corporation has procedures to monitor counterparty credit risk and to obtain collateral when deemed necessary. Accordingly, management believes that the total credit exposure shown below is not representative of the potential risk of loss inherent in the portfolio.

Geographic concentrations are a factor most directly affecting the credit risk of the real estate and emerging markets segments of the Corporation's loan portfolio. The Corporation's real estate portfolio is primarily concentrated in the New York Metropolitan area and in Texas. Its emerging markets portfolio is largely concentrated in Latin American, principally Mexico, Venezuela and Brazil.

Note 22: Fair Value of Financial Instruments

Statement of Financial Accounting Standards No. 107, "Disclosures About Fair Value of Financial Instruments" (SFAS 107), requires the Corporation disclose fair value information about financial instruments for which it is practiable to estimate the value, whether or not such financial instruments are recognized on the balance sheet. Fair value is the amount at which a financial instrument could be exchanged in a current transaction between willing parties, other than in a forced sale or liquidation, and is best evidenced by a quoted market price, if one exists.

Quoted market prices are not available for a significant portion of the Corporation's financial instruments. As a result, the fair values presented are estimates derived using present value or other valuation techniques and may not be indicative of the net realizable or liquidation value. In addition, the calculation of estimated fair value is based on market conditions at a specific point in time and may not be reflective of current or future fair values.

Certain financial instruments and all nonfinancial instruments are excluded from the scope of SFAS 107. Accordingly, the fair value disclosures required by SFAS 107 provide only a partial estimate of the fair value of the Corporation; for example, the values associated with the various ongoing businesses which the Corporation operates are excluded. The Corporation has estimated the values related to the long-term relationships with its customers through its deposit base and its credit card accounts, commonly referred to as core deposit intangibles and

December 31, (in billions)	1994 Distributions				1993 Distributions			
	Total Credit Exposure	% of Total	On-Balance Sheet	Off-Balance Sheet	Total Credit Exposure	% of Total	On-Balance Sheet	Off-Balance Sheet
Consumer	$ 52	20%	$ 31	$21	$ 45	18%	$ 26	$ 19
Real Estate	10	4	8	2	12	5	10	2
Financial Institutions	57	21	43	14	61	24	26	35
U.S. Government and Agencies	25	9	25	—	24	9	24	—
Foreign Governments and Official Institutions	15	6	13	2	15	6	13	2
Brokers and Dealers	36	14	13	23	30	12	11	19
All Other	70	26	33	37	67	26	32	35
Total	$265	100%	$166	$99	$254	100%	$142	$112

credit card relationships, respectively, as well as the value of its portfolio of mortgage servicing rights and its owned and leased premises. In the aggregate, these items add significant value to the Corporation but their fair value is not disclosed in this Note.

The following summary presents the methodologies and assumptions used to estimate the fair value of the Corporation's financial instruments required to be valued pursuant to SFAS 107.

Financial assets

Assets for which fair value approximates book value: The fair value of certain financial assets carried at cost, including cash and due from banks, deposits with banks, federal funds sold and securities purchased under resale agreements, due from customers on acceptances, short-term receivables and accrued interest receivable is considered to approximate their respective book values due to their short-term nature and negligible credit losses. In addition, as discussed in Note One, the Corporation valued loans held for accelerated dispositon at fair value less estimated costs to sell.

Trading assets: The Corporation carries trading assets, which includes debt and equity instruments as well as derivative and foreign exchange instruments, at fair value. The fair value of debt and equity instruments is based on current market value. The fair value of trading assets-risk management instruments is based on the net present value of expected cash flows utilizing prevailing market rates. For the fair value of trading assets, see Note Three.

Securities: Securities held-to-maturity are carried at amortized cost. Securities available-for-sale and interest rate contracts used in connection with the available-for-sale portfolio are carried at fair value. The valuation methodologies for securities are discussed in Note Four.

Loans: The fair value of the Corporation's non-LDC commercial loan portfolio was estimated by assessing the two main risk components of the portfolio: credit and interest. The estimated cash flows were adjusted to reflect the inherent credit risk and then discounted, using rates appropriate for each maturity that incorporate the effects of interest rate changes. Generally, emerging-market loans were valued based on secondary market prices.

For consumer installment loans and residential mortgages, for which market rates for comparable loans are readily available, the fair value was estimated by discounting cash flows, adjusted for prepayments. The discount rates used for consumer installment loans were current rates offered by commercial banks and thrifts; for residential mortgages, secondary market yields for comparable mortgage-backed securities, adjusted for risk, were used. The fair value of credit card receivables was estimated by discounting expected net cash flows. The discount rate used incorporated the effects of interest rate changes only, since the estimated cash flows were adjusted for credit risk.

The estimated fair value of net loans decreased form 104% of carrying value at December 31, 1993 to 101% of carrying value at December 31, 1994, primarily due to the rising interest rate environment in 1994 along with a decrease in the market value of Brady Bonds.

Other: In other assets are equity investments, including venture capital investments, and securities acquired as loan satisfactions. The fair value of these investments was determined on an individual basis. The valuation methodologies included market values of publicly traded securities, independent appraisals, and cash flow analyses.

Financial liabilities

Liabilities for which fair value approximates book value: SFAS 107 requires that the fair value disclosed for deposit liabilities with no stated maturity (i.e., demand, savings and certain money market deposits) be equal to the carrying value. SFAS 107 does not allow for the recognition of the inherent funding value of these instruments.

The fair value of foreign deposits, federal funds purchased and securities sold under repurchase agreements, other borrowed funds, acceptances outstanding, short-term payables and accounts payable and accrued liabilities are considered to approximate their respective book values due to their short-term nature.

Trading liabilities-risk management instruments: In accordance with FASI 39, the Corporation records the gross unrealized losses on derivatives and foreign exchange instruments as trading liabilities-risk management instruments which is included in other liabilities. Such instruments are valued at the net present value of expected cash flows based upon prevailing market rates. For the fair value of trading liabilities, see Note Three.

Domestic time deposits: The fair value of time deposits was estimated by discounting cash flows based on contractual maturities at the average interest rates offered by commercial banks and thrifts.

Long-term debt: The valuation of long-term debt takes into account several factors, including current market interest rates and the Corporation's credit rating. Quotes were gathered from various investment banking firms for indicative yields for the Corporation's securities over a range of maturities.

Unused commitments and letters of credit. The Corporation has reviewed the unfunded portion of commitments to extend credit as well as standby and other letters of credit, and has determined that the fair value of such financial instruments is not material.

The following table presents the financial assets and liabilities required to be valued for SFAS 107.

December 31,(in millions)	1994		1993	
	Carrying Value[a]	Estimated Fair Value[a]	Carrying Value	Estimated Fair Value
Financial Assets:				
Assets for Which Fair Value Approximates Book Value	$ 31,883	$ 31,883	$ 32,065	$ 32,065
Trading Assets:				
Debt and Equity Instruments	11,093	11,093[b]	11,679	11,679[b]
Risk-Management Instruments	17,709	17,709[c]	—[c]	—[c]
Securities:				
Held-to-Maturity	8,566	8,106	10,108	10,288
Available-for-Sale	18,431	18,431	15,840	15,840
Loans, Net	76,287	77,169	72,361	74,918
Derivatives in Lieu of Cash-Market Instruments	97	175	—[d]	—[d]
Other Assets[e]	1,971	2,260	1,670	2,171
Total Financial Assets	$166,037	$166,826	$143,723	$146,961
Financial Liabilities:				
Liabilities for Which Fair Value Approximates Book Value	$120,579	$120,579	$113,202	$113,202
Trading Liabilities-Risk Management Instruments	15,979	15,979[c]	—[c]	—[c]

| | 1994 | | 1993 | *(concluded)* |
December 31,(in millions)	Carrying Value[a]	Estimated Fair Value[a]	Carrying Value	Estimated Fair Value
Domestic Time Deposits	15,675	16,369	16,703	17,050
Long-Term Debt	7,991	7,918	8,192	8,489
Total Financial Liabilities	$160,224	$160,845	$138,097	$138,741

(a) The carrying value and estimated fair value for 1994 include the carrying value and fair value of derivatives used for asset/liability management activities. See the following table for the specific assets and liabilities to which the derivatives relate.

(b) The average fair value of debt and equity instruments held for trading purposes was $11,347 million during 1994 and $8,039 million during 1993. For a further breakout of the fair value of Trading Assets-Debt and Equity Instruments, see Note Three.

(c) The average fair value of Trading Assets-Risk Management Instruments and Trading Liabilities-Risk Management Instruments in 1994 was $17,779 million and $16,143 million, respectively. For 1993, the carrying value and the fair value amounts for Trading Assets-Risk Management Instruments and Trading Liabilities-Risk Management Instruments were reported net in Other Assets. For a further breakout of the fair value of Trading Assets and Liabilities-Risk Management Instruments, see Note Three.

(d) In 1993, the carrying value of derivatives used for asset/liability management was included in Other Assets and in Assets and Liabilities for Which Fair Value Approximates Book Value. The estimated fair value for 1993 excluded the estimated fair value of derivatives used for asset/ liability management, except for those derivatives linked to available-for-sale securities, mortgages held for sale and long-term debt. The carrying value and estimated fair value of the derivatives included in Other Assets and in Assets and Liabilities for Which Fair Value Approximates Book Value at December 31, 1993 was $300 million and $725 million, respectively.

(e) The carrying value and estimated fair value of equity-related investments at December 31, 1994 were $1,899 million and $2,172 million, respectively. At December 31, 1993, the carrying value and estimated fair value of equity-related investments were $1,655 million and $2,140 million, respectively.

Derivatives used for asset/liability management.   The following table presents the carrying value and estimated fair values at December 31, 1994, of derivatives contracts (which are primarily interest rate swaps) used for asset/liability management activities that are included in the above table.

December 31, 1994 (in millions)	Carrying Value[a]	Gross Unrecognized Gains	Gross Unrecognized Losses	Estimated Fair Value
Securities—Available-for-Sale	$542	$ —	$ —	$ 542
Loans	123	145	(175)	93
Derivatives in Lieu of Cash Market Instruments	97	194	(116)	175
Liabilities for Which Fair Value Approximates Book Value	4	—	(18)	(14)
Domestic Time Deposits	20	5	(716)	(691)
Long-Term Debt	26	1	(104)	(77)

(a) The carrying value of derivatives used for asset/liability management is recorded as receivables and payables and are primarily included in Other Assets on the balance sheet, except derivatives used in connection with available-for-sale securities which are carried at fair value and are included in Securities: Available-for-Sale on the balance sheet.

Chapter Sixteen

Taxation of Hedging Transactions

Peter J. Connors
Tax Partner
Baker & McKenzie

L. G. "Chip" Harter
Tax Partner
Baker & McKenzie

INTRODUCTION

Even though a transaction designed to hedge economic risks produces satisfactory results from an economic or accounting perspective, the transaction may not produce symmetric or even acceptable results from a tax perspective. This could be the case with respect to a variety of possible tax issues, any of which could prevent a hedge that is effective on a pretax basis from being effective on an after-tax basis. The tax rules applicable to financial products as well as to underlying transactions are extraordinarily complex. In many cases, whipsaws or mismatches are created so as to prevent taxpayers from adopting certain potentially tax-motivated strategies. As will be discussed below, the tax rules in a number of cases permit taxpayers to obtain synthetic-instrument treatment, thereby permitting taxpayers to obtain tax symmetry and to avoid these whipsaws. In most other cases, only a partial fix has been adopted, thereby leaving the unwary open to a variety of traps that can potentially destroy an otherwise effective hedging strategy. This chapter will review the U.S. federal income tax consequences to corporate taxpayers that hedge interest-rate, currency, or commodity-price risk. Special considerations for dealers and other taxpayers, such as mutual funds and insurance companies, are not addressed.

TAX ISSUES

Financial accounting places a significant emphasis on the timing of income or loss recognition and balance-sheet presentation. Tax accounting for hedging transactions must address a variety of additional issues not relevant in financial accounting. The principal issues are the character of income or expense from hedging transactions and the source of hedging transaction income or expense. These issues of timing, character, and source are reviewed below.

Timing

The general federal-income-taxation rule for financial products is that gain and loss are recognized once there is a realization event. As an example, gain on a U.S.-dollar-denominated bond will not be recognized until the bond is disposed of. The same is true of positions in stock. Some positions are taxed differently. These include (1) positions that are subject to mark-to-market treatment, such as Section 1256 contracts; (2) option premiums which may be deferred until there is a realization event and (3) positions that are subject to either the straddle or wash sale rules.

Section 1256 contracts. Section 1256 of the Internal Revenue Code sets forth special rules requiring the recognition of gain or loss for so-called Section 1256 contracts. This is accomplished by requiring each taxpayer to recognize gain or loss as if the Section 1256 contract were sold at the end of the taxable year. Section 1256 contracts include (1) regulated futures contracts, (2) foreign-currency contracts, (3) listed nonequity options, and (4) dealer equity options. Mark-to-market treatment of Section 1256 contracts may be avoided by making a mixed straddle election under Section 1256(d)[1] or by making a hedging election under Section 1256, which is discussed below.

---

[1]A mixed straddle election is an election out of Section 1256. It operates much like the hedging election discussed in this chapter. A mixed straddle is a straddle (1) at least one of the positions of which is a Section 1256 contract, and (2) with respect to which each position forming

A regulated futures contract (RFC) is any contract the amount of which that is required to be deposited and allowed to be withdrawn depends on a system of daily marking-to-market and which is traded on or is subject to the rules of a qualified board or exchange (i.e., a U.S. exchange regulated by the Securities and Exchange Commission, Commodity Futures Contract Trading Commission, or certain foreign exchanges, including the Mercantile Division of the Montreal Exchange).

A foreign-currency contract is a forward contract (1) that requires delivery of, or the settlement of which depends on the value of, a foreign currency that is a currency in which positions are also traded through regulated futures contracts; (2) that is traded in the interbank market; and (3) that is entered into at arm's length at a price determined by reference to a price in the interbank market. These forward contracts *presently* include interbank forward contracts for the delivery of Canadian dollars, British pounds, German deutsche marks, Swiss francs, French francs, Australian dollars, Japanese yen, and the European Currency Unit. Multiple-payment foreign-currency swaps entered into in the interbank market are not Section 1256 contracts regardless of the currency in which they are denominated.

A nonequity option is any option that is traded on (or subject to the rules of) a qualified board or exchange (i.e., a listed option) and is not an equity option.

An equity option is an option to buy or sell stock or the value of which is determined by reference to any stock (or group of stocks) or stock index (other than an option with respect to any group of stocks or stock index if there is in effect a designation by the Commodities Futures Trading Commission of a contract market for a contract based on such group of stocks or index). A dealer equity option is an option purchased or granted by an options dealer in the normal course of his or her activity of dealing in options.

Options.   Options, such as over-the-counter options, that are not subject to Section 1256 are subject to special rules. Purchasers of options recognize a loss on the lapse of an option. The exercise of a call option has no immediate tax consequences (instead, the holder must adjust its basis). The exercise of a put option results in a taxable sale or exchange for the holder. On the other hand, if the holder sells the option, the taxpayer's gain

part of such straddle is clearly identified before the close of the day on which the first Section 1256 contract is acquired.

or loss is recognized (determined as if it were from the sale of property that has the same character as the property to which the option relates).

By contrast, the writer of an option will recognize gain on the lapse of the option. Similarly, the exercise of a call will result in the disposition of an asset. Gain or loss is recognized. By contrast, the grantor of a put option has no gain or loss on the exercise of the put option (instead the grantor's adjusted basis in the property acquired is reduced by the premium, and gain or loss is recognized on disposition of the acquired property).

The loss-disallowance rules.   Two sets of rules may result in the deferral of losses. The first is the wash-sale rule, under which a loss will be deferred if substantially identical stock or securities are acquired during a period beginning 30 days before or after the position is sold or disposed of.

Second, under Section 1092, in the event the taxpayer has two or more positions in a straddle, losses may be deferred to the extent of offsetting gains in other positions. A straddle is broadly defined as offsetting positions with respect to personal property, even if the personal property is not of the same kind. Personal property is defined as any personal property of a type that is actively traded. A position in turn means an interest (including a futures contract, forward contract, or option) in personal property. The straddle rules also apply to successor positions. A successor position is generally defined as a position entered into within a period beginning 30 days after disposition of the loss position and that offsets a second position that was offsetting with respect to the disposed loss position. The straddle rules take precedence over the wash-sale rules where both rules might otherwise apply.

Income earned by certain foreign corporations.   While normally income earned in a foreign corporation is not subjected to current U.S. taxation, certain types of income will be taxed when requisite levels of ownership are reached. As an example, under the provisions of Subpart F, when more than 50 percent of the vote or value of a corporation is owned by five or fewer U.S. shareholders (that is, a shareholder owning 10 percent of the corporation's voting power), then the corporation's foreign-personal-holding-company income is subject to immediate U.S. taxation. Foreign-personal-holding-company income includes the excess of any gains over losses from Section 988 transactions. If a controlled foreign corporation has net foreign-currency losses for the year, however, such losses do not offset other foreign-personal-holding-company income. Shareholders of controlled foreign corporations may avoid immediate taxation of potential foreign-personal-holding-company income through the use of the hedging elections.

Character

For the corporate taxpayer, the character of hedging gains and losses may well be the most important issue. The character issue is by and large the question of whether income or expense, as well as gain or loss, is recognized as ordinary or capital items. The significance of the distinction is that capital items are treated separately for tax purposes. That is, capital gains and losses are netted, and net capital gains and losses are treated separately. Net capital gains of a taxpayer who is an individual are taxed at a lower rate than ordinary income, but net capital gains of a corporation are taxed at the same rate as ordinary income. Net capital losses of an individual are deductible against ordinary income only to the extent of $3,000 per year. Net capital losses of corporations are not deductible and can only be carried back three years and forward five years to be deducted against net capital gains in such years. In prior years, having a net long-term capital gain entitled a corporation to a favorable rate differential. Since the Tax Reform Act of 1986 eliminated the favorable treatment of capital gains for corporations, all that is left is that corporations are restricted in reducing regular ordinary income with capital losses. In many cases, in many industries—banking, for example—this makes capital losses virtually nondeductible. In others, like insurance, because of the presence of investment assets, this is less of a problem.

General rule with respect to financial products. As a general matter the character of gain or loss with respect to financial products is capital to a taxpayer other than a dealer, unless they are part of a qualified hedging transaction or are foreign-currency transactions governed by Section 988 (this section will be addressed in more detail later on in the discussion). It should also be noted that gain or loss on a Section 1256 contract that is a capital asset in the hands of the taxpayer is treated as 60-percent long-term capital gain or loss and 40-percent short-term capital gain or loss, although the distinction between long-term and short-term capital gains is not significant for the corporate taxpayer.

Treatment of foreign-currency positions. Under Section 988, gains and losses from foreign-currency transactions are ordinary. There are two principal exceptions:

1. *Nonequity Options and Regulated Futures Contracts:* Nonequity
   options and regulated futures contracts subject to Section 1256
   are generally capital. However, a taxpayer may elect to treat such
   gains and losses as Section 988 transactions;[2] and

2. *Capital Gain or Loss Election:* A taxpayer may elect to treat
   gain or loss recognized on a forward contract, futures contract, or
   option contract as capital, provided the asset is a capital asset,
   and neither part of a straddle nor an RFC or nonequity option
   with respect to which an election to treat such contract or option
   as a Section 988 transaction (discussed immediately above) is in
   effect.

Source Issues

General rules.   Source is important for principally two reasons.
First, if payments of U.S. source "fixed or determinable, annual or
periodical gains, profits or income" (FDAP) are made to foreign persons,
they may be subject to withholding tax. Second, U.S. taxpayers whose
foreign source income has been subjected to foreign tax may receive a
credit for foreign taxes paid. The credit is largely a function of the amount
of U.S. tax that would be imposed on that income. To determine the
amount of the credit, it is necessary to identify and categorize items of
income as either foreign or domestic and to allocate or apportion deduc-
tions against such income. The more foreign-source income, in general,
the greater the foreign-tax credit allowed and therefore the greater the
amount of credits that can be used.

Interest expense.   In calculating the foreign-tax credit, interest
expense is allocated among all the taxpayer's assets, under the notion that
interest expense is fungible. As a result, with some exceptions for certain
integrated transactions and nonrecourse debt, interest expense adversely
impacts the foreign-tax credit limitation, regardless of how the proceeds of
the borrowing are actually used so long as the taxpayer has foreign-source
assets. Interest expense is also important for foreign taxpayers that conduct
business in the United States. This is because interest that is paid to related
parties is subject to an earnings stripping limitation under Section 163(j).

---

[2]Treas. Reg. §1.988–1(a)(7).

TAXATION OF HEDGING TRANSACTIONS THAT DO NOT QUALIFY FOR INTEGRATED TREATMENT

The regimes extending integrated tax treatment to hedging transactions are extremely narrow. Current Treasury regulations extend such treatment only to perfectly symmetrical hedges of foreign-currency-denominated debt instruments and certain foreign-currency-denominated executory contracts. Proposed regulations would extend integrated treatment to perfectly symmetrical hedges of dollar-denominated debt instruments. The vast majority of hedging transactions do not fall within these narrow regimes. Hedges of commodity price exposures or equity positions, for example, would not qualify. Hedges that do not perfectly match the cash flows of the position being hedged similarly do not qualify, such as hedges of net foreign-currency positions or hedges of anticipated positions.

The vast majority of hedging transactions are therefore taxed as separate, stand-alone transactions, rather than as direct adjustments to the gain or loss on the transaction being hedged. Thus, the amount, timing, character, and source of the gain or loss on the hedging transaction must be determined and reported on a separate transaction basis.

Given that the entire point of a hedging transaction is to have the gain or loss on the hedge offset the loss or gain on the transaction being hedged, the aim of the applicable tax rules is to allow taxpayers to achieve a character, timing, and source treatment of their hedging transactions that is symmetric with the character, timing, and source treatment of the transaction being hedged. The gains or losses on the hedge can thus be reported on the taxpayer's tax return in a manner that nets out against the losses or gain of the transaction being hedged, achieving a result similar to integrated treatment.

The Need for Taxpayer Identification of Hedging Transactions

A tax regime that provides a different treatment of gains or losses on a transaction, depending on whether the transaction was entered into as a hedge, runs the risk that taxpayers will use hindsight in determining whether to report the transaction as a hedge. Under the case law that preceded the present regulatory regime, for example, a futures transaction entered into with a speculative purpose produced capital gains or losses, whereas a futures transaction entered into in order to hedge ordinary business risks produced ordinary gain or loss. During a period when capital gains were taxed at lower rates than ordinary income, taxpayers were tempted to use the benefit of hindsight in concluding that transactions that had resulted in gains were speculative transactions, producing capital gains, whereas transactions that had resulted in losses were business hedges, producing ordinary losses. In drafting the present regulatory regime, the Treasury Department was careful to limit the ability of taxpayers to whipsaw the system using hindsight. The regulations achieve this end by requiring taxpayers to designate transactions as hedges on the same day the hedges are entered into to receive the benefits of symmetrical tax treatment with the underlying transaction.

In cases where a taxpayer fails to make a timely hedging designation, the resulting asymmetry between the hedge and the underlying transaction generally works against the taxpayer. The regulations further give the IRS the ability to treat a transaction as a hedge even if the taxpayer failed to make a hedging identification, and the regulations provide rules that effectively penalize the identification as hedges of transactions that do not in fact qualify as hedges under the regulations.

The most important element in tax planning for hedging transactions is therefore the compliance with these same-day hedge identification requirements. Taxpayers must be aware of what the relevant hedge identification requirements are, and taxpayers must have procedures in place to ensure that the necessary identifications are made on a same-day basis. The specific identification requirements will be discussed below in the context of the relevant regulations.

Character Rules for Nonintegrated Hedges

As discussed above, the general rule is that gains and losses with respect to financial products (other than foreign-currency transactions subject to Section 988) are capital in character, and capital losses are deductible only against capital gains. Treasury regulations issued under §1.1221-2 provide an exception to this general rule, however, by affording ordinary treatment to gains and losses from a defined universe of hedging transactions ("§1.1221-2 Hedges"). A §1.1221-2 Hedge is defined as a transaction that a taxpayer enters into in the normal course of the taxpayer's trade or business (1) to reduce the risk of price changes or currency fluctuations with respect to ordinary property that is held or to be held by the taxpayer, or (2) to reduce risk of interest-rate or price changes or currency fluctuations with respect to borrowings made or to be made or ordinary obligations incurred or to be incurred by the taxpayer.

To receive ordinary treatment for gains or losses resulting from a §1.1221-2 Hedge, a taxpayer must identify the hedge as a §1.1221-2 Hedge before the close of the day on which the hedge is entered into and must identify the item being hedged on a substantially contemporaneous basis. The regulations provide that in all events the identification of the transaction being hedged must be made on the taxpayer's books and records within 35 days after the date the hedge is established. Both the heding transaction and the transaction being hedged must be identified in every hedging transaction.

Risk-reduction transaction. It is important to note that the regulations require a taxpayer to establish that a transaction was entered into to *reduce* the risks of the taxpayer's business rather than to simply manage those risks. The regulations clearly contemplate that a taxpayer can qualify transactions in which it uses forward contracts, swaps, or other derivatives to lock in fixed future delivery prices of commodities or foreign currency or to lock in a fixed interest rate. What is much less clear is the extent to which a taxpayer can qualify a transaction that substitutes one type of risk for another. It is not clear, for example, whether a taxpayer with long-term fixed-rate borrowings may treat a fixed- to floating-rate interest-rate swap as a hedging transaction because it is not clear that the regulations would treat such a transaction as a risk-reduction transaction.

Although a taxpayer can certainly argue that long-term fixed-rate financing involves a risk that interest rates will fall during the term of the financing, locking the taxpayer into above-market financing, it is not clear that the regulations consider the possibility of such a future opportunity cost a hedgeable risk. The examples in the regulations of fixed-to-floating swaps are all predicated on the assumption that the taxpayer has a floating-rate ordinary asset and that the swap is a risk-reduction transaction because it matches the floating-rate income stream on such asset with a synthetic floating-rate interest liability. One of the key areas of uncertainty as to how these hedging regulations will be administered is the degree to which revenue agents conducting audits will use them in attempts to disqualify fixed-to-floating swaps as hedging transactions.

A second aspect of the requirement that a transaction reduce the risk of a taxpayer's business is that this risk reduction must be measured in light of the facts and circumstances of the taxpayer's entire business. It is not sufficient that a hedge offset and reduce the risks of a particular transaction. Under the requirement that a hedge qualify as a "macro" hedge rather than just as a "micro" hedge, a taxpayer presumably would not, for example, be able to qualify a floating-to-fixed interest-rate swap as a hedge of a floating-rate liability if the exposure with respect to the floating rate interest expense was already offset by a floating-rate income stream.

> *Example:* USCO's debt liabilities consist entirely of fixed-rate long-term borrowings. USCO is concerned that, in the event of a general decrease in market interest rates, it will be locked into above-market financing. It decides to mitigate this risk by entering into an interest-rate swap, under which it pays a floating rate and receives a fixed rate, to effectively convert one-half of its debt to floating-rate debt. USCO concludes that this mixture of fixed- and floating-rate debt provides the best balance of exposure to interest-rate increases inherent in floating-rate debt and exposure to interest-rate decreases inherent in fixed-rate debt. To demonstrate that USCO has a valid hedging strategy, USCO must be able to prove that the swap is "reasonably expected to reduce the overall risk of [USCO's] operations."[3] No such test would have to be satisfied if USCO merely issued floating-rate liabilities in the first place.

Under present Treasury regulations, risk reduction is measured on a corporation-by-corporation basis. A corporation can qualify a hedge as a §1.1221-2 Hedge only if it is a hedge of its own economic exposure; it cannot qualify a hedge of the exposure of a related corporation, even if it files a consolidated tax return with that corporation. If currently proposed regulations are adopted in their present form, this risk-reduction standard will instead be tested on a consolidated group basis, allowing corporations that together file a consolidated federal income tax return to enter into hedges of each other's exposures and qualify those hedges as §1.1221-2 Hedges. The proposed regulations would, however, allow corporations to elect instead to test the risk reduction on a separate corporation basis.

Ordinary property or ordinary obligation. Only hedges of borrowings, ordinary property, and ordinary obligations can qualify as §1.1221-2 Hedges. Ordinary property is generally defined as property that would always give rise to an ordinary gain or loss if sold. Therefore inventory property and receivables from the sale of inventory or the

---

[3]Treas. Reg. §1.1221-1(c)(1)(A)(ii).

provision of services will constitute ordinary property. Supplies that are consumed in a business but that are not inventory, such as aviation fuel used by an airline, are treated as ordinary property for purposes of the hedging regulations if the taxpayer in practice does not resell more than a negligible portion of its supply. Capital assets do not constitute ordinary property. Equity positions, therefore, cannot be hedged, except by dealers for whom the equity positions constitute inventory. Importantly, hedges of foreign subsidiaries (sometimes known in tax folklore as "Hoover Hedges," for the famous case), will not qualify as ordinary assets. The foreign currency gains and losses on such hedges will nevertheless be ordinary in character under the regime for foreign currency instruments discussed below.

An obligation of a taxpayer is treated as an ordinary obligation for purposes of the hedging regulations if the performance or termination of the obligation could never produce a capital gain or loss. An obligation to pay money under a debt instrument will therefore constitute an ordinary obligation of the obligor.

Identification requirements. As discussed above, the hedging regulations have very specific requirements as to identification and record-keeping procedures. To qualify as a §1.1221-2 Hedge, a hedge must be identified by the taxpayer on its books and records as a hedging transaction for tax purposes before the close of the day the transaction is entered into. The taxpayer must also make a "substantially contemporaneous" identification of the exposure being hedged. This identification of the exposure being hedged does not need to be made on the same day that the hedge is entered into, but must in all events be made no more than 35 days after entering into the hedging transaction.

The hedging regulations provide specific requirements for the identification of certain types of hedging transactions. In the case of hedges relating to the anticipated acquisition of an asset, a taxpayer must include in the identification the expected date or dates when it anticipates that the assets will be acquired and the quantity of assets that it expects to acquire on those dates. With respect to hedges of inventory, a taxpayer must specify the type or class of inventory to which the hedge relates. If the hedge relates to specific purchases or sales, the identification must include the expected dates and quantities of the amounts to be purchased or sold.

With respect to hedges of debt obligations issued by a taxpayer, the taxpayer must identify the specific debt issue that is being hedged and the portion of the issue price and the portion of the term of the debt to which the hedge relates. If the hedge relates to debt that the taxpayer anticipates it will issue in the future, the identification must specify the expected issuance date, the expected maturity date, the total expected issue price, and the expected interest provisions. Where a taxpayer is hedging an aggregate position, rather than individual transactions, the hedging designation must include a description of the nature of aggregate risk being hedged and of the overall hedging program under which the hedging transaction is being entered.

In all cases, a hedging designation must be unambiguous and must specifically recite that it is being made for tax purposes. A hedging designation made for financial accounting or regulatory purposes does *not* satisfy the tax regulations unless the taxpayer's books and records specifically state that such identifications are also being made for tax purposes.

Designations by the IRS—Whipsaw Rules. A taxpayer is generally bound by its hedging designation unless it can show that the designation was made as a result of an inadvertent error and the taxpayer consistently corrects the erroneous hedging designations for all open taxable years. If the taxpayer fails to identify a transaction that would otherwise qualify as a hedging transaction, the taxpayer is generally bound to treat the hedging transaction as a capital transaction. If, however, the taxpayer can show that the failure to make the identification was due to an inadvertent error and corrects such errors on a consistent basis for all open years, the taxpayer may treat the transaction as a §1.1221-2 Hedge.

If a taxpayer improperly identifies a transaction that does not qualify as a hedging transaction and cannot demonstrate that such designation was an inadvertent error, a draconian whipsaw regime applies. If a transaction improperly designated as a hedge produces a gain, that gain will be treated as ordinary income. If, however, the transaction produces a loss, that loss will be treated as a capital loss. This rule is applied on a transaction-by-transaction basis and can therefore produce extremely harsh results. If an IRS agent on audit demonstrates that a series of transactions designated as hedges did not in fact qualify under the regulations, he or she can assert a tax adjustment far in excess of the economic gain or loss with respect to the transactions. The gross amounts of gains on individual gain trades is left as ordinary income, whereas the gross amount of losses on individual loss trades is treated as capital loss. The entire gross amount of ordinary income is subject to tax and cannot be reduced by the capital losses from the losing trades. Even if the net gain or loss on the overall hedging account is zero, the inability to deduct the losses on the loss trades against the gains on the gains trades can result in a staggering tax adjustment. This whipsaw rule is designed to provide a powerful deterrent against taxpayers being overly aggressive in their designation of transactions as hedging transactions.

The IRS can apply a similar whipsaw regime where a taxpayer fails to identify transactions that clearly qualify as hedges under the regulations as §1.1221-2 Hedges. If the taxpayer can show no reasonable basis for its failure to identify the hedges, the IRS can treat any gains on the transactions as ordinary while leaving the losses as capital on a transaction-by-transaction basis. This regime for failures to identify qualified hedging transactions is somewhat less draconian than the regime for improper hedge identifications in that it can be invoked by the IRS only in cases where the taxpayer had no reasonable basis for failing to make the hedge identifications. The whipsaw regime for improper identifications of hedging transactions that do not qualify under the regulations, by contrast, applies regardless of whether the taxpayer had a reasonable basis for its erroneous identification.

Related-party hedging issues. As discussed above, the present hedging regulations apply on a corporation-by-corporation basis. For a hedge to qualify under the regulations, the hedging transaction must be entered into by the same corporation that has the exposure being hedged, and the risk-reduction nature of the hedging transaction is tested based on the overall risk profile of that single corporation. Proposed regulations, if adopted in present form, would have the hedging regulations operate on a consolidated group basis. Any member of a group of corporations filing a consolidated federal income tax return could treat a hedging transaction as a §1.1221-2 Hedge if the transaction reduced the overall risk of the consolidated group with respect to borrowings, ordinary property, and ordinary obligations. Groups would be permitted, however, to elect to apply the hedging regulations on a separate corporation basis in the manner they apply under the present regulations.

Character Rules for Foreign-Currency Hedges

A separate statutory regime applies to determine the character of gains and losses from most foreign-currency hedging transactions. In 1986, Congress amended the Internal Revenue Code to provide that foreign-currency gains and losses on Section 988 transactions are ordinary in character. Section 988 transactions include foreign-currency-denominated debt instruments, foreign-currency swaps and options contracts, forward contracts, and futures contracts with respect to foreign currency. Also included are interest-rate swaps in a single foreign currency, such as a swap under which one counterparty pays a fixed-rate yen payment stream in exchange for a floating-rate yen payment stream on the same yen notional principal amount. Section 988 transactions do not include equity positions, even if denominated in foreign currency, or foreign-currency-denominated contracts for delivery of other property, such as a gold forward contract denominated in DM.

Given that most foreign-currency-related derivative transactions—including foreign-currency futures, forwards, options, and swaps—are Section 988 transactions, the gains and losses on such transactions are ordinary in character without regard to whether a hedging designation is made under hedging regulations. As discussed more fully below, however, a different set of hedging designation is often desirable with respect to foreign-currency-denominated derivatives in order to avoid the application of the straddle provisions of the Code.

Time of Recognition of Nonintegrated Hedge Gains and Losses

Recent Treasury regulations issued under Section 446 provide detailed rules as to the time of recognition of gains and losses on nonintegrated hedge transactions. These regulations generally apply to both hedging transactions where character is determined under the hedging regulations and to foreign-currency hedging transactions where character is determined under Section 988.

The matching principle. The general rule of these timing regulations is that a taxpayer must use a method of accounting for hedging transactions that clearly reflects income. The method must reasonably match the timing of gains or losses from hedging transactions with the timing of gains or losses from the item or items being hedged. This general rule overrides the normal, realization-based recognition rules that would otherwise apply to a hedging transaction. This matching principle is relatively easy to apply in cases of separate hedges of individual items of exposure, such as a forward sale of a specific quantity of foreign currency expected to be received on a date in the future.

The application of this matching principle becomes less clear, however, in more complicated hedging scenarios, such as a hedge of an aggregate position. The regulations suggest that one possible method of accounting for aggregate hedges is to mark the position to market at least quarterly and then take the resulting gains or losses into income rateably over the period for which the hedging transaction is expected to reduce risk. Taxpayers must record in their records a description of the accounting method used to report the gains and losses of their hedging transactions. The description of the method used must be sufficiently detailed to show that the clear reflection of income standard is reasonably satisfied.

Hedges of Debt Instruments

The regulations provide that gains or losses from the hedge of a debt instrument must be accounted for by reference to the terms of the debt instrument and the period or periods to which the hedge relates. The gain or loss on a hedge of a debt instrument must be taken into account on a yield-to-maturity basis, with the taxpayer accruing the realized gain or loss in the same periods in which it would be taken into account if the gain or loss adjusted the yield of the instrument over the term to which the hedge relates.

Determining the period to which the hedge relates then is most important. Difficult issues arise when the hedge is for a period longer than that of the instrument being hedged. If the hedge is for a shorter period, the relevant period, after termination of the hedge, is the period to which the hedge would have applied had it not been terminated prior to maturity. The issue is somewhat more murky if one hedges say a 5-year instrument with a 10-year swap.

In the case of a hedge of the interest expense with respect to a debt instrument to be issued in the future, for example, the gain or loss on the hedge is treated solely for timing purposes as if it were an adjustment to the issue price of the debt instrument and accrued over the life of the debt instrument.

Hedges of inventory. The regulations also provide specific guidance on accounting for gains and losses on hedges of inventory. The gain or loss on the hedge of the purchase price of inventory must be taken into account in the same period that it would be taken into account if the gain or loss were treated as an element of the cost of inventory. Thus, a taxpayer hedging a purchase of inventory would recognize the gain or loss on the hedge in the same period that the relevant layer of inventory is deemed sold under the taxpayer's inventory accounting method. If a taxpayer enters into a hedge of the sale of inventory, gain or loss on the hedge is taken into account in the same period that it would be taken into account if the gain or loss were treated as an element of the sales proceeds. The regulations also permit taxpayers to account for inventory hedges on an as-realized basis or a mark-to-market basis, in cases where such accounting methods clearly reflect income.

Application of Straddle Rules to Hedging Transactions

Another statutory regime potentially applicable to hedging transactions consists of the mark-to-market and straddle provisions of Sections 1256, 1092, and 263(g). Taxpayers are able to avoid the imposition of these provisions on transactions that qualify as hedging transactions under Treasury Regulation §1.1221-2 or Section 988. As discussed below, a same-day hedging designation is required under Section 1256(e) to avoid the imposition of these provisions.

Section 1256. Section 1256 of the Code requires taxpayers, including taxpayers who are not dealers, to recognize their gains or losses on Section 1256 contracts on an annual, mark-to-market basis. The taxpayer is treated as if it had sold the contract at the close of its taxable year, realizing gain or loss, and making an appropriate adjustment to its basis in the contract. Section 1256 contracts include all futures contracts traded on domestic regulated futures exchanges, all nonequity options traded on such exchanges, and foreign-currency forward contracts traded in the interbank market for delivery of currencies that are traded on domestic futures exchanges.

In the case of a Section 1256 contract used in a hedging transaction subject to the timing rules of Treasury Regulation §1.446-4 (discussed above), those timing regulations generally override the mark-to-market rules of Section 1256 by instead providing that the recognition of the gains or losses on the hedging transaction will be matched in the same taxable years with the gains and losses on the transaction being hedged. A hedging designation under Treasury Regulation §1.1221-2 will also constitute a hedging designation for purposes of Section 1256(e), which directly overrides the operation of the mark-to-market provisions of Section 1256(a).

Section 1092. The straddle rules of Section 1092 generally provide that where a taxpayer enters into offsetting positions in publicly traded property, the taxpayer may not recognize the loss with respect to one of the positions except to the extent that it exceeds the unrealized gains in other offsetting positions making up the straddle. Because hedging transactions are by definition offsetting positions in property, the straddle provisions of Section 1092 would generally apply by their terms. Sections 1092(e) and 1256(e) provide that this straddle rule does not apply to hedging transactions properly identified as such by a taxpayer on the same day the transaction is entered into. Thus a properly identified hedging transaction is not technically subject to the straddle rules of Section 1092, but the effect of the regulations under Treasury Regulation §1.446-4, which will apply, can result in a similar matching of losses with gains on offsetting positions.

Section 263(g) interest-capitalization rules. The final piece of the straddle regime is Section 263(g). This provision requires a taxpayer that incurs interest expense to acquire or carry personal property that constitutes a position in a straddle to capitalize such interest expense, adding it to the basis of such property. If, for example, a taxpayer borrows money to finance the purchase of gold bullion and then hedges that gold bullion by entering into a 1-year forward contract for the sale of bullion, any interest expense on the borrowing is not currently deductible and must instead be added to the basis of the gold bullion for purposes of calculating the gain or loss on the forward sale. Section 263(g) does not apply to a hedging transaction that has been properly identified as such by the taxpayer. Avoiding the application of this potentially onerous provision is one of the significant benefits of making a hedging designation under either Treasury Regulation §1.1221-2 or Section 1256(e).

Income Earned by Certain Foreign Corporations

We mentioned earlier that income earned by certain foreign corporations may be taxable currently, if the income is foreign-personal-holding-company income. Foreign personal holding company income includes, *inter alia,* interest, dividends, and the excess of foreign currency gains over foreign currency losses for the year for foreign subsidiaries entering into qualified hedging transactions using Section 1256 contracts to identify such hedges under Section 1256(e). For this reason, it is typically advantageous to make an election under Section 1256(e) to avoid mark-to-market treatment. Furthermore, other elections may be helpful in avoiding foreign-holding-company-income treatment of currency gains.

The qualified hedging exception. An additional election is available for foreign currency transactions entered into by controlled foreign corporations for qualified hedging transactions. Qualified hedging transactions include bona fide hedging transactions that are

- Reasonably necessary to the conduct of regular business operations;
- Entered into primarily to reduce the risk of currency fluctuation with respect to property or services sold or to be sold or expenses necessary to be incurred;
- Transactions with respect to "qualified business transactions" (these are transactions that while generating foreign-currency gain, are so related to the taxpayer's business that they are exempt from foreign-personal-holding-company income status);
- Identified within five business days; and
- Transactions for which the amount of currency gain or loss attributable to the hedging transaction is clearly identifiable in the records of the CFC or its controlling shareholder.

The Section 1256 hedging elections. We noted in the preceding pages that an election under Section 1256(e) overrides the operation of both the mark-to-market rules of Section 1256 and the straddle rules of Section 1092. A proper election under Section 1256(e) or Treasury Regulation §1.1221-2 will be operative in the context of a controlled foreign corporation.

Foreign-Tax-Credit-Limitation Effects of Hedging Transactions

The foreign-tax-credit-limitation effect of hedging transactions is yet another area where Treasury regulations prevent taxpayers from exploiting asymmetries between the taxation of a hedging transaction and the transaction being hedged. Because the amount of foreign-tax credits a

U.S. multinational corporation can credit against its federal income tax liability is a function of the amount of its net foreign-source income, such taxpayers generally will seek to maximize their foreign-source income and minimize the amount of expenses allocated against such income.

The general rules for sourcing gains and allocating losses from hedges of debt instruments are not symmetrical with the rules for sourcing interest income and allocating interest expense. The IRS therefore issued regulations that prevent taxpayers from benefiting from the asymmetry between these sets of rules, but generally allow these asymmetries to operate when they are detrimental to taxpayers.

The interest expense of a U.S. corporation must be allocated against both its domestic- and foreign-source income in proportion to the value of assets producing each type of income. Gains on a hedge of interest expense entered into by a U.S. corporation, however, will generally be treated as U.S.-source income, while losses would generally be allocated entirely against U.S.-source income. As a result of the asymmetry between these rules, a taxpayer that hedges its interest expense and incurs a loss on its hedge offset by a decrease in the amount of its interest expense is in a more favorable foreign-tax-credit-limitation position than if it had simply had interest expense equal to the net of its actual interest expense against its hedging loss. The entire amount of the hedging loss is allocated against U.S.-source income, while the offsetting reduction of interest expense reduces the amount of expense allocable against foreign-source income. The taxpayer thus has more net foreign-source income and less U.S.-source income, and therefore has a greater foreign-tax-credit limitation.

Conversely, if the taxpayer has a gain on its interest-rate hedge that offsets an increase in its interest expense, the taxpayer is worse off, because the combination of hedge gain and increased interest expense produces more U.S.-source income and less foreign-source income than would an allocation of a net interest amount equal to the net of the actual interest expense and hedging gain.

To prevent taxpayers from exploiting this asymmetry, Treasury Regulation §1.861-9T(b)(6) provides that *losses* from hedges of interest expense are to be allocated between U.S.- and foreign-source income in the same manner as interest expense. The regulation further provides that if the taxpayer makes a same-day identification of the hedge as a hedge of interest expense, any gain from the hedge will be treated as a direct reduction of interest expense for purposes of the foreign-tax-credit limitation. If a taxpayer makes this hedging identification, the allocation rules function in a symmetrical manner. Both hedging gains and hedging losses are treated as if they were direct adjustments to interest expense for foreign-tax-credit-limitation purposes. If a taxpayer fails to make such a hedging designation, however, it has the worst of both worlds. If the interest-rate hedge produces a gain, the asymmetry inherent in the general allocation and sourcing rules is allowed to work against the taxpayer. If the interest-rate hedge produces a loss, the regulations prevent the asymmetries from working in favor of the taxpayer.

Similar asymmetries are addressed in regulations dealing with foreign-currency hedges. Foreign-currency gains and losses, like gains and losses on interest-rate hedges, are generally U.S.-source gains and losses. If a taxpayer borrows in a strong currency, at an interest rate less than the interest rate prevailing on similar dollar-denominated debt obligations, it will generally anticipate having a foreign-currency loss on repayment of the principal. Under the application of the general sourcing and allocation rules, the taxpayer would be in a better position than if it had borrowed in U.S. dollars at the same financial cost. The reduction in interest expense achieved by borrowing in the strong currency reduces the amount of interest expense allocated against foreign-source income, while the offsetting foreign-currency loss would be allocated entirely against U.S.-source income and not against foreign-source income.

Temporary Treasury Regulation §1.861-9T(b)(2) prevents taxpayers from taking advantage of this asymmetry when a taxpayer borrows in a strong foreign currency, then hedges out all or part of its foreign-currency exposure under the borrowing. This regulation provides that if a taxpayer borrows in a foreign currency at a market rate that is less than comparable U.S.-dollar rates and then enters into a hedge of its foreign-currency exposure with respect to the borrowing, its net foreign-currency loss on the borrowing and the hedge will be allocated for foreign-tax-credit-limitation purposes as if the loss were additional interest expense.

INTEGRATION TREATMENT

There are two types of hedging models. Under the one model, discussed above, the timing and character of the item being hedged is matched with the hedging transaction. Under a second model, the hedge is fully integrated into the transaction being hedged. The separate identity of the underlying transaction is largely lost. Given the goal of hedging, it is no surprise that integrated hedges produce more favorable results.

Integrated treatment is strictly limited. There are two types of transactions that qualify for integrated treatment and they presently are limited to foreign-currency transactions. Proposed regulations would expand the types of transactions eligible for hedge treatment.

Hedges of Nonfunctional Currency Debt

Under limited circumstances, a taxpayer is allowed under Treasury Regulation §1.988-5 to integrate a foreign-currency debt obligation (either an asset or a liability) with a hedge to create a synthetic debt obligation (for example, a U.S.-dollar loan). By integrating the debt obligation and the hedge, the taxpayer is able to avoid (1) the application of the straddle rules and Section 1256 mark-to-market rules, and (2) the rules that treat certain currency and hedge losses as expenses equivalent to interest.

Hedges of Executory Contracts Denominated in Foreign Currency

Treasury Regulation §1.988-5 also allows a taxpayer to integrate an executory contract with a hedge of the executory contract, provided the hedge was entered into after the contract was entered into and before the accrual date of the payable or receivable arising from the contract. An executory contract is generally defined as a contract, denominated in a foreign currency, entered into by the taxpayer to buy or sell goods or services in the ordinary course of the taxpayer's trade or business. If integration applies, amounts paid or received under the hedge by the taxpayer are treated as paid or received under the executory contract, and the taxpayer recognizes no exchange gain or loss on the hedge. In addition, the straddle and mark-to-market rules do not apply.

Example: USCO enters into an agreement with Japan Co., an electronics manufacturer, that requires USCO to purchase depreciable computer equipment for delivery on the first day of each month of 1996. Under the terms of the contract, USCO will pay Japan Co. 150,000 yen for the computer by the end of the month of delivery. USCO is concerned that the yen will appreciate in value and hedges its purchase agreement by entering into a series of forward contracts to purchase yen. If the purchase contract and the yen contract qualify as a hedged executory contract, the forward contract would be integrated with the purchase agreement, thereby determining the basis of the asset purchased. If the yen did appreciate, absent the election, USCO would have a higher cost basis, which it could recover over the life of the equipment, but would also immediately recognize foreign-currency gain on the forward.

Hedges of Declared Dividends, Rent, and Royalty

Proposed Treasury regulations have been issued that would expand the scope of the foreign-currency regime. Proposed Treasury Regulation §1.988-5(d) allows integrated treatment for hedges of qualified payments that are denominated in or determined with reference to a nonfunctional currency. Under the proposed regulations, the hedge and the qualified payment are integrated, so amounts paid or received pursuant to the hedge are treated as paid or received pursuant to the qualified payment. Qualified payments include declared but unpaid dividends and fixed but unaccrued rent and royalty payments. The proposed rules allow a qualified payment to be hedged by means of a deposit of a nonfunctional currency in a hedging account, or by means of a forward contract, futures contract, option (if the option expires by the accrual date and the option is exercised on or before such date), warrant, or similar financial instrument that is denominated or determined by reference to the value of one or more nonfunctional currencies.

Integrated Hedging of Certain Debt Obligations

The IRS has issued proposed regulations that provide for so-called integration treatment in certain situations where a taxpayer hedges a debt instrument that does not result in a currency change with respect to the debt instrument (unlike the Section 988(d) integrated transaction, which must result in a change in the denomination of the instrument). The proposed regulations would apply to hedges of debt instruments that are either assets or liabilities of a taxpayer and are slated to be effective 60 days after they are issued as final regulations.

Hedges of Foreign-Currency Debt Instruments

We now turn to the specifics of integrated tax treatment for hedges of foreign-currency debt instruments.

Integrated economic transaction. In order to constitute a qualifying hedging transaction under Section 988, a number of requirements must be satisfied:

a. All payments to be made or received under the qualifying debt instrument (or amounts determined by reference to a nonfunctional currency) are fully hedged on the date the taxpayer identified the transaction as a qualified hedging transaction such that a yield to maturity in the currency in which the synthetic debt instrument is denominated can be calculated. Any contingent-payment features of the qualifying debt instrument must be fully offset such that the synthetic debt-instrument is not classified as a contingent payment instrument.

b. The hedge is properly identified on or before the date that the acquisition of the financial instrument constituting the hedge is settled or closed.

c. None of the parties to the hedge are related.

d. In the case of a qualified business unit with a residence outside the United States, both the qualifying debt instrument and the hedge are properly reflected on the books of such qualifying business unit through the term of the qualified hedging transaction.

e. Both the qualifying debt instrument and the hedge are entered into by the same individual, partnership, trust, estate, or corporation. In the case of a corporation, the same corporation must enter into both transactions, even if it is part of a group filing a consolidated tax return.

Identification requirements. Before the close of the date the hedge is entered into, the taxpayer must enter on its books and records for each qualified hedging transaction, the following:

a. The date the qualifying debt instrument and the hedge were entered into;

b. The date the qualifying debt instrument and the hedge are identified as constituting a qualified hedging transaction;

c. The amount, if any, that must be deferred under the special rules for legging into a hedge;

d. A description of the qualifying debt instrument and the hedge; and

e. A summary of the cash flows resulting from treating the qualifying debt instrument and the hedge as a qualified hedging transaction.

Tax effect of integration. The income tax effect of treating a qualifying debt instrument and a hedge as an integrated transaction is to create a synthetic debt-instrument. Interest income from a synthetic debt instrument is sourced by reference to the sourcing rules that would apply to the interest on the qualifying debt instrument if it were not part of a hedge. The character for foreign-tax-credit-basketing purposes of interest income from a synthetic debt-instrument is determined by reference to the character of the underlying debt instrument. Interest expense from a synthetic debt-instrument is allocated and apportioned under the general rules relating to interest expense allocation and apportionment. If an integrated transaction results in the elimination of foreign-currency gain—for example, where a Swiss-franc debt instrument has been integrated into a synthetic U.S.-dollar-instrument (as in Figure 16–1)—the income from the transaction no longer runs the risk of generating foreign-currency gain which could produce foreign-personal-holding-company income.

Special rules for legging in and legging out.   There are special rules that apply when a hedge is entered into after the date the qualifying debt instrument is entered into or acquired (legging in), or when a qualifying debt instrument or hedge that is properly identified as a qualified hedging transaction is disposed of, or otherwise terminated prior to maturity of the qualified hedging transaction (legging out).

Legging in: If a taxpayer legs into integrated treatment, exchange gain or loss is realized with respect to the qualifying debt instrument determined solely by reference to changes in exchange rates between the date the instrument was acquired by the holder, or the date the obligor assumed the obligation to make payments under the instrument, and the leg-in date. Such gain is defined and recognized only on the date that the qualifying debt instrument matures or is disposed of.

Legging out: If a taxpayer legs out of integrated treatment, then:

1. The transaction will be treated as a qualified hedging transaction prior to the legging out and during the time it otherwise qualified as a qualified hedging transaction.
2. If the hedge is disposed of or otherwise terminated, the qualifying debt instrument is treated as sold for its fair market value on the date the hedge is disposed of or otherwise terminated (the leg-out date), and any gain or loss (including gain or loss resulting from factors other than movements in exchange rates) from

FIGURE 16–1
Synthetic Dollar-Borrowing

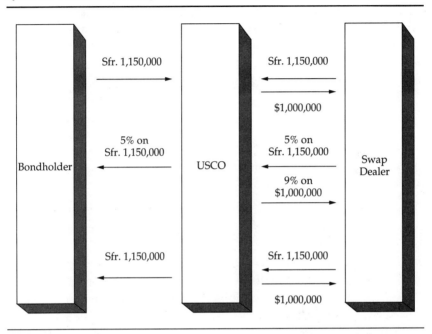

the identification date to the leg-out date is used to determine the taxable gain or loss on the leg-out date.

3. If the qualifying debt instrument is disposed of or otherwise terminated, the hedge is treated as sold for its fair market value on the date the qualifying debt instrument is disposed of or other otherwise terminated (the leg-out date), and any gain or loss from the identification date to the leg-out date is realized and recognized on the leg-out date.

4. A special wash sale rule applies to losses if gain is recognized on the terminated instrument and during the 60 days around the leg-out date (30 days before and 30 days after) a new hedge is entered into.

   IRS' authority. If a person enters into a qualifying debt instrument and a hedge but fails to comply with any of the requirements relating to qualifying hedging transactions and, on the basis of all the facts and circumstances, the commissioner concludes that the qualifying debt instrument and the hedge are, in substance, a qualified hedging transaction, the commissioner may treat the qualifying debt instrument and the hedge as an integrated hedging transaction. The commissioner may identify a qualifying debt instrument and a hedge as an integrated hedging transaction regardless of whether the qualifying debt instrument and the hedge are held by the same taxpayer, if held by related parties.

Hedged Executory Contracts

Basic requirements.   An executory contract and a hedge may be treated as an integrated transaction if the following requirements are satisfied:

a. The executory contract and the hedge are properly identified.
b. The hedge is entered into (or in the case of nonfunctional currency deposited in an account with a bank or other financial institution, such currency is acquired and deposited) on or after the date the executory contract is entered into and before the accrual date (i.e., the date when the item of income or expense, including a capital expenditure, that relates to an executory contract is required to be accrued under the taxpayer's method of accounting).
c. The executory contract is hedged in whole or in part through the period beginning with the date the hedge is identified and ending on or after the accrual date.
d. None of the parties to the hedge are related.
e. Both the executory contract and the hedge are entered into by the same individual, partnership trust, estate, or corporation (even if the corporation is part of a group filing a consolidated tax return).

IRS' authority.   If a taxpayer enters into an executory contract and a hedge but fails to satisfy one or more of the requirements necessary for the transaction to be treated as an executory contract hedging transaction, and based on the facts and circumstances the commissioner concludes that the executory contract is a hedge, then the commissioner may treat the transaction as an executory hedging transaction and may make appropriate adjustments. In addition, the commissioner may treat an executory contract and a hedge as an integrated transaction, regardless of whether the executory contract and hedge are held by the same taxpayer, if they are held by related parties.

Effect of hedged executory contract.   The effect of integrating an executory contract and a hedge is to treat amounts paid or received under the hedge as paid or received under the executory contract, or any subsequent account payable or receivable, or that portion to which the hedge relates. No exchange gain or loss is recognized on the hedge. If an executory contract on the accrual date becomes an account payable or receivable, no exchange gain or loss is recognized on such payable or receivable for the period covered by the hedge.

Synthetic Debt-Instruments

Background.   On December 16, 1994, the IRS issued proposed regulations providing for so-called integration treatment in certain instances where a taxpayer hedges a debt instrument that does not result in a currency change. These proposed regulations are modeled after the regime contained under the rules of Section 988(d) and Treasury Regulation §1.988-5(a), discussed above. They allow for the integration of a qualifying debt instrument and a Section 1.1275-6 hedge. For these purposes, a qualifying debt instrument is either a contingent-payment debt instrument, a variable-rate debt instrument, or an integrated transaction to which the proposed regulations otherwise apply. It is noteworthy that a fixed-rate instrument cannot be a qualifying debt instrument, nor can a tax-exempt obligation of any sort. A Section 1.1275-6 hedge is any financial instrument if the combination of the cash flows on the financial instrument and the qualifying debt instrument result in either a fixed-rate debt instrument, or a variable-rate debt instrument that pays interest at a qualified floating rate. A financial instrument is a spot contract, a forward contract, a futures contact, an option, a notional principal contract, a debt instrument, or similar instrument, or combination or series of financial instruments. Stock is not a hedge for these purposes.

Effect of integrated treatment.   The integrated transaction is generally treated as a single transaction by the taxpayer during the period that it qualifies as an integrated transaction. Thus, the rules that govern the integrated transaction are the rules that would govern the treatment of the qualifying debt instrument.

Requirements for integrated treatment. The requirements for integration closely follow those for integration under Section 988(d). However, under this provision, neither the qualifying debt instrument nor the Section 1.1275-6 hedge can be part of an integrated transaction entered into by the taxpayer that has been terminated under the special legging-out rules.

Chapter Seventeen

Operations Risks

*Antonino Piscitello**
First Vice President
Société Générale

INTRODUCTION

This chapter describes how external factors such as information technology, telecommunications, deregulation, regulation, and multinational trade alliances have redefined financial markets, customer expectations, and marketing strategy. The proliferation of products and risks is also discussed. These forces have given impetus to considerable changes and the reengineering of the organization itself; they have also made it necessary to expedite the time-to-market required to develop new products. Emphasis is given to the prevention and reduction of operation risks while giving particular attention to netting. Finally, the chapter gives considerable coverage to the role of the new professional back office, the importance of which has become more evident with transformation of credit risk to operations risk (see Figure 17–1).

The Back Office—From an Assembly-Line Process to a Value-Added Organization

Advances in information technology, and deregulation of financial and capital markets, have contributed to the globalization of markets, and this in turn has fueled a spectacular growth in transaction volume. Volume isn't all that has grown. New and increasingly complex capital markets

---

*The views expressed in this article do not necessarily reflect the views of Société Générale.

FIGURE 17–1
Counterparty Risk Continuum

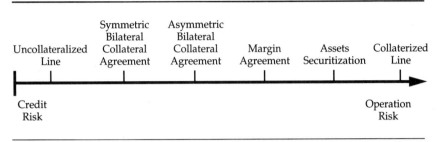

and derivative products are emerging at record speeds, and banks with the back-office sophistication to deliver them will pull ahead of the pack. Product integration and quality service are the keys to becoming a top-tier player. Cross selling, and more important, cross relating of products, must be mirrored at the operations side. Finally, in a financial market acutely aware of the high potential risks of derivative products, the organization must meet the challenge of an increasingly complex set of regulatory controls, both external and internal, and ensure that proper risk discipline is maintained.

To meet the challenges of today's complex derivatives market environment, the organization has to both rethink its approach and retool. This involves developing the skills and experience level of back-office staff, upgrading the computer support systems, and improving communications among the various operations areas. The back office must no longer be reactive and must not play second fiddle to the front office; it needs to be proactive, cooperative, and prepared to meet the challenges of today's dynamic market environment. The ability for the back office to redefine itself is critical to the success of the institution's ability to become a key market player in derivative products and to its ability to control risk.

Creating the Knowledgeable Back Office through Diversity

In staffing up to meet the demands posed by the new capital markets' volumes and complexity, a broader view and perspective is required. The

back-office personnel have to be "market aware" and "product knowledgeable," and must attain a technical level similar to that of the front-
office staff, with strong analytical skills and a command of high-level
math.

Professionals should be recruited from various industry segments—
such as investment banking, insurance, public accounting, and the information technology industry—as well as from traditional commercial
banking areas, and should have a diverse range of experience and expertise. This variety of background broadens the view of the staff and
facilitates the introduction of new and creative approaches in dealing with
new products and new situations. A diverse staff recruited from a variety
of areas represents a cross section of the internal and external parties that
the back office typically deals with.

In addition to supporting outside training and seminars, in-house cross-
training programs are set up to increase understanding and enhance cross-
product opportunities. Regularly scheduled seminars, on topics from
letters of credit to foreign exchange and derivatives, brings together the
commercial, trading, and marketing areas of the bank.

CAPITAL MARKETS—A CHANGING ENVIRONMENT

System Support Evolution

System and technology support has become such an integral part of the
back-office operations that today it would be inconceivable to think of the
back office without taking into account the important role that technology
plays in operations.

The evolution of system support in a way has mirrored the evolution of
the back office itself.

During the 1960s, system support was provided in the form of mainframe computers employing centralized batch data-entry processes to
primarily support general-ledger accounting and statement reporting. At
that time the back office was monolithic, supported centralized data entry,
and was paper-processing-intensive.

The 1970s ushered in the minicomputers supporting on-line terminals,
and as a result the monolithic back-office process was broken down,

allowing individual departments to deploy their own minicomputers. The process was still data-entry oriented and centrally controlled, although the minicomputer contributed to decentralization and specialization along department lines. Mainframe computers were still used for general ledger accounting and statement production while supporting the beginnings of management information reports (MIS). The minicomputers were usually not connected to the mainframe; if they were at all connected, it was through batch processes such as magnetic tape feeds.

The 1980s saw the introduction of databases and improved connectivities between minicomputers and mainframes, which resulted in considerable integration of various systems and improved management information reporting, while on-line or real-time functionalities were also considerably enhanced.

Similarly, the back office started to be concerned with interdepartmental efficiencies and interfaces while still remaining decentralized by individual departments.

The mid-1980s saw the birth of the personal computer (PC), which revolutionized the way that professional workers did their business, particularly on the front-office level. While the integration between minicomputers and mainframes continued, the PC applications remained self-contained with little or no connection with the rest of the enterprise's computers, except for the emergence of local area networks (LANs), which connected PC users with each other. The PC revolution initially bypassed the back office, since it was still organized along the assembly-line model, and staffed by clerical personnel with little incentives to exercise initiative and creativity.

In the 1990s, the revolution continues: More powerful and faster PCs are introduced; new generations of PCs are brought to market in shorter and shorter cycles (less than one year); and powerful reduced-instruction-set-computer (RISC) workstations become commonplace in the trading floor. Client-server technology, which facilitates PC-to-PC and PC-to-minicomputer communication, takes hold; now all elements can be brought together, and diverse units of computer hardware can communicate with each other: mainframes, minicomputers, PCs, and RISC work stations can share resources globally and enterprisewide.

Client-server revolutionized the way of doing business in so far as it was able to support both worlds: customized, dedicated applications along with integrated and shared information resources. It became much easier to tailor-make new products and services while maintaining appropriate risk and management controls.

Enter the back office, which had to retool, become professional, and join the information revolution by becoming part of the business and technology "loop" and by establishing itself as a business partner with the front office while at the same time maintaining its fiduciary and control role.

Today, a typical back office is left with the legacy of this system evolution, which spans the gamut of hardware and software, bringing together legacy systems, minicomputer applications, PC solutions, and new client-server open-system applications that need to be rationalized and interconnected.

For derivative products, support systems have similarly evolved from the back of an envelope to an HP calculator to a PC spreadsheet, a RISC workstation, and finally to a full-scale back-office system (See Figure 17–2). Various vendor software packages as well as internally developed systems are pragmatically integrated to provide consolidated reporting for virtually all capital markets and derivatives activities.

Market Changes

As a result of the deregulation of the financial market and the increased competitive climate, and facilitated by the advances in information technology, markets have become global in scope with unprecedented possibilities for innovation and speed, as well as risk.

Financial products are moving from classical (simple) products to more complex value-added ones (i.e., GICs, CMOs, swaps, options); this is also true for commercial banking activity (i.e., trade finance, project finance, asset securitization). These new value-added products contribute substantially to the bank's profitability. The back office must have the tools to quickly transform itself and adapt, changing from supporting simple processes to more complex ones that require professional-level staff instead of clerical staff. These new complex products typically cannot be supported manually; they require immediate system solutions that must also meet the specific requirements of the local business and the bank clients.

Capital markets and derivative products are subject to a high degree of change and innovation within a short time frame. As a result, the product

FIGURE 17–2
Derivative Systems Evolution

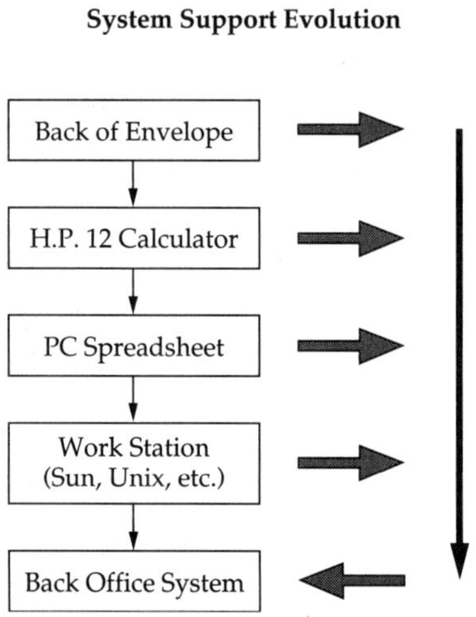

System Support Evolution

life cycle has become compressed and considerably shortened. This realization requires that the product-development and the associated system-development time frames be dramatically reduced and the time-to-market process expedited.

Some products may become obsolete by the time an appropriate system is studied, developed, tested, and implemented in a traditional way.

Globalization, the removal of trade barriers, and deregulation at the national and supernational levels (i.e., EC, NAFTA) have increased the volatility of the financial markets. The ease of participation and the quantum jump in the quality, reliability, and accessibility of information technology, communications, and market data services have created efficient markets—"virtual hypermarkets"—with the obvious consequence of reducing income spreads while increasing risks and competition.

Recent Regulatory Concerns

Because of the banking problems experienced by the United States during the 1980s—such as Latin American lending, highly leveraged transactions (HLTs), real estate loans, the stock market crash of 1987, as well as more recent well-known derivatives losses—continuous regulatory changes are expected for the foreseeable future (i.e., risk-management reporting, fees for daylight overdrafts, disaster recovery requirements). Due to political and economic factors, new requirements may be imposed, such as additional disclosure, mark-to-market accounting for all financial products, transaction taxes for funds transfer, futures, and foreign exchange. Because of money-laundering concerns, the authorities are requiring additional amounts of information for funds transfer records, thus requiring considerable changes in CHIPS, Fed-wire, and other clearing systems. In addition, regulators will be more aggressive in monitoring internal controls and the quality of the back office as a result of some of the recent derivatives debacles, such as the Barings failure, Kidder Peabody's phantom profits, and the Orange County fiasco. These derivatives losses have gained sensationalized coverage by the popular media and generated considerable political sentiment that puts pressure on the regulators to add new layers of regulation.

These regulations—along with recommendations by the Group of 30, the GAO, and the Derivatives Policy Group (SEC, CFTC, OCC, FRB, FDIC)—will add to the complexity and cost of doing business and require further appropriate preparation by the back-office staff.

Product Changes

As we have noted, the market forces and their globalization have not only increased the market volatility but they also demand improved product implementation speed ("product volatility"), and a reduced time-to-market life cycle.

To achieve this goal, the bank must evaluate the cost-versus-benefit opportunities before introducing a new product. The market-related and counterparty-related risks must be evaluated and well understood. In addition, the organization must be ready to assess the various "operations and processing risks" (described later) associated with the support of this new activity.

To properly evaluate these risks, a new-product-development committee must be formed. This committee needs to be represented by various senior support managers—such as operations, technology, accounting/finance, tax, legal, trading management, and risk management—to evaluate the various operations risks (i.e., organization structure risk, technology risk, staff risk) and processing risks (i.e., delivery and settlement risk, valuation risk). A check list describing the new product's characteristics and summarizing its cost/benefit analysis, the system and personnel resources required, and the various risks associated with the new product must be prepared before the product committee's meeting.

When a decision to proceed with a product is reached, then a pragmatic action plan must be developed. This plan will strive to achieve fast implementation while at the same time anticipating and minimizing the various operations and processing risks.

THE COMPETITIVE EDGE

The changing economic environment, and the high speed of change itself, require the organization to stay abreast of market developments and trends and to aggressively develop new products and services that meet the needs and expectation of clients.

Some of the important attributes and approaches that lead to success are discussed below.

Flexibility

Flexibility becomes one of the main constants in this environment. The organization needs to stay nimble and yet focused. In order to take advantage of market opportunities, a flat organizational structure is required where professionals—"knowledge workers"—are encouraged to thrive, unencumbered by a rigid hierarchical structure, and to pursue business opportunities wherever and whenever they emerge.

These professional workers will require communication and information tools that will allow them to stay up-to-date within their field, market, and organization, so that they can form "virtual teams" with colleagues within and outside the organization to collaborate in the development of new products and services, and to find solutions to problems.

Minimum tools required include a PC, with office support software, such as Windows, electronic spreadsheets (Excel, Lotus 1–2-3), word processing software (Microsoft Word, WordPerfect, etc.), and database queries linked to a local area network, as well as wider area networks (WANs) through E-mail and groupware (Lotus Notes).

Information access should include all relevant internal application systems, as well as outside news and market-data information services such as Dow Jones, Reuters, and Telerate.

Organization flexibility, where knowledge workers are configured in flexible teams with specific objectives, will provide the adaptability and incentives to take advantage of new opportunities while at the same time fine-tuning the organization by discarding unprofitable or costly products and services.

System Implementation Strategies

In order to compete with banking counterparts, it is necessary to define a comprehensive system implementation strategy that takes into account corporate systems (long term), transitional systems (middle term), and local systems (short term).

Corporate systems. Corporate systems support mature products and services. They provide benefits of scale, standardization, and consistency across the organization. They should be designed to support an open environment to easily communicate and exchange information with other systems and to maintain a database depository (relational) with standardized data objects. Query tools to generate management-information reports in a timely and flexible way should also be part of the design.

Corporate systems are typically long term in life cycle, and they support the long-term strategy of the organization and the overall corporate management-information needs.

Examples of corporate systems include corporate G/L accounting systems, retail banking systems, global netting systems, counterparty risk systems.

Transitional systems. Transitional systems interface between local and corporate systems, support medium-term solutions, and support products that are in the process of becoming more stable and standardized. Transitional systems are frequently the only mechanism available for consolidating short-term local systems, and integrating them with the corporate systems. In a changing product and system environment, transitional systems often save the day by keeping things going.

Transitional systems eventually are upgraded and rewritten and become an integral part of corporate systems. They bridge short-term solutions and long-term solutions, maintain continuity between local systems and corporate systems, and are managed in a cooperative way by corporate information technology (IT), local IT, and local user organizations such as the back office. They support both local and corporate needs.

These systems are usually neglected because they often require considerable resources to support, are inappropriately considered band-aids and typically are not state-of-the-art solutions; still, they represent a very important stage in the system evolution, which brings together the local IT team and the corporate IT team. Both teams learn to work with each other, understand each other's needs, and embark on implementing realistic, useful projects instead of grandiose and sometimes unrealistic ones, thus limiting the downside financial project risk. These projects foster a common knowledge and teamwork that will later help implement better local and corporate systems.

Examples of transitional systems include P&L reporting systems, desk profitability systems, etc.

Local systems.   Local systems support local products unique to the local market, (i.e., GICs, CMOs). They also support new and rapidly changing products (i.e., derivative products), take advantage of the local business opportunities, speed up the time-to-market process for these opportunities, and provide data-feed to strategic systems.

Local systems are a prerequisite for local business activity. They should be under the control of the back office and front office, depending on their functions. They should support short-term business needs and have a short-term life cycle.

Examples of local systems include interest-rate-swaps systems, mortgage-backed-security systems, GICs system, etc.

Strategic advantages of implementing local systems include: support for strategic business (such as derivative products) and the provision of data feeds and downloads to both local and corporate strategic systems (i.e., risk control, liquidity systems). For the newer high-risk products, local systems are often the only practical alternative to providing meaningful consolidated information—manually prepared information would be a clearly unacceptable choice in those cases. The third advantage is that the experience gained in the local system implementation can be leveraged to develop and implement more robust strategic systems.

It is very important for senior management and business units to "buy in" to this approach if it is to succeed, since it departs from the traditional way that systems are implemented.

The most important consideration in system implementation for derivative products is how quickly reliable systems can be delivered so that the local organization can take advantage of the business opportunities before these opportunities pass by.

Rapid Implementation of Traditional Software Packages

There are various approaches to expediting system development:

- Prototyping
- CASE tools
- JAD and RAD
- Rapid implementation of traditional software packages

Prototyping is based on the approach that before embarking on a major system development effort, a working prototype should be developed first. The prototype will focus on key features and priorities of the system while deliberately omitting many of the noncritical details, using the 20–80 rule. By implementing a working prototype quickly and evaluating its results, one can determine whether to proceed with the full-fledged project, or whether to drop it or modify it before undertaking a lengthy development that otherwise may bring unsatisfactory results and expose the firm to project risk as well as *technology risk.*

CASE tools are based on a new discipline of planning, specifying, standardizing, modularizing, and programming. By properly training the IT staff in CASE tools, the development time frame can be dramatically reduced.

Joint advanced development (JAD) and rapid advanced development (RAD) are new methodologies that depart from the traditional system-development life cycle by bringing together the key stakeholders in the system-development process and empowering them to design, specify, program, and test the system in concurrent segments while working as a team rather than doing these steps sequentially. JAD and RAD applications can result in considerable reduction in implementation time frames.

One very successful overlooked approach is the "rapid implementation of traditional software packages." This approach is pragmatic. It requires no investment in new technology or tools and can be applied concurrently with the techniques described earlier. Rapid development of traditional software packages can be very useful in developing transitional systems. This approach is outlined below:

Rapid implementation of traditional software packages.

- Select reputable vendor.
- Choose software with platform consistent with own shop.
- Pick up modules or system "as is."
- Make system acceptance conditional to software meeting:
  — FASB requirements for accounting.
  — Current accepted market practice for valuation.
- Appoint an independent expert, i.e., a "Big 6" accounting firm, acceptable to software vendor and bank, who will "referee" FASB and current accepted market practice test.
- Implement system.
- Request modification from vendor, as is sometimes required after initial implementation.
- Develop gateway between front and back office systems to reconcile deal input and valuation.

The next figure (Figure 17–3) reflects the product life cycle and the system implementation life cycle dependent on the product maturity.

Concurrent system-strategies summary. To summarize, various development techniques and strategies are available to reduce time-to-market implementation of new products. These techniques and strategies should be adapted concurrently to meet the needs of the organization. These approaches should not be considered to be mutually exclusive but should be adapted in concert to address the particular situation and requirements.

A summary of concurrent strategies and techniques for corporate, transitional, and local systems is given below.

FIGURE 17–3
Product Life Cycle

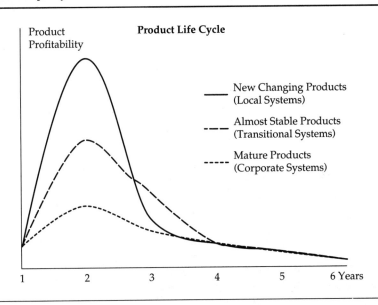

Product Life Cycle

Long-range (corporate) systems—mature products (>4 years)

• Corporate-wide relational data base (Oracle, Sybase, etc.)
• CASE tools
• JAD and RAD
• 4GLs
• SQL
• Open systems architecture
• Object-oriented languages
• Standardized databases and database management

Medium-range (transitional) systems—intermediate products (1½ to 4 years)

• Rapid implementation of traditional software packages
• Batch consolidation

- On-line integration through cross-reference files
- End-of-day relational database extract

Short-range (local) systems—new products (<2 years)

- CASE tools
- PCs (spreadsheets, RDB, etc.)
- LANs
- Workstations (Unix, C, etc.)
- Traditional stand-alone systems
- Rapid implementation of traditional software packages
- Systems that integrate clusters of products
- Uploads/downloads

Client Relationship versus Product Orientation

Traditionally, most banks had a product orientation in marketing. They had mature and well-established products that were processed efficiently though economies of scale. They would structure their organization and particularly their back office in an assembly-line fashion with the main goal being to deliver these products efficiently and profitably.

It was, however, difficult to make customized changes to these products when required. Customization was discouraged because it meant altering the production and controls. The obvious risk was operational—clerical workers were trained for specific tasks and departure from these tasks would likely result in errors. Therefore, customization would result in loss of benefits of scale and thus, profits.

Deregulation, new technology, and advances in communication increased competition from nonbanks—such as mutual funds, investment banks, brokerage houses, and insurance companies. Considerable bank disintermediation took place. Clients were lured away by nonbanks—financial institutions that provided equivalent banking services yet were more customized, flexible, and client oriented.

The banks, conservatively organized with a command and control mentality, were no match to these flexible and aggressive competitors. Unless their internal structure was reengineered to be more flexible and focused through a professional and knowledgeable back office, banks would be at a competitive disadvantage.

It must be noted, however, that some of these nonbank organizations, in their haste to gain market share and sustain ever increasing profits, failed to introduce proper controls and quality and exposed themselves to considerable risks.

It became critical for the marketing team to focus on the overall client relationship in order to provide clients with customized solutions to their financial needs and for the bank to leverage the opportunities to serve the overall client in a more comprehensive manner rather than simply push specific products. However, the client-relationship managers could not deliver on their promises unless their back office could also understand and appreciate the client's requirements and provide effective value-added solutions to the clients' needs, while managing the risks associated to these more complex and customized products and services.

Organizational Changes

Trading operations have recently undergone considerable changes and are still in a transition stage, but the transformation of the back office from an assembly-line process to a professional organization will become reality.

The front office.   In the past, when capital markets were stable and subject to little change, the front office's main concern was to cover the bank's position by hedging or by taking a speculative position based on trading assumptions and trends. The trading products were standard, well understood, and intuitive and, as a result, the traders' position information needs were typically met by the back office, which provided a gap report and other daily activity reports. Because of the intuitive nature of the business, the trader could easily manage the trading activity without sophisticated modeling or risk-management tools.

The back office.   During this early period, the primary function of the back office was to enter the trade tickets into the system, confirm the trade, reconcile the trade against the trader blotter, and make sure that daily activity reports, position reports, and gap reports were prepared by the next morning for the trader. There was very little involvement by the back office with the preparation of profit and loss (P&L) reports since, in most cases, profit and loss was "accrued" rather than marked-to-market; analytical skills were not encouraged.

This type of support was routine and could be performed by dedicated and experienced clerical personnel.

The middle office. The subsequent market changes and the increase in complexity and volatility of new products have made the trading environment more sophisticated and quantitative. This required the introduction of powerful computer and telecommunication systems.

New derivative products were introduced and new regulatory and accounting standards required that the trading P&L be marked-to-market rather than accrued.

These changes, plus the new competitive environment, required more-specialized trader support from the back office. New mark-to-market portfolio valuation, sensitivity analysis, modeling systems, and new risk-management tools were needed, since the traders could no longer rely on instinct for their P&L. The front office needed support staff that could understand, analyze, and communicate these needs.

Attempts were made to use senior clerical back-office personnel to assist the front office with these new tasks. However, it soon became clear that the capabilities, skill set, and training of senior clerical personnel were not appropriate to support these new needs.

A wide gap emerged between the expertise and capability level of the front office and those of the back office. To fill this gap, many organizations established the middle office between the front office and the back office.

The middle office was staffed with skilled employees who usually reported to the front office, and sometimes to the risk-management department. Little attempt was made to reengineer the back office and to upgrade its staff to a professional level.

The middle office, typically, became a go-between, an interpreter between the front office and the back office, and was staffed by "would-be traders" whose loyalty was to the front office where the opportunity to become traders and to receive better bonuses existed. This approach compromised the reporting independence of the middle office and resulted in organizational risk.

It could be argued that the middle office became another organizational layer between the traders and back office without necessarily providing a level of checks and balances. The unintended result was to further slow the conversion of the back office from a clerical to a professional organization. Unwittingly, it may have created disincentives for the back office to better understand the trader's business. It may have also contributed to motivation problems, since the middle office was often considered "elitist" by the back office.

Finally, the organization dedicated additional human resources to the middle office, resources that were not made available to the back office. In fact, a case could be made that the back office was deprived of these professional resources.

A case could be made for the middle office to serve the traders as their support, research, and risk-management arm; however, to the extent that the middle office reports to the front office, its independence is compromised and it cannot fulfill the role of checks and balances normally fulfilled by the back office. The middle office in some organizations reports to risk management, which is usually independent from the front office. In either case, it still makes sense to strengthen the professional level of the back office, since it already fulfills a check-and-balance role vis-à-vis the front office.

The primary role of the middle office is to be a problem solver, but upgrading the staff level of the back office prevents many of the problems from occurring in the first place and, therefore reduces the need for a middle office.

OPERATIONS RISKS

Risks are broadly divided here into two categories: economic risks and operations risks.

Economic risks are the risks that the organization is willing to take when entering into a deal with a given counterparty. These risks are known and evaluated in advance and include: *counterparty credit risk, market risks, country risks, tax risks, political risks.* These risks determine the spread required to enter into the transaction profitably; in other words, they represent the probability of the economic loss the organization is willing to undertake.

What are a lot harder to evaluate are the *operations risks,* which are above and beyond the known economic risk and basically depend on the overall quality and management of the organization itself. They are associated with the execution, management, performance, and control of derivatives deals after the deals are booked. These risks are independent from the *economic risks* the trader undertakes when entering into a deal.

Operations risks are further subdivided into two categories: *firmwide risks* and *processing risks*. Firmwide risks are associated with the quality of the back office as well as other support areas of the organization, while processing risks are exclusively associated with the back office. Operations risks are listed below and further defined later.

Operations Risks

Firmwide risks

- Organizational structure risk
- Staff risk
- Product risk
- System and technology risks
- Model risk
- Accounting risk
- Fraud risk
- Procedure/work-flow risk
- Disaster recovery risk
- Tax risk

Processing risks

- Position risk
- Delivery and settlement risk
- Documentation risk
- Valuation risk
- Collateral risk
- Curve generation risk

Firmwide Risks

Firmwide risks make up a broad category of risk associated with overall operation and support of business activity, which in this case deals with derivatives.

Organizational structure risk. *Organizational structure risk* is the risk that the organization might not have an independent reporting structure between the trading function and the processing, confirmation, valuation, and control of the derivatives process. Appropriate checks and balances and adequate expertise in trading, processing, and control is necessary to avoid conflict of interest. The economic risk, volatility, complexity, newness, and exotic nature of derivatives require a clear separation of duties and responsibilities. It is necessary to introduce checks and balances and ensure that expertise in derivatives is not concentrated in one individual or in a small group of individuals exclusively. This risk can be reduced by making sure that expertise is represented in key functional areas of the organization. This will help to assure that risks are well understood, managed, and properly measured.

It is of fundamental importance that the derivatives business executed in the front office by the traders is independently processed, confirmed, valued, reviewed, and monitored by an independent back office. The back-office organizational structure must not have any reporting lines to the front-office business lines, it must be independent from it in order to avoid conflicts of interest, particularly in the monitoring and reporting of the profit and loss to general management.

The back office must also independently report market and counter-party risk to the bank's general management. An appropriate organizational structure is shown in Figure 17–4.

The above organizational structure, by assigning independent responsibility and expertise, will help to minimize organizational structure risk.

The structure includes the guidelines of Recommendation 8 of the Group of 30 study, which states that market makers " . . . *should have a market risk management function, with clear independence and authority, to ensure that the . . . responsibilities are carried out. . . .* "

Staff risk. Staff Risk is the risk of not having the right professional staffing level, particularly in the back office and other support functions.

Unless the back-office staff has at least a comparable technical level of experience and qualification in the field of derivatives as the traders, then it would be practically impossible for the back office to exercise its supervisory role. Lack of proper expertise could result in the back office becoming a "rubber stamp" to the front office. This situation would be unfortunate, since the back office is the first line of defense to uncover errors and irregularities that may occur in processing derivatives.

Another aspect of staff risk is present when expertise is concentrated in

FIGURE 17–4
Front-Office and Back-Office Reporting Lines

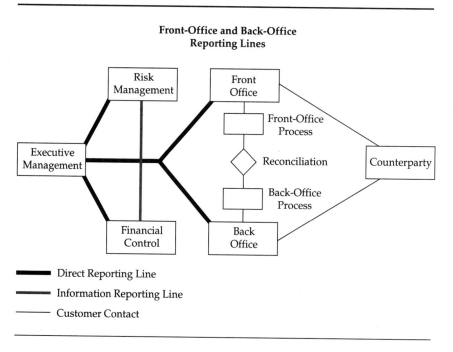

Front-Office and Back-Office
Reporting Lines

only few individuals within the same area. If these individuals leave the organization all at once, they create a dangerous *vacuum of expertise.* Recommendation 16 of the Group of 30 study addresses staff risk as follows:

Recommendation 16: Professional Expertise

Dealers and end users must ensure that their derivatives activities are undertaken by professionals in sufficient number and with the appropriate experience, skill levels, and degrees of specialization. These professionals include specialists who transact and manage the risks involved, their supervisors, and those responsible for processing, reporting, controlling, and auditing the activities.

Product risk.   Product risk is the risk that a new product may be too complex or poorly understood and the organization will not become aware of its economic/operational risks until it is too late. This may include the inability of the back office to process, value, and control this new product because of lack of adequate systems, personnel, and expertise. An important risk to be considered when introducing new derivative products is the *valuation model risk* (described in a later section), which must be clearly understood by the organization.

One mechanism to minimize this risk is to convene a product risk committee with senior representatives from a cross section of the organization, specifically to assess the risk factors associated with new products and to determine the organization's preparedness to enter into this type of activity.

A new-product checklist identifying the various steps to be considered for the new product—such as valuation model, systems, personnel, training, procedures, and various risks—should be prepared by the back office before the product risk committee meets to decide on the new product.

System and technology risks. System risk exists when the organization enters into sophisticated derivatives activity without having in place an adequate system to process, value, and control this new product. More generally, system risk exists when systems are unreliable, inefficient, and experience "bugs."

Technology risk exists when the organization fails to stay up-to-date in technological developments and when the technology fails to support management and regulatory requirements.

Recommendation 17 of the Group of 30 Study address the system and technology risk as follows:

Recommendation 17: Systems

Dealers and end users must ensure that adequate systems for data capture, processing, settlement, and management reporting are in place so that derivatives transactions are conducted in an orderly and efficient manner in compliance with management policies. Dealers should have risk management systems that measure the risks incurred in their derivatives activities including market and credit risks. End users should have risk management systems that measure the risks incurred in their derivatives activities based upon their nature, size, and complexity.

Model risk. Model risk exists where the organization lacks the proper valuation model for sophisticated derivatives. This is particularly important when dealing with a complex product in a market that may not be very liquid. Model risk also exists when valuations used by the front office and back office fail to reconcile with each other.

Accounting risk. Accounting risk exists when faulty accounting treatment that fails to comply with FASB standards or accepted market practice is provided to support derivative products.

This is particularly dangerous, especially when no adequate reconciliation between economic and accounting results exists—which could not only result in unexpected or unexplained economic losses but also in regulatory sanctions.

Fraud risk. Fraud risk exists when dishonest employees manage to assume sensitive trading, processing, and control functions without being detected.

Appropriate checks and balances and independent reporting lines are among the most important deterrents to fraud. It is important to perform background checks on key employees when they are recruited as well as at later stages, particularly when they are moved to sensitive positions.

A strong deterrent, naturally, is a constantly updated audit program with a well-trained audit team that has experience in derivatives products and markets.

Procedures/work-flow risk. Procedures and work-flow risk exist when the process has no written procedures and when the work flow is not structured in a predictable and well-designed manner, with proper audit trails maintained.

The need for well-designed work-flow and written procedures is even greater for more-complex derivative products. Paradoxically, the more complex a product or process is, the less written documentation is maintained.

Because derivative products are subject to continual change, it is critical that the back office review procedures and work flows on a periodic basis.

Disaster recovery risk. Disaster recovery risk exists when the organization has not planned for alternative site, computer resources, communication resources, trading facilities, and other support services in case of disaster.

Because of the market volatility and the product complexities, which make it difficult enough to operate during the normal course of business, it is nearly impossible to continue doing business during a major disaster that may prevent the utilization of the firm's premises, systems, or communications.

It is particularly important for market makers to have alternative remote-trading and technology sites and to be able to recover from "point-of-failure" with minimal disruption. To help achieve this, it is imperative to continually "shadow" or "mirror" critical data to the alternative remote site electronically.

Tax risk. There exist obvious economic risks in not properly taking into account the tax implications of a derivative transaction. In addition, the operations tax risk is the risk of not maintaining detailed tax information associated with each derivative deal. Failure to do so in a timely and explicit manner may result in the tax authorities disallowing the tax advantages for a particular transaction or for a class of transactions.

Processing risks. Processing risks make up a wide category of operation risks associated with the support of derivatives. Processing risk is particularly applicable to the back office, since one of its many functions is to accurately process and maintain the integrity of records. Processing risks include:

Position reporting risk. Position reporting risk exists when the back office cannot provide an accurate position both at the end-of-day and on an intraday basis. Position reporting risk also exists when the back-office position and the front-office position disagree. This may obviously cause economic loss if the trader makes trading assumptions based on positions that may be incorrect or that cannot be easily reconciled with the front office.

Delivery and settlement risk. Delivery and settlement risks are economic risks as a result of the counterparty being unable to deliver its part of the transaction. They become an operation risk if, because of erroneous counterparty position and lack of adequate settlement information, the back office fails to immediately stop payments that are to be made to the counterparty once it is known that the counterparty is in bankruptcy.

Delivery and settlement risk can be both an economic and operational risk depending on the specific situation:

- It can be strictly an economic risk if the counterparty fails to settle or deliver due to credit, liquidity, or political factors.
- It can be both an economic and an operational risk if the counterparty fails and yet the back office may not have the proper clearing and settlement systems to recognize that the counterparty has failed.
- It can be strictly an operational risk if the counterparty *has not* failed, yet the back office because of inadequate systems and procedures fails to make timely deliveries and settlements and therefore incurs compensation costs.

This risk is mitigated by the utilization of timely systems and the adoption of both payment netting and risk netting.

Documentation risk. Documentation risk exists unless derivatives deals are properly covered by well-designed agreements (i.e., an ISDA agreement) that are properly executed and supported by appropriate confirmations in a timely manner. Without appropriate documentation, it may be difficult to have the terms of the deal enforced in case of dispute or bankruptcy.

The legal department and the back office must maintain aging reports showing the status of master agreement and supporting confirmations, with specific explanations and notifications for follow-up. See Figures 17–5 and 17–6. In Figure 17–6 the averages are weighted by "0" for the first business day, "1" for the second business day, "2" for the third business day, etc.

Valuation risk. Valuation risk exists if the back office cannot perform, at least on a daily basis, an independent (from front office) mark-to-market valuation for all derivatives, or if the back-office valuation results differ from those of the front office.

To ensure that proper valuation is done, the back-office must have (1) a professional staff with technical expertise comparable to that of the front office (staff risk), (2) sophisticated real-time on-line systems (system risk), and (3) an automated means to reconcile the daily P&L between the front office and the back office.

FIGURE 17–5
Status of Outstanding Confirmations

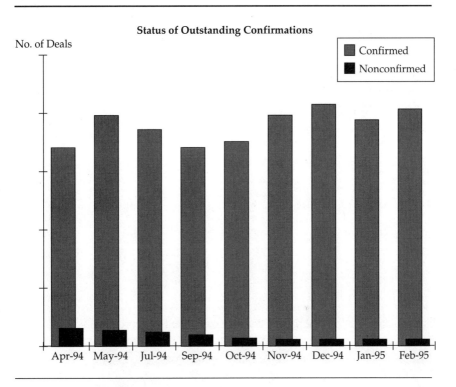

Status of Outstanding Confirmations

Additionally, the back office must obtain objective market rates independent of the front office. For the most liquid and least volatile instruments, these market rates could be obtained directly through market-data-feed vendors (e.g., Reuters, Telerate, Bloomberg). For less-liquid and more-volatile instruments, market rates can be obtained from brokers and market makers or by engaging independent specialists and consultants.

Collateral risk. Although collateral risk is the economic risk of failure of the counterparty to post collateral, it is also an operation risk if the back office fails to have the expertise level and the system to maintain the counterpart position in a timely and accurate manner so that appropri-

FIGURE 17–6
Aging of Confirmations

Average Time Spent to Send a Confirmation		
	This Period	*Last Period*
Same day	20	15
1 business day	15	21
2 business days	5	19
3 business days	2	3
4 business days	1	0
5 business days	0	0
6 business days	0	0
7 business days	0	0
8 business days	0	0
9 business days	0	0
10 business days	0	0
Average	0.81 Day	1.17 Days

ate collateral calculations and margin calls are triggered when due. Otherwise the risk of undercollateralized accounts may translate into economic loss in the event of the counterparty's failure.

Curve generation risk. Curve generation risk is the risk of incorrectly generating the yield curve that is used for valuation. This could transpire due to a faulty model or inaccurate or untimely data (see also valuation risk, above).

This can result in incorrect valuation and misleading reporting of the P&L.

CONFIRMATION MATCHING & NETTING

The recent growth in capital markets, foreign exchange (FX), and money market (MM) activity and the concomitant growth in processing cost and risk exposure demands that netting procedures and systems be instituted (particularly FX netting) in order to reduce operations costs, and to improve quality while reducing counterparty risk and delivery risk.

This is an area of risk control where the back office can play a primary role in enabling the netting process to take place as well as in ensuring its integrity and thus avoiding delivery risk by implementing accurate and timely netting. For this reason, this topic deserves the wider treatment given below.

CHIPS, FedWire, and SWIFT

The majority of the payment traffic is performed with CHIPS and FedWire for U.S. dollars and SWIFT for foreign currencies.

The CHIPS and FedWire systems are communication networks as well as actual clearing and settlement systems. Payments are electronically transmitted, and all balances are maintained by their respective systems. CHIPS end-of-day netting of payments is performed by the New York Clearing House, thus reducing the overall exposure.

SWIFT is a secure electronic financial communication network through which FX confirmations and payment orders are sent; however, it is *not* a payment and settlement system.

Although most FX transactions are confirmed and settled through SWIFT, it is still possible to advise and send payment orders using tested telexes.

Once a trade is executed by the trader, the confirmation (MT3nn's)[1] and payment (MT2nn's) of FX transactions are a country-by-country process that involves a time-consuming and error-prone manual confirmation-matching process followed by payment order instructions sent directly (usually via SWIFT) to each nostro[2] bank for the specific currency. The SWIFT system serves as a network communicating this information among more than 2,400 member banks and participants in more than 115 countries. Since SWIFT is not a clearing house and it does not net payments from its various participants, netting must be performed outside the SWIFT system.

To overcome this problem of multiple confirmations and payments, a number of "netting agents" (FXNET, SWIFT-ACCORD, Multinet, ECHO, etc.) provide specialized services that allow the user to perform the matching (confirmations) and netting (payments) processes.

---

[1]MT represents SWIFT message type. MT3nn represents message type 300 series.

[2]Nostro is the foreign correspondent bank where the foreign currency account is maintained.

Deal Execution and Settlement without Auto-matched Confirmation and Netting

The following is the typical execution and settlement process for executing and settling an FX deal without automatic confirmation matching and netting. Although the process describes an FX trade, the process is similar for other products (money market, FRAs, etc.).

Confirmation of deals. Each day as trades are executed with counterparties by the traders (over the phone, Reuters, Telerate, etc.), the trades are sent to the back office for confirmation. A written confirmation is required from both parties to the transaction. The majority of the deals are also confirmed over the phone, while the rest are confirmed manually matching SWIFT confirmations (MT3nn's) or tested telexes received.

By value date the counterparties exchange payment orders (MT2nn's) usually via SWIFT or tested Telex messages to the respective nostros in order to credit the counterparty in the respective currency.

Confirmation matching. Confirmation matching will ensure that every deal executed by the trader corresponds exactly to the deal executed by the counterparty with the trader.

Confirmation matching independently confirms the activities of the traders and reduces the documentation risk as well as the organizational risk, since deals executed by the front office are independently verified.

Typically, SWIFT confirmations (MT3nn's) received from our counterparties are manually matched against corresponding (MT3nn's) confirmations already sent by the bank to the same counterparty. Discrepancies are brought to the attention of the counterparty and the trader and are resolved promptly.

The above confirmations-matching process is deal-by-deal without netting the payments. It protects the bank from documentation risk insofar as it establishes independently of the traders that the trade on the books exactly matches the trade on the counterparty's books.

Payment orders. By value date, payment orders are sent by the two counterparties to their respective nostros to settle the deal in the relevant currency.

A payment order is sent by the counterparty for each individually confirmed and matched deal, regardless of the fact that for the two counterparties there could be several deals for the same value date and currency, which could net out into a single payment per currency per counterparty.

Netting of these individual payments would reduce dramatically the cost of processing individual payments and similarly reduce the exposure to the counterparties as well as the delivery risk, since each deal is individually handled as if it were independent of another and, therefore, for multiple deals the exposure is grossed up rather than netted.

It has been estimated that, depending on the number of participants and the netting system, settlement risk can be reduced up to 90 percent.

Nostro reconciliation. In order for the bank to reconcile its activities with each nostro and each currency, the nostro sends the bank a nostro daily SWIFT statement (MT950).

The matched confirmations are checked against the various payment orders (MT2nn's) and nostro SWIFT statement (MT950) for a particular value date and nostro. If, for an already matched confirmation, no corresponding payment order or credit to the nostro has been received, then a "fail" has taken place and an appropriate report is produced for the back office to follow up for prompt resolution.

Currently several software packages (SWIFT-NOSTRO 400, CORONA, etc.) are available to reconcile nostro SWIFT statements automatically. Alternatively, in-house systems may be developed to accomplish the same.

Netting payment of currencies. Netting is desirable because it reduces counterparty risk and delivery and settlement risk, and reduces the cost of sending and receiving multiple payments.

Netting standards have not yet been universally established and are still under review by the various central banks and other government authorities. Netting agreements need to be negotiated for each counterparty and must be in written form. An institution can participate in one or more netting services (FXNET, FXMATCH, ECHO, SWIFT-ACCORD, MULTINET, etc.). However, in order to take advantage of netting, the institution *must* interface the netting service to the internal application systems and make modifications to the application and payment systems in order to inhibit these systems from making individual payments for each deal and to execute netted payment in their place.

Automated Solutions

In order to do netting, the first step required is to automate confirmation matching which, in and of itself, is desirable since it reduces the back-office manual process, makes the overall process more efficient, and reduces delivery risk.

Automated matching can be accomplished

- Internally, by upgrading the back-office systems so that they can automatically match confirmations (MT3nn's) received by the counterparty with the corresponding confirmations (MT3nn's) that the bank has sent;
- Externally, by subscribing to vendor services such as SWIFT-ACCORD, as described below.

Automated confirmation matching. After the FX trade is agreed to by the trader with the counterparty, a parallel confirmation exchange takes place on both sides of the deal by the respective back offices; confirmations are usually sent via SWIFT (MT3nn's).

A typical automated confirmation system would intercept all confirmations received and pair them off with reciprocal confirmations sent to the counterparty for the same FX trade. These matched trade pairs are kept on a matched confirmation queue.

An exception report of all confirmations, both sent and received, is produced for the trades that don't have a perfect match. The back office will take prompt corrective action to resolve or repair these instances where no perfect match exists for a trade.

For all matched confirmations, electronic and hard-copy reports are produced daily, periodically, or upon request to monitor the matching activity and resolve problems. An electronic audit trial of confirmations which do not have a match will be maintained to be used later with nostro reconciliation if necessary.

Netting. The matched confirmation queue will be organized by counterparty, value date, deal type (e.g., FX, MM), and currency. A netted report (electronic and hard copy) will be produced providing the details of each trade, such as the net value by currency within counterparty and within value date.

Netting agent.   In order for netting to be effective among the counterparties, it must be achieved through an independent and impartial netting agent such as a clearing house or other trust institution. This agent could act in two different ways:

- It guarantees the accuracy of the netted information transmitted to the counterparties, while the counterparties themselves are responsible for generating the payment orders (e.g., FXNET).
- It guarantees the integrity of the netting information as well as executing the actual settlements (e.g., ECHO).

This netted report or statement (MT97n's or MT950 or equivalent) will represent the netted transactions, one or two days before value (depending on currency). From this report, either electronically or manually, a payment order (MT2nn) will be formatted and sent via SWIFT to the nostro bank in order to make a net payment transfer to the counterparty instead of making individual payments.

Once the electronic netted report is available, netting can be done as follows:

Bilateral Netting

Bilateral payment netting.   In bilateral payment netting, the bank contractually agrees with a counterparty on the terms and conditions of the netting process such as which products and currencies to net and the cutoff time by which to net.

A typical netting system will keep track of the counterparties with whom the bank has netting agreements and the specific terms applicable to the counterparty.

Bilateral netting by novation.   Bilateral netting by novation is similar to bilateral payment netting except that, while payment netting offers improved efficiencies by reducing the number of payments actually exchanged, it doesn't necessarily reduce the counterparty risk, since in case of counterparty insolvency, the courts could "cherry-pick" and could actually order the payment netting void and request funds to be returned to the trustees of the insolvent counterparty.

With bilateral netting by novation both counterparties are protected against this risk. When the bank enters into a new trade (T_1) with the same counterparty, novation has the effect of substituting the contract of an earlier trade (T_o) with a new contract that now includes both trades together $(T_o + T_1)$.

If another trade (T_2) is executed later, again novation replaces the earlier contract with a new (novated) contract $(T_o + T_1 + T_2)$, and so on.

To generalize, if N is the novated contract at any point in time, T_i is the trade (T), and i is the trade sequence number, then the novated contract represents the contract equivalent of the summation (Σ) of all the existing contracts:

$$N = \sum_{i=o}^{n} Ti$$

Multilateral netting. In multilateral netting, the contract substitution is in effect performed by the netting agent (MULTINET, ECHO, etc.), in which case, in order for a bank to net, it must become a participant of a netting organization administered by the netting agent, by agreeing contractually to abide by all its rules and regulations.

In a netting organization, the netting agent will become an intermediary, "back-to-back," individually with the two counterparties. Each counterparty's legal obligation will be with the netting agent and not with each other. The netting agent will net all trades made among all participants by currency and value date and settle them on the value date.

Multilateral netting significantly reduces operation costs, counterparty risk, delivery risk, and settlement risk when compared with the typical process of settling FX deals with each counterparty individually, one deal at a time.

Netting reports provided by the netting agent must include detailed deal and reference information for each deal.

Although corporate customers are not yet part of the SWIFT system, vendor packages are available to convert corporate confirmations to SWIFT (MT3nn's) format and provide confirmation matching. The matching information could then be incorporated into the bank's matching queues.

Even though several organizations provide automatic confirmation matching and netting products or services, in order to take advantage of them, the institution needs to have an integrated system that can easily consolidate various products with the same counterparty. Oftentimes, lack

FIGURE 17–7
FX Deal Execution and Settlement Manual Process

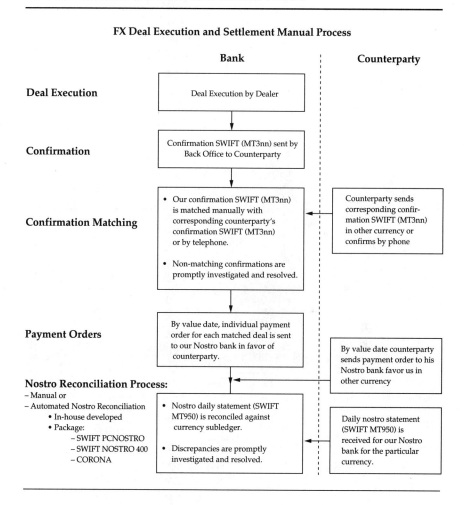

FX Deal Execution and Settlement Manual Process

of a well-integrated system will limit the organization's ability to deploy a netting system, putting it at a great disadvantage vis-à-vis the competition. This is an example of technology risk.

Figures 17–7, 17–8, and 17–9 schematically summarize the automated confirmation and netting process.

FIGURE 17–8
FX Deal Execution and Settlement with Automated Confirmation Matching

FX Deal Execution and Settlement with Automated Confirmation Matching

| | Bank | Counterparty |

Deal Execution — Deal Execution by Dealer

Confirmation SWIFT (MT3nn) sent by Back Office to Counterparty

Automated Confirmation Matching Process:
– In House Developed
– Packages:
  • SWIFT-ACCORD
  • Montran, etc.

• Our confirmation SWIFT (MT3nn) is matched with corresponding counterparty's confirmation SWIFT (MT3nn) or by telephone.

• On-line identifications of "unmatched" and "mismatched" confirmations.

• "Electronic Matched Confirmation Report.

• Non-matching confirmations are promptly investigated and resolved and electronic trail kept.

Counterparty sends corresponding confirmation SWIFT (MT3nn) in other currency or confirms by phone

Payment Orders — By value date, individual payment order for each matched deal is sent to our Nostro bank in favor of counterparty.

By value date counterparty sends payment order to his Nostro bank favor us in other currency

Nostro Reconciliation Process:
– Manual or
– Automated Nostro Reconciliation
  • In-house developed
  • Package:
    – SWIFT PCNOSTRO
    – SWIFT NOSTRO 400
    – CORONA

• Nostro daily statement (SWIFT MT950) is reconciled against currency subledger.

• Discrepancies are promptly investigated and resolved.

Daily nostro statement (SWIFT MT950) is received for our Nostro bank for the particular currency.

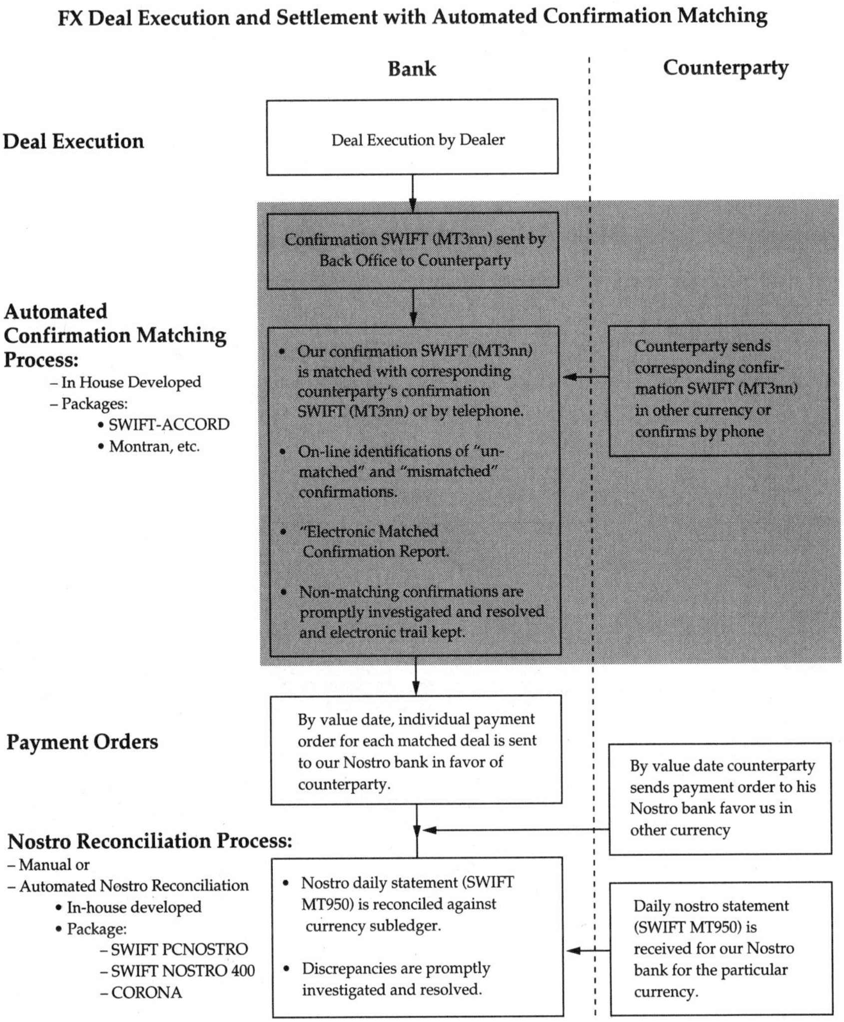

FIGURE 17–9

FX Deal Execution and Settlement with Automated Confirmation Matching and Netting

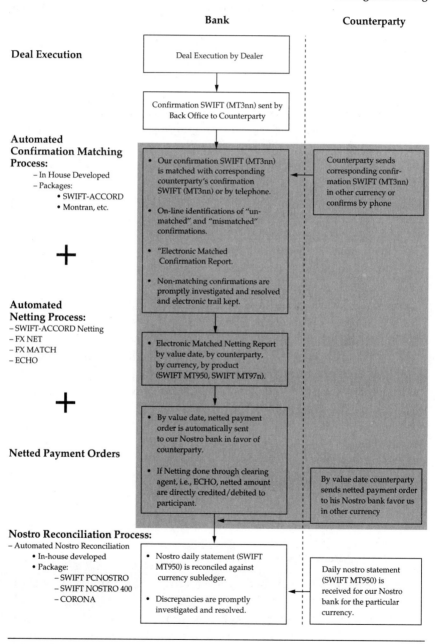

FX Deal Execution and Settlement with Automated Confirmation Matching and Netting

THE PROFESSIONAL BACK OFFICE

The various factors described above have led to a radical change in the structure, organization, skill set, and purpose of the back office.

Traditionally, the back office has been organized as an assembly-line clerical operation that fulfilled a data-entry and bookkeeping role. Very little else was expected; the rest was left up to the traders and the corporate accounting department.

The back office had little appreciation of how their role fit in with the overall business activity of the organization, much less how their efforts affected the client relationship.

This state of affairs may have been tolerated at the time when banking was experiencing little change, products were simple and mature, and markets were protected, at a time when technological changes were measured in decades rather than months and when regulations and market practices made banking predictable and intuitive.

As we have seen, those were the "good old days" when the "3,6,3" rule was the banking norm—borrow money at 3 percent, lend it at 6 percent, and get to the golf course by 3:00 p.m.!

The new banking norm now is no-norm. Change, change, and more change. We are in the age of global markets, or rather "virtual hypermarkets," where the information superhighway takes us many times around the globe in nanoseconds, the 24-hour global book trading is staffed by "rocket scientists" that do not launch space rockets anymore but rather new derivatives that can create "derivative fallout" by potentially setting off systematic risk (as it is repeatedly emphasized in the popular press). Although these fears are in fact exaggerated, certainly this new environment cannot be comfortably and creditably supported by a clerical back office.

A new breed of professional is needed to safeguard the interests of the organization while supporting its participation in the derivative markets— the new back-office professional.

Analytical Skills

The background of the new back-office professional must include analytical and problem solving skills.

The staff must be recruited not only from a traditional commercial banking environment but rather from a broad segment of the financial industry and associated professions such as investment banking, public accounting, information technology, insurance industry, exchanges, and the security industry.

The staff should be capable of using a variety of tools from HP calculators to electronic spreadsheets, as well as sophisticated information technology systems, in order to carry out their responsibilities.

The back-office staff must be market-aware and product-knowledgeable and must be able to perform valuations of capital market products independently from the front office.

The back-office staff must be IT literate and must reach a working-knowledge level of information technology in order to actively participate in the specification, design, and implementation of systems for new products in a variety of platforms in full partnership with the technical IT staff.

The back-office staff must be familiar with current risk measurements, analysis, and statistical techniques in order to be able to provide sensitivity and risk analysis daily or on demand. Variations and exceptions must be promptly researched and explanations provided to traders and management.

A well-prepared and professional back-office staff with independent reporting lines from those of the trading-room management will ensure objectivity and integrity of analysis.

The New Back-Office Professional

The academic preparation of the new back-office professional should include a university degree in finance, engineering, math, or other quantitative discipline. In key areas such as risk monitoring and market valuation, advanced degrees and special certification (e.g., CPA) may be required.

These academic skills and professional experience are basic attributes that will enable the back-office professional to analyze derivative products; design optimal operational process; valuate these products regularly; understand, monitor, and report the various risks; and most importantly, provide the highest level of service to the bank's clients.

Integration Skills

The back-office professional's analytical skills will help to define the various processes, solve problems, and specify new system requirements.

Integration skills are necessary in order to bring together information technology, accounting, mathematics, statistics, banking, economics, and process control. This will create an effective operations environment that facilitates the performance of the business while at the same time monitoring its integrity and reducing the various risks.

Value-Added Organization

The back-office professional must also be able to perform an active role as a partner with the traders and the client-relationship officer in order to enhance client relations by providing first-class service while supporting customized product structures and maintaining appropriate controls.

Independence between the Front Office and the Back Office

Independent organization structure. Academic preparation, professionalism, experience, and in-depth knowledge of the products traded is the first step to ensure independence and confidence in the back office, and it will go a long way to create self-esteem, inspire respect, and enhance communications.

Organization structure risk must be eliminated by ensuring that the back office has independent reporting lines from the trading unit. Within the back office itself, functional separation must exist between processing, settlement, and risk control; yet all these units must have a comparable level of professionalism. They must be knowledgeable and competent enough to understand both back-office and trading activities.

Independence between front-office and back-office systems. This organizational separation must also be reflected in the system structure. The back office must have its own system completely independent from the front office.

The two systems must be independently designed, programmed, installed, and maintained.

Although this may sound contrary to the currently held views that systems should be integrated and unified to avoid duplications and errors, this approach is desirable for over-the-counter derivative products for the reasons given below.

For a typical market-making institution, derivatives are, as we have presented earlier, value-added, low-volume, high-risk products—arguably, at least two orders of magnitude less in volume than most other classical banking products such as funds transfers, FX, or money market products.

Because of their comparatively low transaction-volume and high risk, it is preferable for derivatives to have dual independent systems—one for the front office, one for the back office. This approach will eliminate both model risk and system risk by ensuring that both systems arrive at the same P&L results independently.

Errors in valuation and systems "bugs" may be difficult if not impossible to detect before they could do major damage. Running the back-office and front-office systems concurrently and automatically comparing their results provides a practical and effective way to ensure that the two systems are constantly being "debugged."

An automated daily comparison is performed deal-by-deal to validate transaction integrity and valuation. If the two valuations differ above a given threshold, then the transaction records and valuations for both systems will be analyzed in detail. If the transaction records agree, then the discrepancy in valuation must be caused by either system error (bug) or valuation model error (see Figures 17–10 and 17–11).

Advantages and disadvantages of dual systems are summarized below:

Advantages of dual systems. Having dual systems, followed by automatic deal-by-deal reconciliation, screens out input errors up-front. It greatly reduces the possibility for unwelcome surprises later on in the life of the deals.

Dual valuation, from independently developed software, will also catch errors due to software "bugs" or valuation-methodology differences in either system.

The ability to discover valuation differences is of great importance when dealing with complex derivative products such as swaps and options.

Disadvantages of dual systems:

- Cost of maintaining two different systems instead of one.
- Cost of maintaining two separate reference databases.
- Cost of inputting a deal twice.

It can be argued that dual independent input will not add much to

FIGURE 17–10
Dual Systems

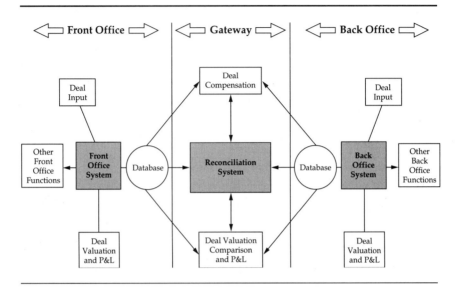

ensuring the integrity of both the front-office and back-office systems, since both inputs depend on the same dealer's ticket. Granting this, it is of fundamental importance that the valuation subsystems remain independent and that they are independently maintained for the reasons given above.

As a practical matter, since the two systems are independently developed and maintained, it may be more expensive to integrate the input modules of both systems than actually separately inputting each deal both in the front and back offices. Given the fact that over-the-counter derivatives are a low-volume business, separate inputs, when handled by a professional back-office staff, could add the extra level of comfort that "two sets of eyes" can provide in the case of unusual situations.

Independent Risk Reporting

Risk reporting and monitoring is a critical function performed by the back office in concert with the risk-management function. In addition to timely

FIGURE 17–11

Interest-Rate Derivatives Desk P/L Summary

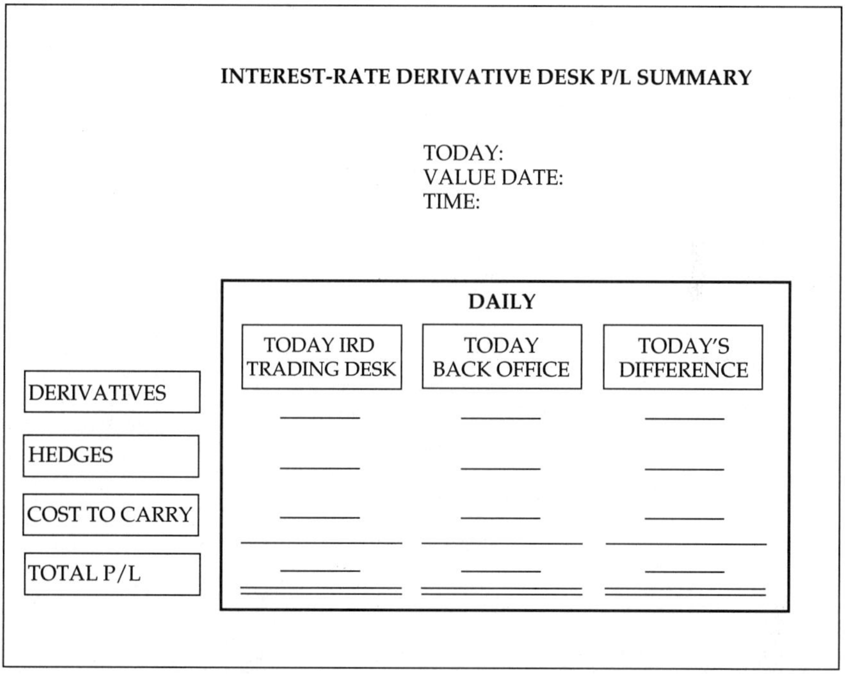

INTEREST-RATE DERIVATIVE DESK P/L SUMMARY

TODAY:
VALUE DATE:
TIME:

	DAILY		
	TODAY IRD TRADING DESK	TODAY BACK OFFICE	TODAY'S DIFFERENCE
DERIVATIVES	————	————	————
HEDGES	————	————	————
COST TO CARRY	————	————	————
TOTAL P/L	————	————	————

---

reconciliations of the bank nostro and custodian accounts in order to ensure that proper settlement and delivery of currencies and securities has taken place as anticipated, discrepancies and fails must be promptly resolved.

Limits reporting must be performed by the back office on a daily basis or on an intraday basis, when necessary, to ensure that the bank properly monitors the amount of market risk it is willing to accept by trader, currency, desk, and product.

For typical overnight market-shifts, one approach is to perform an interest-rate sensitivity analysis by trader, currency, desk, products, and for the entire bank. By subjecting the yield curve to a hypothetical parallel shift, for example, of plus or minus 100 basis points, the bank

FIGURE 17–12
Risk-System Processing Flow

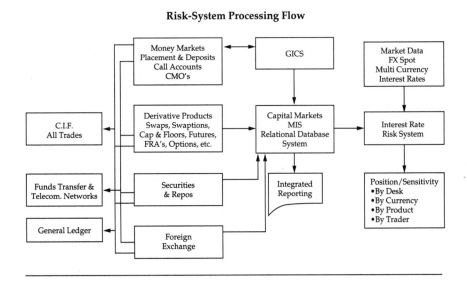

Risk-System Processing Flow

can revalue the portfolio and find out what would be the correspondent loss caused by this 100-basis-point yield-curve parallel shift and then compare it with the corresponding limits (loss) that the organization is willing to tolerate.

A variance report is produced for traders and management and if limits are exceeded, the traders may be instructed to liquidate part of the portfolio to bring the maximum allowed loss within limits. (See Figures 17–12, 17–13, and 17–14.) Analyses and explanations are provided to account for significant variances from one day to the next even if the potential losses are within limits.

For event risks, frequent stress tests must be conducted based on various catastrophic scenarios such as a stock market crash, liquidity problems, systematic risk, and foreign-exchange controls. These stress tests include nonparallel shifts of the yield curve.

FIGURE 17–13
Position Limits

Positions Limits
MONEY MARKET PORTFOLIO

YRS	USD			JPY			GBP			FRF			DEM			OTHER		
	Pos	Lim	Var	Pos	Lim	Var	Pos	Lim	Var	Pos	Lim	Var	Pos	Lim	Var	Pos	Lim	Var
1	—	—	—	—	—	—	—	—	—	—	—	—	—	—	—	—	—	—
2	—	—	—	—	—	—	—	—	—	—	—	—	—	—	—	—	—	—
3																		
4																		
5																		
6																		
7																		
8																		
9																		
10																		

CONCLUSIONS

As we have been made aware by the recent derivatives debacles (Barings, Kidder Peabody), in most instances the weakest link has been their back-office organization, which has lacked the proper level of professionalism and/or independence to recognize and report in a timely manner and at the appropriate level the substantial losses these organizations incurred.

These situations confirm that the back office must evolve from a clerical processing unit that books transactions for the front office into a professional value-added team that is competent in derivative products—a team that can analyze market sensitivity and risks, develop new products in

FIGURE 17–14
Sensitivity Limits

Sensitivity Limits

	Currencies	Limits in Millions	Sensitivity	Variance
Money Market	USD	_____	_____	_____
	FRF	_____	_____	_____
	DEM	_____	_____	_____
	JPY	_____	_____	_____
	GBP	_____	_____	_____
	OTHER	_____	_____	_____
USD Derivatives	USD	_____	_____	_____

partnership with the front office, implement systems, and integrate management information of these products.

The new professional back office, no longer an assembly-line operation, is, in fact, a flexible team delivering quality value-added products and services that support the business relationships and partnerships of the organization.

Throughout this discussion, one crucial ingredient has been assumed to be present: senior management's true commitment and support to the development of the professional back office. Without such endorsement, the organization may be in for some real surprises.

What about Your Organization?

Is your back-office organization flexible and staffed with professionals experienced in derivative products?

Does your IT strategy have separate components for (1) local systems, (2) transitional systems, (3) corporate systems?

Does your back office have a separate and independent reporting line from the front office?

Do your front office and back office have independent valuation systems that are compared daily?

Is P&L reporting independent from the front office?

Does your organization have a senior level new-product-development committee?

Do you have an effective disaster recovery program?

Does your back office use automated confirmation matching?

Does your organization employ netting?

If any of the above answers is no, then your organization may be exposed to significant operations risks.

Chapter Eighteen

Internal Control: Considerations for Derivatives Risk Management

Richard M. Steinberg
Senior Partner
Coopers & Lybrand L.L.P.

INTRODUCTION

The continuing evolution of and complexity surrounding derivatives have made it more important than ever that businesses make sure that derivatives are used only in support of their basic business objectives. In recent years, a number of multinational companies have suffered well-publicized internal control failures resulting in significant losses, leaving top management and directors asking the question, "How could this have happened to us?" More important, how many directors and managers can say today that this could not happen to them? Management and directors subject their companies to significant exposure when they allow subordinates to trade in highly complex and volatile financial instruments without providing the necessary oversight and control.

One of the difficulties in determining which controls should be in place stems from the fact that the concept of internal control can mean different things to different people. That different companies are subject to different operating environments and different risks further complicates the control issues. The solution lies in establishing a carefully crafted internal control structure over derivatives activities that is consistent with the company's culture and meets its operational needs, and in designing and implementing controls to ensure management's directives are carried out in a manner consistent with the company's business philosophy and objectives.

In order to have a common conceptual basis of internal control, we look to what has become the authority on the subject, *Internal Control— Integrated Framework*, issued by the Committee of Sponsoring Organizations of the Treadway Commission. The next few paragraphs outline the definition and components of internal control as set forth in that report, commonly referred to as the COSO Report. Then there follows a discussion of the application of those concepts to derivatives activities.

Overview

Internal control is defined broadly by the COSO Report as a process, effected by an entity's board of directors, management, and other personnel, designed to provide reasonable assurance regarding the achievement of objectives in the following categories:

- Effectiveness and efficiency of operations,
- Reliability of financial reporting, and
- Compliance with laws and regulations.

The first category addresses the entity's basic business objectives, including performance and profitability goals and safeguarding of resources. The second relates to preparation of reliable published financial statements, and the third deals with complying with laws and regulations to which an entity is subject. All three are applicable in creating an effective system of internal control. Depending on the nature of an entity's business, however, one or more of these three broad categories may take on particular relevance.

Within the broad definition of internal control, there are five interrelated components that are derived from the way management runs the business. These components are integrated into the management process, and they build on one another to form an integrated framework that reacts to changing conditions, both internal and external to the organization. These components may take different forms as a result of a company's size, industry, and operating style, but to create a truly effective system of internal control, all five must be present. These components are:

Control environment. The control environment sets the tone of the organization, and is the foundation for all other components of internal control. It focuses on the ethics, integrity, and competence of the entity's people; management's philosophy and operating style; the way management assigns authority and responsibility; and the board of directors' attention and direction to the activities of the organization.

Risk assessment. Risk is present in all entities. Risk assessment addresses the establishment of objectives and assessment of risks, both internal and external, that might prevent achievement of those objectives. It also addresses how relevant risks should be managed and the establishment of mechanisms to address changing risk.

Control activities. Control activities are those policies and procedures by which an entity ensures that it carries out management directives aimed at the identified risks. This component requires action at all levels of an organization and includes activities such as approvals, reconciliations, reviews, security of assets, and segregation of duties.

Information and communication. Information must be captured and communicated in a timely manner in order to enable individuals to carry out their responsibilities. The gathering and dissemination of information must take place across all sectors of an organization. Not only must pertinent information be communicated downward to individuals, but there must be avenues to communicate upstream to top management. This component involves creating awareness of individuals' roles in the internal control system and recognizing how pertinent information affects others in carrying out their responsibilities.

Monitoring. The internal control system must be monitored to assess its effectiveness over time. This is accomplished through ongoing activities of the individuals managing business activities, as well as through separate evaluations by individuals whose responsibility it is to assess the effectiveness of the system and its components, such as an internal audit department. Deficiencies should be reported upward in the organization, with more serious violations being reported to top management and to the board.

These five components are closely linked. With any component either not present or not operating effectively, the integrity of the overall structure is threatened. A key to creating and maintaining an effective internal control structure is to recognize this integrated framework and how these five components traverse an entity's activities and its operations, financial reporting, and compliance objectives. This integrated framework involves active and substantive involvement on the part of management, beginning with the chief executive officer and the board of directors.

CONTROL ENVIRONMENT

The control environment applies to the organization in its entirety, as well as to particular units or functions such as a treasury department that is responsible for derivatives transactions.

The effectiveness of an organization's control environment begins with the integrity, ethical values, and competence of its people. Most larger companies have written codes of conduct, which are useful. Personnel dealing in derivatives must be fully aware of the company's code, and are benefited where the code is specific to derivatives activities. There should be clear direction on the nature of dealers with which the company will do business and the ethical plane on which transactions will be carried out. While a written code, even one tailored to the derivatives activities, contributes to providing direction and establishing a critical tone, there is no guarantee that it will always be followed. Of greater importance are actions of top management in dealing with people and issues related to derivatives transactions. The attitudes and behavior of top management, particularly in dealing with sensitive issues, send an extraordinarily clear message as to what is expected of all personnel.

A company's commitment to a competent workforce is absolutely critical, particularly when it comes to personnel who can subject the company to extraordinary financial exposure. People dealing with derivatives must have the skills and experience to understand operating risks to which the entity is subject, and be able to match the derivatives instruments to best deal with that risk. Perhaps no single weakness has been cited more often as the cause of large derivatives-related losses than a failure to understand the purpose and risks of derivatives instruments.

Personnel must not only be familiar with a wide variety of instruments, but must also have the analytical and quantitative skills to fully understand the linkage between the indices to which instruments are linked and the implications in terms of their nature, amounts, and timing. Accordingly, attention to recruiting, training, promotion, and evaluation of people dealing with derivatives will directly affect the quality and success of the derivatives function. If an entity's size, limited use of derivatives, or other factors preclude it from maintaining the requisite skill-base "in-house," then it becomes essential to bring the necessary expertise to bear on a consulting basis. Companies that presumed that the broker/dealer would automatically be acting as an impartial advisor sometimes have found themselves arguing that position in courts of law.

A company's control environment is also directly affected by the degree to which it provides incentives to its people to achieve targets. Financial incentives have long been successfully used in helping companies achieve their business objectives. With derivatives, however, because of the potential for huge exposure, incentive compensation must be used with extreme care. There have been instances where employees have seized opportunities for tremendous personal gain, creating a "heads I win, tails you lose" proposition. Incentives must be carefully crafted to ensure that the company is not exposed to unwanted risks.

Management's overall philosophy, operating style, and organizational structure are further elements of the control environment. A company might be aggressive, seeking high rewards by accepting high risks. It might, for example, be prepared to take speculative positions in its operating activities by not hedging certain risks. Or, it might use derivatives for purely speculative purposes. Some companies, primarily financial institutions, practice what is called dynamic and portfolio-risk-management strategies. They include taking a view on the market. Here, the institution makes a conscious decision not to hedge the entirety of the existing risks, or it takes a tactical and usually limited speculative position, based on the direction in which it believes the underlying factor, such as interest rates, will move.

Many observers recommend that most companies, particularly commercial/industrial companies, not use derivatives to speculate. They believe that there are better ways to speculate, such as by investing in derivative-related funds run by money managers with ready information and market savvy to provide the best—although far from certain—return. Inasmuch as the majority of businesses strive to use derivatives solely to hedge business risk, this discussion of controls is based on that presumption.

Just as organizational structures vary widely from one company to the next, a derivatives function might be centralized, or spread far and wide to be a part of the operating units whose activities generate the risks that are the subject of hedging. Whatever the structure, it is imperative that management have a strong grasp of all derivatives activities. It is just not acceptable for one or two people in an obscure place in an organization to expose a company's vast resources, unknown to those responsible for running the business. Basic organizational design, management, and oversight functions—the everyday blocking and tackling of managing a business—must be tended to.

A related topic is how a company assigns responsibility and authority for hedging risks. It is more relevant today than ever with the restructuring—whether it is called streamlining, downsizing, or rightsizing—that has occurred in so many businesses. In many cases, the highly complex and critical decisions on the use of derivatives are made at lower levels of an organization without the requisite direction and management. Making decisions closer to the market can be successful, as long as responsibilities and authorities for specified types of transactions and exposure limits are clearly established and enforced.

Finally, the control environment is affected by the board of directors, which has responsibility for oversight of management. The risks associated with derivatives transactions require that directors give significant attention, satisfying themselves that effective controls are in place. Directors must ask the tough questions; they must probe and challenge to ensure that management understands the underlying operating risks and the use of derivatives in hedging those risks, and that accepted risks are prudently and effectively managed. Too many boards have learned too late that they were not sufficiently involved.

Table 18–1 summarizes the activities of management relevant to an effective control environment for derivatives activities.

RISK ASSESSMENT

Every organization faces a number of risks when using derivatives—both internal and external to the organization. The key to effective control is determining which risks are acceptable to the organization, and taking action to maintain risk within established parameters.

TABLE 18–1
Activities Relevant to an Effective Control Environment for Derivatives Activities

---

Integrity and Ethical Values

- Implementation of a code of conduct and other policies regarding acceptable practices, conflicts of interest, or expected standards of ethical behavior, including manner of reporting conflicts that arise with such code of conduct.
- Standards for dealing with employees, customers, investors, securities dealers, etc., in carrying out derivatives transactions.
- Careful use of any performance targets or compensation tied to the achievement of those targets.

Competence

- Formal job descriptions of all treasury function positions.
- Analysis of the knowledge and skill level needed to adequately perform job responsibilities of treasury function personnel.

Management Philosophy and Operating Style

- Clear objectives in investing in derivatives (i.e., hedging operating risks).
- Assessment of level of risk acceptable to management in carrying out derivatives transactions.
- Substantive and timely interaction between senior management and management of the treasury function, particularly when operating in geographically removed locations.

Organizational Structure

- Appropriate organizational structure of the treasury function and its ability to provide necessary information to manage its activities.
- A clear-cut definition of treasury function managers' responsibilities.
- A sufficiently high level of knowledge and experience of treasury managers in light of their responsibilities.

Assignment of Authority and Responsibility

- Assignment of responsibility and delegation of authority commensurate with achieving the treasury function's goals and objectives.
- Effective control-related standards and procedures over the treasury function, including treasury personnel job descriptions.
- People with requisite skills relative to the size and complexity of treasury function activities.

Training and Development

- Policies and procedures over hiring, training, promotion, and compensation of individuals responsible for derivatives activities.
- Appropriateness of remedial actions with employees in response to departures from policies and procedures.
- Adequacy of background checks, particularly with respect to prior treasury function activities.

(continued on page 542)

(concluded from page 541)
- Effective performance evaluations and their relation to the code of conduct and other guidelines.

Involvement of the Board of Directors
- Board's independence from management, such that necessary and difficult questions are raised about management's activities with respect to derivatives transactions.
- Sufficiency and timeliness with which information is provided to the board to facilitate monitoring of management's use of derivatives.

Risk must be assessed on two levels. First is the identification of risks that underlie normal operating activities of the business. These might include fluctuating interest rates, foreign currencies, or commodity prices. It should be recognized that a decision to leave these risks uncovered could be viewed as a prudent business risk, or as a form of speculation. But whatever the decision, it should be based on an understanding of the nature of the risks and the amount of related exposure.

On the second level, if derivatives are used to hedge operating risks, the use of derivatives in and of itself presents different risks. It is these risks inherent in the use of derivatives that are addressed here.

An overriding issue is the possibility that personnel will not fully understand the nature of the derivative instruments or the underlying operating risk, or will not act with the requisite care or in the best interests of the company. These risks are addressed under the control environment, discussed above, as well as in connection with the other components of internal control.

Correlation Risk

Correlation risk is the risk that the derivative intended to serve as a hedge and the hedged item do not move in tandem. Because there is no such thing as a perfect hedge, a gain on a derivatives transaction might not fully offset a loss on the underlying activity, or vice versa. Accordingly, when deciding whether to hedge a risk, it should be determined whether there is an expected high correlation between anticipated changes in the market value of the hedging instrument and the hedged item, and whether the correlation is likely to continue throughout the hedging period. In any event, since the market might not perform as expected, there must be continual tracking of fluctuations during the period.

Basis Risk

Basis risk is the risk that the difference between the spot price of the hedged item and the price of the hedging instrument will increase or decrease over time. The basis is sometimes referred to as the spread. Although one might think that over time the spread should stay fairly constant, that has not always been the case. As witnessed in the financial market upheaval in October 1987, many factors can influence the pricing of hedging instruments and the underlying items being hedged.

For example, the spread between the Standard & Poor's (S&P) 500 futures contracts and the actual S&P 500 Index on October 23, 1987, went from positive to negative and back again, all within 15 minutes. Although some argue that this phenomenon was an aberration, it dramatically illustrates basis risk to holders of S&P 500 futures contracts. Because the spread between futures prices and spot prices is zero on the settlement date of a futures contract, basis risk is usually not significant to the hedger that has the ability and intent to hold the hedge position to maturity.

Credit Risk

Credit risk is the risk that the counterparty to the transaction (e.g., a hedger taking the opposite position, or a broker/dealer or a banker who arranged the transaction) will not honor its commitments. Creditworthiness is particularly important when one is dealing in instruments not traded on a securities or commodities exchange, such as forwards, swaps, and privately negotiated options (i.e., over-the-counter derivatives). Even with exchange-traded instruments, such as futures and publicly traded options, companies need to assess the creditworthiness of the broker.

In addition, a mechanism should be in place for monitoring the counterparty's continued health even for counterparties with prominent names. The extent and frequency with which such procedures are applied will, of course, vary on a case-by-case basis.

Where there is significant credit risk, it is usually prudent to require collateral. In an era when some of the most widely traded instruments are in book-entry rather than physical form, delivery of collateral is quick, easy, and relatively inexpensive. Companies should have procedures to make sure they indeed have possession of the collateral, and that it is adequate relative to the transaction.

Opportunity Cost

In exchange for protection from price fluctuations, hedgers must generally be willing to:

- Give up potential profits when prices move in favor of the initial transaction being hedged,
- Pay a premium on an option for the right to exercise,
- Pay related commissions and fees to a banker or broker arranging the transaction.

An analysis of the total costs associated with a hedging strategy is critical to understanding its economics.

Other risks in the use of derivatives include:

- Political risk: expropriation, regulatory changes
- Liquidity risk: cash flow, funding, investor relations
- Competitive risk: long-term strategy
- Taxation risk: inefficient structures, legislative changes
- Accounting risk: reporting, inefficient hedging
- Cash transmission risk: EDI, funds transfer
- Security risk: data, assets, insurance, fraud
- Model risk: financial models for derivatives
- Operational risk: inadequate systems, human error, or management failure
- Legal risk: inefficient documentation, insufficient authority of a counterparty, uncertain legality, and unenforceability in bankruptcy or insolvency

Indeed, organizations face numerous risks in derivatives transactions. Compounding the difficulty in assessing the significance of each risk is that, depending on market conditions—and regulatory, global, and political events—risks are constantly changing. It is therefore imperative that mechanisms be in place to identify and analyze the risks and that management take effective action to manage them.

Table 18–2 summarizes some of the do's and don'ts of managing derivatives risk.

TABLE 18–2
Some of the Do's and Don'ts of Managing Risk

Do

- Obtain a sound understanding of the financial price risks (foreign currency, interest rate, commodity prices) inherent in your company's operations.
- Understand the various derivatives and financial instrument techniques available to hedge or mitigate these risks. Different instruments and different strategies each carry different risks and rewards.
- Be intimately familiar with the economics of the underlying operating risk and potential hedging instrument.
- Make sure your systems, procedures, and personnel can properly handle derivatives activities.
- Carefully select broker(s) through which to execute listed futures and options transactions and bank(s) or investment bank(s) through which to place forwards and currency and interest-rate swaps.
- Ensure that top management approves the hedging and financial risk-management strategies and related limits over these activities, and that the board provides effective oversight to the process

Don't

Don't assume that:

- Accounting and tax rules will match the economics of a hedging strategy.
- Strategies presented by your banker, investment banker, or commercial banker are most appropriate for your company, or that your existing broker and banker can properly meet all your needs. Ensure that strategies and execution capabilities are evaluated on a comparative basis.
- Top management and the board automatically understand the economics, accounting, tax, treasury, systems, and control aspects of hedging and financial risk management.
- Your existing systems, procedures, and controls can properly handle your selected strategies.
- Hedges will always operate as intended.
- Accounting, tax, and regulatory rules governing your strategies will remain unchanged.

CONTROL ACTIVITIES

Control activities are the policies and procedures that help ensure that management directives are carried out and actions are taken toward achievement of the organization's objectives.

Probably the most important tool for controlling derivatives activities is a clearly defined policy statement. A clear-cut, comprehensive, and unambiguous statement of the objectives and limits of derivatives transactions is essential. The policy statement should cover matters such as:

- Funding
- Investment management
- Foreign-exchange exposure
  - transaction
  - translation
  - economic
- Interest-rate exposure
- Banking relationships
- Counterparty exposure
- Liquidity

To be useful, the policy must be explicit. The terms hedging versus speculation need to be clearly spelled out. A plain-vanilla instrument to one person might be an exotic instrument to someone else. The intentions of management on the use of derivatives—including their purpose, nature, and monetary amounts—need to be spelled out unambiguously.

There is sometimes a tendency when developing a policy statement to consider operating risks in isolation rather than in the context of the company's overall activities. For example, in one case consideration was given to currency-rate movements on debt, but not on expected revenue streams. In another case, a finance director who was carrying out a loosely defined currency-exposure policy to minimize risk was indeed covering 100 percent of the dollar amount of currency exposure. He also, however, was opening significant interest-rate exposure by not matching the timing of hedging cover relative to maturity of the underlying exposure. Neither top management nor the board was aware of either the existence or size of the resulting interest-rate exposure.

The policy should, of course, conform to applicable laws, including the entity's bylaws and the rules and regulations of applicable governmental agencies or self-regulatory organizations. It should define the organizational structure of the derivatives function, responsibilities of its staff, and reporting requirements, and clearly segregate incompatible functions. Trading authorization should be established to make clear who is allowed to trade, the limitations with counterparties, the instruments that can be used, and the monetary limits.

Limits should be set on amounts that may be placed:

- In any one security, maturity, entity, industry, currency, country, credit rating, interest rate, or market.
- With any one investment banking firm, broker/dealer, or counterparty.
- By any one individual.

Criteria for selecting broker/dealers, portfolio managers, or investment advisors with whom the company will deal should typically include:

- Knowledge of financial instruments.
- Long-term experience.
- Research capacity.
- Strategy development.
- Compatibility of the advisor's hedging strategies or techniques with the company's investment, financing, and hedging philosophy and goals.
- Reputation.
- Financial standing within the industry.
- Ability to execute transactions quickly and accurately.
- Integration with and responsiveness to the company's management information needs.
- Clarity and usefulness of reports received from third parties.
- Fees and margin requirements (if any).
- Reinvestment opportunities.

The policy document should be regularly updated to reflect the changing nature of the business and acceptable risks, and it should be formally approved by senior management.

It is often useful to supplement the policy with a more detailed manual outlining specific procedures needed to carry out the policy. These might cover steps required to identify positions, execute transactions, carry out the necessary administrative requirements, effect payments, and account for the transactions. This assigns responsibility and accountability, promotes consistent processes, provides a ready reference source, and is particularly helpful in periods of staff absence or turnover. It also provides a basis from which internal auditors can review adherence to the control standards.

Mechanisms are needed to exist to ensure that the policy and related procedures are properly carried out. For example, companies can set up limits regarding counterparties, but these are pointless unless the system for reporting breaches is effective and timely. The most sophisticated treasury functions, which have overnight and intraday limit-breach reports automatically produced, can lose the value of the control if reports are not reviewed immediately or if satisfactory explanations are not obtained. Where a company has numerous hedges entered into by a number of traders, the daily results of this activity should be independently checked, confirmed, and reconciled.

Further, procedures might require that counterparties be evaluated initially and monitored periodically thereafter by:

- Obtaining and reviewing current financial statements (at least annually and preferably quarterly).
- Requiring that such financial statements be audited (at least annually).
- Establishing standards for the financial statements (e.g., an unqualified audit opinion) and financial tests, including minimum net capital and leverage; this review should be documented and approved by the appropriate levels of management.
- Obtaining internal control letters or similar third-party reviews, if appropriate.
- Reviewing reports from business news services, analysts, and credit-rating agencies such as Moody's and Standard & Poor's.

There should be procedures requiring that changes to the list of authorized brokers and dealers and counterparties be approved in writing. There also should be procedures over the form of agreements for derivatives instruments and procedures related to collateral requirements, margins, and future-settling transactions, with the terms and rights of parties to these agreements clearly defined.

Additional matters that might be addressed in a procedures manual are set out in Table 18–3.

Most of the controls are self-evident, but it is remarkable that many companies have not addressed many of these matters. Weaknesses are particularly common regarding segregation of duties and the adequacy of third-party mandates.

TABLE 18–3
Common Control Activities

Segregation of Duties
- Between trading, funds transfer, accounting, and administration
- Between trade initiators and approvers
- Between operators and systems personnel

Reconciliations
- Bank confirmations to trade records
- Trade slips to accounting records
- Prenumbered trade slip sequence
- Bank account to accounting records

Authorization
- Opening new accounts
- Confirmation of trades
- Position taking
- System amendments
- New limits or counterparties
- Trade amendment

Checking and Review
- Authorized payees
- Systems access listings
- Loan documentation
- Trades performed in the day
- Bank mandates
- Limit monitoring

Segregation of duties: It is too common, even in larger companies, for staff who authorize trades also to transact them, and for staff who transfer funds to account for and report on them. Procedures should be established to effectively segregate duties among individuals responsible for:

- Making investment and credit decisions,
- Custody of securities and collateral,
- Disbursing and receiving funds,
- Record keeping,
- Confirmation of positions, and
- Performing reconciliations.

Adequacy of third-party mandates: Mandates should be issued to banks and other parties with which the derivatives function has a relationship. These are an important backstop in the case of a breakdown in established procedures and controls. Mandates should cover the names of treasury staff approved to trade, limits on trading activities, bank accounts to which funds can be transferred, and the names and positions of those authorized to sign trade confirmations and to whom the counterparty's confirmation letters should be sent. The wording of mandates is often imprecise and subject to misinterpretation. As with the policy statement, it is important that mandates with third parties be clear and unambiguous.

INFORMATION AND COMMUNICATION

Obtaining and transmitting information pertinent to derivatives activities is absolutely critical, from several perspectives.

First, personnel responsible for hedging operating risks must have timely information on business transactions giving rise to those risks. There should be open and clear communication channels from the various operating units, so that the nature and extent of risks can be analyzed, and relevant hedges can be effected.

Second, there must be comprehensive and up-to-date information on the marketplace for derivatives instruments and brokers, dealers, and other intermediaries and counterparties. This is dangerous terrain for the novice or the misinformed.

Third, information on derivatives transactions must be clearly communicated upstream to senior management. Reporting mechanisms must be clear and timely. Information should include the underlying operating risks and the extent to which the risks are matched. The degree of exposure due, for example, to changes in rates must be clearly laid out. This is often best accomplished through sensitivity analyses that cover any reasonably conceivable condition, even conditions that initially appear unlikely. Management does not want a surprise. Most executives are prepared to take business risks where they understand what the company is getting into. They don't appreciate being misinformed, or uninformed, of potentially large exposures.

Fourth, the flow of information must be ongoing, with timely updates. Risks and markets change quickly, and it is imperative that management responsible for assessing or hedging risks is informed of current conditions. If an initial decision was to "go naked" on a risk, that decision should be reassessed. If the risk was hedged or collateral was obtained, the value of the hedge and collateral should be remeasured. And there should be appropriate procedures for reacting to risk that has grown greater than the company wishes to bear.

Fifth, there must be not only the flow of relevant information, but also effective communication. Experienced managers recognize the difference. It is one thing to receive a written report with pertinent information. But it is quite another to be sure that the implications of that information are fully understood. Written reports on derivatives activities frequently need to include analysis and highlighting of particularly relevant data, and it is often important to supplement the written report with face-to-face presentations.

These communications must take place all the way to the board level. As noted, unless exposures are truly minimal, the board of directors should be apprised of how derivatives are used and of related exposures. In one well-publicized case, a company's directors suddenly became aware of huge derivatives exposures, and moved quickly to close out all positions, resulting in losses that brought the company to its knees. Later, the directors were accused of jumping the gun, failing to recognize that the derivatives instruments were proper hedges for underlying operating risks. While the facts have yet to be fully presented, one thing is clear: When a board is surprised, there is the potential for precipitous action.

Finally, there should be channels through which information coming from any of a variety of sources on significant and sensitive problems can flow upstream in an organization. Whether from a clerk in an accounting or operating department, or a broker/dealer or counterparty, the organization should have open channels and be receptive to signals that something might be amiss.

MONITORING

Any control system, particularly where it relates to activities as significant as derivatives, must be monitored to ensure it remains relevant and effective over time. Monitoring is effected in two ways: (1) through normal ongoing managing of a business and its activities, and (2) through separately focused evaluations.

Ongoing Monitoring

Management at all levels is alert to information indicating a potential problem. It is particularly important that management activities related to derivatives transactions or the underlying risks being hedged be alert for any sign indicating that the control system might not be working.

For example, managers should consider whether periodic trade reports show unexpected change in their nature, maturities, amounts, or counterparties; whether new operating risks might not be addressed; whether reports or communications become less frequent or from different sources; or whether explanations or analyses signal misinformation.

In this connection, it should be recognized that an unexpected *gain* from derivatives transactions is as significant as an unexpected loss in terms of its implications for the internal control system.

Managers should be alert to unusual questions or comments from personnel within the organization or from outside. A broker/dealer or counterparty inquiring about a trade or position might be communicating more than what initially meets the eye. Information from internal or external auditors might be telling.

Management must be alert and sensitive to information from these and other sources. While busy schedules are the norm, making it too easy to ignore a sign, it is truly important to pay attention to one's instincts and follow up on potential problems. When it comes to derivatives activities and their related risks, it is foolhardy not to do so.

Separate Evaluations

From time to time, it is important to have a more direct and thorough monitoring of the control system through a separate evaluation.

This involves an in-depth evaluation of each of the other four components—control environment, risk assessment, control activities, and information and communication. The continued applicability of the policies and procedures, relevance to the business's operating activities, and their effective operation should all be addressed.

This separate evaluation will usually involve a company's internal auditors, and is most effective when led by line management with knowledge of the underlying operating activities and risks that are the subject of derivatives transactions, as well as the derivatives activities themselves. It is of particular importance that identified control-weaknesses are addressed, not only the immediate symptom(s), but also the underlying cause. This information should be reported to responsible line managers and corrective action taken. There should be timely follow-up to ensure the needed changes are, in fact, put in place.

This discussion has been presented in the context of the five COSO components, in order to present the relevant control issues in the context of that control framework and common management processes. Related information is presented in the following tables.

Table 18–4 presents recommendations from the Global Derivatives Study Group (G-30) Report for dealers and end users of derivatives as well as for legislators, regulators, and supervisors of financial markets, and Table 18–5 presents a list of questions developed by the American Institute of Certified Public Accountants (AICPA).

TABLE 18–4
*Global Derivatives Study Group (G-30) Report
Recommendations for Dealers and End Users*

GENERAL POLICIES

Recommendation 1: The Role of Senior Management
Dealers and end users should use derivatives in a manner consistent with the overall risk management and capital policies approved by their boards of directors. These policies should be reviewed as business and market circumstances change. Policies governing derivatives use should be clearly defined, including the purposes for which these transactions are to be undertaken. Senior management should approve procedures and controls to implement these policies, and management at all levels should enforce them.

VALUATION AND MARKET-RISK MANAGEMENT

Recommendation 2: Marking to Market
Dealers should mark their derivatives positions to market, on at least a daily basis, for risk management purposes.

(continued on page 554)

(continued from page 553)

Recommendation 3: Market Valuation Methods

Derivatives portfolios of dealers should be valued based on mid-market levels less specific adjustments, or on appropriate bid or offer levels. Midmarket valuation adjustments should allow for expected future costs such as unearned credit spread, close-out costs, investing and funding costs, and administrative costs.

Recommendation 4: Identifying Revenue Sources

Dealers should measure the components of revenue regularly and in sufficient detail to understand the sources of risk.

Recommendation 5: Measuring Market Risk

Dealers should use a consistent measure to calculate daily the market risk of their derivatives positions and compare it to market risk limits.

- Market risk is best measured as "value at risk" using probability analysis based upon a common confidence interval (e.g., two standard deviations) and time horizon (e.g., a one-day exposure).
- Components of market risk that should be considered across the term structure include: absolute price or rate change (delta); convexity (gamma); volatility (vega); time decay (theta); basis or correlation; and discount rate (rho).

Recommendation 6: Stress Simulations

Dealers should regularly perform simulations to determine how their portfolios would perform under stress conditions.

Recommendation 7: Investing and Funding Forecasts

Dealers should periodically forecast the cash investing and funding requirements arising from their derivatives portfolios.

Recommendation 8: Independent Market-Risk Management

Dealers should have a market-risk management function, with clear independence and authority, to ensure that the following responsibilities are carried out:

- The development of risk limit policies and the monitoring of transactions and positions for adherence to these policies. (See Recommendation 5.)
- The design of stress scenarios to measure the impact of market conditions, however improbable, that might cause market gaps, volatility swings, or disruptions of major relationships, or might reduce liquidity in the face of unfavorable market linkages, concentrated market making, or credit exhaustion. (See Recommendation 6.)

- The design of revenue reports quantifying the contribution of various risk components, and of market-risk measures such as value at risk. (See Recommendations 4 and 5.)
- The monitoring of variance between the actual volatility of portfolio value and that predicted by the measure of market risk.
- The review and approval of pricing models and valuation systems used by front- and back-office personnel, and the development of reconciliation procedures if different systems are used.

Recommendation 9: Practices by End Users

As appropriate to the nature, size, and complexity of their derivatives activities, end users should adopt the same valuation and market-risk management practices that are recommended for dealers. Specifically, they should consider: regularly marking to market their derivatives transactions for risk-management purposes; periodically forecasting the cash investing and funding requirements arising from their derivatives transactions; and establishing a clearly independent and authoritative function to design and assure adherence to prudent risk limits.

CREDIT RISK MEASUREMENT AND MANAGEMENT

Recommendation 10: Measuring Credit Exposure

Dealers and end users should measure credit exposure on derivatives in two ways:

- Current exposure, which is the replacement cost of derivatives transactions, that is, their market value, and
- Potential exposure, which is an estimate of the future replacement cost of derivatives transactions. It should be calculated using probability analysis based upon broad confidence intervals (e.g., two standard deviations) over the remaining terms of the transactions.

Recommendation 11: Aggregating Credit Exposures

Credit exposures on derivatives, and all other credit exposures to a counterparty, should be aggregated taking into consideration enforceable netting arrangements. Credit exposures should be calculated regularly and compared to credit limits.

Recommendation 12: Independent Credit Risk Management

Dealers and end users should have a credit risk management function with clear independence and authority, and with analytical capabilities in derivatives, responsible for:

- Approving credit exposure measurement standards.
- Setting credit limits and monitoring their use.
- Reviewing credits and concentrations of credit risk.
- Reviewing and monitoring risk-reduction arrangements.

(continued on page 556)

(continued from page 555)

Recommendation 13: Master Agreements

Dealers and end users are encouraged to use one master agreement as widely as possible with each counterparty to document existing and future derivatives transactions, including foreign-exchange forwards and options. Master agreements should provide for payments netting and close-out netting, using a full two-way payments approach.

Recommendation 14: Credit Enhancement

Dealers and end users should assess both the benefits and costs of credit enhancement and related risk-reduction arrangements. Where it is proposed that credit downgrades would trigger early termination or collateral requirements, participants should carefully consider their own capacity and that of their counterparties to meet the potentially substantial funding needs that might result.

ENFORCEABILITY

Recommendation 15: Promoting Enforceability

Dealers and end users should work together on a continuing basis to identify and recommend solutions for issues of legal enforceability, both within and across jurisdictions, as activities evolve and new types of transactions are developed.

SYSTEMS, OPERATIONS, AND CONTROLS

Recommendation 16: Professional Expertise

Dealers and end users must ensure that their derivatives activities are undertaken by professionals in sufficient number and with the appropriate experience, skill levels, and degrees of specialization. These professionals include specialists who transact and manage the risks involved, their supervisors, and those responsible for processing, reporting, controlling, and auditing the activities.

Recommendation 17: Systems

Dealers and end users must ensure that adequate systems for data capture, processing, settlement, and management reporting are in place so that derivatives transactions are conducted in an orderly and efficient manner in compliance with management policies. Dealers should have risk-management systems that measure the risks incurred in their derivatives activities including market and credit risks. End users should have risk-management systems that measure the risks incurred in their derivatives activities based upon their nature, size, and complexity.

Recommendation 18: Authority

Management of dealers and end users should designate who is authorized to commit their institutions to derivatives transactions.

ACCOUNTING AND DISCLOSURE

Recommendation 19: Accounting Practices

International harmonization of accounting standards for derivatives is desirable. Pending the adoption of harmonized standards, the following accounting practices are recommended:

- Dealers should account for derivatives transactions by marking them to market, taking changes in value to income each period.
- End users should account for derivatives used to manage risks so as to achieve a consistency of income recognition treatment between those instruments and the risks being managed. Thus, if the risk being managed is accounted for at cost (or, in the case of an anticipatory hedge, not yet recognized), changes in the value of a qualifying risk-management instrument should be deferred until a gain or loss is recognized on the risk being managed. Or, if the risk being managed is marked to market with changes in value being taken to income, a qualifying risk-management instrument should be treated in a comparable fashion.
- End users should account for derivatives not qualifying for risk-management treatment on a mark-to-market basis.
- Amounts due to and from counterparties should only be offset when there is a legal right to set off or when enforceable netting arrangements are in place.
- Where local regulations prevent adoption of these practices, disclosure along these lines is nevertheless recommended.

Recommendation 20: Disclosures

Financial statements of dealers and end users should contain sufficient information about their use of derivatives to provide an understanding of the purposes for which transactions are undertaken, the extent of the transactions, the degree of risk involved, and how the transactions have been accounted for. Pending the adoption of harmonized accounting standards, the following disclosures are recommended:

- Information about management's attitude to financial risks, how instruments are used, and how risks are monitored and controlled.
- Accounting policies.
- Analysis of positions at the balance-sheet date.
- Analysis of the credit risk inherent in those positions.
- For dealers only, additional information about the extent of their activities in financial instruments.

(continued on page 558)

(concluded from page 557)

RECOMMENDATIONS FOR LEGISLATORS, REGULATORS, AND SUPERVISORS

Recommendation 21: Recognizing Netting

Regulators and supervisors should recognize the benefits of netting arrangements where and to the full extent that they are enforceable, and encourage their use by reflecting these arrangements in capital adequacy standards. Specifically, they should promptly implement the recognition of the effectiveness of bilateral close-out netting in bank capital regulations.

Recommendation 22: Legal and Regulatory Uncertainties

Legislators, regulators, and supervisors, including central banks, should work in concert with dealers and end users to identify and remove any remaining legal and regulatory uncertainties with respect to:

- The form of documentation required to create legally enforceable agreements (statute of frauds).
- The capacity of parties, such as governmental entities, insurance companies, pension funds, and building societies, to enter into transactions (ultra vires).
- The enforceability of bilateral close-out netting and collateral arrangements in bankruptcy.
- The enforceability of multibranch netting arrangements in bankruptcy.
- The legality/enforceability of derivatives transactions.

Recommendation 23: Tax Treatment

Legislators and tax authorities are encouraged to review and, where appropriate, amend tax laws and regulations that disadvantage the use of derivatives in risk-management strategies. Tax impediments include the inconsistent or uncertain tax treatment of gains and losses on the derivatives, in comparison with the gains and losses that arise from the risks being managed.

Recommendation 24: Accounting Standards

Accounting standards-setting bodies in each country should, as a matter of priority, provide comprehensive guidance on accounting and reporting of transactions in financial instruments, including derivatives, and should work toward international harmonization of standards on this subject. Also, the International Accounting Standards Committee should finalize its accounting standard on financial instruments.

Source: *Derivatives: Practices and Principles,* The Group of Thirty, 1993.

TABLE 18–5
Questions About Derivatives (AICPA)

The AICPA has developed the following specific questions about derivatives activities to help top management and boards of directors of all types of enterprises gain a better understanding of their entities' derivatives activities:

---

1. Has the board established a clear and internally consistent risk-management policy, including risk limits (as appropriate)?
   - Are our objectives and goals for derivatives activities clearly stated and communicated?
   - To what extent are our operational objectives for derivatives being achieved?
   - Are derivatives used to mitigate risk or do they create additional risk?
   - If risk is being assumed, are trading limits established?
   - Is the entity's strategy for derivatives use designed to further its economic, regulatory, industry, and/or operating objectives?

---

2. Are management's strategies and implementation policies consistent with the board's authorization?
   - Management's philosophy and operating style create an environment that influences the actions of treasury and other personnel involved in derivatives activities. The assignment of authority and responsibility for derivatives transactions sends an important message. Is that message clear?
   - Is compliance with these or related policies and procedures evaluated regularly?
   - Does the treasury function view itself, or is it evaluated, as a profit center?

---

3. Do key controls exist to ensure that only authorized transactions take place and that unauthorized transactions are quickly detected and appropriate action is taken?
   - Internal controls over derivatives activities should be monitored on an ongoing basis, and should also be subject to separate evaluations. Who is evaluating controls over derivatives activities?
   - Do they bring the appropriate technical expertise to bear?
   - Are deficiencies being identified and reported upstream?
   - Are duties involving execution of derivatives transactions segregated from other duties (for example, the accounting and internal audit functions)?

---

4. Are the magnitude, complexity and risks of the entity's derivatives commensurate with the entity's objectives?

(continued on page 560)

(continued from page 559)

- What are the entity's risk exposures, including derivatives? Internal analyses should include quantitative and qualitative information about the entity's derivatives activities. Analyses should address the risks associated with derivatives, which include:
  - —Credit risk (the possible financial loss resulting from a counterparty's failure to meet its financial obligations)
  - —Market risk (the possible financial loss resulting from adverse movements in the price of a financial asset or commodity)
  - —Legal risk (the possible financial loss resulting from a legal or regulatory action that could invalidate a financial contract)
  - —Control risk (the possible financial loss resulting from inadequate internal control structure)
- Are our derivatives transactions standard for their class (that is, plain vanilla) or are they more complex?
- Is the complexity of derivatives transactions inconsistent with the risks being managed?
- The entity's risk assessment should result in a *determination about how to manage identified risks* of derivatives activities. Has management anticipated how it will manage potential derivatives risks before assuming them?

---

5. Are personnel with authority to engage in and monitor derivative transactions well qualified and appropriately trained?
   - Who are the key derivatives players within the entity?
   - Is the knowledge vested only in one individual or a small group?
   - The complexity of derivatives activities should be accompanied by development of personnel. For example, do employees involved in derivatives activities have the appropriate technical and professional expertise?
   - Are other employees being appropriately educated before they become involved with derivatives transactions?
   - Does the entity have personnel who have been cross-trained in case of the absence or departure of key personnel involved with derivatives activities?
   - How do we ensure the integrity, ethical values, and competence of personnel involved with derivatives activities?

---

6. Do the right people have the right information to make decisions?
   - What information about derivatives activities are we identifying and capturing, and how is it being communicated?

- The information should address both external and internal events, activities and conditions. For example, are we capturing and communicating information about market changes affecting derivatives transactions and about changes in our strategy for the mix of assets and liabilities that are the focus of risk-management activities involving derivatives?
- Is this information being communicated to all affected parties?
- Are the analysis and internal reporting of risks the company is managing and the effectiveness of its strategies comprehensive, reliable, and well-designed to facilitate oversight?
- The board should consider derivatives activities in the context of how related risks affect the achievement of the entity's objectives—economic, regulatory, industry, or operating. For example, do derivatives activities increase the entity's exposure to risks that might frustrate, rather than further, achievement of these objectives?
- Do we mark our derivatives transactions to market regularly (and, if not, why not)?
- Do we have good systems for marking transactions to market?
- Have the systems been tested by persons independent of the derivatives function?
- Do we know how the value of our derivatives will change under extreme market conditions?
- Is our published financial information about derivatives being prepared reliably and in conformity with generally accepted accounting principles?

Source: *The CPA Letter*, AICPA, July/August 1994.

Chapter Nineteen

Systems to Manage Risk

Colin Southall
Managing Consultant
Ernst & Young

If you can make one heap of all your winnings
And risk it on one turn of pitch-and-toss
And lose, and start again . . .

—Rudyard Kipling, "If"

INTRODUCTION

This chapter provides a guide to the definition of systems architectures for risk management, which can be used as the basis for migration planning when developing a custom-made system, or selecting and implementing a package from an external vendor. In both cases what is needed is a specification of the business and technical requirements that the system must satisfy and a definition of the target systems architecture that can be used as the basis for evaluating the various options available.

There is great competition between system vendors to claim support for risk-management functionality but these packages often meet only part of most users' requirements. An alternative, extending existing management information system (MIS) functionality, also fails to meet users' needs because of the difficulty of obtaining the required source data.

The need to understand how risk-management systems interface and interact with other systems is the key to successful implementation since, unlike product-based trading systems, they perform a task that crosses the normal organization product boundaries and provide a consolidated view of the business. The definition of a target system architecture makes these boundaries explicit and guides the migration-planning exercise required to implement the system. A clearly defined methodology will provide the structure needed to plan and manage this complex process.

ENVIRONMENT

In order to define a target system architecture that can be used to evaluate vendor packages or guide the development of custom-made systems, an organization must understand what the pressures for change are, how they arise, and how they affect the business.

Business Pressures

It is increasingly important for organizations to identify, quantify, and manage their financial risks. As organizations employ more-complex investment strategies, this need increases and the justification for risk-management systems becomes more prevalent. The following business pressures are fueling this trend:

- **Regulators and Market Practice**
  Regulators are looking more closely at capital adequacy requirements, given their concerns about capital preservation in financial organizations. The implementation of the Capital Adequacy Directive in Europe is intended to provide better accounting for the risks associated with derivative products in setting the capital requirements for these organizations.

  The G-30 Report on derivatives, published in 1993, provides a comprehensive survey of the risk-management practices in banks on market risk, credit risk, and management issues. The recommendations made in the G-30 Report have been used as a benchmark to evaluate organizations and as a guide for future actions. In particular, the report highlights the need to establish a culture of control in any institution utilizing derivatives in their investment and hedging strategies.

- **Rating Agencies**
  In 1985 there were 16 AAA-rated banks. Now there are three. The

need to remain attractive to counterparties and to reduce the cost
of funds has led to the establishment of several derivative product
companies that have enhanced capital backing to cover credit
risks. These organizations require sophisticated credit risk-management and modeling systems that use Monte Carlo simulation to
determine capital requirements at the end of each day. The target
is to achieve and maintain a AAA rating.

The models are defined by each organization but are reviewed
with the rating agencies in order to gain initial rating agency approval and are independently audited each month in order to retain
this approval.

Given that the rating agencies can move more quickly than the
regulators, they now assume a greater prominence in determining
the risk-management strategies that are adopted within an organization.

- **Clients/Counterparties**
  The drive to win and retain client business leads an organization
  to seek better product pricing and the ability to offer a wider
  range of products, often specifically tailored to meet client needs.
  In this competitive environment it is important to have an accurate
  view of the organization's exposure to the client and to be able to
  offset this against client assets by managing collateral or making
  margin calls.

  From the clients' side it is important to find a counterparty that
  understands their needs, that can structure products that are suitable for their business, that mitigates the risks to which they are
  exposed in the normal course of business, and that charges a competitive price for this service.

- **Internal Pressures**
  Within an organization there are competing pressures, such as:

  — The need to *allocate capital* to business units in order to
    achieve the highest returns commensurate with the perceived
    risks.

  — The need to *reward traders* for the business that has been
    won, taking into account the capital used and the risks associ-
    ated with this business.

  — The need to *manage positions* in order to offset market risks in
    the most efficient manner and at least cost.

The organization's goals will determine how these needs are reconciled but, whatever the balance struck, there is an underlying need for systems to monitor the implementation of the policies that are defined.

Implications of Increasing Pressure

Two distinct types of organization are considered here:

- *Banks*, whose business is to deal in exchange-traded derivative products, to create OTC products, and to price and manage these products over the life of the contract. For the banks there are two activities that must be covered: taking on risk through trading and writing OTC contracts, and managing the market and credit risk of the resulting portfolio.
- *Corporates*, which are organizations that use derivative products to offset the risks of carrying out their core business activities but which themselves are not traders of derivative products. The prime need of the corporates is to monitor the performance of the contracts that have been entered into against the underlying business that has been hedged.

The business pressures discussed above affect corporates differently from banks.

Corporates are regulated by company law and the application of accounting standards and will be monitored by the rating agencies and analysts. It is the latter who will apply most pressure to the organization if financial performance is low, excessive trading of derivatives is performed, or inappropriate strategies are adopted to cover normal business risks. Downgrading a company's rating makes the company less attractive as a counterparty and so drives up the cost of new contracts. Internal pressures, especially to enhance performance, can lead to a drive to trade derivatives rather than use them as a hedge for business risks. This can work in the short term but, without good internal controls and the necessary systems to monitor performance, is likely to lead to losses in the longer term.

For banks the implications are threefold:

- They will be forced to move to provide more exotic products as margins on vanilla contracts are traded away through increased competition. This means that their systems will become increasingly complex and the possibility of manual computation will be greatly reduced, forcing greater reliance on these systems.

- A product traded by one department will be used as a hedge by other departments to manage their positions. Banks will see pressure to combine all product-processing onto common systems, with trading and position management being handled by business-aligned front-office systems. In practice this leads to complex risk-management systems that must cross organizational boundaries.

- Risk and return calculations will be required for each trade, for the overnight position and for monthly reviews. This information will span all of the business performed by a bank and will be provided in various forms to traders as well as to senior management in order to enable them to meet regulatory and rating agency requirements, allocate capital, and determine the level of trader remuneration.

Together these implications indicate a need for analysis of data concerning all trading activity on a corporate basis and a need for the realignment of front- and back-office systems on a business and product basis, respectively.

USAGE PROFILES

It is useful to be able to identify the requirements that categories of users have of the systems that they use in the normal course of business. Four general categories of user requirements for risk-management systems are shown in Figure 19–1.

Activity Processing

Activity processing can be characterized as providing support for a defined sequence of activities that must be performed in order to complete some business process, for example, trader entry of deal information. The main requirements are that:

- The system should support the user through the completion of the process, e.g., by prompting for missing mandatory information.
- The user interface should be efficient, e.g., by minimizing the number of keystrokes or mouse clicks that are required to complete the activity.

FIGURE 19–1
Usage Profiles

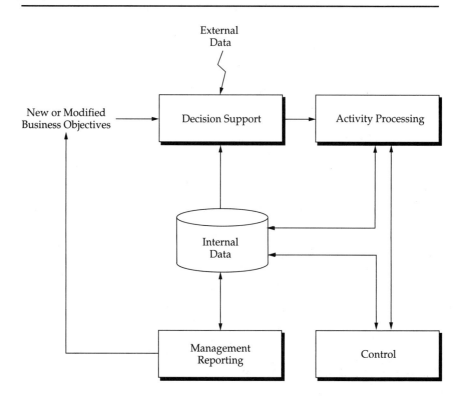

• The system should be able to verify the correctness of the information provided and guide the user in making any required modifications.

Decision Support

Decision-support requirements are more demanding than those for activity processing. The difference lies in the fact that additional information is required to make the decision, and the analysis of this information will not always proceed using the same sequence of steps each time.

For example, pricing a product requires different information and analysis than identifying a suitable hedge for a selected trader's portfolio. Though each is a defined business process, the information required to perform the analysis and the processing required to complete the analysis are more complex than for normal activity processing.

Control

Market-risk limits and credit-risk limits must be set and monitored by the system in order to enforce the defined risk-management policies. Users who modify system controls have a distinct set of requirements:

- They must be able to define and set limits in order to effect the chosen risk-management policies.
- The system must provide adequate security to ensure that these limits cannot be altered or circumvented by unauthorized users.
- The system must monitor business activity against these limits and provide management with warnings of exceptions at the time that they occur. The activity processing aspects of the system will ensure that checks against limits are performed and that exposures are updated as required.

Management Reporting

Senior management and desk heads will use the system in order to review past activity and identify trends that may require changes to the limits that are currently in place. These requirements are similar to the decision support requirements except that they can be performed using precomputed data. Two distinct types of activity must be supported:

- Generation of standard management reports at the end of the day, which will be distributed in paper or electronic form to management.
- Ad hoc queries, which will be used to analyze trading anomalies and changes in market behavior.

ORGANIZATIONAL STRUCTURE

There are many users of risk-management information within an organization. Each has differing needs for this data, which depend on their role and responsibilities. These issues are discussed more fully in Chapter 17 on operations risks.

Bank Organization

Banks typically have a product-based divisional structure with a separate proprietary trading desk covering all products (Figure 19–2). A separate risk-management group monitors overall exposure and reports to senior management, with a credit-risk-management group responsible for counterparty evaluation and credit limit monitoring.

- **Sales**

  Sales staff sell products from stock to new and existing clients. Client requests that cannot be filled from stock are routed to traders for execution. Sales staff require information on stock holdings, clients, and current market activity.

  There is minimal need for risk-management information at this level in the organization, provided that no trading is performed. There is, however, an increasing need for sales staff to ensure that clients buy products that are appropriate to their needs and that they understand the risks that are involved. Sales staff must therefore have a good understanding of risk management.

- **Traders**

  Traders execute client orders and also trade in their own account in one or more markets. Traders can either work in a specified market, e.g., foreign exchange, or can be part of a proprietary trading desk that can trade in any product for the bank's account. Traders need product analytics and pricing algorithms that are responsive to market changes, the ability to identify appropriate hedges for their portfolio, and the ability to execute these trades.

- **Market-Risk Management**

  The market-risk-management group should be independent of the traders and it should report to senior management. This group has the responsibility of assuring senior management that market risks have been properly identified, measured, managed, and priced.

FIGURE 19–2
Bank Organization

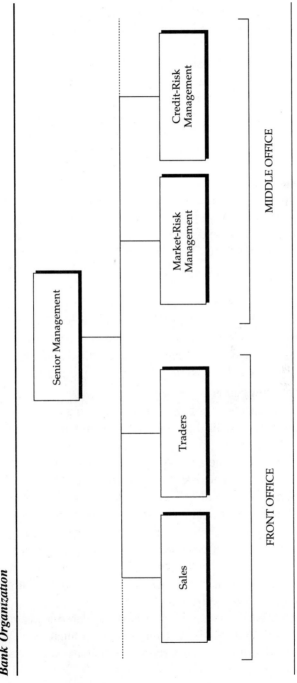

This can lead to tension within the organization, since the group's independence may be compromised by their interrelation with the front office.

This group must define risk limits, set and monitor policy in the risk-management area, develop disaster scenarios and stress test trading portfolios, review and approve new pricing and risk-management models, and review new products. This activity results in revisions to the control aspects of the systems used by traders as well as the need to generate management reports.

- **Credit-Risk Management**

  The credit-risk-management group is responsible for evaluating counterparty credit ratings and for establishing the credit limits for each counterparty and market sector along with other credit limits that may be required. The credit-risk-management group may also have responsibility for monitoring collateral and for tracking the status of legal documentation.

  The credit-risk-management group will provide regular reports to senior management on current limits, utilization of these limits, and exceptions. Changes in credit policy determined by senior management will be fed back to the credit-risk-management group, who are responsible for adjusting the limits accordingly.

- **Senior Management**

  Senior management is responsible for setting policy, for monitoring compliance with the policy, and for monitoring the organization's performance.

  Senior management must be able to identify the type and magnitude of the market risks that have been taken by the bank and to understand the size of the possible losses that might be incurred in normal and exceptional circumstances. Since senior management requires a consistent view across all areas of the business, this information is often provided using value-at-risk measures. On the credit-risk side the need is for senior management to have information on limits, utilization of these limits, and a list of the exceptions that have occurred.

  Overall performance is often now measured using risk-adjusted measures such as RAROC, which allow comparisons of performance between different parts of the business to be made and give

FIGURE 19–3
Corporate Organization

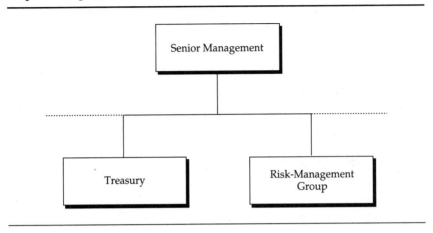

assistance when making capital allocation decisions or setting hurdle rates.

Corporate Organization

Corporates typically have a treasury operation and some form of risk-management group that oversees its activities (Figure 19–3). The organization can obviously become much more complex than shown here, as for example with large multinationals, e.g., oil majors, where trading as well as finance are key elements of the business.

- **Treasury**
  The treasury is expected to fund operations at the lowest cost and risk to the business. There are four parts to this activity:
- Managing cash flow to enable the business to meet its liabilities when they fall due;
- Funding for fixed-asset and working capital;
- Investment of surplus funds; and
- Management of interest-rate risk and currency exposures.

These activities cover all four types of usage profile as treasury staff evaluate funding and investment opportunities (decision support), enter contract details (activity processing), report to senior management, and monitor controls.

- **Risk-Management Group**

  The risk-management group in a corporate is likely to focus more on establishing and operating controls than on the complex evaluation of market and credit risks. At a minimum, the risk-management group should clearly identify who can enter into contracts and the type of contacts that the authority covers, e.g., do not allow historical price rollovers of forward contracts. The risk-management group must also set limits and monitor exposures against these limits, and periodically test the effectiveness of the controls that have been established.

  Most of the larger losses in the derivatives market have been incurred by end users where the lack of these fundamental controls has been a recurrent theme, for example, the losses incurred on oil contracts by Metallgesellschaft's U.S. subsidiary in 1993.

- **Senior Management**

  Corporate senior management requires summary information from the risk-management group that states the limits that have been defined, exposures against these limits, and an evaluation of the controls that have been established. They will also require information on the current position for all contracts.

BUSINESS REQUIREMENTS

The business requirements must define:

- The system scope in terms of the organization units and business activities that must be supported;
- The business processes that must be supported by the target system; and
- The critical success factors (aspects of the business that must be improved) and the associated key performance indicators (metrics that can be used to measure the level of support for each critical success factor).

Risk management, in common with most business activity, can be viewed as having a mix of business process, organization structure, and staff skills requirements that must be balanced against the organization's capabilities in each area. The business process requirements can be divided into four components:

- *Market risk* of current positions, which covers sensitivity to market movements (components of risk), exposures to market movements (value at risk [VAR]), and limit management.
- *Credit risk,* which covers counterparty exposures, collateral management, and credit-limit management.
- *Operations risk,* which covers errors and omissions within the organization in the execution and settlement of a contract.
- *Performance measurement,* which provides a measure of the risk-adjusted return made on the capital employed (RAROC) or on the value at risk (RORAC).

These are further described below.

Obviously, not all requirements will need to be considered in all organizations since existing systems will provide adequate coverage in many cases. These requirements form one element of the evaluation criteria that should be considered when choosing between alternative solutions. Three other aspects that should also be considered are: (1) the technical basis for the solution and the fit with the organization's existing technical infrastructure; (2) the ability of the supplier to implement the proposed solution and, following this, to provide the required level of operations support; and (3) the cost of the proposed solution.

Market Risk

Four aspects of market risk should be considered:

- *Sensitivity* to market movements can be measured in several ways, e.g., absolute price or rate change (delta), convexity (gamma), and volatility (vega). These measures are calculated for individual trades and for portfolios of trades by traders and risk-management staff to monitor and manage their positions. This is categorized as decision support access.
- *Exposure* to market movements is often measured using a value-

at-risk (VAR) approach. This represents the possible loss to the organization based on the following assumptions:

— The expected period for which the position is held;

— The expected volatility of the market; and

— The confidence level associated with the loss, i.e., the frequency with which this level of loss is expected.

VAR calculations require that each element of risk be aggregated and that correlations between these categories be taken into account. For example, USD- and DEM-denominated cash flows are aggregated to form two separate positions. The overall exposure, taking correlation into account, will normally be lower than the simple sum of the two positions.

For positions with limited optionality, Markowitz models provide a fast method of calculating VAR under normal market conditions once the initial positions have been identified. Alternatively, Monte Carlo simulation, which uses probabilities and a large number of randomly generated market scenarios, can be used to identify the distribution of possible outcomes. This is a much more computationally intensive process than the use of Markowitz models.

This information is used by traders and risk-management staff and reported to senior management. The former require decision support access, i.e., on-line calculation, while the latter require management reporting access to end-of-day information.

• *Stress testing* is performed to determine how positions are affected by extreme market movements. In contrast, VAR calculations show expected losses based on historical trends for the market. A range of scenarios can be constructed that consider abnormal price movements coupled with longer holding periods. These scenarios can be run against the current positions and the resulting losses calculated using simulation techniques.

This information is used by risk-management staff, who require decision support access, and reported to senior management, who require management reporting access.

• *Limits* can be set against a range of market risk measures, and stop loss limits can be set against trader P&L. In all cases the current or proposed position will be measured against these limits by the system. This is handled for traders by making these checks an integral part of the activity processing access, and for risk-management staff by providing them with control access to set and modify limits. Risk-management staff and senior management also require management reporting access to review current exposures against the limits that have been set.

Credit Risk

Among the range of credit-risk requirements are the following:

- Calculation of the *current exposure* to a counterparty by summing the mark-to-market value of all contracts that show a profit for the firm.
- Calculation of the *potential exposure* to a counterparty to identify the maximum loss that might be expected for all contracts with the counterparty—calculation of the potential exposure requires the use of statistical models.
- *Limits* can be set for each counterparty for both current exposure and potential exposure. The limits will be set by credit-risk-management staff and will be used and viewed by traders, risk-management staff, and senior management.

Other aspects of credit-risk management that should be considered are the management of *collateral* and the management of *contract documentation*, in particular the tracking of netting arrangements. Both of these functions will be handled by risk-management staff and reported to senior management.

Operations Risk

This covers the cost of failure by the organization through error or omission to perform any of the tasks associated with the management of contracts during their life. Factors that could be considered include staff fraud as well as the ability of the business to continue in operation following natural disaster.

Management of operations risk requires that exceptions to the expected order of processing be reported to management—e.g., missed payments, payments directed to the wrong counterparty, and incorrect contract details sent to a counterparty. It is management's responsibility to ensure that remedial actions are taken to correct these errors.

Performance Measurement

This provides a measure of the return made on a position that has been adjusted for the risks inherent in the position. There are two broad categories of performance measure:

- The risk-adjusted return on the capital employed (RAROC) measures the return made above the risk-free rate on the capital employed, which covers market risks, credit risks, and operational risks. This measure can be used as the basis for determining the level of capital allocated to business units.
- The return on risk-adjusted capital (RORAC) measures the return made on the capital at risk and so provides a hurdle rate that business units are supposed to match or exceed.

These measures are normally provided on a daily basis to risk-management staff and to senior management using management reporting access.

SYSTEM ARCHITECTURE

The main stumbling block in building large systems is our ability to deal with complexity. Methods for reducing the level of complexity that must be mastered in order to define a system or an element of a system have been studied for many years. The current focus is on the use of modules that encapsulate processing and data and that have clearly defined interfaces.

A key property of any system is its internal structure. A good structure makes the system easier to understand and maintain, and enables the system to be extended to cater for new requirements without undue effort. "Good" has two dimensions: the system must support a model of the business that matches users' expectations; and the system must have an internal structure that reduces dependencies between different elements of the system, hides complexity, and is based on the use of appropriate technologies.

Architecture in this context becomes the specification of the concepts and techniques that define the characteristics of all systems that can be created using these concepts and techniques. An architecture methodology consists of:

FIGURE 19–4
Architecture Process

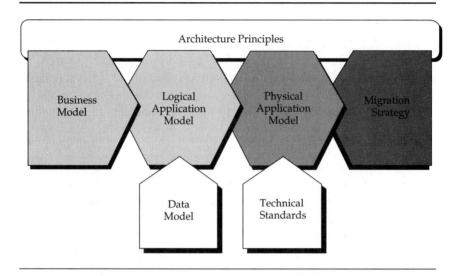

- The specification of the defining characteristics of the approach, e.g., the use of modules;
- The specification of the deliverables and their notations, which are used to define a system that supports these architectural principles; and
- The specification of the processes that can be used to develop these deliverables. Process definitions must be provided for each of the steps involved and also for the overall sequence of steps.

One view of the system architecture process (Figure 19–4) is that it consists of building a number of models that move from the purely business-process view of the requirements to a definition of the modules that must be implemented to support these business requirements and the technical infrastructure that supports these modules. All stages in this process should adhere to a defined set of architecture principles, to a corporate data model, and to corporate technical standards.

- The *business model* defines the business processes that must be supported by the system and identifies the external entities (users of the system and other systems) with which the system must interact. This model defines the system scope and the business requirements that must be satisfied.

- The *logical application model* defines the services that must be provided to implement the required business model and the grouping of services to form modules. This represents the transformation from a business-process view to a modular view. Services are defined by specifying the inputs and outputs of each service and the operations that must be performed. Modules are defined by listing the services provided by each module. The *data model* defines the service parameters and their associated business rules.

- The *physical application model* transforms the logical application model, taking into account implementation constraints such as bandwidth and processing power. The specification of the system is still in terms of the services provided and the grouping of services to form modules, though the groupings may differ or new modules may be defined because of the constraints that have been imposed. The *technical standards* define the environment in which the system will be implemented and the technologies that can be used.

- Implementation of the system will proceed in a number of steps in all but the simplest of cases. Together the sequence of steps makes up the *migration strategy* to be followed. Each step in the migration strategy can be considered to be a separate project that consists of the analysis, design, coding, and testing effort required to implement the specified modules of the physical application model.

The process is iterative. Decisions made—for example, in the definition of the physical application model—may result in changes being made to the business model as a better understanding of the business requirements and technical constraints is obtained.

Business requirements have been outlined in earlier sections of this chapter. The next section discusses technical issues facing risk-management systems and describes three system architectures that could be adopted for implementing these systems, based on the location of processing, data storage, and display functions. Some of the benefits and disadvantages of each approach are also discussed. The important thing to remember is that an ideal architecture does not exist; a range of options should be evaluated and an appropriate solution chosen. In almost all cases an organization is starting from a position where investment in current technology cannot be abandoned. The cost of change is an important factor in the selection of an appropriate migration strategy as are the availability of required staff skills and the impact of change on existing applications.

SYSTEM ISSUES

Business pressures, organization constraints, and business requirements must all be satisfied by risk-management systems. The main system issues for source data (input), processing, and reporting (output) are discussed below.

The overriding system issues are:

- *Connectivity*: the ability to obtain data, perform calculations, and access results using a mix of new and legacy systems.
- *Scalability*: the ability to expand the system to meet increased demand, e.g., to provide more frequent or more complex processing, to hold more detailed data for a wider range of business activities, or to extend access to reports to users in new departments or geographic locations.
- *Flexibility*: the ability to cope with changes in the format and location of input data, modifications to processing algorithms, or the adoption of new report layouts.

These issues are often associated with management information systems, where the need to cross organizational boundaries makes system integration and data access key requirements. The added twist for risk-management systems is the need to provide real-time response and to support the complexity of the modeling algorithms that are employed.

Input

Some of the main issues concerning data acquisition for risk-management systems are:

- *Availability*: the required source data must be identified and suitable access mechanisms provided. Data can be obtained from internal systems as well as from external vendors. In some cases the required data will not exist or will not have the required quality. This leads to the requirement for establishing a system to collect, process, and maintain the needed data, which can then be made available to the risk-management system.

- *Consistency and completeness*: all source data must be complete, otherwise later processing may not be possible. In some circumstances it may be possible to estimate suitable values for the missing data to complete an inferred series. The data must also be consistent: values should be normalized to use the same units and static data, such as counterparty identifiers and currency codes. These should be converted to a standard form, e.g., ISO currency code. In many cases the normalization of static data is a task that requires the often difficult implementation of agreement and roll-out of corporate standards and systems to enforce these standards, e.g., the establishment of a central counterparty register.

- *Timeliness*: data must be available in a timely manner, which will depend on the nature of the processing being performed and on the way in which the results are used. End-of-day prices can be used with overnight processes, which generate position reports for use the following day. Exposures, on the other hand, must be updated at the time that trade information is entered into the system.

- *Quality*: data quality may be an issue; for example, default rates obtained from a rating agency may have missing data items, may not match the organization's requirements closely enough, or may not provide adequate coverage. In these cases it may be necessary to identify a second source for the missing or invalid data that can be used to complete the dataset or to build the required dataset based on data collected from a number of internal and external sources.

- *Cost*: the cost of subscribing to an external data source or providing a connection to an internal system may mitigate against its use. Shared access to source data may be a feasible way of managing this.

- *Access*: data access mechanisms must be identified that limit the number and complexity of the interfaces that must be supported. The cost of constructing and maintaining interface handlers is particularly high. Standard interfaces and access mechanisms for all internal systems are highly desirable as a way of minimizing these costs. External vendors have specialized interfaces that can be hidden by the use of a common data distribution infrastructure that provides a standard interface for user applications.

Processing

Two important issues to consider for processing are:

- Where the processing is to be performed; and
- When the processing is to be performed.

Processing can be performed centrally, on a user's work station, or on one or more servers. The location chosen depends on the existing systems infrastructure and on the needs of the users involved. Processing can be initiated by a user request or can be a timed event that occurs, for example, at the end of each working day. Three possible configurations (centralized processing, work stations, and servers) are discussed below.

- **Centralized Processing**
  A fully centralized system by definition holds all corporate data and perform all processing at a central site on a single system, with the results being made available to users who are either directly connected or who have local or remote access to the system (Figure 19–5).
  The advantage with this approach is that there is a single corporate-data store that holds all information required to support the risk-management requirements. The disadvantages are that the system is not easily scalable, and it is likely that modifications to programs and to the database are complex undertakings.
- **Distributed Processing (Work Station)**
  Distributed systems break the constraint of having a single unit for data and processing. One example of a distributed system (Figure 19–6) is where data is held on multiple systems and all processing is performed on the user's work station, where the results can be viewed.
  The advantages of this approach are that the system is scalable and dependencies between applications are reduced, i.e., the system is more modular. The disadvantages are that the work stations may not be capable of running the required applications, data transfer volumes across the network may prove to be unacceptably

FIGURE 19–5
Centralized Processing

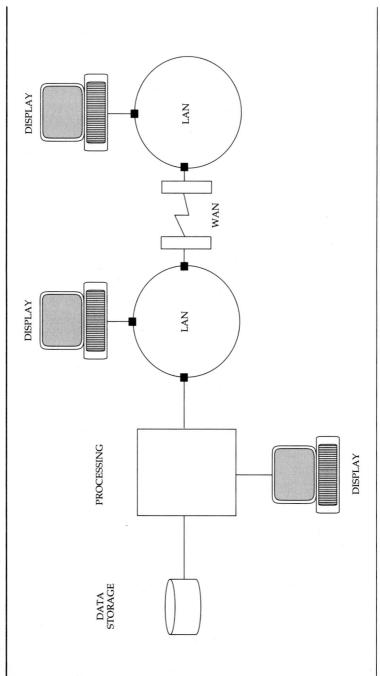

FIGURE 19–6
Distributed Processing (Work Station)

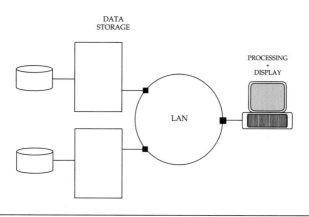

high, and that data are held in several locations and may require normalization before use.

- **Distributed Processing (Server)**
  Another example of a distributed system is where servers are provided to perform processing as well as hold source data and results (Figure 19–7). Processing can be initiated by a user but is performed on one or more servers with the results being viewed on the user's work station.

  The advantages of this configuration are that the system is scalable by the addition of more or larger servers, and that work station constraints are reduced. The disadvantages are that data normalization may still be required and that data transfer volumes may be too high.

  There are many other possible variants on this theme, e.g., three tier architectures which separate presentation, business logic, and data storage functions. The choice of configuration is determined in part by the nature of the processing that must be performed, the demands for access and storage of data, and the user requirements for the manipulation and display of source data and reports. The three examples discussed here provide some indication of the

FIGURE 19–7
Distributed Processing (Server)

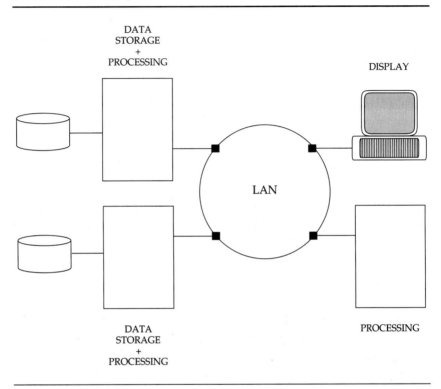

possible range of options that can be considered. Normally, a mixture of these variants is adopted, based on the need to build on the current technical infrastructure and the need to access existing sources of data.

Output

There are two important issues that should be considered in connection with data output:

- *Media*: Media are the forms in which the information is required by the user. Hard-copy reports can be printed centrally and distributed using internal (paper) mail, or the print image can be stored and viewed on a user work station.

- *Type of query*: structured or routine requests for information can be complied with by generating standard reports, which are then available, without the need for repeated processing, to all authorized users. Nonstandard requests must be handled on-line and are best answered by providing the user with a query interface, which provides assistance in building queries and a flexible viewer for the results. In this case it is not necessary that the query should be processed on the user work station. It may be passed to a server, which performs the required processing on behalf of the user and returns the results to the user when the processing is completed.

The storage requirements for these reports and the processing requirements to support the necessary levels of user access must also be considered.

In many cases the demand for output is not what at first sight might be expected. The existing level of demand is often a function of past activity, and a review of distribution lists—or, in more extreme cases, the introduction of charges—will normally result in a marked reduction in demand for reports and the scaling back of system processor and storage requirements.

EXAMPLE

This section provides an example of a server-based distributed systems architecture selected to satisfy the business and technical requirements that have been discussed in this chapter.

One possible logical model of a risk-management system that supports these requirements could be viewed as consisting of 10 modules (Figure 19–8), which are divided into two layers:

- One layer supports user and system interfaces and provides data storage and access; while
- The second layer consists of servers that perform process-intensive operations.

Trading systems are external to the risk-management system and the sources of trade information and provide traders with selected risk-management information. The user roles which the risk-management

FIGURE 19–8
Logical Application Model

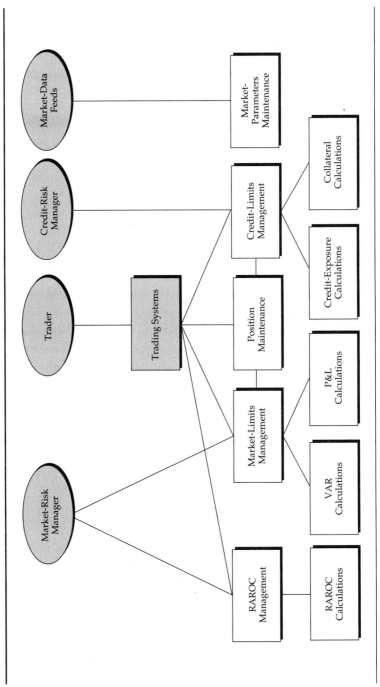

system supports are shown in the ellipses. The lines joining modules define module dependencies and indicate a flow of information or the provision of a service to the caller. In a full specification of the logical architecture model, each module would have a clear definition of its function and the inputs and outputs that it handled.

Moving from the logical application model to the physical application model involves the consideration of implementation constraints. We are looking here to minimize the number of servers while providing adequate processing power for computation-intensive calculations such as Monte Carlo simulation and allow for increased use of the system (*scalability requirement*). We are also seeking to:

- Provide a common mechanism to connect to external systems and provide access to the required source data (*connectivity requirement*); and
- Handle data normalization and the need to incorporate new algorithms into the system at short notice with minimum impact on the system as a whole (*flexibility requirement*).

One possible arrangement of the modules across physical processors is shown in Figure 19–9. There are of course many alternatives that will depend on the technical environment and on the processing and data-storage requirements of the system.

The final task to perform in order to complete the architecture specification is to define the migration strategy that will be used to move from the current environment to the defined target environment. The migration strategy for this example will not be described here but, once defined, it will provide the definition for the projects that must be undertaken to implement the required system. Each project can be considered in turn and an internal development project initiated or an external package selected and implemented. In both cases the migration strategy provides the route map to guide the implementation process, which may consist of many projects spread over several years before the target environment is fully implemented.

CONCLUSION

The pressures that exist in the business environment are forcing banks and corporates to define tighter controls for units using derivative products and

FIGURE 19–9
Physical Application Model

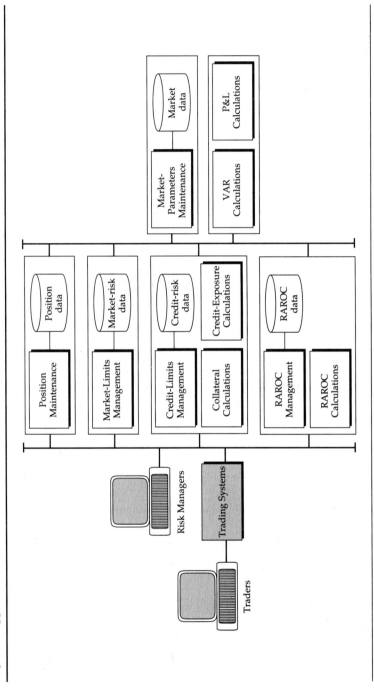

to implement risk-management systems to monitor exposure to financial risk, monitor compliance with the controls, and report exceptions.

What makes these applications more complex than other forms of management information systems are the connectivity, scalability, and flexibility issues that must be satisfied in order to provide workable solutions to meet business requirements.

A key element in the successful implementation of risk-management systems is the definition of a target systems architecture that defines the processing units (modules), the dependencies between modules, and the technical infrastructure that must be implemented to support this processing. The systems architecture can be used to identify and evaluate implementation options based on packages or custom-made development. Following this evaluation a migration plan can be devised that specifies the work that must be performed to move from the current systems environment to the target systems environment.

The complexity of these activities highlights the need for a clearly defined methodology to guide the definition of the business requirements, the specification of the systems architecture, and the definition and evaluation of system options. Some of the elements of one possible methodology have been described here.

LEGAL & REGULATORY

Chapter Twenty

Financial Derivatives
Regulatory Quagmire or Opportunity for Reengineering?

Anthony G. Cornyn, CFA
Director of Risk Management
Office of Thrift Supervision
*Department of the Treasury**

INTRODUCTION

The rapid growth and evolution of the over-the-counter (OTC) markets for financial derivatives pose enormous and varied challenges for bank regulatory agencies. The Office of Thrift Supervision (OTS), the agency created in 1989 to supervise savings and loan associations (S&Ls), initiated a program to monitor the interest-rate risk of savings institutions. A key element of the program is the agency's interest-rate-risk model. The OTS uses the model to conduct a type of scenario analysis known as "stress testing" to measure the vulnerability of S&Ls to different interest-rate environments. A byproduct of the model is that it enables the OTS to address some of the risk-measurement challenges posed by financial derivatives.

This chapter discusses the approach taken by the OTS to supervise and monitor the use of derivatives by savings institutions. The first section

---

*The views expressed here are those of the author and do not necessarily represent the views of the Office of Thrift Supervision or the Department of the Treasury.

discusses the challenges that derivatives pose for the bank regulatory agencies and describes how the OTS is addressing those challenges. The focus is on the challenges posed by end users of derivatives. The second section describes the OTS's interest-rate risk model (referred to interchangeably as the OTS Model or the Net Portfolio Value Model), which the agency uses to measure the interest-rate risk and derivatives exposures of savings institutions. The third section of the chapter illustrates how the OTS Model is used to determine the effect of derivatives on the interest-rate risk exposure of the institutions that use them.

CHALLENGES TO BANK AND THRIFT REGULATORS

The explosive growth and proliferation of financial derivatives presents three key challenges to bank and thrift regulators:

1. Keeping up with the pace of financial innovation in the derivatives markets;
2. Developing the capability to measure the effect of an institution's use of derivatives on its risk exposure; and
3. Ensuring that regulatory policies and practices provide an environment that does not discourage qualified depository institutions from using derivatives.

The Challenge of Keeping Pace with Innovation

Innovation is occurring at an astonishing pace, challenging our ability to follow and comprehend. Relatively new insights in financial theory by Markowitz, Sharpe, Black, Scholes, and others have revolutionized perceptions of financial phenomena, reshaped the financial marketplace, and transformed market participants. Perhaps nowhere is the quickened pace of financial innovation and the challenge it brings more evident than in the world of financial derivatives. When it comes to financial innovation in the 1990s, nearly everyone is playing catch-up.

The steady flow of new derivative products and product variations has presented risk managers with new opportunities and choices. Managers need to understand the new technology and to explore ways in which new derivative products can be converted into economic results. Because major changes in technology can produce major changes in the economics of the industry—in this case by lowering hedging costs, for example, or by facilitating risk transfer, or by providing opportunities to enhance returns—those who neglect the new technology run the risk of losing out to those who exploit it.

The new derivatives technology challenges regulators to climb the learning curve. Financial derivatives have not only changed the risk-management practices of end users, but in some cases have changed the very nature of institutions. In the process, regulators are being driven to review, rethink, and reformulate the way in which institutions under their perview are regulated. Regulators who fail to understand the new technology and its implications can do significant harm if that failure leads to inappropriate regulations or unwarranted intrusions into the activities of regulated entities. At the same time, a failure either to adopt appropriate regulations, if needed, or to provide adequate supervision, where needed, can also be harmful.

The challenge of understanding the new derivatives technology, while daunting, is nevertheless manageable. While the media has made much of the complexity and exotic nature of some derivatives, the products that have gained wide acceptance by end users are generally no more complex and are often considerably less complicated than many conventional financial instruments such as adjustable-rate mortgages, commercial loans, and full-payout leases.

For the most part, savings institutions have confined their use of derivatives to the plain vanilla, instruments such as interest-rate swaps, caps, and floors. In fact, the number of savings institutions that use derivatives to manage risk is relatively small. Only 117 of the 1,822 SAIF-insured savings institutions reported having positions in derivatives as of September 30, 1994, according to OTS data. Of these, 82 had positions in interest-rate swaps, 20 had futures contracts, and 43 had positions in interest-rate options.

Nevertheless, innovation in the derivatives marketplace will continue and the knowledge base of regulators must keep pace. The OTS and the other federal banking agencies have developed extensive training programs on derivatives for examiners, with the goal of providing them with solid understanding of the instruments and of the principles of risk management. The agencies also have specialists who are available to assist examiners in evaluating complex derivatives positions. Specialization alone, however, is not sufficient. The specialists must have the tools they need to measure the risk associated with derivatives.

The Challenge of Risk Measurement

Risk measurement is a key element in bank supervision. While the broad objective of the bank regulatory agencies is to protect the public interest by fostering an environment conducive to sound banking, the essential task of the supervisor is the detection and prevention of excessive risk taking by institutions. To accomplish this, the supervisor must be able to measure risk. Without the ability to measure risk effectively, the supervisor may not detect institutions that are about to fail or those that are imposing excessive risk on the financial system.

The growing use of derivatives has made the financial statements of end users less "transparent." End users often use a variety of financial derivatives and enter into numerous contracts. Although it is obvious that the use of derivatives will alter the risk profile of an institution's portfolio, the direction and degree of alteration may not be readily apparent to the outside analyst. Transparency is diminished. As financial statements become less transparent, the traditional tools of analysis, namely financial ratios, become less useful in measuring risk. And risk measurement by investors, examiners, and other outside analysts becomes more difficult.

While improvements in financial disclosure practices will help, the key to transparency is technology. Just as generals need enhanced radar systems to detect stealth bombers, regulators will need enhanced surveillance systems (i.e., risk-measurement models) to evaluate the risk exposures of depository institutions with complex portfolios of derivatives. Without such systems, the regulator may become overly dependent on the regulated institution's internal assessment of its own risk exposure.

The Challenge of Fostering a Hospitable Regulatory Environment

How can bank and thrift regulators foster an environment in which depository institutions are not discouraged from using derivatives to manage and control risk? Implicit in this challenge is the premise that derivatives are useful financial products and that banks and thrifts should be permitted to use them. While this premise has been challenged, many if not most practitioners agree that derivatives are useful products that have fundamentally changed risk-management practices for the better.

Nevertheless, bank and thrift regulators are faced with a difficult choice when the institutions they regulate begin to use new and potentially risky financial products. The choice is analogous to that faced by officials of the Food and Drug Administration when asked to approve new drugs for the market, which was aptly described by Milton and Rose Friedman in *Free to Choose*. To paraphrase the Friedmans' analysis, a regulator can make two very different mistakes:

1. The regulator can allow banks to use "New Derivative X" to manage their risk exposures, knowing that some banks that use it will fail; or
2. The regulator can refuse to allow banks to use "New Derivative X," knowing that if banks were allowed to use it, several bank failures might be prevented.

Clearly, the regulator that makes the first mistake may become the object of unfavorable media attention. On the other hand, if the regulator makes the second mistake, no one may ever know. Of the two mistakes, which would you be most anxious to avoid, the Friedmans might ask, the one that causes damage to your reputation, or the one that does not?

This bias, whether real or perceived, is commonly thought to influence the behavior of bank and thrift examiners. Some asset/liability managers do not use derivatives to manage risk because they fear their use will invite undue regulatory scrutiny and unfair criticism. While the presence of derivatives will likely draw the scrutiny of examiners, as it should, the important issue is whether examiners will be able to analyze complex derivatives positions and render a fair assessment. Depository institutions need to have confidence that their positions will be reviewed competently. Ensuring that examiners are adequately trained and giving them access to risk-assessment models or other tools that allow them to measure risk with some precision would seem to be the appropriate way to address this concern. Moreover, giving examiners access to models other than those used by the institution itself would go a long way toward raising the examiners' comfort level with derivatives.

In addition, the regulatory agencies must continue to strive for clarity in the regulatory policies and procedures governing the use of derivatives. This too will raise the comfort level of the managers and boards of directors of institutions that are considering the use of derivatives to manage risk.

Finally, regulators can use risk-based capital requirements to influence the use of derivatives by depository institutions. On January 1, 1994, the

OTS added an interest-rate-risk component to its risk-based capital requirements. Under the new framework, an institution's capital requirement is linked directly to its overall interest-rate-risk exposure. Institutions that use derivatives to increase risk exposure face higher capital requirements, while those that use derivatives to reduce risk benefit from lower capital requirements. (Under the prior framework, risk-based capital requirements were based solely on credit risk. Interest-rate risk was not taken into account; and if an institution used derivatives to reduce its interest-rate-risk exposure, its minimum capital requirement would increase.)

OVERVIEW OF THE OTS NET PORTFOLIO VALUE MODEL

What Is Interest-Rate Risk?

For a depository institution, interest-rate risk (IRR) is the risk that changes in market interest rates might adversely affect the institution's net interest income or the economic value of its portfolio of assets, liabilities, and off-balance-sheet contracts.

How OTS Measures IRR

The OTS Model employs an economic value approach to measuring interest-rate risk. The objective of this approach is to gauge how changes in interest rates are likely to affect the estimated net market value of the firm's assets, liabilities, and off-balance-sheet accounts.

Scenario Analysis

OTS uses scenario analysis to evaluate the interest-rate risk exposure of savings associations. Scenario analysis is a tool for thinking about alternative future environments—optimistic as well as pessimistic—in which business decisions may be played out. A scenario is a hypothetical event or chain of events. The goal of scenario analysis is to examine the consequences of a specific business strategy under several possible alternative scenarios. Since the consequences of any strategy will generally vary with each scenario, this type of analysis provides a framework for evaluating the soundness of a strategy.

The advantage in scenario analysis, or stress testing as it is sometimes called, is that it forces management to consider events that they might otherwise ignore. By illuminating the consequences of a decision or a set of decisions in different interest-rate environments, scenario analysis can reduce the possibility of unpleasant surprises. The end result of scenario analysis should be better decision making.

At a typical institution, scenario planning for interest-rate risk management might begin with some "what if" questions. For example, the chief financial officer might ask: What will happen to my institution's earnings and the economic value of its balance sheet if rates rise by 100, 200, 300, or even 400 basis points? What will happen if the yield curve flattens over the next six months? What will happen if the yield curve steepens? The CFO would probably also ask a few key follow-up questions such as: Could my institution survive interest-rate-risk shocks of those magnitudes given its current asset/liability mix? or, How should we restructure our portfolio to ensure greater earnings stability?

Net Portfolio Value

OTS evaluates savings associations' interest-rate risk by estimating the sensitivity of their portfolios of assets, liabilities, and off-balance-sheet contracts to changes in market interest rates. In essence, OTS marks-to-market each institution's balance sheet under several different interest-rate scenarios to determine how the net portfolio value (NPV) of the firm changes in response to changes in interest rates. NPV is defined as as follows:

NPV = the present value of expected net cash flows from existing assets

minus

the present value of expected net cash flows from existing liabilities

plus

the present value of net expected cash inflows from existing off-balance-sheet contracts.

The greater the change in NPV for a given change in rates, the greater the risk exposure of the institution.

The NPV Model takes a snapshot view of the portfolio at each quarter-end and estimates its economic value at that time, and the value of that same portfolio under the alternate interest-rate scenarios.

The model estimates the current, or base case economic value of each type of asset, liability, and off-balance-sheet contract at the end of each quarter.

Then, the model estimates what would happen to the economic value of each type of asset, liability, and off-balance-sheet contract under eight different interest-rate scenarios, which include instantaneous, parallel shifts in the Treasury yield curve of −400, −300, −200, −100, +100, +200, +300, and +400 basis points.

Scenario Analysis of the Thrift Industry

An indication of the sensitivity of the thrift industry to changes in rates as depicted by the OTS Model is shown in Table 20–1.

Table 20–1 shows summary output from the OTS Model for the universe of 1,421 reporting institutions as of September 30, 1994. The sensitivity profile of the 1,421 institutions is typical of what observers of thrift institutions might expect: A rise in interest rates causes NPV to fall, while a fall in rates causes NPV to rise. Notice that an instantaneous interest-rate shock of plus 100 basis points causes a 9 percent decline in net portfolio value from the base case level; a plus-200-basis-point shock causes a 20 percent decline in value; and a 300-basis-point shock causes a 32 percent decline in value. This shows that, as expected, the industry is harmed by rising interest rates.

Table 20–1 also shows the Net Portfolio Value Capital Ratio (or NPV Capital Ratio) of the group for each scenario. The ratio is an indicator of capital strength, calculated by dividing the NPV of the group in each scenario by the present value of the group's assets in that scenario. This mark-to-market leverage ratio changes in each scenario. As shown, the group has an NPV capital ratio of 9 percent in the base case. A 100-basis-point decline in rates from the base-case level causes the NPV Capital Ratio to rise to 9.5 percent; a 200-basis-point decline causes the ratio to rise to 9.7 percent.

Methods for Calculating Economic Value

Discounted cash-flow analysis. A fundamental characteristic of all financial instruments is that they give rise to cash flows. The value

TABLE 20–1
Interest-Rate Sensitivity of Savings Associations Filing Schedule CMR
(as of September 30, 1994) (000's)

Interest-Rate Scenario	Net Portfolio Value			NPV Capital Ratio
	$ Amount	$ Change	% Change	
+400	$38,032	−31,158	−45%	5.3%
+300	47,144	−22,046	−32	6.4
+200	55,562	−13,628	−20	7.5
+100	63,015	−6,175	−9	8.3
0 (Base Case)	69,160	0	0	9.0
−100	73,555	4,366	6	9.5
−200	75,916	6,726	10	9.7
−300	76,062	6,872	10	9.6
−400	76,606	7,416	11	9.6

of any financial instrument can be estimated by projecting the amount and timing of future net cash flows associated with the instrument, and multiplying those cash flows by appropriate discount factors. This procedure for estimating the value of a financial instrument is commonly referred to as discounted cash flow analysis, or present-value analysis.

The NPV Model employs two cash-flow-based techniques to value financial instruments; a static discounted cash flow approach, and an option-based pricing approach. In addition, the model uses a version of the Black-Scholes model to value interest-rate derivatives such as options and interest-rate caps.

Static discounted-cash-flow method. The NPV Model employs the static discounted-cash-flow method to value the following items:

- Multifamily and nonresidential mortgages
- Construction and land loans
- Second mortgages
- Consumer loans

- Commercial loans
- Nonmortgage investment securities
- Time deposits
- Demand deposits
- FHLB advances and other borrowing
- Interest-rate swaps

Under the static discounted-cash-flow approach, the economic value of a financial instrument is estimated by calculating the present value of the instrument's expected cash flows. The present value is determined by discounting the cash flows the instrument is expected to generate by the yields currently available to investors from an instrument of comparable risk and duration. Therefore, to calculate the present value, information is needed about the size and timing of cash flows and about the appropriate discount rate.

Cash flows are estimated under each of the nine interest-rate scenarios evaluated by the model. Under each scenario, a single path of future interest rates is assumed. (This analysis is referred to as static cash-flow analysis because each scenario depicts a single projected path of interest rates, as opposed to numerous paths used by the option-based approach described below.) Cash flows are calculated under each scenario, based on the assumed path of interest rates depicted in that scenario.

Option-based pricing approach. The NPV Model uses an option-based approach to value:

- 1–4 family fixed-rate mortgages
- 1–4 family adjustable-rate mortgages
- Mortgages serviced for others
- Mortgages serviced by others
- Firm commitments to buy, sell, or originate mortgages

The Model's option-based pricing approach makes use of Monte Carlo simulation to value assets with embedded options that have a significant impact on the assets' price sensitivity.

The most significant embedded options, from the perspective of savings associations, are the prepayment options and interest-rate caps and floors contained in mortgages and mortgage-related securities. Prepayment options can introduce significant uncertainty into the timing of mortgage cash flows.

In large part, the value of a prepayment option depends on the volatility of interest rates. When interest-rate volatility increases, there is a greater chance that mortgage rates will fall sufficiently below the rates on existing mortgages to induce prepayments. The proceeds from the prepayments could only be reinvested at the then lower market rates. When interest rates rise, prepayments fall, because it is to the advantage of mortgagors to retain their relatively low-coupon mortgages. This slowdown in prepayments works to the disadvantage of lenders because the mortgages are paying rates of interest below those at which new mortgages could be originated.

Compared to static pricing models, a Monte Carlo model provides improved estimates of the interest-rate sensitivity of mortgage assets by taking interest-rate volatility into account. A Monte Carlo model uses an interest-rate simulation program to generate numerous random interest-rate paths that, in conjunction with a prepayment model, are used to estimate mortgage cash flows along each path. In fact, the option-based approach actually repeats the static cash flow approach many times with different interest-rate paths.

The Black-Scholes model for interest-rate derivatives. The NPV Model uses a version of the Black-Scholes model to value the following instruments:

- Options on interest-rate futures
- Optional commitments to buy and sell mortgages
- Interest-rate caps and floors
- Interest-rate swaptions

OTS MODEL AND DERIVATIVES

As noted earlier, one of the challenges to bank regulators posed by derivatives is that of risk measurement. The use of derivatives at financial institutions has grown dramatically. Balance-sheet complexity has increased, and balance-sheet transparency has decreased. It has become more difficult to analyze the financial statements of derivatives users without the aid of a computer model.

The OTS Model has helped the OTS to cope with the risk-measurement challenges of derivatives. But coping with the challenge of measuring the effect of these instruments on portfolio risk was not easy.

Confronting the Data Problem

In developing the model, we were confronted with the problem of how to collect the data needed to value financial derivatives without imposing an excessive reporting burden on the thrift industry. The crux of the problem was that there were so many different types of derivatives that it was difficult to construct a reporting form that would accommodate all of them.

The OTS Model uses financial data provided by savings institutions on the Consolidated Maturity and Rate Schedule (Schedule CMR) of the Thrift Financial Report. The original reporting form, which was introduced in 1991, did not fully accommodate the variety of financial derivatives used by savings institutions; several types of derivatives were aggregated or lumped together on the form, and as a result, the information needed to value the certain derivatives accurately was not available. In 1993, we revised the reporting form to obtain better information on derivatives.

Coding System for Derivatives

The revised reporting form uses a unique coding system to categorize financial derivatives. This system accommodates the collection of detailed information on nearly 300 different types of derivative instruments. Each derivative contract held by an institution is identified by a four-digit code. The first two digits designate the general type of contract; the last two digits designate the specific type of contract within the general type.

For example, the code 5004 designates a fixed-for-floating interest-rate swap based on 3-month LIBOR. The digits "50" identify a fixed-for-floating swap and the digits "04" identify 3-month LIBOR as the reference index for the floating-rate side of the swap.

The various contract codes used to identify options on futures, for example, are listed in Table 20–2.

In addition to the four-digit code, the notional amount of the position and other pertinent information is collected. This information is used to estimate the cash flows and present values of each derivatives position

TABLE 20–2
Contract Codes for Options on Futures

Long Call	Long Put	Short Call	Short Put	Underlying Instrument
9002	9026	9050	9074	30-day Fed funds rate futures
9004	9028	9052	9076	3-month Treasury bill futures
9006	9030	9054	9078	2-year Treasury note futures
9008	9032	9056	9080	5-year Treasury note futures
9010	9034	9058	9082	10-year Treasury note futures
9012	9036	9060	9084	Treasury bond futures
9014	9038	9062	9086	1-month LIBOR futures
9016	9040	9064	9088	3-month Eurodollar futures

reported on the form. An institution can report each position separately or aggregate positions that are similar. Figure 20–1 shows that section of the reporting form that is used to collect data on off-balance-sheet derivatives.

The four-digit coding system accommodates most types of financial derivatives, but not customized and exotic derivatives. When an institution has financial derivatives that cannot be accommodated by the coding system, an alternative data collection scheme is used that involves a "self-reporting" mechanism. Specifically, the institution must submit estimates of the market values of the "noncodable" derivatives for the nine designated interest-rate scenarios used by the OTS Model. The self-reported estimates for the noncodable derivatives are provided in a special section of the form (see Figure 20–2). These estimates are fed into the OTS Model and used in determining the institution's NPV. To use the self-reporting mechanism, an institution must be able to model the derivatives to generate the market value estimates or obtain them from a third party.

The self-reporting mechanism is particularly useful in addressing the reporting and valuation problems of nonstandard securities such as collateralized mortgage obligations and structured notes. As a general rule, savings institutions should not purchase any derivative securities unless they can comply with the self-reporting requirements of Schedule CMR.

FIGURE 20–1
Dealing with Off-Balance-Sheet Derivatives

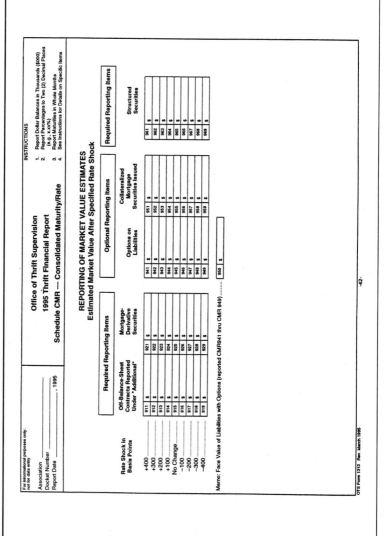

FIGURE 20–2
Dealing with Exotics

For informational purposes only; not for data entry	Office of Thrift Supervision	INSTRUCTIONS
Association _____	1995 Thrift Financial Report	1. Report Dollar Balances in Thousands ($000)
Docket Number _____	Schedule CMR — Consolidated Maturity/Rate	2. Report Percentages to Two (2) Decimal Places (e.g., x.xx%)
Report Date _____, 1995		3. See Instructions for Details on Specific Items

Off-Balance-Sheet Positions

Off-Balance-Sheet Contract Positions

	[1] Contract Code	[2] Notional Amount	[3] Maturity or Fees	[4] Price/Rate #1	[5] Price/Rate #2
Position 1	801	802 $	803 $	804 .	805 .
Position 2	806	807 $	808 $	809 .	810 .
Position 3	811	812 $	813 $	814 .	815 .
Position 4	816	817 $	818 $	819 .	820 .
Position 5	821	822 $	823 $	824 .	825 .
Position 6	826	827 $	828 $	829 .	830 .
Position 7	831	832 $	833 $	834 .	835 .
Position 8	836	837 $	838 $	839 .	840 .
Position 9	841	842 $	843 $	844 .	845 .
Position 10	846	847 $	848 $	849 .	850 .
Position 11	851	852 $	853 $	854 .	855 .
Position 12	856	857 $	858 $	859 .	860 .
Position 13	861	862 $	863 $	864 .	865 .
Position 14	866	867 $	868 $	869 .	870 .
Position 15	871	872 $	873 $	874 .	875 .
Position 16	876	877 $	878 $	879 .	880 .

NOTE: Enter "price" or "rate" in columns 4 & 5 to two decimal places (e.g., "price" = 102.25 or "rate" = 6.12%)

MEMO: Reconciliation of Off-Balance-Sheet Contract Positions Reported

	# of Positions
Reported Above at CMR801-CMR880	901 $
Reported Using Optional Supplemental Reporting	902 $
Self-Valued & Reported as "Additional" Positions at CMR911-CMR919	903 $

OTS Form 1313 Rev. March 1995

-41-

Output: IRR Exposure Reports

Each quarter, the OTS Model generates interest-rate risk exposure reports for individual savings institutions. These customized reports contain information on the interest-rate sensitivity of an institution's assets, liabilities, and off-balance-sheet contracts. Information on the sensitivity of an institution's derivatives positions is available in the off-balance-sheet section of the report. (A sample exposure report is shown in the appendix to this chapter.)

Using Exposure Reports for Derivatives Analysis

When a regulator learns that an institution is using financial derivatives for risk management, questions and concerns are raised. An obvious question is whether the institution is using the derivatives to increase or decrease risk exposures. The exposure reports generated by the OTS Model can be used by supervisory personnel as well as managers and boards of directors of savings institutions to address that question.

In evaluating the interest-rate risk associated with derivatives, the OTS evaluates that risk in the context of an institution's total portfolio. A basic principle of modern portfolio theory is that the risk of any asset should not be judged in isolation but rather in the context of an investor's entire portfolio. This principle also holds true for derivatives. A derivative instrument that looks risky in isolation may, when added to an institution's portfolio, reduce the overall risk of the portfolio. A portfolio approach to risk measurement is the proper framework for evaluating the risk-reward trade-offs of using derivatives. Under the portfolio approach, the relevant consideration is not the risk of a derivative in isolation, but rather how the addition of a derivative to a portfolio alters the firm's risk-return trade-off.

Case Study: XYZ Federal Savings

Is XYZ Federal Savings using swaps to hedge or speculate? An OTS exposure report for XYZ Federal Savings, a hypothetical S&L, is presented in the appendix to this chapter. The report provides a detailed evaluation of XYZ's interest-rate sensitivity. Page 1 of the report provides summary NPV data, while pages 2 though 6 show the interest-rate sensitivity of XYZ's assets, liabilities, and off-balance-sheet contracts. On

TABLE 20–3
Effect of Swap Positions

Rate Scenario	(1) Unhedged NPV	(2) Pay-Fixed Swaps	(3) Pay-Floating Swaps	(4) Unhedged NPV + Col. (2)	(5) Unhedged NPV + Col. (3)	6 NPV
400	−5,364	65,868	−74,366	60,504	−79,730	−13,862
300	41,240	54,472	−61,560	95,712	−20,320	34,152
200	94,717	42,497	−48,104	137,214	46,613	89,110
100	139,196	29,914	−33,961	169,110	105,235	135,149
0	176,642	16,689	−19,092	193,331	157,550	174,239
−100	201,998	2,789	−3,457	204,787	198,541	201,330
−200	212,266	−11,823	12,988	200,443	225,254	213,431
−300	219,024	−27,187	30,234	191,837	249,258	222,071

page 6 of the report, we see that XYZ Federal Savings is using two types of interest-rate swaps.

The question of whether the interest-rate swaps are increasing or decreasing XYZ's risk exposure can be addressed by examining what happens to its NPV with and without swaps over a range of interest-rate scenarios.

Using information from page 6 of XYZ Federal's exposure report, we constructed Table 20–3 to show the effect of the two swap positions on XYZ Federal's NPV over a range of interest-rate scenarios. Column (1) of Table 20–3, which is labeled Unhedged NPV, shows what XYZ's Federal's NPV payoff profile would look like without the two swap positions. In essence, Unhedged NPV represents the net portfolio value of XYZ Federal's core business, (i.e., its total business exclusive of any off-balance-sheet derivatives).

Columns (2) and (3) show the present values of XYZ's two swap positions in the alternative scenarios. Column (4) shows Unhedged NPV plus the pay-fixed/receive-floating swaps, and Column (5) shows Unhedged NPV plus the pay-floating/receive-fixed swaps. Finally, Column (6) shows NPV, which is the sum of Columns (1), (2) and (3).

We can gauge whether the swaps are risk-increasing or risk-reducing for the different scenarios by reviewing the data in Table 20–3. Column

FIGURE 20–3
Unhedged NPV versus Unhedged NPV plus Pay-Fixed Swaps

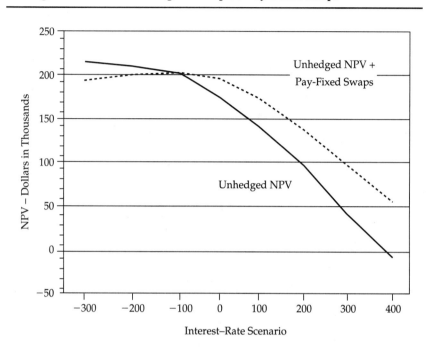

(1) shows that XYZ Federal's Unhedged NPV decreases in the rising-rate scenarios and increases in the falling-rate scenarios. The same general pattern is evident for NPV in Column (6). NPV, however, is lower than Unhedged NPV in the rising-rate scenarios, which suggests that, on balance, the swaps exacerbate XYZ's exposure to rising rates.

Column (2) shows that the pay-fixed swaps have a payoff pattern that should provide XYZ Federal with hedge protection in the rising-rate scenarios. Column (4) shows that adding the pay-fixed swaps to the Unhedged NPV produces smaller losses in the rising-rate scenarios. (See Figure 20–3.)

An examination of Column (3) of Table 20–3, however, reveals that the pay-floating swaps decrease in value in the rising-rate scenarios and

FIGURE 20–4
Unhedged NPV versus NPV Including Pay-Fixed and Pay-floating Swaps

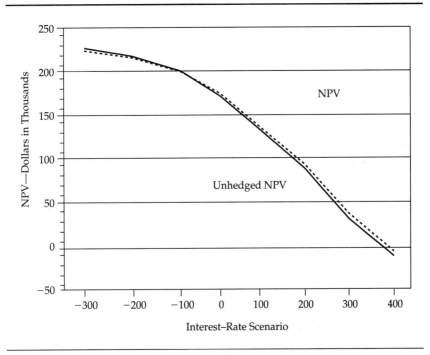

increase in value in the rising-rate scenarios. This position not only does not provide protection against rising rates, it reduces the hedging benefits provided by the pay-fixed swap.(See Figure 20–4.)

Because the pay-floating swaps have a payoff profile that parallels the payoff pattern of Column (1), they increase XYZ Federal's exposure to interest-rate risk. The institution could reduce its exposure to rising rates by closing out its position in the pay-floating swaps at a loss. The existence of those swaps does not necessarily mean that this particular position was initiated to speculate on a possible decline in interest rates. For example, at the time the swap was initiated, XYZ Federal may have a had a significantly different risk profile, or it may have initiated the swap to unwind, or effectively cancel, a pay-fixed swap.

CONCLUSION

Risk measurement is a key element of bank and thrift supervision. The regulator needs to be able to determine whether depository institutions that use financial derivatives are taking excessive risks or are imposing excessive risk on the financial system. Regulators also need to be able to measure derivatives risk on a portfolio basis to ensure that risk-based capital requirements are reasonably risk-based so that institutions that use derivatives to reduce their risk exposure receive the benefit of lower capital requirements. The OTS approach to interest-rate-risk measurement, which employs stress testing of an institution's net portfolio value, has provided OTS with a useful tool to cope with the challenges posed by financial derivatives.

Appendix to Chapter Twenty

Page 1

Interest–Rate Risk Exposure Report of
XYZ Federal Savings, a FSB

DOCKET: 00000 XYZ FEDERAL SAVINGS, A FSB WASHINGTON, DC CYCLE: MAR 1994	OFFICE OF THRIFT SUPERVISION RISK MANAGEMENT DIVISION INTEREST RATE RISK EXPOSURE REPORT (Balances in $000)	DATE: 08/18/94 TIME: 09:17 EDIT: 06/28/94 PAGE: 01

*** INTEREST RATE SENSITIVITY OF NET PORTFOLIO VALUE (NPV) ***

	Net Portfolio Value			NPV as % of PV of Assets	
Change in Rates	$ Amount	$ Change	% Change	NPV Ratio	Change
+400 bp	-13,862	-188,102	-108 %	-0.55 %	-687 bp
+300 bp	34,152	-140,087	-80 %	1.32 %	-500 bp
+200 bp**	89,110	-85,129	-49 %	3.36 %	-296 bp
+100 bp	135,149	-39,090	-22 %	4.99 %	-133 bp
0 bp	174,239			6.32 %	
-100 bp	201,330	27,090	+16 %	7.20 %	+88 bp
-200 bp	213,431	39,192	+22 %	7.56 %	+124 bp
-300 bp	222,071	47,832	+27 %	7.80 %	+147 bp
-178 bp	210,749	36,509	+21 %	7.48 %	+116 bp

** Denotes rate shock used to compute interest rate risk capital component

	03/31/94	12/31/93	03/31/93
*** RISK MEASURES: 200 BP RATE SHOCK ***			
Pre-Shock NPV Ratio: NPV as % of PV of Assets	6.32 %	6.12 %	4.93 %
Exposure Measure: Post-Shock NPV Ratio	3.36 %	4.27 %	3.06 %
Sensitivity Measure: Change in NPV Ratio	-296 bp	-185 bp	-186 bp
*** CALCULATION OF CAPITAL COMPONENT ***			
Change in NPV as % of PV of Assets	-3.09 %	-1.99 %	-1.96 %
Interest Rate Risk Capital Component ($000)	15,007	0	—

DOCKET: 00000
XYZ FEDERAL SAVINGS, A FSB
WASHINGTON, DC
CYCLE: MAR 1994

OFFICE OF THRIFT SUPERVISION
RISK MANAGEMENT DIVISION

PRESENT VALUE ESTIMATES BY INTEREST RATE SCENARIO
(Balances in $000)

DATE: 08/18/94
TIME: 09:17
EDIT: 06/28/94
PAGE: 02

*** Change in Interest Rates ***

*** ASSETS ***	-178 bp	-300 bp	-200 bp	-100 bp	No Change	+100 bp	+200 bp	+300 bp	+400 bp
MORTGAGE LOANS & SECURITIES									
Fixed-Rate Single-Family First-Mortgage Loans & MBS:									
30-Yr Mortgage Loans	193,903	198,627	194,859	189,819	182,941	174,869	166,400	158,053	150,116
30-Yr Mortgage Securities	13,796	14,075	13,846	13,616	13,353	13,001	12,543	12,016	11,466
15-Year Mortgages & MBS	719,095	737,671	722,776	703,743	678,482	649,721	620,312	591,729	564,575
Balloon Mortgages & MBS	122,928	124,801	123,273	121,285	117,805	113,667	109,516	105,492	101,630
Adjustable-Rate Single Family First-Mortgage Loans & MBS:									
Current Market Index ARMs:									
6 Mo or Less Reset Freq	16,247	16,294	16,256	16,208	16,154	16,095	16,033	15,968	15,899
7 Mo to 2 Yrs Reset Freq	469,288	472,205	469,888	466,328	460,810	452,487	441,655	428,725	414,553
2+ to 5 Yrs Reset Freq	27,649	28,114	27,720	27,412	27,066	26,686	26,197	25,567	24,843
Lagging Market Index ARMs:									
1 Mo Reset Freq	–	–	–	–	–	–	–	–	–
2 Mo to 5 Yrs Reset Freq	–	–	–	–	–	–	–	–	–
Multifamily & Nonresidential Mortgage Loans & Securities:									
Adjustable-Rate, Balloon	193,081	194,826	193,369	191,963	190,602	189,280	188,000	186,760	185,559
Adjustable-Rate, Fully-Amort	34,706	35,005	34,756	34,515	34,279	34,047	33,822	33,602	33,389
Fixed-Rate, Balloon	119,745	123,495	120,365	117,336	114,405	111,568	108,822	106,162	103,587
Fixed-Rate, Fully-Amortizing	21,068	22,583	21,312	20,148	19,082	18,103	17,202	16,372	15,606
Construction & Land Loans:									
Adjustable-Rate	26,462	26,496	26,465	26,430	26,402	26,369	26,332	26,307	26,278
Fixed-Rate	29,804	29,979	29,834	29,689	29,546	29,405	29,265	29,127	28,989
Second Mtg Loans & Securities:									
Adjustable-Rate	58,632	58,703	58,641	58,572	58,518	58,457	58,388	58,346	58,295
Fixed-Rate	24,954	25,595	25,060	24,546	24,053	23,579	23,123	22,685	22,264
Other Assets Related to Mortgage Loans & Securities:									
Net Nonperforming Mtg Loans	3,169	3,226	3,180	3,124	3,050	2,964	2,873	2,780	2,688
Accrued Interest Receivable	8,822	8,822	8,822	8,822	8,822	8,822	8,822	8,822	8,822
Advances for Taxes/Insurance	42	42	42	42	42	42	42	42	42
Float on Escrows on Owned Mtg	2,189	1,260	1,988	3,052	4,318	5,518	6,582	7,497	8,286
Less: Value of Servicing on Mtgs Serviced by Others	-150	-141	-149	-154	-159	-164	-168	-171	-172
*Mortgage Loans & Securities	2,085,731	2,121,962	2,092,598	2,056,806	2,009,891	1,954,845	1,896,098	1,836,222	1,777,059

Page 3

```
DOCKET: 00000                          OFFICE OF THRIFT SUPERVISION              DATE:  08/18/94
XYZ FEDERAL SAVINGS, A FSB                RISK MANAGEMENT DIVISION               TIME:  09:17
WASHINGTON, DC                                                                  EDIT:  06/28/94
CYCLE: MAR 1994              PRESENT VALUE ESTIMATES BY INTEREST RATE SCENARIO   PAGE:  03
                                        (Balances in $000)
```

*** Change in Interest Rates ***

*** ASSETS (Cont.) ***	-178 bp	-300 bp	-200 bp	-100 bp	No Change	+100 bp	+200 bp	+300 bp	+400 bp
NONMORTGAGE LOANS									
Commercial Loans:									
Adjustable-Rate	72,020	72,120	72,030	71,929	71,846	71,752	71,646	71,572	71,486
Fixed-Rate	30,308	30,963	30,417	29,883	29,361	28,852	28,354	27,868	27,392
Consumer Loans:									
Adjustable-Rate	41,591	41,572	41,587	41,606	41,629	41,655	41,685	41,717	41,752
Fixed-Rate	27,256	27,958	27,372	26,806	26,261	25,735	25,227	24,736	24,263
Other Assets Related to Nonmortgage Loans & Securities:									
Net Nonperforming Nonmtg Lns .	-891	-898	-892	-886	-880	-874	-869	-863	-858
Accrued Interest Receivable	603	603	603	603	603	603	603	603	603
* Nonmortgage Loans	170,887	172,319	171,117	169,942	168,821	167,722	166,645	165,632	164,638
CASH, DEPOSITS, & SECURITIES									
Cash, Non-Int-Earning Deposits, Overnight Fed Funds & Repos	38,877	38,877	38,877	38,877	38,877	38,877	38,877	38,877	38,877
Equities & All Mutual Funds	–	–	–	–	–	–	–	–	–
Zero-Coupon Securities	–	–	–	–	–	–	–	–	–
Govt & Agency Securities	–	–	–	–	–	–	–	–	–
Term Fed Funds, Term Repos, & Interest-Earning Deposits	14,568	14,583	14,571	14,559	14,547	14,535	14,523	14,511	14,500
Munis, Mtg-Backed Bonds, Corporates, Commercial Paper ...	15,791	16,095	15,842	15,594	15,351	15,113	14,880	14,652	14,428
Mortgage-Derivative Securities:									
Valued by OTS	–	–	–	–	–	–	–	–	–
Valued by Institution	298,676	301,637	299,418	296,044	289,111	279,493	268,620	251,693	242,253
Less: Valuation Allowances for Investment Securities	–	–	–	–	–	–	–	–	–
*Cash, Deposits, & Securities	367,912	371,192	368,708	365,073	357,885	348,018	336,900	319,733	310,058

DOCKET: 00000 XYZ FEDERAL SAVINGS, A FSB WASHINGTON, DC CYCLE: MAR 1994	OFFICE OF THRIFT SUPERVISION RISK MANAGEMENT DIVISION PRESENT VALUE ESTIMATES BY INTEREST RATE SCENARIO (Balances in $000)	DATE: 08/18/94 TIME: 09:17 EDIT: 06/28/94 PAGE: 04

*** Change in Interest Rates ***

*** ASSETS (Cont.) ***	-178 bp	-300 bp	-200 bp	-100 bp	No Change	+100 bp	+200 bp	+300 bp	+400 bp
REPOSSESSED ASSETS	27,608	27,608	27,608	27,608	27,608	27,608	27,608	27,608	27,608
REAL ESTATE HELD FOR INVESTMENT	2,168	2,168	2,168	2,168	2,168	2,168	2,168	2,168	2,168
INVESTMENT IN UNCONSOLIDATED SUBSIDIARIES	3,096	3,145	3,116	3,072	3,056	2,994	2,874	2,688	2,458
OFFICE PREMISES & EQUIPMENT	53,295	53,295	53,295	53,295	53,295	53,295	53,295	53,295	53,295
*Subtotal	86,167	86,216	86,187	86,143	86,127	86,065	85,945	85,759	85,529
MORTGAGE LOAN SERVICING FOR OTHERS									
Fixed-Rate Servicing	1,904	1,719	1,851	2,125	2,496	2,755	2,881	2,937	2,939
Adj-Rate Servicing	–	–	–	–	–	–	–	–	–
Float on Mtgs Svc'd for Others	1,053	889	1,018	1,157	1,280	1,361	1,425	1,489	1,543
*Mtg Ln Servicing for Others	2,957	2,608	2,869	3,283	3,777	4,116	4,306	4,426	4,482
OTHER ASSETS									
Margin Account	–	–	–	–	–	–	–	–	–
Miscellaneous I	89,067	89,067	89,067	89,067	89,067	89,067	89,067	89,067	89,067
Deposit Intangibles:									
Retail CD Intangible	1,856	1,536	1,813	2,039	2,277	2,473	2,665	2,842	3,001
Transaction Acct Intangible	5,567	1,676	4,890	8,381	12,272	16,255	19,977	23,483	26,774
MMDA Intangible	3,612	1,074	3,157	5,565	8,624	12,790	16,825	20,763	24,538
Passbook Account Intangible	1,370	-707	442	6,076	12,749	19,400	25,962	32,105	37,783
Non-Int-Bearing Acct Intang	2,805	1,740	2,631	3,472	4,270	5,026	5,740	6,420	7,067
*Other Assets	104,277	94,386	102,000	114,600	129,260	145,012	160,237	174,680	188,230
VALUE OF FSLIC GUARANTEES REPORTED BY INSTITUTION	–	–	–	–	–	–	–	–	–
*** TOTAL ASSETS	2,817,931	2,848,682	2,823,480	2,795,847	2,755,760	2,705,778	2,650,131	2,586,453	2,529,996

Page 5

```
DOCKET: 00000                    OFFICE OF THRIFT SUPERVISION              DATE:  08/18/94
XYZ FEDERAL SAVINGS, A FSB         RISK MANAGEMENT DIVISION                TIME:  09:17
WASHINGTON, DC                                                            EDIT:  06/28/94
CYCLE: MAR 1994           PRESENT VALUE ESTIMATES BY INTEREST RATE SCENARIO  PAGE:  05
                                   (Balances in $000)
```

*** LIABILITIES ***	-178 bp	-300 bp	-200 bp	-100 bp	No Change	+100 bp	+200 bp	+300 bp	+400 bp
DEPOSITS									
Fixed-Rate, Fixed-Maturity:									
Maturing in 12 Mo or Less	505,396	507,830	505,795	503,807	501,848	499,959	498,086	496,249	494,469
Maturing in 13 Mo or More	351,638	363,561	353,590	344,091	335,016	326,369	318,106	310,208	302,657
Variable-Rate, Fixed-Maturity	1,270	1,270	1,270	1,270	1,270	1,270	1,270	1,270	1,270
Demand:									
Transaction Accts	153,788	153,788	153,788	153,788	153,788	153,788	153,788	153,788	153,788
MMDAs	325,436	325,436	325,436	325,436	325,436	325,436	325,436	325,436	325,436
Passbook Accts	220,954	220,954	220,954	220,954	220,954	220,954	220,954	220,954	220,954
Non-Interest-Bearing Accts	42,239	42,239	42,239	42,239	42,239	42,239	42,239	42,239	42,239
* Deposits	1,600,721	1,615,078	1,603,072	1,591,585	1,580,551	1,570,015	1,559,879	1,550,144	1,540,813
BORROWINGS									
Fixed-Rate, Fixed-Maturity:									
Maturing in 36 Mo or Less	737,787	743,643	738,763	733,965	729,247	724,607	720,044	715,555	711,140
Maturing in 37 Mo or More	117,866	123,645	118,814	114,211	109,823	105,640	101,651	97,845	94,213
Variable-Rate, Fixed-Maturity	118,042	118,275	118,081	117,888	117,695	117,504	117,314	117,124	116,935
* Borrowings	973,695	985,562	975,658	966,063	956,766	947,752	939,008	930,524	922,289
OTHER LIABILITIES									
Escrow Accounts									
For Mortgages	12,848	12,848	12,848	12,848	12,848	12,848	12,848	12,848	12,848
Other Escrow Accounts	–	–	–	–	–	–	–	–	–
Collat. Mtg Securities Issued	–	–	–	–	–	–	–	–	–
Miscellaneous I	27,559	27,559	27,559	27,559	27,559	27,559	27,559	27,559	27,559
Miscellaneous II	–	–	–	–	–	–	–	–	–
*Other Liabilities	40,407	40,407	40,407	40,407	40,407	40,407	40,407	40,407	40,407
OPTIONS ON LIABILITIES	–	–	–	–	–	–	–	–	–
*** TOTAL LIABILITIES	2,614,823	2,641,047	2,619,136	2,598,056	2,577,724	2,558,173	2,539,294	2,521,075	2,503,508

*** Change in Interest Rates ***

```
DOCKET: 00000                              OFFICE OF THRIFT SUPERVISION                    DATE:  08/18/94
XYZ FEDERAL SAVINGS, A FSB                    RISK MANAGEMENT DIVISION                      TIME:  09:17
WASHINGTON, DC                                                                             EDIT:  06/28/94
CYCLE: MAR 1994                        PRESENT VALUE ESTIMATES BY INTEREST RATE SCENARIO    PAGE:  06
                                                   (Balances in $000)
```

				*** Change in Interest Rates ***					
* OFF-BALANCE-SHEET POSITIONS *	-178 bp	-300 bp	-200 bp	-100 bp	No Change	+100 bp	+200 bp	+300 bp	+400 bp
OPTIONAL COMMITMENTS TO ORIGINATE									
FRMs & Balloon/2-Step Mortgages	4,515	6,836	5,220	3,247	39	-3,914	-8,055	-12,078	-15,846
ARMs	283	350	342	294	218	110	-32	-198	-377
Other Mortgages	–	–	–	–	–	–	–	–	–
FIRM COMMITMENTS									
Purchase/Originate Mtgs & MBS	1,112	2,471	1,387	-170	-2,476	-4,943	-7,319	-9,570	-11,694
Sell Mortgages & MBS	–	–	–	–	–	–	–	–	–
Purchase Non-Mortgage Items	–	–	–	–	–	–	–	–	–
Sell Non-Mortgage Items	–	–	–	–	–	–	–	–	–
OPTIONS ON MORTGAGES & MBS	–	–	–	–	–	–	–	–	–
INTEREST-RATE SWAPS									
Pay Fixed, Receive Floating	-8,812	-27,187	-11,823	2,789	16,689	29,914	42,497	54,472	65,868
Pay Floating, Receive Fixed	9,599	30,234	12,988	-3,457	-19,092	-33,961	-48,104	-61,560	-74,366
Basis Swaps	–	–	–	–	–	–	–	–	–
Swaptions	–	–	–	–	–	–	–	–	–
INTEREST-RATE CAPS	–	–	–	–	–	–	–	–	–
INTEREST-RATE FLOORS	–	–	–	–	–	–	–	–	–
FUTURES	–	–	–	–	–	–	–	–	–
OPTIONS ON FUTURES	–	–	–	–	–	–	–	–	–
CONSTRUCTION LIP	–	–	–	–	–	–	–	–	–
SELF-VALUED [CMR911-CMR919]	943	1,733	974	835	824	338	-714	-2,292	-3,936
*** OFF-BALANCE-SHEET POSITIONS	7,640	14,436	9,088	3,538	-3,797	-12,456	-21,727	-31,225	-40,350
*** NET PORTFOLIO VALUE ***									
ASSETS	2,817,931	2,848,682	2,823,480	2,795,847	2,755,760	2,705,778	2,650,131	2,586,453	2,529,996
- LIABILITIES	2,614,823	2,641,047	2,619,136	2,598,056	2,577,724	2,558,173	2,539,294	2,521,075	2,503,508
+ OFF-BALANCE-SHEET POSITIONS	7,640	14,436	9,088	3,538	-3,797	-12,456	-21,727	-31,225	-40,350
*** NET PORTFOLIO VALUE	210,749	222,071	213,431	201,330	174,239	135,149	89,110	34,152	-13,862

Chapter Twenty-One

Portfolio Management and Regulation

The Regulatory Implications for Investment Companies Employing Derivatives

Jeffrey P. Burns
Associate
Morgan, Lewis & Bockius LLP

INTRODUCTION

What a derivative is and how these instruments are employed has increasingly become a focus of the financial media and regulators worldwide. It is estimated that the market for these instruments, however defined, amounts to between $12 trillion and $35 trillion in principal or notional amount. As a result, greater emphasis and interest has been directed to the various derivative instruments and their corresponding markets. For instance, in 1994, several significant losses incurred by commercial entities and registered investment companies caused U.S. regulators, such as the Securities and Exchange Commission (SEC) and, the Commodity Futures Trading Commission (CFTC), to place greater scrutiny on the use of these instruments. During 1993 and 1994, Congress held hearings on the derivatives markets and introduced legislation to regulate the derivatives activities of banks, securities firms, and other unregulated dealers in derivatives. In addition, several reports on this subject noted the need for additional regulation in order to properly monitor various unregulated derivatives dealers. Regulators, however, have up to this point maintained that existing statutes and regulations provide adequate means of addressing and regulating existing derivatives activities.

Accordingly, Congress has deferred to federal financial regulatory agencies the regulation and supervision of the derivatives markets. In this vein, regulators have bolstered their oversight responsibilities with respect to derivatives and now place greater emphasis on examination and inspection programs to determine whether entities such as broker-dealers and investment companies are improperly leveraging their assets to enhance yields to the detriment of investors, market stability, and long-term existence. This chapter briefly summarizes the regulatory structure imposed by the SEC on investment companies investing in derivatives, emphasizing troublesome compliance areas for investment advisors and boards of directors to consider.

INVESTMENT COMPANIES AND THE DERIVATIVES MARKETS

Derivatives Markets

Investment companies or funds engage in trading strategies that employ derivative instruments for the purpose of hedging market risks, obtaining exposure to a variety of differing markets without portfolio liquidation, and/or increasing potential fund yields. Although stock and bond funds' use of derivatives has been limited, tax-free-municipal funds have been heavy users of derivatives. In addition, money market funds are increasingly holding structured financial instruments, characterized by periodic interest-rate adjustments that may not pay out the par value of the instrument at maturity. Both the investment company industry and the SEC are concerned that the imprudent use of derivatives has caused recent fund losses. As a result, the SEC is questioning the adequacy of fund "derivatives" disclosures to shareholders.

Derivatives include a wide array of financial products that derive their value from other assets, such as securities, foreign currencies, and commodities. Certain derivative products—such as options on securities, futures contracts, and options on futures contracts—are listed and traded on various exchanges; others—such as currency and interest-rate swaps, collars, caps, and floors—are customized to suit the needs of institutional investors, and are purchased and sold in the over-the-counter (OTC) market. Derivatives trading is generally a zero-sum game, i.e., for every winner there is a corresponding loser. In effect, derivatives do not create wealth but instead allocate risks in a manner similar to insurance contracts.

Derivatives historically encompassed options, forwards, futures, and other financial instruments with similar characteristics.[1] The term *derivative* is also being used in current parlance to include securities that repackage the ownership of assets, such as mortgage-backed securities, collateral mortgage obligations (CMOs), and asset-backed securities. Moreover, convertible securities and structured securities that may have an imbedded option or future that affects payout of the instrument are also considered derivatives.

The market for derivatives is essentially divided into two types: exchange-traded and OTC. Exchange-traded derivatives consist of standardized futures and options contracts traded in an auction market on the floor of a regulated exchange. These products are guaranteed by the exchange clearing house, which is the counterparty of every contract. Others include, but are not limited to, index and currency warrants, hybrids, and mandatorily convertible bonds or preferred stock. Contrary to the manner in which futures and options are structured, these other exchange-traded products do not have the exchange clearing-house guarantee. Instead, investors must look to the assets or credit of the derivatives dealer or corporate issuer for payment.

The second category of derivative is known as OTC (for a description of notable OTC derivatives, see Appendix A). In the OTC derivatives market, derivatives dealers offer customized products, such as swaps,[2] caps, collars, floors, options, and structured instruments.[3] These products

---

[1] *See* Cohen, "The Challenge of Derivatives," 63, *Fordham Law Review,* 1993 (1995) for a discussion of the term "derivative" and its generally understood meaning. See also Markham, ' "Confederate Bonds," "General Custer," Instruments,' 25, *Seton Hall Law Review 1,* (1994) for a general discussion of the derivatives' market and its recent growth.

[2] A swap is an agreement between two parties to exchange sets of cash flows over a period of time in the future. These contracts are not currently subject to SEC or CFTC regulation and are not traded on a futures or securities exchange (i.e., an OTC instrument).

[3] A cap is an OTC instrument where the buyer pays a single fixed amount and the seller makes periodic payments based on the excess of a given floating rate over a given annual rate. A floor is an instrument where the buyer pays a single fixed amount while the seller makes periodic payments based on the excess of a given annual rate over a given floating rate. A collar is an instrument where a cap and a floor are combined so that one party makes floating rate payments on the

do not have a clearing house, and therefore the credit of the issuer is of paramount concern. In general, OTC products do not have the restrictive requirements imposed by the exchange and the regulators, such as transparency, position limits, duration limitations, and margin and capital requirements. Dealers, however, may require collateral payments similar to a margin system.

Although derivatives help end users to manage financial risks by better matching risk/reward profiles, derivatives may also aggravate the following risks: (1) market,[4] (2) credit,[5] (3) operational,[6] (4) liquidity,[7] and (5) legal.[8] In the case of exchange-traded products, these risks are greatly reduced. Dealer and issuer-type products that are exchange-traded would have greater credit risks due to the absence of a clearinghouse guarantee; however, the listing criteria required by the exchanges help to lessen such concerns.

For OTC products, all of the risks listed above are very real and must be taken seriously by senior management. In particular, credit and operational risks provide the greatest opportunity for failure for end users employing derivatives. Therefore, many derivatives dealers have established high credit-rated derivatives subsidiaries in order to provide greater financial security and stability.[9] It is important to emphasize that end users

---

cap and the other makes floating rate payments on the floor. A structured instrument is one whose interest rate and/or principal value is linked to the movement of the value of certain equities, commodities, interest rates, foreign currencies, or foreign markets.

[4]Market risk is the risk of decline in the value of the derivative arising from adverse movements in the price, index, or rate of the instrument underlying the derivative.

[5]Credit risk is the risk of exposure in the event a counterparty to the transaction defaults, or otherwise fails to perform under the terms of the derivative.

[6]Operational risk is the risk that inadequate internal controls, procedures, human error, systems failure, or fraud can result in unexpected losses.

[7]Liquidity risk is the risk that a financial asset cannot be sold or replaced quickly at its fundamental value.

[8]Legal risk is the risk of loss resulting from the unenforceability of a contract.

[9]A derivative product company (DPC) is a AAA-rated subsidiary of a financial institution or securities firm that provides its parent corporation with a vehicle for participating in derivative product transactions through an increased credit standing. DPCs are given a credit rating by one or more credit rating institutions. Such rating services normally perform an evaluation of each DPC with emphasis on the following areas: portfolio quality, management and operating guidelines, parent-subsidiary relationship, and capital adequacy and risk modeling.

continue to evaluate the dealer-issuer's financial strength since high credit ratings are not a guarantee against failure or financial collapse.

Operational risk is another key risk that senior management must be keenly aware of in the case of OTC derivatives. The complexity of modern derivative products has caused an increase in this type of risk for derivatives dealers and end users. Accordingly, certain internal controls should be implemented to protect against potential losses from operational difficulties.[10]

Derivatives and Investment Companies

A 1994 survey by the Investment Company Institute (ICI) indicated that 475 investment companies held derivatives having a market value averaging approximately 2 percent of net assets and an average notional value of over 15 percent of net assets.[11] In addition, an increasing number of the equity and debt securities purchased by mutual funds have features similar to an embedded option, forward or futures contract, causing prices or yields to vary, at least in part, based on the future value of the securities, the future value of another security, or the future value of a securities index or interest-rate index. In fact, a number of investment companies have been jolted by a precipitous decline in their portfolios as a result of the sudden illiquidity of inverse floaters and similar instruments.[12]

Although no formal action has been taken by the SEC, certain

---

[10]Senior management of both derivatives dealers and end users should include the following areas in connection with the implementation of an internal control program: (1) oversight by informed and involved management; (2) systems; (3) operations, including record keeping, documentation, and confirmation activities; (4) controls to allocate management responsibility; and (5) audit.

[11]ICI, *Derivatives Securities Survey* (February 1994). The survey further indicated that the level of use of derivatives varied according to fund type, with fixed-income funds accounting for 84 percent of total market value of all derivatives held by reporting funds and 62 percent of the total notional amount.

[12]*See, e.g.,* "Bond Fund Sets Disclosure Pact on Derivatives," *The Wall Street Journal,* April 18, 1994, p. C1; "Paying the Piper," *Barron's,* April 11, 1994, p. 15; "Derivatives Undo a Popular Paine Webber Fund, Triggering 4% One-Day Drop in Its Value," *Barron's,* May 16, 1994, p. MW12; "Sinking Funds," *Barron's,* May 16, 1994, p. MW12; "Piper Jaffray Acts to Boost Battered Fund," *The Wall Street Journal,* May 23, 1994, p. C1. In addition, *see infra* Part VI, Section B.

members of the SEC have expressed concern about the increasing use of derivatives by investment companies and have spotlighted the role of independent directors. For example, SEC Chairman Arthur Levitt advised that:

> In overseeing the fund's portfolio management, directors will increasingly have to ask about derivatives and whether they achieve intended results. Directors will have to satisfy themselves that portfolio managers have the expertise to handle them—that their uses are in keeping with the fund's policies—that appropriate limits are set and observed—and that managers are not blinded to the risk.[13]

More specifically, former SEC Commissioner Richard Y. Roberts previously cited four specific measures that fund directors should take with regard to derivatives: (1) review of the disclosure documents to determine whether the risks associated with the fund's investment strategies are appropriately disclosed and to verify whether these risks are compatible with the fund's investment objectives and policy; (2) frequent discussions with the investment advisor to substantiate that each portfolio manager's knowledge (as well as his or her staff) is adequate in connection with the risks associated with the fund's derivatives investment strategies; (3) an understanding that the trading strategies employed by the fund's portfolio managers do not run afoul of the anti-leverage provisions of Section 18 of the Act; and (4) an annual review of the fund's portfolio to ensure compliance with Guide 4 of Form N-1A, which limits an investment company's investment in illiquid investments to 15 percent of its total portfolio.[14]

Although these speeches do not constitute formal action by the SEC, they do constitute statements regarding the possible direction of the agency with respect to derivatives, and therefore deserve careful consider-

---

[13] *See* Remarks of Arthur Levitt, Chairman, SEC, entitled *Mutual Fund Directors: On the Front Line for Investors* before the 1994 Mutual Funds and Investment Management Conference, Scottsdale, AZ, on March 21, 1994. Chairman Levitt added that if a fund employs derivatives, then the directors would be well advised to review pricing and liquidity issues, trading strategies, accounting questions, and internal controls. See also Remarks of Arthur Levitt, Chairman, SEC, entitled *Mutual Fund Directors as Investor Advocates* before the 2nd Annual Symposium for Mutual Fund Trustees and Directors, Washington, D.C. on April 11, 1995.

[14] *See* Remarks of Richard Y. Roberts, Commissioner, SEC, entitled *Emphasis on the Watchdog Role and Responsibilities of Mutual Fund Directors* before the IDS Mutual Fund Conference, Scottsdale, AZ, on February 10, 1994.

ation. Accordingly, these recommendations, and other concerns that should be addressed, are discussed in turn.

THE REGULATORY FRAMEWORK

Section 18 and Leverage[15]

The use of leverage by investment companies originally led to legislation to regulate the investment company industry in 1940.[16] Prior to the passage of the 1940 Act, many investment companies had leveraged their assets to exceedingly dangerous levels through excessive borrowing and through the issuance of excessive amounts of senior securities usually in the form of preferred stock. These leveraged capital structures dramatically increased the speculative nature of investment company securities, a result that Congress viewed as undesirable.

Congress addressed this concern by limiting, in Section 18 of the 1940 Act, the amount and type of borrowings a fund could incur. Section 18 of the 1940 Act prohibits open-end investment companies or mutual funds from issuing any senior security other than bank loans or borrowings. Such borrowings cannot exceed one-third of a fund's assets measured after the borrowing has been made. Closed-end investment companies, on the other hand, have the ability to issue senior debt securities up to one-third of their assets.

The SEC addressed the leverage aspect of derivative instruments and other similar transactions in a 1979 Release, concluding that any arrangement resulting in the leveraging of investment company assets, without any significant limitation, involves the issuance of a senior security in violation of Section 18 of the 1940 Act.[17] Notwithstanding Section 18 of the 1940 Act, the SEC has permitted funds to invest (short or long) in derivative instruments that create senior securities, under certain circumstances, if the fund takes steps to substantially reduce or eliminate the leverage involved. The SEC has identified three ways to permit funds to

---

[15]*See* S. Strauss, Derivatives and Leverage: Considerations Under Section 18 of the 1940 Act, *Investment Lawyer* (August 1994) for a complete analysis of Section 18 under the 1940 Act.

[16]*See Investment Trusts and Investment Companies: Hearings on S. 3580 Before a Subcommittee of the Senate Committee on Banking and Currency*, 76th Cong., 3d Sess. 1029 (1940)(Statement of David Schenker, Chief Counsel, SEC Investment Trust Study).

[17]*See* Investment Company Act Release No. 10666 (April 18, 1979).

engage in such portfolio management techniques: (1) own the instrument or assets underlying the contract; (2) set up a segregated account consisting of cash, government securities, or high-grade liquid debt equal to the contract price (less any initial or variation margin or options premiums already deposited); or (3) own an offsetting position. These steps function as a practical limit on the amount of leverage the fund may undertake and also ensure that there are adequate assets to meet the obligations arising from such activities.[18] Accordingly, through the use of segregated assets or covered positions, investment companies can employ derivatives and avoid the asset coverage restrictions of Section 18 of the 1940 Act.

With respect to the trading of certain derivative products—such as options, futures, and forwards—investment companies generally use segregated accounts in order to comply with Section 18. A segregated account freezes certain assets of the investment company and renders such assets unavailable for sale or other disposition.[19] The chart in Appendix B to this chapter summarizes the legal requirements mandated by the 1940 Act and the SEC in applicable interpretative releases and no-action letters.[20]

Certain derivatives, however, do not create claims against a fund, and, therefore, do not require asset coverage—i.e., mortgage- and asset-backed securities, of which open-end investment companies hold significant amounts. These assets, therefore, have no significant legal limitations on the extent they may be held by funds, other than the diversification requirements imposed by the 1940 Act and the Internal Revenue Code and the restrictions on the amount of illiquid assets that may be held. However, like options, such instruments may be designed to capture (or suffer) market movements augmented beyond that normally achieved using the same amount of capital. The SEC would effectively like to have directors

---

[18]*See, e.g.,* IDS Bond Fund Inc. (April 11, 1983); Montgomery Street Income Securities, Inc. (April 11, 1983); SteinRoe Bond Fund, Inc. (Jan. 17, 1984); Z-Seven Fund, Inc. (May 21, 1984); GMO Core Trust (Aug. 19, 1985); Putnam Options Income Trust II (September 23, 1985); Dreyfus Strategic Investing and Dreyfus Strategic Income (June 22, 1987); Hutton Options Trading L.P. (February 2, 1989); and Stanford C. Bernstein Fund (June 25, 1990). Investment company purchases of options on individual securities, securities indexes, and futures contracts generally do not run afoul of Section 18 of the 1940 Act because of the absence of the leveraging of fund assets. In such cases, the potential loss is limited to the amount of premium paid.

[19]The value of assets in the segregated account must be marked-to-market daily, with additional assets placed in such account whenever the total value falls below the obligation of the derivative instrument.

[20]*See supra* notes 18 and 19; Guide 23 to Form N-1A.

impose limits on the use of these instruments to establish protections not covered by Section 18 but designed to accomplish similar purposes.

Liquidity and Valuation

The SEC imposes limits on the portion of a mutual fund's assets that may be used to purchase illiquid assets.[21] Furthermore, the SEC requires daily computation of net asset values by open-end investment companies so that investors can rely on pricing for purposes of purchase and redemption.[22]

It is essential that an investment company properly value its portfolio securities. As the SEC has stated:

> [V]aluation of portfolio securities by an investment company is . . . critical . . . such valuation largely determines the price at which shares of the company are sold and redeemed and the compensation of the investment advisor where . . . such compensation is based on net assets. Moreover, investors may be misled by the reported performance of an investment company where portfolio securities are not properly valued.[23]

Section 2(a)(41) of the 1940 Act and Rule 2a-4 thereunder require that, in determining net asset value, "securities for which market quotations are readily available" be valued at the market value and that securities for which market quotations are not readily available be valued at "fair value as determined in good faith by the board of directors."[24]

The pricing of complex OTC derivative instruments is particularly troublesome due to the fact that, as previously stated, often only the counterparty or the dealer that structured the product may be willing to make a bid. The recent upheaval in these markets has resulted in underwriters being accused of failing to provide adequate secondary-market support or accurate pricing information.[25] Further, recent press reports have also indicated that the brokerage houses that have created these products have been very reluctant to make markets in such esoteric

---

[21]*See* Guide 4 to Form N-1A; Investment Company Act Release No. 18612 (March 12, 1992), 57 FR 9828.

[22]*See* Rule 22c-1 under the 1940 Act [17 C.F.R. 270. 22C-1 (1994)].

[23]*Winfield & Co., Inc.*, 44 SEC 811, 817 (February 2, 1972).

[24]*See* Section 2(a)(41) of the 1940 Act and Rule 2a-4 under the 1940 Act [17 C.F.R. 270.29-4 (1994)].

[25]Pressman, "Major Buyer of Derivatives Leaves Market, Cites Disclosure," *The Bond Buyer,* September 9, 1993, p. 1.

securities, fearing losses when markets are volatile and unpredictable.[26] Questions have also been raised about the adequacy and accuracy of pricing services, particularly during times of market stress.

In particular, investment company custodians have struggled with developing appropriate accounting, reporting, and valuation systems for OTC derivative instruments.[27] In terms of valuation, the custodian must determine the appropriate price of the derivative, which may vary according to the pricing model employed. Moreover, a more accurate measure of the derivative may at times be the price of the underlying security or asset, the value of the collateral backing the derivative, or the potential value of the underlying security or asset. These valuation issues for custodians in pricing a particular derivative, coupled with the absence of concrete accounting standards and the multi-informational flows among various departments at the fund itself, make pricing a daunting task for most custodial banks.[28]

The SEC has issued two interpretive releases that provide guidance on how to arrive at a carrying value for a fund's portfolio securities when market quotations are unavailable.[29] In Investment Company Act Release No. 5847, the SEC set forth the guiding principle for valuing "restricted securities." Specifically, this release states that the "current fair value of restricted securities would appear to be the amount which the owner might reasonably expect to receive for them upon their current sale."[30] Consistent with this guiding principle, the SEC maintains that boards of directors are ultimately responsible for determining the fair value of each such security in good faith.[31] Accordingly, if a board does not actually value

---

[26]See, e.g., Jereski, "Mortgage Derivatives Claim Victims Big and Small," The Wall Street Journal, April 18, 1994, at C1; C15.

[27]For an investment company, a custodian bank tracks the fund's positions in securities and other instruments as well as provides valuation services for various reporting obligations.

[28]See Kentouris, C. "Global Custodians Struggle with Responsibilities for New Instruments," Redemption Digest and Securities Industry Daily, May 17, 1994.

[29]Investment Company Act Release Nos. 5847 (October 21, 1969), 35 FR 253 and 6295 (December 23, 1970), 35 FR 19986.

[30]Investment Company Act Release No. 5847, supra note 30.

[31]As a result of the variety of securities and other assets held by funds, no particular formula or method of valuing securities or other assets for which market quotations are not readily available exists. In the context of such valuation, a registered investment company must have access to financial information regarding restricted securities and other assets held by the fund for which market quotes are not readily available. See Investment Company Act Release No. 5847, supra note 30.

each security itself, it may determine the *method* of valuing each issue of restricted securities in a fund's portfolio and must continuously review the appropriateness of such method.

In the later release, the SEC emphasized that "it is incumbent upon the board of directors to satisfy themselves (sic) that all appropriate factors relevant to the value of securities for which market quotations are not readily available have been considered and to determine the method of arriving at the fair value of each such security."[32] The SEC did note, however, that there is not a single standard by which an investment company can value its nonmarketable portfolio securities.

Custody of Assets

Section 17(f) of the 1940 Act provides that the securities and similar investments of a registered investment company must be placed in the custody of (1) a bank meeting certain requirements as specified in the 1940 Act, (2) a member of a national securities exchange, or (3) the company itself, in accordance with SEC rules. With respect to futures and commodities transactions, futures commission merchants (FCMs) and commodity clearinghouses do not fit within these categories, and therefore cannot meet the requirements for investment company asset custody.

The SEC, through its no-action procedure, has provided a manner in which investment companies are able to engage in futures transactions.[33] The custody procedure involves the establishment of a segregated account with a third-party custodian to hold the fund's initial margin deposit. The account is maintained in the name of the FCM, who has agreed that the assets will remain at all time with the custodian unless released back to the fund or sold or disposed of pursuant to the terms of the FCM's agreement with the fund. In connection with variation margin, the agreement between the fund and the FCM must provide that the fund will pay to the FCM or the FCM will pay to the fund, an amount equal to any change in the value of the futures contract on a daily basis. The FCM is required to notify the fund after close of trading each business day of the amount of

---

[32] *See* Investment Company Act Release No. 6295 *supra* note 30. In determining fair value, a board may appoint financial experts for assistance. The board is required to closely monitor, supervise, and review these calculations of fair value, paying particular attention to the appropriateness of the method used in valuing securities and other assets that do not have market quotations readily available.

[33] *See* Claremont Capital Corp. (September 16, 1979).

margin owed to or payable by the fund and must pay over any amount owed to the fund on the next business day.[34]

Disclosure

SEC Regulations require that an open-end investment company include in its prospectus, for any investment technique that places 5 percent or more of the fund's net assets at risk, a short description of "the types of securities in which [it] invests or will invest principally" as well as any investment practices or techniques that the fund employs or will employ.[35] For purposes of determining the percent of net assets at risk, the fund must refer to the potential liability or loss that it may incur in connection with the practice, and not simply the amount of assets invested.[36] Part F of the 1994 generic comment letter specifically comments that:

> [I]f more than 5 percent of a fund's net assets are at risk from its involvement in derivative instruments and derivative-based transactions, its prospectus should (1) identify the types of derivative-based transactions in which it will engage; (2) briefly describe the characteristics of such transactions or instruments; (3) state the purpose for which the fund will use derivatives; and (4) identify the risks of derivative instruments and derivative-based transactions.[37]

Former SEC Commissioner Roberts noted that current disclosure is most often boilerplate and not very useful to investors.[38] He asserted that brevity, rather than exhaustiveness, would assist investors' understanding. "Discussion of types of investments that will not constitute Registrant's principal portfolio emphasis, and of related policies or practices, should

---

[34] A proposal by the SEC would permit FCM and clearinghouse custody of investment company margin, subject to conditions designed to ensure the safekeeping of investment company assets. *See* Investment Company Act Release No. 20313 (May 24, 1994), 59 FR 28286. This proposal is still pending with the SEC.

[35] *See* Form N-1A, Items 4(a)(ii) and (b)(ii).

[36] *See* Letter to Registrants from Carolyn B. Lewis, assistant director, Division of Investment Management (February 22, 1993); Instructions to Item 8.4.c. of Form N-2.

[37] Letter to Registrants from Carolyn B. Lewis (February 1994).

[38] *See* Remarks of Richard Y. Roberts, Commissioner, SEC, entitled "Tax-Exempt Derivatives and Mutual Funds," before IBC Quantitative Municipal Investment Management Conference, New York, New York, dated January 27, 1994. Commissioner Roberts further cautioned in his speech that investment companies should clearly explain their derivative activities (i.e., whether investments are for hedging or speculative purposes, or a combination thereof, and roughly indicate such percentage); disclose the objectives of their derivative transactions; discuss the risks; and quantify the percentage of fund assets in derivatives.

generally receive less emphasis."[39] If no more than 5 percent of net assets were at risk in a fund's prior fiscal year, or are intended to be put at risk during the current year, or, in fact, may not be put at risk without violation of fund policies, "disclosure of information in a prospectus about such practice should be limited to that which is necessary to identify the practice."[40]

With respect to risks of using derivatives, the fund must discuss briefly the principal speculative or risk factors associated with investment in the fund, "as well as those factors generally associated with investment in a company with . . . policies . . . or trading markets similar to the Registrant's."[41] The SEC staff has specifically advised those funds investing in derivatives to include clear discussions of the risks associated with such instruments, including that:

1. A hedging technique may fail if the price movements of the securities underlying the derivative do not follow the price movements of the portfolio securities subject to the hedge;
2. The loss from investing in futures contracts is potentially unlimited;
3. Gains and losses in derivatives depends on the portfolio manager's ability to predict correctly the direction of stock prices, interest rates, and other economic factors; and
4. The investment company will likely be unable to control losses by closing its position where a liquid secondary market does not exist.[42]

In addition, the SEC recently amended its rules to require that investment companies discuss in their prospectuses or annual reports any economic factors or investment strategies and techniques that materially affected performance during the most recently completed fiscal year.[43]

Press reports have also stated that the SEC's Division of Investment

---

[39] See Form N-1A, Item 4(b).

[40] Id.

[41] See Form N-1A, Item 4(c) and Guide 21. This discussion concerning risk factors must appear under a caption entitled "Risk Factors." See Letter to Registrants from Carolyn B. Lewis (January 11, 1990). In addition, similar requirements apply to closed-end investment companies. See Form N-2, Item 8.

[42] See Letter to Registrants from Carolyn B. Lewis (February 22, 1990).

[43] See Form N-1A, Item 5A. In response to this item, investment companies should discuss, for example, the effect that market fluctuations and the fund's hedging techniques had on its perfor-

Management is considering new requirements on what is disclosed to fund investors regarding derivatives.[44]

Diversification

Another possible trap in the use of derivatives by registered investment companies is the diversification requirement imposed by Section 5(b) of the 1940 Act on certain companies that are classified as "diversified." Section 5(b) of the 1940 Act requires that with respect to 75 percent of a fund's assets, no more than 5 percent may be invested in securities of a single issuer or in more than 10 percent of the outstanding voting securities of such issuer. Accordingly, for purposes of compliance with Section 5(b), a diversified investment company must determine who is the issuer[45] of each derivative and what is the value of the investment.[46]

Fund of Funds

Derivative securities are complex and include collateralized mortgage obligations and other asset-backed securities. Care must be taken to ensure that any such entity in which a fund invests satisfies the exclusion from the definition of "investment company" offered by Rule 3a-7 under the 1940 Act. Otherwise, the fund may inadvertently run afoul of the prohibition contained in Section 12(d) of the 1940 Act on acquisition of (a) investment company securities having, in the aggregate, a value more than 10 percent of the fund's total assets, or (b) securities of a single investment company

---

mance. *See* Investment Company Act Release No. 17294 (January 8, 1990), 55 FR 1460 (Proposed Amendments to Form N-1A).

[44] *See* Report of the Division of Investment Management regarding Mutual Funds and Derivative Instruments, dated September 26, 1994; King, "Congress May Ask SEC to Study Derivatives in Mutual Funds," *The Bond Buyer,* September 7, 1993, p. 10; Power, "SEC Officials Plan to Require Managers to Report More Data on Mutual Funds," *The Wall Street Journal,* June 27, 1994, p.A 14.

[45] Section 2(a)(22) of the 1940 Act defines an issuer as "*every* person who causes or proposes to issue any security. . . . " [emphasis added].

[46] Registered investment companies must also be aware of the requirements of Subchapter M of the Internal Revenue Code relating to the special tax treatment. Although it is beyond the scope of this chapter, these tax requirements include the "short-short" test, diversification and qualifying income requirements. Of particular concern, especially in the area of compliance, is the "short-short" rule. This rule requires that less than 30 percent of the investment company's gross income be derived from the sale or disposition of assets held for less than 3 months. Accordingly, an investment company must implement internal procedures that adequately track the holding periods for derivatives in order to comply with the "short-short" rule.

of more than 5 percent of its total assets, or (c) more than 3 percent of the outstanding voting securities of another investment company.

Section 12(d)(3) of the 1940 Act and Rule 12d3-1 thereunder generally prohibit mutual funds from purchasing securities issued by broker-dealers except under limited circumstances as noted above. The use of derivatives by mutual funds is accordingly affected by this regulation in two ways: (1) mutual funds must determine whether the derivative qualifies as a security; and (2) mutual funds must determine whether the derivative was issued by the broker-dealer.

Affiliated Transactions

For funds with advisors affiliated with dealers actively participating in the derivatives market, the fund must comply with Section 10(f) of the 1940 Act and Rule 10f-3 thereunder. Acquisition of securities in an offering in which such dealer is the principal underwriter is prohibited unless, among other things, (a) the offering is a firm commitment offering either of securities registered under the 1933 Act or of municipal securities, (b) if not municipal securities, the issuer has three years of operation, and (c) if municipal securities, the issue is highly rated by a nationally recognized statistical rating organization (NRSRO).

Further, if a dealer of derivatives also holds a significant percentage (5 percent or more) of a fund's shares in an omnibus account, it may be an affiliated person of the fund prohibited by Section 17(a) from selling any security or other property to the fund. Moreover, a derivative product that does not have a readily available market cannot be part of an interfund transaction permitted under Rule 17a-7.

CFTC Requirements

Rule 4.5 under the Commodity Exchange Act (CEA) was adopted in order to permit certain institutional investors, such as registered investment companies, to use CFTC-regulated derivatives (i.e., futures and related options contracts). Without this exemptive relief granted by the CFTC in Rule 4.5 with respect to the application of the CFTC's commodity pool provisions, investment companies would, in effect, be prohibited from investing in futures contracts and options on futures.

Rule 4.5 permits the use of futures contracts, options on futures and commodity options for bona fide hedging purposes. Moreover, a registered investment company, if authorized by its investment policies and objectives, is permitted to engage in these instruments for nonhedging purposes as long as such contracts do not exceed 5 percent of the investment company's assets.

Compliance Systems

A careful analysis should be made in connection with each investment in derivatives, especially OTC instruments, in order to determine who will be deemed the issuer or issuers of the instrument for purpose of applicable diversification requirements under Section 5(b) of the 1940 Act and Subchapter M of the Internal Revenue Code and, for money market funds, under Rule 2a-7. A determination must also be made as to the valuation to the fund's investment in the securities of each such issuer.

Appropriate procedures should be in place for evaluating creditworthiness of counterparties in OTC derivatives and for monitoring overall exposure to each counterparty. Credit quality analysis is essential for risk management and, in the case of money market funds, to assure compliance with Rule 2a-7.

Portfolio managers should be permitted to use particular derivatives on behalf of a fund only if senior management of the investment advisor is satisfied that the portfolio manager has the appropriate knowledge and expertise. In particular, management should be comfortable that the portfolio manager fully understands how the derivative is structured and the factors that affect the pricing and returns realized on such derivative instruments, that the portfolio manager will utilize such instruments consistent with the investment objectives and policies of the fund as disclosed in its registration statement and that the instrument has been properly classified as liquid or illiquid.

Moreover, management should also take steps to insure that legal, accounting, and compliance personnel understand the instruments in which the fund invests. In particular, accounting personnel should have the expertise necessary to deal effectively with the unique accounting and tax issues associated with derivatives. These issues include, but are not limited to: identification for book and tax purposes of the nature of income produced by derivatives; when income and gain for book and tax purposes is deemed to be realized and in what amounts; and the manner in which income on derivatives should be calculated for purposes of performance advertising.

Legal and compliance personnel should also be sufficiently familiar with the instruments proposed to be utilized by the fund to be able to adequately evaluate whether their use is consistent with the fund's investment policies and restrictions and the types of risks described in the prospectus.

Procedures should also be in place requiring preclearance of written documentation of derivative transactions prior to actual investment. Particular attention should be directed by legal personnel toward ensuring that the documents properly reflect the economic deal bargained for, that the counterparty is authorized to enter into the transaction, and that appropriate remedies are afforded in the event of a default.

In connection with each OTC derivative transaction, instructions should be provided to the investment company's custodian as to the specific assets to be maintained in custody and whether any margin or other specific arrangements need to be implemented. In addition, if the particular derivative instruments are maintained in book entry form, assurance should be obtained that the book entry system utilized is a qualified system under Rule 17f-4 under the 1940 Act or that a no-action letter or opinion of counsel as to the propriety of the use of such a system has been obtained. In addition, the custodian should be informed as to the nature of the product acquired by the fund, the manner in which payments to be received by the fund are to be calculated, the currency in which it is to be received, the timing of such payments and the extent of the custodian's responsibility, if any, for verifying that payments required to be made under the instrument are properly calculated by the issuer and that the fund receives the payments to which it is entitled under the terms of the instrument.

RECENT DEVELOPMENTS

Since 1993, several reports detailing the OTC derivatives market have been released by various organizations worldwide.[47] A primary focus of these reports is the involvement of various financial institutions in OTC deriva-

---

[47] See *Recent Developments in International Interbank Relations*, Bank for International Settlements, Report prepared by a Working Group established by the Central Banks of the Group of Ten countries, Basle, October 1992; Group of Thirty, Global Derivatives Study Group, *Derivatives: Practices and Principles* (July 1993) ["G-30 Study"]; Report of the CFTC, *OTC Derivative Markets and Their Regulation* (October 1993)["CFTC Report"]; Report Prepared by the House Banking Committee Minority Staff, *Financial Derivatives* (November 1993) ["House Banking Report"]; General Accounting Office, *Financial Derivatives: Actions Needed to Protect the*

tives transactions and whether capital standards are adequate, given the various market and credit risks involved. In addition, these same reports detail the risks both internal and external to end users and dealers as well as call for greater scrutiny by top management through the implementation and monitoring of internal control mechanisms. The most significant of these derivatives reports are summarized in the following section.

Derivatives Studies

Group of Thirty (G-30). The G-30 Study (or "Study") released in July 1993 was written by senior managers of firms acting as end users and dealers of derivatives as well as individuals from related legal, accounting, and academic disciplines. The Study sets forth 20 recommendations for firms engaging in derivatives transactions and 4 recommendations for legislators and regulators. The major contribution of the Study to the derivatives debate has been to define a set of sound risk-management practices for end users and dealers. Accordingly, the guiding principle throughout the G-30 Study is the importance of internal controls established and monitored by senior management rather than direct federal regulation in most areas.[48]

The significant G-30 recommendations indicate that each end user and dealer of derivatives should take the following measures:

1. A determination by top management regarding the scope of involvement in derivatives activities and the specific policies to be applied;
2. Daily mark-to-market valuation of positions;
3. A quantification of market risk under a variety of market conditions (i.e., performance of stress simulations) and forecasts of funding needs;
4. Assessment of credit risks from derivatives transactions based on the risk exposure in relation to firm credit limits;

Financial System (May 1994) ["GAO Report"]; and Technical Committee of the International Organization of Securities Commissions (IOSCO), *Operational and Financial Risk Control Mechanisms for Over-the-Counter Derivatives Activities of Regulated Securities Firms* (July 1994) ["IOSCO Study"].

[48]The Study attempts to encourage dealers and end users of derivative products to develop appropriate systems for measuring and monitoring risks.

5. Use of multiproduct master agreements with netting provisions (such as the ISDA Master Agreement);

6. Assurances that the derivatives transactions entered into within and across jurisdictions are legally enforceable;

7. Establish market- and credit-risk management functions within the firm separate from the dealer function;

8. Authorize only those individuals with the requisite skill and knowledge to transact in derivatives and manage the risks;

9. Establish management information systems sophisticated enough to monitor, manage, and report the risk and exposure of derivatives in a timely and precise manner; and

10. Adopt accounting and disclosure practices for international harmonization and transparency.

In addition, the Study also encouraged legislators and regulators to take the following steps in order to provide a level of certainty without impairing the proper use of derivatives:

1. Recognize netting arrangements and amend the Basle Accord to reflect such benefits in bank capital regulations;[49]

2. Remove the legal and regulatory uncertainties regarding derivatives;

3. Amend inappropriate and disadvantageous tax regulations; and

4. Provide guidance on the accounting and the reporting of derivatives and other financial instruments.

Although the G-30 Study suggests the establishment of a variety of internal control and monitoring systems related to the use and risk expo-

---

[49]Netting is defined as an agreed offsetting of positions or obligations by trading partners or participants in a system. Netting reduces a larger number of individual positions or obligations to a smaller number of positions. In April 1993, the Basle Committee on Banking Supervision issued two proposals to amend the Basle Agreement. The first proposal would amend the existing framework established under the Basle Agreement to permit banks to recognize certain types of netting arrangements for purposes of calculating their capital requirements. The second proposal would broaden the existing framework of the Basle Agreement to require banks to hold capital against the market risk associated with their trading activities. Banking regulators and Congress have taken steps to bolster netting arrangements with respect to swaps and other OTC transactions. See Waldman, "OTC Derivatives & Systematic Risk: Innovative Finance or the Dance into the Abyss," 43 Am. U.L. Rev. 1023 (1994) and Dugan, "Derivatives: Netting, Insolvency, and End Users," Banking L.J. 638 (1995).

sure of derivatives transactions for firms engaged in the OTC derivatives marketplace, the Study falls short of mandating these reforms by legislation and/or regulatory initiative. Instead, the Study relies on the business judgment of individual firms, as well as the discipline of the marketplace, for establishing appropriate capital levels and risk tolerances.

The basic premise of the Report is that there is no need for fundamental regulatory reform or change. This fact is borne out by the forward to the Study, which plainly states:

> The general attitude of the Study toward regulation is plain: derivatives by their nature do not introduce risks of a fundamentally different kind or of a greater scale than those already present in the financial markets. Hence, systemic risks are not appreciably aggravated, and supervisory concerns can be addressed within the present regulatory structures and approaches. Where the official priority should be placed, in the view of the Study, is in clarifying legal uncertainties, and resolving legal inconsistencies between countries, that may impede risk-reduction procedures such as 'netting.'[50]

Therefore, the G-30 Study is a starting point for financial institutions, securities firms, and other participants in the global OTC derivatives market. It provides the framework for sound risk-management practices without imposing unnecessary legislative and/or regulatory measures that could inhibit new product innovation and/or discourage market participants from developing individualized risk-management systems.

General Accounting Office (GAO). The GAO in May 1994 released its long-awaited two-year derivatives study (the "GAO Report" or "Report") commissioned by the Senate and House Banking and Agricultural Committees. A major focus of the Report concerns gaps in the OTC derivatives regulatory framework, notably securities firm and insurance company affiliates. Moreover, the Report also noted with disfavor the absence of federally mandated risk-management systems.

Although GAO acknowledged the utility of derivatives and risk-management products to hedge against the risks of change in interest rates, a falling dollar, or other market parameters, the Report warned that if a large dealer of derivatives " . . . failed, the failure could pose risks to other firms—including federally insured depository institutions—and the financial system as a whole."[51] Accordingly, GAO does not believe that

---

[50] G-30 Study, *supra* note 48, pp. i-ii.

[51] GAO Report, *supra* note 48, at pp. 11–12.

the recommendations set forth by the G-30 Study will be implemented and fully monitored without federal intervention and oversight. To a large degree the differences in approach cited by GAO from the findings embodied in the G-30 Study can be associated with the political environment (exacerbated by the reported derivatives losses experienced by firms during 1994) rather than economic or regulatory reality.[52]

The Report estimated that at year-end 1992, the worldwide volume in derivatives activity amounted to $12.1 trillion in notional amount, although the actual risk or exposure is significantly less than the notional or principal amount of derivatives transactions. For example, GAO found that gross credit risk for the 14 major U.S. financial institutions amounted to 1.8 percent of their notional amount.

The GAO Report specifically recommended the following reforms:

1. All major U.S. OTC derivatives dealers should be federally regulated;
2. SEC responsibility for unregulated entities (securities firm and insurance company derivatives affiliates);
3. Creation of an interagency commission to establish principles and standards for each federal financial regulator in connection with derivatives activities;
4. Improved accounting and public disclosure of derivatives holdings;
5. Development of more stringent capital standards for derivatives dealers;
6. Establish requirements for all major OTC derivatives dealers to submit to independent audit committees and internal control reporting;
7. Internal control reporting by boards, managers, and external

---

[52]In fact, many regulators are not convinced that new regulations are necessary, especially when such regulations could be quickly outdated in the fast-paced derivatives business or even worse, increase the risks. Regulatory initiatives that create an inhospitable U.S. environment for derivatives could have the effect of driving this business offshore. Moreover, some regulators have argued that they should not be in a position to prevent sophisticated market participants from taking risks or engaging in derivatives transactions based on their view of the market. *See* Steven Lipin, "GAO to Join Hot Debate on Derivatives," *The Wall Street Journal*, May 18, 1994, p. C1; C.16. *See also* Testimony of Arthur Levitt, chairman, SEC, Concerning Derivative Financial Instruments before the Subcommittee on Telecommunications and Finance Committee on Energy and Commerce, dated May 25, 1994.

auditors to include assessments of derivatives risk-management systems;

8. Annual examinations of the adequacy of risk-management systems used by major OTC derivatives dealers;

9. Harmonization of disclosure, capital, examination, and accounting standards for derivatives; and

10. Ensure that the Financial Accounting Standards Board (FASB) quickly proceeds to develop and adopt accounting and disclosure requirements for derivatives.[53]

The economic effect of many of GAO's recommendations would clearly increase costs for the securities and commercial banking industries and could as a result decrease the availability of such financial products. Notwithstanding possible legal and jurisdictional challenges, it is unlikely that legislative and regulatory-mandated requirements affecting the internal management of securities firms and other corporations would be adopted.[54] However, informal controls for policing derivatives, such as close federal supervision and voluntary oversight, are much more likely to occur due to the tradition of self-regulatory oversight in the securities industry and the political and legal difficulties involved in legislating government control over the internal management of corporate entities. Moreover, it is highly unlikely that the 104th Congress would be willing to go along with these reforms.

In July 1994, the six major U.S. securities dealers in derivatives and the SEC started to cooperate in order to establish voluntary standards regarding derivatives sales and trading.[55] The SEC indicated its desire to establish standards in the following areas: (1) extent of disclosure relating to certain derivatives operations; (2) capital requirements; and (3) suitability

---

[53]The FASB in October 1994 adopted improved disclosures about derivative financial instruments—futures, forwards, swaps, options, and other financial instruments with similar characteristics. The rule requires additional disclosures about the size, nature, and terms of derivatives. Moreover, corporations holding derivatives for trading purposes must also disclose the average fair or current value balance of positions during the reporting period and net gains or losses from such trading. The FASB Rule did not, however, require companies to inform investors about potential risks to the company of trading in specific derivatives. *See* FASB, "Disclosure About Derivative Financial Instruments and Fair Value of Financial Instruments," (April 14, 1994) [Exposure Draft].

[54]*See Business Roundtable* v. *SEC,* 905 F.2d 406 (1990) and Internal Affairs Doctrine as described in *CTS Corp* v. *Dynamics,* 481 U.S. 69, 107 S.Ct. 1637 (1987).

[55]Taylor and Lipin, "SEC, Six Firms Work to Set Derivatives Rules," *The Wall Street Journal,* July 6, 1994, p. C1; C. 18.

of selling derivatives to users such as cities, pension funds, and mutual funds. Senior SEC staff believe that any agreement on voluntary standards must strengthen the information base for its existing risk-assessment program, better develop methods for evaluating capital adequacy, and ensure that customer protection issues are adequately addressed. Wall Street, however, views voluntary standards as a way of preventing more burdensome legislative efforts.[56]

As a result of the continuing efforts of the SEC, the CFTC, and notable broker-dealers, voluntary guidelines for the oversight of OTC derivatives activities by U.S. regulators have been adopted.[57] These standards focus on four areas: (1) internal controls monitoring derivatives exposures; (2) enhanced reporting to regulators; (3) evaluation of capital given derivatives risks; and (4) the nature of the counterparty relationship. Although these guidelines are nonbinding, it is believed that most broker-dealers in the U.S. will implement a majority of the recommendations.[58]

Derivatives Losses and Litigation

In 1994, several U.S. corporations suffered losses using interest-rate swaps, foreign-exchange derivatives, and various other types of structured derivative products similar to futures and/or options in their payoff scheme. This list includes such notable corporations as Procter & Gamble (P&G), Air Products & Chemical Inc., Atlantic Richfield, Gibson Greet-

---

[56]In 1994, the following bills were introduced in Congress for the purpose of regulating derivatives activities of financial institutions and their nonregulated securities affiliates: (1) H.R. 4170, entitled "Derivatives Safety and Soundness Act of 1994"; (2) H.R. 3748, entitled "Derivatives Supervision Act of 1994"; (3) H.R. 4745, entitled "Derivatives Dealers Act of 1994"; and (4) S. 2291 entitled, "Derivatives Supervision Act of 1994." Congressional leaders in 1995 have reintroduced all of these bills, which are pending in Congress. Specifically, House Banking Chairman James A. Leach (R-Iowa) introduced H.R. 20 entitled the "Risk Management Improvement and Derivatives Oversight Act of 1995;" Henry Gonzalez (D-TX) introduced H.R. 31 entitled the Derivatives Safety and Soundness Act of 1995; Edward J. Markey (D-MA) introduced H.R. 1063 entitled "Derivative Dealers Act of 1995"; and Byron L. Dorgan (D-ND) introduced S. 557 entitled "Derivatives Limitations Act of 1995."

[57]See Derivatives Policy Group, "A Framework for Voluntary Oversight of the OTC Derivatives Activities of Securities Firm Affiliates to Promote Confidence and Stability in Financial Markets" (March 1995).

[58]Similarly, the Federal Reserve Bank of New York, Public Securities Association and other financial trade organizations have released a set of voluntary guidelines entitled "Principles and Practices of Wholesale Financial Market Transactions" (August 17, 1995). These voluntary guidelines relate to the conduct of financial institutions and other appropriate market participants in connection with OTC derivatives.

ings, Dell Computer Corp., and Marion Merrell Dow. For example, P&G announced in April 1994 that it would take a one-time pretax charge of $157 million in order to close out two interest-rate swap contracts.[59]

In the cases of *Gibson Greetings, Inc.* v. *Bankers Trust Co.*[60] and *Procter & Gamble, Inc.* v. *Bankers Trust Co.*[61], the plaintiffs raised issues of suitability and fraud in the sale of swaps and other derivatives. In *Gibson Greetings*, the plaintiff sued Bankers Trust Co. (Bankers) for $23 million in compensatory damages and $50 million in punitive damages, alleging that Bankers misrepresented the risks of the swaps and thereby took advantage of their customer.[62] The *Gibson* case is particularly noteworthy, because it is the first time that an end user of derivatives claimed a lack of sophistication as a basis for its suit. This suit was settled by the parties at a cost to Bankers of $14 million. Moreover, both the SEC and the CFTC instituted administrative proceedings against Bankers, which have been settled without admitting or denying the findings. As part of this settlement, Bankers agreed to pay a fine of $10 million, as well as hire an independent consultant to conduct a review and make recommendations on internal management controls.[63]

The P&G case involves a transaction where P&G agreed to sell put options on 30-year Treasury bonds to Bankers while receiving a floating rate equal to the prevailing commercial paper rate in year one and the commercial paper rate plus a spread over the remaining years of the swap

---

[59]See Lipin, Bleakley, and Granito, "Portfolio Poker: Just What Firms Do With 'Derivatives' Is Suddenly A Hot Issue," *The Wall Street Journal,* April 14, 1994, p. A1; A7

[60]No. C-1-94-620 (S.D. Ohio 1994).

[61]No. C-1-94-735 (S.D. Ohio 1994).

[62]The transaction at issue was for a term of five years in which Gibson would receive a fixed interest rate and pay a floating interest rate based on the square of six-month LIBOR. At maturity, Gibson would pay Bankers $30 million and Bankers would pay the lesser of $30.6 million or an amount determined by the yields on 2-year and 30-year Treasury bonds. When interest rates increased in February 1994, Gibson incurred a loss of $8 million, which subsequently became $17.5 million. Gibson claims that Bankers forced it to then enter into closing transactions that capped the losses at $27.5 million.

[63]See In Re BT Securities Corporation, Securities Exchange Act Release No. 35136 and CFTC Docket No. 95-3 (December 22, 1994). The basis for the action by the SEC was premised on Bankers' material misrepresentations in the sale of the "derivative" to Gibson. The SEC recharacterized the swaps as securities, maintaining that both transactions were options based on underlying Treasury yields. Accordingly, Section 10(b) of the 1934 Act and Rule 10b-5 thereunder formed the heart of the SEC's case. Alternatively, the CFTC brought its enforcement action against Bankers in terms of its obligation as a commodity trading advisor (CTA). Therefore, the alleged advisory relationship between Bankers and Gibson became the basis of the CFTC's case for fraudulent misrepresentation and omission.

from Bankers. The strike prices of the put options were determined, however, by yields of 5-year Treasuries. P&G was essentially gambling that U.S. interest rates would remain stable or decrease. As interest rates rose in early 1994, P&G incurred losses amounting to approximately $157 million. P&G brought its case against Bankers, focusing on fraudulent sales practices, the advisory relationship, and unenforceability of contract. This case is still pending.

The case of Barings PLC illustrates how the absence of properly implemented internal controls and supervision by senior management can lead to disastrous results if a rogue trader is permitted to go unchecked. In Barings PLC, a Singapore-based derivatives trader, Nicholas W. Leeson, managed to accumulate losses of approximately $950 million from futures and options on futures trading in the Nikkei-225 Index, Japanese government bonds and short-term Euroyen securities. In effect, Mr. Leeson speculated that both the Japanese stock market and interest rates would increase, which turned out to be a disastrous wager. These losses ultimately led to the collapse of Barings PLC, the oldest investment firm in the United Kingdom, founded in 1767.

Barings PLC apparently permitted Leeson to have full control over his trading as well as settlement activities without supervision. This combination of desk trading and back-office operations proved fatal and should provide senior management in the future with a textbook case of what not to do in terms of internal control procedures. Although the trading by Leeson was not in exotic derivatives, the tragic debacle nonetheless points to the fact that all financial instruments, whether plain vanilla or exotic can be deadly if used improperly without adequate management oversight and control.[64]

---

[64] Another case that illustrates the dangers of not having appropriate internal control procedures is the Orange County, California, Investment Pool. In December 1994 the county and its investment funds were forced to file for protection under Chapter 9 of the Federal Bankruptcy Code. The county's investment pool incurred losses estimated to be $1.5 billion (out of a pool of approximately $8 billion) due to highly leveraged trading strategies involving reverse repurchase agreements as well as investment in structured notes such as inverse floaters. Reports of the Orange County affair indicate that the ex-treasurer of Orange Country, Robert L. Citron, had full discretionary authority to invest the county's funds. The lack of supervision and of adequate internal control procedures by the county's Board of Supervisors is largely to blame for these losses to a fund that in all respects should have been conservatively managed consistent with its "public" nature. *See, e.g.,* Floyd Norris, "In Orange County, Strategies Sour," *The New York Times,* December 5, 1994, p. D1; Laura Jereski, G. Bruce Knecht, Thomas T. Vogel, Jr., and Andy Pasztor, "Orange County, Mired in Investment Mess, Files for Bankruptcy," *The Wall Street Journal,* December 7, 1994, p. A1, A6; and Andrew Bary, "Peter Pan Portfolio," *Barron's,* December 5, 1994, p. 17–18. Similarly, in a recent case, bond trader Toshihide Igushi cost Daiwa Bank Ltd. up to $1.1 billion from losses associated with "unauthorized trades" in U.S. Treasury securities over

These large derivatives losses raise serious questions concerning whether top management and boards of directors of end users of OTC derivatives fully understand the risks, whether the manner in which such products are sold by dealers to corporate end users is appropriate, and whether corporate disclosures of OTC derivatives positions are adequate. Accordingly, with each subsequent announcement of corporate losses attributable to the unsuccessful use of OTC derivatives, the level of concern is heightened at the appropriate regulatory agencies and on Capitol Hill.

Several investment company/investment advisor complexes have come under fire for losses resulting from investments in derivatives (most notably mortgage derivatives).

In October 1993, a shareholder class action was filed against Hyperion Asset Management and Hyperion 1999 Term Trust and its interested directors and underwriters. The complaint alleged that a 25 percent drop in net asset value during 1993 resulted from the investment of approximately one-third of the fund's assets in interest only (IO) strips of mortgage-backed securities. Purchasers of IOs will invest in these instruments with the expectation that interest rates will rise. During the period of time alleged, interest rates fell and the fund's shares plummeted in value. The complaint alleges, among other things, that the risks of investing in the fund, including the use of IOs, not only were not sufficiently disclosed; they " . . . constituted a reckless and mistaken gamble that interest rates, which had been declining prior to the inception of Hyperion 1999 in June 1992, would reverse themselves . . . instead of continuing to decline." The prospectus is alleged to have been materially misleading.[65] The U.S. District Court for the Southern District of New York recently ruled, however, that the offering materials for the three Hyperion trusts investing in mortgage-backed securities properly disclosed the investment and attendant risks.[66]

The Hyperion litigation was followed by a number of other incidents

---

an 11-year period. Like Leeson, Mr. Igushi was head of securities trading and back-office operations, thereby enabling him to keep the scheme undetected by top management. See Sapsford, Sesit and O'Brien, "Toxic Trading," *The Wall Street Journal,* September 27, 1995, pp. A1, A6.

[65] *Olkey* v. *Hyperion 1999 Term Trust,* S.D.N.Y. (Mukasey J.) (October 18, 1993). The case is still pending. Immediately after its original filing, approximately 10 additional plaintiffs joined the fray. All of these complaints have now been consolidated into one (large) complaint. *In re Hyperion Securities Litigation*, Civ. Action No. 93-Civ. 7179 (MBM), S.D.N.Y., February 22, 1994. The consolidated complaint describes Hyperion as a "massive fraud."

[66] *In re Hyperion Securities Litigation,* Civ. Action No. 93-Civ. 7179 (MBM), S.D.N.Y. July 12, 1995.

that raised the public sensitivity level to the risks of investments in derivatives. Huge losses were reported by well-known hedge fund managers such as Michael Steinhardt and George Soros, who were caught, along with many others, going the wrong way when bond prices in Europe and Japan plunged and interest rates, which move in the opposite direction of bond prices, climbed about one full percentage point.[67]

Other recent developments concerning investment company/derivatives litigation are discussed in turn.

Paine Webber Short-Term U.S. Government Fund declined in value almost 6 percent in 1994 due to declines in the value of mortgage derivatives held by the fund. Paine Webber agreed to reimburse investors in the fund for losses incurred by the fund attributable to its investment in mortgage derivatives. The amount of such reimbursement is estimated to be $33 million. In addition, Paine Webber has agreed to buy back from the Fund approximately $50 million in IO and principal only (PO) mortgage derivatives held by the Fund to reduce volatility. These actions were taken by Paine Webber as part of an agreement in principle to settle a class action lawsuit brought by some investors in Paine Webber's Short-Term U.S. Government Income Fund.

The Piper Funds Institutional Government Income Portfolio's net asset value declined approximately 24.6 percent between January 1, 1994, and May 6, 1994. The decline was in large part attributable to the fund's investments in inverse floaters and POs. A class action was filed against the fund, its manager, underwriter, and inside directors, attacking the fund's alleged failure to adequately disclose the risks associated with the fund's derivatives investments.[68] In February 1995, Piper Jaffray agreed to settle this case for approximately $70 million in order to compensate investors in the Institutional Government Income Fund. A separate shareholder class-action in Minnesota state court has also been settled for $2 million.[69] These settlements draw to a close the largest litigation to arise

---

[67]Greenwald, "The Secret Money Machine," *Time* Magazine, April 11, 1994, pp. 28, 30–31. The article noted that " . . . institutions like banks, insurance companies and brokerage houses now hold billions of dollars of unregulated derivatives contracts that are not recorded on their books. Thus, no one, including the firms themselves, knows just what pressures may be building up."

[68]*Rodney* v. *Piper Funds, Inc.,* et al., Civ. No. 3-94-587 (D. Minn.), May 9, 1994. Other plaintiffs also brought suits against Piper, which were consolidated into one complaint. *In Re: Piper Funds, Inc. Institutional Government Income Portfolio Litigation.*

[69]"Piper Jaffray Agrees to $2 Million Accord on Shareholder Suit," *The Wall Street Journal,* September 11, 1995, p. 35.

from a disastrous investment strategy dominated by mortgage derivatives.[70]

In July 1994, a class action was filed in the United States District Court for
the Southern District of New York against the TCW/DW Trust 2000 and
TCW/DW Term Trust 2003, alleging, among other things, that the Trusts'
registration statements and prospectuses were false and misleading; that they
misrepresented the character, composition, and safety of the Trusts; failed to
disclose that certain securities held by the Trusts were high risk; and
generally mislead investors as to the emphasis the Trusts would place on so-
called exotic mortgage derivatives.[71] The complaints demand monetary and
punitive damages against all defendants. This case is pending resolution.

In another important development, several managers of money market
funds have bailed out their funds in the face of losses from investments in
derivatives and other unusual instruments. The majority of these losses
have resulted from fund holdings of floating-rate securities whose returns
are linked to or derived from various interest-rate indexes. The most
notable of these bailouts have included BankAmerica Corp's Pacific
Horizon Prime Money Market Fund and the Zweig Cash Fund.[72] The
motivation for a bailout of these funds by the manager or advisor is to
maintain investor confidence and loyalty, which could be damaged by
derivatives losses that cause a money market fund's net asset value per
share to fall below the $1.00 level.[73]

CONCLUSION

A primary focus of the 1940 Act and regulations adopted thereunder by
the SEC has been the use of leverage by investment companies.[74] The use
of derivatives by an investment company—to hedge the effects of market

---

[70]*See* Knecht, "Piper Reaches $70 Million Pact to Settle Suit," *The Wall Street Journal*, Feb-
ruary 16, 1995, p. C1.

[71]*Sheppard* v. *TCW/DW Trust 2000, et al.*, 94-Civ-5404 (S.D.N.Y.), July 22, 1994.

[72]*See* Calian and Jasen, "Managers Prop Up Money-Market Funds with Quiet Bailouts in Face
of Losses," *The Wall Street Journal*, June 10, 1994, p.C1; C13; Anderson, "SEC Chief Levitt
Warns Mutual Funds to Be Cautious in Handling Derivatives," *The Wall Street Journal*, June 21,
1994, p. C17; and McGough and Calian, "Adviser Puts Cash in Zweig Cash Fund to Compensate
for Losses in Derivatives," *The Wall Street Journal*, June 13, 1994, p. C10.

[73]The bailout in these cases either consists of a buyback of the instrument at par or face value
or the payment of cash to cover the fund losses.

[74]Section 1(b)(7) of the 1940 Act states that the public interest and the interest of investors is
adversely affected . . . "when investment companies by excessive borrowing and the issuance of

volatility, to re-allocate its investment portfolio, or for enhancing the return of such portfolio—may create leverage that artificially magnifies profits and losses. As a result, senior management of investment advisors and boards of directors of investment companies must be diligent to adequately ascertain whether portfolio managers and other investment professionals are properly trained and experienced; that the use of derivatives by the fund is consistent with its policies and objectives; whether management has implemented and followed appropriately defined limitations; and whether the risks inherent in derivatives are recognized and properly monitored.

Although derivatives may be more complex than traditional financial instruments, the identical evaluation is performed in order to determine appropriateness for investment (i.e., valuation, volatility, market risks, creditworthiness, and limits). Moreover, senior management of the advisor and directors should question why derivatives are needed and whether the strategies employed are achieving their intended result. It is clear from the number of large losses stemming from derivatives trading during 1994 that continuous oversight and supervision by top management and investment company boards of directors is necessary to control the imprudent use of these complex financial instruments.

Appendix 21–A

The four basic building blocks of traditional derivatives are the:

- *Forward Contract:* An agreement to purchase or sell a specific quantity of a commodity, security, or other instrument at a specified price, with delivery at a specified future date.
- *Futures Contract:* A standardized agreement, traded on an exchange or board of trade, to purchase or sell a specific amount of a commodity or financial instrument at a particular price on a specified future date.
- *Option Contract:* A contract that grants the right, but not the obligation, for or during a specified period, to buy or sell a commodity, security, or other financial instrument at a specified date in exchange for an agreed-upon sum.

---

excessive amounts of senior securities increase unduly the speculative character of their junior securities."

- *Swap:* A contract between two parties to exchange or swap a stream of cash flows under an agreed-upon set of terms.

There are a wide variety of OTC derivatives, and in many instances such derivatives are custom-tailored to particular investors and thus can involve virtually any type or degree of risk such investors are willing to assume. For purposes of this appendix, I have separated OTC derivatives into four general categories: mortgage derivatives, structured instruments, money market derivatives, and tax-exempt derivatives.

- *Mortgage Derivatives.* A mortgage derivative is an instrument generally created by pooling mortgages and dividing interests therein into multiple series or classes of individual securities (tranches) each of which has different coupon rates, expected maturity, payment expectations, and risk/return characteristics. This is accomplished by allocating cash flows on the underlying mortgages in various ways. The most common tranches in connection with mortgage derivatives include:
  — *Inverse Floaters.* An inverse floater is a security that pays a coupon rate that moves in a direction opposite to the changes in a designated interest-rate index. A rise in interest rates will cause a drop in the coupon rate of an inverse floater, while a decline in interest rates will cause an increase in its coupon rate. The coupon rate on an inverse floater typically changes at a multiple of the changes in the relevant index (i.e., the coupon rate moves up or down by more than 1 basis point for every 1-basis-point increase or decrease in the index). Consequently, a degree of leverage is generally embedded in an inverse floater.
  — *Principal-Only Securities.* Principal-only securities (POs) receive only principal payments made on the underlying mortgages. POs have a face value and typically are purchased at a price deeply discounted to that face value. The face value of a PO is ultimately received through scheduled payments and prepayments on the underlying mortgages. If interest rates fall, POs generally will increase in value. This is because prepayments on the underlying mortgages typically will accelerate, leading to a more rapid return of principal. However, if interest rates increase, POs generally will decline in value. This is because prepayments on the underlying mortgages typically will subside, thus lengthening the time period in which principal value will be received.
  — *Interest-Only Securities.* Interest-only securities (IOs) receive only the interest payments on underlying mortgages. Unlike POs, these securities have no face value. Rather, they have an assumed principal value (notional principal amount) which is used to calculate the amount of interest due. IOs are bought at deep discounts to their notional principal amount. The notional principal amount is reduced by scheduled

payments and prepayments of principal on the underlying mortgages, and as that amount is reduced, cash flow on the IO declines. IOs increase in value when interest rates rise and prepayments slow. This is because the notional principal amount will be reduced at a slower rate, thereby extending the period of time over which interest payments are received. If interest rates decline, however, and prepayments increase, IOs will decline in value. This is because the notional principal amount will be reduced at an accelerated rate and, accordingly, the interest stream will be received for a shorter period of time than projected. A very rapid rate of prepayment may result in an investor in an IO actually receiving back less than its original investment.

— *Z Tranches.* In certain mortgage derivatives there is a tranche that receives all payments after all the tranches have been paid. The final tranche of certain of these mortgage derivatives is known as a Z tranche. Until all other tranches are paid off Z-tranche holders receive no cash. Instead, like a zero-coupon bond, "accrued interest" is applied to increase the face value of the security. Once all tranches are paid off, Z-tranche holders start to receive cash payments that include both principal and continuing interest. Z tranches tend to be volatile instruments.

• *Structured Notes.* Structured notes are debt securities whose principal value at maturity or whose interest rate during the term of the security is linked to or depends on the performance of currencies, interest rates, stock indices, or other benchmarks (the "Reference Index"). The interest rate and/or the principal amount payable at maturity may be increased or decreased depending upon changes in the Reference Index. Such increases or decreases may be at a multiple of changes in the Reference Index. Structured notes may be issued by U.S. government agencies or instrumentalities or by domestic or foreign private issuers. Often they are custom-designed to accommodate the desires of particular investors.

• *Structured Equity.* Structured equity typically takes the form of preferred stock convertible mandatorily or at the option of the issuer or the holder into common stock of the issuer. These instruments generally offer a higher yield than that available from traditional convertible preferred but also normally require the investor to forego a portion of the appreciation potential on the underlying common stock, while assuming full downside risk with respect to the underlying common.

• *Money Market Derivatives.* Various instruments with adjustable interest rates have been developed for money market funds. Rule 2a-7 permits money market funds to purchase long-term instruments with stated maturities of longer than one year if they have floating or variable interest rates and the instrument can reasonably be expected to have a market value that approximates its par value upon adjustment of the interest rate. The adjustable-rate instruments that have been newly developed for money market funds qualify under Rule 2a-7 as eligible investments for such funds but involve greater risks than the more traditional floating- or variable-rate instruments of not returning to par at the time of an interest-rate adjustment. Certain of the new type of adjustable-rate instruments have interest rates tied to medium- or long-term interest rates. Another type of instrument (known as a range note) pays above-market interest rates as long as interest rates remain within a certain range, but the interest rate resets to zero on any day when the interest rate falls out of the range.

Another type of adjustable-rate instrument is one whose interest rate is linked to an index that resets relatively infrequently and therefore significantly lags changes in short-term rates. The lag has the effect of causing the instrument to trade at a premium or discount to par.

- *Tax-Exempt Derivatives.* Structured derivatives have been developed for the tax-exempt market that incorporate many of the features associated with taxable derivatives and involve similar types of risks. These include primary and secondary derivatives.

- Primary tax-exempt derivatives are issued directly by a state or local government or by a conduit acting on its behalf. Examples of primary derivatives include the following instruments:

    — *Inverse Floaters.* These are tax-exempt bonds that bear an interest rate that moves in a direction opposite to that of market rates. Typically, the interest rate is equal to the difference between a base rate and a market rate fixed through periodic auctions or based on an interest-rate index.

    — *Derivative-Rate Bonds.* These are tax-exempt bonds that bear a variable interest rate, which is adjusted in accordance with a specified formula. The formula typically includes a fixed-rate component linked to an interest-rate index and a supplemental component resembling a swap or cap.

    — *Tender Option Bonds.* These are long-term tax-exempt bonds that are effectively converted into short-term tax-exempt bonds through an agreement with a third-party financial institution pursuant to which the third party grants bondholders the right, at periodic intervals, to sell to such third party the bonds at their face value. In exchange for such agreement, periodic payments are made by the bondholders to the third-party institution (which reduce the effective interest rate paid to bondholders) in an amount equal to the difference between the interest rate on the bond and short-term tax-exempt market rates. Net of such payments, bondholders receive interest at prevailing short-term rates.

    — *Stripped Tax-Exempt Bonds.* These are instruments that represent an interest in particular payments or portion of payments on an underlying tax-exempt bond.

APPENDIX 21–B Collateral Requirements for Derivatives

Instrument	Release 10,666	No-action Letters*	Guide 23 of Form N-1A
Caps and Floors	Although the SEC has not addressed the status of caps and floors under Section 18 of the 1940 Act, industry practice provides for a segregated account in an amount at least equal to the fund's obligations with respect to such caps or floors determined on a daily basis.		
Foreign Currency Forward Contracts Hedging an Underlying Foreign Security Position			**Initial Hedge Position** does not require a segregated account of cash or high-grade liquid securities. If the position subsequently is determined to be "unhedged" or "speculative," then a segregated account of cash or high-grade liquid debt securities is required with a value, marked-to-market daily, at least equal to the portion of the contract that is no longer sufficiently covered by the **Initial Hedge.**
Foreign Currency Forward Contracts–Short Positions		*Maintenance of a segregated account:* Cash or high-grade liquid debt securities, with a value, marked-to-market daily, in an amount at least equal to the market value of the underlying foreign currency, reduced by any margin payments.	

(continued)

Instrument	Release 10,666	No-action Letters*	Guide 23 of Form N-1A
Foreign Currency Forward Contracts–Long Positions		**Maintenance of a segregated account:** Cash or high-grade liquid debt securities with a value, marked-to-market daily, at least equal to the dollar amount of the fund's obligation under the contract on settlement date, reduced by any margin payments.	
Futures Contracts–Long Positions		**Maintenance of a segregated account:** Cash or high-grade liquid debt securities with a value, marked-to-market daily, at least equal to the dollar amount of the fund's obligation on the futures contract, reduced by any margin payments.	
Futures Contracts–Short Positions		**Maintenance of a segregated account:** Cash or high-grade liquid debt securities, with a value, marked-to-market daily, in an amount at least equal to the market value of the instruments underlying the contract, reduced by any margin payments.	
Index Futures Contracts–Long Positions		**Maintenance of a segregated account:** Cash or high-grade liquid debt securities with a value, marked-to-market daily, at least equal to the dollar amount of the fund's obligation on the futures contract, reduced by any margin payments.	

Instrument	Release 10,666	No-action Letters*	Guide 23 of Form N-1A
Index Futures Contracts–Short Positions		**In lieu of maintaining a segregated account of high-grade liquid assets or employing options on futures as cover, a fund may appropriately cover by holding a portfolio of securities with characteristics substantially similar to the underlying index or stock index comprising the futures contract. As a result of imperfect correlation between a fund's portfolio of securities and index futures contracts used as a hedge, a fund may buy or sell index futures contracts and related options in greater or less than the dollar amounts than the dollar amount of the securities being hedged based on the historical volatility relationship or "Beta" value. See Z-Seven Fund, Inc., SEC No-Action Letter (April 20, 1984).**	
Mortgage Derivatives	N/A—Potential loss is limited to the initial investment.		
Options on Futures–Long Positions	**No segregated account is imposed because the potential loss is limited to the amount of premium paid (leveraging concerns do not exist).**		

(continued)

Instrument	Release 10,666	No-action Letters*	Guide 23 of Form N-1A
Options on Futures–Short Calls		**Maintenance of segregated account:** Cash or high-grade liquid debt securities, with a value, marked-to-market daily, at least equal to the market value of the instruments underlying the contract (but not less than the exercise price), reduced by any margin payments.	
Options on Futures–Short Puts		**Maintenance of segregated account:** Cash or high-grade liquid debt securities, with a value, marked-to-market daily, at least equal to the dollar value of the strike price of the put option, reduced by any margin payments.	
Options on Securities–Long Positions	**No segregated account is imposed because the potential loss is limited to the amount of premium paid (leveraging concerns do not exist).**		
Options on Securities–Short Calls		**Maintenance of segregated account:** Cash or high-grade liquid debt securities, with a value, marked-to-market daily, at least equal to the market value of the instruments underlying the contract (but not less than the exercise price), reduced by any margin payments.	

Instrument	Release 10,666	No-action Letters*	Guide 23 of Form N-1A
Options on Securities–Short Puts		**Maintenance of segregated account:** Cash or high-grade liquid debt securities, with a value, marked-to-market daily, at least equal to the dollar value of the strike price of the put option, reduced by any margin payments.	
Reverse Repurchase Agreements	**Maintenance of a segregated account:** Cash or high-grade liquid debt securities with a value, at least equal to the dollar amount of the fund's obligation to repurchase securities.		
Short Sales	**Maintenance of a segregated account:** Cash or high-grade liquid debt with a value, marked-to-market daily, at least equal to the greater of the current market value of the securities sold short or the value of such securities at the time they were sold short, reduced by any margin payments. **Guide 9 to Form N-1A**		
Structured Securities	N/A—Potential loss is limited to the initial investment.		

(continued)

Instrument	Release 10,666	No-action Letters*	Guide 23 of Form N-1A
Swaps	Although the SEC has not addressed the status of swaps under Section 18 of the 1940 Act, industry practice provides for a segregated account in an amount at least equal to the net amount of any excess of the fund's obligations over its entitlements with respect to each swap, determined on a daily basis.		
When-Issued Purchases and Forward Commitments	**Maintenance of a segregated account:** Cash or high-grade liquid debt securities with a value, marked-to-market daily, at least equal to the dollar amount of the fund's obligation on settlement date.		

*SEC no-action letters have expanded the analysis in Release No. 10,666 to certain financial instruments and transactions that leverage a fund's assets inconsistent with Section 18 of the 1940 Act.

Chapter Twenty-Two

Litigation Involving Derivatives

William J. McSherry, Jr.
Partner

Jordan E. Yarett
Partner

Paul A. Straus
Associate
Battle Fowler LLP

BACKGROUND

Although the complete dimensions of the problem are not yet known, it is clear that losses resulting from the purchase of derivatives are widespread and very large. Since 1992, large multinational corporations, municipalities, mutual funds, and individual investors have reported billions of dollars of losses resulting from the purchase of a wide variety of derivatives. Derivatives dependent on interest-rate indices caused enormous losses when interest rates rose in late 1993 and 1994. Derivatives have also caused losses resulting from the bond market slump, from sharp turns against the dollar in currency trading, and from increases in stock market indices. In addition to these large publicly reported losses, there are believed to be far greater losses in the portfolios of private companies, pension plans, and hedge funds that have not been publicly acknowledged.

Not surprisingly, these losses have engendered considerable finger-pointing—at the treasurer, controller, or investment manager who decided to purchase the derivatives and at the broker or banker who sold the product. Equally unsurprisingly, this finger-pointing has led to the filing of derivatives-related litigations and arbitrations, largely against the commercial banks and brokerage firms that created or "sold" the types of derivatives that have most drastically declined in value over the last two to three years. Some of this litigation is an attempt to recover a loss, while some litigation has been brought to recover a trading profit from a contractual counterparty. Ancillary litigation has also been filed, such as shareholder actions against corporate directors and officers who allowed these derivative purchases to occur; litigation against investment advisors and managers that purchased derivatives for their clients; and, in at least one well-publicized instance thus far, in governmental proceedings against one of the most prominent professionals in the derivatives marketplace.

From a litigation perspective, it is useful to draw a distinction between those derivatives that have the traditional characteristics of an investment, such as mortgage- or other asset-backed securities, strips, interest-only (IO) or principal-only (PO) securities on the one hand, and swaps, futures contracts, or forward contracts, which are ordinarily not entered into for investment purposes, on the other hand. An important practical difference is that losses in investment derivatives are generally market losses, whereas losses on swaps and similar products generally produce a gain for another party; i.e., the latter represent a zero-sum game, while the former do not.

Perhaps the most unusual aspect of the recent litigation activity involving derivatives is the identity of some of the plaintiffs. As one would expect, there are on file several class actions brought on behalf of individual investors against the issuers of securities that have declined in value, including the issuers of trust participations and mutual funds that suffered losses as a result of their purchases of derivatives. However, there also are a number of actions pending that have been brought by quite untraditional securities-action plaintiffs such as the State of West Virginia; Orange County, California; Procter & Gamble; Marion Merrell Dow, Inc.; and Gibson Greetings, Inc.

While the litigations involving losses from derivatives that have been filed in the last year involve different facts and relationships, at one level or another they all involve assertion(s) (1) that the derivative products created risks that were concealed from the purchaser or investor, or were inadequately disclosed, or (2) that the derivative products were unsuitable for the end user or purchaser. What differentiates these claims from more traditional securities-law claims is not just the identity of some of the plaintiffs, but also the facts that the plaintiff-purchaser often employs professional(s) with some experience with complex financial products, and that the plaintiff-purchaser's professionals presumably have a far greater understanding of the business needs of the client/customer than the professionals employed by the banker or broker. Indeed, in many instances, it was the losing side's "professional" who originally sought the type of product at issue in the litigation, sometimes being involved in the structuring of the derivative in an effort to meet the needs of the client/customer.

In an attempt to circumvent their own professionals' generalized sophistication, some of these institutional plaintiffs have asserted that the derivatives they purchased were so complex and difficult to analyze that their own professional(s) could not assess all of the risks (few corporate treasurer's offices possess the software needed to analyze completely the risks of the most complex derivative products). Consequently, it is alleged, the customer became unusually dependent on the bank or broker to assess the risk for the customer, not only at the time of sale, but after the sale in the secondary market as well.

It is this alleged dependence on the bank or broker—a dependence created by the complexity of the product—that differentiates recent litigation activity over derivatives losses from litigation over losses engendered by more traditional, less complex securities, commodities, and contractual relationships—like plain vanilla swaps, options, and similar products—some of which might nonetheless properly be characterized as derivatives. This alleged dependence is often complicated by the fact that the customer may believe that it is relying on the professional counterparty for advice, but then enters into the transaction directly with the professional as its counterparty. This combination of roles, it has been alleged, gives rise to a higher duty on the part of the professional counterparty executing a derivatives contract than the duty ordinarily imposed by law on a broker, dealer, or lender executing a more traditional, less complex product with more easily calculable risk and value.

In response, the professionals point out that if this argument were accepted as the law, then the seller of a complex derivative product would in effect become a guarantor of the success of an investment or hedging strategy that is often suggested or sought after by the customer in the first instance.

In addition to arbitrators and the courts, legislators, regulators, and industry representatives are attempting to deal with the universe of disclosure, regulatory, suitability, and liability issues that the continued marketing of complex and intricate derivative products presents.

Introduction

The first part of this chapter describes the litigation that has already been commenced that involves losses stemming from derivatives. The second part of the chapter addresses some of the legislative, regulatory, and industry proposals advanced thus far to deal with the legal and business issues created by the relatively new and largely unregulated marketplace for complex derivatives. The third part addresses various litigation theories advanced by claimants and identifies other theories that the authors expect to be advanced by claimants in the future.

Litigation Already on File—Consumer/Individual Investor Claims

Most of the litigations and arbitrations involving derivatives losses that have been filed have been brought by individual investors (or their IRA account trustees) against the brokerage industry. Virtually all of these claims have been asserted as arbitration demands against brokerage firms before the National Association of Securities Dealers (NASD), The New York Stock Exchange (NYSE), other stock exchanges, or the American Arbitration Association (AAA). To date, the tracking mechanisms of the bar associations and the securities industry have published no statistical or analytical data singling out the success or failure of those claimants seeking to recover losses from derivatives.

Most of these individual investor claims are premised on traditional theories of recovery in such proceedings, with a familiar focus on small investor "suitability" issues. Virtually all of these individual investor claims involve investment derivatives rather than index or hedging derivatives. Analytically, these individual investor claims are no different from claims with which these arbitration tribunals have had long-standing experience over the years: claims involving options, commodities, junk bonds, and international stocks and bonds which have produced investment losses that were allegedly the result of inadequate disclosure of the risks, or that were allegedly unsuitable investments.

There is generally no question about the relative sophistication of the individual investor and the broker, since most individual investors are not nearly as knowledgeable about derivatives as their broker. Some of these arbitrations present ERISA issues as well as issues under the securities laws, but none has resulted in any precedent differentiating the duties of a seller or broker of derivatives from the purveyors of other financial or investment products.

Shareholder Litigation against Mutual Funds and Other Purchasers of Derivatives

Also as noted above, there have been some class actions filed against mutual funds, closed-end investment companies, and their advisors that purchased such derivative securities as IOs or inverse floaters and that suffered large losses in net asset value. For example, in September 1993, investors in trusts managed by Hyperion Capital Management, Inc. (Hyperion) filed several class actions.[1] In their consolidated complaint, the investors alleged that they relied on representations in prospectuses that gave the impression that the funds would invest only in securities "of the highest credit quality."[2] The complaint in the *Hyperion* class action alleges that the purchase by the funds of hundreds of millions of dollars of IOs constituted a "reckless and mistaken gamble" on the direction of interest rates.[3]

Similar class action claims have been filed against affiliates of Piper Jaffray Funds, Inc. (Piper Jaffray) based on the purchases by Piper Jaffray (for mutual funds it advised) of inverse floaters tied to LIBOR and other interest-rate indices.[4] The Hyperion trusts suffered their losses as interest rates declined in 1992 and early 1993 (causing the prepayment and refinancing of the mortgages underlying the IOs),[5] whereas the inverse floaters in the Piper Jaffray mutual fund portfolios declined as interest

---

[1]*In Re Hyperion Securities Litigation*, No. 93 Civ. 7179 (S.D.N.Y. October 18, 1993). These consolidated cases will be referred to herein as the "Hyperion Securities Litigation."

[2]*Id.* Specifically, the plaintiffs allege that "Hyperion's stated investment strategy was to assemble investment portfolios with offsetting reactions to interest-rate fluctuations, thereby creating an overall balance that would attempt to neutralize the losses suffered by any individual portfolio component. The Hyperion Trusts, however, engaged in a dramatically different investment strategy, and for their investors, the results were disastrous." Plaintiffs' Memorandum Opposing Defendants' Motions to Dismiss The Second Consolidated Amended Class Action Complaint at 1–2, dated February 8, 1995 (referred to herein as "Hyperion Plaintiffs' Mem. on Dismissal Motions").

[3]*Id.* at 3–6.

[4]*In Re Piper Funds, Inc. Institutional Government Income Portfolio Litigation No. 3-94-587* (D.Minn. May 5, 1994). These consolidated cases will be referred to herein as the "Piper Funds Litigation."

[5]Amended Complaint, Hyperion Securities Litigation, at paragraphs 2, 14.

rates rose in late 1993 and 1994.[6] There are other similar class actions involving derivatives that have been filed against trusts, banks, mutual funds, and their advisors.[7] As often happens with large class actions, these cases, even those outstanding for two or more years, have been primarily focused to date on motion practice addressed to the adequacy of the pleadings or to the propriety of the action being maintained in a particular forum or as a class action.[8] So far, these class actions have added little or nothing to existing jurisprudence under the federal securities laws or other laws as they may specifically relate to derivatives. Even though the complaints in these cases sometimes characterize the derivatives as "exotic" or as "toxic waste," all of these class actions premise their claims on traditional theories of recovery under the federal and state securities laws.[9] Most of these cases challenge the adequacy of the disclosure in a prospectus, or in "roadshow" or other statements by the issuer or seller which are contrasted with the actual derivatives purchased by the trusts, mutual funds, or other defendants.[10]

---

[6]Amended Complaint, Piper Funds Litigation, at paragraphs 34–37, 39.

[7]See, e.g., *Schwabach* v. *Mutual Savings Bank,* No. 95-CV-71590 DT (E.D. Mich.); Richard A. Lockridge and Gregg M. Fishbein, *Shareholder Lawsuits Involving Derivatives,* 893 PLI/CORP 63 (May 1995) (this article identifies several pending cases: *Hosea, et al.* v. *The Managers Funds, et al.,* (inverse floaters and POs); *Fleck* v. *The Managers Fund, et al.*; *Gordon* v. *American Adjustable Rate Term Trust 1998 and 1999*; *Sandusky County* v. *Government Securities Corp. of Texas* (settled by purchasing derivatives at full purchase price); *Sedrak* v. *Government Fund*; *Hahn* v. *Investors Trust Government*; and *In re Paine Webber Short-Term U.S. Government Income Fund Securities Litigation*).

[8]See, e.g., Hyperion Securities Litigation, *supra,* note 2.

[9]See, e.g., Amended Complaint, Hyperion Securities Litigation.

[10]See, e.g., Hyperion Plaintiffs' Mem. On Dismissal Motions, pp. 19–25. On July 14, 1995, the complaint in the Hyperion Securities Litigation was dismissed with prejudice for failure to allege material misrepresentation or omissions. *In re Hyperion Securities Litigation,* No. 93 Civ. 7179 (S.D.N.Y. July 14, 1995). The Court held that the Trusts' prospectuses, which expressed Hyperion's objectives in terms of "expectation, not assurance," "candidly" discussed the Term Trusts' strategy and risks posed by interest-rate fluctuations. *Hyperion,* slip op. at 10, 12. The court noted, in *dicta,* that Hyperion's articulation of the damaging consequences that declining interest rates might have on the portfolios as a whole was probably more extensive than the federal securities laws require, because investors could weigh the risks themselves based on the Trust's description of the various securities and their individual interest-rate characteristics. *Hyperion,* July 14, 1995, slip op. at 13. In other words, federal securities laws do not appear to impose any greater disclosure burden on derivatives than is imposed on any other type of security. *Id.*

Untraditional Plaintiffs in the Litigation Arena

Of considerably more interest to the corporate or municipal treasurer or pension plan administrator are those cases filed by institutions that purchased derivative products directly from a professional counterparty. While most of these cases are still making their way through the courts and none has yet resulted in a judicial decision that distinguishes investment derivatives from other investment products, the facts of these cases do serve to illustrate the unusual circumstances that have brought about these large losses for relatively sophisticated purchasers of volatile derivatives.

The derivatives litigation that has received the most publicity was the action brought by Gibson Greetings, Inc. (Gibson) against Bankers Trust Company (BT) and its securities affiliate, B.T. Securities Corporation (BT Sec.).[11] Gibson alleged in its complaint that BT and BT Sec. recommended extremely highly leveraged derivatives transactions without adequately disclosing the risk, despite knowing that Gibson's intention was to enter into interest-rate transactions solely for hedging purposes. The derivatives involved in *Gibson* included so-called wedding band options (which provided for significant payments by Gibson if interest rates were to move out of a specified band or spread), a knock-out call option (which provided that if at any time during the life of the option the yield on the 30-year Treasury security dropped below 6.48 percent, the option expired or was knocked out), and several other complex swaps, spread lock, and periodic-floor agreements.

The *Gibson* complaint alleged fraudulent and negligent misrepresentations and breach of fiduciary duty under the common law. In addition, Gibson alleged violations of Sections 4(a) and 40(1) of the Commodities Exchange Act as well as a violation of Section 32.9 of the Rules of the Commodities Futures Trading Commission (CFTC).

Gibson is believed to be the only case alleging violations of the Commodities Exchange Act's antifraud provisions in connection with a swap transaction. The Commodities Exchange Act's principal antifraud provision (Section 4(b)) was not relied upon by Gibson, presumably because that section premises liability on a principal/agency relationship. The Gibson swaps were negotiated between Gibson and BT Sec. securities as principals. The *Gibson* complaint did not rely on alleged violations of

---

[11] *Gibson Greetings, Inc.* v. *Bankers Trust Co., et al.*, No. 1-94-620 (S.D. Ohio Sept. 12, 1994).

the federal securities laws, presumably because there was no support at that time for the claim that an interest-rate swap is a security within the meaning of the federal securities laws.[12]

Discovery in the *Gibson* case revealed one of the problems inherent in the unregulated marketplace for complex derivatives such as the swaps and other products sold to Gibson. There was no established market for many of the types of derivatives sold to Gibson; consequently, the value of Gibson's open positions was established by BT itself, which used sophisticated computer models to advise its customer of the value of the position. However, as was subsequently revealed in discovery (from audio tapes maintained by BT of its internal conversations as well as its conversations with customers), BT significantly understated Gibson's losses in its communications with Gibson, which allegedly led Gibson to report incorrect financial information to the Securities and Exchange Commission (SEC) and contributed to Gibson's decision to purchase additional derivatives. The values provided by BT to Gibson allegedly differed in some cases by as much as 50 percent from those generated by the computer models used by BT.[13]

BT's apparent deception of Gibson led to a disciplinary action against BT by the Federal Reserve Board, which settled its charges against BT in an agreement that imposed extensive and novel disclosure and valuation requirements as well as supervision of the bank's derivatives procedures by independent counsel.[14] BT and BT Sec. reportedly agreed to settle the civil suit brought by Gibson by reimbursing $14 million of Gibson's reported $20 million in derivatives losses.[15]

The SEC[16] and the CFTC[17] also commenced separate disciplinary

---

[12]Mark A. Horwitz, "Swaps Ahoy! Should Regulators Voyage Into Unknown Waters?" 1 *Indiana Journal of Global Legal Studies,* 515, n.65 (1994).

[13]John F. X. Peloso and Stuart M. Sarnoff, "What Next For Derivatives," *N.Y. Law Journal,* Feb. 16, 1995 at 6 (hereinafter, Peloso).

[14]Written Agreement between Bankers Trust New York Corp., Bankers Trust Corp., BT Securities Corp., and the Federal Reserve Bank of New York, dated Dec. 5, 1994.

[15]See Brett G. Fromson, "Derivatives Case May Set Precedent; Bankers Trust Said To Near Settlement," *The Washington Post,* Dec. 15, 1994. See also Richard R. Lockridge and Gregg M. Fishbein, "Shareholder Lawsuits Involving Derivatives," included in *Management and Avoidance of Derivatives Litigation,* Practicing Law Institute, 1995 at 70.

[16]*In the Matter of BT Securities Corp.,* Admin. Proc. File No. 3-8579, Securities Act Release No. 7124, Exchange Act Release No. 35136 (Dec. 22, 1994).

[17]*In the Matter of BT Securities Corporation,* CFTC No. 95-3, 1994 LEXIS 340 (CFTC Dec. 22, 1994).

proceedings against BT Sec. under the antifraud provisions of the federal securities laws (for the SEC) and under the CFTC's rules governing commodities futures advisors (for the CFTC). The question of whether interest-rate swaps and derivatives tied to interest-rate indices constitute "securities" was thought to be settled prior to the institution of these disciplinary actions. The SEC, however, took the position in its settlement with BT Sec. that certain of the interest-rate-based swaps and contracts sold to Gibson were "securities" within the meaning of the federal securities laws.[18]

Gibson acted as a spawning ground for other derivatives litigation. Shortly after the *Gibson* case was filed, Procter & Gamble commenced a similar action against BT.[19] Gibson's losses evoked shareholder litigation by Gibson shareholders against Gibson's board and management.[20] Notwithstanding Gibson's seemingly successful settlement with BT, these shareholder actions were set for trial this fall.[21]

Litigation has also been instituted by banks or brokerage firms when the customer/counterparty refuses to pay its obligations under a derivative contract. In 1994, Lehman Brothers brought such an action against a Chinese trading company, Minmetals International Non-Ferrous Metals Trading Company (Minmetals) and certain affiliates.[22] Lehman Brothers sought $55 million, which Minmetals had lost in foreign currency and other trading that included derivatives. In its answer, Minmetals filed counterclaims against Lehman Brothers, claiming that Lehman Brothers violated Rule 10b-5 promulgated by the SEC by recklessly recommending that Minmetals purchase $50 million worth of Thai bond repurchase agreements as well as interest-rate swaps and foreign-currency contracts.

Minmetals is a Chinese company based in Beijing. Minmetals claims that the derivatives sold to its 31-year-old trader were not suitable investments, were not authorized by Minmetals' parent company, were too

---

[18]See *supra*, n. 16; Exchange Act Release No. 35136 (December 22, 1994).

[19]*The Procter & Gamble Co.* v. *Bankers Trust Co., et al.*, No. 94-0735 (S.D. Ohio Western Div.). See Derivatives Litigation Reporter, Andrews Publications, May 3, 1995, p. 14 (hereinafter, "Andrews").

[20]*In re Gibson Greetings Securities Litigation*, No. C-1-94-445 (S.D. Ohio Western Div.).

[21]*Andrews*, May 3, 1995, p. 11. Since the trial date was set, the trial judge passed away; the new trial date is not set at this time.

[22]*Lehman Bros.* v. *Minmetals Int'l Non-Ferrous Metals Trading Co., et al.*, No. 94-Civ-8301, 1995 WL 380119 (S.D.N.Y. June 26, 1995).

complex for the trader to understand, and that they violated Chinese law that allegedly bars certain trades without government permission.[23] As noted above, the complex nature of some derivatives has given rise to the claim that even a very sophisticated purchaser can be misled. Minmetals is directly pitting the expertise of its 31-year-old trader against the Lehman Brothers brokers who sold these products.

This case squarely presents the related questions of the reasonableness of the Minmetals trader's alleged reliance on Lehman's advice and the extent of the duty owed to Minmetals by Lehman, its trading counterparty and alleged advisor. Given the nature of foreign-currency desks at institutions like Lehman, it is reasonable to assume that Lehman entered into transactions with others as a result of its trades with Minmetals. Thus, if Lehman proves to be unable to recover from Minmetals, it could well be exposed to losses in other transactions it entered into in order to offset its contracts with Minmetals.

Ultra Vires Claims

Minmetals' reliance on Chinese law concerning its alleged lack of authority to engage in these transactions is obviously a defense that will not ordinarily be available to domestic commercial entities that have lost money in derivatives transactions. Illegality or *ultra vires* claims are usually unavailing when a purchaser of derivatives is a commercial entity, but they have become relatively commonplace when the purchaser is a governmental entity.

For example, Orange County, California—which lost more than $2 billion as a result of highly leveraged reverse repurchase agreements and derivatives—sued Merrill Lynch Pierce Fenner & Smith, Inc. (Merrill Lynch), claiming that Merrill Lynch "illegally extended credit to the county . . . as part of a massive and unauthorized investment scheme."[24] California Government Code 25256 provides that debts or liabilities that violate the state's statutory provisions are *ultra vires* (literally, in Latin, "beyond the power"). California law also prohibits counties from taking

---

[23]*Id.* On June 26, 1995, Judge Keenan granted Minmetals' motion to dismiss the claims against Minmetals' parent company on guaranty theories, finding that Lehman Brothers did not even allege in its complaint that there was a guaranty executed by the parent company. *Andrews*, June 21, 1995 at p. 13.

[24]*In re County of Orange, et al.* v. *Merrill Lynch & Co., Inc., et al.*, Adv. SA 95-0-1045-JR (within 1995 WL 331412 (Bankr. C.D. Cal. 1995), Complaint at 7.

on more annual debt than they generate in revenues without the approval of two-thirds of the voters. It has been reported that brokerage firms other than Merrill Lynch declined to do business with Orange County because they were aware of possible restrictions on Orange County's authority to enter into these types of transactions in such large amounts.[25]

Orange County is not the first governmental entity to seek to avoid a losing contract by using *ultra vires* arguments. In 1990, a California federal court ruled in *City of San Jose* v. *Paine Webber, et al.* that the City of San Jose did not have the authority to purchase reverse repurchase agreements, including some that were similar to those involved in the Orange County debacle.[26] The City of San Jose reportedly lost $60 million as a result of its purchase of these reverse repos and is reported to have ultimately recovered $26 million from 13 brokerage firms, including Merrill Lynch.

In 1987, the state of West Virginia lost millions of dollars by purchasing interest-rate-sensitive when-issued 7-year Treasury notes, reverse repurchase agreements involving the Treasury notes and a put option on 10-year Treasury notes. In 1992, a West Virginia state court awarded the State of West Virginia summary judgment in a suit against Morgan Stanley & Co., Inc. (Morgan Stanley), which had sold the derivatives to the state.[27] On March 3, 1995, on remand from the West Virginia Supreme Court, the trial court held that the basis for Morgan Stanley's liability was an implied cause of action under West Virginia Code 12-6-2, a provision of the Investment Management Law. The trial court entered judgment for the full amount of the state's losses on the when-issued notes and the reverse repo used to finance the purchase ($25,809,708) as well as the put transaction ($6,768,571). In explaining its 1992 ruling, the trial court found that "the Investment Management Law in effect at the time prohibited speculation with public funds, that the Board of Investments and its staff were fiduciaries, and that, prior to engaging in these transactions, Morgan had both constructive and actual knowledge that it was dealing with fiduciaries and that speculation was specifically prohibited by West Virginia law . . . the above-listed transactions were speculative and, therefore, illegal or

---

[25] Andy Pasztor and Laura Jereski, "Orange County Sues Merrill For $3 Billion," *The Wall Street Journal,* Jan. 13, 1995, at A3.

[26] *City of San Jose* v. *Paine Webber, et al.,* No. C-84-20601, 1991 WL 352485 (N.D. Cal. June 6, 1991).

[27] *State of West Virginia* v. *Morgan Stanley Group, Inc.,* No. 89-C-3700 (W.Va. Cir. Ct. March 15, 1992).

ultra vires in the sense that they violated an express statutory prohibition against speculation with public funds."[28] On June 5, 1995, the West Virginia Supreme Court reversed the lower court's decision and directed that a trial be held.[29]

"Warnings" by Brokers of Excessive Risk

One of the many interesting problems for Orange County in its case against Merrill Lynch arises from the fact that in 1993 Merrill Lynch brokers allegedly warned the former Orange County treasurer, Robert Citron (the architect of the Orange County Investment Pools), that his portfolios were excessively vulnerable to interest-rate movements. Indeed, before the precipitous increase in interest rates in late 1993 and early 1994, Mr. Citron is alleged to have rejected a Merrill Lynch offer to purchase all of the derivatives in the Orange County portfolio. The Orange County portfolio was heavily leveraged (with more than $13 billion in borrowings) and, when interest rates were forced even higher in 1994, the portfolio suffered huge losses, which were exacerbated by this leverage.

Merrill Lynch's alleged warning to its customer and its offer to purchase the derivatives are not unique. Many brokers and banks warned their customers that they were overexposed or had too much risk in their portfolios, especially those customers that had purchased or were purchasing derivatives with intrinsic leverage. Documented pretransaction warnings about excess risk should insulate a broker from criticism as well as liability; whether warnings "after the fact" (i.e., after the broker sold the derivatives to the customer) satisfy or mollify a broker's duty to warn a customer is an open question. Whether an after-the-fact warning serves to insulate the broker from liability for losses incurred after the date of the warning also remains to be seen.

Other Governmental-Entity Derivatives Litigation

Orange County is far from the only governmental entity that has sued to recover losses resulting from derivatives transactions. In March 1994, the

---

[28]Findings and Conclusion, filed March 3, 1995, West Virginia Supreme Court, in *State of West Virginia v. Morgan Stanley & Co., Incorporated*, No. 89-C-3700, 1995 WL 329574 (W.Va. March 5, 1995).

[29]*State of West Virginia v. Morgan Stanley & Co., Incorporated*, 1995 WL 329574 (W.Va. June 5, 1995).

County College District for Cook County, Illinois, filed an action in Illinois federal court against West Capital Government Securities Inc.[30] The complaint in that action alleges the unauthorized purchase of approximately $100 million of POs and support class POs by the College District treasurer. The plaintiff college district alleges that its broker/counterparty knew that the district was restricted by statute and board resolution from purchasing the derivatives, but nonetheless recommended them to the district treasurer, thereby impliedly representing that they were suitable investments and misleading the treasurer as to the nature and risk of the securities. The College District seeks rescision of these transactions on the grounds of lack of authority and based on alleged misrepresentations and omissions that induced the treasurer to purchase the securities.

On September 2, 1994, a complaint was filed by county commissioners of Charles County, Maryland, against Liberty Capital Markets Inc. and other brokers.[31] Charles County alleges that its treasurer, who invested almost $30 million of county funds in mortgage-backed derivatives, lacked the authority to do so and that the transactions were *ultra vires.*

The authors have uncovered no United States case dealing with a derivatives obligation (or even an interest-rate swap or option) where the defense of lack of authority or *ultra vires* has been successfully used to shield a commercial party—as opposed to a governmental party—from its obligations. The *City of San Jose* and *State of West Virginia* cases are not, however, the only cases in which a court has found a lack of authority on the part of a governmental unit as a ground for voiding an obligation after it has resulted in losses.[32]

There are also decisions in a United Kingdom case in which an English court and the House of Lords have held that interest-rate swap contracts entered into by a local government exceeded the local government's authority and therefore were *ultra vires* and void.[33] In 1991, the House of

---

[30] *County College District #508, County of Cook and State of Illinois* v. *West Cap Government Securities Inc.,* No. 94-C-1920, 1994 WL 530849 (N.D. Ill. Sept. 29, 1994).

[31] *County Commissioners of Charles County Maryland* v. *Liberty Capital Markets Inc.,* No. DKC 94-CB-2188 (D. Md. Sept. 2, 1994).

[32] See, e.g., *Chemical Bank* v. *Washington Public Power Supply System,* 666 P.2d 329 (Wash. 1983) (en banc).

[33] *Hazell* v. *Hammersmith and Fulham London Borough Council,* [1990] 2 QB 697, 3 ALL E.R. 33 and [1992] 2 AC 1, [1991] 1 ALL E.R. 545. *See also* 2 W.L.R. 372 (House of Lords 1991).

Lords shocked the financial markets with that decision. The House of
Lords examined 592 swap transactions, mostly straightforward interest-
rate swaps and options, entered into by a London borough (a local
governmental authority) with Midland Bank Plc.; Security Pacific National Bank, N.A.; Chemical Bank, N.A.; and others from 1987 to 1989.
An independent auditor challenged the transactions on the ground that the
Council's power to enter into the transactions was not created expressly or
impliedly by the statute that enabled the Council to incur debts. The banks
asserted that the swaps were executed "in conjunction with" debt obligations and, thus, constituted "parallel contracts," for the replacement of
debt, or "reprofiling" transactions changing the proportion of fixed- or
floating-rate debt. The House of Lords rejected the banks' arguments and
determined that the early swaps entered into between the borough and the
banks were "speculative," and therefore unauthorized, because their
"success" was predicated on a forecast of future interest rates.[34]

A 1993 study[35] of derivatives practices concluded that business corporations are not likely to be able to raise an *ultra vires* defense, since the
doctrine of *ultra vires* acts has largely been abolished by modern corporation law.[36] Aside from the *Minmetals* case, as yet there are no known
claims by business corporations that the purchase of a derivative was *ultra
vires*. Whether such claims will be asserted by business entities other than
corporations—such as trusts or partnerships—remains to be seen.

In the United States, there are various ways in which governmental
organizations deal with the authority of officials to engage in derivative
transactions. Although there are two basic types of enabling statutes, the
so-called laundry-list approach and the so-called prudent-man-standard
approach, there are states, municipalities, districts, authorities, and other
public bodies with a wide range of enabling statutes and regulations,
sometimes combining both statutory approaches.[37] Obviously, a derivatives dealer should be cautious when doing business with a governmental
entity and should determine in advance, with the help of counsel, the
authority of the entity to enter into the transaction. Equally obviously, if a

---

[34] 2 W.L.R. at 375, 378.

[35] Global Derivatives Study Group of The Group of Thirty, Derivatives Practices And Principles, Appendix I: Working Papers (1993) (hereinafter, "Group of Thirty").

[36] See, e.g., Revised Model Business Corporation Act 3.04 (1984).

[37] See, e.g., David M. Lynn, "Enforceability of Over-the-Counter Financial Derivatives," *The
Business Lawyer,* Nov. 1994 at 310 n. 103.

governmental entity has suffered a loss from a derivative product, its authority to enter into the transaction should be thoroughly examined.

Cases Involving Investment Guidelines

A claim that has been asserted by commercial entities that is somewhat akin to the *ultra vires* claims by governmental units is the claim that the purchase of derivatives was precluded by the terms of an investment management agreement, or by investment guidelines provided to the seller of the derivatives or to the money manager who purchased derivatives for the customer's account. For example, in *Marion Merrill Dow, Inc.* v. *Askin Capital Management L.P.,* a major American pharmaceutical company sued its outside money manager, alleging breach of the investment management agreement, fraud, and breach of the advisor's fiduciary duty.[38]

Marion Merrill Dow, Inc. (MMD), alleges that its advisor represented that it would maintain a safe, "market-neutral," and "risk-balanced" portfolio, but instead invested in derivative products that speculated on interest rates. These claims are very similar to those filed in the class actions referred to above, except that MMD relies on a separate investment management agreement in addition to the federal and state securities laws and the common law of torts.

Claims Relating to the Secondary Market

In addition to complaining about the securities that were purchased on its behalf by its investment manager, MMD also alleges that its manager misrepresented the manner in which the portfolio would be valued and hedged, and its liquidity maintained, in the secondary market. MMD alleges that it suffered losses of $11 million to $14 million when interest rates rose, the market for these instruments became illiquid, and the value of its derivative holdings fell.

MMD claims that its manager undertook responsibilities to maintain an orderly market for these derivatives and that the failure to maintain a secondary market contributed to the loss. MMD couches these claims as affirmative misrepresentations at the time of the purchase. Whether there

---

[38] *Marion Merrell Dow, Inc.* v. *Askin Capital Management, L.P.,* No. 94-0341-CV-W-2 (W.D. Mass. April 12, 1994).

were affirmative misrepresentations at the point of sale or not, the fact remains that much of the loss from certain types of derivatives has been caused by the illiquidity of the position and the inability (or refusal) of the originating broker/professional to maintain a secondary market in a rapidly declining market.

Although many of the prospectuses issued in connection with original-issue CMOs and other asset-backed derivatives recite warnings about the illiquidity of the secondary market, in fact, dealers in derivatives of all types are alleged to have promised their customers that the firm that underwrote the original issue, or that structured the transaction, would in effect become a market maker and would assure an orderly secondary market. Whether or not such promises were made, the absence of an orderly secondary market for some types of derivatives cannot be denied. For example, the sudden rise in interest rates in early 1994 quickly resulted in a drying up of the secondary market for many inverse-interest-rate-derived products. The absence of a meaningful secondary market, coupled with a deluge of sales of huge portfolios of such derivatives in the hands of Askin, Kidder Peabody, and others (and a tarnished image for such derivatives in the investment community) caused the value of derivatives such as inverse floaters to plummet, leaving customers with an illiquid investment and with a market value that has been as low in some cases as 20 percent of the original cost of the derivative.

Thus far, *MMD* and *Gibson* are the only cases challenging the broker's conduct in the secondary market. As will be discussed in the third part of this chapter, future claims based on disputes over pricing, valuations, breakage statistics, and other activities in the secondary market are virtually certain to erupt into litigation.

Review of the Past Year's Derivatives Cases

Since the *Gibson* case was filed, there have been some private settlements of claims by brokers and investment managers before litigation was filed and there have been some reported arbitration decisions. Some banks and brokers have reportedly made an effort to appease customers' complaints about derivatives losses by working with the customers to mitigate the loss, or by compensating the customers directly, or indirectly in a separate transaction. Judging from the relatively large number of cases still pending, however, it is also clear that some customers and some banks and brokers are taking a firm or hard-line position and are litigating or arbitrating rather than settling. Given the large amount of money at stake and the novelty of some of the claims being asserted, it is likely that the wave of litigation spawned by *Gibson* will roll on, at least until the courts have decided some of these cases and resolved the open issues described in this chapter.

There is some evidence that pension plans that suffered losses in derivatives are contemplating suing their investment managers, or the brokers that sold them derivatives. There is also the potential for additional shareholder derivatives litigation and for governmental litigation against those responsible for permitting these investments (such as ERISA fiduciaries or directors of regulated businesses like insurance companies, savings banks). As noted above, Procter & Gamble and Gibson are facing derivatives suits brought by shareholders against their directors.[39] The complaints in both of those actions allege that the board of directors was negligent in permitting the corporate treasurer to invest in derivatives. Similar claims could be asserted by plan participants under ERISA, or by bondholders or investment trust beneficial owners against trustees or other fiduciaries.

None of the litigations or arbitrations filed to date has produced a judicial decision or arbitration award that focuses specifically on the nature of derivatives as creating new or different duties for sellers of such products. The theories advanced by sophisticated purchasers of these products—such as the theory that the complexity of the product creates a greater disclosure duty, or that it creates an advisory rather than a counterparty relationship, or that this complexity obviates the need to prove reliance—have not as yet been tested in court in the context of complex derivative products.

In determining respective rights and obligations between sophisticated purchasers and sellers of derivatives, the courts will have to analyze the derivative itself, an analysis that should determine whether the particular derivative is a security or a commodity within the meaning of federal securities laws and federal commodities laws, as well as state securities laws. The courts will also have to deal with the fact that many of the derivatives that produced the largest losses were created by the seller in response to the request of the purchaser for such a product. A typical

---

[39] *Drage* v. *Procter & Gamble, et al.*, No. A9401999 (Court of Common Pleas, Hamilton County, Ohio, April 25, 1993); *In Re Gibson Greetings Securities Litigation*, No. C-1-94-455 (S.D. Ohio).

scenario is a request by a corporate treasurer, pension fund manager, or municipal controller for some type of derivative product to increase yield or to hedge interest rates, currency values, or some other variable, with the treasurer or similar official later claiming that the particular derivative chosen by the dealer was not what the treasurer wanted, or that the treasurer did not understand the risks inherent in the product.

In an unregulated market, with no prospectuses issued for most of these derivatives, many of these litigations will likely turn on "who said what to whom" at the time the derivatives were sold. If the conversations were recorded and these recordings are admissible, then the judicial or arbitration fact-finding process will be facilitated by a contemporaneous record. If there is no admissible contemporaneous record, however, and there is a factual dispute as to what occurred at the point of sale, such cases will not be suitable for summary judgment or other summary disposition and a trial will be necessary.

Conclusion

In sum, "derivative" has become a generic dirty label for a wide variety of products. Some straightforward, traditional hedging products—such as interest-rate swaps—have produced large losses and are considered derivatives. Although some interest-rate swaps can become quite complex, most of these products are understood by the average professional corporate treasurer or money manager.

Nonetheless, some derivative products—even some swaps, options, and other hedging contracts—are, by any objective standard, pushing the edge of the envelope of even the above-average financial or risk manager's ability to appreciate and understand all of the risks involved. Exotic products like knock-out options and wedding bands, can sometimes be sufficiently complex that a full appreciation of the risks of such products could not have been gleaned by a purchaser/end user that lacked the necessary software and expertise without substantial input from a professional.

There may well be different results in court cases involving derivatives depending upon the complexity of the particular derivative and upon the ability of an in-house treasurer/controller to appreciate the risk of the derivative under various possible market scenarios. It is the complexity of some derivatives that gives rise to the uncertainty surrounding the duties, liabilities, rights, and obligations of the participants in these markets. Absent sufficient complexity to raise doubts as to the ability of the customer to understand the risk and intelligently evaluate whether or not to acquire the position or contract, there is no reason to impose any new, greater, or different duty on a derivatives dealer than is imposed on any other dealer. Since there are already cases of record involving quite complex derivatives and at least one is scheduled for trial in the near future, answers to some of these questions about the duties of derivatives dealers selling complex derivatives may be forth-coming shortly.

PROPOSED LEGISLATIVE, ADMINISTRATIVE, AND OTHER INSTITUTIONAL RESPONSES TO DERIVATIVES PROBLEMS

Legislators, regulators, and other governing officials, alarmed by the public's perception of experiences such as those of Orange County, Gibson and Barings, have raced to propose solutions to the "derivatives problem."[40] Suggestions have ranged from increased disclosure, to applying existing securities laws to derivative transactions, to prohibiting the use of derivatives by banks except for hedging purposes. The result is a patchwork of proposed legislation and regulation that varies in the definition of derivative, in the scope of the parties affected, and in the remedies for noncompliance. The following highlights some of the recent proposals that may be of interest to litigants, potential litigants, and participants in the derivative markets.[41]

---

[40]For a recent illustration of the legislative concerns regarding Orange County, Barings, and other derivatives experiences, as well as responses by cooler heads, see the debate on the defeated Markey Amendment to the Securities Litigation Reform Act (H.R. 1058), which would have ex-empted derivatives from the act. (141 Cong. Rec. H2818-01 [daily ed., March 8, 1995]).

In addition to Orange County, Barings, and the other well-publicized derivatives experiences, legislators have cited the recent fall of Capital Corporate Credit Union, a large corporate credit union that lost heavily in CMOs and was taken over by federal regulators. (141 Cong. Rec. S3964-01 [daily ed., March 15, 1995]) (statement of Sen. Dorgan).

Several legislators have analogized derivatives to government securities, which were largely unregulated until the Government Securities Act was passed. (E.g., 141 Cong. Rec. E35-02 [daily ed., February 27, 1995]) (statement of Rep. Markey) (citing the "many similarities between the pre-1986 Government securities market and today's derivatives markets").

[41]For a detailed outline of regulatory and legislative proposals and developments regarding derivatives as of December 1994, see Ernest T. Patrikis, et al., *Managing Risk Exposure in Deriv-*

Congress

The GAO Report. Much of the congressional activity relating to derivatives has responded to a report of the General Accounting Office entitled "Financial Derivatives—Actions Needed to Protect the Financial System," dated May 18, 1994 (the GAO Report). The GAO Report examined the nature and extent of derivatives use, the risks derivatives pose, internal risk-control mechanisms, the extent of existing regulation of derivatives, the adequacy of existing accounting rules, and the implications of the international use of derivatives.[42]

The GAO Report estimated that the notional amount[43] of derivatives outstanding globally as of the end of 1992 was at least $12.1 trillion. This represents an increase of approximately 145 percent from the end of 1989, the earliest year for which comparable data is available.

The GAO Report identified four principal risks of derivatives: credit risk, market risk, legal risk, and operations risk. Credit risk is the risk that the counterparty will fail to meet its financial obligations. The GAO Report concluded that, while the amount of derivatives-related credit exposure tends to be smaller than, for example, banks' lending-related credit exposure, derivatives-related credit risk is more difficult to manage, because the amount of exposure can change rapidly.

Market risk is the exposure to potential financial loss resulting from unfavorable movements in interest and currency rates, as well as equity and commodity prices, on which derivative instruments' values are based. Measuring market risk can be complex and is often dependent on a dealer's on-line link with the market and computer software employing advanced mathematical, statistical, and database techniques. Because over-the-counter (OTC) derivative products lack centralized markets, dealers must rely on sophisticated mathematical models to compute values, often using assumptions for a number of variables.

Legal risk is the risk that a particular derivative instrument will be invalidated or held unenforceable by a court or legislative or regulatory

---

atives: How to Deal with Recent Regulatory and Legislative Developments, 873 PLI/CORP 69 (December 8, 1994).

[42]GAO Report at 5.

[43]The notional amount of a derivative instrument is generally not a meaningful measure of the actual risk involved, since in most derivative instruments the amount actually at risk is only a percentage of the notional amount. GAO Report at 29.

body. Dealers attempt to manage legal risk through internal legal review and occasionally by requiring legal opinions confirming a counterparty's authority to enter into the derivative transaction.

Operations risk is the exposure to possible financial loss resulting from inadequate systems, management failure, faulty controls, fraud, or human error. In effect, operations risk is the danger that the other three risks will be inadequately managed, either because of a flaw in the dealer's internal management controls or through deception by a counterparty.

Notwithstanding the massive scale of derivatives activity and the tremendous risks inherent in derivatives, the GAO Report found that "no comprehensive industry or federal regulatory requirements existed to ensure that U.S. OTC derivatives dealers followed good risk-management practices."

The GAO Report issued several recommendations to financial regulators, including (1) facilitating centralized current information concerning counterparty concentrations and sources and amounts of earnings, which would be accessible to all regulators; (2) a consistent set of capital standards; (3) specific requirements for independent audits and internal control reporting by derivatives dealers; and (4) leadership in working with other countries' regulators to harmonize requirements. Further, the GAO Report recommended that SEC registrants establish requirements for derivatives reporting, including assessments of derivatives-risk management systems. Finally, the GAO Report recommended that the Financial Accounting Standards Board (FASB) issue an exposure draft providing comprehensive rules for derivative products, including expanded disclosure requirements, and consider a market-value accounting model for all financial instruments, including derivative products.

Proposed Legislation. In an attempt to address the risks and recommendations identified in the GAO Report, four bills were introduced in Congress in 1994. None was passed.[44] However, the events of late 1994 and early 1995—including Orange County, Gibson Greetings, and Barings—have resurrected congressional concern. Three of the 1994 bills, as well as one new bill, were introduced in 1995 in response to what some legislators continued to perceive as the "derivatives crisis."

On February 27, 1995, Representative Markey (D-Mass.) introduced

---

[44]*Peloso* at 6 and n.4.

the "Derivatives Dealers Act of 1995."[45] Originally introduced in 1994,[46] partly in response to the GAO Report, the legislation was designed to "close the most glaring legal gap affecting the derivatives markets—the presence of virtually unregulated OTC derivatives dealers in the market."[47]

The bill defines derivative as "any financial contract or other instrument that derives its value from the value or performance of any security, currency exchange rate, or interest rate (or group or index thereof)."[48] The definition expressly *excludes* securities traded on national securities exchanges or automated interdealer quotation systems, forward contracts with maturities of 270 days or less, commodity futures subject to the Commodities Exchange Act, and bank deposits.[49]

The bill would amend the Securities Exchange Act of 1934 (the 1934 Act) to require all "derivatives dealers" to register with the SEC.[50] The bill would apply all the prohibitions of the 1934 Act to derivatives dealers even if the jurisdictional requirement of the use of the mails or any means or instrumentality of interstate commerce is not met.[51] The bill would also empower the SEC to adopt rules with respect to transactions in derivatives relating to financial responsibility safeguards, financial reporting, and record keeping, and would enable the SEC to enforce its rules by revoking a derivatives dealer's registration.

The bill does not contain language providing an express private right of action. However, the bill would add "derivative" to the definition of "security" in Section 3(a)(10) of the 1934 Act. As a practical matter, therefore, the bill should extend existing implied liability for violation of provisions like Section 10(b) to instruments not previously considered securities, such as interest-rate swaps.[52]

---

[45] H.R. 1063, 104th Cong., 1st Sess. (1995).

[46] H.R. 4745, 103d Cong., 2d Sess. (1994).

[47] 140 Cong. Rec. E111469-03 (daily ed., July 13, 1994) (statement of Rep. Markey).

[48] H.R. 1063, 104th Cong., 1st Sess. 2 (1995).

[49] *Id.*

[50] *Id.* at 101. The bill defines derivatives dealers as persons other than financial institutions who buy, sell, or enter into derivatives for their own account as part of a regular business. *Id.* at 2.

[51] H.R. 1063, 104th Cong., 1st Sess. 101 (1995).

[52] The bill would not expand the definition of "security" in the 1933 Act. Presumably, therefore, the causes of action under Sections 11 and 12(2) of that act would still not apply to instruments that have not traditionally been held to be securities.

In addition to derivatives dealers, banks are a significant target of the latest wave of proposed legislation. On March 15, 1995, Senator Dorgan (D-N.D.) introduced a bill titled the "Derivatives Limitations Act of 1995," seeking to prohibit banks and other federally insured financial institutions from engaging in speculative derivatives trading on their own accounts.[53] That bill would amend the Federal Deposit Insurance Act (FDIA)[54] and the Federal Credit Union Act (FCUA)[55] to prevent federally insured banks and credit unions from engaging in any transaction involving a "derivative financial instrument" for their own account *except* for hedging and other specifically enumerated transactions.[56] The bill defines "derivative financial instrument" as "an instrument the value of which is derived from the value of stocks, bonds, other loan instruments, other assets, interest or currency exchange rates, or indexes, including qualified financial contracts," as well as any other instrument determined to be a derivative by the appropriate federal banking agency. Thus, banks would be permitted to use derivatives in the normal course of business to reduce the risk of price changes, currency fluctuations, interest-rate changes with respect to the loans, and other assets and investments in their portfolios.

Banks are also the principal target of a bill introduced on January 4, 1995, by Representative Gonzalez (D-Tex.). Titled the "Derivatives Safety and Soundness Supervision Act of 1995," this bill addresses the perceived need for uniform regulation of derivatives activities by federal regulators.[57] The bill would require a number of federal agencies, including federal banking agencies—the SEC, the CFTC, the Secretary of the Treasury, and the Federal Reserve, among others—to establish "substantially similar" standards relating to minimum capital requirements, accounting, disclosure, comprehensive risk management systems, and suitability with respect to derivatives transactions entered into by banks, brokers, investment companies, insurance companies, and other financial

---

[53]S. 557, 104th Cong., 1st Sess. (1995); see 141 Cong. Rec. S3964-01 (daily ed., March 15, 1995) (statement of Sen. Dorgan). A version of this bill was also introduced in 1994. S. 2123, 103d Cong., 2d Sess. (1994).

[54]12 U.S.C. 1811 *et seq.* (1989)

[55]12 U.S.C. 1781 *et seq.* (1989)

[56]S. 557, 104th Cong., 1st Sess. 2 (1995).

[57]H.R. 31, 104th Cong., 1st Sess. (1995). Rep. Gonzalez had introduced a substantially similar bill on May 26, 1994, that was not passed. H.R. 4503, 103d Cong., 2d Sess. (1994).

institutions.[58] The act would empower federal regulatory agencies to require quarterly disclosures of both *quantitative* information with respect to all derivatives—including gains, losses, and gross notional amounts of derivatives held—and *qualitative* information, including the purposes of all derivative transactions and the institution's investment strategies and accounting policies.

The bill would require all financial institutions engaging in derivatives activities to file written management plans approved by the appropriate agency to ensure that the activities are adequately supervised within the institution and consistent with the institution's risk-management and business strategy, as well as with uniform risk-management standards. The failure of any institution to comply, or to engage in derivatives activities without adequate expertise may be considered an unsafe or unsound practice.

The bill would also require the Secretary of the Treasury to propose a joint study with representatives of "the other major industrialized countries" concerning the need for *international* regulation and supervision of derivatives activities.

There is one new bill proposed in 1995 that would apply to both banks *and* securities dealers, but that would establish a very different scheme with respect to each. The proposed "Risk Management Improvement and Derivatives Oversight Act of 1995," introduced on January 5, 1995, by Representative Leach (R-Ia.),[59] would create a Federal Derivatives Commission to establish standards for regulatory supervision of financial institutions engaged in derivatives activities. That bill delegates the definition of a derivative to the new commission, defining "derivative financial instrument" only as "any securities contract, commodity contract, forward contract, swap agreement or any other similar agreement or instrument" that the new Federal Derivatives Commission determines to be a derivative financial instrument for purposes of the act.[60]

The proposed new Federal Derivatives Commission would be composed of the heads of various existing federal agencies and departments, including the chairman of the Board of Governors of the Federal Reserve

---

[58]H.R. 31, 104th Cong., 1st Sess. 101 (1995).

[59]H.R. 20, 104th Cong., 1st Sess. (1995).

[60]H.R. 20, 104th Cong., 1st Sess. 102 (1995).

(who would also chair the new commission), the Comptroller of the Currency, the chairman of the FDIC, and the chairmen of the SEC and the CFTC. The new commission would be required to establish uniform standards for capital requirements, leverage limits, accounting, disclosure, sales practices, and other controls. In turn, the various federal agencies would implement the new standards by adopting their own substantially similar regulations. The commission would make recommendations to the agencies relating to capital requirements, comprehensive risk-management systems, regulatory examinations of banks, internal management supervision of derivatives activities, use of collateral, credit-risk reserves, legal-risk precautions, minimum prudential practices for municipalities and pension funds using derivatives, and enhanced disclosure to mutual fund customers of risks posed to mutual funds that purchase derivatives. The bill would also provide that the failure of an institution-affiliated party to have adequate technical expertise may be deemed by the appropriate federal agency to constitute an unsafe or unsound banking practice for purposes of the FDIA.[61]

The bill contains a second proposed act named the "Derivatives Dealer Self-Regulation Act of 1995," which, as its name suggests, would authorize the Board of Governors of the Federal Reserve to require a system of self-regulation among financial institutions dealing in derivatives. The self-regulation act covers only financial institutions dealing in derivatives which are not already registered as securities brokers or dealers or futures commission merchants. The definition of "derivative" for purposes of this act would be left to the board.

The act contemplates the registration of national derivatives associations, which would establish rules designed to prevent fraudulent and manipulative acts and practices, promote just principles of trade, and facilitate derivatives transactions. The associations' rules must also provide fair procedures for disciplining members, denying membership, and other enforcement measures.

The act would make it unlawful to effect any transaction in or induce or attempt to induce the purchase or sale of any derivative financial instrument unless the dealer is a member of a registered national derivatives association. The act would provide criminal penalties for violation of the

---

[61] 12 U.S.C. 1818 (1989).

act, including the false statement in any application, report, or document, of up to a $2.5 million fine (up to $1 million for natural persons) and/or 10 years imprisonment.

The 1994 failure of three of the currently pending bills, as well as the virulent opposition to new regulation by agencies such as the SEC and the Federal Reserve,[62] may not bode well for the pending legislation. However, experiences such as Barings—and perhaps more importantly, the ongoing public perception of those experiences—will not likely go away. Each publicized loss—particularly those in instruments such as interest-rate swaps, which are currently unregulated—will impose greater pressure on legislators to respond.

Office of the Comptroller of the Currency (OCC)

Banks and other federally insured financial institutions have already received guidance with respect to their derivatives activities through a series of OCC publications. In October 1993, the OCC issued a circular providing that banks should establish procedures to ensure that particular derivatives are appropriate for particular customers, that customers are aware of the risks, that the terms of the contract are compliant with laws and regulations, that risk is managed and measured at least daily, and that the hedging of physical commodities is limited.[63]

In May 1994, the OCC responded to questions concerning Circular 277. The OCC indicated that, while Circular 277 did not prohibit unsuitable transactions, a bank should inform a customer before engaging in a transaction that the bank believes is inappropriate.[64]

Finally, in October 1994, the OCC issued a handbook on a bank's use of derivatives.[65] The handbook provides for the oversight of derivatives policies by management and the board of directors, for an analysis of customer appropriateness (including obtaining information regarding the customer's business and purposes for the derivative transaction), and establishes guidelines for netting arrangements.

---

[62]*E.g.*, 141 Cong. Rec. H2818-01 (daily ed., March 8, 1995) (statement of Rep. Cox).

[63]*Risk Management of Financial Derivatives*, OCC Banking Circular No. 277 (Oct. 27, 1993) ("Circular 277").

[64]OCC Bulletin 94-32, *Questions and Answers For BC-277: Risk Management of Financial Derivatives* (May 1994).

[65]*The Comptroller's Handbook, Risk Management of Financial Derivatives* (October 1994).

Particularly significant for litigation purposes is the OCC's focus on customer suitability. Although the OCC's chief concern in this area was the legal and credit risk posed to banks when derivative instruments are unsuitable for the customers who purchase them, these guidelines could be employed as evidence of a standard of care in actions under state law. Moreover, whatever the OCC's intent, the fact that the OCC recognizes a need for banks to ensure that the derivative instruments they offer are suitable for their customers underscores the fact that the complexity of derivative instruments often forces customers to rely on banks and brokers to recommend suitable derivative financial products. The fact that such reliance is necessary may persuade courts to find that banks and brokers owe greater duties to their customers with respect to these complex transactions than would otherwise pertain to a more fully arm's-length relationship.

FASB

One arena that has already seen changes take effect—and that could create derivatives-related liability—is the set of standards governing financial accounting. The FASB has recently attempted to deal with the problem of off-balance-sheet risk that occurs when entities hold derivative financial instruments.[66] FAS 119 defines "derivative financial instrument" as "a futures, forward, swap or option contract, or other financial instrument with similar characteristics."[67] FAS 119 requires entities that hold or issue derivative financial instruments for trading purposes to disclose information such as the average fair value of the instruments and the net gains or losses from trading activities. FAS 119 requires entities holding derivative financial instruments for activities *other* than trading, such as hedging, to disclose information such as their objectives and strategies in purchasing the instruments and descriptions of the transactions whose risks the derivatives are intended to hedge.

---

[66]*Disclosure About Derivative Financial Instruments and Fair Value of Financial Instruments,* Statement of Financial Accounting Standards No. 119 (Financial Accounting Standards Board 1994) ("FAS 119"). FAS 119 amends two earlier statements, FAS 105 and FAS 107, both of which dealt with off-balance-sheet risk, but did not focus on derivatives.

[67]FAS 119 at 2. The definition excludes on-balance-sheet receivables and payables that are typically included in definitions of derivative securities, such as mortgage-backed securities, interest-only and principal-only obligations, and indexed debt instruments. *Id.*

Although it does not provide its own cause of action, FAS 119 may provide a weapon for parties who have been injured by derivatives losses. As with all FASB pronouncements, FAS 119 is part of GAAP and must be followed by all reporting entities. Therefore, publicly held corporations that fail to disclose the extent and nature of their derivatives positions—as well as an accurate analysis of the risks—as required by FAS 119, and suffer losses in those positions may find themselves subject to suits by investors under the federal securities laws for material misstatements and omissions in their financial statements.

The SEC, the CFTC, and Attempts at Self-Regulation

As discussed above, the SEC has not taken a position generally on whether OTC derivatives such as interest-rate swaps constitute securities for purposes of the securities laws. Similarly, the CFTC has washed its hands of many derivative contracts that might be considered commodities.[68]

On March 9, 1995, the SEC and the CFTC announced that they had received the report of a group of the six broker-dealers with the largest OTC derivatives affiliates, known as the Derivatives Policy Group (DPG).[69] The report, titled "Framework for Voluntary Oversight," proposed a self-regulating framework for OTC derivatives, including internal risk-management and monitoring programs, enhanced quantitative reporting to the SEC and the CFTC, a framework for the evaluation of risk in relation to capital, guidelines on relationships between professionals and

---

[68]*Peloso* at 3, 6. For example, Rule 35.1(b)(2)(xi) exempts from regulation swaps entered into by persons (including individuals) exceeding $5 million in net worth or $10 million in total assets. Marc A. Horwitz, "Swaps Ahoy! Should Regulators Voyage into Unknown Waters?" 1 *Indiana Journal of Global Legal Studies* 515, at n. 84 and accompanying text (1994). In the *Bankers Trust* administrative proceeding discussed above, the CFTC avoided the issue of whether derivative instruments constituted commodities by premising its jurisdiction on BT's close relationship with Gibson stating that the relationship fell within the agency's rules governing futures advisors. (Peloso at 6) The SEC was more direct, finding that "certain" of the derivative instruments sold to Gibson by Bankers Trust were securities. *In re BT Securities Corp.*, Admin. Proc. File No. 3-8579, 58 S.E.C. Docket 1145 at 4 (December 22, 1994). The SEC took the position that, while the one of the instruments at issue was called a "swap," it was in actuality a "cash-settled put option that was written by Gibson and based initially on the 'spread' between the price of the 7.625% 30-year U.S. Treasury security maturing on November 15, 2022, and the arithmetic average of the bid and offered yields of the most recently auctioned obligation of a two-year Treasury note." *Id.* at 4 n. 6. It remains to be seen whether this classification by the SEC will be extended to garden-variety interest-rate swaps and other OTC derivative instruments.

[69]*SEC News Digest* 95-46 (March 9, 1995).

nonprofessional counterparties, and processes for internal review of written material used in connection with OTC derivatives transactions.[70] In a joint press release, the SEC and the CFTC stated that the report should be viewed as part of an ongoing process by the SEC and CFTC to address the OTC derivatives activities of nonbank dealers. "With this information, the Commissions have an opportunity to analyze in an improved fashion the firms' OTC derivatives activities and their implications for systemic risk."

The future of derivatives legislation and regulation is unclear. Despite well-publicized problems, attempts at legislation and regulation have been vigorously opposed. Arthur Levitt, chairman of the SEC, testified before the Senate in January 1995 that

> [I]t would be a grave error to demonize derivatives and blame them for the loss in Orange County. Derivatives are not inherently bad or good. They are a bit like electricity, dangerous if mishandled, but bearing the potential to do tremendous good.[71]

Whether and in what ways legislators and regulators will attempt to prevent the mishandling and harness the good in derivatives remains to be seen. While this proposed legislation and regulation may have no direct bearing on pending or future litigation involving derivatives, the courts and arbitration panels that must grapple with the existing law will necessarily be influenced by this ongoing public debate. Indeed, as noted above, some of the releases and advisory statements already issued recognize the existence of potential abuses and focus on the tension in defining legal relationships and duties that the complex nature of derivatives present for the courts, the industry, and for the regulators.

LIABILITY THEORIES

Nontraditional plaintiffs and complex financial arrangements promise to make litigation over losses from derivatives trading and investments a fertile and stimulating field for the next few years. As noted above, an important case involving a large multinational corporation and one of the

---

[70]For a synopsis of this report see Wilmer, Cutler & Pickering, "Bank Securities and Investment Services Alert" (April 1995) at 2-3.

[71]Quoted at 141 Cong. Rec. H2818-01 (daily ed., March 8, 1995) (statement of Rep. Cox).

world's largest packagers of complex derivatives (BT Sec.) which ws originally scheduled for trial in the fall of 1995 has been postponed.[72]

Starting with the filing in September 1994 of Gibson's lawsuit against BT, a wave of derivatives litigation has washed up onto the courts and the arbitration panels of the securities industry. For decades, corporate America stood shoulder to shoulder with its bankers and brokers, fighting the plaintiff securities bar together. Now, faced with large losses on products that were not in existence when most of the applicable laws were enacted, the earlier reluctance of corporate America to do battle with its bankers and brokers has waned for some corporate end-users of derivatives who suffered large losses.

The prospect of shareholder or taxpayer litigation against a management that has incurred losses from derivative transactions is another complication facing the corporate manager or governmental official. Shareholder litigation against Gibson was expected to go to trial in the fall of 1995. With alert shareholders and their counsel watching, management facing significant derivative losses is obliged to evaluate its own legal position as well as the legal position of the entity they manage before deciding whether or not to pursue a claim against the seller of a derivative that has caused a loss.

Although the wave of derivatives-related litigations is for the most part well under a year old, and is in its embryonic stages from a jurisprudential perspective, some legal theories have already emerged with sufficient frequency to bear noting. The rest of this chapter summarizes the principal theories that have surfaced thus far, without regard to their utility as a defensive measure or as an offensive weapon.

Lack of Capacity/Authority

Ultra Vires. As noted above, this theory is ordinarily not available to business corporations, but it has been successfully asserted by some governmental units and is the subject of several ongoing cases. Most of the pending cases that present authority issues involve school districts, counties, and other governmental entities, but the theory may be available to noncorporate business entities, such as business trusts and partnerships,

---

[72] A status conference is scheduled in the Proctor & Gamble action for October 6, 1995 at which time a new trial date is expected to be established.

and may also be available to pension plans that have declarations of trust or investment guidelines that establish the parameters of permissible investments.

Individual Authority. Since most derivatives activity by customers is performed by one person or a few persons within the organization, it has been claimed that this human center of derivative activity lacked the actual or apparent authority to bind the entity. There are hints of this type of claim in the Orange County litigation and in the reports about the Barings trader, and may prove to be a subplot in some of the pending cases.

Lack of Binding Contract

Even assuming authority, there may be insufficient writings to satisfy the applicable statute of frauds. The several forms of master agreement established by industry associations tend to indicate that a writing is required to evidence a trade.[73]

Defenses designed to avoid the terms of a written contract would include duress—a rarely successful defense in a dispute between sophisticated business people, and one that would rarely be available to avoid an initial derivatives transaction (absent some preexisting relationship that could provide commercial or other leverage sufficient to coerce a party into entering into the initial transaction). However, given the reality of the derivatives marketplace, it is likely that some end users will assert that continuing large losses, the absence of liquidity, and the need to stop losses left the end user with no choice but to enter into a subsequent transaction with the same counterparty. Such an end user would claim that its assent to the subsequent transaction was not free and, thus, that the contract for the subsequent transaction should not be binding.

Similarly, fraud may be asserted to try to avoid a contractual obligation where, for example, the seller of the derivative has misled the buyer, or omitted to disclose something that the end user should have known in order to make an informed decision. The latter situation was alleged in *Gibson* and is often asserted in tandem with fraud claims under federal and state securities laws.

---

[73]See, e.g., Int'l Swaps and Derivatives Ass'n, Inc., *Master Agreement* (Local Currency-Single Jurisdiction) (1992); Int'l Swaps and Derivatives Ass'n, Inc., *Confirmation of OTC Bond Option Transaction* (1993).

Federal Securities Laws

As noted above, the SEC has generally avoided regulating swaps and other similar "noninvestment" derivatives, but did take the position in its administrative settlement with BT Sec. that one of the interest-rate contracts that BT Sec. sold to Gibson was a "security."[74] While swaps and similar contracts have never been held by a court to be a security for purposes of the 1933 Act or the 1934 Act, some derivatives are clearly understood to be securities, including CMOs and their derivatives.[75] Where there has been a public offering of a new issue of derivatives, such as CMOs or other asset-backed securities, the prospectuses and selling literature will be governed by the same laws, regulations, and case law as any other security. Derivatives that qualify as government securities will also be covered by the provisions of the Government Securities Act. 15 U.S.C. 78o(c)1.

The Investment Company Act of 1940 (the 1940 Act) regulates investment companies and, among other things, precludes a registered investment company from changing from its investment policy without the vote of a majority of its security holders.[76] The Investment Advisors Act of 1940 (the Advisors Act) regulates the activities of investment advisors.[77] One of the issues to be resolved by the courts in these derivatives litigations is whether the dependence of some derivatives customers on their contractual counterparty gives rise to an implied or *de facto* "advisory" relationship under the common law or under the Advisors Act.

Commodity Exchange Act (CEA)

In order for a derivatives transaction to give rise to a claim under the CEA, the contract must be a futures contract or a commodity option, and the activities of the dealer must be wilfully deceptive or involve a series of acts of fraud or cheating. The *Gibson* case was apparently the first case in

---

[74]*In the Matter of BT Securities Corp.*, Admin. Proc. File No. 3-8579, Securities Act Release No. 7124, Exchange Act Release No. 35136 (Dec. 22, 1994).

[75]See, e.g., *Elysian Federal Sav. Bank* v. *First Interregional Equity Corp.*, 713 F. Supp. 737 (D.N.J. 1989) (denying summary judgment dismissing federal securities law claims based on sale of CMOs).

[76]Section 13(a)(3) of the 1940 Act.

[77]Investment Advisors Act of 1940, 15 U.S.C. 806-1 *et. seq.* (1981).

which an end user asserted a private claim under the CEA in a derivative transaction.[78] In the CFTC's administrative proceeding against BT Sec., the CFTC alleged that BT Sec. acted as a "commodities trading advisor" and that its acts constituted a scheme or artifice to defraud within the meaning of the CEA.[79]

RICO

The Racketeer Influenced and Corrupt Organizations Act (RICO) creates civil liability arising out of an enterprise conducted through a pattern of racketeering activity.[80] "Racketeering activity" includes such activities as federal securities fraud, mail fraud, and wire fraud, among other conduct.[81] On September 1, 1995, Procter & Gamble moved to amend its complaint against BT to assert a RICO claim, apparently the first such claim in a case involving derivatives.[82] Whether the court will permit Procter & Gamble to assert its RICO claim has not been decided. Whether a derivatives dealer can be successfully charged with a pattern of racketeering remains to be seen, but the availability of treble damages under RICO suggests that Procter & Gamble will not be the only derivatives plaintiff to try to fit a derivatives dealers' activities into the framework of the RICO statute. If the court were to permit Procter & Gamble's amended pleading to be filed—and the pleading were to survive a motion to dismiss—then the "stakes" for BT will increase dramatically in the Procter & Gamble case itself and, due to the collateral estoppel consequences of an adverse result on the merits, in other actions as well.

---

[78] *Gibson Greetings, Inc.* v. *Bankers Trust Co., et al.*, No. 1-94-620 (S.D. Ohio, Sept. 12, 1994).

[79] *In the Matter of BT Securities Corporation*, CFTC No. 95-3, 1994 LEXIS 340 (CFTC Dec. 22, 1994).

[80] 18 U.S.C. §§1961–1968.

[81] 18 U.S.C. §1961.

[82] Both Procter & Gamble and BT have sought to seal documents filed in connection with Procter & Gamble's motion for leave to amend Procter & Gamble's complaint. As this chapter went to press, the details of Procter & Gamble's proposed amended complaint and specifically the factual allegations of its proposed RICO claim were not available. Indeed, in an extraordinary ruling, the trial court enjoined *Business Week* from publishing an article apparently based on information filed under seal in this action. Separately, Proctor & Gamble has been trying to force BT to produce certain documents relating to regulatory reviews of BT's derivatives practices. BT and the Federal Reserve Board have resisted this discovery, and the dispute over the discoverability of these materials remains unresolved at this time.

ERISA

The Employee Retirement Income Security Act (ERISA) applies to retirement or pension plans that invested in derivatives, and it may impose liability on fiduciaries who purchased derivatives in breach of their ERISA responsibilities to act prudently and to diversify the investments under their management.[83]

State Laws

Most state securities laws are patterned on, and are often coordinated with, the federal securities laws. Allegations against a dealer or issuer of a security that would state a claim under the federal securities laws will often also state a claim under analogous state securities statutes. It is at least theoretically possible that a derivatives transaction could be effectuated without the use of the mails or other instrumentalities of interstate commerce and, thus, be subject only to state laws concerning the sale of securities.

Most states have enacted deceptive trade practices laws that may apply to the method and content of the marketing of some derivative products. Although swaps are exempt from state laws regulating or prohibiting gambling or the operation of a bucket shop (under the "swap exemption" to the Futures Trading Practices Act of 1993[84]) some derivatives may not be covered by this swap exemption and thus may fit within the literal definition of prohibited conduct under these statutes.

"Suitability" Claims

There is currently no direct SEC suitability requirement for securities brokers and dealers; all broker-dealers, however, are required by the 1934 Act to be members of a self-regulatory organization, like the NYSE and the NASD, each of which has adopted "know your customer," or suitability, rules.[85]

---

[83]29 U.S.C. 1002 (21)(A)(1995); 29 U.S.C. 1109(a)(1995).

[84]17 C.F.R. 35.1(b)(2)(xi) (1992).

[85]See, e.g., NYSE Rule 405; NASD Rules of Fair Practice, Article III, Sections 2(a) and 2(b) (for "non-institutional customers"). In 1995, the NASD submitted to the SEC a proposed interpretation of section 2(a), which attempts to delineate the suitability obligations of a dealer to an

The CFTC also does not directly regulate suitability. There are, however, CFTC regulations governing the activities of futures commission merchants (FCMs) (Reg. 1.55), commodity trading advisors (Reg. 4.31), and commodity pool operators (Reg. 4.21), and the National Futures Association has a "know your customer" rule (Rule 2-30).

The DPG (discussed above) established voluntary standards applicable to OTC derivatives, which imposes a good-faith obligation on the part of so-called professional intermediaries to clarify the nature of the relationship should the professional intermediary become aware that a "nonprofessional counterparty" believes ("incorrectly") that the "professional intermediary" has assumed advisory or similar responsibilities toward the nonprofessional counterparty. This voluntary guideline addresses the central question that some of the pending derivative litigations must resolve, i.e., does there come a point in time when the derivatives professional, either overtly or impliedly, becomes a *de facto* advisor to the nonprofessional counterparty, and, if so, how does this alter the legal relationship of the parties?

National banks and federally licensed branches and agencies of foreign banks, bank holding companies, state-chartered banks in the Federal Reserve System, and state-licensed branches and agencies of foreign banks have received a number of different circulars and supervisory releases, the principal concern of which is to protect the bank, not the counterparty, with respect to derivatives transactions, but when a transaction has been entered into with a bank, these policy statements should be reviewed by both sides of the dispute.[86] Similarly, the bank anti-tying act (12 U.S.C. 1972) should be reviewed when a derivative transaction is related to an extension of credit.

---

institutional customer in transactions involving equity and debt securities. Of interest here is a provision of the proposed interpretation that deals with "new" products with "significantly different risk or volatility than investments generally made by the customer." The NASD has also issued a policy statement that as "new financial products" are introduced, each broker-dealer should "familiarize" itself with each customer's financial situation, trading experience and risk-taking ability. Hybrid securities and index warrants are also the subject of specific guidelines.

[86]See, e.g., *OCC Handbook on Risk Management of Financial Derivatives* (Oct. 24, 1994); OCC News Release 95-33. *Examining Risk Management and Internal Controls for Trading Activities of Banking Organizations*, Supervisory Release 93-69 (Dec. 20, 1993); Federal Reserve Board Trading Activities Manual (Feb. 1994). See also: E. Patrikis and D. Virzera, *Derivatives Activities of Banking Organizations: Initiatives for Supervisors, Enhanced Disclosure, and Legislation*, American Bar Assn. Committee on Futures Regulation, Key West Panel (Feb. 3, 1995).

Fraudulent Misrepresentation

In *Gibson,* it was alleged that BT Sec. cheated Gibson by misrepresenting the amount of gain on the termination of one swap and that BT Sec. proposed transactions to Gibson without disclosing all material facts related (a) to the nature of their dealings, i.e., the so-called "advisory" relationship described herein; and (b) to the risks of the transactions.[87] Procter & Gamble has made similar allegations against BT and BT Sec.[88] As indicated above, these claims, like most fraud claims, are inherently fact-intensive and, at least in Procter & Gamble's case, it appears that it will require a trial to determine BT's exposure to this claim.

Reckless or Negligent Misrepresentation

Somewhat easier for a plaintiff to establish than fraud (due generally to the absence of the need to establish scienter or fraudulent intent) are claims of negligent misrepresentation. Both Gibson and Procter & Gamble have asserted that BT Sec. negligently and/or recklessly provided false information to them in violation of applicable state law (in those cases, Ohio).

Carlton Financial Services has also sued BT Sec. in New York federal court alleging, among other things, that BT Sec. owed a duty to Carlton to provide accurate information and that the information provided to Carlton (concerning Carlton's own requirements) was false or incorrect.[89]

Given the nature of some of the investment derivatives sold in unregulated markets and the absence of a meaningful secondary market for some derivatives, claims like that asserted in *Carlton* could be asserted against a broker, dealer, or bank that regularly undertook to provide market quotes or open position values with respect to derivatives as part of its regular activities. (See, e.g., Restatement 2d, Torts 552.) Other than the *Carlton* case, we are not aware of any derivatives customer asserting such a claim. However, there will certainly be litigation over the accuracy of market value quotes, bids, or offers when a broker or dealer that sold a customer a derivative is offering to buy back the security from the customer.

---

[87] See *supra*, n. 11.

[88] *See supra*, n. 19.

[89] *Carlton Financial Securities* v. *BT Securities Corporation,* No. 94-CIV-7172 (S.D.N.Y. Oct. 3, 1994).

Breach of Fiduciary Duty

Gibson, Procter & Gamble, and Carlton all have alleged that BT Sec. owed them a fiduciary duty that was breached. As indicated above, the exact nature of the duty owed to the end user/customer/purchaser of a derivative by a broker, dealer, or seller is a fundamental question that remains unresolved. It is possible to posit a duty that falls short of a fiduciary duty, but that nonetheless imposes a greater obligation on the part of the professional than has generally been applied to the sale of less complex products.

The more complex the product, and the more reliant the customer is on the counterparty to understand the customer's needs and to structure an appropriate product, the more the relationship resembles an investment advisory relationship. If the facts of a case were to approach such a characterization, then the duty of the professional counterparty could more closely resemble the obligations of an advisor than those of a mere contractual counterparty, the latter of which is the position that the securities industry has steadfastly advanced.

It is this gray area that has prompted the OCC and NASD to issue its cautionary releases and interpretations to the banking and brokerage industry, as described above. How the courts will view these legal relationships remains to be seen.

CONCLUSION

Exactly how the courts, arbitrators, legislators, and regulators will end up addressing this fundamental gray area and ancillary liability issues is not known. With trials set in the near future in high-profile cases involving untraditional, well-represented plaintiffs and with large investment losses in different types of derivatives continuing to appear in the press, some judicial or other precedential guidelines for future purchasers, sellers, and dealers in derivatives should be forthcoming. Meanwhile, the continuing losses from derivatives will undoubtedly result in more and more litigation.

Chapter Twenty-Three

Voluntary Efforts to Provide Oversight of OTC Derivatives Activities:
Are They Enough?

Sheila C. Bair and Susan Milligan[1]

INTRODUCTION

For nearly a decade, the over-the-counter (OTC) derivatives market developed largely outside the ken of regulators and Congress. In the early 1990s, regulators and legislators exhibited a growing desire to know more about OTC derivatives as the notional value of these transactions surpassed the $5 trillion mark. This curiosity led to a spate of studies focusing on the potential systemic risks posed by OTC derivatives and the possible existence of regulatory gaps, especially with regard to the OTC derivatives dealer affiliates of registered broker-dealers.[2] These studies, in turn, led members of Congress to consider legislation to address systemic-risk

---

[1]The views expressed in this chapter are those of the authors and do not necessarily reflect those of the Commodity Futures Trading Commission.

[2]General Accounting Office, *Financial Derivatives: Actions Needed to Protect the Financial System* 10–12 (May 1994); Commodity Futures Trading Commission, *OTC Derivatives Markets and Their Regulation* 6 (October 1993). *Cf.* Group of Thirty, Global Derivatives Study Group, *Derivatives: Practices and Principles* 1 (July 1993) ("The general attitude of the Study towards regulation is plain: derivatives by their nature do not introduce risks of a fundamentally different kind or of a greater scale than those already present in the financial markets. Hence, systemic

concerns and regulatory gaps identified by the studies.[3] Federal financial regulators were united in their opposition to immediate legislation. Both to forestall legislation and to respond to concerns identified by the studies, a flurry of activity regarding OTC derivatives by the members of the President's Working Group on Financial Markets ensued.[4]

The pressure for legislation to address OTC derivatives increased as well-publicized losses involving these products mounted. Stunning losses by Metallgesellschaft, Procter & Gamble, and Gibson Greetings, among others, increased the scrutiny trained on OTC derivatives dealers by Congress, federal financial regulators, and the media.[5] Eager to thwart legislation, OTC derivatives dealers joined in voluntary efforts to address the concerns expressed in these quarters. The fruits of those voluntary efforts are the focus of this chapter. The chapter will provide an overview of the Derivatives Policy Group's (DPG) Framework for Voluntary Oversight and the draft Principles and Practices for Wholesale Financial Market Transactions (Principles) developed by OTC dealers. The chapter will also examine whether these efforts are likely to succeed in forestalling further regulatory and congressional action on OTC derivatives.

---

risks are not appreciably aggravated, and supervisory concerns can be addressed within present regulatory structures and approaches.")

[3]S. 2291, *Derivatives Supervision Act of 1994*, 103d Cong., 2d Sess., 140 Cong. Rec. 9171 (July 18, 1994)(Riegle); S. 2123, *Derivatives Limitations Act of 1994*, 103d Cong., 2d Sess., 140 Cong. Rec. 5836 (May 17, 1994)(Dorgan); H.R. 4503, *Derivatives Safety and Soundness Supervision Act of 1994*, 103 Cong., 2d Sess., 140 Cong. Rec. 4164 (May 26, 1994)(Gonzalez and Leach); H.R. 4745, *Derivatives Dealers Act of 1994*, 103 Cong., 2d Sess., 140 Cong. Rec. 5655 (July 13, 1994)(Markey).

[4]Letter from Secretary of the Treasury Lloyd Bentsen to President of the Senate Albert Gore (October 19, 1994) (discussing the activities of the Working Group on Financial Markets with emphasis on the members' individual and collective actions regarding OTC derivatives).

Consistent with the recommendation of the CFTC's report on OTC derivatives, *supra* at note 2, in early 1994, Secretary Bentsen asked the members of the Working Group to consider the "increasing importance of the OTC derivative market." Letter from Secretary Bentsen to Acting CFTC Chairman Barbara Holum (Jan. 3, 1994). The members of the Working Group are the Secretary of the Treasury and the chairmen of the Board of Governors of the Federal Reserve, the CFTC, and the SEC.

[5]Marc Levinson, "Exiled on Wall Street," *Business Week,* Nov. 14, 1994, at 49; Randall Smith and Steven Lipin, "As Derivatives Losses Mount, Industry Fights to Avert Regulation," *The Wall Street Journal,* Aug. 25, 1994, at 1, col. 6.

DERIVATIVES POLICY GROUP INITIATIVE

The DPG's Framework for Voluntary Oversight (the Framework) had its genesis in the GAO's May 1994 report to Congress regarding derivatives markets.[6] That report found, among other things, that basic regulatory safeguards did not apply to many major U.S. derivatives dealers.[7] In particular, the GAO singled out the derivatives affiliates of security firms, which are beyond the reach of most SEC regulatory requirements, including examination and capital requirements.[8] These affiliates are required to file quarterly risk-assessment reports regarding the notional amount and replacement costs of their derivatives positions.[9] However, the GAO found that the reports do not contain "sufficient information for detecting potential credit risk problems" to permit the SEC "to anticipate and quickly respond to a crisis involving derivatives at these firms."[10] The GAO concluded that regulatory gaps in OTC derivatives oversight heightened systemic risk. It recommended that Congress bring the unregulated derivatives activities of securities firms and others under the purview of an existing federal financial regulator.[11]

Congressman John Dingell (D-Mich.), who was then chairman of the SEC's House oversight committee, requested the views of SEC chairman Arthur Levitt regarding GAO's report.[12] In his response, Chairman Levitt embraced the view of the Working Group on Financial Markets that existing regulatory authorities were sufficient to deal with issues pertaining to OTC derivatives oversight, and that legislation was neither necessary nor desirable at the present time.[13] Levitt's response went on to summarize a variety of initiatives the SEC had undertaken to address such

---

[6]See note 2, *supra*.

[7]GAO report, *supra* note 2, at 10.

[8]*Id*. at 88.

[9]*Id*. at 87.

[10]*Id*. at 88.

[11]*Id*. at 14–15. The GAO was politic enough not to recommend which among the various federal financial regulators should be given jurisdiction over OTC derivatives.

[12]Letter from the Honorable John Dingell, Chairman, Committee on Energy and Commerce, House of Representatives, to SEC Chairman Arthur Levitt (May 23, 1994).

[13]See Letter from SEC Chairman Arthur Levitt to Honorable John Dingell, Chairman, Committee on Energy and Commerce, House of Representatives (July 18, 1994).

areas as disclosure, information access, and capital requirements.[14] He also referenced ongoing efforts by SEC staff to work with major OTC derivatives dealers to develop an oversight program to enhance existing reporting requirements; to design sales-practice standards; and to explore whether proprietary models could be incorporated into capital standards.[15]

A month later, at the suggestion of Chairman Levitt,[16] the DPG was formed. The membership of the DPG includes principals of six major, SEC-registered broker-dealers that conduct significant OTC derivatives activity through unregistered affiliates.[17] E. Gerald Corrigan, chairman of the International Advisors, Goldman Sachs; and John Heimann, chairman, Global Financial Institutions, Merrill Lynch serve as co-chairmen of the DPG. Ironically, Corrigan, when president of the Federal Reserve Bank of New York, was among the first to raise regulatory concerns about OTC derivatives activity in a highly publicized 1992 speech.[18]

The DPG's self-professed objective was to design a voluntary oversight framework to respond to public policy issues that had been raised by Congress, regulators, and others regarding risks associated with OTC derivatives activity. The DPG divided its work into four major components: management controls, enhanced reporting, evaluation of risk in relation to capital, and counterparty relationships. In March of 1995, after the expenditure of an extraordinary amount of time and effort by the principals and staffs of the six firms involved, as well as by the SEC and CFTC, the Framework was publicly released. In accepting the Framework, Chairman Levitt and Chairman Schapiro hailed it as "a positive step forward in addressing the important financial activity occurring in the unregistered affiliates of broker-dealers."[19] Levitt and Schapiro went on to say that the Framework "should be viewed as part of an ongoing process by the SEC and CFTC to address the OTC derivative activities of nonbank

---

[14]*Id.* at 1–2.

[15]*Id.*

[16]Shortly after the DPG's inception, CFTC Chairwoman Mary Schapiro joined Chairman Levitt as a principal regulatory contact for the DPG.

[17]The members of the DPG are: William Bowden, CS First Boston; Jacob Goldfield, Goldman Sachs; Peter Karches, Morgan Stanley; David Komansky, Merrill Lynch; John Macfarlane, Salomon Brothers; and Thomas Russo, Lehman Brothers.

[18]Remarks of F. Gerald Corrigan, president, Federal Reserve Bank of New York, 64th Annual Mid-Winter Meeting of the New York State Bankers Association (January 30, 1992).

[19]Joint SEC/CFTC news release, *SEC and CFTC Receive Derivatives Policy Group Report Calling It a "Positive Step in Improving Derivatives Oversight"* (March 9, 1995).

dealers" and that it would enable both agencies to "analyze in an improved fashion the firms' OTC derivative activities and their implications for systemic risk."[20]

Management Controls

The Framework's treatment of management controls addresses the need for systems and processes to measure, monitor, and control risk, as well as the need for clear lines of accountability to ensure compliance with such processes.

Specifically, the Framework would require each firm's board, or equivalent body, to adopt written guidelines addressing: the scope of permitted OTC derivatives activity; acceptable levels of credit and market risk; and the structure and appropriate independence of the firm's risk-monitoring and risk-management processes and related organizational checks and balances. The Framework would also require that an annual report be prepared by an external auditor regarding the firm's compliance with its written guidelines. This report would be made available to the SEC and the CFTC.[21]

Enhanced Reporting

In developing a comprehensive reporting format, the DPG sought to draw upon the methodologies actually used by firms to measure credit risk. Its primary goal was to develop a series of reports to provide regulators with meaningful information about credit-risk concentration, a profile of the credit risk of the reporting entity's OTC derivatives portfolio, and information regarding net revenues generated by OTC derivatives and related activities.

The Framework provides for reporting credit-risk concentration by separately identifying the firm's top 20 net exposures, counterparty by counterparty. The credit-risk profile of the firm's portfolio is to be reported by aggregating, by counterparty, the net exposure, the aggregate net replacement value, and the gross replacement value. These figures must then be organized by credit rating category, industry, and geographic location. Monthly net revenue data must also be provided, as well as

---

[20]*Id.*

[21]Framework at 22.

consolidated financial statements regarding the notional amount of out-standing OTC derivative transactions and current net credit exposures.[22]

Evaluation of Risk in Relation to Capital

In developing a framework for the evaluation of risk in relation to capital, the DPG decided that the best approach was to rely on firms' own quantitative models. However, because the models are proprietary and differ from firm to firm, the DPG had to develop standards and verification techniques to ensure that the performance characteristics of all models used would be broadly similar and rigorous. The Framework notes that this is the first time such common standards have been developed for such a purpose.[23]

The DPG also had to devise a common approach for calculating estimates of exposure or risk of loss associated with a given derivatives portfolio. In this regard, it adopted—as a reasonable estimate of capital at risk—the maximum loss expected to be exceeded by a given portfolio once in every 100 biweekly intervals.[24] The Framework notes that a "one percent/two-week threshold" appears to be gaining acceptance in the international supervisory community.[25]

It should be emphasized that the Framework does not, in itself, specify a capital standard. Rather, it provides guidelines for estimating market and credit risks to facilitate a firm's own evaluation of such risks in relation to its capital position. In this regard, the Framework states that,

> [O]ver the next several months, the SEC and CFTC will begin to receive from the participating firms enhanced quantitative reports, estimates of capital at risk, stress scenario data . . . [and] estimates of current and potential credit exposures [as well as] model verification data on a recurring basis . . . . In light of this dramatically improved flow of information to the SEC and the CFTC, the DPG has concluded that, at this time, the implementation of a capital adequacy standard involving the use of rigid formulas linking capital at risk . . . to capital levels should be avoided.[26]

---

[22]Framework at 25.

[23]Framework at 6. The minimum standards are laid out at pages 29–31 of the Framework.

[24]Framework at 28.

[25]Framework at 7.

[26]Framework at 9.

Counterparty Relationships

The counterparty relationships component of the Framework proceeds from the premise that the OTC derivatives market is predominantly an arms-length market in which each counterparty has a responsibility to review and evaluate transactions and to obtain necessary information or professional assistance.[27] The focus of the Framework is to articulate guidelines for firms acting as professional intermediaries in the OTC derivatives market to employ in their relationships with nonprofessional counterparties.[28]

The Framework's guidelines for professional intermediaries address: promotion of public confidence; the use of a generic risk disclosure statement; the nature of the relationship between the professional dealer and the nonprofessional customer; the use of marketing materials; the development of specific transaction proposals; the provision of scenario, sensitivity, or other analyses to nonprofessional counterparties; the terms of transactions; and the valuation of transactions.

These guidelines hold the professional intermediary to a standard of good faith and nonmisleading behavior. In several instances, the Framework urges the professional to offer or seek additional information where it appears that the nonprofessional may not understand the information provided. The Framework identifies these situations as those where: (1) confusion as to the nature of the relationship arises,[29] (2) particularly complex or significantly leveraged transactions are involved,[30] or (3) valuation information may be unclear.[31]

The Framework also provides guidance on the professional intermediary's internal policies, controls, and supervision of personnel. Areas addressed include: legal capacity, authority, and creditworthiness; supervision and controls; legal documentation review; record keeping; training; and special situations "involving OTC derivatives that may present a heightened risk of contract repudiation or raise other concerns."[32]

The section of the Framework dealing with counterparty relationships

---

[27]Framework at 9.

[28]*Id.*

[29]Framework at 37.

[30]Framework at 38.

[31]Framework at 39.

[32]Framework at 40.

was influenced by the global nature of the OTC derivatives market.[33] The Framework urges the development of uniform guidelines regarding counterparty relationships by all OTC derivatives dealers "regardless of institutional function or geographic location."[34] The adoption of such guidelines would "eliminate competitive inequalities and would facilitate consensus on a broader body of agreed practices in the OTC derivatives market."[35] The implication is that the DPG might have acted more proactively in this area but for the competitive pressures they felt.

The Framework is clearly a positive first step toward improving SEC and CFTC oversight of OTC derivatives. As both the members of the DPG and the two agencies recognized, the Framework is "part of a process, not an event" that needs to continue over time.[36] For example, needed progress toward capital standards should be based on the Framework's observations concerning the evaluation of risk in relation to capital. Actual sales practice standards should be developed based on the general guidelines provided by the Framework. Additional areas that should be explored include reducing potential systemic risk by improving payment and settlement systems, and perhaps even the development of an OTC clearinghouse. If these developments occur, the DPG effort will be a positive one for the members of the DPG, their customers, and the SEC and CFTC.

DRAFT PRINCIPLES AND PRACTICES FOR WHOLESALE FINANCIAL TRANSACTIONS

In the summer of 1994, representatives of trade groups composed of dealers in the OTC market, under the auspices of the Federal Reserve Bank of New York, met to develop a code of conduct applicable to trading in the wholesale OTC financial markets.[37] This group did not confine its efforts to discussions regarding OTC derivatives but addressed a broader

---

[33] Framework at 9.

[34] Framework at 9.

[35] Framework at 41.

[36] Framework at 1.

[37] The groups involved in drafting the Principles were the Emerging Markets Traders Association, the Foreign Exchange Committee of the Federal Reserve Bank of New York, the International Swaps and Derivatives Association, the New York Clearing House Association, the Public Securities Association and the Securities Industry Association.

category of transactions than the DPG. However, the group did limit its focus to wholesale transactions, while the DPG included retail transactions. In January of 1995, the group's drafting committee released a draft "Code of Conduct" for comment by other dealers. In March of 1995, a new draft, now entitled, Principles and Practices for Wholesale Financial Market Transactions (Principles), was released for comment by end users as well as dealers. The final document, little changed from the March 1995 draft, was released in August 1995.

Section One—Purpose of Principles and Practices

Section One of the Principles discusses their purpose, delineates their applicability, and describes their nature. The Principles are "intended to provide guidance for the conduct of wholesale transactions in the OTC financial markets between participants" in the United States.[38] Transactions are not limited to swaps, but also include, among other things, OTC foreign-exchange transactions. The term "participant" is defined quite broadly and includes any institution or governmental entity "that engages regularly in one or more types of" wholesale OTC transactions.[39] Individuals are not covered by the Principles.

In the Nature of Principles section, the Principles are described as "confirm[ing] the arms-length nature of transactions" and "articulat[ing] a set of best practices that participants should aspire to in connection with their transactions."[40] Over time, the Principles "will continue to evolve," especially those concerning the policies and procedures of participants contained in Section Three.[41] Adherence to the Principles is described as voluntary, and policies or procedures implemented based on the Principles "should be appropriate for the size, nature and complexity of the participant and its transactions as well as its business activities generally."[42]

Only with time will it become clear whether all members of the groups that formulated the Principles will endorse and adhere to those Principles. Some dealers may see competitive advantages to distancing themselves

---

[38]Principles and Practices for Wholesale Financial Market Transactions §1.1 (March 20, 1995 Draft). [hereinafter Principles].

[39]Principles and Practices §1.1.

[40]Principles §1.2.

[41]Principles §1.2.

[42]Principles §1.2.

from the Principles, especially the controversial provisions concerning relationships between participants. This section will be discussed in detail later.

The Principles contain an interesting warning to participants. They state that it "should not be assumed" that participants, as defined, necessarily adhere to the Principles.[43] However, participants are put on notice that other participants "will make certain assumptions about the nature of the relationship between participants."[44] These statements increase the likelihood that entities that choose not to adhere voluntarily to the Principles— in many cases, end users—will, in effect, be forced to abide by them.

Section Two—Participants—Financial Resources

Section Two of the Principles advises that a participant should have adequate financial resources to meet its commitments under transactions covered by the Principles.[45]

Section Three—Participants—Policies and Procedures

Section Three of the Principles provides guidance on the policies and procedures that participants should have in place. The Principles recognize that policies should "be appropriate to the nature, size and complexity of the participant and its transactions."[46] The topics covered by this section include: supervision and training of employees;[47] control and compliance;[48] risk management;[49] independent risk monitoring;[50] credit risk;[51] and legal capacity and authority to transact.[52] The guidance offered in these sections is generally consistent with the G-30 recommendations and the reports of the CFTC and GAO.

---

[43] Principles §1.2.

[44] Principles §1.2.

[45] Principles §2.1.

[46] Principles §3.1.

[47] Principles §3.2.

[48] Principles §3.3.

[49] Principles §3.4.

[50] Principles §3.5.

[51] Principles §3.7.

[52] Principles §3.8.

Section Three also contains general guidance to participants regarding the valuation of transactions.[53] Participants should maintain policies and procedures "for valuation of transactions at intervals appropriate for the type of transaction in question."[54] If a participant lacks the internal capability to value a transaction and no value for the transaction is readily available, the participant should seek a valuation from an external source "at intervals appropriate for the type of transaction."[55] This section will apply almost invariably to nondealer end users of derivatives. When seeking a valuation from an external source, such a participant should specify the type of valuation that it desires, e.g., midmarket, indicative, or firm price.[56] When assessing the usefulness of a valuation from an external source, the Principles state that it is essential for the participant to consider whether the valuation was obtained from a counterparty, how long it took the source to provide the valuation, and whether the participant paid for the valuation.[57] Any participant that provides valuations of transactions should have policies and procedures governing how it does so, including "requiring the participant to clearly state the characteristics of any valuation provided."[58]

The valuation section of the Principles puts the onus on end users to produce or seek valuations "at appropriate intervals," rather than requiring dealers to provide such valuations. Thus, this section of the Principles differs from the reporting regimen imposed under the Commodity Exchange Act[59] for futures and options transactions and for the valuation of managed futures investments.[60] The CEA reporting regimen requires the market professional—the futures commission merchant, introducing broker, or commodity pool operator—to provide valuations of positions. Customers are not required to produce or seek such valuations. The CEA regimen seems the more logical of the two approaches, especially for valuing complex or customized transactions. A prudent end user might

---

[53]Principles §3.6.

[54]Principles §3.6.1.

[55]Principles §3.6.2.

[56]Principles §3.6.2.

[57]Principles §3.6.3.

[58]Principles §3.6.4.

[59]7 U.S.C. §1 *et seq.*

[60]See 17 C.F.R. §1.33; 17 C.F.R. §4.7(a)(2)(ii); 17 C.F.R. §4.22.

choose to value its own transactions, for its own purposes, but it should not
be forced to do so.

Section Four—Relationships between Participants

Sections Four and Five of the Principles, which focus on the relationship
between counterparties to a transaction, are the most controversial sections of the document. Section 4 describes relationships between participants. Participants "should" act honestly and in good faith with regard to
all aspects of transactions. They "should" also exhibit professional cour-
tesy and consideration to counterparties.[61]

The Principles presume that all transactions are arms-length in nature
with no reliance by either counterparty. As a result, each participant
should satisfy itself that it has, or can obtain from an independent party,
the capability to understand and make independent decisions about all
aspects of its transactions. A participant should understand that its
counterparty will assume that it has this capability absent a written
agreement to the contrary.[62] Further, a participant's governing body or
management is responsible for determining the character and level of risk
that is desirable for the participant, in accordance with "any applicable
statutory or regulatory constraints, based on an evaluation of the totality of
its particular circumstances and objectives."[63]

The Principles warn participants not to treat or construe communications from another participant as recommendations or investment advice
and not to rely on them absent a written agreement or applicable law or
regulation "that expressly imposes affirmative obligations to the contrary."[64] These communications include written or oral "ideas or suggestions regarding potential transactions."[65] Any participant that wants to
rely on a counterparty should inform its counterparty in writing, prior to
entering the transactions, that it desires to so rely; the counterparty has
agreed in writing to permit the reliance; and the relying participant "has
provided the counterparty with accurate information regarding its financial objectives and the size, nature and condition of its business sufficient

---

[61]Principles §4.1.

[62]Principles §4.2.1.

[63]Principles §4.2.2.

[64]Principles §4.2.2.

[65]Principles §4.2.2.

to provide recommendations."[66] The Principles state that the obligations of a counterparty permitting it "to provide recommendations and investment advice will then be determined by the written agreement and applicable law."[67]

The Principles urge participants to identify and reach agreement on all material terms and conditions of a transaction. A participant with less than a full understanding of the risks of the transaction, or its fit, given the participant's risk profile, "should" ask its counterparty or an independent advisor questions about these issues. A counterparty "should" respond to such questions in good faith.[68] The Principles put a participant on notice that if it does not ask questions, its counterparty will assume that it has all the information it needs to make decisions about transactions.[69]

The Principles make a participant aware that its counterparty may take positions in transactions that are "identical or economically related" to those entered with the participant, or may have commercial relationships with the issuer of an instrument underlying the transaction.[70] A participant that generally acts as a "broker" should notify both parties if it is acting in another capacity in a particular transaction. A participant that generally acts as a principal may act as an agent for one counterparty on occasion. Such a participant "should avoid misusing its knowledge of the terms on which the counterparty is prepared to execute a transaction to take unfair advantage of the [other] counterparty," but the Principles contain no duty to inform the counterparty of its agency role.[71]

Transactions should be handled in confidence. Information regarding the identity of the counterparty to a transaction should not be discussed or disclosed without express permission, or as required by law, or required or requested by a regulatory authority.[72]

Section Four's emphasis on defining the parameters of the participants' relationship prior to the execution of a transaction is commendable. Advance agreement by counterparties about the nature of their relation-

---

[66]Principles §4.2.3.

[67]Principles §4.2.2.

[68]Principles §4.2.3.

[69]Principles §4.2.3.

[70]Principles §4.2.4.

[71]Principles §4.2.5.

[72]Principles §4.3.

ship would allow each counterparty to better understand its responsibilities and would likely lessen the possibility of litigation between counterparties. The most controversial aspect of Section Four is the presumption that end users can only rely on dealers when the end user requests permission to do so in writing and the dealer agrees. The sticking point is that this presumption exists in spite of the advertisements of dealers seeking trust and emphasizing relationships; their much vaunted, expert, and highly compensated OTC derivatives staff; and their obvious information advantages regarding highly complex and customized products of their own design. Clearly, not every OTC derivatives transaction involves a reliance relationship between the dealer and end user, nor should it. However, a more balanced approach than the Principles would be for the market professional—the dealer—to accept the responsibility to enter each customer relationship with an open mind about its nature, and to negotiate, rather than dictate, its terms with the customer.

Section Five—Considerations Relating to Relationships between Participants

Section Five of the Principles describes a number of "considerations relating to relationships between participants." Unlike Section Four, which uses the recommendatory "should" throughout, Section Five primarily uses the weaker, suggestive "may wish to."[73]

The Principles state that participants, particularly those that are dealers, should adopt policies and procedures designed to address potential misunderstandings or disputes that pose reputational, relationship, or litigation risk.[74]

A participant, for its own protection, also may wish to make an assessment, based on information in hand, of the decision-making capability of its counterparty. Among the factors to be considered in such an assessment are: the nature of the counterparty's business; the financial size and condition of the counterparty; the counterparty's prior dealings or experience in transactions; and the nature, complexity, and risks of the proposed transaction.[75] A participant that, for its own protection, under-

---

[73]Compare Principles §§4.1, 4.2, 4.3, 4.4 with §§5.1, 5.2, 5.3, 5.4.
[74]Principles §5.1.
[75]Principles §5.2.

takes to assess the decision-making capability of a counterparty may then wish to adopt procedures for dealing with exceptional situations. Exceptional situations include those in which a counterparty does not have the capability to understand and make independent decisions regarding proposed transactions, or does have independent decision-making capability but the transaction clearly involves a disproportionately high risk to the counterparty.[76] These procedures could include providing or obtaining additional information to or from the counterparty; involving additional qualified personnel from either or both participants; entering into a written agreement regarding reliance by the counterparty; or not entering into the transactions. The Principles state that other steps also might be appropriate in specific situations.[77]

For its own protection, a participant may wish to inform its counterparties of its view of the nature of their relationship.[78] Providing a copy of the Principles to all counterparties seems like a logical way to accomplish this goal.

For its own protection, a participant may wish to provide more information to its counterparties to assist them in their decision making than is typically provided where a transaction involves a particularly complex payment formula or a significant leverage component. Such information might include, for example, loss scenarios. Where loss scenarios are provided, the participant "should attempt in good faith to use assumptions that provide information that is reasonable under the circumstances."[79]

It is unclear why the suggestions of Section Five concerning forward-looking policies and procedures,[80] assessing counterparty decision-making capability,[81] and providing additional information to counterparties[82] were not included as recommendations in Section Four. These provisions would have strengthened the Principles and moved them closer to the stated goal of "articulat[ing] a set of best practices."[83] A prudent end-user might choose to enter OTC derivatives transactions only with those

---

[76]Principles §5.2.

[77]Principles §5.2.

[78]Principles §5.3.

[79]Principles §5.4.

[80]Principles §5.1.

[81]Principles §5.2.

[82]Principles §5.4.

[83]Principles §1.2.

dealers that intend to follow the Section Five suggestions. Abiding by these provisions would appear to be in the best interests of all concerned.

Section Six—Mechanics of Transactions

Section Six of the Principles deals with the mechanics of transactions. The topics covered are: when transactions are binding;[84] confirmations;[85] payment and settlement instructions;[86] documentation;[87] and complaints and settlement of differences.[88] None of these provisions of the Principles has been controversial.

Section Seven—Standards for Transactions

Section Seven of the Principles is entitled "Standards for Transactions."[89] In reality, this section outlines basic levels of acceptable conduct by participants. It prohibits the following: misuse of market terminology;[90] manipulative practices;[91] bribes and outside fees and commissions;[92] rumors and false information;[93] and money laundering and other criminal activities.[94] Like Section Six, these provisions have not been controversial.

The value of the Principles is that they provide a starting point for discussion between the counterparties to OTC derivatives transactions. The flaw of the Principles is that the starting point is a framework that was developed by one set of counterparties—dealers. Apparently, because they perceived it to be to their advantage, the dealer-drafters created Principles devoid of any distinction between dealers and end users. There is some recognition that not all "participants" are involved in the same levels of activity in "transactions," but this acknowledgement has not translated

---

[84]Principles §6.1.

[85]Principles §6.2

[86]Principles §6.3

[87]Principles §6.4

[88]Principles §6.5

[89]Principles §7.

[90]Principles §7.1

[91]Principles §7.2

[92]Principles §7.3

[93]Principles §7.4

[94]Principles §7.5

into a recognition that different types of participants are likely to have different levels of resources, expertise, and information regarding "transactions." This failure permeates the Principles and probably could have been avoided only by involving end users in the drafting process right from the beginning.

At this point, it is unclear whether end users will accept the assumptions of the Principles. If they do so, the Principles can be expected to evolve little, if at all, over time. If, however, end users, either individually or as a group, refuse to accept the Principles, revisions to them will necessary. These revisions, made with end-user input, would likely achieve a more balanced approach to the issues that arise between dealers and end users in the OTC derivatives market than the existing Principles. Under this scenario, the Principles would be useful for OTC counterparties in their dealings with each other, federal financial regulators, and Congress.

CONCLUSION

The DPG's Framework for Voluntary Oversight and the draft Principles and Practices for Wholesale Financial Market Transactions developed by OTC dealers have had some success in forestalling regulatory and congressional action on OTC derivatives. The DPG Framework has provided greater information to the SEC and the CFTC concerning the largest category of dealers often identified as "unregulated." The Principles have opened a window into the perspectives of dealers regarding their relationships with end users. They have also provided a useful framework for discussions between counterparties. Both of these efforts, commendable though they are, have fallen short. Later iterations of the DPG's Framework need to address directly the issue of sales practices. Later editions of the Principles need to describe more realistically the proper relationship between counterparties. Without these modifications, both efforts are vulnerable to being superseded by further regulation and legislation in the wake of some future major OTC derivatives failure.

Chapter Twenty-Four

CFTC Exemption Procedures For Novel Derivative Transactions*

A. Robert Pietrzak and Michael S. Sackheim

T he Futures Trading Practices Act of 1992 (1992 Act) amended and added new provisions to the Commodity Exchange Act, as amended (CEA or Act).[1] Among other changes, the 1992 Act authorized the Commodity Futures Trading Commission (Commission or CFTC) to exempt any agreement, contract, or transaction (or class thereof) that is otherwise subject to the CEA, either unconditionally or on stated terms and conditions or for stated periods, either retroactively, prospectively, or both, from any of the requirements of the CEA (except for CEA section 2(a)(1)(B))[2] if the Commission determines that such an exemption is consistent with the public interest.

The Commission is granted exclusive jurisdiction under CEA section 2(a)(1)(A)(i) over commodity futures contracts and options on commodity

---

*An earlier version of this chapter was published at 26 Rev. Sec. & Comm. Reg. 121 (July 1993). It has been updated and published with the permission of Standard & Poor's, a division of McGraw-Hill, Inc. This chapter is accurate as of April 1995.

[1]The CEA is set forth at 7 U.S.C. section 1, et seq. (1988 and Supp. IV, 1993. Rules and regulations promulgated by the CFTC are set forth in 17 C.F.R. section 1, et seq. (1993). The 1992 Act, which amends and supplements the CEA, is set forth in Pub. L. 102-546, 106 Stat. 3590 (1992).

[2]Section 2(a)(1)(B) of the CEA is a result of a 1982 jurisdictional accord reached between the Commission and the Securities and Exchange Commission (SEC), and is referred to as the CFTC-SEC Accord.

futures contracts, and under CEA section 4c(b)[3] over commodity options. Prior to the 1992 Act, CEA section 4(a) required that all commodity futures contracts and most types of commodity options be traded on boards of trade that have been designated by the Commission as "contract markets" (customarily referred to as commodity exchanges). The 1980s, however, witnessed the development of innovative derivative instruments that contained many of the indicia of regulated commodity instruments but were not transacted on a commodity exchange. In many attempts to render greater legal certainty in order to facilitate the development of innovative financial transactions, the Commission had issued case-by-case interpretative or enforcement no-action letters permitting the marketing of these instruments,[4] as well as various statutory interpretations providing guidance as to when an instrument could exist free of regulatory interference under the CEA.[5] CEA section 4(a)(1), as amended by 1992 Act section 502(a), now provides the Commission with the authority for the first time to exempt futures transactions from the mandatory exchange-trading requirement.

This chapter examines the exemptions already granted, and the procedures for obtaining or qualifying for further exemptions, under CEA section 4(c), for novel commodity instruments—including swap agreements, hybrid instruments, and forward or commercially acceptable transactions—so as to permit such instruments to be transacted either free of the CEA's exchange-trading requirement or in a relatively unregulated manner.

---

[3]CEA section 4c(b) provides that commodity options may not be entered into by any person contrary to any rule, regulation, or order of the Commission prohibiting any such transaction or allowing any such transaction under such terms and conditions as the Commission shall prescribe.

[4]See, e.g., CFTC Interpretative Letter No. 88–10, Comm. Fut. L. Rep. (CCH) ¶24,262 (June 20, 1988) (CFTC approval of Yen-denominated debt instrument with incidental futures-like elements), and CFTC Interpretative Letter No. 88-16, Comm. Fut. L. Rep. (CCH) ¶24,312 (Aug. 26, 1988) (debt instrument with coupon indexed to an inflation factor).

[5]See, e.g., 54 Fed. Reg. 1139 (CFTC, Jan. 11, 1989) (hybrid instruments); 54 Fed. Reg. 30694 (CFTC, July 21, 1989) (swap transactions); 55 Fed. Reg. 39188 (CFTC, Sept. 25, 1990) (forward contracts). See also CFTC Off-Exchange Task Force Interpretative Letter No. 90-1, Comm. Fut. L. Rep. (CCH) ¶24,583 (Jan. 18, 1990) (collar agreements). A thorough survey of the pre-1992 Act interpretations is contained in Hiden & Crawshaw, *Hybrids and the Commodity Exchange Act*, Sec. and Comm. Reg. at 223 (Dec. 20, 1989).

SWAP TRANSACTIONS

1992 Act section 502(c)(5)(B), which added a new CEA section 4(c)(5)(B), authorized the Commission to exercise promptly its new exemptive authority to grant exemptions for certain swap agreements, as defined in section 101 of the U.S. Bankruptcy Code, that "are not part of a fungible class of agreements that are standardized as to their material economic terms, to the extent that such agreements may be regarded as subject to the provisions of this Act." Any exemption for swap agreements granted pursuant to this authority is subject to such terms and conditions as the Commission may deem appropriate, must be consistent with the public interest, must be entered into solely between appropriate persons, and the exemption must not have a material adverse effect on the ability of the Commission or any contract market to discharge its regulatory or self-regulatory duties.

Definition of Swap Agreement

Commission rule 35.1(b)(1) adopts the definition of swap agreement as specifically set forth in the Bankruptcy Code at 11 U.S.C. section 101(55). The Commission found that the use of the same definition as in the Bankruptcy Code will help to create greater certainty in the marketplace for swaps, given the extent to which market certainty has been advanced by the exemption of swap agreements as defined in the Bankruptcy Code from the automatic stay and other provisions of the Bankruptcy Code.

Exemptive Criteria

Under Commission rule 35.2, a qualifying swap agreement is exempt from all provisions of the CEA, and any person or class of persons offering, entering into, rendering advice, or rendering other services with respect to such agreement is exempt for such activity from all provisions of the CEA (except, in each case, specified antifraud and antimanipulation provisions and the CFTC-SEC Accord). The rule provides an exemption for swap agreements that

(i) are entered into solely between eligible swap participants;

(ii) are not part of a fungible class of agreements that are standardized as to their material economic terms;

(iii) the creditworthiness of any party having an actual or potential obligation under the swap agreement is a material consideration; and

(iv) are not entered into and traded on or through a multilateral transaction execution facility, although arrangements or facilities between parties that provide for netting of payment obligations resulting from such swap agreements are permitted.

Eligible Swap Participants

Rule 35.2(a) requires that an exempt swap must be entered into between appropriate persons, eligible swap participants (ESPs). The ESP requirement is determined at the inception of the swap transaction. There is no requirement that a swap agreement be terminated if an ESP, subsequent to the inception of the swap agreement, no longer qualifies as such. ESPs are limited by Commission rule 35.1 essentially to

(i) a bank or trust company (acting on its own behalf or on behalf of another eligible swap participant);

(ii) a savings association or credit union;

(iii) an insurance company;

(iv) an investment company or a foreign person performing a similar role or function subject as such to foreign regulation, provided that such investment company or foreign person is not formed solely for the specific purpose of constituting an ESP;

(v) a commodity pool or a foreign person performing a similar role or function subject as such to foreign regulation, provided that such foreign person or commodity pool is not formed solely for the specific purpose of constituting an ESP and has total assets exceeding $5 million;

(vi) a corporation, partnership, proprietorship, organization, trust, or other entity not formed solely for the specific purpose of constituting an ESP that meets specified financial and/or risk management requirements;

(vii)   an employee benefit plan or a foreign person performing a similar role or function subject as such to foreign regulation with total assets exceeding $5 million;

(viii) any governmental entity;

(ix)   a broker-dealer or a foreign person performing a similar role or function subject as such to foreign regulation;

(x)   a futures commission merchant, floor broker, or floor trader, or a foreign person performing a similar role or function subject as such to foreign regulation; or

(xi)   any natural person with total assets exceeding at least $10 million.

Under the rule, the most significant distinctions between an ESP and an appropriate person are the following:

(i)   a natural person would qualify as an ESP only to the extent that his or her total assets amounted to at least $10 million;

(ii)   categories of registered and regulated entities and persons that qualify as ESPs include foreign persons performing a similar role or function subject to foreign regulation;

(iii)   partnerships, proprietorships, organizations, trusts, or other entities that meet other specified financial and/or risk management criteria, and that are "not formed solely for the specific purpose of constituting an eligible swap participant" qualify as ESPs. To qualify as an ESP, the person or entity participating in the swap must be acting on its own behalf or on behalf of another ESP as a counterparty of the swap. The Commission has advised that "investment companies, commodity pools, or entities that are collective investment vehicles formed solely for the specific purpose of constituting an eligible swap participant to enter into swap agreements will not be considered eligible swap participants under the exemption."[6]

Nonfungibility and Nonstandardization

Commission rule 35.2(b) requires that an exempt swap agreement not be part of a fungible class of agreements that are standardized as to their

---

[6]Comm. Fut. L. Rep. (CCH) ¶25,539 at 39,591.

material economic terms. The phrase "material economic terms" encompasses provisions that define the rights and obligations of the parties and may affect the value of the swap at origination or thereafter. The Commission has advised that this condition is designed to ensure that the exemption does not encompass the establishment of a formal market structure for swap agreements, the terms of which are fixed and are not subject to negotiation, that functions essentially in the same manner as an exchange except for the bilateral execution of the transaction.[7] Nonmaterial economic terms include definitions, representations, warranties, and default and remedy provisions. The Commission has advised that the use of certain forms and master agreements published by various associations "facilitates communication and negotiations, but does not mean the provisions themselves are not subject to substantial negotiation."[8] Furthermore, a swap agreement would not be considered fungible or standardized by virtue of being subject to a netting system or arrangement, provided that the economic material terms are subject to individual negotiation by the parties.

Creditworthiness

Commission rule 35.2(c) requires that the creditworthiness of any party having an actual or potential obligation under the swap agreement be a material consideration in determining the terms of the swap, including pricing, cost, or credit enhancement terms. The exemption does not encompass transactions that are subject to a clearing system in which credit risk of individual counterparties who are members of the system is effectively eliminated and replaced by a system of mutualized risk of loss that binds members generally, regardless of whether they are counterparties to the original swap transaction. Such a mutualized risk system would constitute a clearing system similar to a futures-exchange clearing house mechanism. However, bilateral arrangements for the netting of obligations to make payments or transfers of property, including margin or collateral, are permitted. Multiparty netting arrangements are also permitted, provided that the underlying gross obligations among the parties are not extinguished until all netted obligations are fully performed.

---

[7]Comm. Fut. L. Rep. (CCH) ¶25,539 at 39,592-93.

[8]Comm. Fut. L. Rep. (CCH) ¶25,539 at 39,592 n. 27.

Multilateral Transaction Execution Facilities

Commission rule 35.2(d) provides that the swap agreement may not be entered into and traded on or through a multilateral transaction execution facility (MTEF). An MTEF is a physical or electronic facility in which all market makers and other participants can simultaneously execute transactions and bind both parties by accepting offers that are made by one member and open to all members of the facility.[9] Effectively, the Commission's definition of an MTEF precludes the use of a futures-exchange type of trading mechanism, regardless of whether the trading is done by on-floor open outcry or through a screen-based computerized trading system. The prohibition of the use of an MTEF does not preclude participants from engaging in privately negotiated bilateral transactions, even where participants use information transmittal or other electronic facilities such as broker screens to communicate with other participants as long as they do not use such systems to enter orders to execute transactions. However, although the Commission advised that a computer-based trading system for swap agreements (as opposed to a computer-based information-providing system) may not be used for an exempt swap agreement, such a computer-based trading system may be the proper subject of the Commission's future exercise of its authority under section 4(c). The Commission has invited applications for exemptive relief for such facilities.

Policy Considerations

In issuing its final exemption rules, the Commission determined that the public interest was served because the legal and financial risk within the financial markets would be reduced, and because legal certainty contributes to the financial integrity of the markets. The Commission believes that the final exemption rule will promote innovation in the swap markets by allowing participants to negotiate and structure transactions that most effectively address their economic needs, and will assist U.S. financial institutions to compete with foreign rivals.[10]

The Commission also determined that because the futures markets and swap markets are linked, with swap-market participants using certain exchange-traded futures as hedging vehicles, the creation of a more

---

[9]Comm. Fut. L. Rep. (CCH) ¶25,539 at 39,593.
[10]Comm. Fut. L. Rep. (CCH) ¶25,539 at 39,594.

certain legal environment for swaps reduces the potential for systemic risk, thereby benefiting U.S. futures markets,[11] and that the issuance of the final swap exemption rule did not raise any significant anticompetitive issues.[12]

Under CEA section 4(c), the Commission may issue further exemptive relief for swap agreements that do not qualify under rule 35.2, upon application by any person, including futures exchanges, for agreements, transactions, or contracts, including classes thereof, not encompassed by the final swap exemption rule. The Commission has indicated that it will also respond to proposals for an MTEF or clearing system, including mutualized risk or multiparty netting of payment obligations for swap transactions, pursuant to its authority under CEA section 4(c).[13]

HYBRID INSTRUMENTS

A hybrid instrument combines characteristics similar to those of a futures or commodity option contract with securities or depository instruments such as a bond or note with a floating interest rate tied (directly or inversely) to a commodity index (such as the price of oil). A debt instrument whose principal is similarly tied to the price of a commodity could also be a hybrid instrument. The commodity-related components of such hybrid instruments may arguably constitute the equivalent of futures contracts or commodity options.

---

[11]Comm. Fut. L. Rep. (CCH) ¶25,539 at 39,594-95. Parties engaging in exempt swap agreements must nevertheless comply with applicable CEA antifraud provisions. See, *In the Matter of BT Securities Corporation*, Docket No. 95-3 (Commission Order, Dec. 22, 1994) (commodity trading advisor antifraud provision). The Commission has requested comments on whether the ESP qualifications should be changed and the Part 35 rules amended to provide for stand-alone prohibitions on fraud and price manipulation. 59 Fed. Reg. 54139 (CFTC, Oct. 29, 1994).

[12]Comm. Fut. L. Rep. (CCH) ¶25,539 at 39,595.

[13]Comm. Fut. L. Rep. (CCH) ¶25,539 at 39,592 n. 30 and 39,596. Swap transactions that do not qualify as exempt under rule 35.2 may nevertheless qualify for an alternative safe harbor from CEA requirements under the Commission's 1989 Policy Statement Concerning Swap Transactions, 54 Fed. Reg. 30694 (July 21, 1989). The safe harbor requires

    (i)   individually tailored material terms;
    (ii) no exchange-style offset;
    (iii) the absence of a clearing organization or margining system;
    (iv) that the swap must be undertaken in conjunction with a line of business; and
    (v) that the swap may not be marketed to the public.

An early suggestion of the CEA issue surfaced in a 1985 letter of the Commission's Office of General Counsel that found that separable gold warrants, initially issued as part of a unit of preferred stock, were equivalents of commodity options that could only be traded on a designated contract market.[14] The jurisdictional issue was brought to a head by the 1986 public offering by The Standard Oil Company of units including detachable notes with payments tied, in part, to an oil index. The Commission staff questioned whether the indexed notes constituted commodity options that could be traded only on a designated contract market. Although the Commission ultimately did not pursue the matter, apparently because the commodity option component did not predominate,[15] the mere fact that the issue was raised led to uncertainty in the debt markets respecting indexed instruments. This regulatory uncertainty was exacerbated by the Commission's 1987 enforcement action against a major banking institution with respect to gold-indexed certificates of deposit.[16]

Before discussing the recent Commission actions, it is important to look at the prior regulatory efforts respecting hybrids, particularly because the adopting release for the 1993 Part 34 rules noted that participants may continue to rely on the Statutory Interpretation for existing and new hybrid instruments.[17]

The 1987 Advance Notice

In December 1987, the Commission issued the Advance Notice seeking comments concerning a proposed Commission regulatory framework for hybrid instruments. The Commission sought comment concerning

(i) hybrid instruments that may possess de minimus futures or commodity option characteristics, and therefore could

---

[14]CFTC Interpretive Letter No. 85-4, reprinted at Comm. Fut. L. Rep. (CCH) ¶22,802 (Sept. 17, 1985).

[15]See generally Gilberg, *Regulation of New Financial Instruments Under the Federal Securities Laws*, 39 Vand. L. Rev. 1599, 1665-66 (1986).

[16]*CFTC v. Wells Fargo Bank, N.A.*, No. 87-07792 (C.D. Cal., Nov. 18, 1987). See generally Sackheim & Schwartz, *Regulation of Commodity-Indexed Deposit Products*, Rev. Fin. Serv. Reg. at 197 (Nov. 18, 1987).

[17]58 Fed. Reg. 5580 (CFTC, Jan. 22, 1993), reprinted at Comm. Fut. L. Rep. (CCH) ¶25,538 at 39,578 n. 2; see also Proposing Release, Comm. Fut. L. Rep. (CCH) ¶25,510 at 39,455. The current Part 34 supersedes the pre-1993 rule, although the enactment of the new provisions was not intended to affect instruments previously issued pursuant to the rule.

be deemed to be excluded from the jurisdiction of the Commission;

(ii) hybrid option instruments that are within the jurisdiction of the Commission, but because of the incidental nature of their commodity option components and their regulation by another agency may warrant exemption from general compliance with the regulations of the Commission; and

(iii) certain commercial transactions that have elements of contracts for forward delivery of a cash commodity in conjunction with aspects of futures contracts as to which prospective no-action treatment might be appropriate.

By suggesting that there might be a CEA regulatory issue with respect to transactions where such an issue was not evident (such as indexed bank deposits, exchangeable preferred stock, annuities, pensions, mortgages, leases, and swaps), the Commission raised a degree of uncertainty as to the legality of such transactions, at least until it acted further to remove the issue (as it indicated it was likely to do). In the interim, which lasted more than a year, market participants were left to rely on informal advice previously given by the Commission staff (the 30- to 35-percent rule) and occasional no-action letters.[18]

The 1989 Statutory Interpretation and the Pre-1993 Rule

In January 1989, the Commission published the Statutory Interpretation relating to hybrid instruments that have the characteristics of futures contracts or commodity options (reissued in April 1990). In July 1989, the Commission also adopted exemptive rules relating to hybrid instruments that may have the characteristics of options contracts, i.e., the pre-1993 rule. Both the Statutory Interpretation and the pre-1993 rule provided that the Commission could consider granting exemptions to certain hybrid instruments on a case-by-case basis.

The Statutory Interpretation and the pre-1993 rule take a quantitative approach to economic equivalence by focusing on the relative balance of an instrument's commodity-independent payments and commodity-

---

[18]See letters of the Task Force on Off-Exchange Instruments cited in the Statutory Interpretation, Comm. Fut. L. Rep. (CCH) ¶24,805 nn. 19 and 24.

dependent payments. A commodity-independent payment is any payment pursuant to a hybrid instrument that is not calculated by reference to the price of a commodity, and a commodity-dependent payment is any payment pursuant to a hybrid instrument calculated by reference to the price of a commodity. The Statutory Interpretation provides that hybrid instruments with futures or options components that satisfy certain criteria, including that such instrument has a significant commodity-independent yield, are excluded from the coverage of the CEA and the regulations thereunder. The pre-1993 rule provides an exemption from the requirements of the CEA and regulations thereunder for hybrid instruments with options components with only limited commodity-dependent payments.

In order to qualify for the exemption provided by the pre-1993 rule or to rely on the Statutory Interpretation, certain common requirements (the Common Requirements) needed to be satisfied:

   (i) the commodity-dependent payment cannot be separately tradeable;

  (ii) the hybrid instrument cannot be marketed as a futures contract or a commodity option; and

 (iii) the hybrid instrument cannot provide for settlement in the form of a delivery instrument specified in the rules of a designated contract market.

The exclusion from application of the CEA based on the Statutory Interpretation continues to be available for hybrid instruments that

   (i) are debt securities or preferred equity securities within the meaning of section 2(1) of the Securities Act of 1933 (the Securities Act), or time deposits, demand deposits, or transaction accounts within the meaning of 12 C.F.R. 204.2(b)(1), (e), and (c)(1) offered by certain qualifying financial institutions and marketed and sold directly to a customer;

  (ii) are indexed to a commodity on no greater than a one-to-one basis;

 (iii) limit the maximum loss on the commodity-dependent component;

 (iv) have a significant commodity-independent yield; and

  (v) fulfill the Common Requirements.

One-to-one indexing limitation. For hybrid instruments offering a coupon or interest rate indexed to the price of a commodity, the percentage change in such coupon or interest rate for any payment period may not exceed (but may be less than) the percentage change in the commodity price to which the coupon or interest payment is indexed. For hybrid instruments having a face value so indexed, the percentage change in the commodity-dependent payment may not exceed (but may be less than) the percentage change in the commodity price to which the face value is indexed. However, the commodity-dependent payment must be adjusted for any repayments of the face value prior to maturity. In the case of hybrid instruments having a face value and a coupon or interest so indexed, the percentage change in each of the commodity-dependent payments must meet the applicable requirements stated above. As an example, the Statutory Interpretation states that the change in the value of a commodity-dependent payment that is indexed to the face amount of an instrument may not exceed the change in value of an amount of the commodity whose value at the time of issuance equals the face amount of the hybrid instrument at the time of issuance.[19]

The Statutory Interpretation specifies that

(i)   each periodic commodity-dependent payment must be indexed to a commodity on no greater than a one-to-one basis, not just the sum of such payments to the maturity of the underlying hybrid instrument;

(ii) if both the interest payments and the principal of a hybrid instrument are indexed to a commodity, the interest payments and the principal payment must each independently satisfy the one-to-one indexing requirement; and

(iii) the one-to-one indexing requirement applies to all percentage changes, including negative changes.

Maximum loss on the commodity-dependent payments. If a hybrid instrument offers a coupon or interest indexed to the price of a commodity, the maximum loss on each coupon or interest payment may not exceed the commodity-independent interest. If a hybrid instrument has a face amount so indexed, the maximum loss to the purchaser may not

---

[19]Comm. Fut. L. Rep. (CCH) ¶24,805 at 36,823.

exceed the face value or purchase price of the hybrid instrument, whichever is greater. If a hybrid instrument has both a coupon or interest and face value so indexed or calculated, the maximum loss may not exceed the respective limits stated above. In any event, the issuer must receive full payment for the instrument upon its issuance, and the provisions of the instrument cannot require the purchaser or any subsequent holder to pay additional out-of-pocket funds or consideration during the life of the hybrid instrument or at its maturity.

The issuer of a hybrid instrument must receive payment in full for such instrument, and cannot require additional payments during the life of such instrument, although payments such as those to cover transfer fees, taxes at maturity, or deferred payment option premiums are permissible. The exclusion is not limited to instruments providing for periodic cash payments, and is available for hybrid instruments in the form of zero-coupon securities or that provide for the issuance of additional securities in lieu of cash interest payments.

Commodity-independent yield.   In order to limit the commodity-dependent yield, it must equal at least 50 percent, but no more than 150 percent, of the estimated annual yield at the time of issuance for a comparable nonhybrid debt, preferred equity, or depository instrument issued by the same or a similar issuer. The Statutory Interpretation notes that as a result of this requirement, for example, no more than half of the issue price of a hybrid-coupon par bond of long maturity could be attributable to the value of its commodity-dependent component, and the commodity-independent yield paid over the life of the instrument would be required to be at least one-half of what would be paid on a conventional debt, preferred equity, or depository instrument. If the commodity-dependent yield is indexed to the Consumer Price Index or other broadly based inflation measures, the estimated annual yield of a comparable nonhybrid instrument would be the estimated real rate of interest calculated as the bond-equivalent yield of the most recently issued one-year Treasury bill less the most recently announced annualized percentage change in the Consumer Price Index. The Commission stated that any time the commodity-dependent payments are denominated in or indexed to a foreign currency or currencies, the comparison to a comparable dollar-denominated nonhybrid rate should be on a dollar-equivalent basis. Such a comparison should make up for variations in interest rates for foreign-currency-denominated hybrid instruments due to an expected appreciation or depreciation of foreign currencies relative to the

U.S. dollar, while comparable nonhybrid instruments have a return rate based solely on the domestic U.S. market. Comparison on a dollar-equivalent basis should result in foreign-currency-denominated hybrids meeting the yield test, when competitively priced.[20]

Interest-rate instruments. The Commission noted in the Statutory Interpretation generally that lending or deposit instruments in which the interest payments are measured by reference to published interest rates such as the prime rate, the London Interbank Offered Rate (LIBOR), and Treasury bill rates are beyond the purview of the CEA. The Commission also believes that indexed bank loans made directly to a commercial customer for the purpose of providing funds for use by the customer in its business, as well as loans to foreign governments or political subdivisions thereof, would be beyond the purview of the CEA.[21] These concepts have been further clarified in the Commission release accompanying the new Part 34, to categorize as beyond the purview of the CEA a floating-rate security in which interest payments are calculated solely by reference to interest rates (or indices thereof), the principal of which is returned upon maturity or redemption.

1993 Part 34 Exemption Rules

Pursuant to section 4(c)(5)(A) of the 1992 Act, on January 14, 1993, the Commission adopted a new Part 34, entitled "Regulation of Hybrid Instruments," concerning hybrid instruments entered into on or after October 23, 1974, that are debt or equity securities or depository instruments.[22] While the former Part 34 applied only to instruments with option components because of the then-existing limit on Commission exemptive authority, the new rules apply to instruments with either or both futures and options components.[23] Under the new Part 34, a test is used to

[20]Comm. Fut. L. Rep. (CCH) ¶24,805 at 36,823.

[21]Comm. Fut. L. Rep. (CCH) ¶24,805 at 36,824 n. 32; see also 58 Fed. Reg. 5580 (CFTC, Jan. 22, 1993), reprinted at Comm. Fut. L. Rep. (CCH) ¶25,538 at 39,584.

[22]58 Fed. Reg. 5580 (CFTC, Jan. 22, 1993), reprinted at Comm. Fut. L. Rep. (CCH) ¶25,538. Part 34 is retroactive. As a result, the exemption is available regardless of when (after October 23, 1974) the instrument may have been entered into.

[23]As with the Part 35 exemption, the Commission has found that the legislative history of the 1992 Act does not require it to determine affirmatively that it has jurisdiction over the hybrid instruments exempt by Part 34. Comm. Fut. L. Rep. (CCH) ¶25,510 at 39,454 n. 2.

determine the predominant nature of the instrument. A debt or equity security or depository instrument for which the sum of the commodity-dependent components is less than the commodity-independent value of the commodity-independent component is exempt from most Commission regulations,[24] including the CEA's exchange-trading requirement, if it meets other specified criteria. The 1992 Act and the Commission have referred to this as the predominant purpose or predominance test. The theory is one of functional regulation—only those hybrid instruments that are "predominantly" commodity options or futures instruments should be subject to the CEA's exchange-trading provisions.

To qualify as an exempt hybrid instrument under the new Part 34, the following conditions must also be satisfied:

(1) An issuer must receive full payment of the hybrid instrument's purchase price, and a purchaser or holder of a hybrid instrument may not be required to make additional out-of-pocket payments to the issuer during the life of the instrument or at maturity;[25]

(2) The instrument may not be marketed as a futures contract or commodity option, or, except to the extent necessary to describe the functioning of the instrument or to comply with applicable disclosure requirements, as having the characteristics of a futures contract or a commodity option;

(3) The instrument may not provide for settlement in the form of a delivery instrument that is specified as such in the rules of a designated contract market;[26] and

---

[24]The Commission cannot exempt a transaction from the provisions of CEA 2(a)(1)(B)(v), e.g., single-equity futures products may not be the subject of a section 4(c) exemption. See Letter of Acting Commission Chairman Bair to SEC Chairman Levitt, dated September 22, 1993. It is the Commission's position, however, that single-equity products with futures characteristics that meet the requirements of the Statutory Interpretation do not violate CEA Section 2(a)(1)(B)(v). Id. (addressing "ELKS" and "DECS"); see also CFTC Interpretative Letter No. 94-32, Comm. Fut. L. Rep. (CCH) ¶26,042 (Feb. 4, 1994); and CFTC Interpretative Letter No. 94-93, Comm. Fut. L. Rep. (CCH) 26,249 (July 27, 1994).

[25]This requirement replaced the maximum loss provisions of the Statutory Interpretation and the 1992 proposed Part 34, which limited the amount of interest losses to interest received, and the amount of principal loss to the face value of the instrument. This new formulation is intended to provide greater flexibility in the structuring of hybrid instruments through the allocation of indexed returns between principal and interest. Comm. Fut. L. Rep. (CCH) ¶25,538 at 39,583-84.

[26]This requirement, while in the pre-1993 rule, was not included in the initial proposal for the current Part 34.

(4) The instrument must be initially issued or sold subject to applicable federal or state securities or banking laws to persons permitted thereunder to purchase or enter into the hybrid instrument.[27]

Predominance. The means of determining predominance has been the subject of extensive commentary by the Commission and others.[28] In essence, the predominance analysis of Part 34 envisions a world in which all indexed returns can be seen in terms of options contracts. In this world, a floating interest rate on an instrument that increases with an increase in an index from a given point (the strike price) can be seen as a long call held by the purchaser of the instrument. Similarly, an interest rate that increases or decreases with an increase or decrease in an index from a given point, much as a futures contract does, can be viewed as both a long call and short put position of the purchaser.

Having decomposed the instrument into its options equivalents, the premiums for the options (which reflect the perceived amount of risk they involve) must be determined. If an options pricing model were utilized in the pricing of the overall instrument, the premiums from that method of valuation should be utilized in the Part 34 analysis. If the overall instrument were not so priced, any "commercially reasonable valuation method" may be used to price the implied option components.[29] The Commission has stated that an issuer may rely on a Part 34 options pricing analysis by the underwriters or other advisors as long as it has a reasonable basis for believing that the instrument complies with Part 34.[30]

Appropriate persons. Using the authority granted the Commission by section 4(c)(3)(K) of the 1992 Act to broaden the statutory specification of "appropriate persons" between which an exempt hybrid

---

[27]The express provisions of Part 34 do not have a provision like that in the pre-1993 rule requiring that any commodity-dependent payment not be separately tradeable. The proposing and adopting releases, however, indicate that any futures or options components that are later to be severed must be separately analyzed, at the time of issuance, to determine if they each meet the requirements of Part 34. Comm. Fut. L. Rep. (CCH) ¶25,510 at 39,459; Comm. Fut. L. Rep. (CCH) ¶25,538 at 39,581-82.

[28]See, e.g., Statement Regarding Certain Aspects of Title III of S.207, Cong. Rec. 54312 (Apr. 11, 1991).

[29]Comm. Fut. L. Rep. (CCH) ¶25,538 at 39,582.

[30]Id. at 39,585.

transaction must take place, the Part 34 exemption permits an exempt hybrid to be "sold subject to applicable federal or state securities or banking laws to persons permitted thereunder to purchase or enter into the hybrid instrument." The proposing release and other aspects of the regulatory scheme of Part 34 (including the eligibility of exempt securities for exemption under Part 34) indicate that this requirement is met by any person with respect to whom the instrument is sold pursuant to the requirements of or an exemption provided by applicable federal or state securities or banking laws.[31]

EXCLUSION FROM CEA REGULATION

Pursuant to the releases concerning Part 34, transactions not intended to fall within the regulatory sphere of the CEA include, in general, nontransferable life insurance contracts, indexed annuities or pensions, adjustable-rate mortgages, employment agreements, leases, and similar agreements.[32] Similarly, no commodity-dependent payment will be deemed to exist for transactions structured to replicate instruments denominated and paid in one currency, with spot translations from and into another currency on purchase and then at payment.[33] Finally, floating-interest-rate instruments (including securities) are not generally subject to the CEA. This is true regardless of the character of the formula or calculation used to determine the interest payment, provided it is determined solely by reference to interest rates (or indices thereof) or relationships between a constant and one or more interest rates (or indices thereof) rather than to another commodity, and the principal is returned upon maturity or redemption. It is even true if multiples of interest rates, rate indices, or spreads are utilized.[34] The releases are less clear as to whether principal indexed to interest rates would be within the regulatory scope of the CEA. The

---

[31] Comm. Fut. L. Rep. (CCH) ¶25,510 at 39,460. Securities initially sold outside the United States, which are subsequently resold in the United States to U.S. persons in compliance with applicable securities or banking laws, are eligible for the Part 34 exemption. See CFTC Interpretative Letter No. 93-68, Comm. Fut. L. Rep. (CCH) ¶25,259 (June 23, 1993).

[32] Comm. Fut. L. Rep. (CCH) ¶25,510 at 39,456 n. 8.

[33] Comm. Fut. L. Rep. (CCH) ¶25,538 at 39,584 n. 24.

[34] Comm. Fut. L. Rep. (CCH) ¶25,510 at 39,456 n. 8; Comm. Fut. L. Rep. (CCH) ¶25,538 at 39,584.

proposing release suggests it would, while the adopting release raises the issue again but does not clearly answer it.

Commodity-indexed securities, including debt instruments, and depository instruments may thus qualify for an exemption from the exchange-trading requirements and other provision of the CEA through compliance with either the Commission's 1990 Statutory Interpretation or Part 34 of the Commission's regulations adopted in 1993, or by the Commission's consideration on a case-by-case basis of a new exemption.

FORWARD CONTRACTS AND OTHER COMMERCIAL TRANSACTIONS

A 1990 judicial decision created concern among the international oil trading community that commercial oil transactions that infrequently resulted in physical delivery because of a commercially acceptable cash settlement mechanism could be attacked in the future as constituting transactions in violation of the CEA.[35] In authorizing the Commission to exercise its new exemptive authority with respect to forward transactions, the Congressional Conferees cited the *Transnor* case and concluded that "[m]any markets of this nature are international in scope; foreign parties are already engaging in such transactions free of restraints imposed by the Act that may create competitive disadvantages for U.S. participants."[36] The Congressional Conferees encouraged the Commission to "review this type of trading to determine whether exemptive or other action should be taken."[37]

Within days of the enactment of the 1992 Act, on November 16, 1992, a

---

[35]The decision in *Transnor (Bermuda) Ltd.* v. *BP North America Petroleum*, 738 F. Supp. 1472 (S.D.N.Y. 1990) (hereinafter "Transnor"), created legal uncertainty with respect to commercial entities engaging in certain 15-day Brent Oil market transactions which almost never resulted in the physical delivery of oil but were routinely settled out between the parties. The court concluded that because the 15-day Brent Oil transactions were routinely settled by means other than delivery, were relatively standardized, and were entered into with high levels of speculation, the transactions constituted off-exchange futures contracts. As futures contracts rather than forward contracts, the transactions could not lawfully be engaged in other than on a regulated exchange.

[36]H.R. Rep. No. 102-978, 102d Cong., 2d Sess. (1992) ("Conference Report") at 82. The Congressional Conferees also directed the Commission to conduct a study to be concluded by October 1993 concerning the future regulatory structure for off-exchange derivatives trading. Conference Report at 83-84.

[37]Conference Report at 82.

group of entities, including producers, processors, and merchandisers of crude oil, natural gas, and other products derived from crude oil or natural gas, which also included at least one Wall Street commodity trading house, filed an application (Energy Application) with the Commission for exemptive relief pursuant to CEA section 4(c) with respect to certain contracts for the purchase and sale of crude oil and other energy-related commodities.[38]

In April 1993, the Commission published an Order entitled "Exemption for Certain Contracts Involving Energy Products" (Energy Order).[39] The Commission understood that the commercial arrangements as set forth in the Energy Application are common in the energy cash market; are standard commercial practices to avoid and/or minimize transaction costs, noneconomic payments, and product movements; and are used for reducing the number of transactions necessary to perform obligations between earned energy-product participants. The Commission concluded that the issuance of an exemption for such transactions would further the policies, purposes, and objectives of the CEA.[40] The Commission noted that the Energy Application did not appear to raise any significant competitive issues, the issuance of the exemption would improve the legal certainty of the agreements and transactions at issue, the exemption would reduce the risk that the physical market might be disrupted, and granting the exemption could result in expanded participation by foreign and domestic energy companies in the transactions at issue.[41] Pursuant to its exemptive authority under CEA section 4(c)(1), the Commission's Energy Order exempted from the exchange trading and other provisions of the CEA, including the CEA's antifraud provisions (except from the CFTC-SEC Accord and provisions that prohibit the manipulation of the market prices of commodities), contracts for the purchase and sale of specified energy products that meet the following very specific criteria:

- The initial agreements (termed "Energy Contracts") impose binding delivery obligations on the parties and do not provide either

---

[38]*Application for Exemptive Relief in Connection with Contracts for the Purchase and Sale of Physical Commodities* (Nov. 16, 1992) (on file with the Commission's Secretariat).

[39]58 Fed. Reg. 21286 (CFTC, Apr. 20, 1993). Congress specifically directed the Commission to consider exemptive relief for the crude-oil market. Conference Report at 81-82. The Energy Order is limited to markets related to energy products. Parties engaging in similar transactions for other commodities may find it prudent to seek exemptive relief from the Commission.

[40]58 Fed. Reg. 21286 at 21292 and 21294.

[41]58 Fed. Reg. 21286 at 21292.

party with the unilateral right to offset the contract or to discharge
its obligation under the contract by a cash payment, except pursuant to a *bona fide* term of the contract permitting the unilateral
termination of the contract for *force majeure*, insolvency, or bankruptcy of one of the parties, default or other inability to perform,
unexpected at the time the contract is entered into.

- Energy Contracts are entered into between principals and their
  material economic terms (including, in particular credit terms) are
  subject to individual negotiation between the parties. Parties to
  Energy Contracts may establish bilateral collateral or other credit
  protection arrangements, such as a letter of credit or other documentation of funds availability, to address credit issues.

- Parties to Energy Contracts may satisfy or otherwise settle their
  obligations through several types of commercially acceptable arrangements, not limited to the seller's passage of title and the purchaser's payment and acceptance of the commodity underlying the
  contract.

- Two parties to an Energy Contract may enter into a bilateral netting or other similar agreement, subsequent to the execution of an
  Energy Contract. Under such an agreement, the two parties agree
  to net or book out the obligations imposed under two or more
  Energy Contracts that provide for delivery of the same commodity
  at the same delivery location and during the same delivery period,
  and thus cancel each other. Such a netting agreement can be entered into at the time that the canceling Energy Contract is originated, or subsequently, through a different agreement, at a time
  prior to when performance on the contracts otherwise would be
  due.

- The parties to the Energy Contract may enter into a subsequent
  agreement that provides for settlement in a manner other than by
  physical delivery. The second contract, however, cannot stand
  alone as an independent transaction–it must be incidental to a preexisting, *bona fide* Energy Contract. Moreover, the establishment
  of the second contract cannot be made a precondition of the initial
  Energy Contract. Accordingly, the second contract must be a separately negotiated agreement and, if the counterparty subsequently
  does not agree to the second contract, the parties must remain

obligated in accordance with the binding delivery requirements imposed under the initial Energy Contract.

- Three or more parties, upon finding that they form a chain, or a string or circle within a chain, to satisfy their obligations under an Energy Contract, whether or not title passes or is deemed to pass, through a subsequent, separate agreement, with unanimous consent of the parties, to book out and satisfy their obligations through separately negotiated bilateral cash payments or other mutually acceptable terms.[42]

The exemptive relief in the Energy Order is specifically limited to crude oil and other energy products. The appropriate persons—termed "eligible participants"—who may enter into exempt transactions pursuant to the Energy Order are limited to commercial participants who in connection with their business activities

(i) incur risks, in addition to price risk related to the underlying physical commodity;

(ii) have a demonstrable capacity or ability, directly or through separate bona fide contractual arrangements, to make or take delivery under the terms of the contracts;

(iii) are not prohibited by law or regulation from entering into such contracts;

(iv) are not formed solely for the specific purpose of constituting an eligible entity to enter into the exempt transaction;

(v) qualify as

(a) a bank or trust company,

(b) a corporation, partnership, proprietorship, organization, trust, or other business entity meeting certain financial threshold tests,

---

[42]Energy Order, 58 Fed. Reg. 21286 at 21293-94. The Commission has advised that the use of brokers and other third parties to facilitate bilaterally negotiated book-outs of chain energy contracts does not constitute a clearing system. Energy Order, 58 Fed. Reg. 21286 at 21294 n. 27. The Commission has expressed similar views with respect to communication and matching facilities on other markets. CFTC Interpretive Letter No. 91-8 (Division of Trading and Markets, 1991), reprinted at Comm. Fut. L. Rep. (CCH) ¶25,156 (spot-foreign-currency computerized matching system); and 58 Fed. Reg. 5587 at 5591 (swap-market computerized broker screens).

(c) an SEC-regulated broker-dealer, or

(d) a Commission-regulated futures commission merchant. The Energy Order also permits governmental entities to qualify as eligible entities to engage in exempt energy products transactions.[43]

The Commission's Energy Order rendered a degree of legal certainty to the cash marketplace for cash energy products.[44] The acting commission chairman concluded that the new exemptive authority "frees the Commission from the constraints of the futures/forwards dichotomy. In this regard, the exemptive authority allowed the Commission to approach situations on a case-by-case basis."[45] Pursuant to this approach, the very same Brent Oil transactions that were found to be futures contracts in *Transnor*, and were subsequently concluded to be excluded forward contracts by the Commission's 1990 Statutory Interpretation, now qualify simply as exempt energy product transactions.

In a dissent, one Commissioner pointed out that "proceeding with an exemption from our jurisdiction, as opposed to describing a class of excluded transactions, demonstrates implicit recognition that some of the transactions which we are exempting could indeed be futures . . . . The contracts are standardized, there is a large amount of speculative activity, and the overwhelming majority of transactions do not result in delivery, but are cash settled."[46] Commissioner Bair also concluded that exempting the parties who engaged in the energy contracts from the CEA's antifraud provisions was unnecessary, and set a dangerous precedent for future exemptive relief under CEA section 4(c).[47]

---

[43]Energy Order, 58 Fed. Reg. 21286 at 21294.

[44]The Commission has noted that the issuance of the Energy Order does not preclude the concurrent applicability to the transactions exempted thereunder of the forward contract exclusion set forth in the Commission's *Statutory Interpretation Concerning Forward Transactions*, 55 Fed. Reg. 39188 (Sept. 25, 1990). Energy Order, 58 Fed. Reg. 21286 at 21289 n. 8.

[45]58 Fed. Reg. 21286 at 21294.

[46]Energy Order, 58 Fed. Reg. 21286 at 21295.

[47]Id. The Energy Order's exemption of the energy contracts from the CEA's antifraud provisions, principally section 4b, has been severely criticized by certain members of Congress as "irresponsible." See "Lawmaker Tells Albrecht to Resign over Forward Contract Exemption," *Securities Week,* May 3, 1993, at 1. Such public congressional anger may have the effect of impeding future exemptions with respect to novel commercial transactions. For an argument for the inapplicability of the CEA's antifraud provisions to cash commodity transactions, see Nathan, "The Statutory Definition of a 'Future,' " *Futures International Law Letter* (Apr. 1992) at 8-12.

True commercial transactions engaged in by commercial participants providing for the future delivery of a commodity should fall squarely within the CEA's forward-contract exclusion and therefore not be regulated under the CEA or require an exemption from the Commission. Commercial commodity transactions calling for the future delivery of a commodity that, through custom or subsequent negotiation, rarely result in delivery, may nevertheless qualify for an exemption from CEA regulation, but only upon application to the Commission. This form of exemption may be especially important with respect to commercial and/or financial transactions involving an intangible, such as a stock index, that results in cash settlement rather than physical delivery of the intangible. It is within the context of the forward contract/futures contract dichotomy that the most frequent invocation of the Commission's exemptive authority will probably arise, with respect to the development of novel commercial and financial transactions that infrequently or never result in the delivery of a commodity.

PROPOSED INSTITUTIONAL DERIVATIVES MARKET

On October 24, 1994, the Commission proposed new rules to permit certain transactions to be traded on contract markets free of many of the traditional regulatory approval procedures and trading requirements (the Proposal).[48] Proposed Part 36, entitled "Exemption of Section 4(c) Contract Market Transactions," was issued in response to petitions filed in 1993 by the Chicago futures exchanges for the approval of less onerously regulated central markets for innovative derivative instruments.

Pilot program.   Pursuant to proposed Rule 36.1(a), the Commission will implement the exemption for section 4(c) contract market transactions pursuant to a three-year pilot program. Thereunder, each board of trade on which a section 4(c) contract-market transaction is to be traded must be a contract market designated and regulated as such by the Commission, subject to many but not all of the provisions of the CEA and

---

[48] 59 Fed. Reg. 54,139 (CFTC, October 1994). As of the date of the publication of this book, the Commission has not adopted any rules under Part 36.

Commission regulations, including the requirement of utilizing a clearing facility subject to Commission oversight. However, the transactions will be exempt from CEA provisions that are specifically inconsistent with the Part 36 exemption. To be designated as an exempt contract market, the board of trade must submit its rules relevant to governance, disciplinary proceedings, financial requirements, and other trading and customer protection rules, to the Commission for approval. Exempt section 4(c) contract market transactions will be required to comply with trading rules, listing of transaction rules, reporting requirements, registration requirements, risk disclosure requirements, and antifraud and antimanipulation provisions set forth in Part 36, in lieu of the provisions of the CEA and Commission regulations that generally apply to traditional commodity futures and options contracts traded on futures exchanges regulated by the Commission.

Appropriate persons. Exempt section 4(c) contract market transactions may only be transacted by eligible participants, as defined in Part 36. An eligible participant may be (i) a depository institution; (ii) an insurance company; (iii) a registered investment company or regulated commodity pool, or a foreign analog, provided that such entity is not formed solely for the purpose of constituting an eligible participant and has total assets exceeding $5 million; (iv) a business entity not formed solely for the purpose of constituting an eligible participant, which has total assets exceeding $10 million or has a net worth of $1 million and enters into the transaction in connection with the conduct of its business or for risk-management purposes; (v) an employee benefit plan with total assets exceeding $5 million and whose investment decisions are made by a bank, trust company, insurance company, investment company, investment advisor, or commodity trading advisor; (vi) a governmental entity (with comments sought as to whether a municipality should be included); (vii) an SEC-regulated broker-dealer or a CFTC-registrant; and (viii) any natural person with total assets exceeding $10 million.

Types of transactions. Proposed rule 36.2 provides that exempt transactions must be settled either in cash or by means other than the transfer or receipt of any commodity. This requirement would permit settlement by the delivery of a subsequent contractual agreement, such as a subsequent swap agreement. Exempt section 4(c) contract-market transactions must be cleared through a Commission-regulated clearing organization that settles accounts for positions on a daily basis and are separately identified on a clearing association's books. Transactions in agricultural commodities, except for contracts based on a broad-based index of agricultural commodities, will not be permitted to be the subject of an exempt transaction. Exempt section 4(c) contract-market transactions must reasonably be distinguished from commodity futures or options on futures contracts approved by the Commission for trading on a traditional futures exchange in relation to the exempt section 4(c) contract's hedging functions and/or pricing basis. The Commission has advised that it contemplates that a broad array of contracts would be eligible for section 4(c) exempt status, including (i) newly issued 30-year U.S. Treasury bonds, which are cash-settled based on either cash transaction prices or firm quotes obtained from electronic information vendors; (ii) 6-month LIBOR instruments, which are cash-settled; and (iii) 2-year interest-rate swaps, which are cash-settled based on a survey of swap dealers. So-called flexible commodity options, which are already traded on certain futures exchanges, would be permitted to be traded as section 4(c) transactions. Foreign-currency forward futures contracts and options thereon may be traded as exempt section 4(c) contract market transactions. Under proposed section 36.2(a)(5), any transaction subject to the provisions of the CFTC-SEC Accord as set forth in CEA section 2(a)(1)(B), will not be within the scope of the Part 36 exemption rules.

Applicable regulations for exempt transactions.   Exempt section 4(c) contract-market transactions will be permitted to be traded either on a trading floor or off the floor, i.e., not subject to existing CEA competitive trade execution requirements. The transactions will be subject to immediate post-trade reporting and clearing requirements. Part 36 will require exempt contract-market transactions to comply with special record-keeping, audit trail, customer protection, transparency, financial integrity, and antifraud provisions. Proposed rule 36.3(g) specifically provides that trades entered into in compliance with section 4(c) contract-market trading rules will not be in violation of the usual CEA antifraud provisions "based solely on having been executed noncompetitively." The Commission advised that by permitting noncompetitive off-floor trading, "the futures exchanges' ability to draw institutional participants to the more transparent exchange (as opposed to OTC) markets will be enhanced."

Exemption approval procedure.   A board of trade that meets the traditional requirements of the CEA for approval as a contract market and that seeks an exemption for section 4(c) contract-market transactions must submit the terms and conditions of each proposed exempt transaction to the Commission at least 10 days prior to the proposed effective date. Exempt transactions may begin trading 10 days after submission, unless the Commission has notified the board of trade that the submission does not meet the conditions of Part 36. This procedure contrasts with the Commission's much lengthier approval process for a traditional commodity futures contract or option on futures contract, which is begun with the filing by the exchange of a petition detailing the economic interest, hedging utility, price discovery function, and public interest purposes to be served by the trading of the contract.

APPENDICES

The Role of the Board of Directors and Senior Management in the Derivatives Business

Jeffrey L. Seltzer
Managing Director, Financial Products
CIBC Wood Gundy

S et forth below is a summary of best-practices recommendations related to the role of the board of directors (the "Board") and senior management in the derivatives business as promulgated by certain regulators and industry groups. It also summarizes proposed legislation and refers to relevant judicial decisions. This outline is current as of September 1, 1995. Readers are advised to refer to the text of the documents described herein for a full description of the actual recommendations and their context.

I. Regulatory Agencies

A. *Office of the Comptroller of the Currency Circular on Risk Management for Financial Derivatives (BC-277 [November 1993] and Q&A Supplement [May 1994])*

   1. Derivative activities must be subject to effective senior management supervision and oversight by the Board:

      a) The Board doesn't need operating expertise in derivatives but must have sufficient understanding of the products and risks to approve the bank's derivatives business strategy, to limit the amount of earnings and capital at risk, and to review periodically the results of derivatives activity.

2. Senior management must maintain comprehensive written policies and procedures to govern use of derivatives:

    a) The Board should review adequacy in light of activity and market conditions at least annually.

    b) Policies and procedures should identify:

        i) Managerial oversight and responsibilities,

        ii) Scope of activities,

        iii) Risk limits,

        iv) Risk measurement and reporting processes,

        v) Operational controls.

3. Senior management approval should be sought for new products or risk types and/or products for which the bank has no relevant experience or for which liquidity is uncertain. Unusual types of transactions may require specific approvals. Senior management should determine appropriate approving personnel.

4. Senior management must establish an independent unit for measuring and reporting risk exposures.

5. Senior management must maintain comprehensive risk-management systems commensurate with the scope, size, and complexity of activities and risks:

    a) Systems should be subject to effective management supervision and oversight by the Board.

    b) Reports to senior management and board should accurately present the nature and levels of risk taken and compliance with approved policies and limits.

6. Senior management must provide for audit coverage to ensure timely identification of internal control weaknesses and/or system deficiencies.

7. Senior management of the U.S. office of a foreign bank may be the U.S. branch management rather than senior management of the head office if the head office has outlined

appropriate risk limits and other controls within which the branch must operate and has established effective reporting and audit functions.

8. Banks that are limited end users must have risk-measurement systems. They must be able to document that the use of derivatives reduces risk. New personnel are not required for risk measurement but these people must be independent of sales and trading.

B. *Federal Reserve Board Examination Memo on Risk Management and Internal Controls for Trading Activities of Banking Organizations (December 1993)*

1. The Board and senior managers must be aware of their responsibility and adequately perform their role in risk management.

2. The Board approves all significant policies, which should be consistent with organization's broader business strategies, capital, expertise, and risk tolerance.

3. The Board should be regularly informed of risk exposure and regularly evaluate policies and procedures in light of such risk.

4. The Board must conduct and encourage discussions between it and senior management regarding risk-management process and risk exposure.

5. Senior management must ensure that there are adequate policies and procedures on both a long-term and short-term basis.

6. Senior management must provide for clear delineations of authority, adequate systems, risk limits, independent risk-management functions, effective internal controls, and comprehensive risk reporting.

7. Senior management must ensure that procedures are in place (including independent risk-management functions) and actively discuss them with traders.

8. Senior management must ensure that activities are allocated sufficient staff to manage and control risks.

C. *SEC/CFTC/SIB Joint Statement on OTC Derivatives Oversight (February 1994)*

1. Policies should be promulgated by the Board and reviewed as business and market circumstances change.

2. Valuation procedures and techniques, risk-management, and information systems should be designed to ensure adequacy of management information and external reporting.

3. Define appropriate levels of delegated authority.

4. Appropriate expertise should be maintained at all levels of the firm.

5. Establish credit- market- and legal-risk units independent of trading personnel, which report directly to senior management.

6. Utilize risk-reduction techniques such as master agreements and credit enhancements.

D. *Federal Deposit Insurance Corporation Examination Guidance for Financial Derivatives (May 1994)*

   1. Each member of the Board and executive management must be fully cognizant of the existing and proposed strategy for derivatives; the extent of current activities; and potential risks:

      a) Each Board member and executive is not expected to have significant technical knowledge but must be fully aware of the risks. However, technical experts must be retained and appropriate supervision exercised.

   2. Derivatives management must prepare an executive document, in language suitable for the technical knowledge of the whole Board, which details the exact nature of the planned involvement and the levels of risk to be incurred. Risk parameters should be expressed in terms of likely and worst-case scenarios and specific board approval obtained.

   3. The Board must fully discuss the overall business strategy, costs, benefits, and especially the risks of the activities.

E. *Basle Committee on Banking Supervision Risk Management Guidelines for Derivatives (July 1994)*

   1. The Board should approve all significant policies related to the management of all risks throughout the institution:

   a) Policies must be consistent with the organization's broader business strategies, capital strength, management expertise, and overall willingness to take risk;
   b) Policies must identify risk tolerances of the board and clearly delineate lines of authority and responsibility for managing the risk of these activities;
   c) The Board must be regularly informed of the risk exposures;
   d) The Board must regularly reevaluate significant risk-management policies and procedures, with special emphasis on those defining risk tolerances;
   e) The Board must conduct and encourage discussions between it and senior management, as well as between senior management and the rest of the institution, regarding the institution's risk-management process and risk exposure.

2. Senior management should be responsible for ensuring that there are adequate policies and procedures on both a long-run and day-to-day basis by ensuring:

   a) Clear delineations of lines of responsibilities for managing risk;
   b) Adequate systems for measuring risk;
   c) Appropriate risk limits (exceptions should be reported to senior management and approved by authorized personnel);
   d) Effective internal controls;
   e) Comprehensive risk-reporting process.

3. Management must ensure that all appropriate approvals are obtained and that adequate operational procedures and risk controls are in place prior to engaging in derivative activities for the first time.

4. Any subsequent changes in such activities or any new activities should be approved by the Board or by an appropriate level of senior management as designated by the Board:

   Senior management and all relevant personnel (risk management, internal control, legal, accounting, and auditing) must understand the product and be able to integrate the product into risk measurement and control systems prior to becoming involved in the product at significant levels.

5. Senior management should regularly evaluate risk-management procedures to ensure that the procedures are appropriate and sound:

   a) Foster and participate in active discussions with the Board, the staff of risk-management functions, and with traders regarding procedures for measuring and managing risk;

   b) Ensure that derivatives are allocated sufficient resources and staff to manage and control risks.

6. Ensure that compensation policies, especially in risk-management, control, and senior management functions, are structured in a way to be independent of the performance of trading activities to avoid potential incentives for excessive risk taking.

7. Maintain independent risk-management functions with an independent system for reporting exposures to senior management and the board. Independent risk-management personnel must have a complete understanding of derivative risks with appropriate personnel:

   a) Reports must be able to be easily read and understood by senior management and directors using a common conceptual framework for measuring and limiting risk;

   b) Regularly review and evaluate the various components of the risk-management process.

F. *International Organization of Securities Commissions Operational Financial Risk Management Control Mechanisms for OTC Derivatives Activities of Regulated Securities Firms (July 1994)*

   1. The Board must oversee the framework of risk-management policies and procedures and management controls, which should address:

      a) Measurement of market risk and credit risk, including aggregate exposures against risk-tolerance objectives;

      b) Acceptability criteria for counterparties, strategies, and products;

      c) Risk-monitoring procedures and exception reporting criteria;

      d) Personnel policies (including expertise, training, and compensation);

      e) Separation of trading and risk-management functions;

      f) Establishment of management control and checks over accounts, trades, operational staff, and systems.

  2. This framework should be communicated to all concerned and should be reviewed as business and market circumstances changes.

G. *Federal Reserve Board Supervisory Memo on the Purchase of Structured Notes (August 1994)*

  1. Board-approved policies that address the goals and objectives expected to be achieved with such products and that set limits on the amount of funds that may be committed to them.

  2. Management must fully understand the risks these instruments can present, including their potentially reduced liquidity in secondary markets and the price volatility that any embedded options, leveraging, or other characteristics can create.

  3. Maintain adequate information systems and internal controls for managing the risks under changing market conditions.

  4. Maintain clear lines of authority for making investment decisions and for evaluating and managing the institution's securities activities that involve such instruments.

H. *Office of the Comptroller of the Currency Advisory Letter on Purchases of Structured Notes (August 1994)*

  1. Bank management should understand the risks of structured notes and be able to explain how such securities accomplish strategic portfolio objectives.

  2. Maintain risk-measurement systems to evaluate possible impact from adverse changes in market conditions.

  3. Establish limits for degree of acceptable price risk.

  4. Redemption-linked notes or notes that contain leverage should be specifically authorized in written policy.

I. *Federal Deposit Insurance Corporation Examination Guidance for Structured Notes (August 1994)*

1. Banks that invest in structured notes should have effective senior management supervision and oversight by the Board to ensure that activities are conducted in a safe and sound manner.

2. Specific written policies and procedures must be in place that address:

   a) Managerial oversight and responsibilities,

   b) Risk limits,

   c) Reporting requirements,

   d) Investment strategies,

   e) Procedures to measure and monitor risks,

   f) Internal controls.

3. Structured-note strategies must be consistent with overall business and risk management strategies.

J. *Office of the Comptroller of the Currency Examination Manual on Risk Management of Financial Derivatives (October 1994)*

1. The Board must establish a written policy and control framework for the use of derivatives that ensures proper identification and evaluation of risk exposures. The level of detail should be commensurate with the complexity and volume of derivatives activities. Policies must keep pace with the changing nature of the business. Significant changes to policies should be reviewed and endorsed. The general framework should:

   a) Reflect the Board's risk appetite and its risk profile;

   b) Be consistent with underlying strategic and business objectives;

   c) Provide sufficient managerial and operational resources to conduct the activity in a safe and sound manner;

   d) Ensure appropriate structure and staffing of key risk-control functions, including internal audit (independence is paramount);

   e) Detail requirements for the evaluation and approval of

new business or product initiatives (the product assessment and approval process);

f) Establish guidelines for dealing with affiliates;

g) Outline approved derivative products and authorized activity;

h) Limit the aggregate level of risk exposure expressed as earnings or capital at risk. Such limits should be reviewed and approved by the Board, or a committee thereof, at least annually. Other appropriate measures of risk should be used commensurate with the volume and complexity of activity;

i) Provide a comprehensive limit structure that addresses key risk factors. These limits should be consistent with bank strategies, historical performance, and the overall level of earnings or capital the board is willing to risk;

j) Describe the limit exception approval process;

k) Require stress testing of risk positions;

l) Require accurate and validated risk measurement methodologies.

2. The Board must adequately hold senior management accountable for performance by reviewing:

a) The consistency of performance against strategic and financial objectives over time;

b) Internal and external audit results;

c) The level of compliance with policy, procedure, and limits;

d) The quality and timeliness of communication to the Board.

3. The Board, either through the bank's asset and liability management committee or other appropriate policy forum, must establish an independent risk-control function, which is designed to limit the bank's vulnerability to foreseeable risks. The risk control unit must:

a) Report independently from those individuals directly responsible for trading decisions and trading management;

b) Be adequately staffed with qualified individuals;

    c) Be fully supported by the Board and senior management and have sufficient stature within the organization to be effective;

    d) Have been provided with the technical and financial resources, corporate visibility, and authority to ensure effective oversight.

4. The Board must require and provide for a strong audit function, which evaluates internal controls, validates the integrity of data, and reviews new products.

5. The Board must ensure that compliance with applicable federal, state, and foreign laws and regulations is periodically verified through a compliance function.

6. The Board must establish mechanisms for effective assessment of capital, accounting, and legal exposures.

7. The Board and senior management must establish a mechanism through which new products are captured and reported. A uniform product assessment process should form part of the overall risk-management function. Depending on the magnitude of the new product or activity and its impact on the risk profile of the bank, senior management and, in some cases, the Board should provide the final approval.

8. The Board must be provided with material sufficient to understand the bank's financial derivatives activities. This documentation should include:

    a) A clear statement of derivatives strategy and the success thereof;

    b) Ongoing educational material and information regarding major activities;

    c) Reports indicating compliance with policies and law;

    d) Internal and external audit reports;

    e) Reports indicating level of risk;

    f) Reports detailing performance of trading, positioning, and hedging activity.

9. Standard Board reports should include:

    a) Market risk

        i) Trends in aggregate market risk exposure

      ii) Compliance with Board-approved limits

      iii) Summary of performance versus objectives

      iv) Risk/return information

  b) Credit risk

      i) Trends in overall counterparty credit risk

      ii) Compliance with Board-approved policies, procedures, and counterparty limits

10. Standard senior-management reports include:

  a) Market risk

      i) Trends in exposure to applicable market variables

      ii) Compliance with aggregate limits by major businesses/regions

      iii) Summary of performance vs. objectives that articulate risk vs. return

      iv) Major new product developments or business initiatives

  b) Credit risk

      i) Trends in counterparty credit risk

      ii) Credit concentrations

      iii) Credit reserve summary

      iv) Compliance with policies, procedures, and counterparty limits

      v) Trends in credit exceptions

      vi) Periodic reports on credit-risk-model development and model validation review

K. *Bank Negara Malaysia Statement on Applications by Commercial Banks to Offer or Trade in Derivative Instruments (January 1995)*

  1. Proposed derivatives activity must be approved by the Board or a committee designated by the Board to oversee such activities.

  2. The Board must:

    a) Be fully aware of the activity and products as well as the potential risk exposure;

b) Ensure that the bank's involvement is properly approved;

c) Put in place an adequate risk-management process that integrates prudent risk limits, sound measurement procedures and information systems, continuous risk monitoring, and frequent management reporting, along with comprehensive internal controls and audit procedures.

L. *Hong Kong Monetary Authority Derivatives Trading Internal Control Review (March 1995)*

1. Chief executives should be asking themselves questions such as the following:

   a) Is senior management of the authorized institution fully aware of the trading strategy of its dealers and is that strategy consistent with the policy guidelines laid down by management and the board of directors?

   b) Is senior management able to exercise effective control over trading activities conducted in separate subsidiaries? Are reporting lines from such subsidiaries to the authorized institution clearly defined?

   c) Is senior management fully aware on a daily basis of the risk exposures incurred by its dealers? Does it have the ability to monitor the growth in gross positions as well as in net exposures and to react promptly to sudden changes in the former?

   d) Is senior management able to monitor separately trades for the institution's own account and those for customers? Is it aware both of trades on licensed exchanges and over-the-counter trades?

   e) Is there adequate segregation of duties between the trading function (front office) and the confirmation, settlement, and accounting functions (back office)?

   f) Is there a separate risk and credit controller who reports independently on trading activities to senior management?

   g) Does senior management monitor the funding by the institution of trading activities, including margin payments, in subsidiaries or sister companies? Are limits set on such funding? Are there procedures for prompt investigation of breaches of limits and/or sudden growth in the volume of such funding?

h) Does senior management have effective means of ensuring that the effectiveness of internal controls is reviewed in a timely manner by internal auditors with the appropriate expertise? When was the last such review conducted? Have the recommendations of that review been implemented?

M. *Federal Reserve Board Letter on Evaluating the Risk Management and Internal Controls of Securities and Derivative Contracts Used in Non-Trading Activities (SR 95–17) (March 1995)*

1. The Board should:

a) Approve overall business strategies and significant policies that govern risk taking, including those involving derivative contracts. Particular attention should be paid to those policies identifying managerial oversight and articulating risk tolerances and exposure limits and they should be reviewed periodically;

b) Monitor actively the performance and risk profile of the institution and its derivatives portfolios;

c) Review, at least quarterly, information that is sufficient in detail and timeliness to allow them to understand and assess the risks facing the institution as a whole and derivatives positions in particular;

d) Encourage discussions between its members and senior management, as well as between senior management and others, regarding the risk-management process and risk exposures.

2. The Board and senior management should be informed of the institution's total credit-risk exposures no less than quarterly.

3. The Board, or a committee thereof, should set limits on the amounts and types of transactions authorized for each firm. They should also periodically review and reconfirm the list of authorized dealers, investment bankers, and brokers.

4. The Board should approve market-risk exposure limits in terms of specific percentage changes in the economic value of capital and in the projected earnings of the institution under various market scenarios. Similar and complementary limits on the volatility of prices or fair value should be established at the appropriate instrument, product-type, and portfolio levels based on the institution's willingness to accept market risk.

5. Market-risk exposure should be reported to the Board no less than quarterly. Their evaluation should assess trends and performance in terms of established objectives and risk constraints and identify compliance with limits and exceptions.

6. The Board and senior management should be aware of liquidity risks and should address them in the institution's liquidity plan and the broader context of the institution's liquidity-management process.

7. Senior management should:

   a) Maintain clear lines of authority and responsibility for acquiring instruments and managing risk, appropriate risk limits, adequate risk-measurement systems, acceptable standards for valuing positions and measuring performance, effective internal controls, and a comprehensive risk-reporting and risk-management review process;

   b) Review reports that provide both good summary information and sufficient detail to assess the sensitivity of positions to change in credit quality, market prices, and rate of liquidity conditions;

   c) Review periodically the organization's risk management procedures;

   d) Encourage and participate in active discussions with the Board and risk-management staff regarding risk measurement, reporting, and management procedures;

   e) Ensure that activities are conducted by competent staff with technical knowledge and experience consistent with the nature and scope of the institution's activities.

Resources should be sufficient to effectively manage and control risks.

N. *Office of the Superintendent of Canadian Financial Institutions' Derivatives Best Practices (May 1995)*

1. Written policies and procedures must be developed which address business strategy, risk management, accounting standards, and internal allocation of capital to support the risk of the business.

2. Each type of derivative should be subject to a product authorization from senior management which designates units or individuals authorized to buy or sell the product and the uses to which the product will be put.

3. Senior management should review, at least annually, the adequacy of written policies and procedures in light of the institution's activities and market conditions.

4. Senior management should ensure that activities are allocated sufficient resources and staff.

5. Board or a committee thereof should approve and periodically review all significant policies. Board should consider its level of risk tolerance, capital resources, business strategy, and level of expertise of senior management and trading staff.

6. Board must have, and ensure that senior management has, a good understanding of risk management processes, derivatives in use, and risk exposures arising from such derivatives.

7. Board should conduct and encourage discussions between its members and senior management, as well as between senior management and others in the institution.

8. Management should incorporate the derivatives business into its Board approved internal global policy limits on the combined market risk of all financial instruments. These limits should be consistent with the Board's view of the maximum amount of capital that should be put at risk.

9. Senior management must provide for an independent credit risk management functions. They should receive reports that

document credit risk by counterparty along with all other exposures the institution might have to a particular counterparty.

O. *Bank of England's Board of Banking Supervision Inquiry into the Collapse of Barings Bank (July 1995)*

1. Management teams have a duty to understand fully the businesses they manage.

2. Responsibility for each business activity has to be clearly established and communicated.

3. Clear segregation of duties is fundamental to any effective control system.

4. Relevant internal controls, including independent risk management, have to be established for all business activities.

5. Top management and the audit committee have to ensure that significant weaknesses, identified to them by internal audit or otherwise, are resolved quickly.

II. Trade Association Guidance

A. *Group of Thirty Recommendations (July 1993)*

1. Ensure that derivative policies are approved by the board of directors and are consistent with overall risk-management policies of the firm.

2. Policies should be clearly defined and reviewed regularly.

3. Senior management should approve procedures and controls to implement the board of directors' policies.

B. *American Institute of Certified Public Accountants Financial Instruments Task Force Detailed Questions About Derivatives (June 1994)*

1. The Board must establish a clear and internally consistent management policy (including risk limits).

2. Management's strategies and implementation policies must be consistent with the Board's authorizations.

3. Key controls must exist to ensure that only authorized transactions take place and that unauthorized transactions are quickly detected and appropriate action taken.

4. Magnitude, complexity, and risks of the entity's derivatives transactions must be commensurate with the entity's objectives.

5. Personnel with authority to engage in and monitor derivatives transactions must be well qualified and appropriately trained.

6. The right people must have the right information to make decisions.

C. *Government Finance Officers Associations Recommended Procedures for Use of Derivatives by State and Local Governments (July 1994)*

1. Use of derivatives by government entities should receive particular scrutiny.

2. Understand that state and local laws may not specifically address the use of derivatives, which therefore requires extra care.

3. Be aware of the risks.

4. Establish internal controls for each type of derivative to ensure that these risks are adequately managed, including:

   a) Written statement of purpose and objectives,

   b) Written procedures for monitoring,

   c) Sufficient expertise of management and technical resources to oversee derivative programs with periodic training of staff,

   d) Record-keeping system sufficiently detailed to allow auditors to determine if program is functioning in accordance with established objectives,

   e) Regular reports by management to their governing body with appropriate disclosure made,

   f) Exercise caution in dealing with brokers, dealers and investment managers.

D. *Investment Company Institute Memorandum on Investments in Derivatives by Registered Investment Companies (August 1994)*

1. The Board's responsibility is to review and approve policies developed by the investment advisor and other service providers and to oversee the performance of their duties.

2. Review existing practices of the fund and its advisor to determine whether derivatives are appropriately addressed in the areas of investment oversight, compliance, and operational monitoring and disclosure to investors:

   a) Derivatives should be analyzed in the context of a fund's entire portfolio and should not be allowed to overshadow more significant risks that funds may take in conventional securities market.

3. The Board, depending upon context and the particular circumstances of the fund (including the level, types, and objectives of a fund's derivative instruments), should:

   a) Understand generally the type of instruments and nature of associated risks;

   b) Request, receive, and review information from the investment advisor about the advisor's overall strategy with respect to derivatives;

   c) Review the fund's valuation procedures;

   d) Consider the adequacy of disclosure;

   e) Obtain assurances from the advisor as to the derivatives expertise of its portfolio managers and analysts, its operational capacities, and its internal controls (including how risk-management responsibilities are allocated and how risk- management principles are applied).

E. *The Association of Corporate Treasurers (U.K.) Guide to Risk Management and Control of Derivatives (1994)*

   1. The following checklist applies to the Board and senior management:

      a) Has the Board approved the use of derivative transactions, including their strategic use, the explicit policies, and the related procedures?

      b) Is this approval specific as to purpose (e.g., hedging or trading), product type and market and credit risk limits?

      c) Have the terms used in these policies been adequately defined in order to avoid ambiguity over the correct interpretation?

      d) Are these risk policies integrated into the company's overall management policies?

e) If responsibility for policy has been delegated to senior management has the Board formally endorsed these policies?

f) Does senior management have an adequate level of understanding of derivatives such that at least they can explain simply the key issues and risks to the relevant board members?

g) Have the approved strategies, policies, and procedures been adequately communicated to the treasury and all dealing staff and have they been acknowledged formally?

h) In the case of banks, securities firms, and any organization for which derivatives are part of their business, has management satisfied itself that it has properly quantified the capital at risk and that adequate capital is in place or rapidly available?

i) Has the Board or senior management approved the company's risk-management approach?

j) Does the Board or senior management regularly review risk management and other treasury activities to assess compliance of derivative transactions with approvals granted?

k) Has someone responsible for derivative activities made a presentation (including the strategic issues and advantages of using derivatives, the controls, and the management information process) to senior management or the Board?

l) Do procedures ensure that only authorized persons can commit the company to derivative transactions?

m) Are these arrangements unambiguously documented in the mandates with all counterparties with whom the organization deals?

n) Has an independent risk-management function been established?

o) Does the risk-management activity incorporate stress scenarios to measure the impact of extreme market conditions on the portfolio?

p) Have overall risk limits been developed to monitor transactions and positions?

q) Have individual authority limits been established to cover all financial exposures?

r) Are the limits placed on each individual trader related to expertise and experience?

s) Are trading limits established for geographical locations, recognizing that certain geographical areas pose more risk than others?

t) Are counterparty position limits in place?

u) Are stop-loss limits established by the company?

v) Does the company limit open positions by product type?

w) Does the trading manager or treasurer have a real-time method of monitoring exposure against limits?

x) Are persons responsible for compliance with limits independent of the dealing function?

y) If limits need to be exceeded, is the proper level of authorization obtained, in writing, before the trades are executed? (On rare occasions the treasury will need to exceed limits. To ensure the credibility of the original limits, a policy must be in place requiring approval, by an appropriate level of management, before the transaction is done.)

z) Is there a regular, timely, and independently produced derivatives management report, covering

   i) commentary on derivatives activities,

   ii) valuations, position balances,and market exposures by product type,

   iii) earnings at risk exposures,

   iv) credit exposures,

   v) the amount of unhedged market exposure,

   vi) breaches of limits,

   vii) cash balances, borrowings, and forward liquidity requirements.

aa) Has the company established appropriate and independent performance measures for its derivatives activities?

bb) Are these measures prepared on a risk- adjusted basis?

cc) Is the performance report reconciled to what management expected the exposures and profit/loss to be?

dd) Is the performance report distributed to the appropriate levels of management?

ee) Are staff assigned only to tasks for which they have adequate experience and training?

ff) Are staff required to keep up-to-date by attending training on derivatives developments such as new systems, revisions to risk management policies, new products and market developments, regulatory requirements, and accounting or tax issues?

gg) Are derivative operations subject to periodic reviews from an appropriate professional advisor?

hh) Are pricing models reviewed independently of the trading desk by outside professional advisors or an independent risk manager within the organization?

ii) Does the internal audit department perform reviews of the derivative operations with appropriate frequency?

jj) Is internal audit staffed with personnel with sufficient skill and experience?

kk) Does internal audit have special procedures for new products/activities?

ll) Do the examinations cover all areas of the derivative operations, including the trading limits, trade execution and processing, valuation, accounting, and tax?

F. *Derivatives Policy Group Framework for Voluntary Oversight (March 1995)*

1. The OTC derivatives activities of a firm should be conducted pursuant to general authorizing guidelines reviewed and approved by the firm's governing body, a committee of such governing body, or a committee designated by the governing body for the purpose of approving such guideline.

2. The authorizing guidelines should be in written form as adopted by the firm's authorizing body.

3. Factors to be considered include the firm's overall business strategies and product lines, its tolerance for risk and its general risk management philosophy, its past performance and experience, its financial conditions and capital levels, its internal expertise and experience, and the sophistication of its risk monitoring and management systems.

4. Authorizing guidelines should address:

   a) The scope of authorized activity or any nonquantitative limitation on the scope of authorized activities;

   b) Quantitative guidelines for managing the firm's overall or constituent risk exposures;

   c) Scope and frequency of reporting by management on risk exposures;

   d) Mechanisms for reviewing the guideline.

5. Firm management should ensure that control procedures are consistent with the authorizing guidelines, including, in particular, procedures with respect to the following matters:

   a) Measurement of risk consistent with prescribed guidelines;

   b) Establishment of risk guidelines for business units;

   c) Data collection and synthesis;

   d) Policies for valuation methodology;

   e) Establish a process for identifying and managing deviations from risk guidelines.

III. Congress

A. *General Accounting Office Report on Financial Derivatives (May 1994)*

   1. a) Financial regulators, with respect to financial institutions, and the SEC, with respect to SEC registrants, should establish specific requirements for independent, knowledgeable audit committees and internal control reporting for all major dealers;

      b) Internal control reporting by boards of directors, managers, and external auditors should include assessments of risk-management systems. The FDICIA Model is recommended.

2. The Board should be responsible for approving the risk-management policies and controls that management proposes. The Board should look to independent risk-monitoring unit and external auditors for analysis before approvals. The Board is ultimately accountable for risk assumed by the firm.

3. Senior management should implement the approved policies and controls to ensure that risks are:

   a) Within limits approved by the Board;

   b) Properly analyzed before transactions are undertaken;

   c) Monitored on an ongoing basis;

   d) Comprehensively reported on in a timely manner.

B. *Proposed "Derivatives Safety and Supervision Act of 1995" (Gonzalez)*

1. Effective senior management supervision and oversight by the board of a financial institution to ensure that derivative activities are conducted in a safe and sound manner and are consistent with the board's overall risk-management philosophy and the institution's business strategy.

2. Must have a written management plan, approved by the board of directors, that ensures that such activities are:

   a) Conducted with appropriate direct oversight of the directors and the senior executive officers (as defined in Sec 32(f) of the Federal Deposit Insurance Act);

   b) Conducted in a safe and sound manner;

   c) Consistent with the overall risk management philosophy and the business strategy of the management of the institution;

   d) Establishes prudential standards for the management of the risks involved in such activities and a framework for internal controls with respect to such activities.

3. All financial institutions, acting as a dealer or active end-user, must have a sufficient number of directors who are familiar with the risks associated with any class of derivatives and the total current credit exposure with respect to such class and the activities of the institution with respect to such class.

C. *Proposed "Risk Management and Derivatives Oversight Act of 1995" (Leach)*

   1. A Federal Derivatives Commission will be established that will promote principles and standards, including the requirement of effective senior management supervision and oversight by the board of a financial institution to ensure that derivative activities are conducted in a safe and sound manner and are consistent with the Board's overall risk-management philosophy and the institution's business strategy.

IV. Legal Analysis of Corporate Director's Duty

A. *Business Judgment Rule*

   1. Presumption that decisions by a Board that are informed and made in good faith shall not be reviewed by a court even if the consequences of such decisions indicate that the choice was unwise.

B. *Affirmative Duty to Hedge?*

   1. *Brane v. Roth* 590 N.E. 2d 587 (Ind.Ct.App. 1992).

   2. *In re Compaq* 848 F. Supp. 1307 (S.D. Houston).

C. *Waste of Corporate Assets Resulting from Derivatives*

   1. *Drage v. Procter & Gamble* (Hamilton County, Ohio 1994)

Global Advanced Technology: FirstDerivative

Thomas S.Y. Ho, Ph.D.
Founder and President
Global Advanced Technology

Global Advanced Technology (GAT) is a fixed income research, consulting, and analytics firm based in New York City. GAT combines leading edge fixed-income research with advanced computer technology.

GAT was founded in 1987 by Dr. Thomas S.Y. Ho and Mark Wainger. Dr. Ho is best known as the developer of the "Ho-Lee Model," an arbitrage-free rate movement framework published in the *Journal of Finance*, 1986, while he was a professor of finance at New York University's Stern School of Business.

From Dr. Ho's research, GAT has introduced the Integrative Bond System (OAS-based portfolio analytics) and GAT Precision (CMO analytics), two fixed-income analytical products. GAT has also developed several approaches to portfolio management including Key Rate Durations, and Linear Path Space that have been incorporated into its products.

FIRSTDERIVATIVE

FirstDerivative is GAT's new system for dynamically pricing and analyzing derivative securities. As part of GAT's new generation of software, FirstDerivative is designed to provide state-of-the-art standards for delivering theoretically-consistent analytics to investment professionals. The system is easy to use, powerful, and directly integrated with GAT's new fixed-income software. FirstDerivative is designed to provide dynamic analytics to sophisticated financial managers who do not have time to write their own computer programs or design complex spreadsheets.

FIGURE B–1A
FirstDerivative's 3-Dimensional Approach to Valuing Derivatives

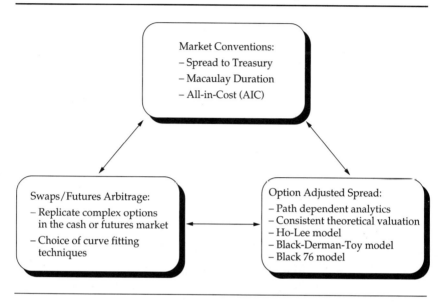

This system answers all these questions for professionals working with the derivatives market:

- What are the risks in your portfolio?
- Do you have a complete picture of your hedging strategy?
- Is your dealer giving you a fair level on a bid or offer for a derivative?
- Can you design and price complicated securities?
- Can you tie out your pricing methodology with the swap market?
- Can you have an open architecture system that allows for easy integration with accounting packages?
- Is your system dynamic enough to permit true interactive analysis?

APPLICATIONS

Market Convention Analytics Allow Replication of Dealer Pricing

FirstDerivative incorporates conventional market analytics (such as All-in-Cost) and the swap/Eurodollar futures arbitrage. The user can replicate dealer pricing and then use theoretical valuation to investigate arbitrage strategies.

Powerful Models Provide Risk/Cheap Analysis

FirstDerivative uses GAT's approach to arbitrage-free analytics. The user chooses between one of three option-pricing models: 1) Ho-Lee, 2) Black-Derman-Toy, and 3) Black 76. Path-dependent derivatives can be valued along GAT's Linear Path Space (LPS), a probability-based interest-rate-sampling approach that replaces the time-consuming Monte Carlo simulation. LPS allows fast, accurate valuation of such complex path-dependent securities as index-amortizing swaps, knock-outs, and look-backs.

FirstDerivative is fast. GAT's experience in advanced software development and financial innovativeness ensures that pricing and interest-rate-scenario testing are virtually instantaneous. Most existing derivatives software requires a lot of time to perform arbitrage-free analytics. GAT analytics provide a consistent valuation framework which enables the user to perform accurate rich/cheap analyses on a swap or derivative.

Flexible and Dynamic Analytics for Accurate Risk Measurement

FirstDerivative provides a complete menu of interactive analytics for risk evaluation in line with the Group of 30 recommendations on managing derivative risk, including Marking to Market, Value at Risk, Market Valuation, Profit and Loss Component Analysis, and Stress Testing.

GAT's unique Key Rate Duration analytics measures the sensitivity of a security to nonparallel shifts in the yield curve. Static risk-measurements such as duration, convexity, and the Greeks are also provided.

FirstDerivative's menu of both static and dynamic risk-measurements allows for comprehensive evaluation of risk in derivatives. Dynamic,

FIGURE B–1B

interactive analytics are vital to accurate risk measurements of complex derivatives. For instance, it gives the user the option of pricing caps and floors using forward volatilities and forward-forward volatilities. Results of static versus dynamic measures can be compared using GAT's interest-rate-scenario modeling.

The *OAS* screen provides the user with such OAS-based risk measurements as effective duration, convexity, and Key Rate Durations. OAS allows the user to choose between the following option-pricing models: Ho-Lee, Black-76, Black-Derman-Toy, and the Linear Path Space for path-dependent options. The user will be able to choose the appropriate valuation approach for the derivative's structure.

FIGURE B–1C

Security Coverage of Virtually All Swaps and Derivatives

FirstDerivative covers a wide range of instruments, including standard swaps, index-amortizing swaps, CMT swaps, caps/floors/collars, swaptions and options. Flexibility is included in the swap analysis by allowing for the input of different payment, reset, and stub periods. The Swaptions/Options analysis handles generic and off-market swaps, and American and European options.

The user can easily structure, replicate, or analyze any number of derivatives offered in the market. Flexibility in setting exact transaction terms means increased accuracy in analysis.

The *Swap Calculator* screen allows the user to define virtually any type of swap. It is designed to handle both standard and nonstandard swaps using US

FIGURE B–1D

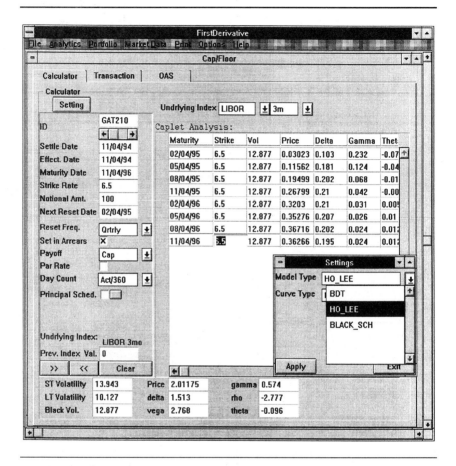

and certain foreign curves. Flexible set-up allows the user to custom-build a transaction with any combination of terms including Day Count, Reset Frequency, Amortization Schedules, Call Schedules, etc.

The *Cap/Floors/Collars* screen provides analytics that are specifically designed to analyze caps, floors, and collars on a wide range of instruments. Unique to FirstDerivative is the ability to break down caps, floors, and collars into component "caplets" and "floorlets" for more detailed analysis.

FIGURE B–1E

Screen: FirstDerivative — File Analytics Portfolio Market Data Print Options Help

Forward/Future Markets

Implied Forward Tsy Rates

	1m	3m	6m	12m
1m	5.16	5.64	6.21	6.77
3m	6.1	6.46	6.84	7.09
6m	7.06	7.22	7.3	7.32
12m	7.25	7.28	7.33	7.42
2..	7.51	7.54	7.59	7.75

Implied Forward Swap Rates

	1m	3m	6m	12m
1m	5.67	5.84	6.22	6.73
3m	6.04	6.33	6.64	7.06
6m	6.83	6.95	7.12	7.45
12m	7.54	7.65	7.78	7.96
2..	8.10	8.10	8.24	8.35

Option Volatilities

	Cap/Flr	Swptn
1Yr	18.00	16
2Yr	18.125	17
3Yr	18.00	17.5
4Yr	17.75	17.7
5Yr	17.625	17.6
7Yr	16.50	17
10Yr	15.625	16.5

Treasury Vol

	Tsy	LIBC
Short	25.31	25.3
Long	10	10

InfoDate: 11/01/94

Eurodollar Futures

	Price	Rate	3Mo	6Mo	12Mo
12/19/94	94	6	5.97	6.35	6.83
03/13/95	93.51	6.48	6.68	6.9	7.26
06/19/95	93.02	6.97	7.13	7.31	7.61
09/18/95	92.66	7.33	7.48	7.65	7.86
12/18/95	92.33	7.66	7.81	7.91	8.04
03/18/96	92.23	7.76	8	8.08	8.14
06/17/96	92.09	7.9	8.16	8.17	8.24
09/16/96	91.98	8.01	8.18	8.2	8.31
12/16/96	91.86	8.13	8.21	8.3	8.38
03/17/97	91.86	8.13	8.39	8.43	8.43
06/16/97	91.8	8.19	8.47	8.45	8.49
09/15/97	91.75	8.25	8.43	8.44	8.53
12/15/97	91.63	8.36	8.44	8.52	8.58
03/16/98	91.66	8.33	8.6	8.64	8.63
06/15/98	91.61	8.38	8.67	8.65	8.68
09/14/98	91.55	8.44	8.63	8.63	8.72
12/14/98	91.45	8.54	8.62	8.71	8.77
03/15/99	91.48	8.51	8.79	8.82	8.84
06/14/99	91.43	8.56	8.86	8.84	8.89
09/13/99	91.37	8.62	8.81	8.86	8.92

Market Data Access and Integrity Provides Accurate Data

FirstDerivative's Market Database is updated nightly as part of GAT's market data service. GAT's market database contains all of the data for the fixed-income markets. FirstDerivative supplies all of the data as specified by International Swap and Derivatives Association, Inc. (ISDA) for derivative transactions.

The user does not need to collect, format, or input any market data into the system to produce sound market-based analytics or to comply with regulatory transaction and reporting requirements. The data is displayed in a familiar, spreadsheet-like format that allows the user to input new data if the markets change dramatically during the day.

The *Market Data* screen accesses FirstDerivative's extensive database of current market information, historical market data, and GAT proprietary term structure information. Proprietary processed information includes spot curves, forward curves, volatilities, Eurodollar strip curve, and swap curves.

Complete Portfolio Evaluation Capabilities

FirstDerivative allows for "portfolio within a portfolio" structures, in which the derivative transaction is modeled as a single security and the underlying portfolio of securities is modeled as another security. Portfolio capabilities provide for interest-rate-risk reports, position limits with issuers, and other reports for an entire portfolio of derivatives.

"Portfolio within a portfolio" capabilities are especially important for companies complying with FAS 115 (mark to market and segregation of portfolios) and FAS 91 (amortized cost-accounting method) standards. For example, a portfolio manager could maintain an entire CMO portfolio in the system along with the interest-amortizing swaps used to hedge the portfolio.

User-Friendly Multiple Display Screens

The screens use the latest graphical user interface (GUI) technology that allows the user to move easily between screens or display multiple screens at one time. Object-oriented programming enables GAT to add new features quickly as new derivatives or reporting requirements come to the market.

The user can structure a derivative, view the analytics and resulting cash flows, leave the cash flow screen open, and then reconfigure the derivative to suit his or her needs.

UPCOMING CAPABILITIES

More Exotic Securities, Foreign Market Data, Full Portfolio Ability

FirstDerivative's capabilities are currently being expanded to cover the following instruments: CMO swaps, range floaters, lookback and knock-out options. The next expansion phase will cover a full range of currency swaps, differential swaps, two-color rainbow swaps, and swaps on equity indices.

System updates will include "drag and drop" features for customizing security design, and the inclusion of real time market information (current data is close of prior business day).

Foreign yield curve, currency, and currency volatility information will be added in order to handle multicurrency and interest-rate transactions. All foreign rate information will conform to information standards as specified in the *1991 ISDA Definitions* handbook: Japanese yen rate indices (JPY-LIBOR-ISDA, JPY-LIBOR-BBA, JPY-LIBOR-Reference Banks); deutsche mark rate indices (DEM-LIBOR-ISDA, DEM-LIBOR-BBA, DEM-LIBOR-Reference Banks, DEM-FIBOR-ISDB, DEM-FIBOR-FIBO, DEM-FIBOR-Reference Banks); and, pound sterling rate indices (GBP-LIBOR-ISDA, GBP-LIBOR-BBA, GBP-LIBOR-Reference Banks).

Expanded portfolio capability for FirstDerivative will support the following capabilities:

- Creation of portfolios for security positions or holdings.
- Tracking transaction data including trade/settlement dates, size, and origin/destination of all transactions.
- Top down analysis for portfolios within a master portfolio by allowing individual portfolios to be modeled as single securities within a larger portfolio. This capability is invaluable for analyzing and implementing portfolio optimization and hedging strategies.

TECHNICAL FEATURES

Object-Oriented Design for Greater Flexibility

GAT is using an object-oriented design method for the new product. Object-oriented design allows developers to create "objects" that encapsulate both data and processes associated with real-life entities like securities, portfolios, and transactions. The result is an application closely modeled on end-user actions. Object-oriented systems are also easy to maintain, easy to extend, and easy to customize. Well-designed objects result in code re-use, which helps avoid redundancies in the system architecture. User-defined indices are an example of the benefits of this design. For instance, one of the problems with many other derivatives packages is that indices cannot be customized, so a nonstandard swap cannot be accurately priced. Object-oriented design allows FirstDerivative users complete flexibility in choosing interest-rate indices that act as objects. Currently, a user can use many of the readily available data series in GAT's database. In the future, the user will be able create his or her own "objects" or series by specifying a security or a series of rates (basically any time series for a security or index).

Compatibility with Industry Standard Relational Database-Management Systems and Back-Office Systems

Portfolios and securities in FirstDerivative are stored in industry standard relational database-management systems (RDBMS) like Oracle or Sybase for retrieval of security holdings and will provide the user with extensive reporting capabilities. Interaction with relational databases will provide the user with an open and extendable environment in which to interact with GAT's New Windows version of Integrative Bond System (IBS) framework or link into other systems that the user may already use, such as in-house accounting or risk-management systems.

Most accounting, back-office, and custom inventory-systems use Structured Query Language (SQL). GAT is writing the new application to be ODBC-compliant (Open Database Connectivity), and to use all major SQL databases. FirstDerivative supports all major SQL and relational databases (including the industry standards such as Sybase, Oracle, Informix). This compatibility allows the sharing of portfolio or security-specific information with any software package that has SQL technology (specifics on fields are given in the FirstDerivative users' manual).

Operability across All Major Platforms

It is available and operates the same across all major platforms including UNIX systems (such as Sun, HP, Alpha), and WindowsNT.

Appendix B–2

INSSINC (Investment Support Systems, Inc.): ORCHESTRA

Raj Patel
Senior Vice President
Sales and Marketing
INSSINC

There are a large number of suppliers of risk-management systems in the market today. Choosing the right system could be a major undertaking. It is important to be aware of some key issues before embarking on this process, some of which are the:

- Expertise in risk management and technology issues
- Stability and experience of the supplier in providing such a service
- Size and satisfaction of the existing customer base
- Functionality of the system, including:
  - Usability
  - Instruments supported—exchange traded and/or OTC
  - Integration of front and back office functions
  - Availability of advanced pricing models and sensitivity information
  - Ability to interface with existing systems
  - The ability to maintain a product-development program
- Technical support

INSSINC provides integrated systems for trading-room decision support, financial risk-management, and back-office systems.

Founded in 1983 by Elie R. Zabal, president and chief executive officer and William G. Johnson, chairman, INSSINC has been characterized since its inception by a heavy emphasis on market-specific functionality.

INSSINC is best known for its premiere product line, FUTRAK, which integrates all front and back office transaction processing and accounting for derivatives. FUTRAK is characterized by its modularity, which supports the full range of off-balance-sheet and synthetic-investment products.

INSSINC has developed a new product line: the GUI-based ORCHES-TRA. The ORCHESTRA NT/Windows-based interest rate front office is designed to provide traders and risk managers with analytical decision-support tools and techniques when managing their positions in a full range of financial instruments, including futures, caps and floors, swaps and swaptions, as well as listed and OTC options. This front office is fully integrated to the FUTRAK middle and back offices.

ORCHESTRA has been available on a UNIX-based platform as a development environment. However, the direction for all of INSSINC's packaged products is to operate on 32-bit architecture on the Windows/NT platform, allowing for database independence but targeted for the SYBASE relational database.

SYSTEM INTRODUCTION

Front Office Overview: ORCHESTRA & FACTS

The Front Office offers portfolio analysis, sensitivity, and hedge management, as well as individual deal pricing. Users can add simulated trades to a "live" book and perform what-if analyses. Some highlights include:

- On-line portfolio valuation
- User-defined pricing grids
- Portfolio analysis (value 01, delta, gamma, vega, theta, eta)
- Analysis of real and simulated trades
- User choice of foreign-currency option models
- Solve features (i.e., solve for strike/volatility, zero cost, etc.)

In addition, the Front Office has its own reporting capabilities, including:

- Mark to Market

FIGURE B–2A

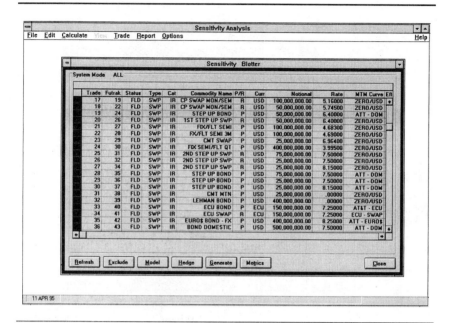

- Cash Flow
- Portfolio Matrix Sensitivity

The user has complete flexibility in grouping trades together, such as by book, instrument type, strategy, currency, and trader.

ORCHESTRA functionality. ORCHESTRA provides calculations for the full set of derivatives. It offers sensitivity analysis for movements in underlying securities, market rates, volatility and the zero curve, with state-of-the-art, 3D graphical displays. Further, any trade can be captured into a portfolio as a simulation, allowing the user to create what-if scenarios for risk analysis.

The following instrument types are supported:

- Portfolio Risk-Management
- FRAs
- Interest-Rate Futures

FIGURE B–2B

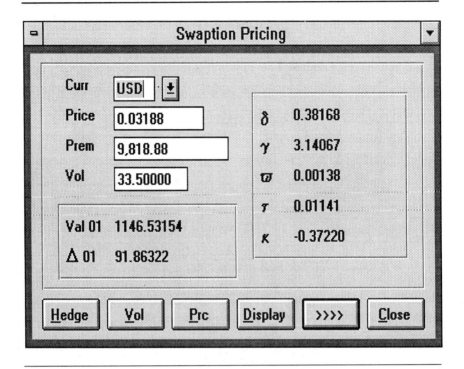

- Interest-Rate Options
- Swaps
- Swaptions
- Caps/Floors/Collars/Corridors
- Bonds
- Loans and Deposits/Cash Flows

FACTS functionality.   FUTRAK's Advanced Currency Trading System (FACTS) is a powerful tool for the currency trader. It gives the user the opportunity to perform comprehensive and in-depth analyses of both single-option and portfolio trading opportunities. The trader is able to model scenarios based on real positions or to simulate hypothetical scenarios.

FACTS is available on a total system license or with the FUTRAK Back Office, and can handle the following instrument types:

- FX OTC Options
- FX Exchange Futures
- FX Exchange Options
- Spot & Forward

Some of this system's functionality include:

- Modeling based on either Black & Scholes (lognormal), Cox-Ross (binary) or Quadratic (analytic)
- User-defined single-option and portfolio matrices
- Portfolio sensitivity analysis of live and simulated transactions that can be viewed in either tabular or graphic form, on screen or via printed reports
- Maturity ladder analyses within user-defined time frames

Front office option models. INSSINC Front Office pricing models, whether for interest rate or foreign currency, are supported by empirical tests, with results that have proven to be sound. The system utilizes modified Black-Scholes and Cox-Ross option pricing models. However, INSSINC also can provide advanced pricing models, such as Ho-Lee, Hull-White, Black Derman Toy, Heath Jarrow Morton, and Farshid Jamshidian, on request.

FUTRAK Overview: Middle & Back Office

FUTRAK is a comprehensive PC-based software package designed to manage the full range of foreign-exchange and interest-rate derivatives. Both the Middle and Back Office can operate either independently from the Front Office or integrated with it.

The Middle Office, as it is often termed, can provide credit limit and exposure analysis together with regulatory reporting (Bank of England, MOF, Federal Reserve, etc.)

The Back Office tracks the transaction from input, through on-line margin reconciliation with exchanges and brokers, to full accounting and reconciliation. FUTRAK's reporting capabilities include approximately 120 standard reports and a customized Report Writer called SCULPTOR, as well as trade confirmations, including FRABBA, BBAIRS, ISDA, and user defined.

Some system highlights and standard reports include:

- Complete Today's Activity Report
- Upcoming Events Diary Report
- Rate Settlement and Interest Payments
- Total Book Mark to Market, by Trader, Portfolio, Broker/ Counterparty
- On-line or End of Day Confirmation Generation
- On-line Margin Display
- Position
- P&L—Today's, Month to Date, Year to Date

Back office: Internal reporting structure & general ledger. The FUTRAK Back Office Portfolios are determined by the Organizational Hierarchy, which allows the user to define the levels at which information, such as P&L, positions, balances, transactions, etc., is to be classified and displayed. The structure is illustrated as follows:

FIGURE B–2C
FUTRAK Hierarchy

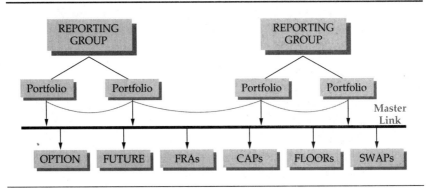

The Reporting Group is the broadest classification of financial trading areas within the FUTRAK user's institution. Reporting Groups are typically profit or cost centers and may include departments such as foreign exchange and interest rate. FUTRAK allows for up to 50 Reporting Groups.

The Commodity Group is a category which cuts across all sections of the structure. It is a means of subdividing the chart of accounts by specific instruments traded throughout the company. The Commodity Group demonstrates the system's ability to differentiate between types of commodities handled by a particular Reporting Group or Portfolio. A Commodity Group, for example, ensures like types of transactions, such as swaps, FRAs, futures, options, etc., can be grouped for reporting purposes.

Master Link Codes group open trades within a portfolio specifically for mark to market and position reporting purposes. The Master Link does not have an effect on the chart of accounts.

In addition, FUTRAK allows the user to associate different instruments into groups, defined either for hedging or strategy purposes.

Commodity specification, broker, agent, and counterparty tables.   All commodity specifications (i.e., instrument definitions such as USD/FRA, USD/FUT/LIF and USD/DEM/OTA), Brokers (exchange), agents (OTC), and counterparty tables are defined in the base operating system by the user at installation.

The commodity specification allows the user to define:

- All commodity types
- Naming and numbering conventions for each commodity
- Master Link Codes for mark to market and position analysis
- P&L currency, first currency (i.e., that which is to be the "foreign currency"), base settlement currency, and FX settlement currency contract size.
- Maximum/minimum prices for internal check
- Formula/GL entry for contingency accounting
- Exchange symbol for option margin calculations (i.e., associaiton of risk arrays for SPAN margining)
- Futures contract delivery dates
- Option expiration dates

FUTRAK's accounting support.   Accounting information includes:

- Unrealized P&L (mark to market) on open positions
- Realized P&L from paired (closed) contracts
- Option premiums paid and received

- Receivables and payables
- Commissions
- Interest accruals
- Contingencies
- Retained earnings

FUTRAK provides contingent financial accounting facilities on both the Portfolio and Commodity levels or, alternatively, allows the user to post all contingencies to a single account corresponding to the type of transaction.

The system also offers both single and multicurrency reporting capabilities for tracking P&L, and "intercurrency" accounts may be utilized to balance multi-currency postings.

P&L for hedges involving cash, futures and options may be posted directly to the Income Statement or to the Balance Sheet, then amortized on a straight-line basis to coincide with the tenor of the asset or liability being hedged. Users can also split profits and losses into separate P&L accounts.

Reporting. FUTRAK provides the user with the ability to track trading activities and validate trade inputs, whether trades are outright or spread, or associated with a hedge or strategy, through a series of on-line displays, on-line generated reports, and end-of-day reporting.

On-line screen displays include:

- Overall Summary Position
- Exchange Traded Positions and P&L (Futures & Options)
- Open Trades
- Today's Trades
- Display Fixing Dates for FRAs
- Securities on Deposit
- Option Expiration Schedule
- Current Margin Accounts for self & client

FUTRAK's generation and end of day report facility is extensive and can be supplemented with the SCULPTOR module, user-defined reports and on-line inquiries.

Appendix B–3

Midas-Kapiti International: CMark

David Dixon
Business Development Manager
Midas-Kapiti International

INTRODUCTION

The derivatives market moves swiftly. New types of trades are continually invented and offer profitable margins for those who are there first. Traders' needs therefore take high priority within an institution. Expensive, flexible systems which price trades and manage portfolios help traders keep up with new instruments.

These systems tend to be developed rapidly and installed with little concern for conventional software development techniques. Pricing algorithms are invented by "rocket scientists," often with little peer review. In many cases, the systems are written and maintained by inexperienced programmers in the trading room, with minimal documentation, limited regard for change or version control, and with only a small amount of testing. Some systems are constructed using spreadsheets, giving traders the ability to override formulas "on-the-fly," without any form of auditing or control. Conditions such as these present considerable risk to an institution. The underlying assumption is that the "back office" will provide the checks and controls necessary to manage risk. Unfortunately, that is not always the case.

Furthermore, by focusing on traders in the "front office," emphasis is on the deal only up to the point it is executed. There is little consideration for the deal's ongoing maintenance. Many derivatives, however, remain on the books for five years or more, requiring regular rate setting and settlement, daily mark-to-market, and conventional risk management such as hedging. Long-term administrative costs for the life of a trade can significantly affect its profitability.

This appendix examines some of the risks of the trading room and considers how they can be contained, at a reasonable cost, by back office systems and controls.

TYPES OF RISK

The risks discussed here are not new, but are sometimes overlooked. It is easy to think of recent examples where institutions have reported losses, or even gone out of business, because they did not have the necessary controls in place.

Formula Risk

Many pricing formulas have been published over the years. Often they have known restrictions, so users develop their own enhancements or correction factors. With so much variation in the market, it is important to ask if the pricing formula used for a specific trade is correct and appropriate. Common sources for errors include:

- *Miscoding the algorithm*
  For example, an algorithm that works for semiannual and quarterly coupons might not work for monthly coupons, due to a simple programming mistake. This type of error should be detected by thorough system testing. However, the fast-paced environment of the trading room does not always allow time for such detailed testing.
- *The formula may not represent market practice*
  Even though a formula is theoretically correct, it may not reflect the way the market works.
- *The formula may be inappropriate for the instrument*
  For example, bond-option pricing algorithms normally assume that a bond price may go above or below 100. However, this is unsuitable for zero-coupon bonds, where the price will never rise above 100.

In widely-used software, which is already tried and tested, the chance of an error remaining undetected is small. And, because the algorithms are in use at many sites, they can become de facto market standards.

Careful software design ensures the appropriate formula is used. Back office systems should allow users to enter full trade details, and automatically produce confirmations from the data—so the counterparty can verify that the details are correct. Once the system has all the trade data, it can select the correct pricing algorithms.

Pricing Risk

Even if formula risk is eliminated, a valid price will only be obtained if the formula's input data are correct. Input data, however, may not be correct. For example, there could be simple data-entry errors, or data might be deliberately misstated to alter the value of a position.

Good back-office computer systems prevent these errors by taking prices directly from market feeds. In addition, systems should enforce authorization controls for users who enter prices manually (perhaps with second-user verification) and produce daily journals. By using these techniques, the system is capable of providing auditable valuations.

Reporting Risk

When formula risk and pricing risk are eliminated, the next question to ask is, "Does the organization know all the deals that have been done?"

An institution must reconcile incoming trade confirmations and statements to ensure that all trades are accurately recorded in its internal systems. These systems must in turn be capable of reporting the trades and risks. Reporting must be timely, will quite likely require consolidation across different branches, and may need to be consolidated internationally. Computerization can help reduce the time scale and cost of the process, and may be the only way to meet these requirements.

Integration Risk

Formula risk, pricing risk and reporting risk do not represent the entire problem. Institutions typically have a number of systems installed to support different business units. If these systems are not integrated, there is no way for the organization to obtain an overall picture of its position. Therefore, any system (whether computerized or manual) must be capable of linking to others. If this linking is incomplete, or not timely, the institution is at risk.

Administration Risk

A trade can live for many years after it has been executed, and must be properly processed throughout its life. Typically, back-office staff establish manual administrative procedures to handle new type of trades as they arise. If these staff leave the company, they may take all knowledge of the procedures with them. Institutions must take precautions to minimize this risk.

In practice, it is difficult to ensure all procedures are fully documented. Comprehensive computer systems, which process trades automatically, are a better solution for avoiding administration risk.

Client Disclosure Risk

Recent events have made it clear that, when selling an instrument, a bank must do its utmost to ensure the counterparty is fully aware of the risks. Equally important, the bank must be able to demonstrate that the risks were adequately explained. This is not always easy to achieve, especially because it may not be in the trader's interest to make all risks clear.

One approach is for a bank to require its clients to use an independent third-party analysis tool. By entering trade details and performing 'what-if' analyses and stress tests in an independent system, clients are far less likely to be surprised by a trade's subsequent behavior. As a further step, it is possible to electronically download trade details from the bank into the client's system, to ensure that the correct data is available to be analyzed.

MIDAS-KAPITI INTERNATIONAL'S SOLUTION

The best way to manage the numerous risks banks and corporate treasuries face today is to have a strong back-office computer system in place. CMark from Midas-Kapiti International is designed precisely for that purpose.

CMark counters the problems of the back office. It processes derivatives throughout the life of a trade: it produces confirmations (in ISDA and SWIFT formats) at trade inception; performs full accounting daily (including revaluations, accruals and amortizations); automates rate setting (and also produces standard rate-set advices); calculates settlements and generates SWIFT payments; provides an extensive range of standard reports—diaries, P&L, regulatory requirements such as capital adequacy, etc.; enables users to write their own reports; and offers security features such as daily journals, second-user verification and password-protected functions.

In addition, CMark has been designed to integrate with other systems—to update other systems including general ledgers, risk-management systems, payment systems and cash-management systems. Its reporting structures are parameter-driven to match an institution's internal structure. And its accounting is also parameter-driven, allowing CMark to meet different standards and cope with different requirements such as those for hedging and trading.

Equally important, CMark is designed as a modular product because the derivatives market is dynamic and growing. CMark is designed for easy installation—an institution need only purchase support for the specific instruments it trades, and can add support for other types later. In addition, CMark is a scaleable system and will grow with a business. The same software is installed at small installations with under 100 open trades as well as larger sites with over 20,000 trades.

SUMMARY

Historically, catering to the needs of the fast-moving trading room has always been a top priority. This approach has allowed businesses to grow rapidly, but has increased risk in the front office, while neglecting the long-term costs of back-office trade administration.

As trading volumes grow, it is more critical than ever to implement back-office computer systems that provide complete support for the life of a trade, manage risks, limit costs, and provide the comprehensive management reporting necessary to succeed in a fiercely competitive environment.

Appendix B–4

Enterprise Technology Corporation: The Compliance Monitor™

Joseph Rosen
Managing Director
Enterprise Technology Corporation

Developed in conjunction with one of Wall Street's largest firms, ETC's Compliance Monitor™ software package is designed to perform periodic testing of portfolios to ensure compliance with applicable investment guidelines, whether mandated by federal or state laws, fund prospectuses, clients or by internal policies, or any combination of these.

The Compliance Monitor™ performs the necessary mathematical calculations and screening to ensure that the percentage of a portfolio in each type of security or asset class does not move above (or below) the specified maximums (or minimums) for each portfolio, and checks to see that the portfolio does not invest in prohibited securities.

The Compliance Monitor™ also highlights for the Compliance Officer all securities for which positions have been established for the first time. This enables the Compliance Officer to research the new positions to make certain that they are properly classified and tested against the guidelines.

The various calculations and tests are built into the Compliance Monitor™. However, the user (normally the Compliance Officer) can easily indicate to the system which guidelines apply to each portfolio. An on-line screen allows the user to associate guidelines with portfolios using a "point-and-click" approach.

Compliance Reports

The key feature of the Compliance Monitor™ is a set of three reports that it prepares regularly for the Compliance Officer:

- Compliance Exception Report
- Portfolio Compliance Analysis
- New Securities Report

The Compliance Exception Report highlights all apparent violations and near-violations of a portfolio's investment guidelines. It is normally run daily. The Portfolio Compliance Analysis Report provides a full analysis of every portfolio, indicating where each portfolio stands in respect to every applicable guideline, whether or not it is in or near violation. The New Securities Report lists all securities for which positions have been established for the first time, so that they can be properly researched.

Compliance Database

At the heart of the Compliance Monitor™ is a Compliance Database which drives the classification of securities and the testing of portfolios. This database, which is controlled by the Compliance Department, is completely independent of the securities databases maintained by the Operations/Accounting Department and/or the trading desk. Securities holdings which are fed from the trading and/or accounting system, and which are not already found in the Compliance Database, are reported on the New Securities Report so that the Compliance Officer may research them and make certain that they are accurately categorized and entered into the Compliance Database.

Timing and Consistency

The design philosophy behind the Compliance Monitor™ is that compliance with investment guidelines can only be accurately tested at a single, consistent point in time—at the close of business. Systems which test for compliance at the time that trades are entered are partially helpful, but they are not sufficient—a portfolio can be knocked out of compliance by the changes in the market, without any new trades. Furthermore, many if not most of the typical guidelines are based on the total market value of the portfolio, which can be most meaningfully and readily calculated as of the close of business.

Investment Guidelines Supported

The Compliance Monitor™ includes tests for the following types of investment guidelines:

- Maximum/Minimum Percent of Portfolio in an Asset Class
- Prohibited Class of Security or Market/Contract
- Maximum/Minimum Market Concentration
- Maximum/Minimum Geographic Concentration
- Maximum Duration
- Maximum/Minimum Maturity
- Maximum Percent of Portfolio in One Industry
- Maximum/Minimum Issuer Rating
- Maximum Percent of Portfolio in Single Issue/Issuer
- Maximum Allowable Short Position by Class of Security

Restricted Securities List

The Compliance Monitor™ also keeps track of your firm's Restricted Securities List, and prepares a periodic report of trades executed in restricted securities.

Flexibility

The Compliance Monitor™ is designed to be as flexible as possible. It is table-driven, so that the user can control the categories of asset classes, markets and geographic regions, for example. The investment guidelines themselves are parameterized as well.

Technical Environment and User Interface

The Compliance Monitor™ runs on IBM-compatible PCs (either stand-alone or networked on a LAN) under Microsoft Windows. It utilizes a very friendly, easy-to-use "point-and-click" user interface.

Feed From Trading/Portfolio System

The Compliance Monitor™ is designed to accept a feed of portfolio holdings and trades data from your trading/portfolio management or accounting system. This is normally done daily. There is generally some custom programming work necessary at the outset to set up the feed for the first time.

Customization

The Compliance Monitor™ can be customized to meet the specific needs of an organization.

About Enterprise Technology Corporation

Founded in 1978, Enterprise Technology Corporation is a New York City based consulting and software development firm specializing in the analysis, design, implementation and support of financial applications systems. Its primary clients are large, well-known banks, insurance companies, and trading and investment firms. Typical projects have included securities trading, portfolio management, investment analysis and accounting systems, global electronic data transfer systems, and specialized applications to support sophisticated, "leading edge" banking and finance programs.

Super Computer Consulting Corporation: ConvB and ExoticOp

Izzy Nelken
President
Super Computer Consulting Corporation
440 N. Wabash Ave. #4909
Chicago, IL 60611 USA
Phone/fax (312) 527-6127

In the past few years, financial markets have grown in sophistication and complexity. A great number of products are offered, often with complicated risk/reward characteristics. It is even more difficult to consider a portfolio of instruments. Risk management, interpretation and control have become quite complex.

Super Computer Consulting Corporation provides sophisticated financial expertise, training, and software.

The company currently offers two software products.

1. ConvB—our Convertible Bond evaluation system
2. ExoticOp!—our exotic options portfolio manager

ConvB

Convertible bonds are bonds which can be converted into a pre-determined number of common shares at the holder's option. Since they typically may also include call and put options, they are very difficult to analyze correctly. Traditionally, convertible bonds have been analyzed as a combination of a bond and equity options. Although this approach makes sense for very low and very high share prices, it fails when share

FIGURE B–5A

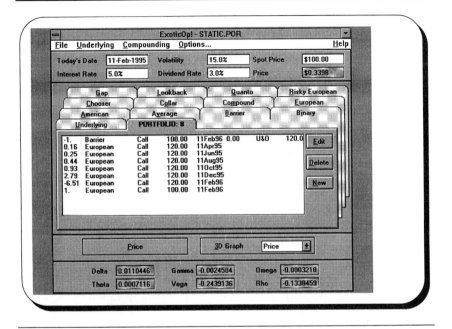

prices are at an intermediate range. However, this is exactly the range where most of the opportunities are in the markets.

In a July 1994 article, "Costing the Converts" in *Risk Magazine,* Super Computer Consulting proposed to use a two factor model which treats both share prices and interest rates as stochastic variables. It first developed a binomial tree for share prices and another binomial tree for interest rates. These trees were developed to fit current market data, such as the yield curve and volatility of rates, the current stock price and its volatility, etc. It then combined the two binomial trees to form a quadranary tree (or "quadro tree") in which every node has four descendants. These represent four possible states of the world (stock up, rates up; stock up, rates down; stock down, rates up; and stock down, rates down). Although this approach is more correct in a theoretical sense, there are several technical difficulties with it. First, the quadro tree must be built so it is "recombining." If it is not, the algorithm will be intractable. Also, the probabilities of each move must be correct. Finally, a fast algorithm is required.

Through ConvB all of these problems have been solved. ConvB, can be

FIGURE B–5B

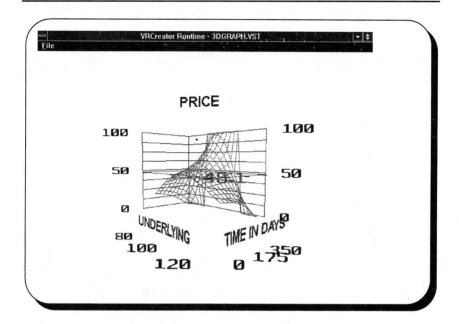

FIGURE B–5C

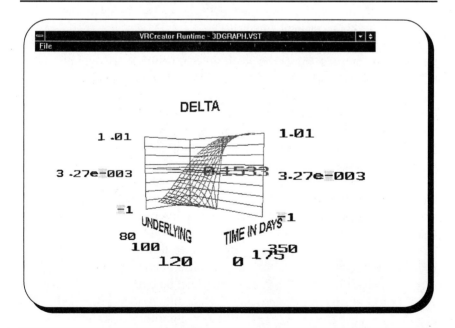

used to price convertible securities and also compute their sensitivities to stock price and interest-rate movements (e.g. Delta, Functional Duration etc.).

ConvB is used by sell-side firms which advise issuers as to the terms of an upcoming convertible deal. It is also used by buy-side firms such as portfolio managers and traders who deal in convertible bonds.

ConvB is available for PC Windows or Unix based environments or as an add-on to Lotus 123, Excel, and a variety of other programs and data bases.

ExoticOp!

ExoticOp! is an exotic options portfolio manager. It is used to analyze options on equities, commodities, and currencies. The user inputs a portfolio of options. These can be either regular options (American or European expiry) or any of more than thirty types of exotic options. These may include: barrier options, binary (all-or-nothing) options, chooser options, lookback, Quanto, and Asian options. Each type of option has a special input screen to which the user types in the details of the particular options. Extensive on-line documentation is also included so the users always have "help" at their fingertips.

After entering a portfolio of options with possible both long and short positions, the program prices the portfolio. The program also computes the various sensitivities (known as Delta, Gamma, Omega, Theta, Vega and Rho), see figure B–5A. ExoticOp! also comes with an optional 3-D virtual reality graphics utility. With this utility, the user can obtain a 3-Dimensional graph of the price of the portfolio vs. the level of the underlying and the time to expiry, see figure B–5B. In addition, the user can obtain a 3-D graph of any of the sensitivity parameters. For example, in figure B–5C we show a graph of Delta vs. the spot price of the underlying and the time to expiry. These 3-D graphs are actual virtual reality objects. The graphs can be rotated, manipulated and viewed from many possible angles and distances.

Ernst & Young's International Capital Markets Group

Colin Southall
Senior Consultant
Ernst & Young

With the proliferation of new and complex financial products, Ernst & Young have assembled an International Capital Markets Group who specialize in providing audit and consulting services on such instruments. Services include:

• **Risk Management and Operations Reviews.** The ability of back-office systems and procedures to control derivative products should be confirmed periodically. This review should include an assessment of the adequacy of risk management and related controls, operational accounting systems and controls, trading systems and controls, and management and financial reporting capabilities.

• **Pricing and Valuation.** Valuation procedures must be established and, using established quantitative models, the effectiveness of pricing methodologies should be reviewed periodically.

• **Using Technology for Performance Enhancement.** Ernst & Young's services range from scoping systems and resources to control derivatives and conceptual systems design, to identifying technology-based process reengineering solutions. The Ernst & Young Fusion methodology provides an integrated approach to planning and managing all elements of process improvement and system implementation work.

• **Managing Tax Risk and Tax Arbitrage Opportunities.** Based on the firm's knowledge of local and international taxation, Ernst & Young can identify solutions to mitigate tax risks, and to take advantage of tax opportunities, associated with both trading and hedging activities.

- **Capital Adequacy.** Ernst & Young have advised clients on the financial and systems implications of new capital regulations such as those contained within the EU Capital Adequacy Directive and the new Basle proposals. The firm has worked with both clients and regulators in addressing regulatory concerns relating to derivatives activities, and can therefore help provide insight into how an organization's structure would stand up to regulatory examination.

- **AAA-Rated Subsidiaries.** Ernst & Young has helped clients evaluate various financing and collateral-based structures and considered the operational, regulatory and logistical issues in establishing them. The firm has also been involved in the due-diligence process required by rating agencies.

- **Training.** Ernst & Young has conducted customized seminars to meet the specific needs and interests of our clients. These have been aimed at various levels of management and include both the basic concepts underlying derivative transactions, as well as more complex products and risk management.

Ernst & Young's International Capital Markets Group

NEW YORK (Country code 1)
Accounting and Audit Services:

Edwin Pisani	(212)-773-2712
Eileen Garvey	(212)-773-3434
Stephen Howe	(212)-773-3258
Peter Desmond	(212)-773-3181
Kevin Reilly	(212)-773-2074

Tax Services:

Michael Costa	(212)-773-2813
Harris Horowitz	(212)-773-1911

Management Consulting Services:

David Shpilberg	(212)-773-2527

LONDON (Country code 44)
Accounting and Audit Services:

David Cannon	(71) 931-1180
Tony Clifford	(71) 931-2250

Tax Services:

Stephen Barrett	(71) 931-1348

Management Consulting Services:

Edward Collier	(71) 931-3250

AMSTERDAM (Country code 31)

Kees De Lange	(20) 549-7222
Herman Hulst	(20) 549-7278

DUSSELDORF (Country code 49)

Jo Epperlein	(211) 93-52-225

PARIS (Country code 33)

Jean-Marie Galichon	(1) 46-93-67-18
Patrick Gounelle	(1) 46-93-66-22

SYDNEY (Country code 81)

Sean Van Gorp	(2) 248-4819

TOKYO Country code 81)

Shigeru Fujita	(3) 3503-1283
Michiyoshi Sakamoto	(3) 3503-1272

TORONTO (Country code 1)
Accounting and Audit Services

Bill Rupert	(416)-943-3664
Peter Blaiklock	(416)-943-3375

Treasury Consulting Services:

Bill Vanderburgh	(416)-943-3573

Tax Services:

John Van Ogtrop	(416)-943-3138

ZURICH (Country code 41)
Accounting and Audit Services:

Martin Frey	(1) 286-33-38

Tax Services:

Rudolf Sigg	(1) 286-31-35

Management Consulting Services:

Ivan Wagner	(1) 286-36-23

Infinity Financial Technology: Montage®— Financial Toolkits and Applications

Jeffrey L. McIver
Director of Financial Engineering
Infinity Financial Technology, Inc.

A robust software system for trading derivative products must be successful on two fronts. First, it must offer flexible applications for structuring profitable deals, effectively managing risk and processing deals efficiently. Second, it must provide an open technology platform for custom development and the integration of existing systems. Infinity's Montage is designed to give financial institutions a competitive advantage on both fronts. It does this by combining a full suite of applications for trading, risk management and operations with powerful software toolkits. Montage delivers sohisticated software solutions for today's competitive market, while ensuring a continued return on investment as the market evolves.

MONTAGE TOOLKITS

Infinity's software toolkits are designed to enable financial institutions to fully exploit object-oriented programming and relational database technology in their own custom development efforts. The software toolkits

---

Montage is a registered trademark and Montage Data Model and Fin++ Class Library are trademarks of Infinity Financial Technology, Inc. Montage can be ported to object database management systems.

FIGURE B–7A

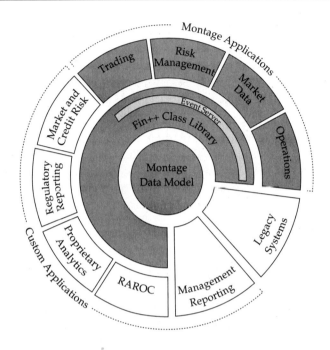

Montage includes front-end applications for trading, risk management and operations, as well as software toolkits which provide a technology platform for custom development and the integration of existing systems. Montage is based on object-oriented programming and integrates the flexibility of open systems with the power of relational database technology.

include the Montage Data Model and the Fin++ Class Library. Both are designed expressly for capital markets and treasury operations. The Data Model and the Fin++ Class Library provide an advanced development platform which enables financial institutions to enhance, customize, and control their trading systems from front to back office.

Montage Data Model

The Montage Data Model employs sophisticated relational modeling techniques to organize and warehouse treasury-related data in a centralized, extensible repository. Working in conjunction with relational database management systems such as SYBASE and ORACLE, the Model is designed to enable Infinity's clients to consolidate front to back office data across currencies and instruments. The Montage Data Model can support a wide variety of applications, from simple reporting to exotic options trading. Instrument coverage includes money markets, bonds, swaps, futures, options, caps, floors, FRAs, foreign exchange, bond options, swaptions, futures options, captions and repurchase agreements.

In addition to helping financial institutions manage market risk, the Model offers a broad range of benefits by providing direct access to critical management information. With the Montage Data Model, banks are better equipped to monitor the profitability of trading operations, meet regulatory requirements, track return on capital and capital adequacy, and manage credit exposure.

Fin++ Class Library

The Fin++ Class Library is an extensive collection of tested C++ objects that encapsulate both the financial analytics and database interaction functions for a derivatives trading operation. Fin++ financial classes ensure consistent analytics for pricing, hedging, cash flow projections, sensitivity measurement, and market data management. Database interaction classes manage the update, modification and retrieval of financial information stored in the Montage database. The Fin++ Class Library can be used as-is for custom application development, and can be modified and extended to accommodate proprietary financial analytics.

Because Fin++ is designed to enable new derivative products to be incorporated quickly into the system of record, traders can execute newly customized deals in line with the bank's overall risk management efforts. The net benefit to a financial institution is a reduction in development costs and an increase in trading profits.

MONTAGE APPLICATIONS

Montage offers a full suite of applications for managing a derivatives trading operation of swaps, caps/floors, FRAs, bonds, futures, futures options, swaptions, OTC bond options, money markets, foreign exchange and repurchase agreements. Montage applications combine an intuitive graphical user interface with a powerful financial engineering approach to deliver flexible and easy-to-use tools to traders, marketers, risk managers, and operations professionals.

Trading and Deal Capture

Montage trading applications provide standard pricing, hedging, and deal capture in a few key-strokes, as well as comprehensive parameter definition and cash flow editing for structuring complex deals. With Montage, traders can model and capture a variety of financial instruments such as basis swaps, average-rate resetting swaps, inverse floaters, LIBOR in arrears swaps, and swaps and caps with complex amortizing structures, including index amortizing swaps. Montage provides graphical screens to handle spot and forward FX and FX swaps; futures trading and position-keeping; government bond pricing and trade capture; repos pricing, trade capture, and rolling; pricing and exercise of swaptions, futures options and OTC bond options; and transaction of money market instruments. Complex transactions combining instruments of different types can be captured and saved to the centralized Montage database for risk management and operations processing. Montage trading applications support copy and paste from spreadsheet programs.

Risk Management

For head traders and risk managers, Montage offers portfolio and risk management tools to help mitigate risk over the life of a multi-currency, multi-instrument portfolio. The system provides broad range of reports and sensitivity measures. In addition to generating predefined reports, the system allows users to build complex customized scenarios modeling various market conditions. Scenarios are built by combining portfolios, sensitivity measures, curves, and reports into a sequence of events. Scenarios are used to perform ad hoc 'what-if' analyses as well as official end-of-day procedures. Generated reports can be saved to the Montage database, providing an institution with the ability to integrate Infinity's risk management capabilities into its proprietary risk reporting system.

Montage supports Value at Risk (VaR) according to J.P. Morgan & Co.'s Risk Metrics™ methodology and data set. Infinity's RiskMetrics implementation uses transaction and market data stored in the Montage

Data Model. The product includes functionality for importing the J.P. Morgan & Co. data files, creating cash flow maps, performing the VaR and Daily Earnings at Risk (DeaR) calculations, and delivering the results.

Market Data Management

Montage provides flexible tools to model a term structure of interest rates, volatility and basis spreads. Curves can be constructed from a set of underlying instruments, from a simple set of data points, or through a function of other curves. Curve utilities allow users to quote indicative levels for swaps and FRAs. Other utilities are included for shifting curves, and for displaying curves as forwards, yields, discount factors and zeros. The system supports on demand update of rates from real-time market data feeds, as well as copy and paste functions in conjunction with a spreadsheet application.

Operations

The Montage Back Office provides application functionality for deal capture, rate resets, confirmations, advices, payments, and general ledger accounting. Montage automates trade capture, initial trade date confirmations, and general ledger entry production, and is fully integrated with the front office. A single, consolidated SQL relational database provides open access to data, front to back. By capturing data in a fully documented, open relational database schema, Montage provides the framework for supporting not only operations groups, but the full complement of back office departments, including audit, compliance, and legal.

MONTAGE SYSTEM ARCHITECTURE

Montage uses a client/server architecture and runs on a variety of hardware platforms in standard graphical user interfaces. A generic object broadcasting architecture allows applications to publish and subscribe to events on a network. The current version of the Montage database is SYBASE and ORACLE compatible, including triggers and stored procedures. Montage is designed for portability to other relational and object database engines. Direct interation with the Montage database can be performed with many off-the-shelf software packages.

Platforms
   SUN SPARCstation (Solaris 1.x, 2.x)
   HP 9000/700 Series (HP-UX)
   IBM RS 6000 (AIX)
Graphical User Interfaces
   Motif
   Microsoft Windows
RDBMS
SYBASE SQL Server
ORACLE 7

Off-the-shelf software packages available for direct interaction with the Montage database include the following:

SQL Windows
Uniface
SYBASE APT Workbench
Any ODBC compliant Windows application, including:
   Lotus 1-2-3 DataLens
   Microsoft Access
   Microsoft Excel
   dBase 5.0
   Paradox
   Q+E
and other off-the-shelf software packages

THE COMPANY

Since Infinity's founding in 1989, the cornerstone of the company's strategy has been to provide a technology platform that empowers clients to continuously adapt their systems to the rapidly changing requirements of the market. A pioneer in developing object-oriented client/server toolkits for derivatives, Infinity is now a leading provider of adaptive open systems used by the world's premier financial institutions.

Appendix B–8

Capital Market Risk Advisors, Inc.:
Software Products and Services

Capital Market Risk Advisors, Inc. (CMRA) is a risk-management advisory firm located in New York City. CMRA's assignments range from independent risk-assessment, upgrading risk policies, controls and procedures to best practice, evaluating troubled positions and developing exit strategies, developing strategies for entering or exiting financial products businesses, and educating boards of directors and senior managers in risk management and risk measurement. The firm is comprised of 20 professionals with backgrounds in capital markets, corporate finance, financial engineering, interest rate, currency, equity and commodity derivatives, mortgage-backed securities, asset allocation, and cutting-edge risk management and measurement techniques.

CMRA's clients include supranational and national regulatory bodies, global investment and commercial banks, regional banks, corporations, and institutional money managers including mutual funds, public and private pension funds, and insurance companies.

OPTION VALUATION

CMRA has developed extensive software programs designed to assist clients in the valuation of their complex portfolios. Options that can be valued range from plain vanilla caps and floors to the more complex path-dependent options. These software programs are proprietary; however, a description of them is presented below:

Options Valuation Models

Each of CMRA's internal option pricing models uses one of three general approaches.

- Closed form solution models
- Binomial Tree Models
- Monte Carlo Simulation Models

Mortgage-Backed Securities, Structured Notes and Derivatives Valuation Models

CMRA has developed extensive modeling capability to value fixed rate and floating rate mortgage-backed pass throughs and mortgage-backed derivatives. These structures range from the more plain vanilla CMOs to the more complex IOs, inverse floaters, and kitchen sink bonds.

RISK ASSESSMENT

CMRA also provides cutting edge independent risk-assessment services that allow clients to upgrade their methods for valuing and forecasting their transactions and portfolios. Listed below are the primary independent risk assessment services that CMRA provides.

Value-at-Risk Valuation Models

CMRA provides services to implement Value-at-Risk. CMRA advises clients on the tradeoffs and implications of the many policy issues that must be addressed to successfully institute a VAR approach. CMRA also advises on all aspects of the system selection process.

Portfolio Valuation and Stress Testing

CMRA provides transaction and portfolio valuation services on both plain vanilla and heavily engineered instruments.

Model Calibration and Stress Testing

CMRA also provides a model calibration service whereby a client's models are reviewed, calibrated, and anlyzed. In turn, the model is compared to others used in the marketplace. CMRA also stress tests models to determine the model's sensitivity to changes in the underlying assumptions.

Appendix B–9

Centre Trading Partners L.P.:
The Capital Adequacy Model^{SM}

Lisa M. Raiti, CFA L.P.
Centre Trading Partners

Centre Trading Partners L.P. is a risk-management company specializing in state-of-the-art simulation models for global risk analysis of traditional asset and derivative portfolios. The Capital Adequacy Model^{SM} is one of Centre Trading's several proprietary simulation models designed to measure risk exposure and to evaluate the amount of capital required to protect a portfolio against loss. This Model, as well as several other simulation models designed by Centre Trading, generates large numbers of market and default "what if" scenarios over a wide range of potentially adverse conditions. The user gains the advantage of an "early warning system" to alert him to possibilities of otherwise unforseeable loss. For derivatives in particular, the combination of varying exposure, market dynamics, and default incidents make these simulation models critical tools for predicting complex portfolio and risk behavior profiles.

Centre Trading Partners' risk-management software can be used by insurance companies, dealers, end-users, and other capital market participants to quantify customer default risk, market risk, investment risk or underwriting risk. The Capital Adequacy Model^{SM} and related models are adaptable for both valuation and simulation analysis of a wide variety of assets, liabilities and businesses in the financial services and insurance industries. They can identify risk positions in traditional investments and derivative holdings of insurance and reinsurance companies, banks, securities firms, corporate and industrial entities, municipalities, mutual funds, investment managers and pension funds. One major market includes dealers and end-users seeking to determine capital adequacy against their books, maintain or enhance their credit ratings, measure value-at-risk exposures or complement risk management.

Centre Trading Partner's customized simulation models can:

- Answer new calls for "value at risk" and stress simulations at high levels of certainty to determine risk-adjusted capital needs in financial and insurance derivatives portfolios;
- Measure default risk and market risk exposures in portfolios of traditional assets, structured transactions, and derivative products;
- Independently verify internal risk management calculations;
- Identify portfolio risk-return trade offs for asset-liability management;
- Indicate the relative level of stress a portfolio can sustain to help promote business, rating agency or regulatory objectives;
- Provide access to credit enhancement by demonstrating capital adequacy to a joint venture partner, rating agency, insurer or guarantor;
- Design Triple-A solutions and quantify optimal capital for Triple-A derivative product companies and structured investment vehicles;
- Evaluate balance sheet "spin-off" strategies such as securitization, investment or acquisition opportunities.

The Capital Adequacy Model[SM] is a Monte Carlo simulation model used to determine potential losses in a portfolio due to adverse market conditions and entity defaults over medium- to long-term time horizons. The model can analyze traditional assets such as stocks and bonds, structured transactions such as collateralized mortgage obligations, and both listed and over-the-counter (OTC) derivative products. The model has been specially designed to consistently analyze both simple and complex structures of multi-currency interest-rate, foreign exchange, equity and commodity derivative contracts.

The Capital Adequacy Model[SM], as a simulation model, distinguishes itself by emphasizing stress simulations and scenario analyses for a large matrix of variables related to counterparty default risk, underlying market risk, insurance underwriting risk, portfolio dynamics, operating guidelines and risk management policies. This comprehensive simulation approach is far more complex than a deterministic approach. In a deterministic approach, such variables are pre-specified. It is a relatively simple approach

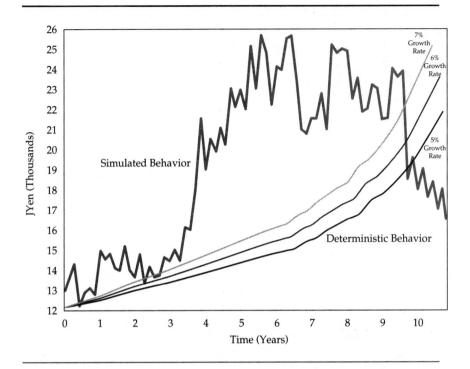

and should suffice for short-term scenario analysis or limited variability projections. However, when the deterministic approach is used *alone* to manage risk, it misses a wide range of variability and volatility in the projected market behavior of the underlying index and derivative contract value. Furthermore, if another factor is introduced into a risk model, such as counterparty default risk, the number of relevant risk variables to specify grows geometrically. A seemingly "easy" deterministic approach then becomes extremely difficult to implement, especially for a large number of possibilities.

The example shown in Figure B–9A of market behavior of the Nikkei 225 stock index underlying a derivatives contract illustrates the need for simulation models. The simulated Nikkei 225 value has been generated by a mathematical relationship based on such factors as the index value's initial value, volatility and correlation with other worldwide stock indices. The deterministic scenarios have been calculated by three alternative continuous growth curves, compounded at growth rates of 5%, 6%, and 7%. As the graph shows, if only the deterministic curves are used, a wide range of behavior is not captured, especially over the ten year period.

Clearly, simulation modeling becomes even more important when analyzing derivatives risk and the large number of variables affecting a contract's value over a long time horizon. Both simulation and deterministic approaches have their place in risk management. The good news is that The Capital Adequacy Model^{SM} and related models can evolve both simulated and specified deterministic scenarios desired by the client.

With respect to market behavior, Centre Trading's models use a Monte Carlo two-factor methodology to evolve the term structure of interest rates. This means that the yield curve does not simply undergo parallel shifts but is allowed to twist and invert. Financial scenarios are simulated consistent with historical exchange rate, interest rate, interest rate and pricing information for calculated correlations and volatilities. A Monte Carlo path can be viewed as a possible outcome of the world as it is relevant to a portfolio. The result of a simulation is many Monte Carlo paths where these paths are chosen consistent with historical price data. Once these paths are laid out, any information of interest can be reported.

Counterparty or borrower default or credit risk scenarios are simulated consistent with historical rating behavior for given rating categories. Portfolio dynamics, operating guidelines and business restrictions in OTC as well as listed products are also simulated. Terms and characteristics of the financial instrument are analyzed. For example, cash flow and prepayment characteristics of the asset or derivative contract, netting treatment and collateral arrangements are included.

The Capital Adequacy Model^{SM} allows for custom-designed reporting capability for senior management, as well as front-, middle-, back-office dealer, end-user and insurer functions. The Capital Adequacy Model^{SM} customized output reports include statistical distributions of the portfolio's or financial instrument's market exposure, capital usage, and change in market value. Sensitivity and "what if" scenario analysis on the impact of varying any input parameters are provided at any desired stress level specified by confidence interval or rating category.

Centre Trading's risk management software products are programmed in C++, can operate on a stand-alone or integrated basis, employ distributed processing, and run on hardware using such operating environments as UNIX OS/2, NT, NextStep, and Windows 95, with adaptability to DOS/Windows. Centre Trading offers the user assistance with in-house system integration, on-site training and on-going technical support. Centre Trading's end products can perform global risk analysis to complement the user's risk measurement, management, and reporting.

Index